A CONTEMPTIBLE LITTLE
FLYING CORPS

A Contemptible
Little
Flying Corps

Being a definitive and previously non-existent
roll of those Warrant Officers, N.C.O.'s and
Airmen who served in the Royal Flying Corps
prior to the outbreak of the First World War.

I. McInnes and J. V. Webb

The London Stamp Exchange
MCMXCI

A CONTEMPTIBLE LITTLE FLYING CORPS

© 1991
Copyright The London Stamp Exchange Ltd.

PUBLISHED 1991 BY

THE LONDON STAMP EXCHANGE Ltd.
The Military & Naval Book Specialists
5 BUCKINGHAM STREET
STRAND
LONDON WC2N 6BS

DESIGNED AND SET IN
12 POINT MONOTYPE VAN DIJCK LEADED 1 POINT
BY
LANGLANDS EDITION
LOUGHBOROUGH

Printed and bound by Antony Rowe Ltd, Eastbourne

ISBN 0 948130 98 9

List of Contents

General Illustrations in the Text

Excluding photographs relating specifically to individuals.

The line drawings of aeroplanes are all to the same scale with the exception of the Handley Page O/100, which is reduced to two-thirds scale.

The photographs on pages 13 & 14 are from the R. A. Lynes Collection.

The photographs on pages 49 & 50 of the medals to J. Baxter are by R. C. Cornish, from the R. A. Lynes Collection.

They call us 'THE EYES OF THE ARMY,'
   For we scout for the foe far and wide.
And with all information worth having,
   We keep the powers fully supplied.
There are Corps who bear much longer records
   For brave deeds, yet History will find
      That in the great fight,
      For the cause of the right,
   WE AIRMEN were not FAR BEHIND.

Foreword

THE CREATION of this book was due to the purchase of two groups of medals, one of which began with a Queen's South Africa Medal whose clasps included 'Defence of Ladysmith,' where the recipient served with the Balloon Section, Royal Engineers, the group continuing with a 1914 Star named to '18, RFC,' and the other, to number 296, started with a 1914 Trio and finished with an Army (GVI) Meritorious Service Medal and a Royal Air Force Long Service and Good Conduct Medal (GV).

Seeking some information regarding those 'founder members' of the Royal Flying Corps, it seemed logical to both purchasers to look for a list of these original Flying Corps men in the Public Record Office, that source of (nearly) all knowledge. Amazingly, there was no such list in the Public Record Office, the RAF Museum at Hendon, or even at the Ministry of Defence (Air), the only references to these men being scattered through thousands of documents in the Public Record Office, and in the *London Gazette*.

At the time it seemed that it would be a fairly simple task to collect the names and numbers from these documents, but the scope of the list has widened steadily over the last few years, as more and more information has been garnered.

Since a cut-off date or service number had to be chosen, the outbreak of war in 1914 seemed a logical finale, when twelve Reservists (Nos. 558-569) were recalled, with the first few war-time volunteers included, including a number of NCO members of the original Air Battalion Reserve, (five in all, Nos. 1369-1372 and No. 1376), to bring the number up to round figures, *viz.* 1,400. We have then added the first 25 Special Reservists. Of the 1,425 men only perhaps two names are missing. (However, readers should note there are two men with the No. 555.) These pre-war regular Other Ranks are the 'first of the many,' the men who serviced the earliest military aircraft, and who were the spiritual ancestors of the millions of 'erks' who have served in the Air Services during the last eighty years. This list is a slight, if belated, tribute to their work, in the hope that it will keep alive the memory of those men who laid the foundations of today's supersonic Royal Air Force.

There are still countless details which can be added to this list, but at least a numerical roll now exists. An experienced publisher (with four years experience) remarked, on seeing the manuscript, 'Is that all there is of it? Anyone could have done that,' but the fact remains, that in the last seventy years, no-one has done it, and it thus stands, with all its shortcoming, as the only roll known to the present writers to record the earliest other ranks of the RFC.

Finally, and most importantly, the authors' most grateful thanks must be offered to the staff of the Public Record Office, both the clerical and production sides, without whose unfailingly cheerful and willing help, this book, quite simply, could not have come into being.

In dedication to all those who have served in the Air Battalion, in the RFC and the RAF, the following poem by John Magee, an American pilot in the Royal Canadian Air Force, is quoted:—

'HIGH FLIGHT'

Oh! I have slipped the surly bonds of earth
    And danced the skies on laughter-silvered wings;
Sunward I've climbed, and joined the tumbling mirth
    Of sun-split clouds – and done a hundred things
You have not dreamed of – wheeled and soared and swung
    High in the sunlit silence. Hovering there,
I've chased the shouting wind along, and flung
    My eager craft through footless halls of air.
Up, up the long, delirious, burning blue
    I've topped the wind-swept heights with easy grace
    Where never lark, nor even eagle flew.
And, while with silent, lifting mind I've trod
    The high untrespassed sanctity of space,
    Put out my hands, and touched the face of God.

John Magee flew Spitfires of 412 Squadron. He was killed in action on 11 December, 1941 aged 19.

A Short Historical Introduction

WHEN MENTION is made of the Royal Air Force (and its predecessor, the Royal Flying Corps) one tends to visualise the air arm as it was at the Armistice, nearly 300,000 strong, with a multiplicity of aircraft, and with strong traditions of its own which owed little or nothing to its parents the Army and the Navy.

It comes, therefore, as a shock to realise that this mighty machine had been born barely six years earlier, its strength less than that of an infantry battalion, and in the teeth of hostility and ridicule from the traditionalist 'cavalry types' in the War Office and in the Army itself.

Although there was strong support from the more progressive military tacticians for the idea of using the new air vehicles for military purposes, it must have taken considerable enthusiasm on the part of a professional soldier to transfer to a new and untried unit, for although the majority of its officers were only attached from their parent regiments, the other ranks were required to become permanent members of the Royal Flying Corps.

The R.F.C. was formed from the Air Battalion, Royal Engineers, the RE having been investigating aerial techniques for over thirty years, the first balloon experiments having been carried out by the RE at Woolwich in 1878. Within a year of this beginning the RE had built five balloons, and in spite of difficulties caused by the lack, in those days, of suitable materials and manufacturing techniques, the Bechuanaland Expedition of 1884 took with it a balloon, given the name 'Sepoy,' under the command of Lt. Trollope (rather unexpectedly a Grenadier Guardsman).

This was the first of a series of such balloons, used exclusively for enemy spotting, and invariably working at the end of a cable on a winch. These observation balloons enabled the local commander to detect enemy concealed behind trees or, literally, 'on the other side of the hill,' and in the year following the Bechuanaland trial the troops at Suakin, on the Red Sea, took a balloon section, under Major Templer, RE, much to the alarm of the Arab insurgents.

By the end of the century, at the outbreak of the Boer War, balloon techniques had advanced considerably, and four balloon sections were in operation in different sectors of the campaign. Three of the balloons were as follows:—

'Tamar' under Major Heath in Ladysmith,
'Thrush' under Major Blakeney at Fourteen Streams.
'Thames' under Capt. Phillips at Potgieter's Drift.

Although it really comes outside the scope of this work, medal collectors may need to be reminded that two Distinguished Conduct Medals were won by members of the Balloon Sections in South Africa. One was awarded to 23362 Sgt W. H. Pearce and the other to 22671 Sgt W. J. Wellman, both 1st Balloon Section.

TRIO OF MEDALS TO SGT W. J. WELLMAN, D.C.M.

THE BALLOON GAS FACTORY AT FORT KNOKKE

LAYING OUT THE BALLOON

FILLING THE BALLOON

UP AND AWAY

In addition the RE had:—

'Tugela' under Major McDonald in China,
'Empire' under Lt. Spaight in Australia,
'Fly' (Training Section) under Major Trollope.

By 1903 balloons were taken sufficiently seriously to be allowed on the annual Army Manœuvres, the strength of the Balloon Section being given as:—

4 officers,
38 NCOs and men, dismounted,
20 NCOs and men, mounted,
6 civilian drivers.

In 1907 the Balloon Companies, RE, were formed into the Balloon School (divided into three companies) (War Office letter 34/379, dated 9.8.1907), with the objective of producing two Balloon Companies in peacetime, and a third in the event of war. The NCOs and men were to train at the school for two years, and then return to their units. An innovation at the school in 1907 was the introduction of the Cody Man-lifting kite, as a more easily operated vehicle for spotting purposes.

As the first heavier-than-air machine ever used by the Army, this kite is an important landmark in the pre-history of the R.F.C..

Three years later, on the 16th May 1910, the 1st and 3rd Balloon Companies were amalgamated into the 1st Balloon Company, while the 2nd Company and the Balloon School became the 2nd Company.

In 1910 the Mobilization Returns show an interesting break-down of the ballooning department, particularly piquant when compared with the figures eight years later:—

Balloon School (Dismounted)	1st Coy	20	
	2nd Coy	20	
	3rd Coy	18	
1st Balloon Coy (Mounted)		9	
2nd		9	
3rd		9	
		85	ORs

By 1912 the Mobilization Returns show the 1st and 2nd Balloon Companies as having increased to 28 and 26 OR respectively, still a minute proportion of the Army as a whole. However, in 1911 a far-reaching change had been made, in that on the 1st of April, of that year the Air Battalion RE had been formed, in an attempt to bring the British

NO. 1 AEROPLANE SECTION, AIR BN. R.E., BULFORD CAMP, C. 1912. S/SGT THOMAS, LATER NO. 7 RFC IN CENTRE.

Army more into line with its continental counterparts. This Air Battalion comprised Airship, Kite Balloon, and Aeroplane Companies, and an HQ, all remaining part of the Royal Engineers, but drawing many of its officers on attachment from other regiments.

In November, 1911 the Air Battalion Reserve was formed, consisting of civilian pilots who engaged to serve in the event of war, but who did no peace-time training.

The same month saw the Royal Navy, which had begun experiments with airships, establish a naval and aeroplane base at Eastchurch, for although they were officially 'The Naval Wing, R.F.C.,' the Admiralty did its best to ignore the Army connection, and from early days described its air branch as 'Royal Naval Air Service.'

A War Office Committee which sat at the end of 1911 to examine the future of air organisation reported early in 1912, most of its recommendations being adopted with commendable speed. A Military Wing of the Royal Flying Corps was formed by Special Army Order on 15th April, 1912, to absorb the Air Battalion by 13th May 1912. This Military Wing was to be made up of:—

Wing HQ, an Airship and Kite Squadron (with the dirigibles Beta, Gamma, Delta, Zeta and Eta), seven Aeroplane Squadrons, and a Workshop Unit (later called 'Flying Depot, Lines of Communication').

The Central Flying School was formed on the same day.

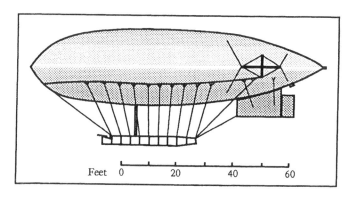

Feet 0   20   40   60

AIRSHIP 'BETA'

The following are extracts from *'From the Ground Up.'*

'The Committee felt also that the lives of those who fly aeroplanes depend to an important degree on the skilful and conscientious manner in which the mechanics of the Royal Flying Corps carry out their work of examination and adjustment of the various parts of an aeroplane, and they wish to bring to the notice of the Lords Commissioners of the Admiralty and the Army Council the importance of ensuring that as large a number as possible of the mechanics of the Royal Flying Corps are adequately trained without delay to perform their duties in an efficient manner.'

'The Committee realise that the organisation of the Royal Flying Corps, when matured, will render possible the training of the requisite numbers, but they suggest that during the present stage of its development, to supplement the training establishment of the Royal Flying Corps, two or three skilled mechanics from each squadron should be specially engaged for a time to act as instructors and to set a standard of technical workmanship while advantage should be taken of the facilities afforded to private firms, both at home and abroad, for teaching men in their workshops.'

Having obtained the men they then proposed they would be employed at the Royal Aircraft Factory (R.A.F.) for about four months to be taught the basics of aircraft maintenance, including erection, servicing and stripping of aviation engines and fitting them. Their object was to rate their capabilities and weed out the unsuitable types of tradesmen, from a service point of view. It was suggested they be offered a better-than-average rate of pay and be given conditions more in keeping with their para-military status.

Requirements for the training of mechanics were more realistically appraised. The R.F.C., on the day after its formation, asked for tradesmen, both skilled and semi-skilled, priority being given to:

> Men who had served as apprentices, or improvers, in general mechanical engineering and had also served in a petrol motor engineering works, including engine test work, or as an engine mechanic. They were required to have a general knowledge of motor engineering, the principles of magneto and coil ignition and be able to make intelligible sketches of machinery details and rough calculations.

These men were to be the technical cream of the expansion and on selection by the O.C. Military Wing could be instantly promoted to sergeant to fill existing vacancies. They would be on probation for one year and if unsuitable be liable for discharge.

A second class of men was required to pass a trade test, and if successful were graded as 1st Class Air Mechanics from the date they completed their basic training. They were eligible for promotion. A third class of men was needed who could be recruited into semi-skilled trades such as machinist, chauffeur, wireman, plumber's mate and motor fitter. The

TWO PERMANENT EXHIBITS AT THE R.A.F. MUSEM, HENDON

physical standards were not clearly defined, except for a detailed requirement of chest measurement, and expansion related to height and an age group of 18 to 30. Height was at a minimum of 5ft 2in (158cm) and the average chest expansion for the grading of height was 2in (50mm). The average physique of men at the turn of the 20th century was well below today's average, consequently the standards had to be made to suit. The terms of service were for four years with the Colours and four years in the Reserve. Men of other arms of the services who elected to transfer to the R.F.C. had to have their service adjusted so that they would also complete four years with the R.F.C. plus the four years reserve. These transferred men were on probation for six months. Senior N.C.O.s (Sergeant and above) who transferred had to agree that they would accept the minimum rank of Sergeant. For other ranks it was conditional that all transfers had to accept the rank of private from leaving their regiment or corps. The class of recruit who was accepted consisted of men of above average intelligence, with a certain amount of education equivalent to the standard of a 3rd class school certificate. The rates of pay for the four ranks of the R.F.C. of 1912 (there was no corporal) were:

Rank	Daily Pay	Messing	Quarters	Rations
Warrant Officer	9s 0d (45p)	3d (1p)	1s 11d (10p)	6d (2.5p)
Sergeant	6s 0d (30p)	3d (1p)	9d (4p)	6d (2.5p)
1st Class Air Mechanic	4s 0d (20p)	3d (1p)	9d (4p)	6d (2.5p)
2nd Class Air Mechanic	2s 0d (10p)	3d (1p)	9d (4p)	6d (2.5p)

The creation of the Royal Flying Corps, the first major British technical service of the 20th century, attracted many young men, products of Britain's highly organised industrial background and enthusiastically drawn by the magic of flight. Such was the response that the R.F.C. was able to expand without too much difficulty, or at least without breaking down, when the testing time of war finally came.

At the same time the Naval Wing, R.F.C., was formed and took over all the military airships in October, 1912. All the Army airships officers (with one exception) and 46 OR were attached to the Naval Wing, causing various inter-service disciplinary problems. To compensate the Military Wing for the loss of its Airship Squadron, an eighth aeroplane squadron was authorised. The Kite Balloon Section was transferred to HQ, and totalled seven officers and 70 OR.

In a document dated 18th June, 1913, the R.F.C. numbers were given as 102 officers and 569 OR, plus five officers and five OR at Central Flying School. The parts of the Military Wing were as follows:—

HQ and No. 1 Sqn (Airships) formed 13.5.12 at S. Farnborough
No. 2 Squadron (Aeroplanes)   13.5.12 at S. Farnborough
No. 3 Squadron   13.5.12 at Bulford
No. 4 Squadron   16.12.12 at Farnborough
                                      (later moved to Netheravon
No. 5 Squadron   26.7.13 at Farnborough
                                      (moved to Gosport 1/7/14)
No. 6 Squadron   31.1.14 at Farnborough
No. 1 (New Aeroplane) Squadron   1.5.14 at Farnborough
No. 7 Squadron   1.5.14 at Farnborough

An interesting statistical table gives the number and origins of the OR serving on:—

	31.12.12	31.12.13	10.8.14
Transferred from Air Bn	87	92	92
Tfd. from rest of Army	159	267	324
Directly enlisted to R.F.C.	224	640	941
Total	*470*	*999*	*1357*

(Including recruits, Special Reserve, etc.)

It is, perhaps, noteworthy that on 1st April, 1914, only four months before the outbreak of the war, the strength of the Military Wing had actually dropped slightly, to 984 OR, from the December, 1913 strength.

A long-running argument developed over the employment of boys in the R.F.C., their training and their number. As early as 20th July, 1912, Major Sykes was writing to the War Office, suggesting an establishment of nine boys per squadron, plus ten for the Airship Squadron and four for the Flying Depot, receiving on 10th April, 1913, from the Director of Military Training authority (dated from 1st April, 1913) to enlist 25 boys in the Military Wing. In fact, the numbers serving on the 28th February, were 15 in the Aeroplane Squadrons, three in the Airship Squadron, three in the Flying Depot, and four at CFS.

War Office instructions regarding the terms of enlistment of boys were not received until 16th June, 1913, the first four boys to join under these terms being 845 J. Eley, 842 G. Graham, 844 E. Salter and 843 J. Welch. In September, 1913 the enlistment of six more boys was approved, making a total of 31, at the expense of six men, in order to keep the OR establishment total unchanged.

By the 4th May 1914, the provision in Army Estimate for 1914-15 was made for 41 boys, distributed as under:——

8 squadrons to have 4 boys each	32
Aircraft Park	3
Central Flying School	6
Total	41

In this roll are to be found the names of 44 boys.

Ten years after the first appearance of Army balloons at the Annual Manœuvres of 1903, the R.F.C. in the 1913 Army Exercise provided its HQ, its Airship Squadron, three Aeroplane Squadrons, and the Flying Depot. The one squadron not present, No. 2, was left out in view of its distance from the exercise, being stationed at Montrose. However, it flew to the Irish Manœuvres of 1913, probably the first time that the R.F.C. had crossed the open sea.

Another innovation was the establishment of a 'Category A Special Reserve, RFC' authorised under Part I. Peace Establishment, 1913-14. This Reserve was to consist of 20 Sgts, 180 1AMs, and 50 2AMs, a total of 250. However, no enlistments took place during 1913.

The Category 'C' Special Reserve, RFC' (announced in Army Order 229 of July, 1913) authorised the enlistment of up to 200 men as 1AMs but as with Category 'A' Reserve there were no enlistments in 1913.

The appointment of Flight Sergeant, to rank between Sgt and Warrant Officer, and the rank of Corporal, between Sgt and 1AM, were sanctioned in May 1914. Another development in the organisation of the R.F.C. was the re-naming, early in 1914, of the 'Flying Depot' as the 'Aircraft Park.'

On the outbreak of war, No. 7 Squadron was in process of formation, a process temporarily suspended until 29th Sept. 1914, its personnel providing the men necessary for bringing up to War Establishment the senior Squadrons.

By 12th August, 1914, the R.F.C. serving with the BEF consisted of HQ, four Aeroplane Squadrons, and an Aircraft Park. A Squadron at that time was made up of an HQ and three flights, (each of four planes), the total man-power of a squadron being 24 officers (including observers), and 131 OR.

An individual note may not be inappropriate in this historical outline. On the 22nd August, 1914, whilst flying as an observer, Sgt-Major Jillings (No. 9 in the R.F.C.) was hit in the leg by a German rifle bullet, thus gaining the unwelcome distinction of being the first British soldier to be wounded by enemy action while in the air.

The official figures of the R.F.C. detachment that proceeded by air and sea to France are given as 105 Officers, 755 other ranks, 73 aeroplanes and 95 M.T. Vehicles. However, readers must not assume that these last were conventional military vehicles. The HQ stores lorry of No. 5 Squadron was an enormous red van bearing the inscription, in stark black lettering, Bovril The lorry containing bombs carried the unsoldierly label, Lazenby's Sauce (The World's Appetizer). Other warlike stores likewise paraded ashore under misleading titles, such as Peek Frean's Biscuits, Stephen's Blue-Black ink, etc. Truly an incongruous miscellany.

Indeed the aircraft too were a distinctly mixed assembly. When No. 3 Squadron was moved in June, 1913 from Larkhill on Salisbury Plain to Netheravon it numbered amongst its aircraft 50hp Avros, Henri Farmans, 50hp Blériots, two BE4s and a 70hp Blériot. The mix was not dissimilar fourteen months later when the Squadron went to war on 12th August, 1914. To illustrate just how an R.F.C. airman earned his 1914 Star it is perhaps useful to consider the following list of towns from which No. 3 Squadron aircraft flew in those hectic first thirteen weeks of the war:—

Amiens	14 August
Maubeuge	17 August
Le Câteau	25 August
St. Quentin	26 August
Compiègne	27 August
Chantilly	31 August
Juilly	2 September
Serris (S.E. of Paris)	
Pezarches	
Coulommiers	
Fère en Tardenois	
Abbeville	October, 1914
St. Omer	and finally in November
Chocques	where they remained until the armistice in November, 1918.

Very soon after the outbreak of the war a small number of men (46) with specialist knowledge of airships were transferred into the Royal Naval Air Service and most earned 1914 Stars in that branch of the service. They were all given new numbers in the range 657 to 702. When transferred back to the Royal Air Force they were again re-numbered, as all ex RNAS men were, by having '200' added before their ex-RNAS number 37 (R.F.C.) (Arvoy B.) became 672 (RNAS) then 200672 RAF.

It would be interesting to know his reaction. (A numerical list of their original R.F.C. numbers follows:—

6, 13, 16, 20, 24, 37, 44, 67, 74, 81, 82, 83, 85, 89, 113, 214, 222, 271, 282, 294, 301, 304, 324, 325, 340, 360, 366, 390, 396, 421, 425, 446, 451, 455, 462, 463, 487, 499, 508, 515, 532, 708, 720, 788, 945, 989.)

An Explanation of the Items in the Roll

I T WILL be seen that the recipients of eight of the early numbers have not been identified, there being, apparently, no reference to them in any existing document. Apart from the HQ Daily Routine Orders, there is virtually no paperwork surviving from before the beginning of 1913, and the most probable explanation for these nameless numbers is that the men concerned left the RFC within a few weeks of joining, either by buying themselves out under King's Regulations 392 (v) (See Appendix 5), or by being discharged by the authorities as being 'unlikely to become an efficient soldier.' However, we have traced perhaps seven names for which we have no confirmed number so have almost achieved success. See No. 88 for details.

NAME

One of the difficulties of making an accurate list of names has been the habit of RFC clerks of using not only different spellings of surnames but of giving sometimes wildly differing initials to the same man on successive rolls. Even the 1918 Muster Roll (see below), is not infallible, and in the cases of men whose names do not appear on that roll, only the appearance of their medals, or information from their descendants, will settle some of the queries which arise.

RANK

The initial rank shown is normally that held at the outbreak of war, with the obvious exception of men who left the service before August, 1914, and those few men at the end of the list who did not enlist until a day or two after the 4th of August.

With the rapid expansion of the RFC as soon as hostilities commenced, many men were promoted within a week or two of the 4th of August, and some will have a higher rank on their 1914 Star than is shown on this list, having been promoted before leaving England. Unlike the 1914-18 War and Victory Medals, the 1914 and 1914-15 Stars show the rank held by the man concerned when he first entered a theatre of war.

SQUADRON

The remarks in the previous paragraph apply also to the men's squadrons, No. 7 in particular being rapidly denuded of its personnel in order to bring other squadrons up to War Establishment strength, particularly as the various units prepared to move to France.

Many of the men who were sent on courses at the Central Flying School do not appear on squadron rolls, and account in some instances, for a lack of entry in this section.

DATE OF JOINING

In most cases this date is the date of joining the Army, either directly into the RFC or (particularly in the earliest days) in a previous unit, but in a few cases this date would seem to be that of transfer to the RFC. It could be significant that the Muster Roll of April, 1918 uses the phrase 'date of joining' and not 'date of enlistment.'

PREVIOUS UNIT

As will be seen, many of the first 70–80 men of the RFC were from the Air Battalion, RE, after which the intakes to the Corps were a mixture of recruits from civilian life and transfers from other Army units, with a surprising proportion from the Brigade of Guards.

RANK AT 1ST APRIL, 1918

On the formation of the Royal Air Force on 1st April, 1918, a Muster Roll (PRO reference AIR 1/819/BOX) was published giving details of every ranker then serving in the new force who had previously served in the RFC or the RNAS. The ex-RFC men retained their original numbers, but as the RNAS numbering had also started at No. 1, all RNAS men transferred to the RAF had 200000 added to their original numbers, a fact which can often be seen when the Star of an RNAS/RAF man is compared with his War and Victory Medals.

Since this Muster Roll listed only those men serving in the ranks on 1st April, 1918, it follows that there are gaps in the numbering, for various reasons. Many men had gained commissions, some had died or been discharged through wounds or sickness, and numbers of unskilled men had been compulsorily transferred to the Army, particularly at the end of 1917 and the beginning of 1918.

A new system of ranks was introduced (see Appendix 6), with many men receiving promotion under the new organisation.

The 1918 Muster Roll also indicates the date of the last promotion. In a few cases this is marked with the symbol meaning 'reverted,' presumably from an earlier, higher rank.

TRADE AT 1ST APRIL, 1918

As with the rank system, the names and pay of the various trades were widely altered on the creation of the RAF, sometimes to avoid friction between men of the two original services, who had been doing similar work, but under different nomenclature and rank structures.

NOTES

The main information gleaned refers to promotions, casualties and gallantry awards, before, during, and after the war, although no category can hope to achieve anything like completion.

Explanations for pre-war discharges are given in Appendix 'A,' where para. 392 of *King's Regulations* is summarised.

With regard to men with remarks after their names, many, as already explained, probably gained commissions, but as the *London Gazette* announcements of their first commissions give no details of their service in the ranks it is impossible, with comparatively common names, to be certain that the new 2/Lt had, in fact, been a particular ranker of the RFC. We have, therefore, put in as 'possible' the commissioning dates of RFC officers whose surnames and initials agree with men missing from the April, 1918 Muster Roll, and here again the medal group may be the only way of confirming the commission of any individual. The Army Medal Forms, now available at the PRO are a useful, but not invariable, source of information.

The list of honours must always remain incomplete although we have searched through (among other lists) 115,000 Military Medals where the RFC was usually classed in the Honours Lists as an Army unit, with recipients named alphabetically, and not in regimental order. The D.C.M. and M.S.M. awards are however believed to be a complete record.

Mention is made in the text of the 'Silver War Badge.' The following Army Order, number 56 of 1917, explains who was entitled to this silver lapel badge, designed to identify those, now in civilian clothes, who had served their country since the outbreak of war in the armed forces:—

> 'His Majesty the King has approved of the Silver War Badge granted under Army Order 316 of 1916, being issued to officers and men of the British, Indian and Overseas Forces who have served since the 4th August, 1914, and who, in the case of officers, have retired or relinquished their commissions, or, in the case of men, have been discharged from the Army, on account of old age, wounds or sickness, such as would render them permanently unfit for further military service, provided their claims are approved by the Army Council.'

In 1922 the RAF started to compile a list 'Airmen Died in the Great War' similar to that produced by the Army, but despite the small numbers involved, compared with the Army's losses, the governmental economies of the Geddes Axe decreed that the country could not afford the few thousand pounds required to print such a work. As in 1945, post-war government put financial economy before honour to the men who had so recently been hailed as heroes, thereby making a complete and accurate list of deaths a near-impossibility. However, we are very grateful to the staff of the Commonwealth War Graves Commission for the help they gave us in establishing the details which are included in this work relevant to fatalities.

Acknowledgements

We should like to acknowledge the help and interest of the following, who supplied information, photographs and valued advice during the preparation of this book. Without them it would have been incomplete and much less interesting:—

Mr. Eric C. Shrewsbury (Formerly No. 979, R.F.C.)
Mr. A. F. Cormack, R.A.F. Museum, Hendon
Mr. Frank Olivant
Wing Commander J. Routledge
Squadron Leader G. J. Coldron
Mr. Chris Bate
Mr J. M. Hawkins, J.P.
Mr. Mike Blackburn
Mr. Richard Lynes
Mr. Robert Lynes
Flight Lieutenant P. W. Philips
Mr. Mark Abbott
The Revd. B. P. R. Pegg
Mr. Bernard Austerberry
Squadron Leader W. B. Sowerby, M.V.O.
Mr. Jack Bruce
Mr. Stewart Leslie

Messrs. G. Allsop, D. J. Barnes, D. J. Blackmore, J. Bradshaw, E. Boxall, M. Carter, R. Cornish, H. Cuming, M. Cutler, H. Carr, M.B.E., M. Dalzell, D. W. Davison, Mrs. J. Done, Messrs. S. W. Edwards, N. A. Gilham, N. G. Gooding, M. Hills, R. Keay, P. Kemp, D. Langham, L. Langlade, A. Langweiler, G. Moss, A. A. Mount, A. N. McClenaghan, Sqn. Ldr. G. Newbury, Messrs. P. Oliver, R. Perkins, J. C. Prior, S. Pile, N. Rigg, I. Rowbottom, A. Stanistreet, A. Stevens, F. Stevens, J. Taylor, E. J. Warren and G. W. Whitehead.

Our thanks go also to two others without whose work we might never have started—or finished; Miss Fiona McInnes, who typed all the early manuscripts and tabulations, and Jim Balmer of Langlands Edition, whose company styled the book. His help and advice were invaluable.

29

GROUP PHOTOGRAPH NO. 1

CONCENTRATION CAMP AT NETHERAVON

Rear, standing, left to right:—
984 SGT.-MAJ. WILFORD, 182 F/SGT. LACY,
202 F/SGT. BROCKBANK, 118 F/SGT. HILLIAR, 9 F/SGT. JILLINGS,
107 F/SGT. BRUCE, 26 F/SGT. RIDD, 241 F/SGT. CARTER,
119 F/SGT. NICHOLLS, 8 SGT.-MAJ. UNWIN.

Front, seated, left to right:—
7 SGT.-MAJ. THOMAS, 808 SGT.-MAJ. PARKER,
3 SGT.-MAJ. RAMSEY, COLONEL SYKES (Commanding Officer
RFC), 4 SGT.-MAJ. FLETCHER, 12 SGT.-MAJ. MEASURES,
2 SGT.-MAJ. STARLING.

GROUP PHOTOGRAPH No. 2

(See key for identification of numbers)

CONCENTRATION CAMP AT NETHERAVON

(1) LG. ART. MCKENNA, (2) 9 F/SGT. JILLINGS, (3) 984 SGT.-MAJ. WILFORD, (4) 8 SGT.-MAJ. UNWIN, (5) 808 SGT.-MAJ. PARKER, (6) LG. ART. POWELL, (7) 3 SGT.-MAJ. RAMSEY, (8) COL. SYKES (Commanding Officer), (9) LT. BARRINGTON-KENNETT (Adjutant), (10) 4 SGT.-MAJ. FLETCHER, (11) 7 SGT.-MAJ. THOMAS, (12) 12 SGT.-MAJ. MEASURES, (13) LG. ART. BEEBY, (14) 2 SGT.-MAJ. STARLING, (15) 119 F/SGT. NICHOLLS, (16) 149 F/SGT. LONG, (17) 64 SGT. MULLEN, (18) 901 SGT. MITCHELL, (19) 816 SGT. SAYWOOD, (20) 107 F/SGT. BRUCE, (21) 202 F/SGT. BROCKBANK, (22) 118 F/SGT. HILLIER, (23) 132 SGT. BULLEN, (24) 77 SGT. HUDSON, (25) 11 SGT. BAXTER, (26) 116 SGT. BULLOCK, (27) 241 F/SGT. CARTER, (28) 26 F/SGT. RIDD, (29) 61 SGT. MCCUDDEN, (30) 437 SGT. TRAILL, (31) 224 SGT. STREET, (32) 260 SGT. METHERY, (33) 251 SGT. KEMPER, (34) 56 SGT. KESZLER, (35) 10 SGT. WADDINGTON, (36) 247 SGT. BATEMAN, (37) 197 SGT. ELLARD, (38) 257 SGT. VALSEY, (39) SGT. MILES (ASC), (40) SGT. SMITH (RE), (41) 14 SGT. EDWARDS, (42) 254 SGT. PORTER, (43) 752 SGT. PAGE, (44) 333 SGT. BAUGHAN, (45) 34 SGT. LITTLE, (46) 108 SGT. SMITH, (47) 18 SGT. CULLEN, (48) 605 SGT. FELSTEAD, (49) 259 SGT. COX, (50) 652 SGT. MOTTRAM, (51) 1112 SGT. FULTON, (52) 150 SGT. BULLOCK, (53) 306 SGT. TINDALE, (54) 16 SGT. BARNES, (55) 751 SGT. FARRER, (56) 266 SGT. ASPINALL, (57) 334 SGT. LAWS, (58) 1191 SGT. PETCH, (59) 279 SGT. KING, (60) 1232 SGT. HARGREAVES, (61) 957 SGT. PATTERSON, (62) 307 SGT. ARCHBOLD, (63) 25 SGT. GOODCHILD, (64) 21 SGT. SLADE, (65) 442 SGT. MCCARTHY, (66) 261 SGT. SEDGER, (67) 163 SGT. O'REILLY, (68) 142 SGT. MCEVOY, (69) 29 SGT. TAYLOR, (70) 69 SGT. SPENCER, (71) 15 SGT. HUGHES, (72) 716 SGT. MILLETT, (73) 36 SGT. GROU, (74) 297 SGT. ANGELL, (75) 152 SGT. JAMES, (76) 41 SGT. BREADING, (77) 296 SGT. HOFFMAN, (78) 255 SGT. HAYWARD, (79) 445 SGT. CAMPBELL, (80) 54 SGT. JONES.

GROUP PHOTOGRAPH No. 3

SECOND SQUADRON R.F.C, MONTROSE

Top row:—
SERGTS. KEMPNER (251), KESZLER (56), MEAD (270),
BORNE (450?), MULLEN (64), NETHEY (104), HATCHETT (28).

Second row:—
SERGTS. ASPINALL (266), SMITH (108), BAXTER (11), JILLINGS (9),
RUMBOLD (162), FELSTEAD (605).

Third Row:—
SERGT.-MAJ. FLETCHER (4), LIEUT. MacLEAN, CAPT. TUCKER,
CAPT. BECKE, MAJ. BURKE, C.O., CAPT. LONGCROFT,
CAPT. MacDONELL, LIEUT. HARVEY,
SERGT.-MAJ. MEASURES (12).

Sitting on ground:—
LIEUTS. DAWES, MARTYN, and CAPT. WALDRON.

.

In due course, the authors intend to publish an
addendum listing additional information and details of
more extant medal groups as they surface.
With this in mind, we would be very pleased to hear,
from any source, of new sightings or fresh data on any of
the men in this book.

Abbreviations of Ranks, Trades, etc.

* An asterisk before the number denotes that the man was entitled to the 1914 Star

A/	Acting	Clk	Clerk (1st, 2nd & 3rd Class)
A/Comm	Air Commodore		
Acet Wdr	Acetylene Welder	CM	Chief Mechanic
Act	Acting	CMM	Chief Master Mechanic
AE	Aero Engines		
Aer Gnr	Aerial Gunner	Cpl	Corporal
A.F.C.	Air Force Cross	Cpl/M	Corporal/Mechanic
A.F.L.	Air Force List	CPO1, 2 or 3	Chief Petty Officer (1st, 2nd or 3rd class)
A.F.M.	Air Force Medal		
Air Bn	Air Battalion, RE (1911-12)		
		Cprsm	Coppersmith
AM	Air Mechanic (1st, 2nd & 3rd Class)	D.C.M.	Distinguished Conduct Medal
1, 2, 3AM	Air Mechanic (!st, 2nd & 3rd Class)	Discip	Disciplinary Branch
		D.S.M.	Distinguished Service Medal
A.M.O.	Air Ministry Order		
A.O.	Army Order	D.S.O.	Distinguished Service Order
A/Pk	Aircraft Park		
A/S Det	Airship Detachment	Dvr MT	Driver, Mechanical Transport
A/Ship	Airship		
AOC	Army Ordnance Corps	Dvr (P)	Driver, Petrol
		Electn	Electrician
Armr	Armourer	Equip Offr	Equipment Officer
ASC	Army Service Corps	Fab Wkr	Fabric Worker
AVM	Air Vice Marshal	F/Clk	Flight Clerk
BEF	British Expeditionary Force	F/Sgt	Flight Sergeant
		Ftr Aero	Fitter, aeroplanes
Blksm	Blacksmith	Ftr Eng Er MT	Fitter, (Engine) Erector (MT)
C&J	Carpenter & Joiner		
Carptr	Carpenter	Ftr Gen	Fitter, general
CEO	Commissioned Engineering Officer	Ftr MT	Fitter, motor transport
CFS	Central Flying School	FTS	Flying Training School
Ch Mech	Chief Mechanic	G/Capt	Group Captain
Ch Mr Mech	Chief Master Mechanic	GD	General Duties
		Hyd Wkr	Hydrogen Worker
		Inst Repr	Instrument Repairer

KBS (BP)	Kite-Balloon Section (Balloon Party)	RFA	Royal Field Artillery
K.I.A.	Killed in Action	RGA	Royal Garrison Artillery
K.R. 392	King's Regulations, para. 392 (see Appendix 5)	Rgr Aero	Rigger, aeroplanes
		RHA	Royal Horse Artillery
Lab	Labourer	RNAS	Royal Naval Air Service; officially 'RFC, Naval Wing'
L.G.	London Gazette		
L.S.&G.C.	Long Service & Good Conduct Medal	RTC	Royal Tank Corps
		S/Major	Sergeant Major
M.C.	Military Cross	Sgt	Sergeant
M.I.D.	Mentioned in Despatches	Sgt/M	Sergeant Mechanic
		SM1 & 2	Sergeant Major, 1st & 2nd Class (April 1919)
M/Cycl	Motor Cyclist		
Misc	Miscellaneous		
MM	Master Mechanic	SMW	Sheet Metal Worker
M.M.	Military Medal	SWO	Station Warrant Officer
Mr Clk	Master Clerk		
M.S.M.	Meritorious Service Medal	(T)	Technical
		T/	Temporary
MT	Mechanised Transport	Techn	Technician
		Tel Op	Telephone Operator
NCO	Non Commissioned Officer	Temp	Temporary
		Tin SMW	Tinsmith & Sheet Metal Worker
Obsvr	Observer		
OR	Other Rank(s)	V.C.	Victoria Cross
P/Driver	Petrol Driver	W/Comm	Wing Commander
Photogr	Photographer	*w.e.f.*	With effect from
PO	Petty Officer (RNAS)	Winch D/F	Winch Driver & Fitter
POW	Prisoner of War	W.O.	War Office
PRO	Public Records Office	WO	Warrant Officer
		WO1	Warrant Officer Class 1
Pte1 & 2	Private, 1st & 2nd Class	WO2 (Air)	A naval commissioned rank, not a warrant officer in the Army sense but a junior officer.
RAFVR	Royal Air Force Volunteer Reserve		
RAMC	Royal Army Medical Corps		
RE	Royal Engineers	WO(T)	Warrant Officer (Technical)
Rec Dep	Recruits Depot		
Res Aero Sqn	Reserve Aeroplane Squadron	W/Op	Wireless Operator

The Roll

★ An asterisk infront of the number denotes that the man was
entitled to the 1914 Star

When I Was a Boy

(Tune: 'When I Was a Boy' from 'HMS Pinafore' by
Gilbert and Sullivan.)

When I was a boy I went to war
As an Air Mechanic in the Flying Corps,
I dished out dope and I swung the prop,
And I polished up my talents in the Fitters' Shop;
And I did my work so carefully,
That now I'm a General at the Ministry.

As an Air Mechanic I made such a name,
A Sergeant-Major I soon became,
I wore a tunic and a Sam Browne belt
And my presence on parade was most acutely felt.
My presence was felt so overwhelmingly,
That now I'm a General at the Ministry.

As a Sergeant-Major I made such a hit,
That I demanded further scope to do my bit.
Of my lofty ways there was never any doubt.
And they sent me up in a Nieuport Scout.
I flew so well over land and sea,
That now I'm a General at the ministry.

I flew in France with such amazing zest,
That the King grew tired of adorning my chest,
People boosted McCudden, Bishop and Ball,
But readily agreed that I out-soared them all;
My merits were declared so overwhelmingly,
That now I'm a General at the Ministry.

So mechanics all, wherever you be
If you want to climb to the top of the tree,
If your soul isn't fettered to a pail of dope,
Just take my tip – there's always hope.
Be smart in the Strand at saluting me,
And you'll all be Generals at the Ministry.

Part 1
Numbers 1 to 103
May—June 1912

The men transferred from other Corps and Regiments of the Army. These are mainly from the Royal Engineers (Air Battalion) and joined the RFC in May or June, 1912.

1. H. EDWARDS

Joined the Army in 1895 and subsequently served in the Airship Detachment of the Royal Engineers. Was appointed a Sergeant Major in the RFC on 13 May 1912. Court Martialled and reduced to Sergeant 15 August, 1913. Discharged at his own request 16 October, 1913, and after 18 years service, with a view to a pension.

★ 2. J. STARLING

A member of the Royal Engineers from 1895 prior to his transfer to the RFC. Serving at South Farnborough from 29 July, 1912 and was living in married quarters at Farnborough Common in October, 1913. Mentioned by McCudden V.C. in *'Flying Fury.'* His Army L.S.&G.C. medal awarded in Army Order 117 of April, 1913 was named to him as Quarter Master Sergeant RFC. He earned a 1914 Star with the Aircraft Park, in France from 16 August, 1914. Commissioned Lieutenant and Quarter Master 1 March, 1915. Mentioned in despatches *London Gazette* 15 June, 1916, and 11 December, 1917. Promoted Temp Lieutenant Colonel 15 December, 1917. Promoted Hon Captain 1 March, 1918. In the 1924 Army List he is shown as a Temp Lieutenant Colonel in the Army on retired pay and as having earned a Queen's South Africa medal with clasps Cape Colony, Orange Free State and Relief of Ladysmith, and King's South Africa medal. (Group photographs 1 and 2.)

★ 3. JOHN RAMSEY

As 1015 Cpl 9 Coy RE, he earned a Queen's South Africa Medal, and later transferred to the Air Battalion when he was a Sergeant in 2 Balloon Company, later was CSM, 2 Company Balloon School. His promotion from Corporal to Sergeant was due to saving the *'Nulli Secundus'* Airship during a storm at Crystal Palace on 10 October, 1907 when it broke away from its mooring and Cpl Ramsey, after opening escape valves, found it too slow so split the nose using a knife tied to the end of a long pole.

NULLI SECUNDUS

Sergeant Major RFC from 13 May 1912 on Salisbury Plain. Mentioned by McCudden V.C. in *'Flying Fury.'* A keen motorcyclist. At Netheraven in 1913. He served in France from 12 August, 1914 initially with 3

Squadron. He was awarded his Military Cross as *Sgt Major* RFC in *L.G.* 1 January, 1915 (see also No. 808 Parker), mentioned in despatches 19 October, 1914, 1 January, 1915 and 1 January, 1916. Commissioned Lieutenant and Quarter Master 1 March, 1915 he was later promoted to Temp Captain and QM RFC. His medal group is known to be in a private collection. (Sold Spink and Son 1966 for £65 and Glendinings 1973 for £90). (Military Cross, Queen's South Africa Medal (Cape Colony, Orange Free State, Transvaal, South Africa 1901 – Cpl RE). 1914 Star and bar trio with M.I.D. oak leaf (*S Maj* RFC and Captain RFC). Not in 1921 *Air Force List.* (Group photographs 1 and 2.)

⋆ 4. ALBERT FLETCHER

Born Plumstead, Kent January, 1881. Enlisted 1899 into the RE as a driver. Previously served in the Air Battalion RE in 1911 was a CQMS. Sgt Major RFC *w.e.f.* 13 May 1912 at Montrose. He was awarded Royal Aero Club Aviators' Certificate No. 519 on 16 June, 1913 in a Maurice Farman at that station. Earned his 1914 Star and bar as Sergt Major Aircraft Park in France from 16 August, 1914. Commissioned Lieutenant and

QM 23 August, 1914. Awarded M.C. in 1917. Promoted Hon Capt 30 August, 1917. In 1918 Air Force list is shown as Temp Brigadier General *w.e.f.* 1 April, 1918. Order of St Michael and St George (Companion) and Order of British Empire (Commander) both 1919. In 1921 *A.F.L.* was Wing Commander C.M.G., C.B.E., M.C. commanding the Aircraft Park in Iraq. He was promoted Group Captain 30 June, 1922, Deputy Director of Organisation Air Ministry 1928-30, and retired 1 July, 1930 an Honorary Air Commodore. Deputy Director of Personnel at Air Ministry 1939-43, AOC-in-C Admin. Transport Command 1943-44, again retired 1945, when he was Deputy Senior Air Staff officer as liaison between Transport Command and BOAC. Died, aged 74 at Neasden, Middlesex in 1955. At Seaby's in 1969 his C.M.G., C.B.E., M.C. and British War Medal and Victory medal (named to Lt Col RFC) were sold for £47.10.0. They are now in the same collection as No. 3. (Group photographs 1, 2 and 3.)

5. W. E. MOORE

Enlisted 9 December, 1889. As 24407 2nd Cpl RE earned Queen's South Africa Medal (clasps Johannesburg, Cape Colony, Orange Free State, and South Africa 1901) with 1 Balloon Section RE. Awarded Edward VII Army L.S.&G.C. in December, 1907, and at the mobilisation of the Air Battalion was Sergeant 1 Balloon Company (Dismounted) and later with 3 Company, Balloon School. He transferred to RFC 13 May 1912 and was Sergeant Major at South Farnborough from 17 August, 1912, and is noted as living in married quarters on Farnborough Common in October, 1913. At the outbreak of WW1 was Sergeant Major 6 Squadron and earned a 1914/15 Star trio, serving abroad from 12 December, 1915. He was mentioned in despatches in the *London Gazette* of 4 January, 1917 and 1 January, 1919. For services in the war he was awarded a French Médaille d'Honneur en vermail in August, 1918, an RAF Meritorious Service

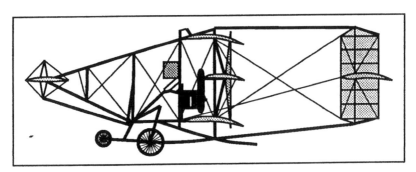

CODY CATHEDRAL

Medal (*L.G.* 1 January, 1919) and a Rumanian Barbatie Si Credenta when in 9 Squadron (*L.G.* 15 July, 1919). In the first RAF Nominal Roll he is shown as a Disciplinary Sergeant Major 1st Class. He came from Bournemouth. His Star is known in a private collection.

★ 6. GEORGE JAMES SQUIRES

Enlisted 1895. As 28462 Corporal 1 Balloon Section RE he earned a Queen's South Africa Medal (clasp South Africa 1901). He was Sergeant (No. 28009) at the Balloon School on the mobilisation of the Air Battalion. On 13 May, 1912 he transferred to the RFC from No. 8410 Sergeant Major. He was a Sergeant Major at South Farnborough from 25 November, 1912 when he earned his Army L.S.&G.C. in Army Order 117 of April, 1913. With Sergeant Majors Starling, Moore and Thomas he was one of only four RFC non-commissioned men living in married quarters on Farnborough Common in October, 1913. He earned a 1914 Star and bar as Sergeant Major, Airship Detachment, then on 18 October, 1914 transferred to RNAS at Dunkirk as No. 661 CPO (Mech). Promoted WO2 25 November, 1914 and WO1 RNAS 30 June, 1917. He was commissioned Lieutenant RAF 1 April, 1918 (Technical Branch). In the November, 1921 *A.F.L.* he is shown as a Flying Officer with an Air Force Cross (*L.G.* 10 October, 1919) and was at the Aircraft Depot Hitchin *w.e.f.* 4 February, 1921. By 1931 he was discharged and employed by the RAF Works and Building Staff Dept as a Civil Engineer.

★ 7. WILLIAM THOMAS

Born Godalming, 31 October, 1883. Formerly 21613 Staff Sergeant RE, he transferred on probation to the RFC 13 May, 1912. He was awarded Royal Aero Club Aviators' Certificate No. 276 still in the Royal Engineers on 3 September, 1912 on Salisbury Plain in a Short. On 25 November, 1912 he was promoted Sergeant Major RFC at the same station. Sergeant Major (Pilot) at Farnborough in 1913. (See group photograph on following page). He was one of four RFC Sergeant Majors living in married quarters on Farnborough Common in October, 1913. As Sergeant Major 4 Squadron he went to France 12 August, 1914 and earned a 1914 Star. He was commissioned Lieutenant and Quarter Master RFC

29 August, 1915 and was mentioned in despatches and awarded a Military Cross in *L.G.* 1 January, 1917. In the April, 1918 *Air Force List* he is shown as Captain RAF. In 1921 *A.F.L.* he was Squadron Leader (T) *w.e.f.* 1 November, 1919 at Central Flying School Upavon from 12 August, 1919. After 15 September, 1928 he served at No. 1 Stores depot, Kidbroke (February, 1938 *A.F.L.*). See *'Cross and Cockade,'* Volume 7 No. 3 page 135, Group Photographs 1 and 2.

★ 8. FREDERICK HENRY UNWIN

Born London 22 February, 1882. Formerly 21259 Staff Sergeant Air Battalion RE he transferred to RFC on 21 February, 1913 and was promoted Sergeant Major 18 April, 1913 on Salisbury Plain. He earned his 1914 Star *w.e.f.* 12 August, 1914 as Sergeant Major 3 Squadron nine days after gaining his Royal Aero Club Aviators' Certificate (No. 862) in a Maurice Farman at Netheravon. Awarded a French Médaille Militaire for gallantry 21 to 30 August, 1914, in *London Gazette* 9 November, 1914. He was commissioned Lieutenant and Quarter Master 1 March, 1915. Wounded in June, 1915 he was promoted Captain 1 March, 1918. In the 1918 *A.F.L.* he is shown as Major ('Technical). In 1921 *Air Force*

639 YATES, 208 HUNTER, 7 THOMAS

List was a Squadron Leader (Technical) O.B.E. *w.e.f.* 26 April, 1920 at Aircraft Depot Egypt. In 1931 he was a Wing Commander at RAF Cairo on Engineering Staff Duties from 19 April, 1929 with Seniority of 1 January, 1926. In 1938 he was a Technical Officer, Wing Commander (Retd) at RAF Cardington. Group Photographs 1 and 2.

* 9. DAVID SAMUEL JILLINGS

Born June, 1881. Next of kin, father, Alfred Jillings, Hanley Place Brook St, Brentwood Essex (a substantial residence, Brook St was a village on the Chelmsford Road to Warley Barracks). Enlisted 11 November, 1899 initially for three years, and nine on the reserve. Lance Sergeant December, 1902. Passed cookery course at Aldershot January, 1905 and the Hythe Musketry course (Distinguished) August, 1907. Promoted Sergeant February, 1907 having passed for promotion in August, 1903. Re-engaged for 21 years November, 1908. Transferred to the RFC 21 January, 1913. Formerly 8410 Sergeant 3/Grenadier Guards. Flight Sergeant in May 1914. Appointed 11 August, 1914 Sergeant Major 2 Squadron. Earned 1914 Star and bar in France from 12 August, 1914.

Wounded by enemy rifle fire from the ground in the upper extremity of the thigh, whilst flying as an observer 22 August, 1914, with Lieutenant M. Noel, near Maubeuge. Driven to Paris by 480 Alderton rather than report to a First Aid Station. As a Sergeant Major, recommended for a Victoria Cross. One vital distinction still preserved when the idea of accepting acts of duty as eligible for the award of the Cross was adopted,

156 WRIGHT, 224 STREET, 61 McCUDDEN

was that the person concerned could be regarded as a free agent. This was, of course, before the institution of the new Warrant which was read as covering acts of duty, but the same reasoning was clearly at work in the rejection of the recommendation of a V.C. for Sergeant Major Jillings, who since he was serving as the observer in his aircraft, it was 'not considered that he was sufficiently free agent for it to be established that ... he was acting on his own initiative.' (taken from the initial set of recommendation for the V.C. made by Sir John French from France in 1914, (391 PRO, WO 32/4993)). He was recommended to receive the D.C.M. but then the M.C. was introduced and one was awarded to him.

Mentioned in despatches in the *London Gazette* 8 October, 1914, 4 December, 1914, 1 January, 1915 and 4 August, 1915. Commissioned 2 Lieutenant 11 December, 1914. Military Cross *L.G.* 1 January, 1915. (See also No. 808 Parker). Royal Aero Club Aviators' Certificate No. 1178 on 15 April, 1915. Later Captain West Yorkshire Regiment and RFC. 1918 *A.F.L.* Flight Lieutenant. 1921 *A.F.L.*, *w.e.f.* 1 June, 1920 at RAF (Cadet) College, Cranwell. Retired (Acting Squadron Leader) 1 October, 1926. In the Reserve of Air Force Officers in this rank 1 February, 1936. In 1937 *A.F.L.* was Honourary Squadron Leader M.B.E., M.C. Personnel Staff 2 (Bomber) Group HQ Andover Hants. No. 02194 in 1946 *A.F.L.* (Retd) still Squadron Leader. Group Photographs 1, 2 and 3.

★ 10. WILLIAM JAMES WADDINGTON

Born Longsight, Manchester, 20 September, 1882. Attested 22 January, 1900 at Bury, a plumber by trade. Served originally in the Volunteers and fought in South Africa as No. 8807, No. 1 Volunteer Service Company, Lancashire Fusiliers and was the senior NCO. Went out again in 1901 with No. 3 Company. Later 10482, Sgt 3/Grenadier Guards he transferred to the RFC on 29 January, 1913. Royal Aero Club Aviators' Certificate 573 on 28 July, 1913 at Upavon in a Short. Earned 1914 Star and bar as Sgt 4 Squadron, in France from 9 September, 1914. Mentioned in despatches as *Sgt Major L.G.* 22 June, 1915. Commissioned Hon Lieut (QM) 13 August, 1915. 1918 *A.F.L.* Captain temp Major (Technical) November, 1921 *A.F.L.*, Squadron Leader, O.B.E. at the Stores Depot, Egypt from 29 May 1920. 1938 *A.F.L.* Squadron Ldr (E) (Retd) seniority

1 January, 1921. His medal group is known in a private collection:—
O.B.E. (*L.G.* 3 June, 1919 as Captain RAF), Queen's South Africa Medal
Cape Colony, Orange Free State, Transvaal, Laings Nek, South Africa
1901, South Africa 1902. (Sgt Vol Company Lancashire Fusiliers). 1914
Star and bar (Sgt RFC) British War Medal and Victory Medal (Captain
RFC). See group photograph No. 2.

* ii. J. Baxter

Enlisted into the Royal Engineers in 1896. Earned Queen's South Africa
Medal with clasps including Defence of Ladysmith serving with the
Balloon Company. Was 29281 Sgt No. 1 Balloon Company on mobilisation
of the Air Battalion and earned his Army L.S.&G.C. Medal as Sgt RFC
in Army Order 99 of April, 1914. He went to France on 13 August, 1914
as Flight Sgt. 2 Squadron and earned his 1914 Star trio. Awarded Royal
Aero Club Aeronauts' Certificate No. 98 on 12 October, 1916 as Sergeant
Major and commissioned 2 Lieut RFC the same day. In 1918 *A.F.L.* was

Lieutenant RAF (Balloon Section). In 1937 *A.F.L.* is shown as Flight
Lieutenant (E) (ret). (See group photographs 2 and 3.)

★ 12. ARTHUR HAROLD MEASURES

Born 20 February, 1882 at Upton, Nottingham. Educated Southwell Collegiate Grammar School, Nottingham. Married 1906. Enlisted into RE (Air Battalion) 1912. Was Sgt Major RFC *w.e.f.* 7 February, 1913 at Montrose. Earned Royal Aero Club Aviators' Certificate No. 520 on 16 June, 1913 in a Maurice Farman at that station. In France as Sgt Major 2 Squadron *w.e.f.* 12 August, 1914 earning a 1914 Star trio. French Médaille Militaire for Gallantry 21-30 August, 1914 in *L.G.* 9 November, 1914. Commissioned Lt and QM 1 March, 1915 and promoted Captain 1 March, 1918. In 1918 *A.F.L.* shown as Major temp Lieut Colonel, O.B.E. Retired June, 1930. In 1937 *A.F.L.* shown as Squadron Ldr O.B.E. (Retd) acting Wing Commander with seniority to 1 April, ·1918. No 01205 1946 *A.F.L.* (Retd) Wing Commander (acting). To Imperial Airways as Divisional Engineer, East Africa (1932). Operations Manager, India (1933) Railway Air Service, (1934). Manager Scottish Airways (1937), later Director Isle of Man Air Services and then 1946-56 Board Member British European Airways Corporation. O.B.E. 1945. Lived Ewell, Surrey and died 12 June, 1969. (See group photographs 1, 2 and 3.)

★ 13. ALLEN LANMAN

Entitled to Queen's South Africa Medal (clasps Cape Colony and South Africa 1902) as Sapper then L/Cpl Balloon Repair Factory. Was 1679 Cpl 1st Balloon Company RE (Dismounted) on mobilisation of Air Battalion. To RFC 13 May 1912. Earned both Royal Aero Club Airship Certificate No. 9 and Royal Aero Club Aeronauts' Certificate No. 23 on 2 July, 1912 as a Sergeant. Earned 1914 Star and bar as Flight Sgt Airship Detachment. Transferred to RNAS on 18 October, 1914 as No. 660 CPO2 (Mech), and promoted WO2 (RNAS) 17 April, 1915. Awarded RN L.S.&G.C. Medal (GV) (Warrant Officer Class 2).1918 *A.F.L.* Lieutenant (Airships). Flying Officer A.F.C. (1919) (Airship Officer) in November, 1921 *A.F.L.* Employed at RAF Airship Base, Howden from 16 March, 1920. M.B.E. 1927. Retired 17 April, 1930. 1937 *A.F.L.* Flight Lieut (Retd) and in 1946 *A.F.L.* as Flying Officer, A.F.C., M.B.E. (retired, General Duties). Group known: A.F.C., M.B.E., Queen's South Africa Medal (Cape Colony and

South Africa 1902), 1914 Star (660 CPO2 RNAS) War and Victory Medals, RN L.S.&G.C. (GV).

⋆ 14. FRANK EDWARDS

Enlisted 31 July, 1895. 28579 Cpl Balloon School on mobilisation of Air Battalion. Transferred to RFC 13 May 1912 as Sgt Airship Detachment. Army L.S.&G.C. *A.O.* 99 of April, 1914. 1914 Star. To RNAS 18 October, 1914, WO2 (RNAS) 20 December, 1914, WO1 (RNAS) 30 June, 1917. In 1918 *A.F.L.* was Lieutenant, and was acting Captain 4 July, 1918. In November, 1921 *A.F.L.* was Flying Officer, HQ Command Tavistock Place London WC1 on Stores Staff Duties from 11 December, 1919. Retired 31 December, 1921 as Captain. In 1937 *A.F.L.* was Flying Officer (Retd) serving at No. 1 Royal Air Force Depot Uxbridge, as Captain (RAF ret.) Asst Barracks Officer. See group photograph No. 2.

⋆ 15. T. HUGHES

Enlisted 26 January, 1897. Formerly Cpl 2nd Balloon Company (Dismounted) RE, on 11 July, 1910 then Sgt 2 Company Balloon School (Dismounted) on mobilisation of Air Battalion RE. As a Sgt, Aircraft Park in France from 16 August, 1914 earned 1914 Star trio. Awarded D.C.M. as Flight Sgt *L.G.* 23 June, 1915 'For conspicuous zeal and devotion to duty, and the noticably efficient manner in which he has carried out his responsible duties.' Army L.S.&G.C. as Sgt RFC in *A.O.* 125 of April, 1917. He had been promoted Tech WO 19 August, 1916 and in the 1918 RAF Muster Roll was Chief Master Mechanic. See group photograph No. 2.

⋆ 16. A. A. BARNES

Sapper, Balloon School, on mobilisation of Air Battalion. He earned both Royal Aero Club Airship Certificate No. 14 and Royal Aero Club Aeronauts' Certificate No. 28 on 2 September, 1912 as a Sergeant. Transferred to RFC as Sergeant and in this rank served in France from 14 August, 1914 with 5 Squadron. Transferred to RNAS 18 April, 1915 as No. 670 and promoted temporary WO2 (RNAS) 18 January, 1917. 2 Lieutenant in 1918 RAF List (Technical). See group photograph No. 2.

★ 17. E. MALLETT

Enlisted 16 October, 1899. Was 3863 Cpl Balloon School RE on mobilisation of the Air Battalion. Sgt No. 5 Squadron in France from 14th August, 1914. Mentioned in despatches *London Gazette* 24 February, 1917 as Flight Sergeant (Acting/Sergeant Major) (Disciplinarian) from 1 June, 1916. Army L.S.&G.C. as Sgt RFC in *A.O.* 125 of April, 1918. In RAF Muster Roll 1 April, 1918 was SM1.

★ 18. CHARLES EDWIN CULLEN

Enlisted 31 December, 1896. Formerly 574 Corporal 3 Balloon Company RE (Dismounted) 11 July, 1910. Had served as a Bugler RE in South African War with Balloons. 1914 Star for service as Flight Sergeant with 2 Squadron in France from 12 August, 1914. M.I.D. *L.G.* 19 October, 1914 and 11 July, 1919. Army L.S.&G.C. in *A.O.* 134 of April, 1915 as Flight Sergeant RFC. Commissioned 2 Lieutenant 9 October, 1917. In November, 1921 *A.F.L.* was Flying Officer (Stores) seniority 20 July, 1920. Employed from 23 December, 1919 at Air Pilotage School (Cadre) Andover. Retired 30 October, 1927. In 1937 *Air Force List* Flight Lieutenant (E) (Retd) (seniority 1 January, 1924), serving then in Equipment Branch, Reception Depot, West Drayton, Group in Webb collection Queen's South Africa Medal (Bugler RE) clasps Defence of Ladysmith, Orange Free State, Laings Nek, Belfast, Cape Colony and South Africa 1901, 1914 Star and bar trio, Defence Medal and GV Army L.S.&G.C. See group photograph No. 2.

19. H. E. VAGG

Born Islington 18 February, 1881. Formerly 3209 Corporal No. 1 Balloon Company RE on mobilisation of Air Battalion then 2 Company Balloon School (Dismounted). Royal Aero Club Aviators' Certificate No. 443 on 18 March, 1913 as Sergeant RFC on Salisbury Plain (CFS) in a Short. Earned 1914/15 Star trio with service overseas from 2 April, 1915. Commissioned 2 Lieutenant RFC and Somerset Light Infantry 8 October, 1915 'for services in the Field.' Mentioned in despatches *London Gazette* 15 June, 1916. Promoted Major 1 May, 1917.

★ 20. HUGH McGRANE

Born Athboy, County Meath 11 February, 1880. As 3259 Sapper No. 4 Balloon Section RE earned China 1900 medal. Was Corporal 1 Balloon Company RE (Dismounted) on mobilisation of Air Battalion. Earned Royal Aero Club Aeronauts' Certificate No. 26 and Royal Aero Club Airship Certificate No. 12 on 30 July, 1912 as a Sergeant, and at Central Flying School Upavon in a Maurice Farman as a Flight Sergeant awarded Royal Aero Club Aviators' Certificate No. 861 on 30 July, 1914. Earned 1914 Star as Flight Sergeant Aircraft Park in France from 16 August, 1914. To RNAS as No. 659 18 April, 1915, WO2 (Airships) 19 April, 1915 and WO1 (Airships) 31 December, 1917. In 1918 was RAF (Dirigible Officer). 1921 (November) *Air Force List* was Flying Officer (Airships) employed from 16 March, 1920 at RAF Airship Base, Howden. It is possible that if his mixed Army and Navy service was allowed to count he may have been entitled to a Naval L.S.&G.C.

★ 21. E. SLADE

Enlisted 21 February, 1901. Formerly 7825 2nd Corporal Balloon School RE on mobilisation of Air Battalion. *Sgt Aircraft Park RFC BEF France* from 16 August, 1914, earning 1914 star trio. Sgt Major from 1 June, 1917.

M.I.D. *L.G.* 13 March, 1918 as Temp SM 'For valuable services in the War' (U.K.). Also mentioned in the *Times* 'B' List 16 March, 1918. In 1918 RAF Muster Roll was SM1 (Discip). RAF L.S.&G.C. *w.e.f.* 26 February, 1919 (see No. 28). See group photograph No. 2.

22. WILLIAM GEORGE STAFFORD

Born Truro, Cornwall 22 November, 1879. As 1939 Sapper No. 4 Balloon section earned a China 1900 medal having enlisted in 1898. In July, 1910 was a 2nd Cpl with No. 2 Balloon Company (Dismounted) and was at the Balloon School on mobilisation of the Air Battalion. He was awarded his Royal Aero Club Aviators' Certificate No. 438 on 18 March, 1913 on Salisbury Plain in a Maurice Farman and was shown as a 2nd class flyer *w.e.f.* 23 October, 1913. He served overseas from 8 November, 1915 earning a 1914/15 star. In the *L.G.* 16 May, 1916 his D.C.M. was awarded (14 Squadron RFC) 'Flight Sgt (A/SM). For consistent good work in connection with the care and repair of aeroplanes.' His Army L.S.&G.C. is in *A.O.* 125 April, 1917 (Sgt RFC). Commissioned 2 Lieutenant RFC 12 October, 1917 he was awarded a Military Cross in *L.G.* 8 August, 1917. In the 1918 *A.F.L.* he is shown as Lieutenant and in *L.G.* 2 September, 1924 Flying Officer Stafford was awarded the Order of El Nahda by the King of Hedjaz. He served in Arabia with Captain T. E. Lawrence giving air support to the Arab Forces under Sherif Feisal, in 14 Squadron, with four old B.E. machines under Major Ross RFC. Stafford's M.C. appeared in the same gazette as Lawrence's C.B. and Ross's D.S.O. Stafford and his mechanic almost died when lost in the desert for some days until rescued by Bedouins. Post War he was attached to the Marine and Armament Experimental Establishment (RAF) Isle of Grain from 1

February, 1921. 1921 (November) *A.F.L.* was Flying Officer seniority 1 August, 1919, and retired a Flight Lieutenant in 1927. He died a year later. His group of eight medals was sold for £2,200 at Christies in March, 1988:— M.C. (Engraved Lieut. Wm. G. Stafford RFC 3.6.17), Distinguished Conduct Medal (GVR. 22 Fl. Sgt. No. 14 Sgt. RFC), China 1900 no clasp (Sapr RE), 1914/15 Star (S. Maj. RFC), British War Medal and Victory medal, M.I.D. oakleaf (Lieut RAF), Army L.S.&G.C. Medal GVR (22 Sjt RFC), Hedjaz, Order of El Nahda, Fourth Class neck badge silver and enamels.

* 23. JOHN WILKINSON

Enlisted 7 February, 1903. Transferred from the Air Battalion, RE to the RFC on 13 May, 1912. He was promoted Sgt Major 3 October, 1914 and was in France with 6 Squadron from 6 October, 1914, earning a 1914 Star and bar trio. Mentioned in despatches *L.G.* 22 June, 1915. In the 1918 RAF Muster Roll he is listed as CMM. Awarded an RAF L.S.&G.C. *w.e.f.* 7 February, 1921 as SM1, he then served in Kurdistan (Nos 6, 30 and 63 Squadrons RAF 19 March, to 18 June, 1923), earning a General Service Medal with that clasp and an RAF Meritorious Service Medal (*L.G.* 11 June, 1924, page 4664), where he was again mentioned in despatches (*L.G.* 6 November, 1924).

24. BERTRAM SCOVELL

He earned a Queen's South Africa Medal prior to his enlistment into the Balloon Sections RE as 13081 Sapper on 27 October, 1903. He transferred from Balloon Company RE (2nd Cpl) in July, 1910 to Balloon School and from the Air Battalion to RFC 13 May, 1912. As a Sergeant, awarded both Royal Aero Club Airship Certificate No. 13 and Royal Aero Club Aeronauts' Certificate No. 27 on 3 September, 1912. As a Sergeant, Airship Detachment, transferred to RNAS as No. 657 18 October, 1914 and was WO2 18 January, 1917. May have been awarded Royal Naval L.S.&G.C. Awarded Air Force Cross as Pilot Officer in *L.G.* 3 June, 1919. 1921 *A.F.L.* (November), Flying Officer A.F.C. (Airships), from 12 April, 1920 employed at RAF Airship Base, Howden. Retired 16 August, 1922. 1938 *A.F.L.*, Flying Officer (Retd) seniority 1 October, 1919.

* 25. H. GOODCHILD

Enlisted as No. 190 RE 27 July, 1896. 2/Corporal 1 Balloon Company RE on mobilisation of Air Battalion in 1911. Sergeant by July, 1914. Earned

1914 Star and bar trio as Flight Sergeant *w.e.f.* 10 August, 1914. He was mentioned in despatches, 8 October, 1914 and 9 December, 1914, and reported as a Prisoner of War in November, 1915. In 1918 RAF Muster Roll he is shown as Flight Sergeant Kite Balloon Section (Balloon Party). Served with 47 Squadron in South Russia in 1919 and was awarded the Medal of Zeal with the ribbon of St. Stanislas (for services at Taranorog in November, 1919) in March, 1920. See group photograph No. 2.

★ 26. FRANK RIDD

Born Plymouth 2 April, 1884. Enlisted 17 July, 1903, and was formerly No. 12859, was L/Corporal 3 Balloon Company RE (Dismounted) in July, 1910 and transferred to the Air Battalion then RFC. Awarded first ever Royal Aero Club Aviators' Certificate No. 227 to an 'other rank,' as 2/Corporal RE 4 June, 1912, on Salisbury Plain in a Bristol. As Sergeant RFC was the first NCO Pilot in the Corps. Described by A.C.M. Sir Philip Joubert de la Ferté as 'my Flight Sergeant, a little slow and rather too gentle.' As Flight Sergeant 3 Squadron he earned a 1914 Star and bar from 12 August, 1914 and is then listed as a Prisoner of War, as

SGT. RIDD, THE FIRST N.C.O. IN THE BRITISH ARMY TO GAIN A PILOT'S CERTIFICATE, SEEN IN A MAURICE FARMAN

Temporary Sergeant Major (Technical) which rank he reached in March, 1916. In 1918 RAF Muster Roll is a Chief Master Mechanic (Technical). See Group Photographs 1 and 2.

27. J. RIGBY

Transferred from the Air Battalion to the RFC and was a Flight Sergeant in 1914. Commissioned 2 Lieutenant 12 October, 1916.

* 28. W. HATCHETT

Enlisted 3 April, 1900 and as a Boy RE earned Queen's South Africa Medal (clasp Cape Colony) and as a Sapper in the Balloon Repair Factory added the clasp South Africa 1901. Via the Air Battalion he was a Sgt in 2 Squadron in France from 12 August, 1914 earning a 1914 Star and bar trio. Promoted QMS 1 May 1918 he was awarded an RAF L.S.&G.C. as Master Mechanic (Tech) *w.e.f.* 3 April, 1918. (*A.O.* 1123 of October, 1919 which listed the first six RAF L.S.&G.C.s awarded) (the other five were Nos. 21. 30, 273, 835 and 1009, of which men Hatchett was the senior by length of service). See Group Photograph No. 3.

* 29. J. TAYLOR

Enlisted 9 November, 1903. Was No. 13112 L/Cpl with 3 Balloon Company RE (Dismounted) in July, 1910 and transferred to the RFC from the Air Battalion. In 1914 was a Sergeant in the Aircraft Park and was awarded a French Médaille Militaire. Promoted Flight Sgt (Rigger) 1 February, 1917, Chief Mechanic 1918 RAF Muster Roll. RAF L.S.&G.C. *w.e.f.* 9 November, 1921 as Flight Sergeant. See group photograph No. 2.

* 30. W. JONES

Enlisted 12 November, 1900. Home town Littlehampton. Formerly 7114 RE and served in South Africa. Was L/Cpl 2 Balloon Company (Dismounted) July, 1910 and with 2 Company Balloon School on mobilisation of the Air Battalion. Sgt 3 Squadron RFC in France from 13 August, 1914 (Star and bar). Mentioned in Despatches *L.G.* 8 October, 1914 and promoted Temp Sgt Major from 1 June, 1916. Awarded Serbian Cross of Karageorge (1st Class) *L.G.* 15 February, 1917 (148 Squadron). Chief Master Mechanic in 1918 RAF Muster Roll. RAF L.S.&G.C. awarded *w.e.f.* 12 November, 1918 (see No. 28) RAF Meritorious Service

Medal in *L.G.* 3 June, 1919. His group of medals were noted as extant in 1986:— Queen's South Africa Medal, 1914 Star and bar trio (M.I.D.), RAF M.S.M., RAF L.S.&G.C., Karageorge with Swords.

31. HENRY TOM HAMILTON COPELAND

Born 3 August, 1889. 13764 L/Cpl Balloon School on mobilisation of Air Battalion. Re-engaged 22 May 1913 to complete 21 years. Sgt in 1914, 2 Lieut. 4 September, 1917. November, 1921 *A.F.L.* Flying Officer *w.e.f.* 1 August, 1919 (Stores Officer) No. 3 Squadron No. 2 India Wing. 1937 *Air Force List:*— Flight Lieut (E) (Retd) seniority 1 July, 1926 serving as 2 Apprentice Wing, Equipment Officer, No. 1 School of Technical Training, Halton Camp, Aylesbury. Retired 3 August, 1934. Recalled 3 September, 1939 to 16 April, 1945. Squadron Leader 1 June, 1940. (No. 10076 1960 *A.F.L.* Squadron Ldr (Equipment Officer) Ret'd).

32. W. H. MORGAN

Enlisted 23 April, 1908 as 17396 RE. In July, 1910 was Spr in No. 3 Balloon Company (Dismounted) and was L/Cpl Balloon School on mobilisation of Air Battalion. Transferred to RFC 13 May, 1912. To France 18 June, 1915 (1914/15 Star) as Flight Sgt (Carpenter) *w.e.f.* 23 August, 1914. 1918 RAF Muster Roll, Chief Mechanic. RAF L.S.&G.C. *w.e.f.* 23 April, 1926 as Flight Sgt.

★ 33. FREDERICK CARTON GRIFFIN

No. 17747 Sapper 1 Balloon Company RE (Dismounted) on mobilisation of Air Battalion. Sergeant in HQ (France) in 1914. Mentioned in Despatches *L.G.* 24 February, 1917 as Sgt Major. Also mentioned in *Times* 'B' List 27 March, 1917. Commissioned 2 Lieutenant 3 September, 1917. November, 1921 *A.F.L.*, Flying Officer (Stores List) seniority 20 July, 1920 from 19 July, 1921 serving at Aeroplane Experimental Establishment

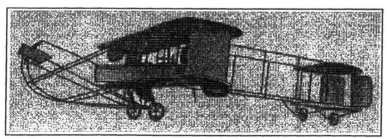

MAURICE FARMAN 'LONGHORN'

Ipswich. 1931 (February) *A.F.L.* was Flight Lieutenant (Qualified in Explosives) employed from 4 May 1930 at No. 2 Store (Ammunition) Depot Altrincham, Cheshire. 1937 *A.F.L.* Flight Lieut. (E) (Retd) seniority 1 July, 1929, employed as Equipment Officer, 2 Flying Training School Brize Norton.

★ 34. LAWRENCE LITTLE

Enlisted 29 March, 1909, was 18718 Sapper Balloon School on mobilisation of Air Battalion. F/Sgt 6 Squadron to France 6 October, 1914. In England when 24 Squadron was being formed at Hounslow in September, 1915, returned to France February, 1916. Promoted Temp SM 1 July, 1916. Left 24 Squadron 13 July, 1916. Chief Master Mechanic in 1918 Muster Roll. Group of four medals sold Christies 1987:—1914 Star and bar (F/Sgt) British War Medal and Victory (SM1 RAF), and RAF L.S.&G.C. (awarded *w.e.f.* 29 March, 1927 as Sgt Major 1st Class). 20th senior RAF Warrant Officer, still serving in 1931. See group photograph No. 2.

34 LITTLE (2nd from left), 1212 WAKELING (3rd from left)

★ 35. A. BENTON

Although he enlisted on 24 June, 1908 a transferee to the RFC, he was still an Air Mechanic 1st Class, with the Aircraft Park in France from 16 August, 1914 (1914 Star). Sometime Flight Sgt he reverted to Sgt

(Coppersmith) *w.e.f.* 12 January, 1918. Sgt Mechanic in 1918 RAF Muster Roll. RAF L.S.&G.C. *w.e.f.* 24 June, 1926 as Flight Sgt.

36. R. A. GROU

Enlisted 11 September, 1906. No. 16018 Sapper No. 3 Balloon Company RE on mobilisation of Air Battalion. Transferred to RFC 13 May 1912. Sergeant by July, 1914. Earned 1914/15 Star as Sgt in Kite Section from 21 March, 1915. Promoted Flight Sgt (Fabric Worker) 1 August, 1916. RAF L.S.&G.C. *w.e.f.* 11 September, 1924 still Flight Sgt. Recalled in WW2 and served in UK as a Warrant Officer (seniority 1 February, 1940) earning Defence and War medals. Retired a second time in September, 1946. See group photograph No. 2.

* 37. B. ARVOY

Enlisted 11 August, 1909, was 19416 Sapper 2 Company Balloon School RE on mobilisation of Air Battalion. To RFC 13 May 1912. 1AM Airship Detachment for 1914 Star and bar. Transferred to RNAS 18 October, 1914 as No. 672, Petty Officer. Awarded Distinguished Service Medal *L.G.* 12 May 1917 as CPO3 RNAS. Master Mechanic on transfer to RAF. Later Sgt Major 1st Class (Rigger Airships) in RAF, No. 200672.

38. ARTHUR ERNEST ATTREE

Born in Brighton. Enlisted 11 February, 1909. Formerly 18511 Sapper, Balloon School RE on mobilisation of Air Battalion. Sergeant when posted overseas 6 December, 1915. Served in India 1915 to 1918, then in Egypt (1914/15 trio). T/Sgt Major 1 August, 1917 SM1 (Discip), 1918 RAF Muster Roll. In 1925 he was on the North West Frontier of India earning one of only perhaps 275 India General Service Medals clasp Waziristan 1925. This clasp was almost exclusively awarded to the RAF at HQ Tank (25), with 5 Army Co-op Squadron (83), at Miramshah with 27 Bomber Squadron (73) or with 60 Squadron (80 medals). RAF L.S.&G.C. Medal awarded *w.e.f.* 11 February, 1927 as SM2. Appointed WO1 5 January, 1930 and released on pension in 1933. His group of five medals is known in a private collection:— 1914/15 trio (Sgt RFC and SM1 RAF), India General Service Medal (Waziristan 1925, F/Sgt RAF) and RAF L.S.&G.C.

39. JOHN BELL

Enlisted 16 September, 1899. As 3426 Sapper Balloon Repair Factory he earned his Queen's South Africa Medal (clasps Cape Colony and South Africa 1901). In July, 1910 he was a Sapper in No. 3 Balloon Company RE and transferred to the Air Battalion in 1911. He went overseas 11 April, 1915 as AM1 earning his 1914/15 star trio and in the 1918 RAF Muster Roll is shown as a Master Mechanic having been promoted QMS on 1 July, 1916. His Army L.S.&G.C. was not promulgated until Army Order 145 of April, 1923 when he is shown as WO2.

★ 40. EDWARD BOLT

Enlisted 6 August, 1909. Formerly 19124 Sapper 3 Balloon Company RE on mobilisation of the Air Battalion. Transferred to RFC 13 May 1912. He was a Cpl on 16 August, 1914 when he went to France with the Aircraft Park (Kites). On a riggers course at CFS September, 1914. M.I.D. as Actg. Sgt Major in *L.G.* 24 February, 1917. Also mentioned in *Times* 'B' List 27 March, 1917. RAF L.S.&G.C. *w.e.f.* 6 August, 1927 as SM 1st Class. His quartet of medals are in the RAF Museum at Hendon. 1914 Star and bar (Cpl RFC), British War Medal and Victory (M.I.D.) (F/Sgt RFC) and RAF L.S.&G.C. (Serving in 1931).

★ 41. G. S. BREADING

Enlisted 22 August, 1910. Served in the Air Battalion. Sgt. 5 Squadron RFC in France from 14 August, 1914. Chief Master Mech (Tech) in RAF Muster Roll (1918) *w.e.f.* 1 October, 1917. RAF L.S.&G.C. *w.e.f.* 22 August, 1928 as SM 2nd Class. See group photograph No. 2. Medals known in a private collection.

★ 42. T. H. BRIGHT

Enlisted 18 May 1910. Served in the Air Battalion. RE. 1AM 4 Squadron in France from 12 August, 1914. Sgt 1 January, 1916. In 1918 RAF Muster Roll as Chief Mechanic (Fitter General).

★ 43. M. CAULFIELD

Enlisted 26 April, 1911. Transferred from Air Battalion to RAF 13 May -1912. 1AM 5 Squadron in France from 14 August, 1914. Sgt from 1 October, 1917. Chief Mechanic (Carpenter) in 1918 Muster Roll. RAF L.S.&G.C. *w.e.f.* 22 August, 1928 as SM2.

★ 44. ARTHUR CHIVERS

Enlisted 13 March, 1909. Transferred from Air Battalion to RFC 13 May 1912. 1AM Airship Detachment in August, 1914. To RNAS 18 October, 1914 as No. 671. Entitled to 1914 Star. Killed 21 April, 1917 in loss of Airship C17, as Coxwain, CPO3 (Mech), off North Foreland. (From Pulham Airship Base).

45. A. C. EASTLEY

Enlisted 26 September, 1910. Served in the Air Battalion. 1918 RAF Muster Roll Chief Mechanic (Driver). Promoted Flight Sgt 1 June, 1917.

46. F. EVANS

Transferred from Air Battalion to RFC 13 May 1912. 1AM Airship Detachment. Discharged 11 August, 1914 under *K.R.* 392 (XXV) 'Services no longer required.'

★ 47. FREDERICK JOHN PARSONS GEARD

Born 1892. Enlisted originally in September, 1910. Served in the Air Battalion RE prior to transfer to RFC. In 1913 shared a room with No. 71 W. V. Strugnell and 979 E. W. Shrewsbury. Served in France from 16 August, 1914 as a Corporal with No. 5 Squadron. Accidentally killed in an aeroplane crash 18 August, 1914, near Péronne. His pilot was Lieut Smith-Barry who survived the crash though both his legs were broken (He recovered and later commanded the School of Special Flying at Gosport.) They were flying in a BE8 serial No. 391.

Geard's body was buried in the Péronne Communal Cemetery Index No. France 510.

The register entry reads:

On the left hand side of the centre path, opposite the 1870 Memorial is the grave of a soldier from the United Kingdom who fell in August, 1914.

'Geard, Cpl. F J P., 5th Squadron RFC

Formerly Royal Engineers, killed whilst returning from reconnaissance (crashed) 18 August, 1914, age 22. Born at Mottingham,
son of John and Emily Geard, of 36, Lascelles Road, Maxton,
Dover.'
A short biography from the Marquis de Ruvigny Roll of Honour
states:—

Corporal No. 47, Royal Flying Corps, 2nd Son of John Geard
of 45 Lascelles Road, Maxton, Dover, Stone Mason, by his wife,
Amelia Emily, daughter of the late William Parsons of Chislehurt,
Kent: b. Mottingham, near Eltham, Kent, 1 Sept. 1892: educ.
Herne Bay. Enlisted in the Royal Engineers at Woolwich, 1 Sept
1910, and after going through a course of training at Chatham was,
in Jan. 1911, posted to the Balloon Section R.E. at Aldershot. He
then belonged to No. 1 Aeroplane Section (R.E.) was appointed
Airman Rigger in Sept. 1911, and the following year transferred to
the RFC. He was killed, while on active service in an aeroplane
accident at Péronne, France, 18 August, 1914; unmarried.

48. C. GRAHAM

Enlisted 18 January, 1894. Formerly 27946 Sapper 2 Company Balloon
School RE (Dismounted) on Mobilisation of Air Battalion. Awarded
George V, 1911 Coronation Medal, and the Army L.S.&G.C. in Army
Order 333 October, 1913 as 1AM RFC. Re-engaged March, 1914 beyond
21 years. Corporal 7 Squadron went overseas 3 April, 1915 (1914/15 star
trio). 1918 RAF Muster Roll Sergeant Clerk. Storeman (*w.e.f.* 1 February,
1915).

* 49. J. P. GUILLE

Enlisted 4 May, 1911. Transferred from the Air Battalion to RFC 13 May,
1912. 1AM Aircraft Park, France, 16 August, 1914. Promoted Sergeant
1 June, 1916 (Kite Balloon Section-Balloon Party). In 1918 RAF Muster
Roll shown as Sergeant (Labourer).

50. WILLIAM HERBERT HARRISON

Born 21 April, 1890. Transferred from the Air Battalion to RFC. Overseas
from 11 October, 1915, earning 1914/15 Star trio. Commissioned 2
Lieutenant (Equipment Officer) 14 March, 1917. 1921 (November) *Air
Force List*, Flying Officer at Instrument Design Establishment, Biggin Hill.
Flight Lieutenant 1 January, 1929 from 31 March, 1928 at No. 1 Stores

Depot, 21 Group, Kidbrooke, London SE3. Retired 21 April, 1935. In 1937 *Air Force List* shown as No. 10101 Flight Lieutenant (E) (retired). Working as Flight Lieutenant (Retd) Air Ministry, Civil Assistant Directorate of Equipment. Recalled 1 November, 1939 to 29 October, 1943. Squadron Leader 1 September, 1941. Last noted in April, 1960 *Air Force List.*

RFC Communiqué No. 21 26 November, 1915

2 Lieutenant O'Malley and Flight Sergeant Harrison (BE2c 13 Squadron) returning from escort to reconnaissance, observed an Aviatik about 7000 feet below. From behind at 25 yards they fired half a drum. Steam came from the engine of the hostile machine which dived into the clouds at 2000 feet just over the line at Fricourt.

RFC Communiqué No. 22 28 November, 1915

With the same pilot he engaged a Fokker near Bapaume. Harrison's Lewis gun jammed three times. Correcting the jams twice he was subjected to heavy fire from the Fokker, and the fight was abandoned.

* 51. THOMAS HENRY CHARLES HINDS

Enlisted 2 September, 1910. Transferred from Air Battalion to RFC. Mentioned by McCudden V.C. in *'Flying Fury.'* A lorry driver 1AM who took many risks driving. 1AM 2 Squadron in France from 13 August, 1914 (1914 Star and bar). SM1 (Disciplinarian) *w.e.f.* 1 January, 1918. In RAF Muster Roll 1918. RAF L.S.&G.C. September, 1928.

* 52. CHARLES ALBERT HOBBY

Born Leatherhead, Surrey, 5 February, 1890. Enlisted 30 July, 1910. Transferred from Air Battalion to RFC. Royal Aero Club, Aviators' Certificate No. 757, 27 March, 1914 at Upavon CFS in a Maurice Farman. Sgt, Aircraft Park, France from 16 August, 1914. Flight Sgt and 2nd Class Pilot from 1 March, 1916 and Chief Mechanic (Pilot) in 1918 Muster Roll. Mentioned in the *Times* 'B' Press Release List 29 August, 1919. General Service Medal (Iraq) as SM2, (6, 30, 55, 63 or 84 Squadron RAF – 10 December, 1919 to 17 November, 1920). RAF L.S.&G.C. as Flight Sgt *w.e.f.* 30 July, 1928.

★ 53. HENRY VAUGHAN JERRARD

Born London 4 November, 1893. Gained his Royal Aero Club Aviators' Certificate No. 538 as a 1AM RFC on 2 July, 1913 at Netheravon in a BE. Cpl 4 Squadron France 13 August, 1914. 2 Lieut 4 June, 1916. Lieutenant 12 August, 1916. 1918 *A.F.L.* – Lieutenant (A and S) RAF. Flight Lieutenant (Stores Officer) 1 August, 1919.

★ 54. JAMES CORAM JONES

Enlisted 21 July, 1910. Transferred from Air Battalion to RFC 13 May 1912. 1AM Aircraft Park, France, 16 August, 1914. Military Medal as Flight Sgt *L.G.* 30 May, 1916. Temp Sgt Major *w.e.f.* 1 March, 1916. Distinguished Conduct Medal *L.G.* 1 January, 1917, citation *L.G.* 13 February, 1917 'A/S.M. M.M. For conspicuous gallantry and devotion to duty. His energy and example have materially contributed to the increase of output of the Aeroplane Repair Section.' 1918 RAF Muster Roll – Chief Master Mechanic (Technical). RAF L.S.&G.C. *w.e.f.* 21 July, 1928 as SM1. December, 1937 *A.F.L.* still shown as WO *w.e.f.* 8 July, 1918. From 1 October, 1935 was Station Warrant Officer 11 Flying Training School, Whitteringham Peterborough. In March, 1938 *A.F.L.* was the 14th senior RAF Warrant Officer and the last on the list with seniority going back to WW1. In the November, 1941 *A.F.L.* he was the ninth most senior, and in October, 1944 he was fourth. See group photograph No. 2.

★ 55. H. T. KENDRICK

Enlisted 30 May 1910. Transferred from Air Battalion to RFC 13 May 1912. 1AM Aircraft Park, France from 16 August, 1914. Flight Sgt, KBS (BP) from 1 January, 1917. 1918 RAF Muster Roll – Flight Sgt (Labourer). Mentioned in the *Times* 'B' Press Release List 29 August, 1919. RAF L.S.&G.C. *w.e.f.* 30 May 1928 as SM2.

* 56. LAURIE A. KESZLER

Enlisted 28 March, 1907. Formerly 16213 Boy, 3 Balloon Company RE July, 1910, then Sapper 2 Company Balloon School (Dismounted) on mobilisation of Air Battalion. Sgt. 2 Squadron in France from 12 August, 1914. Observer/Gunner from 14 September, 1915. Temp SM (D) 1 January, 1917. 1918 RAF Muster Roll, SM1 (Discip). See group photograph Nos. 2 and 3.

* 57. A. KIDD

Enlisted 26 September, 1910. Transferred from the Air Battalion to the RFC 13 May 1912. 1AM with the Aircraft Park in France from 16 August, 1914. Cpl from 1 April, 1916. RAF Muster Roll, 1918, Cpl Mechanic (Blacksmith). (See No. 979.)

* 58. W. LANGTON

Enlisted 15 September, 1910. Transferred from the Air Battalion to the RFC 13 May 1912. 1AM with Aircraft Park in France from 16 August, 1914. Reverted to Cpl 11 March, 1917. In RAF Muster Roll, 1918. Cpl Mech. (Fitter, General).

* 59. J. LONGHURST

Enlisted 15 June, 1911. Transferred from Air Battalion to the RFC 13 May, 1912. 1AM with Aircraft Park to France from 16 August, 1914. Appointed SM1 (Discip) 1 January, 1917. Army M.S.M. *L.G.* 4 June, 1917, 'for Valuable Services in France and Flanders' as Flight Sgt. SM1 in 1918 RAF Muster Roll.

* 60. H. G. MARCHMONT

Enlisted 8 August, 1910. Formerly Air Battalion. 1AM with Aircraft Park to France from 16 August, 1914. Promoted Flight Sergeant (Kite Balloon Section – Silicol Plant) 1 September, 1916. He is shown as Chief Mechanic, (Hydrogen Worker) in the 1918 RAF Muster Roll. He died of heatstroke in Iraq with 84 Squadron 14 August, 1921. He was not entitled to a General Service Medal (Iraq), being posted after the last qualifying date (17 November, 1920). Next of kin, father, 9 Hansdown Road, Swinton. His Victory Medal (only) is in the Webb Collection. (See No. 525.)

* 61. WILLIAM THOMAS JAMES McCUDDEN

Born Chatham 3 April, 1891. (Older brother of McCudden V.C. No. 892). Enlisted into RE July, 1905 aged 14. Formerly 14715 Sapper Balloon School (3 Company) RE. Transferred to RFC May 1912. Royal Aero Club Aviators' Certificate No. 269, 13 August, 1912 on Salisbury Plain in a Bristol as Air Mechanic. Posted from 3 Squadron to

Flying Depot, 3 January, 1913. At Farnborough in 1913, a Sergeant Pilot (see group photograph under No. 7). As Sergeant 3 Squadron went to France 13 August, 1914 and earned 1914 Star and bar trio. Accidentally killed whilst flying at Chatham as Flight Sergeant (Instructor), 13 Squadron, on 1 May, 1915, aged 24. Buried Chatham Cemetery, Kent. Son of the late William Henry and Mrs. Amelia E McCudden of 'Pitlochry,' 37 Burton Road, Kingston-on-Thames. See group photograph No. 2.

62. G. McCLENAGHAN

Enlisted 24 July, 1903 (No. 12869) into Royal Engineers. Born Randalstown, Co. Antrim 21 June, 1885. Transferred from Air Battalion to RFC 13 May, 1912. Served overseas from 7 September, 1915 earning 1914/15 trio. Promoted Corporal (Rigger) 1 July, 1916. Corporal Mechanic (Rigger-Aero) in 1918 RAF Muster Roll. RAF L.S.&G.C. *w.e.f.* 24 July, 1921 as Flight Sergeant. Promoted to SM2 24 March, 1928. Discharged 23 September, 1930 when serving in 41 (Fighter) Squadron. Joined the Air Ministry Constabulary. Died 17 February, 1971 in Southampton. His group of five medals are in the family (1914/15 Star trio, Defence medal and RAF L.S.&G.C.).

★ 63. A. E. LEWIS

Enlisted 28 March, 1907, formerly 16214 Sapper, 3 Balloon Company RE on mobilisation of the Air Battalion. Then he was with 3 Company at the Balloon School. As 1AM 2 Squadron he went to France on 13 August, 1914 and then to Egypt. There he was mentioned in despatches in *London Gazette* 13 October, 1916 as Flight Sergeant and *London Gazette* 16 January, 1918 as Sergeant Major. Awarded Army M.S.M. in *London Gazette* of 12 March, 1917. Promoted Temporary Sergeant Major (Technical) 1 November, 1916. In 1918 RAF Muster Roll shown as CMM (Tech).

★ 64. CHARLES MULLEN

Born Garveyhullian, Co. Tyrone, Ireland. Formerly 22162, 56 Company RE. Joined the RFC 12 March, 1913. Obtained his Royal Aero Club Aviators' Certificate (No. 522) on the 16 June, 1913 at Montrose in a Maurice Farman. A Sergeant in 2 Squadron in France from 13 August, 1914. Awarded Army M.S.M. in *L.G.* 1 January, 1917 as A/Sgt Major 'For Valuable Services with the Army in the Field.' Commissioned 10 April, 1917. See group photographs Nos. 2 and 3.

★ 65. C. NASH

Enlisted 14 March, 1910 and transferred into Air Battalion. As 1AM was with Aircraft Park in France from 12 August, 1914. Promoted Temp *Sgt* Major 1 February, 1918 and in 1918 RAF Muster Roll was A/CMM (Tech). Awarded India General Service Medal (Waziristan 1921-24) and RAF L.S.&G.C. *w.e.f.* 14 March, 1928 as Flight Sergeant.

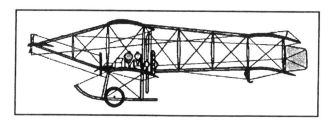

BRISTOL BOXKITE

★ 66. T. OLDERSHAW

Formerly 18882 Sapper, 1 Company Balloon School RE (Dismounted) on mobilisation of Air Battalion. Transferred to RFC 13 May, 1912 and a Corporal in the Aircraft Park in France from 16 August, 1914. He was discharged 16 February, 1915 as unfit.

★ 67. EDWARD JOHN PROTHEROE

Enlisted 10 March, 1911 into the Air Battalion and gained both Royal Aero Club Aeronauts' Certificate No. 36 and Airship Certificate No. 21 on 11 November, 1913 as 1AM. He went to France as a Corporal with the Airship Detachment in 1914 and was transferred as No. 676, Petty Officer (Mech.) into the RNAS. Commissioned Flying Officer 26 November, 1917, he is shown as Lieutenant (Airships) in the 16 April, 1918 *A.F.L.* 1921 (November) *A.F.L.*, Flying Officer (Airships) from 22 June, 1921 under instruction as Pilot or Observer No. 4 Flying Training School Palestine. Promoted Flight Lieutenant (No. 13228) *w.e.f.* 1 July, 1926, from 4 October, 1930 at RAF Worthy Down and he was posted on 8 December, 1936 to the No. 2 Balloon Training Unit, Rollestone Camp, Salisbury 9 (*vide* March, 1938 *A.F.L.*).

68. G. A. SIMMONS

As 2AM transferred from Air Battalion to RFC 13 May 1912. Discharged 10 December, 1912 under King's Regs. 392 (x) 'Having been convicted by the Civil Power.'

★ 69. R. SPENCER

Enlisted 1 April, 1909, formerly 18716 Sapper RE. With the Balloon School on mobilisation of Air Battalion. Sgt 3 Squadron to France 13 August, 1914 (1914 Star and bar). Promoted Temp Sgt Major (Disciplinarian) 1 February, 1916 and in 1918 RAF Muster Roll as SM1 (Discip). See group photograph No. 2.

70. P. C. STRICKLAND

As No. 16017, Sapper No. 1 Balloon Company on mobilisation of Air Battalion. To RFC 13 May, 1912. Discharged medically unfit 8 July, 1913.

★ 71. WILLIAM VICTOR STRUGNELL

Born 23 July, 1892 in Southampton. Was at school with McCudden V.C. In training saw Staff Sergeant Wilson crash (No. 92). Served with the Air Battalion RE and took his Royal Aero Club Aviators' Certificate No. 253 on 24 July, 1912 on Salisbury Plain in a Bristol and for a while was 1AM (Pilot). With 5 Squadron to France 14 August, 1914. Was a Sergeant Pilot with No. 3 Squadron in 1915. Commissioned 2 Lieutenant Hampshire Regiment and RFC.

RFC Communiqué No. 2

On the 29 July, 2 Lieutenants Strugnell and Anderson, 1 Squadron, encountered four hostile machines South-East of Lille. Three of the machines were of the Scout type – with planes similar to the Bristol Scout.

RFC Communiqué No. 29 5 February, 1916

Lieutenant Strugnell (Morane Scout, 1 Squadron) attacked and drove off an LVG South-East of Armentières. Later during patrol an Aviatik was sighted at 9000 feet going towards its own lines. The Morane Scout overhauled it and opened fire at 400 feet range, eventually closing to much closer range. Tracer bullets were seen to hit the wings and fuselage and apparently the pilot, who appeared to fall forward. The hostile machine then nose dived very steeply into the clouds, not under control.

Awarded M.C. in *London Gazette* 3 June, 1916 as Captain 56 Squadron, and a bar to the Military Cross in *London Gazette* 26 July, 1917. 'For conspicuous gallantry and devotion to duty. Whilst leading an offensive patrol he attacked and brought down a hostile machine, later on the same patrol he brought down a second machine.' By this date he had accounted for five machines and a kite balloon (he finished the war with seven victories). Major RFC 1 September, 1917. Squadron Leader 1921 (November) *Air Force List* (seniority 1 August, 1919) from 21 March, 1921 at No. 1 Flying Training School Netheravon. In February, 1931 *Air Force List* was Wing Commander (1 July, 1928) from 1 September, 1928 at No. 9 (Bomber) Squadron Boscombe Down. He was then posted as Officer Commanding No. 1 Armoured Car Company in Mosul, Iraq. By 1 July, 1934 was a Group Captain and *w.e.f.* 26 July, 1935 was Station Commander RAF Station Manston 24 (Training) Group. Awarded both the 1935 Silver Jubilee and 1937 Coronation Medals. Retired 7 June, 1945.

WING COMMANDER, IRAQ 1932; WESTLAND WAPITI.

Shown as 'retired' in 1946 *Air Force List* onwards as Group Captain (General Duties). Died 7 January, 1977.

★ 72. F. F. ('FREDDIE') TRAYLOR

Enlisted 9 August, 1909. Served in the Air Battalion, formerly Sapper 19128 Balloon School. To France as Cpl 2 Squadron 13 August, 1914 and mentioned in despatches as Sgt 22 June, 1915. Promoted Temp SM (T) 1 March, 1916. In 1918 RAF Muster Roll CMM (Technical).

★ 73. ARTHUR C. WARD

Enlisted 15 July, 1910 formerly 17267 Sapper, Balloon School Air Battalion. Transferred from 6 Squadron to Aircraft Park as Cpl 12 August, 1914 and went with that unit to France 16 August, 1914. He was an Aerial Gunner with No. 6 Squadron during 1915. On 15 October, 1917 promoted Temp Sgt Major (Tech). In 1918 RAF Muster Roll was CMM (Tech). Mentioned in despatches 28 October, 1921 as SM1 in Mesopotamia.

★ 74. S. H. WHITTAKER

Enlisted 15 June, 1911 into the Air Battalion. Transferred to RFC 13 May 1912. 1AM with Airship Detachment when he earned 1914 Star. Transferred to RNAS 18 October, 1914 as No. 674. Promoted to Petty Officer 1 June, 1915. In 1918 was No. 200674 Sgt. Mech. (Carpenter) in RAF, however after 19 years service he was awarded his RAF L.S.&G.C. Medal in the rank of Leading Aircraftman *w.e.f.* 24 June, 1930. (See also

No. 689, the only other pre-war airman to receive an L.S.&G.C. Medal still as an airman.)

★ 75. F. V. WELLS

Enlisted 2 June, 1907. Transferred from the Air Battalion to RFC 13 May 1912. Went to France 14 August, 1914 with 5 Squadron. Was 1AM Fitter (Aero Engines) *w.e.f.* 1 August, 1917 and still in this rank and trade in April, 1918 RAF Muster Roll (See also No. 302).

76. S. F. CROFT

Enlisted 30 June, 1908 into 2/Royal Sussex Regt and as No. 9081 Corporal transferred to RFC HQ on 24 June, 1912. He was promoted Sergeant Major 1 February, 1916 and in the 1918 RAF Muster Roll is listed as SM1 (Discip).

★ 77. THOMAS HUDSON

Transferred to RFC HQ from 3/Grenadier Guards as No. 13307 Lance Sergeant on 27 June, 1912, was drill sergeant, No. 5 Squadron. Was the NCO responsible for allocating RFC numbers to the initial members of the Corps. Was the first secretary of No. 1 RFC Royal Army Temperance Branch on 9 April, 1913. There is a photograph of Sergeant Hudson and the first RATA in the RFC in the April, 1913 *'On the March'* and another of the very first meeting in the May 1913 Edition. As sergeant with the Aircraft Park went to France on 16 August, 1914. He was commissioned 2 Lieutenant on 19 January, 1917 into 19 Squadron RFC. Retired as a Squadron Leader. Alive in 1979 in St. Albans, Herts (15, Thomas Sparrow House, Wheathamstead). See group photograph No. 2.

Extracts from letters received from members of No. 77 Tom Hudson's family:—
    'Father was on Trenchard's staff because having been commissioned *on the field* after the Battle of the Somme, he went to GHQ as a Staff Captain. This was at the time, in 1917, I believe when H.R.H. The Prince of Wales was serving with them. I know that Dad was well known to their lordships Trenchard and Gort, particularly by virtue of his service with the Grenadier Guards from which he transferred to become the *first recruiting Sergeant of the RFC.'* [*Comment:* This would explain why Tom Hudson 'dished out' the numbers.]

'He told of early days of preparing aircraft for Col Cody at Farnborough. Dad was the first to reach Col Cody when he crashed and was killed.

'He mentioned how, in the days prior to the development of the Constantine gear for synchronising of machine gun fire through the propeller, and how they had to lay on the wing and fire.'

'Father also told of Lord Trenchard forming the RFC with a few Officers and Men (then serving with various regiments) gathered together. He outlined his aims. He then stuck a union jack in the ground and said 'We will call ourselves THE ROYAL FLYING CORPS.'

'In 1912 father was all-round champion of the British Army at home including Lt/heavyweight champion of the Brigade of Guards (the same night that Bdr Billy Wells won his title). The same year he got his Football International Cap. A member of the Roberts Cup Shooting Team and winner of the coveted silver spoon at Bisley. This sporting prowess he carried with him to the RFC/RAF. He was Captain of a RFC cricket team who played W. G. Grace's team on Fry's ground at Bristol! Dad made 140 and believed that W. G. Grace was so impressed with the performance of the RFC that he sportingly deliberately gave a catch to draw the match.'

'In 1918 father was CO at Dronfield Woodhouse Aerodrome. Released in 1919. At the outbreak of WWII he rejoined the RAF,

COLONEL CODY

assisting with initial training. In 1940 was seconded to General Sikorsky as Adjutant in the formation of the Polish Free Fighter Sqn at Gloucester, later serving as Sqn/Ldr at Torquay and Newquay. Released in 1946.'

(See also 1169 James Hudson, his brother. They were two of twelve children.)

78. O. LATIMER

Formerly 7613 Lance Corporal 1/Somerset L.I., transferred to RFC HQ 24 June, 1912. Was a Sergeant in 1914 and commissioned Lieutenant 12 October, 1916 and Captain 15 June, 1917.

⋆ 79. FRANK G. PREEN

Enlisted 1 May, 1907 and transferred as 8066 Lance Corporal from the King's Royal Rifle Corps Depot at Winchester to RFC HQ 20 June, 1912. As 1AM 3 Squadron he went to France on 12 August, 1914 being entitled to 1914 Star and bar. Shown on 1918 RAF Muster Roll as Flight Clerk (Gen) having been promoted to Flight Sergeant on 1 August, 1916. He served with No. 1 Squadron in India in 1920 and in Mesopotamia in 1921-22 and 23. His group of four medals is known in a private collection consisting of 1914 Star and bar trio, and RAF L.S.&G.C. Medal. This last award *w.e.f.* 1 May, 1925 as Flight Sergeant. Warrant Officer Class 1, 1 August, 1929. Serving in 1931.

80. E. FOWLES

Enlisted 25 August, 1909 and served in the Air Battalion RE. Promoted Acting Sergeant Major (Disciplinarian) 1 January, 1916 and awarded Army M.S.M. in *L.G.* 1 January, 1917 'for Valuable Services with the Army in the Field' as Sergeant (Acting Sergeant Major). In 1918 RAF Muster Roll listed as SM1 (Disciplinarian).

81. FREDERICK STRODE CHAPMAN

Enlisted 16 June, 1908 and transferred to RFC from 19 Hussars on 1 July, 1912. A corporal in 1914, he transferred to RNAS 18 October, 1914 as No. 664 and was promoted WO2 (RNAS) on 7 May, 1917. In 1918 RAF List he is shown as 2 Lieutenant (Technical) being promoted to Flying Officer on 1 October, 1919. 1921 (November) *A.F.L.*, Flying Officer from 16 March, 1920 at No. 1 School of Technical Training (Boys), Halton. Retired 20 September, 1922. He is shown in this rank as retired in both the 1937 and 1946 Air Force Lists.

CAP BAND OF NAVAL WING

★ 82. W. CLAYTON

Enlisted 26 September, 1910 and transferred from 4 Dragoons to RFC on 1 July,1912. Earned 1914 Star and bar as Corporal with the Airship Detachment in 1914 and transferred to RNAS 18 October, 1914 as No. 673 Leading Mechanic. Promoted to CPO3, 1 August, 1916. He was a Flight Sergeant (Discip) in the RAF No. 200673. Awarded RAF L.S.&G.C. Medal *w.e.f.* 26 September, 1928 as SM2.

★ 83. CECIL W. HARRISON

Served throughout the Boer War with No. 2 Company, 3/Grenadier Guards. Entitled to Queen's South Africa Medal (Belmont and Modder River). Transferred from 3/Grenadier Guards as 5608 Private to RFC 1 July; 1912. As Cpl Aircraft Park went to France 16 August, 1914 and earned the 1914 Star and bar. He transferred to RNAS on 18 April, 1915 as No. 703 and was later A/Lieutenant RAF.

★ 84. G. H. POWELL

Enlisted 17 February, 1908. Transferred from Grenadier Guards to RFC 1 July, 1912. 1AM with HQ in France from 12 August, 1914. As a Cpl earned French Médaille Militaire in 1914 and was mentioned in despatches for Italy in *L.G.* 6 January, 1919 as Temp Sgt Maj, which rank he attained 8 July, 1917. In the RAF Muster Roll (April, 1918) he is listed as SM1 (Disciplinarian).

★ 85. G. H. PRICE

Enlisted 13 February, 1907. Transferred from 1st Grenadier Guards to 1 Squadron RFC 27 June, 1912. 2AM with the Airship Detachment when he earned his 1914 Star. Transferred to RNAS 18 October, 1914 as No. 662. Promoted to P.O. 1 March, 1916. Awarded Distinguished Service Medal in May, 1918 as Petty Officer Mechanic. He was later Sgt Mechanic (Airship Rigger) in RAF No. 200662.

86. F. S. WILLIAMS

Enlisted 5 November, 1906. Formerly 12951 Pte 1/Grenadier Guards, transferred to RFC 1 July, 1912. Flight Sgt 1 December, 1917. Shown in 1918 RAF Muster Roll as Flight Clerk (Gen). RAF L.S.&G.C. *w.e.f.* 5 November, 1924 as Flight Sgt. Serving as a WO in a crashed aircraft recovery unit in 1939.

★ 87. A. W. WARD

Formerly 9323 Pte 2/Welsh Regt. Transferred to 1 Squadron RFC 24 June, 1912. As Sgt, went to France with 6 Squadron on 6 October, 1914. 2 Lieutenant RFC 12 November, 1917.

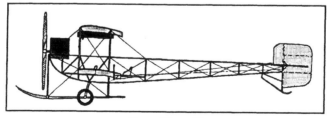

AVRO TYPE D

88. NOT TRACED

(See also 92, 149, 182, 197, 260, 261, 450) Probably bought out, transferred back to unit or discharged as unsuitable before any permanent appointment into RFC. However, the names of seven NCOs have been noted for whom no positive number is recorded. These men: Wilson, Long, Lacy, Ellard, Methery, Sedger and Borne, are possibly seven of the eight not traced.

★ 89. A. R. BROCK

Enlisted 12 March, 1912. Formerly 6263 at Depot RAMC. Transferred to RFC No. 1 Squadron 24 June, 1912. As 2AM (Airship Detachment) earned 1914 Star and bar. To RNAS 18 October, 1914 as AM1 No. 668. Promoted to Leading Mechanic 1 June, 1915. Later in RAF as Corporal Mechanic (Driver), No. 200668, in April, 1918 RAF Muster Roll.

★ 90. C. S. CARDEN

Enlisted 5 June, 1908. Formerly 13749 1/Grenadier Guards. To 2 Squadron RFC 27 June, 1912. As Corporal No. 2 Squadron went to France 12 August, 1914. Promoted 1 December, 1916 to Temp Sergeant Major (Technical). Awarded RAF M.S.M. 'For Valuable Services in Italy' in this rank in *L.G.* 3 June, 1918. In 1918 RAF Muster Roll listed as CMM (T). Came from Enfield. Awarded RAF L.S.&G.C. *w.e.f.* 4 November, 1926 having reverted to the rank of Flight Sergeant.

91. WILLIAM HEDLEY BUTT

Born Bristol 18 August, 1891. Enlisted 18 May, 1910. Earned Royal Aero Club Aviators' Certificate No. 673 as 1AM in a Maurice Farman at Central Flying School Upavon. Mentioned in despatches 42 Squadron 15 May, 1917 as Flight Sergeant (Temp Sergeant Major) (Disciplinarian) which rank he had held since 1 April, 1916. RAF Muster Roll (April, 1918) SM1. RAF L.S.&G.C. *w.e.f.* 4 November, 1926 in same rank. Serving in 1931 15th Senior RAF Warrant Officer.

92. (SEE 88)

It is possible that this number was allocated to Staff Sergeant R. H. V. Wilson who earned Royal Aero Club Aviators' Certificate No. 232 on 18 June, 1912 in a Bristol at CFS Salisbury Plain. This made him the second only NCO pilot in the British Army. However, he was killed in a Flying accident on 5 July, 1912, again on Salisbury Plain, when a passenger in a Nieuport monoplane (70 h.p. Gnome engine) flown by Captain E.P. Loreine. In a tight turn the machine side-slipped and fell 1400 feet to the ground killing both men. He was the first other rank flying casualty in the RFC. (See '*The Forgotten Ones*'). Born Andover, 12 March, 1883.

* 93. J. W. MASKERY (OR MASKENEY)

Born Mickleover, Derby, 8 February, 1887. Enlisted 1 October, 1908. Formerly 13976 Private 1/Grenadier Guards transferred to No. 2 Squadron RFC 27 June, 1912. Earned 1914 Star and bar as 1AM in 4 Squadron from 12 August, 1914. Royal Aero Club Aviators' Certificate No. 3273 on 25 July, 1916 as a Flight Sergeant. Promoted further, but reverted to Flight Sergeant *w.e.f.* 18 February, 1918. In 1918 RAF Muster Roll was Chief Mechanic (Carpenter). RAF L.S.&G.C. *w.e.f.* 1 October, 1926 as Flight Sergeant.

* 94. E. THAKE

Enlisted 22 October, 1908. Formerly 52648 Gunner 4 Depot RFA. To 2 Squadron 27 June, 1912. 1AM 4 Squadron to France 9 September, 1914 earning 1914 Star and bar. In 1918 RAF Muster Roll was Chief Mechanic (Rigger Aero).

* 95. FREDERICK SHELTON

Enlisted 5 October, 1908 as No. 13987 into 1/Grenadier Guards and transferred as Lance Corporal on 3 June, 1912 into RFC. He was posted to 2 Squadron on 27 June, 1912. As 1AM (Airframe Fitter) with 2 Squadron he earned a 1914 Star and bar arriving in France on 13 August, 1914. Promoted Temporary Sergeant Major (Disciplinarian) 1 April, 1916 and was SM1 in 1918 RAF Muster Roll. Served in Kurdistan after WW1 and earned RAF L.S.&G.C. *w.e.f.* 5 October, 1926 as SM1. As the 16th senior RAF Warrant Officer he retired from the Royal Air Force in October, 1932. In June, 1988 his two surviving sons donated his group of five medals to the RAF Museum at Hendon. They are:— 1914 Star and bar trio (all named RFC), General Service Medal (Clasp Kurdistan) and RAF L.S.&G.C. (These last two named to SM1 RAF).

* 96. F. HILLS

Enlisted 1 October, 1907. As 13402 Pte 1/Grenadier Guards awarded George V, 1911 Coronation Medal. Posted to 2 Squadron RFC 27 June, 1912. As 2AM 4 Squadron served in France from 9 September, 1914. Promoted Sergeant (Disciplinarian) 1 July, 1917. Still held this rank in 1918 RAF Muster Roll.

* 97. HENRY AUSTIN

Enlisted 9 December, 1908 and as 9574 Lance Corporal transferred to 3 Squadron RFC from 1/Loyal North Lancs Regiment on 24 June, 1912. As Sergeant 6 Squadron posted to France from 12 October, 1914. Promoted Temporary Sergeant Major (Disciplinarian) on 1 May, 1917 and shown as SM1 (Disciplinarian) in 1918 RAF Muster Roll. Awarded RAF L.S.&G.C. *w.e.f.* 9 December, 1926 as SM1. Serving in 1931.

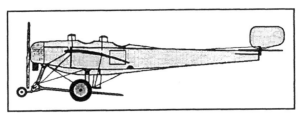

BRISTOL 80h.p. MILITARY MONOPLANE

★ 98. EDWIN FREDERICK PALMER

Enlisted 4 January, 1909. In September, 1909 after training as a Sapper at the RE Training Battalion, Chatham, he was drafted to the Balloon School, Farnborough. He flew as engineer in the airship 'Beta.' As Corporal transferred from the Air Battalion RE to RFC on 13 May, 1912. Posted as 1AM to France with the Aircraft Park on 16 August, 1914. Promoted Flight Sergeant 1 May, 1916 he is shown as Chief Mechanic (Winch Driver and Fitter) in 1918 RAF Muster Roll. Awarded RAF L.S.&G.C. *w.e.f.* 4 January, 1927 as Flight Sergeant. Promoted WO1 5 March, 1930. Serving in 1931. (see 'The Forgotton Ones').

★ 99. C. F. ALLEN

Enlisted 13 June, 1906. Formerly 12742 Private in 2/Grenadier Guards he transferred to 3 Squadron RFC on 27 June, 1912. As 1AM 3 Squadron served in France from 12 August, 1914. Was at Hounslow in September, 1915 when 24 Squadron was formed. Served with them in France from February, 1916. Left 11 June, that year. Promoted Sergeant (Storeman) 18 December, 1916 and shown as Sgt. Clerk (Storeman) in 1918 RAF Muster Roll, earning RAF L.S.&G.C. *w.e.f.* 13 June, 1924 as Flight Sergeant.

★ 100. WILLIAM HENRY BURNS

Born Bethnal Green. As a Cpl in 3 Squadron RFC posted to France 13 August, 1914. (See No. 194 for rescue attempt). He died of wounds received on 6 October, 1915 from shrapnel on the second day of the Battle of Loos when a Flight Sergeant still in 3 Squadron. He was taking part in the battle 'armed' with an Aldis Lamp acting as signaller with Major Furse to RFC observers (Sgt Watts and Cpl Roberts) flying overhead. He is described as a giant of a man and was nicknamed 'Tiny.' Buried Etaples Military Cemetery (III.C.8A) aged 27. Son of William and the late Emily Selina Burns, husband of Elizabeth Burns of 225 Grosvenor Buildings, Manisty Street, Poplar, London.

★ 101. W. A. PEAD

Enlisted 11 September, 1909 as a Boy soldier. Awarded George V, 1911 Coronation Medal. Formerly 14458 Pte 1/Grenadier Guards. Posted to 3 Squadron 27 June, 1912 on transfer to RFC. 2AM 3 Squadron in France from 13 August, 1914. Promoted Sergeant 1 August, 1917 and in 1918 RAF Muster Roll is shown as Sergeant Mechanic (Fitter, Aero).

★ 102. ARTHUR CLAUD ROBINS

Born London 18 December, 1889. Enlisted 22 November, 1911 trained as a rigger and earned his Royal Aero Club Aviators' Certificate No. 793 as Corporal 21 May 1914 at Netheravon Central Flying School in a Maurice Farman. He passed for 2nd Class flyer on 25 June, 1914. As a Sergeant in 3 Squadron he flew to France as a passenger to Lieut Prettyman on 13 August, 1914. He was promoted Temp SM (D) on 1 March, 1916 and was SM1 (Discip) on RAF Muster Roll. Mentioned in the *Times* 'B' Press Release 29 August, 1919. Left the RAF in 1919 and joined de Havillands in Canada. Died in the late 1950's in Swindon. (See *'The Forgotten Ones'*).

103. F. RUTTERFORD

Enlisted 28 December, 1905. Formerly 12518 Pte 2/Grenadier Guards he was posted to 3 Squadron on 27 June, 1912 on transfer to RFC. As 2AM with RFC HQ went to France 2 April, 1915 and earned 1914/15 Star trio. Promoted Sergeant (Storeman) 1 August, 1917 and was a Sergeant Clerk in the 1918 RAF Muster Roll.

RFC Recruiting Song

(Tune: 'The Lowther Arcade and the Tin Gee-Gee')

I was walking in the town up Regent Street
When I saw the RFC
I thought to myself, Now they look neat,
I think that would suit me.
So I strolled inside, and carefully lied
About my carpentry,
But when I came out, I swaggered about—
For I was in the RFC.

They sent me down to Salisbury Plain
To a place they call Larkhill.
The sergeants they bullied with might and main
And made us do some drill.
All the fellows they were 'risky', they smoked naught
        but de Reske
When going to the YM hut.
And they didn't do us badly—tho' we weren't from
        Pope and Bradley*
For we were the Flying Corps—Tut! Tut!

* One of the earliest tailoring firms to specialise in RFC
'maternity' jackets, as these were popularly known.

Part 2
Numbers 104 to 515
June—December 1912

Mainly the men who enlisted into the RFC direct from civilian life from June to 31 December, 1912. However there are some men who transferred from other Army units during this period.

---

* 104. A. F. NETHEY

Served in Cape Mounted Rifles in the Second Boer War and earned the Queen's South Africa Medal. He was a Sergeant in 2 Squadron on 12 August, 1914 when he went to France. After being mentioned in despatches as Flight Sergeant/Acting S/Major in *L.G.* 13 May 1917 was awarded a Military Medal in *L.G.* 28 September, 1917 still serving in 2 Squadron. He had been acting Sergeant Major since 1 January, 1916 and was commissioned 2 Lieutenant on 16 September, 1917. His group of five medals is in the Webb collection:— M.M. (Flight Sgt RFC), Queen's South Africa Medal (clasp Cape Colony 3857 Pte Cape M.R.), 1914 Star (Sgt RFC), British War Medal and Victory Medal (2 Lieutenant RAF). He came originally from Bath. See Group Photographs 2 and 3, and note against Number 260.

105. A. DUDLEY

Enlisted 17 June, 1912 directly into RFC. Sergeant 7 Squadron to France 17 September, 1915 earning 1914/15 trio. Discharged 'sick' 4 September, 1916. Silver War Badge No. 7426.

★ 106. G. J. LANGFIELD

Enlisted 18 June, 1912 directly into RFC. As a Cpl 6 Squadron he went to France on 9 August, 1914 earning a 1914 Star and bar. He was therefore the first RFC Other Rank to land in France, no doubt accompanying an Officer on some reconnaissance duty. On 12 August, 1914 he joined the Aircraft Park. As a Flight Sergeant he was awarded an Army M.S.M. in *L.G.* 12 March, 1917 'for Valuable Services with the Armies in the Field.' He was promoted Temp SM (D) on 1 May 1917, and was SM1 (Discip) in 1918 RAF Muster Roll. RAF L.S.&G.C. *w.e.f.* 18 June, 1930 as Flight Sergeant.

★ 107. WILLIAM ROBERT BRUCE

Born London 11 July, 1881. Took his test for Royal Aero Club Aviators' Certificate (No. 467) as a Sergeant 23 April, 1913 on Salisbury Plain in a Maurice Farman. Was a Flight Sergeant in July, 1914. As a Sgt Major in 5 Squadron went to France on 14 August, 1914. He was commissioned Lieutenant and Quarter Master 1 March, 1915 and was Hon. Captain in RAF List 1918 *w.e.f.* 1 March, 1918. November, 1921 *A.F.L.*, Squadron Leader O.B.E. *w.e.f.* 17 June, 1920 (Stores Officer) from 13 May 1920 at 1 Group HQ Kenley. In February, 1931 *A.F.L.* Group Captain, Deputy Director of Equipment, Air Ministry from 1 January, 1930. See group photographs 1 and 2.

★ 108. G. F. SMITH

Enlisted 26 June, 1912 directly into RFC. At the outbreak of war he was Sergeant in 2 Squadron and was promoted to Flight Sergeant prior to proceeding to France on 12 August, 1914. He was promoted WO1 2 March, 1913 and was CMM (Tech) on 1918 RAF Muster Roll. See group photographs Nos. 2 and 3.

109. REGINALD COLLIS

Born Dorking 31 January, 1894. Obtained his Royal Aero Club Aviators' Certificate (No. 412) on 4 February, 1913 as a 1st Class Air Mechanic in a Maurice Farman at CFS Salisbury Plain. He was designated 2nd Class Flyer *w.e.f.* 22 October, 1913. Served overseas from 26 May 1915 earning 1914/15 Star trio. Commissioned 2 Lieut 29 June, 1915.

RFC Communiqué No.7 27 August, 1915

2 Lt Collis and Lt G.A. Parker on a BE2c when flying over Ypres attacked and chased an Aviatik which, upon being fired at, dived and appeared to land. A second machine, a German Scout, attacked them near Hooge and, hitting the wireless set, succeeded in breaking it. After a good deal of ammunition had been expended the German machine flew away towards Roulers.

RFC CommuniquéNo.8 28 August, 1915

2Lt Collis and Lt Parker when on a BE2c carrying out artillery registration near Hooge, saw a hostile machine coming to attack them from the direction of Roulers. Turning to meet it, they fired fifty rounds and then manœuvred round again to get into a more favourable position. Having expended most of their ammunition, a wireless message was sent for a Scout to come out, but on firing the last few rounds, the German machine dived steeply.

The observer then signalled to say that the German had gone.

The registration was continued, and was interrupted twice by hostile machines which, however, when approached showed no fight.

RFC Communiqué No.31 19 March, 1916

2Lt R. Collis and Flt Lt Emergy (FE), while flying over the channel at 8000 feet, saw a hostile machine being shelled over Dover. They gave chase, but could not get within range. Presently they saw another machine making for Deal. They flew up channel and met this hostile aeroplane on its return. Lt Collis was then at 8000 feet and the hostile machine at 4000 feet. Planing down with engine throttled back until within 150 yards, the observer opened fire immediately behind. The hostile machine did not return the fire and made no attempt to manœuvre out of range. After a drum had been expended the enemy was observed to plunge down towards the sea with a steep right-hand bank and with irregular puffs of smoke coming from the engine. Lt Collis now experienced some difficulty with his engine and during the time that he was changing over the petrol to the service tank, he lost sight of the hostile machine, which was last seen at 1500 feet diving steeply.

110. J. E. HODGES

Transferred to RFC from RE 15 July, 1912. Nothing further has been traced on this man.

111. A. BENNETT

Enlisted 25 November, 1912. Posted to 2 Squadron. Discharged 9 January, 1913 under *K.R.* 392 (ix) as Sergeant. 'Unfitted for the duties of the Corps.'

★ 112. S. JENKINS

Enlisted 26 June, 1912 directly into RFC. 1AM 5 Squadron at the outbreak of WW1. Promoted Cpl 10 August, 1914, proceeded to France with the squadron 14 August, 1914. Awarded French Médaille Militaire in *L.G.* 9 November, 1914 'for Gallantry 21-30 August, 1914.' Promoted Temp SM (T) 1 April, 1917 and shown as CMM. (Technical) in 1918 RAF Muster Roll.

★ 113. A. W. WILSON

Enlisted 26 June, 1912 into KRRC (?). 1AM in 2 Squadron to France 14 August, 1914. Royal Aero Club Aviators' Certificate No. 1789 on 24 September, 1915. He was then a Sergeant *w.e.f.* 1 May 1915 and was appointed 1st Class Pilot. In 1918 RAF Muster Roll shown as Sgt Mech (Pilot).

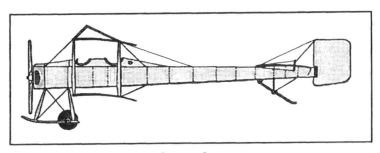

SHORT S.45

⋆ 114. J. H. HAMILTON

Enlisted 28 June, 1912. Transferred from RE to RFC 15 July, 1912. Earned 1914 Star and bar in 5 Squadron as 1AM from 14 August, 1914. Promoted Sergeant (Rigger) 1 June, 1917, and shown in 1918 RAF Muster Roll as Sgt Mech (Rigger Aero). Was alive in July, 1977. Address 22 Gaddesby Road, Kings Heath, Birmingham.

⋆ 115. R. F. STANBROOK

Enlisted 28 June, 1912 into RE and transferred to RFC 15 July, 1912. 2 AM at outbreak of war and earned 1914 Star and bar with Airship Detachment transferring to RNAS on 18 October, 1914 as AM1 No. 682. Promoted to Petty Officer 15 December, 1916. In 1918 RAF Muster Roll is shown as 200682 Sgt (Discip).

⋆ 116. H. C. S. BULLOCK

As Sgt 2 Squadron served in France from 13 August, 1914. Mentioned in despatches and awarded Military Medal 3 June, 1916 as Sgt Major, he was commissioned 2 Lieutenant 19 October, 1916 and awarded an M.B.E. 1 January, 1918, and was Lieutenant (Technical) in 1918 *Air Force List*. (See group photograph No. 2.)

117. D. MARTIN

Transferred from RE to RFC 15 July, 1912. Discharged 24 April, 1913 under King's Regulations 392 (ix) 'unfitted for duties in the Corps.'

⋆ 118. GEORGE A. HILLIAR

Flight Sergeant in July, 1914. Earned 1914 Star for service as Sergeant Major with the Aircraft Park from 12 August, 1914. Commissioned 2 Lieutenant 13 February, 1916, and Captain 26 May, 1917. However in the 1918 RAF *Air Force List* he is shown as substantive 2 Lieutenant (Technical). Squadron Leader from 17 June, 1920. 1921 *A.F.L.* Stores Officer RAF Cranwell from 21 January, 1921. He retired on 1 July, 1927 a Wing Commander (Engineering) and in December, 1937 was serving as (Retd) Equipment Officer at RAF Station Cranfield, Bletchley (No. 1 Bomber Group). Still a retired officer in 1946 *Air Force List*, in this rank.

⋆ 119. JOHN R. NICHOLLS

Born 9 April, 1878. Enlisted circa 1898 but his service prior to being a Flight Sergeant with No. 4 Squadron in France, from 9 September, 1914 earning a 1914 Star and bar is unknown. However in Army Order 121 of April, 1916 he was awarded his Army L.S.&G.C. as Sergeant Major RFC. Commissioned 2 Lieutenant (Equipment Officer) RFC on 18 March, 1917 and in April, 1918 *Air Force List* shown as Lieutenant. Promoted Acting Captain 3 May, 1918. He was promoted to Flight Lieutenant (Engines) on 30 June, 1922 at No. 1 Stores Depot Kidbrooke London. He retired 19 November, 1924 and is still shown as a retired officer in this rank in 1960 *Air Force List*. (See group photographs 1 and 2).

120. W. SHARP

No details prior to his being noted as a Sergeant with No. 3 Squadron in August, 1914. He did not earn a 1914 or 1914/15 Star. As a Sergeant earned an Army M.S.M. in *L.G.* 16 August, 1917, for 'Valuable Services with the Armies in the Field.' However he had already been commissioned 2 Lieutenant *w.e.f.* 12 October, 1916. Shown as Lieutenant (A and S) in *Air Force List* of April, 1918.

121. G. HARRISON

Re-transferred as a Sergeant to 2/Grenadier Guards 1 December, 1912.

⋆ 122. R. W. WARE

Born 26 March, 1894. Enlisted 26 June, 1912. As 1AM No. 3 Squadron earned 1914 Star and bar from 13 August, 1914. Promoted Flight Sergeant, (Driver M.T.) on 1 January, 1917. In 1918 RAF Muster Roll is Chief Mechanic (Driver). He earned an RAF L.S.&G.C. as SM2 *w.e.f.* 26 June, 1930. Awarded 1935 Silver Jubilee Medal. Commissioned No. 31100 Flying Officer 8 January, 1937. Flight Lieutenant 8 January, 1940. Served as a Wing Commander in WW2. Retired 12 March, 1949. No. 979 E.W. Shrewsbury met him in July, 1975 in Limpsfield.

⋆ 123. P. N. LEE

Enlisted 2 July, 1912. 1AM Aircraft Park, in France from 12 August, 1914. Promoted Sergeant (Rigger) on 1 September, 1916. In 1918 Muster Roll he is listed as Sergeant Mechanic (Rigger Aero). Served in Middle East in 1928 and earned a General Service Medal (clasp Southern Desert, Iraq). See No. 1160. RAF L.S.&G.C. as SM2 *w.e.f.* 2 July, 1930. His group of six medals including 1935 Silver Jubilee medal is known in a private collection.

★ 124. G. E. MORGAN

Enlisted in June, 1912 directly into RFC and earned 1914 Star as 1AM 4 Squadron. Promoted Sergeant, but died of a self-inflicted wound on 3 January, 1916, aged 22. Son of Sophia and William Godfrey Morgan of 9 Walsham Rd, New Cross London. Buried Villens-Bocage Communal Cemetery Extension (B.11).

★ 125. J. R. SMALLBONE

Enlisted 27 June, 1912, directly into RFC. 1AM, 3 Squadron in France from 13 August, 1914. Promoted Flight Sgt (Carpenter) 1 February, 1917. Ch Mech (Carpenter) in 1918 RAF Muster Roll.

★ 126. J. WAELAND

Enlisted 28 June, 1912, directly into RFC. Cpl 3 Squadron in France from 13 August, 1914. Promoted Flight Sergeant (Rigger) 1 September, 1915. Awarded RAF M.S.M. in this rank, for services in France, in *L.G.* 3 June, 1918. In 1918 RAF Muster Roll listed as Ch Mech. (Aero Rigger). Came from Canning Town.

⋆ 127. HENRY GILES AYLEN

Enlisted 17 November, 1906. Formerly 45207 Gunner 43 Battery RFA. Transferred 27 June, 1912 to 3 Squadron RFC. As 1AM 3 Squadron earned 1914 Star and bar, in France from 13 August, 1914. Promoted Temp SM (Tech) *w.e.f.* 1 March, 1916. In 1918 RAF Muster Roll listed as Chief Master Mechanic (Tech). Awarded RAF L.S.&G.C. as SM1 *w.e.f.* 17 November, 1924, in 1931 was 12th senior RAF Warrant Officer. In December, 1937 *Air Force List* shown as Warrant Officer, from 20 August, 1935 with 24 (Communications) Squadron at Hendon NW9. In March, 1938 *A.F.L.* with seniority dating only from 28 February, 1920 was 16th senior RAF Warrant Officer. In November, 1941, he was the tenth most senior RAF Warrant Officer. Commissioned during WW2 personal No. 45849; shown as retired in 1946 *Air Force List*.

128. W. G. TURNER

Enlisted 12 April, 1907. Formerly 45357 Gunner, 55 Battery. RFA. Transferred to 3 Squadron RFC 24 June, 1912. Served overseas from 26 July, 1915 and earned 1914/15 Star trio. Mentioned in despatches three times, 4 January, 1917 and 13 May, 1917 (both times as Flight Sergeant) and in *L.G.* 30 May, 1918 (as Sergeant Major) for 18 April, 1918 in Italy. Was promoted Temp SM (T), 1 March, 1916. In 1918 RAF Muster Roll listed as Ch. Mr Mh (Technical). Awarded RAF M.S.M. in *L.G.* 1 January, 1919 (for Italy as Chief Master Mechanic). Originally from Plumstead.

⋆ 129. J. HURST

Enlisted 15 September, 1911. Formerly 67036 Gunner 137 Battery. RFA. Transferred to 2 Squadron 27 June, 1912. As 1AM in 2 Squadron earned 1914 Star. Promoted 1 June, 1917 to Temp SM (D). SM1 (Disciplinarian) in 1918 RAF Muster Roll.

⋆ 130. ALBERT EDWARD BELL

Enlisted 1 July, 1912 directly into the RFC. With the coincidence of so many men on this short list of 1425 sharing the same surname, (and especially the confirmation of the two McCudden brothers) it is interesting to speculate on the relationship of some of the other pairs of men with identical surnames. Perhaps No. 39 John Bell brought his younger brother with him upon transfer from the Air Bn to RFC.

Whatever happened previously we know that No. 130 Bell went to France as a Cpl with 6 Squadron and earned a 1914 Star and bar. He was promoted Temp SM (D) on 1 May, 1917 and is shown as SM1 (Discip) in the 1918 RAF Muster Roll. He was awarded an RAF L.S.&G.C. Medal *w.e.f.* 1 July, 1930 as SM1. In the December, 1937 *Air Force List* is shown as serving at No. 7 Flying Training School, Peterborough, Northants from 25 February, 1935. In March, 1938 he was the seventh senior RAF Warrant Officer and in November, 1941 and October, 1944 he was the fourth. When he retired in 1946 he was the senior WO in RAF. His group of eight medals is in the RAF Museum at Hendon:— 1914 Star and bar (Cpl, RFC); British War Medal and Victory Medal (Flight Sergeant, RFC); Defence Medal; War Medal 1939-45; Silver Jubilee Medal, GV 1935; Coronation Medal, GV1 1937 (these last four un-named as issued); RAF L.S.&G.C. Medal (GV) (SM1 RAF).

★ 131. P. UPHILL

Enlisted directly into RFC on 1 July, 1912. Posted as Cpl, 3 Squadron, to France 13 August, 1914. On 1 February, 1917 was promoted Flight Sgt. In 1918 RAF Muster Roll is listed as Chief Mech. (Carpenter).

★ 132. THOMAS FRANCIS BULLEN

Born 2 February, 1887. First record of him is as a Sergeant at Netheravon in July, 1914. F/Sgt, 5 Squadron in France from 14 August, 1914. In the *London Gazette* of 9 November, 1914 he is shown as *Sgt Major* and was awarded the French Médaille Militaire, for services between 21 and 30

August, 1914. Commissioned 2 Lieut RFC 8 October, 1915, 'For Services in the Field' Major RFC 1 January, 1918. Squadron Leader, November, 1921 *A.F.L.* with O.B.E., seniority 1 August, 1919, from 29 May 1921 Commanding Engine Repair Depot, Egypt. From 17 April, 1929 22 Group HQ South Farnborough. Retired 8 August, 1933, RAFVR 1 September, 1939 to 26 August, 1945. In the 1969 *Air Force List* he is shown as 01126 Squadron Ldr (Retd) O.B.E. (E). Not in 1970 *A.F.L.* See group photograph No. 2. (See No. 337.)

133. H. W. CARTER

Formerly 17528 Driver RE he joined 1 Balloon Company on mobilisation of the Air Battalion. He was a 2AM in 5 Squadron when on 12 May, 1914, he was killed in a mid-air collision at 500 feet at Farnborough. Captain E. V. Anderson was the pilot of the Sopwith three-seater, tractor bi-plane (80 h.p. Gnome) and both were killed instantly. Lieutenant C. W. Wilson, the other pilot, was injured but survived.

SOPWITH DI No. 324 IN WHICH H. W. CARTER WAS KILLED

★ 134. CHARLES R. GALLIE

Born Shipton Yorks 4 February, 1892. As 1AM at Central Flying School, Upavon, gained his Royal Aero Club Aviators' Certificate (No. 559) on 12 July, 1913 in a Maurice Farman. On 8 October, 1914 as a Sergeant, 6 Squadron, he flew a BE2 to France earning his 1914 Star trio. He was commissioned 2 Lieut RFC and Royal Scots Fusiliers (his previous regiment?) 'For Services in the Field' on 20 June, 1915 (see *L.G.* 27 July, 1915). He was K.I.A. 22 August, 1915.

★ 135. REGINALD DAVID GORRIE MACROSTIE

Born 1 January, 1890. Mentioned by McCudden V.C. in *'Flying Fury.'* A Corporal in 3 Squadron when he went to France on 12 August, 1914 and earned a 1914 Star and bar. He was commissioned 2 Lieutenant in the Royal Dublin Fusiliers 28 October, 1917. He transferred to RAF at the end of WW1 and was later awarded M.B.E. 1921 November, *A.F.L.*, Flying Officer, M.B.E. *w.e.f.* 20 July, 1920. From 20 May 1920 Stores Officer No. 2 Flying Training School, Royston. Flight Lieutenant February, 1931 *A.F.L.*, seniority *w.e.f.* 1 July, 1926 from 15 December, 1929 at No. 4 Stores Depot Ruislip. Squadron Leader (E) 1 February, 1935. From 30 January, 1937 was Equipment Officer at Manston (1937 *A.F.L.*) Still serving in 1946 as No. 10122 Squadron Leader. Retired 21 April, 1948. Noted in April, 1975 *A.F.L.* but not in the next year's.

★ 136. H. GREEN

Enlisted 16 August, 1909. Served in the Air Battalion. 1AM 2 Squadron in France from 12 August, 1914. Awarded Distinguished Conduct Medal in *L.G.* 27 July, 1916 as Flight Sergeant, No. 21 Reserve Squadron 'For consistent good work. By his perseverance and application he has, though very shorthanded, never failed to have aeroplanes ready for reinforcement.' Promoted Flight Sergeant (Rigger) 1 June, 1916. M.I.D. *L.G.* 25 September, 1916. Awarded Army Meritorious Service Medal *L.G.* 11 November, 1916 'Valuable Services with the Army in the Field.' All three awards are believed to be for Egypt. In the 1918 RAF Muster Roll he is listed as Chief Mechanic (Rigger Aero).

★ 137. W. G. PLUNKETT

Enlisted originally 26 July, 1909. Formerly 19080 Spr 57 Company RE he transferred to RFC in August, 1912 and was posted to 3 Squadron on 28th. 1AM 3 Squadron he went to France 13 August, 1914. Promoted Flight Sergeant 1 August, 1916. In 1918 RAF Muster Roll listed as Chief Mech (Rigger Aero).

⋆ 138. R. STREET

Enlisted 16 January, 1908 into 2/Grenadier Guards. As 13556, Private, was posted to RFC HQ 24 June, 1912. 2AM 5 Squadron to France on 14 August, 1914 earning 1914 Star and bar. Then as Sergeant was awarded a French Médaille Militaire the same year. He was promoted Flight Sergeant on 1 June, 1916 (Driver M.T.) and in the 1918 RAF Muster Roll was Chief Mechanic (Driver). Mentioned in the *Times* 'B' Press Release, 29 August, 1919.

⋆ 139. E. PARSONS

Formerly No. 14360 Pte 3/Grenadier Guards, transferred to 2 Squadron RFC 24 June, 1914. To France 12 August, 1914 as 2AM 2 Squadron. Discharged under *K.R.* 392 (xvi) 'no longer physically fit for war service.' Silver war badge 50562.

140. W. T. HARE

Enlisted 8 April, 1907. Formerly 16218 Driver 3 Balloon Company RE on mobilisation of the Air Battalion. As 2AM served overseas from 7 December, 1914 earning 1914/15 Star trio. Promoted Sergeant 1 January, 1917 and was Sergeant Mechanic (Driver) in 1918 RAF Muster Roll. Entitled to Indian General Service Medal (Clasp Afghanistan, N.W. Frontier, 1919) as Sergeant.

⋆ 141. H. GOLDSTONE

Enlisted 15 August, 1905. Formerly 14542 Sapper 3 Balloon Company RE in July, 1910. At the Balloon School (Mounted) on mobilisation of the Air Battalion. 2AM 3 Squadron to France 12 August, 1914. Promoted Sergeant 1 July, 1917. In 1918 RAF Muster Roll as Sgt/Mech (Rigger/ Aero).

⋆ 142. E. McEVOY

As Sergeant in 3 Squadron he earned a 1914 Star and bar serving in France from 12 August, 1914. Commissioned 2 Lieutenant Oxfordshire & Buckinghamshire LI 27 February, 1916. See group photograph No. 2. Trio of medals in a private collection.

* 143. J. M. KNIGHT

Transferred to RFC HQ from 1/Rifle Brigade 24 June, 1912. 1AM Aircraft Park, in France from 16 August, 1914. M.I.D. *L.G.* 4 January, 1917 and 7 November,1917, both times as Sgt Major. Commissioned 2 Lieutenant 1 February, 1918. See *'Cross and Cockade'* Volume 6, No. 2, page 85, where he is noted as a pilot in No. 10 Reserve Squadron.

144. WILLIAM SMITH

Born Dulwich, London, 18 April, 1889. Enlisted 19 August, 1907. Formerly 2246 Cpl Rifle Brigade, transferred to HQ 27 June, 1912. Royal Aero Club Aviators' Certificate No. 579 on 5 August, 1913 as 1AM at Upavon (C.F.S.) in a Maurice Farman. As Corporal, with the Aircraft Park earned 1914/15 star trio. Promoted Temp S.M.(T) 1 March, 1916. M.I.D. *L.G.* 30 November, 1915 and 1 June, 1916 also 'mentioned' for services at the Air Ministry *L.G.* 22 January, 1919, and next day in the *Times* 'B' List. Chief Master Mech (Tech) in 1918 RAF Muster Roll. His medals were returned to RAF Records Office 27 June, 1929 (deceased?).

* 145. CHARLES RAMPLIN

Enlisted 10 September, 1906. Formerly 4023 L/Cpl 1/Rifle Brigade when transferred to 1 Squadron RFC on 4 July, 1912. 1AM Aircraft Park in France from 16 August, 1914. On a Riggers course at CFS September, 1914. Temp SM (T) from 1 April, 1917. Chief Master Mech (Tech) in RAF Muster Roll (1918). Awarded RAF M.S.M. in *L.G.* 28 October, 1921 as SM1 for service in Iraq/Mesopotamia. (Of 872 RAF MSMs awarded only 29 were for this theatre (1921-24)). Awarded General Service Medal (Iraq) and then RAF L.S.&G.C. Medal *w.e.f.* 12 September, 1924 as SM1. Retired 1931.

* 146. W. G. SCALES

Enlisted 2 December, 1909. Formerly Suffolk Regt, transferred to RFC 6 July, 1912. As 1AM Aircraft Park to France 16 August, 1914. Promoted Sergeant 1 August, 1917. 1918 RAF Muster Roll Sergeant (Disciplinarian).

* 147. T. J. MOUNTFORD

Enlisted 18 February, 1911. Formerly 5317 Pte No. 3 Company RAMC transferred to RFC No. 1 Squadron, 24 July, 1912. To France 12 August, 1914 as 1AM with RFC HQ earning 1914 Star and bar. Promoted Sergeant (Wireless Operator) 1 June, 1917. Recommended for M.S.M. 15 March, 1917 'For continuous good works as squadron wireless Sergeant, July, 1916 to February, 1917' by Brig. Gen. C. A. H. Longcroft. Not approved. Distinguished Conduct Medal in *L.G.* 3 June, 1917 with 15 Squadron 'For continuous gallantry and devotion. He has performed good work consistently throughout, and has at all times set a fine example to his men.' 1918 RAF Muster Roll, Chief Mechanic (Wireless Operator).

* 148. HARRY JENKINS

Enlisted 2 May, 1907. Formerly 8068 Rifleman 1/KRRC, transferred to No. 2 Squadron 2 July, 1912. 1AM with 2 Squadron earning 1914 Star and bar in France from 12 August, 1914. Awarded French Médaille Militaire as Corporal in 1914. Temp SM (Discip) 1 January, 1917. April, 1918 RAF Muster Roll SM1 (Discip). Mentioned in the *Times* 'B' Press Release of 29 August, 1919. General Service Medal (Kurdistan) as SM1. RAF L.S.&G.C. Medal w.e.f. 2 May, 1925, as SM1. Still serving in 1931. *Vide* RFC Communiqué No. 43, 20 June, 1916 Cpl Jenkins was driver of a winch with No. 1 Kite Balloon Section. Seven rounds of HE burst within 20 yds. He moved the winch, under fire, slowly up the road, with the balloon at 600 feet above it.

149. (SEE 88)

However, this might be Flight Sergeant Long. See group photograph No. 2. Not traced elsewhere.

* 150. JOHN BULLOCK

Formerly 7519 L/Cpl 1/Somerset L.I. transferred to 3 Squadron RFC 27 June, 1912. As a Transport Sergeant, 5 Squadron, went to France 13 August, 1914. Commissioned 2 Lieutenant 14 December, 1916. 1921 (November) *A.F.L.* was Flying Officer (T) (Flying and Observer Officer) seniority 1 August, 1919 from 21 February, 1921 at Coastal Command Aircraft Depot Dunfermline. Retired as Flight Lieutenant 1 January, 1929. In 1937 *Air Force List*, shown as Equipment Officer (Flight Lieut (ret)) RAF Station Pembroke Dock. See group photograph No. 2.

★ 151. ALFRED WILSON

Enlisted 14 September, 1905. Formerly 6632 Rifleman 1/KRRC. On transfer to RFC posted to 3 Squadron 2 July, 1912. Was a Sergeant in 3 Squadron when he went to France 13 August, 1914. Mentioned in despatches *L.G.* 10 October, 1914 as Sergeant. Royal Aero Club Aviators' Certificate No. 3883 on 23 November, 1916 as a Sergeant Major. Was a Sergeant Pilot, with 11 Squadron but reverted to Corporal (1st Class Pilot) 22 March, 1917. Reported missing, flying an FE2B. Prisoner-of-war 1 April, 1917. In 1918 RAF Muster Roll shown as Corporal Mechanic (Pilot).

★ 152. FRANK JAMES

Born Barrow-on-Soar, 19 February, 1888. Enlisted 6 January, 1908. Formerly 7595 Private 1/Coldstream Guards. Posted to Central Flying School 27 June, 1912. As a Sergeant earned Royal Aero Club Aviators' Certificate No. 864, on 28 July, 1914 at CFS Upavon in a Maurice Farman. Earned 1914 Star and bar as a Sergeant in 4 Squadron, in France from 9 September, 1914. Mentioned in *L.G.* 30 November, 1915 as a Sergeant still with 4 Squadron and promoted Temp SM (Discip) on 1 January, 1916. French Médaille Militaire *L.G.* 24 February, 1916.

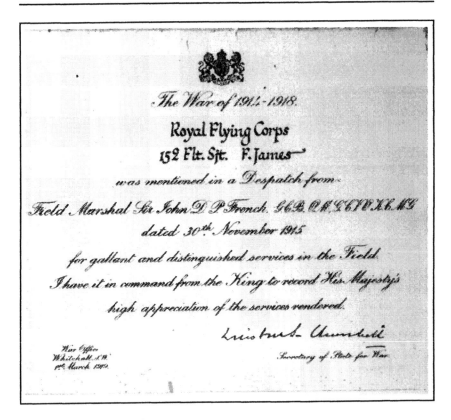

London Gazette 24 February, 1916:—

The President of the Republic has bestowed the decoration 'Médaille Militaire' on the undermentioned Warrant Officers, Non-Commissioned Officers and Men in recognition of their distinguished services during the campaign:

152 Flight Sergeant Frank James, R.F.C.
251 Sergeant Major Joseph Kemper, R.F.C.
555 Sergeant Archibald Augustus James Beer, R.F.C.

SM1 (D) in 1918 RAF Muster Roll. Awarded RAF M.S.M. as Master Clerk in *London Gazette* 1 January, 1919. RAF L.S.&G.C. as SM1 *w.e.f.* 6 January, 1926. In the February, 1931 *A.F.L.* he is the 6th senior RAF Warrant Officer. Also served in WW2 and awarded M.B.E. His medal group is known to be in a private collection:— M.B.E. (2nd type, military ribbon), 1914 Star and bar trio (152 Sgt RFC with oakleaf), Defence and War medals (1939-45), RAF M.S.M. (GV), RAF L.S.&G.C. (GV) and French Médaille Militaire. See group photograph No. 2.

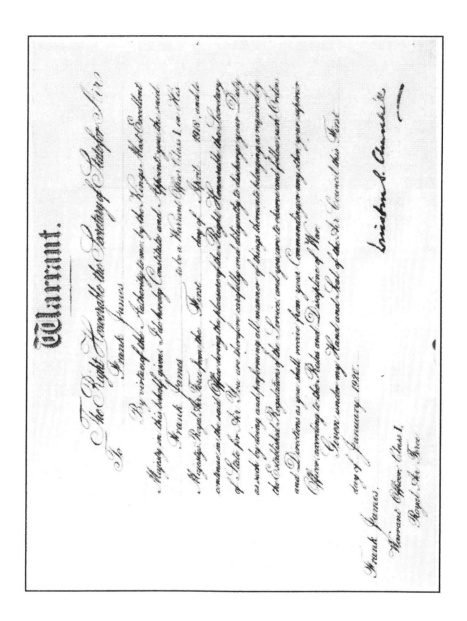

* 153. THOMAS WARREN

Born Loughborough 20 January, 1890. Enlisted 27 January, 1908. Formerly 7646 Corporal 1/Coldstream Guards. Was 17831 Sapper RE 2 Company Balloon School (Dismounted) on mobilisation of the Air Battalion. When transferred to RFC was posted to CFS on 27 June, 1912. Awarded Royal Aero Club Aviators' Certificate No. 748 on 26 February, 1914, as a 1st class Air-Mech in a Maurice Farman at CFS. As a Corporal 6 Squadron. earned 1914 Star and bar from 6 October, 1914. Acting WO (T) from 1 January, 1918. Act. Chief Master Mechanic in 1918 RAF Muster Roll.

154. O. WILLIAMS

A Sergeant in 1912. Discharged 31 March, 1914 under *K.R.* 393 (ix) 'Unfitted for the duties of the Corps.'

* 155. C. H. HEARNE

Enlisted 5 July, 1912 and was a 2AM in 2 Squadron in France from 12 August, 1914. Promoted Flight Sergeant (Rigger-Aero) 1 November, 1917, and was Chief Mechanic in 1918 RAF Muster Roll.

* 156. H. C. WRIGHT

Born Evesham Worcester, 20 September, 1889. Transferred from 87 RAMC Depot to RE in 1912 prior to transfer to RFC. Royal Aero Club Aviators' Certificate No. 456 on 11 April, 1913 as a Sergeant in a Short at CFS Upavon. Appointed 2nd class flyer *w.e.f.* 6 November, 1913. Sergeant (Pilot) at Farnborough in 1913. As a Sergeant, served in 6 Squadron earning 1914 Star and bar in France from 16 August, 1914 (*N.B.* 6 Squadron not in France as a unit until October, 1914, thus he must have been on the strength of 2, 3, 4, or 5 Squadron.). Discharged as unfit on 11 January, 1915. See *'Cross and Cockade,'* Volume 7, No. 3, page 135 and photograph under No. 7. He may be the Sergeant front left in the photograph on Page 10.

157. H. J. BANNISTER

Enlisted 8 July, 1912. Served overseas from 3 February, 1915, as a Sergeant in 1 Squadron. Promoted Temp SM (T) on 1 March, 1918 and was Acting Chief Master Mechanic 1918 RAF Muster Roll. His 1914/15 star British War Medal and Victory medal are known in a private collection, all named to Sergeant.

★ 158. GEORGE DUNVILLE

Enlisted July, 1912, directly into RFC. Was 1AM in 3 Squadron in France from 12 August, 1914. Earned Royal Aero Club Aviators' Certificate No. 5144 on 17 August, 1917. Killed in Action as Sergeant 5 September, 1917, aged 23. Son of Mr. and Mrs. Dunville of Shankhill Road, Belfast. Husband of Susannah Vance (formerly Dunville) of 184 Grosvenor Road, Belfast. Buried Carnmony Cemetery, Co. Antrim, Ireland (Row B, Grave 56).

159. CHARLES EDWARD JARVIS

Born Harwich, 14 October, 1882. From Pewsey close to CFS Salisbury Plain on enlistment 9 July, 1912 directly into RFC. Awarded Royal Aero Club Aviators' Certificate No. 524 on 17 June, 1913 as a Sergeant at CFS Upavon in an Avro. He served overseas from 20 December, 1915 earning a 1914/15 star trio as a Warrant Officer. Appointed WO 12 March, 1915. Chief Master Mechanic in 1918 RAF Muster Roll. Awarded RAF M.S.M. in this rank in *London Gazette* 1 January, 1919 (pages 99-101). RAF L.S.&G.C. Medal *w.e.f.* 9 July, 1930. He had been appointed WO1 on 1 October, 1928. Served in WW2. In November, 1941 *A.F.L.* he was the

35th senior RAF Warrant Officer, though then his seniority was shown as from 1 December, 1931.

* 160. A. N. ARMSTRONG

Served in 111 Battery, RFA prior to transfer to RFC 10 July, 1912. As 1AM Aircraft Park in France from 16 August, 1914. Mentioned in Despatches as Sergeant 5 Squadron in *L.G.* 1 January, 1916. Commissioned 2 Lieutenant 15 November, 1916. Shown as Lieutenant ('Technical) in first *Air Force List* (April, 1918). Discharged prior to 1921. In November, that year serving in the Department of Civil Aviation at the Air Ministry as a civilian junior assistant to the Controller of Communication.

* 161. WALTER FRANK BRYANT

As a Sergeant with 4 Squadron in France from 12 August, 1914 earned 1914 Star and bar. As Sergeant Major was commissioned 2 Lieutenant (RFC and Royal West Surrey Regt) on 16 May 1916 'For Services in the Field.' Flight Lieutenant (Stores Staff Duties) *w.e.f.* 31 July, 1920 serving at HQ Mediterranean Group Valetta, Malta. In February, 1931 was a Wing Commander in the Stores Branch (seniority 1 July, 1930) (Qualified at Commissariat Course) and was Officer Commanding No. 4 Stores Depot 21 Group, Ruislip, Middlesex. Retired 11 September, 1931. In 1937 he was employed as Equipment Staff Officer, Northern Area Observer Corps at Hucknall, Notts. Recalled in June, 1942 he served the remainder of WW2 as Wing Commander, (No. 49879).

* 162. R. RUMBOLD

Sergeant, 2 Squadron in France from 12 August, 1914. M.I.D. *L.G.* 1 January, 1916 in 2 Squadron but had been commissioned 2 Lieutenant 8 October, 1915 'For Services in the Field.' See group photograph No. 3.

* 163. T. O'RIELLY

Formerly 46949 acting Bombadier 86 Battery RFA, posted to Central Flying School 20 June, 1912 on transfer to RFC. A Sergeant on 26 June, 1914 assumed his real name of Walter Walker Reilly (*K.R.* para, 1901). Sergeant, RFC HQ in France from 12 August, 1914. Commissioned 2 Lieutenant 22 September, 1914. See group photograph No. 2.

★ 164. O. P. ARIES

Enlisted 17 August, 1909. Formerly 9134 Private 2/Oxfordshire & Buckinghamshire L.I. posted to 3 Squadron 24 June, 1912 on transfer to RFC. 2AM RFC HQ, France from 12 August, 1914. Promoted Corporal (MT Driver) 1 September, 1917, and retained that rank in 1918 RAF Muster Roll.

165. P. H. SAUNDERS

As 2AM discharged 13 June, 1914 under *K.R.* 392 (xiv) on payment of £18. He was therefore not a recruit but a long-service man wishing to leave the Army.

★ 166. J. G. O'GIOLLAGAIN

Formerly 10480 L/Cpl Royal Irish Fusiliers he transferred to 1 Squadron RFC 3 July, 1912. As 1AM 6 Squadron served in France from 5 October, 1914. Royal Aero Club Aviators' Certificate 1299 on 1 June, 1915. Sergeant Pilot from 9 October, 1915. Wounded 7 December, 1915. Commissioned 2 Lieutenant 21 December, 1915. Accidentally killed 5 September, 1917 serving with 11 Squadron.

★ 167. ALFRED ROBERT MAY

Born Woolwich 24 November, 1891. Enlisted originally 7 March, 1906, aged 14. Formerly 32655 Gunner, 17 Company RGA, posted to 3 Squadron 3 July, 1912 on transfer to RFC. Royal Aero Club Aviators' Certificate No. 863 on 4 August, 1914 as a Sergeant at Netheravon in a Maurice Farman. As a Sergeant in 3 Squadron earned 1914 Star and bar in France from 12 August, 1914. Promoted Temp SM (D) w.e.f. 1 August, 1916. M.I.D. *L.G.* 1 July, 1916 for Egypt and *L.G.* 25 September, 1916. SM1 in 1918 RAF Muster Roll. RAF M.S.M. in *L.G.* 3 June, 1918 as Flight Sergeant (Temp S.M.), 47 Squadron, for services in Salonika. RAF L.S.&G.C. w.e.f. 7 March, 1924, as SM1. Still serving, when the 22nd senior WO1 in 1931. Originally from Plumstead. However, he must have been discharged then re-called in WW2 for in November,

1941 *A.F.L.*, he was the 48th senior RAF Warrant Officer with seniority from 1 August, 1933.

* 168. A.L . WOOLSEY

Enlisted 28 October, 1907, formerly 10227 Bandsman 2/Durham L.I. transferred to RFC (Regt. Order 19, December, 1912). A Corporal in 2 Squadron in France from 12 August, 1914. Promoted Q.M.S. (T) 1 April, 1916. Awarded Military Medal on 14 September, 1916 when serving with No. 1 Wing RFC. Master Mechanic (Tech) in 1918 RAF Muster Roll. Awarded RAF L.S.&G.C. Medal as SM2 *w.e.f.* 28 October, 1925.

* 169. GEORGE BAKER

Enlisted 13 June, 1910. Formerly 20201 Sapper 39 Company RE. Posted to Flying Depot 2 July,1912 on transfer to RFC. As 1AM, 2 Squadron earned 1914 Star and bar in France from 12 August, 1914. Promoted Temp S.M.(D) w.e.f 1 July, 1917 and listed as SM1 in 1918 RAF Muster Roll. Awarded RAF L.S.&G.C. Medal w.e.f. 13 June, 1928 as SM1. Serving in 1931 when he was 21st Senior WO in RAF. Served in WW2, as Squadron Leader (No. 11020) in 1944. His medals are known in a private collection (1914 trio, named to 1AM and T.S.M., Defence, War and L.S.&G.C. Medals).

* 170. J. DANGERFIELD

Enlisted 19 July, 1912 directly into the Corps. 1AM in 2 Squadron in France from 13 August, 1914. Royal Aero Club Aviators' Certificate No. 4223 on 11 February, 1917. Promoted Sergeant (1st Class Pilot) 22 March, 1917. Shot down and taken Prisoner of War when Sgt/Pilot 16 Squadron 20 April, 1917. Left 4.10 pm to patrol Avion-Willerval in BE2 No. 2553 with 2AM Harvey as observer. Sergeant Mech (Pilot) in 1918 RAF Muster Roll (presumably still a P.O.W.). His 1914 Star is known in a private collection.

* 171. EDWARD MATTHEW LING

2AM Aircraft Park in France from 16 August, 1914. Discharged under *K.R.* 392 (xxv) 'His services no longer required.' But commissioned 2 Lieutenant 25 November, 1917. Flying Officer (T) *w.e.f.* 24 October, 1919 stationed at No. 1 School of Technical Training (Boys) Halton, from 16 March, 1920.

★ 172. A. PALMER

Enlisted 10 July, 1912. Formerly at the RE Depot and transferred to RFC 25 July, 1912. Earned 1914 Star and bar in France as 1AM with the Aircraft Park from 16 August, 1914. Promoted Temp SM (T) from 1 August, 1917 and shown as Chief Master Mechanic (Tech) in 1918 RAF Muster Roll.

★ 173. S. J. PAYNE

Enlisted in 1903 into Somerset L.I. Served with 3 Squadron at Netheravon in 1913. Serving on a riggers course of instruction at Central Flying School in September, 1914, as Sergeant. In France from 7 October, 1914 as Sergeant Major, 6 Squadron. Commissioned Lieutenant and Quarter Master 1 June, 1915 and was in charge of No. 5 Park. Mentioned in despatches *L.G.* 22 June, 1915 (as Sergeant Major) and 24 February, 1917. Awarded Belgian Croix de Guerre. Shown as Major (Tech) in 1918 *Air Force List*. Died in 1919. His Croix de Guerre, Next of Kin Plaque and service papers are known in a private collection.

★ 174. JAMES MCCRAE

Born Glasgow 16 May, 1887. Formerly 5938 Lance Sergeant, 2/Scots Guards. Transferred to RFC 15 July, 1912. Awarded Royal Aero Club Aviators' Certificate No. 691 on 24 November, 1913 at Upavon in a Short of Central Flying School, when a Sergeant. Appointed 2nd Class flyer *w.e.f.* 17 December, 1913. Earned 1914 Star and bar, in France as Flight Sgt, 4 Squadron from 12 August, 1914. Mentioned in despatches *L.G.* 15 June, 1916, as Sergeant Major. Commissioned 2 Lieutenant 2 August, 1916. Was Temporary Major, Park Commander on 22 August, 1917.

Awarded M.B.E. as Lieut. Col. RAF. In November, 1921 *A.F.L.* shown as Squadron. Ldr. M.B.E. (Tech) seniority 1 August, 1919 on the non-effective list from 11 July, 1921. In the February, 1931 *A.F.L.* is shown as Wing Commander (Seniority 1 July, 1928) serving at RAF Home Command HQ, Uxbridge, Middlesex on Personnel Staff Duties from 23 April, 1929. Group Captain *w.e.f.* 1 July, 1934 and Commanding Officer *w.e.f.* 15 March, 1935, Home Aircraft Depot, Henlow Camp, Beds.

Awarded both 1935 Silver Jubilee and 1937 Coronation Medals. In 1946 *A.F.L.* shown as Group Captain (retired). See photograph in Appendix 2.

* 175. CECIL EDGAR MARTIN

Enlisted 1 May, 1908. Formerly 17435 Sapper Field Company RE. Serving with 2 Company Balloon School RE (Dismounted) on mobilisation of the Air Battalion RE. On transfer to RFC was posted to 1 Squadron 2 July, 1912. 1AM RFC HQ in France from 12 August, 1914 earning 1914 Star and bar. Promoted Temp SM (D) on 1 November, 1916. SM1 in RAF (1918) Muster Roll. Awarded RAF M.S.M. in *L.G.* 3 June, 1919 as Sgt Major for services in France with 74 Squadron. Awarded Order of Chevalier of Léopold II of Belgium and Belgian Croix de Guerre in *L.G.* 15 July, 1919. Awarded RAF L.S.&G.C. Medal as SM1 *w.e.f.* 1 May, 1926. Still serving in 1931 (35th senior RAF WO at that time). Originally from Peckham London S.E.

176. A. E. BOOTH

Enlisted 8 November, 1904. Formerly 21665 Gunner, 38 Company, R.G.A. Posted to 3 Squadron on 4 July, 1912 on transfer to RFC. Served overseas from 7 November, 1915 earning 1914/15 Star trio. Promoted Flight Sergeant 1 June, 1917 and was Chief Mechanic (Aero-Rigger) in 1918. RAF L.S.&G.C. *w.e.f.* 30 December, 1921 as Flight Sergeant (17 yrs and 7 weeks) so presumably had boy service prior to November, 1904 which was allowed to count. Believed to have flown as an observer on 15 July, 1916 with 2 Lieutenant Mathewson of 25 Squadron and brought down a Fokker.

* 177. JAMES HENRY WINCH

Born 13 June, 1889. Formerly 18835 Sapper 'E' Company RE. Posted to RFC HQ 8 July, 1912 on transfer to the Corps. As a 1AM with HQ served in France from 12 August, 1914. Recommended for a D.C.M. in No. 6 Squadron November, 1915 but not approved. Commissioned 10 July, 1916. Flying Officer in November, 1921 *Air Force List* (T) seniority 1 August, 1919, serving at School of Technical Training (Men) Ramsgate from 1 April, 1921. Flight Lieutenant in February, 1931 *Air Force List* (GD Branch, Qualified at Specialist Engineering Course) seniority 1 July, 1924. From 18 February, 1930 serving at Home Aircraft Depot, Henlow Camp, Beds (posted for Engineering Duties). Squadron Leader *w.e.f.* 1

April, 1935, serving at No. 3 Flying Training School at South Cerney, from 24 April, 1935 in 1937 *Air Force List*. Wing Commander *w.e.f.* 1 July, 1940, Group Captain 1 March, 1941 (05031), retired 15 April, 1944. Still in 1960 *Air Force List* as Group Captain (T).

178. JOHN ROLAND GARDINER

Born 19 February, 1886 in Portsmouth. Formerly with 'E' Company RE. Posted to CFS 4 July, 1912. Royal Aero Club Aviators' Certificate No. 707 on 11 December, 1913 as a Sergeant in a Short of CFS at Upavon. Reputedly flew to France as a passenger with Lieutenant Joubert de la Ferté (See *'Flying Fury'* by McCudden V.C.) but is shown as being entitled to only the 1914/15 Star for service overseas from 23 July, 1915. Recommended for Military Medal July, 1916, not approved. However, awarded Army M.S.M. in *L.G.* 11 November, 1916 as Flight Sergeant (24 Squadron, commanded by Major L. G. Hawker, V.C.) for 'Valuable Services with the Army in the Field.' Commissioned 2 Lieutenant 2 January, 1918. Flying Officer in November, 1921 *Air Force List* seniority 20 July, 1920, Stores Officer at No. 2 Flying Training School, Royston from 1 August, 1921. No. 4 Armoured Car Company, Iraq, 1925/27. Flight Lieutenant in 1931 (February) *Air Force List* serving at the Air Ministry from 12 September, 1928 (Supply and Research) for the Directorate of Equipment, seniority as Flight Lieutenant 1 January, 1927. Retired 19 February, 1931. In the 1937 *Air Force List* shown as Flight Lieutenant (E) (Retd) (No. 10094) but is known to have been recalled on 25 August,

1938 and served as a Wing Commander, from 1 June, 1942 to 9 September, 1944. Last noted in April, 1960 *Air Force List*. His Medal group is known in a private collection:— 1914/15 Star trio, Defence and war medals and Army M.S.M. (Fl. Sgt. No. 24 Sqn, RFC).

179. J. McDONALD

Formerly 20126 Lance Corporal RE. Posted to No. 2 Squadron 6 July, 1912 on transfer to RFC from Training Battalion RE. In 1914 was 1AM with No. 4 Squadron and earned 1914/15 Star trio for service overseas from 11 October, 1915. Commissioned 2 Lieutenant 6 May, 1917.

★ 180. A. F. J. HOLDER

Enlisted 21 April. 1911. Formerly 9687 Lance Corporal 2/Royal Sussex Regiment when posted to No. 1 Squadron on 6 July, 1912 on transfer to RFC. 1AM, Aircraft Park, France from 16 August, 1914. Reverted to Sergeant (Rigger) 10 January, 1917 and shown as Sergeant Mechanic (Rigger-Aero) in 1918 RAF Muster Roll. Mentioned in the *Times* 'B' Press Release of 29 August, 1919. RAF L.S.&G.C. *w.e.f.* 21 April, 1929 as Flight Sergeant. Awarded India General Service Medal (N.W. Frontier 1930/31).

★ 181. IVOR FRANK CHAMBERS

Born 15 August, 1892. Enlisted 15 July, 1912, directly into RFC. 1AM No. 4 Squadron when he was posted to France with B.E.F. 12 August, 1914. Temp Sergeant Major (T) 1 September, 1917. Chief Master Mechanic (Technical) in 1918 RAF Muster Roll. Promoted WO1 15 March, 1929. RAF L.S.&G.C. *w.e.f.* 15 July, 1930. Commissioned Engineer Officer (Flying Officer) *w.e.f.* 18 May, 1937 (No. 35055) and posted to No. 3 Flying Training School, South Cerney, Cirencester. Posted 20 November, 1937 to RAF Kalaframa, Malta. Final Promotion to Squadron Leader (1 June, 1941) and retired 23 October, 1946. Last noted in April, 1978 *Air Force List*. His medal group was sold by Glendinings in 1990: 1914 Star & bar trio, 1939/45 and Africa Stars, Defence and War Medals, 1935 Jubilee Medal and RAF LS&GC (W.O.).

182. (NOT TRACED, SEE 88)

However, this might be Flight Sergeant Lacy. See Group Photograph No. 1 not traced elsewhere.

* 183. S. A. JONES

Enlisted 16 July, 1912 into RFC. 2AM, Aircraft Park, in France from 16 August, 1914 with B.E.F. Corporal Rigger *w.e.f.* 1 May, 1915 and Corporal Mechanic (Rigger-Aero) in 1918 RAF Muster Roll.

* 184. J. STOREY

Enlisted 16 July, 1912 into RFC. 1AM No. 4 Squadron in France from 9 September, 1914. Mentioned in Despatches in the *London Gazette* of 15 June, 1916 as Flight Sergeant and already promoted Temp Sergeant Major (T) *w.e.f.* 1 June, 1915. Chief Master Mechanic in 1918 RAF Muster Roll.

* 185. VICTOR COLIN HIGGINBOTTOM

Born Warwick, 30 March, 1887. Enlisted 26 February, 1908. Formerly 17256 Sapper 'L' Company RE posted to Central Flying School on transfer to RFC on 26 June, 1912. Royal Aero Club Aviators' Certificate No. 317 as 1AM on 15 October, 1912, on Salisbury Plain in an Avro of CFS. Appointed 2nd Class flyer (1AM) *w.e.f.* 22 October, 1913. To France with BEF as 1AM in No. 2 Squadron on 12 August, 1914. Thus he was a 1st Class Air Mechanic Pilot in France. Placed on a charge in mid-August, for killing a chicken. He was punished and his fitter and rigger who ate the bird philosophically observed 'one learns from one's mistakes.' Promoted Temp Sergeant Major (T) 1 May, 1916 and was Chief Master Mechanic in 1918 RAF Muster Roll.

186. J. C. McNamara

Formerly 20332 Sapper 'L' Company RE when posted to CFS on transfer to RFC, on 26 June, 1912. Royal Aero Club Aviators' Certificate No. 445 on 1 April, 1913 as 1AM in a Maurice Farman of CFS on Salisbury Plain. Appointed 2nd Class flyer *w.e.f.* 4 November, 1913. Was still 1AM in 1914. Served overseas from 19 December, 1915 earning 1914/15 trio. Commissioned 2 Lieutenant 23 March, 1917. Killed in Action 2 June, 1917 serving in 4 Squadron. Born Pietermaritzburg, South Africa, 31 October, 1886.

* 187. A. R. Seabrook

Enlisted 13 June, 1911. Formerly 21685 Sapper RE ('L' Company) to Central Flying School 26 June, 1912 on transfer to RFC. Corporal 6 Squadron, when posted to France 5 October, 1914. Promoted to T/SM 1 April, 1917. C.M.M. (T) in 1918 RAF Muster Roll. Mentioned in Despatches for services at home in *L.G.* 14 June, 1918, and next day in the *Times* 'B' List.

188. Ernest Edward Copper

Born 14 May, 1892 in London. Enlisted 29 April, 1911. Formerly 21459 Sapper 'L' Company RE. (to C.F.S. 26 June, 1912) Royal Aero Club Aviators' Certificate No. 674 as 1AM on 1 November, 1913 at CFS Upavon in a Maurice Farman. (No record of 1914 nor 1914/15 star.) Promoted 1 January, 1916 to Temp SM (T). RAF M.S.M. *L.G.* 3 June, 1918 with No. 54 Squadron. RAF L.S.&G.C. Medal *w.e.f.* 29 April, 1929 as SM1. Originally from Beckenham, Kent. Probationary Flying Officer (Stores Branch) No. 21142 5 January, 1931. Awarded 1935 Silver Jubilee Medal. Flight Lieutenant *w.e.f.* 1 September, 1937 stationed at RAF Dishforth, Thirsk, Yorks. with Warrant Officer G.W. Hepple

(No. 780). Squadron Leader 1 August, 1939. Retired 29 June, 1942. Re-employed 30 June, 1942 to 24 May, 1948. Noted in April, 1963 *A.F.L.*, not in 1964 *A.F.L.*

★ 189. S. E. HODGSON

Enlisted 22 February, 1910. Formerly 19891 Sapper 'L' Company RE. To CFS 26 June, 1912 on transfer to RFC. To France, 12 August, 1914 with 2 Squadron as 1AM. Promoted TSM (D) 1 July, 1917. SM1 (Discip.) in 1918 RAF Muster Roll. RFC Communiqué No. 20, 10 November, 1915. 'As Sgt (Observer) flying with 2 Lt. Sanday, 2 Squadron in a BE2c on artillery registration at 4500 feet saw an LVG at 8500 feet. They attacked it with rifle fire. It dived for Lens.'

★ 190. FREDERICK DISMORE

Born East Ham, Essex, 26 May, 1893. Enlisted 26 June, 1911. Formerly 21698 Sapper 'L' Company RE. To CFS 2 July, 1912 on transfer to RFC. Royal Aero Club Aviators' Certificate No. 580 as 1AM on 5 August, 1913 at CFS Upavon in a Short. To France 6 October, 1914 with 6 Squadron as a Corporal. Promoted T.SM (T) 1 May 1917. As a pilot, 2 Squadron, crashed 29 April, 1917. Chief Master Technician (Tech) in 1918 RAF Muster Roll. Belgian Order of Léopold II (Chevalier) *L.G.* 15 April, 1918 still in 2 Squadron.

★ 191. WALTER GEORGE WEBB

Formerly 18601 'L' Company RE. Served in No. 1 Balloon Squadron. Farnborough. Mentioned by McCudden V.C. in *'Flying Fury.'* Posted to 1 Squadron 6 July, 1912 on transfer to RFC. Joined 3 Squadron November, 1913. Aerial photographer. Flew with de la Ferté. To France 16 August, 1914 as 1AM with 3 Squadron. Royal Aero Club Aviators' Certificate No. 1330 of 11 June, 1915. Mentioned in despatches *L.G.* 22 June, 1915 as a Sergeant. Killed in action 26 January, 1917 as Flight Sergeant Pilot (45 Squadron). Buried Menin Communal Cemetery, Belgium. See *'Cross and Cockade,'* Volume 5, No. 3, page 137, and *'The Forgotten Ones.'*

192. J. WYATT

Formerly 9102 L/Cpl 3/Coldstream Guards. Posted to Flying Depot on transfer to RFC on 9 July, 1912. Discharged 22 May, 1913 on conviction by Civilian Powers for felony.

193. F. B. JANSON

To RFC from 3 Dragoon Guards 16 July, 1912. As a 2AM was Court Martialled on 7 December, 1912 'For using violence to his superior officer' and was returned to 6 Dragoon Guards on 13 February, 1913.

* 194. JOSEPH LESTER COSTIGAN

To France, 13 August, 1914 as Sergeant 3 Squadron. Accidentally killed 12 March, 1915, loading Melinite bombs, at Merville Aerodrome, onto Lieut Cholmondeley's Morane which was destroyed , when a Flight Sergeant. (see also Nos. 534, 582, 589, 872, 1171 and 1192.) Aged 26, son of Joseph Phillip and Julia Costigan of 19, Wynne Rd, Erdingon, Birmingham. Born Putney, London, 1889. (No. 100 Sgt Burns led the rescue. In all 11 men were killed and two badly injured.) Buried Chocques Military Cemetery (I,A,37).

195. D. BENYON

Enlisted 5 June, 1906. Formerly 5819 Pte 3 Dragoon Guards. Posted to CFS on transfer to RFC 4 July, 1912. No record of 1914 nor 1914/15 Star. Promoted 22 January, 1916 to Temp SM (T). CMM (Technical) in 1918 RAF Muster Roll. RAF L.S.&G.C. Medal as SM1 15 June, 1924.

* 196. J. H. ROSE

Formerly 14252 33 Company RE. Transferred to Flying Depot 24 June, 1912. As Sergeant, Aircraft Park posted to France 16 August, 1914. Royal Aero Club Aviators' Certificate No. 964 on 7 November, 1914. Died in UK 28 January, 1916 when SM1 (27 Squadron). His 1914 Star and British War Medal only are known in a private collection. (Sold Capital Medals 1988 £75). Son of Mr. H. Rose 'Brookside' Steyning Road, Rottingdean, Sussex. Buried St. Margarets Churchyard, Rottingdean.

197. (NOT TRACED, SEE 88).

Possibly the Sergeant Ellard not recorded elsewhere but noted in Group Photograph No. 2. See also Nos. 967 and 696.

198. FREDERICK WHILTON

Born 25 January, 1887. Formerly 6579 L/Sgt 3/Coldstream Guards. Posted to CFS 9 July, 1912 on transfer to RFC. One of the first three other ranks posted to No. 7 Squadron on its formation 1 May, 1914. Earned 1914/15 Star trio for service overseas as a Sergeant from 7 December, 1915. Mentioned in Despatches 1 July, 1916 with the Egyptian Expeditionary Force. Awarded Distinguished Conduct Medal in *L.G.* 27 July, 1916 in 17 Squadron when a Sergeant Major 'For consistent good work. His devotion to duty has been invaluable in promoting the efficiency of the Squadron.' M.I.D. *L.G.* 25 September, 1916 for Salonika. Awarded Army Meritorious Service Medal as Sgt Maj. 'For valuable services with the Armies in the Field' in *L.G.* 11 November, 1916. Commissioned 2 Lieutenant 8 October, 1917. M.I.D. *L.G.* 5 June, 1919 for Egypt as 2 Lieut RAF. After promotion to Flying Officer 20 July, 1920, when he was serving as Stores Officer 230 Squadron Coastal Command Felixstowe (from 25 July, 1921), promoted to Flight Lieutenant 1 January, 1924. In 1931, still Flt. Lt. employed from 8 February, 1927 on Stores Staff Duties at RAF Coastal Command HQ Tavistock Place, London WC1. Retired 31 March, 1931. In 1937 *A.F.L.* shown as Flight Lieutenant (Retd) employed at Marine Aircraft Establishment (Experimental) Felixstowe. RAFVR 1 September, 1939 to 27 July, 1945. Noted in April, 1969 *A.F.L.* but not that of 1970.

BLERIOT XI

★ 199. F. W. CLARK

Enlisted 16 June, 1911. Formerly 5990 Pte 4 Dragoon Guards. To 2 Squadron RFC on probation 6 July, 1912. Finally transferred per Regimental Orders 19 December, 1912. As 1AM 2 Squadron in France from 12 August, 1914 earning 1914 Star and bar. Promoted Quarter Master Sergeant 1 May 1916. Was Master Mechanic in 1918 RAF Muster Roll.

★ 200. H. STEED

Enlisted 12 August, 1909. Formerly 10218 Pte 2/Welsh Regt. Posted to 3 Squadron 24 June, 1912 on his transfer to RFC. As 2 AM 3 Squadron to France 13 August, 1914, earning 1914 Star and bar. Promoted Sergeant (Batman) 1 February, 1917 and held that rank and trade in 1918 RAF Muster Roll.

★ 201. C. F. W. EVERITT

Enlisted 16 July, 1912 directly into the Corps. 1AM 5 Squadron, to France 14 August, 1914. Reverted to Sergeant Fitter (Aero Engines) from 8 March, 1918.

★ 202. P. J. WAGHORN

Enlisted 22 September, 1908. Formerly 17921 Sapper 3 Balloon Company RE in July,1910. Balloon School (Mounted) on mobilisation of the Air Battalion. As 2AM 2 Squadron, served in France from 12 August, 1914. Promoted Flight Sergeant Driver (MT) 1 April, 1916. Mentioned in despatches for Egypt 12 January, 1918, as Flight Sergeant. Chief Mechanic (Driver) in 1918 RAF Muster Roll.

★ 203. CHARLES JOSEPH BROCKBANK

Sergeant at Farnborough Flying Depot in May 1913 in charge of aircraft maintenance. Flight Sergeant, Aircraft Park in France from 16 August, 1914. Commissioned 2 Lieutenant 7 December, 1916. He was awarded the M.B.E. in *L.G.* 3 June, 1918. Shown as Lieutenant (T) in 1921 *A.F.L.* seniority 1 November, 1919 with O.B.E. From 1 April, 1918 serving at Records Office, Ruislip. Acting Squadron Leader when he retired 22 May, 1929. See group photographs 1 and 2.

* 204. J. BUCKINGHAM

Formerly 4317 Rifleman 1/Rifle Brigade when posted to 3 Squadron 2 July, 1912 on transfer to RFC. As 2AM 5 Squadron to France with BEF 14 August, 1914 earning 1914 Star and bar. Discharged unfit 21 April, 1916.

205. L. A. WILLSHIRE

Enlisted 5 September, 1911. Formerly 4321 Rifleman 1/Rifle Brigade when transferred to RFC (CFS) on 9 July, 1912. Served overseas from 11 December, 1915 earning 1914/15 trio. Promoted Sergeant (Gen. Fitter) 1 September, 1916. Sergeant Mechanic (Fitter) in 1918 RAF Muster Roll.

* 206. A. S. CARDNO

Enlisted 16 July, 1912 directly into the Corps. As 1AM RFC HQ posted to France 12 August, 1914. Mentioned in despatches as Flight Sergeant *L.G.* 4 January, 1917. Reverted to Sergeant (1st Class Pilot) 16 May, 1917. Sergeant Mech (Pilot) in 1918 RAF Muster Roll. Missing (later confirmed as K.I.A.) 6 May, 1918 as Sergeant Pilot 29 Squadron. See '*Cross and Cockade,*' Vol 2, No. 4, pages 102 and 114.

207. WILLIAM BOYLE POWER

Born Plymouth 15 December, 1888. Earned Royal Aero Club Aviators' Certificate No. 838 on 1 July, 1914 as 1AM at Upavon (CFS) in a Maurice Farman. Served overseas in Egypt as Cpl from 19 November, 1914 earning 1914/15 Star. Sgt Major Instructor January, 1916 at Royal Aircraft Factory (see McCudden V.C. '*Flying Fury*'). Promoted 2 Lieutenant 30 May, 1916.

* 208. ALBERT HUNTER

Awarded Royal Aero Club Aviators' Certificate No. 137 on 19 September 1911 when a civilian. At Farnborough in 1913, a Sergeant Pilot As Sergeant in 4 Squadron earned 1914 Star and bar in France from 13 August, 1914. M.I.D. *L.G.* 30 November, 1915 as Acting Sergeant Major

11 Squadron. Commissioned 2 Lieutenant RFC and W. Yorks. Regt. 5 March, 1916. Awarded French Croix de Guerre 9 March, 1917. Awarded O.B.E. as Major RAF. Flight Lieutenant (T) O.B.E. seniority 1 August, 1919 from 26 January, 1921 employed at Aircraft Depot, India. He was acting Squadron Leader when he retired 18 April, 1930. See '*Cross and Cockade*,' vol 7, No. 3, page 135 and photograph under No. 7.

★ 209. LOUIS HECTOR METZ

Enlisted 7 February, 1910. Formerly 32646 A/Bombardier 57 Company RGA transferred to RFC HQ 19 July, 1912. As Corporal 4 Squadron earned 1914 Star and bar in France from 12 August, 1914. Promoted Temp SM (D) 1 January, 1916. Awarded Army M.S.M. as A/SM in *L.G.* 1 January, 1917, 'For Valuable Services with the Armies in the Field.' The recommendation states 'For continuous good service and dedication to duty. Has served continuously in the BEF since August, 1914 and had proved himself at all times a highly reliable and efficient NCO.' In the 1918 RAF Muster Roll listed as SM1 (Discip) (Awarded RAF L.S.&G.C. Medal *w.e.f.* 7 February, 1928 as SM1) Seventh senior WO in the RAF in 1931. His group of five medals is known in a private collection:— 1914 Star and bar trio, (Cpl & T/SM RFC) Army M.S.M. and RAF L.S.&G.C. Medal (GV).

★ 210. T. L. GLIDDEN

Enlisted 18 July, 1912. As Corporal 3 Squadron earned 1914 Star and bar in France from 13 August, 1914. Awarded French Médaille Militaire for gallantry 21-30 August, 1914, see *L.G.* 9 November, 1914. Flight Sergeant (Fitter Engines) from 1 October, 1916. Chief Mechanic in 1918 RAF

Muster Roll. Awarded RAF M.S.M. in *L.G.* 1 January, 1919. Originally from Kensal Rise London N.W.

★ 211. CHARLES ALEXANDER CORNELIUS FIDLER

Born 9 August, 1892. Formerly 8558 Pte 2/Wilts Regt. Posted to Flying Depot 15 July, 1912 on transfer to RFC. Awarded Distinguished Conduct Medal as Flight Sergeant (Acting Sergeant Major) when at 'X' Aircraft Park in *L.G.* 31 May, 1916 'For conspicuous good work in connection with the care and repair of aeroplanes.' Commissioned 2 Lieutenant (T) RFC 29 October, 1917. In November, 1921 *A.F.L.* was Flying Officer seniority 1 August, 1919, stationed at RAF Flying School, India from 23 August, 1920. Flight Lieutenant (E) in February, 1931 *A.F.L.* seniority 1 January, 1928 stationed at Home Aircraft Depot, Henlow Camp, Beds., from 24 January, 1929. Retired 19 February, 1933. In the 1937 *A.F.L.* he is shown as Flight Lieutenant (Retd) working at Reception Depot, West Drayton and was recalled in WW2, 13 October, 1939, being promoted Squadron Leader 1 September, 1940 and Wing Commander (No. 03250) on 1 September, 1942. Retired 31 December, 1947. Last noted in April, 1965 *A.F.L.*

212. ROBERT JOHN SLADDEN

Formerly 44256 Gunner 148 Battery RFA he was posted to the Flying Depot 16 July, 1912 on transfer to RFC. At the outbreak of WW1 he was still there, 1AM, but was posted overseas to Egypt as A/Sergeant Major on 30 November, 1915 earning a 1914/15 Star in that rank. He was the senior Warrant Officer in Darfur in the Sudan in 1916. Awarded Distinguished Conduct Medal in *L.G.* 31 May 1916 as Flight Sergeant (Acting Sergeant Major) 17 Squadron. 'For consistent good work in connection with the care and repair of aircraft.' Posted back to UK before being commissioned 2 Lieutenant 6 April, 1917. Promoted Acting Captain RAF on 4 March, 1919 he was awarded an M.B.E. in *L.G.* 3 June, 1919 as Lieut A/Captain. In the November, 1921 *A.F.L.* he is shown as Flying Officer (Stores) seniority 20 July, 1920 serving at the No. 1 Technical Training School (Boys) at Halton. He retired in this rank on 2 November, 1921. Still shown thus in 1937 *A.F.L.* His medal group is known in a private collection:— M.B.E. (1st type), D.C.M. (GV Fl. Sgt.), 1914/15 Star (S. Maj), British War Medal and Victory Medal (WO. Cl. 1) Khedive's Sudan Medal (1910) (Darfur 1916 Sgt. Maj. RFC). (see also No. 1083)

213. CLARANCE TREMAINE DAVIS

Formerly 8760 Private 1/Coldstream Guards, he was posted to CFS 15 July,1912 on transfer to RFC. Posted overseas 25 June, 1915 as Cpl earning 1914/15 trio. Awarded Army M.S.M. as Temp SM in *L.G.* 16 August, 1917 'For Valuable Services with the Armies in the Field.' Commissioned 2 Lieutenant 18 October, 1917. Flying Officer in November, 1921 *A.F.L.* (Stores List) seniority 20 July, 1920 serving at the RAF Depot, Uxbridge, from 1 June, 1920. Flight Lieutenant in February, 1931 *A.F.L.* seniority 1 January, 1927 serving at Station HQ, RAF Upavon, from 7 December, 1927.

★ 214. HAROLD D. JACK

Enlisted 22 September, 1908. Formerly served in 2/Connaught Rangers and transferred to RFC 20 July, 1912. He was a 1AM with the Airship Detachment when he earned his 1914 Star and bar. He was posted to RNAS 18 October, 1914 as 677 AM 1st Class, probationary Flying Officer 19 March, 1917, and was promoted WO2 (Airships) 1 October, 1917. (A commissioned rank in the Navy) He was 2 Lieutenant RAF 25 October, 1918.

★ 215. JOHN H. KERR

Enlisted 11 August, 1910. 1AM at Aircraft Park in France from 16 August, 1914, earning 1914 Star and bar. Promoted Flight Sergeant (Driver M.T.) 1 February, 1918. Awarded RAF M.S.M. as SM1 in *L.G.* 10 October, 1919, for services in France. (Promoted SM1 12 June, 1918) RAF L.S.&G.C. Medal as SM *w.e.f.* 11 August, 1920. Still serving in August, 1934, retired the following month.

★ 216. GEORGE HENRY LEIGHTON METCALFE

Enlisted 13 September, 1906. Formerly 1588, Pte, 4th Hussars as G. Kitchen to 2 Squadron RFC 12 July, 1912, assumed his true name of George Henry Leighton Metcalfe 3 July, 1914. 1AM with Aircraft Park, in France from 12 August, 1914 earning 1914 Star and bar. Promoted Flight Sgt (Fitter Gen) 1 June, 1916 and was Ch Mech (Fitter) in 1918 RAF Muster Roll. M.I.D. for India *L.G.* 3 June, 1919. RAF L.S.&G.C. as SM2 *w.e.f.* 13 September, 1924.

★ 217. DANIEL HENRY NEWTON

Born 22 November, 1891. Enlisted 22 July, 1912 directly into RFC. 1AM Aircraft Park, to France 16 August, 1914 earning 1914 Star and bar. Mentioned in despatches as Flight Sergeant 15 June, 1916. Awarded Army M.S.M. as F/Sgt in *L.G.* 11 November, 1916 'For Valuable Services with the Armies in the Field.' Promoted T/SM (Technical) 1 February, 1917 and was CMM (T) in 1918 RAF Muster Roll. RAF L.S.&G.C. *w.e.f.* 22 July, 1930, as SM1. In 1931 *A.F.L.* as 45th senior RAF Warrant Officer. Commissioned Engineering Officer (Flying Officer) on 11 September, 1933 and shown in 1937 *Air Force List* as having been awarded an M.B.E. and from 28 February, 1935 being stationed at the Aircraft Dept, Karachi, India. Promoted to Squadron Leader 1 September, 1940. In 1946 *Air Force List* was Wing Commander (No. 35007) seniority 1 December, 1941. Retired 6 March, 1947. Died 11 June, 1978.

218. GEORGE BUCHAN

Enlisted 4 November, 1910. Formerly 33839 Gunner 108 Heavy Battery RGA, posted to Central Flying School 12 July, 1912 on transfer to RFC. No record of issue of either 1914 or 1914/15 Stars. Promoted T/Sergeant Major (T) 26 January, 1916, and was CMM (Technical) in 1918 RAF

Muster Roll. Awarded RAF L.S.&G.C. November, 1928 as Warrant Officer. Retired November, 1934.

★ 219. R. RAYNBIRD

Enlisted 11 October, 1909. Formerly 59551 Driver, 122 Battery RFA. Transferred to No. 2 Squadron 12 July, 1912. 1AM, No. 2 Squadron to France 12 August, 1914. Promoted Temporary Sergeant Major (Technical) 1 March, 1917. Chief Master Mechanic (Technical) in 1918 RAF Muster Roll. The trio is in a private collection: 1914 Star (1AM), British War Medal and Victory Medal (Flight Sgt. RFC).

★ 220. HENRY HARRY CUMMINS

Enlisted 22 July, 1912 directly into RFC. 1AM No. 2 Squadron, France from 12 August, 1914, earning 1914 Star and bar. Promoted Temporary Sergeant Major (Technical) 1 August, 1917 and was Chief Master Mechanic (Technical) in 1918 RAF Muster Roll. RAF L.S.&G.C. 22 July, 1930 as SM1. In 1931 *A.F.L.* was WO1. Awarded 1935 Silver Jubilee Medal. In March, 1938 *Air Force List* shown as serving at RAF Hornchurch Essex from 28 March, 1933 when 10th senior RAF Warrant Officer. Not in 1941 *Air Force List*. Still serving in 1944. (See also Nos. 632 and 1174.)

★ 221. A. A. ENTICKNAP

Enlisted 23 July, 1912 directly into RFC. 1AM, No. 2 Squadron, in France from 12 August, 1914. Flight Sergeant (Fitter Aero Engines) *w.e.f.* December, 1915. Chief Mechanic in 1918 RAF Muster Roll.

★ 222. W. COLLIN

Earned 1914 Star as Sergeant Airship Detachment. Transferred to RNAS 18 October, 1914 as No. 679. Chief Petty Officer 1st Class (Engineer) 1 August, 1916. In 1918 RAF Muster Roll was 200679 Chief Master Mechanic (Fitter Aero).

223. A. TURNER

A Sergeant at the Central Flying School was discharged 27 March, 1913 under *K.R.* 392 (xvi), 'No longer physically fit for war service.'

★ 224. E. J. STREET

Born Wells, Somerset, 6 April, 1878. Transferred to RFC from Coldstream Guards. Awarded Royal Aero Club Aviators' Certificate No. 439 on 18 March, 1913 as Sergeant in a Maurice Farman of Central Flying School at Salisbury Plain. Sergeant Pilot at Farnborough in 1913. Still a Sergeant but with No. 4 Squadron he served in France from 12 August, 1914. As Observer near Merville, to Lieutenant Harvey-Kelly he drove down a Rumpler Taube on 26 August, 1914, and they landed to try to capture it and fly it back. But the Army burnt the enemy machine  before they could get to it. The previous day the same pilot had attempted the same act and he was subsequently recommended for a Victoria Cross. He was awarded a D.S.O. instead. As Sergeant awarded French Médaille Militaire for Gallantry between 21-30 August, 1914. See *London Gazette* 9 November, 1914. In January, 1915, was Sergeant Major No. 1 Reserve Squadron. Commissioned 2 Lieutenant 10 July, 1916. Lieutenant (Technical) in April, 1918 *Air Force List*. (See 'The Forgotten Ones'). See group photograph No. 2 and photograph under No. 7.

★ 225. J. LAWRENCE

Enlisted 16 September, 1907. Formerly 9511 Private 2/Welsh Regiment. Posted to No. 2 Squadron 24 June, 1912 on transfer to RFC. 1AM, No. 2 Squadron in France from 12 August, 1914. Temporary Sergeant Major (Disciplinarian) *w.e.f.* 1 March, 1917. Sergeant Major 1 (Disciplinarian) in 1918 RAF Muster Roll.

★ 226. W. MORRIS

Enlisted 3 March, 1910. Formerly 18951 Sapper 17 Company RE. Posted to No. 3 Squadron 2 July, 1912 on transfer to RFC. Corporal, No. 5 Squadron in France from 14 August, 1914. Promoted Temporary Sergeant Major ('Technical) 1 June, 1917. Chief Master Mechanic (Technical) in 1918 RAF Muster Roll.

★ 227. W. H. JOWITT

Enlisted 24 February,1910. Formerly 19910 Sapper 17 Company RE. Posted to Flying Depot 2 July, 1912 on transfer to RFC. Posted overseas from 17 April, 1915 earning 1914/15 Star trio. Promoted Flight Sergeant 1 January, 1918. Was Chief Mechanic (Fitter Aero) in 1918 RAF Muster Roll.

★ 228. W. E. LEE

Formerly 20233 Sapper 59 Company RE to Flying Depot 4 July, 1912 on transfer to RFC. Corporal, No. 2 Squadron in France from 13 August, 1914 earning 1914 Star and bar. As Flight Sergeant was wounded 7 December, 1915 and had a foot amputated. He was discharged 30 September, 1916 under *K.R.* 392 (xvi). His Silver War Badge was numbered 14356.

★ 229. HUGH JONES

Formerly 20619 Sapper 17 Company RE. Posted to No. 2 Squadron 2 July, 1912 on transfer to Corps. As 1AM No. 2 Squadron earned 1914 Star and bar in France from 13 August, 1914. Commissioned 2 Lieutenant 10 July, 1916. In 1921 *Air Force List* was Flying Officer (Stores List) seniority 20 July, 1920 serving at School of Technical Training Ramsgate from 16 August, 1920. In 1931 *Air Force List* he is a Flight Lieutenant seniority 1 July, 1924 serving at Station HQ, RAF Tangmere from 5 November, 1929. In 1938 he was retired and was an Assistant Administrative Officer, Directorate of Civil Aviation at the Air Ministry. He had an M.B.E.

MAURICE FARMAN 'SHORTHORN'

★ 230. O. R. ROWE

Enlisted 24 September, 1910. Formerly 20574 Sapper 17 Company RE. Posted to Flying Depot 2 July, 1912 on transfer to Corps. 1AM with Aircraft Park, in France from 16 August, 1914. Promoted Flight Sergeant (Carpenter) 1 December, 1916 and was Chief Mechanic in 1918 RAF Muster Roll. RAF L.S.&G.C. Medal as Flight Sergeant *w.e.f.* 24 September, 1928 (A.M.O. 834/1928). Rowe was mentioned in an Air Ministry Press Release of 29 August, 1919 and also in the *Times* 'B' Press Release the same day. He wore an oakleaf on his Victory Medal. His group of five medals is known in a private collection:— 1914 Star and bar (230 2 AM O.R. Rowe RFC), British War Medal and Victory medal (F. Sgt RFC), Indian General Service Medal (3 clasps Afghanistan NWF 1919, Waziristan 1919-21 and Waziristan 1921-24 – Flight Sgt RAF) and RAF L.S.&G.C. Medal (F. Sgt.) The 3-bar IGS combination of bars occurs only three times in 4,561 medals issued to the RAF, two to officers and this one, unique to an Other Rank. (He is also shown on the Waziristan, 1925 roll but could not of course have this clasp and that for 1921-24.)

★ 231. J. NEWMAN

Enlisted 4 July, 1910. Formerly 20275 Sapper, 17 Company RE. Posted to Flying Depot 2 July, 1912 on transfer to RFC 1AM with Aircraft Park, in France from 16 August, 1914. Promoted Sgt (Painter) 1 February, 1918. Sgt Mech in 1918 RAF Muster Roll.

★ 232. B. BILLINGS

Enlisted 3 June, 1908. Formerly 17553 L/Cpl 59 Company RE. Posted to 1 Squadron 4 July, 1912 on transfer to RFC. As Cpl 6 Squadron served in France from 6 October, 1914. T/SM (T) *w.e.f.* 9 October, 1915. CMM (Tech.) in 1918 RAF Muster Roll. Awarded RAF M.S.M. as T/SM 20 Squadron in *L.G.* 3 June, 1918 for Service in France. Died in 1919 and posthumously mentioned in despatches in *L.G.* 11 July, 1919. Originally from Bury St. Edmunds.

★ 233. E. DAVIS

Enlisted 23 July, 1912, directly into RFC. 1AM with Aircraft Park in France from 16 August, 1914. Promoted Flight Sergeant (Fitter, Aero Engines) 1 February, 1918 and was Chief Mechanic in 1918 RAF Muster Roll.

234. J. BAKER

Discharged as Sergeant 15 July, 1913 under *K.R.* 392 (ix) 'Unfitted for duties in the Corps.'

★ 235. A. E. SCOTT

Enlisted 16 December, 1908. Formerly 18230 L/Cpl 5 Signalling Company RE. Posted to Flying Depot, 2 July, 1912 on transfer to Corps. Corporal, Aircraft Park, in France from 16 August, 1914. D.C.M. *L.G.* 11 January, 1916 as Sergeant No. 1 Aircraft Park 'For conspicuous devotion to duty and resource. Throughout the campaign he has always exhibited great technical ability and untiring energy, and has been in no small measure responsible for the efficiency of the planes sent out to squadrons.' Promoted T/SM (T) 1 August, 1917 and mentioned in despatches 13 March, 1918 as Sergeant Major (For Valuable Services in the War (United Kingdom)). Also mentioned in the *Times* 'B' List 16 March, 1918. Was CMM in 1918 RAF Muster Roll.

236. L. W. JONES

Formerly 17213 Sapper 5 Signalling Company RE. Posted to Flying Depot 2 July, 1912. As 1AM discharged by purchase under Article 1130 (i) of the Pay Warrant on 1 June, 1914.

237. E. KIRBY

Possibly 25848 Corporal 4th Balloon Section RE in China, 1900. However was 'returned to unit' 30 September, 1912 under Daily routine Orders of 1 Squadron of 1 October, 1912.

238. FRANK PRATT

Born Leamington 22 July, 1889. Formerly 8299 L/Sgt 1/D.C.L.I. posted to 3 Squadron 27 June, 1912 on transfer to RFC. As 1AM earned Royal Aero Club Aviators' Certificate No. 541 on 3 July, 1913 in a Bristol Aircraft of the RFC on Salisbury Plain. Pratt was an extremely clever chap, well educated, but with a gift for running into minor disciplinary troubles. For example he returned from leave wearing boots with toe-caps – against orders. For this 'crime' Major Brooke-Popham gave him three days' confinement to camp. He got his own back a short time later. He was a good vocalist and something of a calypso singer, since he improvised his own lyrics. Performing at a camp concert, his song being the 'Army Alphabet,' he came to the letter 'O.' Wagging his finger at Brooke-Popham, who was sitting in the front row, he chanted:

> *'O' stands for orders,*
> *Some of which are brutes.*
> *Never come off Easter leave*
> *Wearing toe-capped boots!*

'Brookham' – bless his heart – nearly fell out of his chair with laughter, while the squadron, most of whom knew of Bill's punishment nearly lifted the roof in their enjoyment of this apt retort to authority. A simple little episode, perhaps, but then No. 3 under 'Brookham's' command was a happy squadron. Still 1AM in August, 1914. Proceeded overseas 29 January, 1915 earning 1914/15 Star. Commissioned 2 Lieutenant 1 October, 1916.

★ 239. WILLIAM JOHN BURTENSHAW

Formerly in the Air Battalion RE. Transferred to the RFC 13 May, 1912. 1AM, with the Aircraft Park in France from 16 August, 1914. In England (Hounslow) September, 1915 when 24 Squadron were formed. Served with them in France, as Sergeant, 2 February, to 27 August, 1916. Awarded Royal Aero Club Aviators' Certificate No. 3894 on 28 November, 1916. Was Killed in Action, a Sergeant Pilot of 25 Squadron 28 April, 1917. Buried Lapugnoy Military Cemetery (iv. F. 4.).

240. F. W. LIGHTFOOT

Enlisted 24 February, 1910. Formerly in the Air Battalion RE. Transferred to RFC 13 May, 1912. No trace of entitlement to 1914 nor 1914/15 Stars nor British War Medal nor Victory Medal. Promoted Sergeant Photographer 1 December, 1916. Sergeant Mech (Photographer) in 1918 RAF Muster Roll.

★ 241. LEWIS EDWARD CARTER

Formerly 4613 Sergeant 21 Lancers. Transferred to RFC 19 July, 1912, and posted to 1 Squadron. Served in France from 9 September, 1914, as Flt Sgt, 6 Squadron. (*N.B.* 6 Squadron served in France as a unit from November, 1914; he must have been detached.) Earned 1914 Star and bar. Awarded D.C.M. in *L.G.* 13 February, 1917 as A/Sgt Major 'For conspicuous gallantry and devotion to duty. He has shown great courage and initiative throughout the campaign, and has been in continuous service since the commencement of hostilities.' Posted to UK 3rd Army Aircraft Park and commissioned 30 May, 1917. 2 Lieutenant (Tech.) in 1918 *A.F.L.* Was Flying Officer (Stores List) seniority 17 June, 1920 in November, 1921 *A.F.L.* serving at No. 1 Stores Depot, Kidbrooke, London, from 1 April, 1918. Promoted Flight Lieutenant (E) 1 January, 1924 and retired 28 March, 1928. Last noted in 1937 *A.F.L.* His group of four medals is in the RAF Museum at Hendon: D.C.M. (A/SM RFC), 1914 Star and bar (Flight Sergeant), British War Medal and Victory medals (T/WO1 RFC). See group photographs 1 and 2.

242. CHARLES WILLIAM ATTWOOD

Born 1 September, 1891. Formerly 18217 Sapper 17 Company RE. Posted to Flying Depot 2 July, 1912 on transfer to RFC. As Corporal, 7 Squadron at outbreak of WW1 served overseas from 2 April, 1915 earning 1914/15 trio. Gained Royal Aero Club Aviators' Certificate 4259 of 17 February, 1917 when a Sergeant. Flying Officer in November, 1921 *A.F.L.* from 1 August, 1919 (GD 'Aeroplane Officer') serving with 100 Squadron at Clondalkin, Ireland, from 13 April, 1921. Saw active service in Kurdistan as Flight Lieutenant. In 1931 (February) *A.F.L.* still Flight Lieutenant (GD) seniority 1 January, 1923. (Qualified in Specialist Signalling Course), serving in a signalling role at the Ismailia Wireless Station, Middle East. Promoted Wing Commander 1 July, 1937 and from 19 May 1937 was Chief Signals Officer No. 16 Reconn. Group, Coastal Command, Lee on Solent. Group Captain 1 June, 1940. Retired 1 September, 1941. Re-employed to 15 May, 1945. He is shown as a retired Group Captain in the 1946 *A.F.L.* No. 05038. His group of seven medals is known in a private collection:— 1914/15 Star (Sgt RFC), British War Medal and Victory Medal (2 Lieut RAF), General Service Medal (clasp Kurdistan. Flight Lieutenant RAF), Africa Star, Defence and War Medals. Noted in April, 1969 *A.F.L.*, but not that of 1970.

★ 243. N. CARLYLE

Enlisted 30 November, 1910. As 1AM with 3 Squadron served in France from 12 August, 1914, earning 1914 Star and bar. Promoted T/SM (T) 1 September, 1917 and was Chief Master Mech (Tech) in 1918 RAF

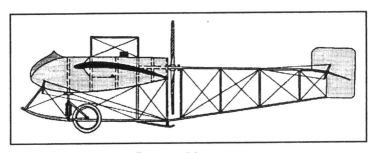

BLERIOT MILITARY

Muster Roll. Listed in the *Times* 'B' Press Release 29 August, 1919. 1914 Star (1AM) and British War Medal (Cpl) sold June, 1989 £150.

244. E. COLE

Formerly 16617 a long-serving NCO 'I' Battery, Royal Horse Artillery. Posted to Central Flying School 25 June, 1912 on transfer to RFC. As a Sergeant discharged 1 September, 1913 undr *K.R.* 392 (xv) 'Free after ... years service, under article 1130 (ii) Pay Warrant. Having completed 12 or 18 yrs with RHA he had re-engaged for a short period, to leave the service at short notice.

245. ALFRED EDWIN LINDON

Born 20 March, 1889. Formerly 32016 Sapper, 'B' Signalling Company. RE. Posted to 2 Squadron 2 July, 1912 on transfer to the Corps. Proceeded overseas 23 November, 1915 earning 1914/15 Star trio. Commissioned Lieutenant 10 October, 1917. Then Captain RAF. In November, 1921 *A.F.L.* was Flying Officer (GD) seniority 1 August, 1919 serving from 15 August, 1921 at School of Technical Training (Men) Ramsgate. In 1931 *A.F.L.* (February) was Flight Lieutenant (GD) seniority 1 January, 1926, having been awarded an M.B.E., qualified at both Specialist Engineering Course and Specialist Photographic Course. From 10 February, 1930, he was serving as a pilot with No. 4 Flying Training School, (flying Atlas, Avro, Bristol Fighter and Vimy machines) at Abu Sueir, Middle East. Retired 25 December, 1933. Shown as retired in April, 1968 *A.F.L.* (No. 04109).

246. CHARLES WILLIAM BAKER

Born 28 April, 1891. Enlisted 28 March, 1911. Formerly 21352 Sapper, 'B' Signalling Company RE. Posted to 3 Squadron 2 July, 1912 on transfer to RFC. Served overseas from 8 November, 1915 earning 1914/15 Star trio. Promoted T/SM (T), 1 October, 1916 and mentioned in despatches in *L.G.* 28 June, 1917 for services in Egypt. C.M.M. (Tech) in 1918 RAF Muster Roll. Awarded RAF Meritorious Service Medal for services in Egypt in *L.G.* 3 June, 1918 as T/Sgt. Major. He originally came from Pewsey, Wilts., very close to the very early Air Battalion Camps of the Royal Engineers, no doubt encouraging him to enlist into an aerial career. Awarded RAF L.S.&G.C. *w.e.f.* 28 March, 1929 as SM1. In February, 1931 was the 28th senior WO in RAF. He was awarded an M.B.E. in the King's Birthday Honours of 1934 and was commissioned (CEO – Flying Officer)

No. 35014 21 July, 1934. Awarded 1935 Silver Jubilee Medal. Stationed at the Aircraft Depot, Dhibban, Iraq in March, 1938. Promoted to Squadron Leader 1 September, 1940. Wing Commander 1 December, 1941. Retired 29 April, 1946. Last noted in 1975 *A.F.L.*

★ 247. FREDERICK GEORGE BATEMAN

Born London 1 June, 1884. Obtained Royal Aero Club Aviators' Certificate No. 712 as a Sergeant on 20 December, 1913 at Netheravon in a Maurice Farman of the RFC. As a Flight Sergeant with 4 Squadron he earned a 1914 Star. He died in the UK on 7 September, 1915 still a Flight Sergeant. Buried Deptford Cemetery, London. (Row 1. Grave 1852) See group photograph No. 2.

★ 248. H. WOODS

Enlisted 9 January, 1899 and served in the Air Battalion RE. As a Sergeant 6 Squadron earned 1914 Star and bar in France from 6 October, 1914. Mentioned in despatches in *L.G.* 1 January, 1916 and promoted Warrant Officer (Disciplinarian) on 11 March, 1917 and shown as SM1 (D) in 1918 RAF Muster Roll. Mentioned again in *L.G.* 14 June, 1918. He was awarded an Army pattern L.S.&G.C. Medal in A.O. 305 of October, 1918. (The RFC was of course still a part of the army in January, 1917 when he became eligible for the award).

249. C. WEBB

He deserted 6 June, 1913 when 1AM. He was discharged 25 October, 1913 under *K.R.* 392 (ix) 'Unfitted for duties in the Corps.'

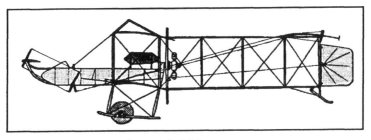

SHORT S.38 MILITARY

* 250. H. T. GASTON

Enlisted 25 July, 1912. As 2AM 5 Squadron served in France from 14 August, 1914. Recommended for, but not awarded Army M.S.M. October, 1915 97 Squadron, 83 Wing. Acting WO (D) 1 January, 1918 and Acting SM1 (paid) in 1918 RAF Muster Roll. However he was awarded his RAF L.S.&G.C. as SM2 and *w.e.f.* 27 April, 1931, nine months later than the 18 years required normally.

* 251. JOSEPH ('JOEY') KEMPER

Born Hull, 10 July, 1887. Awarded Royal Aero Club Aviators' Certificate No. 444 on 1 April, 1913 in a Maurice Farman of CFS on Salisbury Plain when a Sergeant. Was a Flight Sergeant 2 Squadron in France from 13 August, 1914. Refused offer of a commission September, 1914. Appointed Sergeant Major 12 March, 1915. Awarded French Médaille Militaire 24 February, 1916 and commissioned 2 Lieutenant, South Lancs Regt and RFC 'For Services in the Field.' Seniority 1 August, 1916 in *L.G.* 23 August, 1916. Mentioned in Despatches in December, 1917. Promoted Major RFC 15 November, 1917, and held the same rank in April, 1918 *Air Force List.* Awarded M.B.E. *L.G.* 3 June, 1918. In November, 1921 *A.F.L.* was listed Squadron Leader (T) (General List) M.B.E., seniority 1 August, 1919 and serving at Aircraft Depot, Middle East Area, Egypt from 26 April, 1920. He retired on 1 September, 1930 and is shown in the 1937 *A.F.L.* as Flight Lieutenant (Hon, Squadron Ldr.). Reserve of Air Force Officers serving as an Engineering Officer at RAF Station Calshot from 2 November, 1936. See group photographs Nos. 2 and 3.

* 252. D. MARTIN

Enlisted 22 February, 1904. Was Cpl 3 Squadron in France from 13 August, 1914. Flight Sergeant T/SM (T) 11 October, 1915. An observer with 7 Squadron from 4 April, 1916. Awarded Military Medal as Flight Sergeant *L.G.* 11 October, 1916. Mentioned in despatches *L.G.* 7 December, 1917. Chief Master Mech (T) in 1918 RAF Muster Roll. Awarded RAF M.S.M. in that rank in *L.G.* 1 January, 1919. He died 24 February,

1919 and is buried in his home village of Shrewton, Wiltshire. He was twice posthumously mentioned in despatches on 3 June, 1919 and again on 11 July, 1919.

★ 253. W. J. SMYRK

In his school days he had experimented with gliding aero models and with kites. Having served his time as an apprentice press tool-maker, he enlisted as a mechanic in the RFC in July, 1912. During the celebrated August, 1912 Military Trials of aircraft suitability for war, he took the opportunity of a flight with S.F. Cody in his *Cathedral* which surprisingly won the trials. It was built of bamboo struts lashed together with string between every knot and painted with shellac. The string was to prevent the bamboo from splitting.

He had an amusing recollection of the Commanding Officer at No. 3 Squadron, Major H.R.M. Brooke-Popham, who had a passion for looking after his own motor car. Someone had walked off with one of his small adjustable spanners colloquilly known as a 'King Dick' but Brooke-Popham searched in every shed and enquired of all and sundry for what he called his 'King Willie.'

Though an engine fitter, he did rigging too and this involved making up spare flying and landing wires. At that time stranded wire was used, considerable skill being needed for splicing and binding and attaching to the turn-buckle or connecting joint. (The above quotations are from the P. H. Liddle archives.)

As Cpl 6 Squadron served in France from 7 October, 1914. He was a Sergeant in No. 60 Squadron in 1915 and was responsible for servicing the aero engines. When the major overhauls (100 hours) were required, the engines had to be taken to Pont de l'Arche on the Seine. T/SM (T) 1 January, 1916.

The following is an extract from *'Sixty Squadron RAF'*:—

> 'The technical sergeant-major, Smyrk by name, was a wizard with an internal combustion engine. He had been employed at the Gramophone Co.'s factory at Hayes in civil life before joining the R.F.C. in 1912, and had a gift for teaching fitters their business. During almost all the war, two fitters a month had to be sent home to assist in the manning of new units, while the squadrons in the field had, in consequence, always to carry a percentage of untrained or partially trained men, who had to be made into experts on the engines with which they were equipped. The technical sergeant-major had to train these men, and was also the specialist who was

called in whenever one of the flights had an unusually refractory engine which had baffled both the flight commander and his flight sergeant. Smyrk was always equal to every call upon him, and a long line of pilots should, and no doubt do, remember him with gratitude, for, after all, the degree of efficiency with which the engine was looked after often meant the difference between a landing in Hunland and getting home.'

Awarded Army M.S.M. in *L.G.* 1 January, 1918. (A/Sgt. Maj.) (Recommended October, 1916, serving with 60 Squadron) 'For Valuable Services with the Armies in the Field.' Chief Master Mech (Tech) in 1918 RAF Muster Roll. From Islington. (See also No. 266.)

* 254. EDWARD ERNEST PORTER

Born Merridge, Somerset, 15 February, 1890. Enlisted 24 October, 1906. Formerly 12876 L/Sgt 3/Grenadier Guards. Posted to RFC HQ 25 July, 1912 on transfer to the Corps. Royal Aero Club Aviators' Certificate No. 549 of 9 July, 1913 as a Sergeant in a Maurice Farman of CFS at Upavon. Serving at Montrose Scotland with 6 Squadron in August, 1913. As Flight Sergeant 6 Squadron earned 1914 Star and bar in France from 6 October, 1914. SM1 12 March, 1915. Mentioned in despatches in *L.G.* 3 June, 1916. Awarded D.C.M. as Sergeant Major in *L.G.* 21 June, 1916 'For consistent good work. He has shown great zeal and has never failed to carry out his duties successfully.' Commissioned 2 Lieut 11 March, 1917 'For Services in the Field.' Awarded M.B.E. Flying Officer (Stores List) 1 August, 1919, stationed from 23 December, 1919 at Electrical and Wireless School (No. 7 Group) at Winchester (November, 1921 *A.F.L.*). He commited suicide on board the SS *Varsova* bound for Karachi on 19 May, 1927. His group of five medals is known in a private collection:— M.B.E. (1st type, military ribbon), D.C.M. (GV 254 S. Mjr RFC), 1914 Star and bar (Fl. Sgt) British War Medal and Victory medal (with oakleaf. Captain RAF). See group photograph No. 2.

* 255. W. C. HAYWARD

Formerly 13819 Corporal 3/Grenadier Guards. Posted to 3 Squadron 25 July, 1912 on transfer to RFC. Was a Sergeant in 3 Squadron when he earned 1914 Star and bar in France from 12 August, 1914. Distinguished Conduct Medal in *L.G.* 23 and 30 June, 1915 'For conspicuous zeal, devotion to duty, and the noticeably efficient manner in which he has carried out his responsible duties' (as Flight Sergeant). Mentioned in despatches *L.G.* 15 June, 1916. Awarded Army M.S.M. *L.G.* 1 January, 1917 (Sgt, A/Sgt. Major). Commissioned 2/Lt 19 February, (see *L.G.* 22 March, 1917). His group of five medals was sold by J.B. Hayward and Son in 1973 for £190:— D.C.M. (F. Sgt RFC), 1914 Star and bar (Fl Sgt RFC), British War Medal and Victory Medal, (Oakleaf, Lieut RAF), Army M.S.M. (Sgt A/SM). See group photograph No. 2.

* 256. R. E. NORMAN

Enlisted 28 January, 1908. Formerly 49833 acting Bombardier 'E' Battery RHA. A corporal with the Aircraft Park in France from 16 August, 1914. T/SM (T) 1 December, 1915. Chief Master Mech (Tech) in 1918 RAF Muster Roll. Awarded RAF L.S.&G.C. Medal *w.e.f.* 28 January, 1926 as SM1. In the November, 1941 he was the sixth senior WO and in the 1946 *Air Force List* he was then the 3rd Senior WO in RAF. However he enlisted over 4 years prior to the senior WO (130 A. E. Bell). He should have been awarded a bar to his L.S.&G.C. Medal in 1944. Retired January, 1948.

* 257. HERBERT HENRY JOHN VAISEY

Enlisted 30 January, 1907. Formerly 43930 Shoeing-Smith 'E' Battery, Royal Horse Artillery. Posted to 2 Squadron 24 June, 1912 on transfer to RFC. Sergeant, (*w.e.f.* 7 July, 1913) 4 Squadron in France as Fitter AE 13 August, 1914 to 14 August, 1915 earning 1914 Star and bar, and from 16 January, 1916 to 29 May, 1918, Flight Sergeant 3, January, 1915 Acting WO1 August, 1915. WO (T) 19 December, 1916. CMM (Techn) in 1918 RAF Muster Roll. RAF L.S.&G.C. *w.e.f.* 30 January, 1925 as SM1. Qualified as an instructor in shoesmithing and carriage smithy. Discharged 28 June, 1928 (21 yrs 151 days service). See group photograph No. 2.

258. C. BUSHELL

Formerly 54712 Driver 'D' Battery RHA posted to Flying Depot 3 July, 1912 on transfer to RFC. As 2AM was discharged 1 April, 1914 under *K.R.* 392 (xvi) 'No longer physically fit for war service.'

* 259. B. G. COX

Enlisted 8 April, 1909. Formerly 1836 Pte 16 Lancers. Posted to 3 Squadron 4 July, 1912 on transfer to Corps. Sergeant, 5 Squadron, in France from 14 August, 1914 earning 1914 Star and bar. Appointed QMS 1 May, 1916 and was Master Mechanic (Technical) in 1918 RAF Muster Roll. Mentioned in *'Flying Fury'* by McCudden V.C. as a Sergeant Major in August, 1917 touring the front lines recovering crashed aircraft – Allied and German. See group photograph No. 2.

260. (NOT TRACED, SEE 88)

Possibly the Sergeant Methery not recorded elsewhere but noted on group photograph No. 2. However, this may be 104 Nethey.

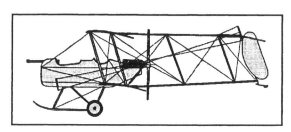

VICKERS MILITARY BIPLANE

261. (NOT TRACED, SEE 88)

Possibly the Sergeant Sedger not recorded elsewhere but noted in group photograph No. 2. However, this may be 705 Ledger.

★ 262. W. WHITMARSH

Enlisted 3 August, 1912. 1AM in 3 Squadron in France from 13 August, 1914. Sergeant (Fitter, General) 1 August, 1916. Sergeant Mech (Fitter, General) in 1918 RAF Muster Roll.

263. HAROLD VICTOR ROBBINS

Born Kenilworth, 25 October, 1887. Awarded Royal Aero Club Aviators' Certificate No. 463 as Sergeant on 22 April, 1913, at Upavon CFS, in a Maurice Farman. Appointed 2nd class flyer *w.e.f.* 23 October, 1913. Still a Sergeant in August, 1914. Served overseas from 5 September, 1915 earning 1914/15 Star trio. He was mentioned in despatches *L.G.* 15 June, 1916 as Sergeant Major. Commissioned 2 Lieutenant 17 August, 1917. In November, 1921 *A.F.L.* shown as Flying Officer seniority 1 April, 1920, at Inland Area Command HQ Uxbridge on Technical Staff Duties (allotment of Motor Transport Aeroplanes etc). Promoted Flight Lieutenant (Stores Branch) 1 August, 1924 and retired 6 October, 1930. In 1937 *A.F.L.* shown as Flt Lieut (E) (Retd) as Equipment Officer at Flying Training School, Leuchars, Fife, Scotland. (No. 21069) Last noted in 1946 *A.F.L.*

★ 264. A. C. HILL

Enlisted 4 February, 1905. Formerly 25521 Gunner 26th (Heavy) Battery, RGA. Posted to 3 Squadron, 31 July, 1912 on transfer to RFC. 1AM (promoted Cpl 10 August) 5 Squadron earning 1914 Star and bar in France from 14 August, 1914. Sergeant Observer on 21 October, 1915, flying with Sergeant F.T. Courtney. Wounded by Anti-Aircraft fire then shot down by Lieutenant Max Immelmann. Promoted QMS 1 November, 1916. Commissioned 3 August, 1917. He is however shown in 1918 RAF Muster Roll as Master Mechanic but this entry was subsequently deleted.

265. ERNEST WILLIAM LAWRENCE

Formerly 5664 L/Cpl., (a Storeman) Tidworth Section, No. 2 Company.
Army Ordnance Corps. Posted to RFC HQ 18 July, 1912 on transfer. A
Corporal at HQ in August, 1914. No record traced of award of either 1914
or 1914/15 Star. Commissioned 2 Lieutenant 22 December, 1916. In
November, 1921 *A.F.L.* was Flying Officer (Stores List) seniority 17 June,
1920, from 8 February, 1921 serving at Stores Depot, Middle East Area,
Egypt. In February, 1931 *A.F.L.* he is shown as Flight Lieutenant
seniority 1 January, 1926 Qualified at Explosives Course, serving from 16
October, 1930 with 45 (Bomber Squadron) (Fairey 111 Fs) at Heiwan,
Middle East. He was shown as retired in January, 1938 *A.F.L.* when he
was Barrack Officer at RAF Andover, Hants.

* 266. J. A. ASPINALL

Enlisted 31 July, 1905. Formerly 6276 L/Cpl 3 Coldstream Guards. Posted
to 2 Squadron 1 August, 1912, on transfer to RFC. As a Flight Sergeant
with 6 Squadron he earned 1914 Star and bar in France from 6 October,
1914. Promoted Warrant Officer (Disciplinarian) 12 October, 1916, but
was awarded Army M.S.M. in *London Gazette* 4 June, 1917 'For Valuable
Services in France and Flanders' as Flight Sergeant (Acting Sergeant
Major 60 Squadron) (See also No. 253). Was SM1 (Disciplinarian) in 1918
RAF Muster Roll. RAF L.S.&G.C, awarded *w.e.f.* 31 July, 1923 as SM1.
P.H. Liddle records that he required a formality out of accord with the
more easy going relationships necessary in a workshop. See group
photographs Nos. 2 and 3.

The following is an extract from *'Sixty Squadron RAF'*:—

> Major F. Waldron, known to his friends as 'Ferdy,' was the first
> commander of the new unit. He had previously commanded No.
> 1 Reserve Aeroplane Squadron at Gosport, and was a cavalry officer
> who had been seconded from his Hussar regiment (the 19th), some
> time before the war, to the R.F.C. He was one of the earlier military
> aviators. He had been an instructor at the Central Flying School
> at Upavon and was a first-class pilot.

> Usually a new squadron received its machines in England at its
> home station and flew them over to France. 60 Squadron, however,
> was to be equipped with Moranes, French machines which were
> not built in England at that time. Consequently the squadron, with
> its motor transport, stores, etc., crossed to France by sea, and went
> to St. Omer, where its equipment was completed.

An R.F.C. squadron had two sergeant-majors: one disciplinary, the other technical. Waldron, when forming 60, chose these warrant officers with considerable discretion. Sergt.-Maj. Aspinall, an old Guardsman brought into the Flying Corps by Basil Barrington-Kennet in the very early days, was the disciplinary warrant officer. He had qualified as a rigger and had tried to learn to fly, but it was as a disciplinarian that he really shone. He played no inconsiderable part in the achievement of whatever success the squadron may have had. He was a first-class soldier, and his instructions to flight commanders in the form of little typewritten lectures were gems of their kind. It should be remembered that at times the casualties in the squadron were very heavy, and officers became flight commanders at an age which would have been regarded as absurd before the war. 'The Great Man,' as we called him, would explain with profound respect to a captain promoted, most deservedly, at the age of nineteen the necessity for assuming a judicial demeanour when an air mechanic was brought up before him on some minor charge; he would, further, instruct the young flight commander most carefully in the punishments appropriate to each offence, and all this without in the smallest particular transgressing that code of military etiquette which regulates so strictly the relations between commissioned and warrant officers. Only his successive commanding officers know how much of the tranquillity and contentment of the men was due to 'the Great Man.' He was also the captain of the Squadron soccer team.'

267. R. A. MILES

Enlisted 20 April, 1907. Formerly 56994 Driver, 132 Battery, RFA. Posted to 1 Squadron 29 July, 1912 on transfer to RFC. Discharged sick (1AM) 18 May, 1915, No overseas service. Silver War Service Badge No. 88927. Re-enlisted in Army Service Corps 9 April, 1917.

★ 268. HARRY THOMAS WARR

Enlisted 15 January, 1910. Formerly 6584 Pte AOC (Aldershot) (Stores Branch). Posted to 3 Squadron 18 July, 1912 on transfer to RFC. Corporal 5 Squadron, to France 14 August, 1914. Acting Warrant Officer (Disciplinarian), 1 April, 1916. SM1 (Disciplinarian) in 1918 RAF Muster Roll. RAF L.S.&G.C. Medal *w.e.f.* 15 January, 1928 as SM1. Noted as

WO1 in 1931 *Air Force List*. Retired May, 1934. However, he was recalled in WWII and in the 1941 (November) *Air Force List* he was then the 14th Senior RAF Warrant Officer with seniority from 1 December, 1923. In October, 1944 he was the fifth most senior.

* 269. WILLIAM PERCY PARKER

Born Woolwich 8 June, 1889. Enlisted 5 April, 1910. Formerly 6648 Lance Corporal AOC (Aldershot) (Stores Branch) when transferred to RFC. Royal Aero Club Aviators' Certificate No. 850 on 21 July, 1914 as 1AM in a Maurice Farman of CFS at Upavon. As 1AM (Pilot) 2 Squadron went to France 12 August, 1914 earning 1914 Star and bar. Awarded French Médaille Militaire as Corporal for Gallantry 21-30 August, 1914, gazetted in 9 November, 1914. Acting Warrant Officer (Disciplinarian) 1 February, 1918 and Acting SM1 (paid) in 1918 RAF Muster Roll. Served post-war in Northern India and Afghanistan. His group of five medals sold by J.B. Hayward and Sons in 1972 for £40:— 1914 Star and bar (1AM), British War Medal and Victory Medal (Flight Sergeant) Indian General Service Medal (2 clasps, Afghanistan North West Frontier 1919 and Waziristan 1919-21 SM1) and French Médaille Militaire.

* 270. JOHN MEAD

Born 1 June, 1885 in South Tynham, Dorset. To 2 Squadron 18 July, 1912. Royal Aero Club Aviators' Certificate No. 475 on 2 May, 1913 as a Sergeant at Montrose in a RFC Maurice Farman. As Flight Sergeant served with the Aircraft Park in France from 16 August, 1914. Mentioned in despatches in *London Gazette* 22 June, 1915 as a Sergeant Major. Commissioned Lieutenant 13 August, 1915. Awarded Military Cross in *L.G.* 1 January, 1917 as Lieutenant and Quarter Master. Listed as Major (Technical) in the 1918 RAF (April) *Air Force List*. In the 1921 (November) *Air Force List* he is shown as Wing Commander C.B.E. M.C.

seniority 1 January, 1919. He retired on 14 March, 1923. He is still shown as retired Wing Commander in 1975 *Air Force List*, (No. 1089), but not in that of 1977. See group photograph No. 3.

★ 271. SIDNEY ERNEST STORRAR

Born 1 April, 1895 at Leigh-on-Sea, Essex. Enlisted 5 August, 1912 directly ito RFC. Earned 1914 Star and bar as 2AM with the Airship Detachment. Transferred to RNAS 18 October, 1914 as Air Mechanic 1st Class No. 681. Commissioned 2 Lieutenant Oxfordshire & Buckinghamshire Light Infantry, and RFC (Observer Officer) 25 October, 1916. Lieutenant RAF 1 April, 1918 (Aeroplane Officer). Flying Officer in 1921 (November) *A.F.L.* seniority 7 June, 1920 still a Pilot, flying with 100 Squadron of the 11 (Irish) Wing at Clondalkin from 9 March, 1921. Flight Lieutenant in 1931 (February) *A.F.L.* seniority 1 July, 1924 (GD Branch) flying with 207 (Bomber) Squadron (Fairey 111 F aircraft) Wessex Bombing Area, Bircham Newton, King's Lynn, Norfolk from 6 October, 1930. Squadron Leader 1 August, 1934, p.s.a. (Graduate of RAF Staff College) in December, 1937 *A.F.L.* stationed *w.e.f.* 3 September, 1937 at the Directorate of Organisation at the Air Ministry. Promoted Wing Commander in 1938, Group Captain on 1 June, 1943. Director of Organisation (Establishments) at Air Ministry 1942-44, C.B.E. in 1944. From 1944 to 1947 he was Air Officer i/c Administration (Transport) firstly as Acting Air Vice-Marshal from 4 September, 1944 then with War Substantive AVM rank from 4 September, 1945. Retired 9 September, 1947. Director of Civil Aviation Palestine then Malaya. Died March, 1969 at his home at Queen Camel, Yeovil, Somerset.

★ 272. E. J. P. KELLY

Enlisted 20 November, 1901. Formerly 9733 L/Cpl Air Battalion RE. Served in 3 Balloon Company RE prior to that. A Corporal in the Aircraft

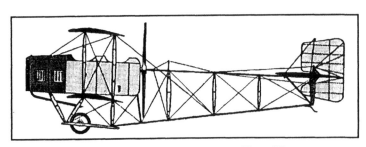

GRAHAME-WHITE MILITARY TYPE VI

Park he served in France from 16 August, 1914. Mentioned in despatches twice, as Sergeant in *L.G.* 22 June, 1915 and as Flight Sergeant in *L.G.* 12 January, 1916. Promoted T/SM (Discip) 1 June, 1917. Was SM1 in 1918 RAF Muster Roll. RAF L.S.&G.C. Medal *w.e.f.* 20 November, 1919 as SM1. Medals known in a private collection (1914 Star trio and RAF L.S.&G.C. Medal).

★ 273. W. A. WELLS

Enlisted 16 April, 1901. Formerly 8713 Sapper 2 Company Balloon School (Dismounted) RE on mobilisation of the Air Battalion. He was 1AM with the Aircraft Park in France from 16 August, 1914. T/SM (D) 1 October, 1916 and SM1 in 1918 RAF Muster Roll. RAF L.S.&G.C. *w.e.f.* 16 April, 1919 as SM1 (one of the first six awarded, see No. 28 above, of which Wells was the Senior by rank).

274. G. BATES

Enlisted 5 January, 1909. Formerly 6320 Pte, 6th Company AOC (Stores Branch). Posted to CFS 18 July, 1912 on transfer to Corps. Posted overseas 16 December, 1915, a T/SM (D) from 12 December, earning 1914/15 Star trio. He was mentioned in despatches 15 May 1917 as Flight Sergeant A/SM. SM1 in 1918 RAF Muster Roll.

★ 275. R. KIRK

Enlisted 30 October, 1908. Formerly 62 Company AOC (Stores Branch) transferred to RFC 7 August, 1912. Served in France from 3 November, 1914 earning 1914 Star and bar. Promoted Flight Sergeant (Carpenter) in 1918 RAF Muster Roll. 'Mentioned' for services at the Air Ministry 22 January, 1919 and next day in the *Times* 'B' List. Indian General Service Medal (clasp Afghanistan NWF 1919) as Sergeant.

276. M. WEARE

Enlisted 6 August, 1912, directly into RFC. Corporal in 7 Squadron in August, 1914. Posted overseas 3 April, 1915 earning 1914/15 Star trio. Flight Sergeant Observer 4 April, 1916. Awarded Military Medal *L.G.* 30 May, 1916. Reverted to Sergeant (1st Class Pilot) 27 August, 1916. *RFC Communiqué No. 68, 27 December, 1916.*

'A German aeroplane which was attacked by 2 Lt. Copeland and Sgt. Weare 7 Squadron, was driven down out of control between Pys and

Miraument.'

Wounded 7 October, 1917 as Sergeant/Pilot 55 Squadron. Sgt/Mech/ Pilot in 1918 RAF Muster Roll.

277. H. GIBLETT

Recruited directly into RFC as 2AM with 1 Squadron. Discharged 25 October, 1912 on payment of £10. (*K.R.* 392 (v)).

* 278. WILLIAM BROWN

Enlisted 17 February, 1910. Formerly 10331 Pte 2/Welsh Regt. Posted to 3 Squadron 30 July, 1912 on transfer to RFC. 1AM with 3 Squadron in France from 12 August, 1914 earning 1914 Star and bar. Sergeant (Carpenter) 1 May, 1916. Sergeant Mech in 1918 RAF Muster Roll. Appointed WO1 4 June, 1930. No trace of the award of an RAF L.S.&G.C. Medal found. Awarded 1935 Silver Jubilee Medal. In 1937 *A.F.L.* had been Station Warrant Officer, Home Aircraft Depot, Hemlow Camp, Biggleswade from 11 February, 1933. In March, 1938 *A.F.L.* was 36th senior RAF Warrant Officer. Not shown amongst RAF WO's in November, 1941 *A.F.L.*

* 279. C. E. KING

Enlisted 9 August, 1912 directly into RFC. As Sgt 5 Squadron in France from 14 August, 1914. Promoted WO (T) 3 March, 1917. Awarded D.C.M. in *L.G.* 9 July, 1917 as Flight Sergeant (A/SM), 'For conspicuous gallantry and devotion to duty. He salved an engine out of a wrecked machine under extremely dangerous conditions, and has at all times set a fine example.' CMM (Technical) in 1918 RAF Muster Roll. Mentioned in despatches 20 May, 1918 as Sergeant Major. See group photograph No. 2.

* 280. R. M. MANDEVILLE

Directly into RFC 9 August, 1912. As 1AM with Aircraft Park earned 1914 Star and bar in France from 16 August, 1914. Sergeant (Driver MT) 1 June, 1916. Sergeant Mech (Driver) in 1918 RAF Muster Roll.

★ 281. W. STUBBINGTON

Direct entry into RFC 9 August, 1912. As 1AM in 4 Squadron in France from 12 August, 1914. Flight Sergeant (Sailmaker) 1 April, 1916. Flight Sergeant (Fabric Worker) in 1918 RAF Muster Roll.

★ 282. VICTOR EDWARD PUNTER

Direct entry into RFC 9 August, 1912. As 2AM Airship detachment earned 1914 Star and bar transferring to RNAS 18 October, 1914 as No. 701 Air Mechanic 1st Class. Ch P.O. (3), 1 September, 1917. Chief Mechanic (Rigger Airships) No. 200701 in 1918 RAF Muster Roll. Awarded RAF L.S.&G.C. Medal as SM2 *w.e.f.* 9 August, 1930. Awarded 1935 Silver Jubilee Medal. Appointed Warrant Officer Class 1, 1 February, 1937. Serving in November, 1941 (*A.F.L.*) and by October, 1944 was the 73rd most senior RAF WO.

★ 283. JAMES HART

Enlisted 17 February, 1908. Formerly 49962 Acting Bombardier 141st Battery RFA. Posted to 2 Squadron 5 August, 1912 on transfer to Corps. As Corporal 6 Squadron in August, 1914 he earned a 1914 Star and bar, serving in France from 10 September, 1914. Promoted T/SM (T) on 1 February, 1917 and was CMM (T) in 1918 RAF Muster Roll. Listed in the *Times* 'B' Press Release 29 August, 1919. His 1914 Star and bar trio, named to Corporal and Flight Sergeant RFC is known in a private collection.

HENRI FARMAN BIPLANE

★ 284. A. V. SMITH

Enlisted directly into RFC 9 August, 1912. As 2AM 2 Squadron earned 1914 Star and bar trio in France from 13 August, 1914. Promoted Flight Sergeant (Photographer) 1 April, 1916 he was Chief Mech (Photographer) in 1918 RAF Muster Roll.

★ 285. A. O. S. WHITEHEAD

Enlisted 2 November, 1907. Formerly 48620 Gunner, 53 Battery, RFA. Posted to Flying Depot 5 August, 1912 on transfer to RFC. As 2AM with 4 Squadron served in France from 12 August, 1912 earning 1914 Star and bar. Promoted Flight Sergeant (Fitter-Aero Engines) 1 June, 1917 and shown as Master Mechanic (Fitter AE) in 1918 RAF Muster Roll. Awarded RAF L.S.&G.C. Medal *w.e.f.* 2 November, 1925 as Flight Sergeant.

286. E. M. BUSH

As 1AM 2 Squadron posted to France 24 November, 1914 earning 1914/15 Star. Commissioned 2 Lieut. 31 October, 1915. M.I.D. 1 January, 1916. Subsequently Squadron Leader. Still alive in July, 1977, then living at 4 Jackson's Court, Hazelmere, High Wycombe, Bucks.

★ 287. E. L. BISHOP

Enlisted 1 September, 1905. Formerly 23676 Gunner 48 Heavy Battery RGA. Posted to 3 Squadron 26 June, 1912. As 1AM, 3 Squadron served in France from 12 August, 1914. Promoted Flight Sergeant (Fitter, Turner) 1 October, 1915. Was a Chief Mechanic in 1918 RAF Muster Roll. Listed in the *Times* 'B' Press Release, 29 August, 1919. His recollections were tape recorded for the files of P.H. Liddle. His photograph is in the collection of the RAF Museum.

★ 288. G. W. WHITE

Enlisted 6 December, 1907. Formerly 7560 Pte 3 Coldstream Guards. Posted to Flying Depot 7 August, 1912 on transfer to Corps. As Corporal 3 Squadron earned 1914 Star and bar in France from 13 August, 1914. Promoted T/SM (T) 22 January, 1916 and was Chief Master Mech (Tech) in 1918 RAF Muster Roll. His 1914 Star only is in the Olivant collection.

289. A. V. COLLETT

Enlisted 12 August, 1912 directly into Corps. Served with 2 Squadron at Montrose in Spring 1913. Weather conditions were very bad in the winter at Upper Dysart so the powers that be built an aerodrome just outside Montrose. Airmen still had to mount guard at Dysart for some time, and Collett says he will never forget the night when he was on guard, pitch dark, snowing, swish of canvas, clanking of chains, banging of tie rods. Suddenly a huge figure in an Inverness cape, long white beard covered in snow, with six enormous shaggy dogs, loomed up out of the darkness. 'Blimey,' he thought, 'this is it!' 'I quietly and quickly drew my Webley Mk.4 pistol, I thought I would shoot the dogs first and use the pistol as a club on 'Old Nick,' as I was certain that's who it was. I challenged him and much to my surprise he answered, 'Friend,' in a very strong Scots accent.

'After talking for a few minutes, he told me he was the Laird of Lunan taking his dogs for a walk. He shook hands with me on leaving and I felt something in my hand. After a few seconds I saw it was 3s 6d, then he called out, 'That is for a bottle of Johnnie Walker to keep yourself warm.'

Was 1AM 7 Squadron when posted overseas 3 April, 1915 earning 1914/15 Star. Promoted Sergeant (Rigger-Aero) 1 August, 1916 and was Sergeant Mech in 1918 RAF Muster Roll. RAF L.S.&G.C. awarded as SM2 *w.e.f.* 12 August, 1930 when he was serving in India. Entitled to Indian General Service Medal (Clasp NWF 1930-31). (Brother to 413 C. I. Collett. Alive in 1960 and living in Blackpool.) He says in *'The Forgotten Ones'*:—

> 'On the outbreak of war, I volunteered for flying duties and was posted to Farnborough. On 13th of August, we took off for France in a B.E.2a. Lieutenant Emmett, a South African, was the pilot.
>
> My armament consisted of a short butt Lee-Enfield rifle, 150 rounds of .303 in a canvas bandolier, a Webley Mk. 4 pistol and fifty rounds of ammunition.
>
> We landed at Shoreham to refuel, took off for Dover, on coming in to land the engine cut out and we crashed badly on landing; the pilot had his right thumb broken, but I received serious injuries and was taken to Dover Cliff Hospital.
>
> On discharge later in the year, I was posted to 'C' Flight No. 7 Squadron, Longreach, Dartford, Kent. Later we rejoined 'A' and 'B' Flights at Netheravon, and proceeded to France where we were based at St. Omer. We lost all our aircraft through various causes and were re-equipped with the French Voison [sic], a wonderful aircraft, a pusher type with 4-wheel undercarriage, with hand-

operated brakes on the rear wheels. You could not turn this machine on the ground as the undercarriage would fold up. Mechanics had to bear down on the rear booms, so lifting the front wheels off the ground, and then pushing it round into the required heading.'

Subsequently Collett served in two of the aircraft depots in France and finished the war in very unhappy circumstances. He had been invalided home owing to an attack of poisoning, and because he had gained wide experience of engines and aircraft during his previous years of service, he was, on discharge from hospital, posted to No. 1 School of Military Aeronautics at Reading. He writes with feeling about this place, and I, having known the personnel there employed on administrative duties, am forced to agree with his strictures on the way the School was run. He writes:

'I tried my damnedest to avoid this posting but it was no use – I went. Every technical N.C.O. was scared stiff of being posted to No. 1 S. of M.A. and very soon I knew why. The officers and N.C.O.s from the C.O. downwards were exceedingly strict. 95% of the administrative duties were thrown on to the technical WOs and N.C.O.s who also had their own duties to carry out. One was placed on a charge for the least thing. I stopped four reprimands in a month for crimes I didn't know I had committed. We had every nationality under the sun as trainees, so you can guess we had our work cut out, without having to carry out stupid admin. duties all hours of the day and night. Three officers were relieved of their command whilst I was there, and there were two cases of suicide, besides outbreaks of spinal meningitis, measles, etc.

Towards the end of 1917 we had quite a number of ex-soldiers from all regiments sent to us as trainees. These men had been wounded and maimed and transferred to RFC for lighter duties. They were treated so badly that 400 of them formed up and were determined to march to Windsor Castle and see the King. Heaven only knows how they were stopped!

I know the senior admin's Sergeant-Major met a crowd of 'Aussies' on a bridge one night and was promptly thrown into the River Kennet.'

There was a D.H.4 housed in a portable hangar in a field close to the School. The River Kennet ran at the end of this field. Every night an armed guard was mounted on the hangar. Once the river over-flowed and flooded the field to a depth of three feet. In spite of this, guard was still mounted, its members having to wade to their post. Collett once waded with water up to his armpits, carrying his equipment on his head until he reached the hangar. On another occasion the water was so deep that a punt had to be fetched to ferry the guard back to dry land. How silly can orders and routine become!

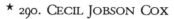

★ 290. CECIL JOBSON COX

Born York, 13 June, 1890. Enlisted 12 August, 1912 directly into RFC. As Cpl 5 Squadron served in France from 14 August, 1914. He was promoted Flight Sergeant 1 May, 1915 and awarded Royal Aero Club Aviators' Certificate No. 3160 on 2 July, 1916. He was then classified as 1st Class Pilot. He was wounded 26 January, 1917 as Flight Sergeant Pilot with 20 Squadron. Chief Mechanic (pilot) in 1918 RAF Muster Roll. Awarded Air Force Medal in *L.G.* 1 January, 1919. See *'Cross and Cockade'* Volume 4, No. 1, page 34.

★ 291. JOHN FRANK CLARK

Formerly 21684 Sapper 30 Company RE and Air Battalion. Posted to 2 Squadron 5 July, 1912 on transfer to RFC. As Corporal 6 Squadron served in France from 6 October, 1914. As Sergeant (Acting Sergeant Major) 25 Squadron awarded Army M.S.M. in *L.G.* 4 July, 1917. 'For Valuable Services in France and Flanders.' Commissioned 2 Lieutenant 3 September, 1917. In 1921 (November) *A.F.L.* was Flying Officer (T) seniority 1 August, 1919, under instruction as Pilot at No. 4 Flying Training School, Middle East Area, Palestine, In February, 1931 *A.F.L.* was Flight Lieutenant (E) seniority 1 January, 1927, from 13 February, 1929 serving at RAF M.T. Depot (21 Group) Shrewsbury. In 1937 was Adjutant RAF Station Hucknall (2 Bomber Group), Squadron Leader 1 December, 1941 No. 03183. Last noted in 1946 *A.F.L.*

★ 292. W. W. J. FILER

Enlisted 18 May, 1911. Formerly 21563 Sapper 30 Company RE. Posted to 1 Squadron 25 July, 1912 on transfer to RFC. 1AM, Aircraft Park, in France from 16 August, 1914. Promoted Flight Sergeant (Acetylene Welder) 1 January, 1917 and was Chief Mechanic in 1918 RAF Muster Roll.

★ 293. W. INGLESON

Enlisted 23 May, 1911. Formerly 21572 Sapper 30 Company RE posted to 3 Squadron 25 July, 1912 on transfer to RFC. As 1AM 3 Squadron served in France from 12 August, 1914. Promoted Flight Sergeant (Blacksmith) 1 December, 1916 and was Chief Mech in 1918 RAF Muster Roll.

★ 294. A. V. WHITTLE

Enlisted 30 January, 1911. Formerly 21073 Sapper 30 Company RE. Posted to 1 Squadron 25 July, 1912 on transfer to Corps. As 1AM Airship Detachment earned 1914 Star and bar, and transferred to RNAS 18 October, 1914 as No. 678, Air Mechanic 1st Class. Petty Officer (Engineer) 1 August, 1916. In 1918 RAF Muster Roll was Sergeant Mechanic (Winch Driver and Fitter) No. 200678.

★ 295. J. H. CAIRNS

Enlisted 30 July, 1907. Formerly 9760 Pte Royal Irish Fusiliers. Posted to 2 Squadron 5 August, 1912 on transfer to Corps. As 1AM 2 Squadron served in France from 12 August, 1914. Flight Sergeant Rigger (Aero), 1 October, 1917 and Chief Mechanic in 1918 RAF Muster Roll.

★ 296. R. G. F. HOFFMAN

Enlisted 20 August, 1906. Formerly 8565 Lance Sergeant 2nd King's Own Border Regiment. Posted to 3 Squadron 8 August, 1912 on transfer to RFC. As Sergeant with 3 Squadron served in France from 13 August, 1914 earning a 1914 Star only (the bar on his medal, see under, is of the slide on type and probably self awarded as many were post WW1). Promoted Quarter Master Sergeant (SM 2nd Class) 1 November, 1915 and given the rank of Master Mechanic (SM2) in the newly formed Royal Air Force on 1 April, 1918. He was promoted to SM1 15 March, 1921 and was awarded his RAF L.S.&G.C. Medal in Air Ministry Order No. 21 of January, 1925 *w.e.f.* 20 August, 1924. This was the 200th such award. He retired in 1930 having 12 years service in the RAF and 12 years in the Army. His name was placed on the Register for an annuity Meritorious Service Medal (WO101 series at PRO) and was listed under King's Own Border Regiment. However the statutes changed before his annuity was awarded and all 5000 or more retired senior NCOs of various Corps and Regiments of the Army, some quite old men who had served Queen

Victoria, were awarded the medal only under Army Order 156 of 3 December, 1953 *vide A.O.* 98 of 1953 'Those registered before 1 January, 1951 shall be eligible for the award of the M.S.M. not with standing that they have not yet been selected for the award of an annuity.' The medals were issued in 1953 when Hoffman would have been aged approximately 65. Quite young compared with some noted. His group of five medals is in the McInnes collection consisting of 1914 Star and slide-on bar (296 Sgt RFC), British War Medal and Victory Medal (SM2 RAF), Army M.S.M. (GVI 2nd type) (296 WO Border Regt) (*N.B.* His original Army Unit but his RFC/RAF number) and RAF L.S.&G.C. Medal (GV) (296 SM1 RAF). See group photograph No. 2.

[Examples of transfers between the Army and the Royal Air Force resulting in the Award of a Standard 'Annuity' Issue of an Army M.S.M. in later life occur occasionally. One such is No. 957 Patterson D. (see below) and another one noted is as follows: O.B.E. (2nd type, military ribbon *L.G.* 1 January, 1946 to 166114, A. Franklin RAF), 1914/15 Star trio (CSM then WO2 E Surrey Regt), 1939/45 and France and Germany Stars, Defence and War Medals. RAF L.S.&G.C. Medal (GV SM1 RAF) (Transferred to RFC in June, 1917) and Army M.S.M. (GV1 2nd type named to WO in East Surrey Regt)].

★ 297. JOHN GROVES PATRIC BEAZLEY ANGELL

As Sergeant 3 Squadron served in France from 12 August, 1914. Mentioned in despatches with 3 Squadron in *L.G.* 1 January, 1916 and as Sergeant Major awarded French Médaille Militaire. However this was not gazetted until 1 May, 1917, and he had been commissioned 2 Lieut from 19 October, 1916. Flight Lieut (General List) (T) – November,

1921, *A.F.L.* seniority 1 August, 1919, from 16 March, 1920 stationed at No. 1 School of Technical Training (Boys) Halton. He retired 22 July, 1929. Recalled in WW2 from retired list and promoted to Squadron Leader 1 March, 1941. See group photograph No. 2. Medals known in a private collection (1914 Star trio, Defence and War Medals and Médaille Militaire).

298. W. WELDON

As 2AM discharged 2 October, 1913 under *K.R.* 392 (xi) 'After sentence of court martial.'

★ 299. THOMAS BELL

As Flight Sergeant with the Aircraft Park, served in France from 16 August, 1914. Still Flight Sergeant was mentioned in despatches in June, 1916 and awarded Military Medal in *L.G.* 3 June, 1916. He was commissioned 2 Lieutenant 3 April, 1917. In November 1921 *A.F.L.* was Flight Lieutenant, Seniority 17 June, 1920 (Stores List). From 1 May, 1919 he had been stationed at No. 3 Depot (7 Group) Steventon. Squadron Leader 1 July, 1924, in February, 1931 stationed from 6 June, 1929 at RAF M.T. Depot (21 Group) Shrewsbury. In 1937 *A.F.L.* shown as Squadron Ldr (Retd) employed as Equipment Officer, RAF Station Aldergrove.

★ 300. C. H. HILL

Enlisted 26 April, 1907. Formerly 33968 Gunner 24th (Heavy) Battery RGA. Posted to 3 Squadron 27 June, 1912 on transfer to RFC. As 1AM in 3 Squadron earned 1914 Star and bar in France from 12 August, 1914. Promoted TP. SM (D) 1 July, 1917 and was SM1 (Discip) in 1918 RAF Muster Roll.

★ 301. G. F. MCALLISTER

Enlisted directly into the RFC 14 August, 1912. As 1AM with the Airship Detachment earned 1914 Star and bar. Transferred to RNAS 18 October, 1914 as No. 697 Air Mechanic 1st Class. Leading Mechanic (Driver) 1 January, 1915. In 1918 RAF Muster Roll was No. 200697 Corp/Mech (Driver – Petrol). Awarded Indian General Service Medal (clasp Waziristan 1921/24). Awarded RAF L.S.&G.C. Medal as Sergeant *w.e.f.* 14 August, 1930.

302. J. W. PORTER

Enlisted 3 January, 1911. Formerly 63581 Gunner 37 Battery, RFA. Posted to 4 Squadron 12 August, 1912 on transfer to RFC. 2AM 4 Squadron in August, 1914. Posted overseas 7 March, 1915 earning 1914/15 Star. Certainly one of the most poorly paid of those RFC men with previous Army service prior to its formation and who survived the war. He was promoted 1AM 1 December, 1915 and was a Private 1st Class (earning 1/8d per day) in RAF Muster Roll of April, 1918. (See also Nos. 75, 317, 342, 447, 456, 510 (who joined in 1903), 560 (who joined in 1902), 567 (who joined in 1900) (these last two were recalled reservists), 674, 677, 702, 813, 844 (who was an ex-Boy), 987, 1045, 1072, 1073, eighteen in all, none of them earning less than poor Porter).

★ 303. A. W. MEPSTEAD

Enlisted 26 May, 1911. Formerly 4244, Rifleman 3/Rifle Brigade. Posted to 1 Squadron as 2AM on 8 August, 1912. As 1AM in 4 Squadron he went to France on 12 August, 1914. Promoted Sergeant (1st Class Pilot) 21 January, 1918 and was Sergeant Mech (Pilot) in 1918 RAF Muster Roll.

★ 304. WALTER ROBERT MAYES

Born 10 October, 1893. Enlisted 10 August, 1912 directly into Corps. As 1AM Airship Detachment earned 1914 Star and bar being posted to RNAS 18 October, 1914 as Leading Mechanic No. 695. Chief Petty Officer (2nd Class) (Rigger Airships) 30 April, 1917. Awarded Distinguished Service Medal in May, 1918 as Chief Petty Officer 2 Class although by that date in 1918 RAF Muster Roll he is listed as 200695 Master Mechanic (Rigger

HENRI FARMAN HF22

153

Airships). As SM2 he was awarded an Air Force Medal in *London Gazette* 23 August, 1919 for his part as First Coxswain in the Airship R.34's double crossing of the Atlantic from Scotland on 2 July, 1919 to New York and returning by 13 July, 1919. Later in *London Gazette* 4 June, 1921 he was awarded a bar to his Air Force Medal for services in the Airship R.36 flying over Bath when the rudder and elevators broke loose and he and Flight Sergeant S. J. Heath A.F.M. climbed on top of the ship and repaired damage. (Only five bars to the A.F.M. were awarded from 1918 to 1939.) On 16 April, 1925 in a fierce westerly gale, he was one of a skeleton crew of 20 who on board the R.33 at Pulham were carried away from their mooring and spent 30 hours battling the elements over the North Sea before bringing the airship back to her base. Promoted WO1 1 October, 1928. Awarded his RAF L.S.&G.C. *w.e.f.* 10 August, 1930. He was commissioned Flying Officer (Commissioned Engineering Officer) with seniority from 19 September, 1933. In the 1937 *Air Force List* he is shown as an Equipment Staff Officer at Fighter Command HQ, Stanmore, Middlesex. Personal No. 35006. Awarded 1937 Coronation Medal. Squadron Leader 1 September, 1940 with an O.B.E. Promoted Wing Commander (Technical) (E) 14 January, 1944 and in 1946 *Air Force List* shown as Group Captain O.B.E., D.S.M., A.F.M., and bar. Retired 22 October, 1945. (see also Nos. 599 and 785). Last noted in April, 1961 *Air Force List*.

305. WILLIAM EDWARD SURMAN

Enlisted 22 November, 1909. Formerly 9217. Pte 1/Royal Berkshire Regt. Posted to CFS 10 August, 1912. A sergeant in August, 1914. Served overseas from 3 March, 1915 earning 1914/15 Star. Reverted from Flight Sergeant to Sergeant (1st Class Pilot) 14 December, 1916. Awarded his Royal Aero Club Aviators' Certificate No. 4434 on 2 April, 1917. Listed as Sergeant Mech (Pilot) in 1918 RAF Muster Roll.

* 306. THOMAS GEORGE TINDALE

Enlisted 10 February, 1910. Formerly 9283 Pte 1/Royal Berks Regiment. Posted to 3 Squadron 10 August, 1912 when transferred to RFC. As Sergeant in 5 Squadron was posted to France on 10 August, 1914.

Awarded D.C.M. in London Gaztte 22 June, 1915 'For conspicuous zeal and devotion to duty, and the noticeably efficient manner in which he has carried out his responsible duties.' Promoted Temporary Sergeant Major (Technical) 1 April, 1916 and listed as CMM (Technical) in 1918 RAF Muster Roll. Mentioned in the *Times* 'B' Press Release of 29 August, 1919. Awarded RAF L.S.&G.C. *w.e.f.* 10 February, 1928 as SM1. In the 1931 *Air Force List* he is shown as the 14th senior RAF Warrant Officer. See group photograph No. 2.

★ 307. CUTHBERT LEOPOLD ARCHIBOLD

Born 12 August, 1887. A Sergeant with the Aircraft Park in France from 16 August, 1914. Commissioned 2 Lieutenant 12 October, 1916. Promoted Captain in May 1917. Squadron Leader in November, 1921 *Air Force List* with seniority of 17 June, 1920 serving from 14 February, 1921 on Stores Staff Duties Middle East Command HQ, Cairo. Wing Commander in February, 1931 *A.F.L.* with seniority of 1 January, 1928 serving at Aden Command HQ, Steamer Point Aden on Stores Staff Duties from 8 October, 1929. In the 1937 *A.F.L.* he is shown as Group Captain O.B.E. (E) seniority of 1 January, 1937 serving as O.C. Equipment Section, Coastal Command HQ, Lee-on-Solent. Awarded 1935 Silver Jubilee Medal. Retired 25 April, 1946. Last noted as Group Captain (Retd) with the rank of Air Commodore in 1962 *A.F.L.*, with a C.B.E. See group photograph No. 2.

308. F. CHENNEY

As 2AM discharged in December, 1913 under *K.R.* 392 (ix), 'Unfitted for the duties of the Corps.'

★ 309. THOMAS BOSWORTH

Enlisted 22 December, 1905. Formerly 32674 Gunner, 108 (Heavy) Battery, RGA. Posted to 3 Squadron 6 August, 1912 on transfer to RFC. Corporal 6 Squadron, in France from 6 October, 1914. On 1 May, 1915 promoted Flight Sergeant (Fitter-Turner). CM (Turner) in 1918 RAF Muster Roll. RAF L.S.&G.C. Medal awarded *w.e.f.* 22 December, 1923 as SM2. Promoted WO1 1 May, 1929. Still serving in 1931. Retired November, 1933.

310. L. REYNOLDS

Transferred back to 118 Battery RFA (No. 52350) 30 January, 1913 after serving some six months in Corps.

★ 311. T. S. WYNNE

A Corporal with RFC HQ in France from 12 August, 1914. Recommended for a commission in September, 1914 becoming 2 Lieutenant in Suffolk Regt.

★ 312. A. E. DAYMOND

Enlisted 16 August, 1912 directly into RFC. As 1AM in Aircraft Park served in France from 16 August, 1914. Promoted Corporal (Storeman) 1 April, 1917 and was Corporal Clerk on 1918 RAF Muster Roll.

★ 313. WILLIAM CHARLES ATTRILL

Enlisted 28 April, 1906. Formerly 43052 Gunner 86 Battery, RFA. Posted to 2 Squadron, 15 August, 1912 when transferred to Corps. Cpl, 2 Squadron earned 1914 Star and bar in France from 13 August, 1914. Promoted T/SM (T) 1 January, 1917 and was CMM (Tech) in 1918 RAF Muster Roll. Awarded RAF M.S.M. in *L.G.* 20 May, 1921 for services in Mesopotamia as SM1. Awarded General Service Medal (clasp Iraq). Awarded RAF L.S.&G.C. *w.e.f.* 28 April, 1924 as SM1.

314. T. BELL

Died in an accident 18 August, 1914.

315. A. E. SHARPE

Enlisted 21 August, 1912, directly into RFC. No record of any overseas service. Awarded Royal Aero Club Aviators' certificate No. 1247 on 19 May, 1915. Promoted T/SM (T) 1 January, 1917. Was CMM (T) in 1918 RAF Muster Roll.

★ 316. T. H. PERRY

Enlisted 10 October, 1908. Formerly 9282 Pte 2/Essex Regt. Posted to No. 1 Squadron 16 August, 1912 on transfer to Corps. As 2AM served with Aircraft Park in France from 16 August, 1914. Sergeant (sailmaker) 1 October, 1916 and Sergeant (Fabric Worker) in 1918 RAF Muster Roll.

⋆ 317. C. V. BEARD

Enlisted 18 March, 1912. Formerly 36781 Gunner with 28 Company RGA. Posted to 3 Squadron 20 August, 1912 on transfer to Corps. As 2AM with 3 Squadron he earned 1914 Star and bar in France from 13 August, 1914. Not promoted 1AM (Fitter-General) until 1 March, 1916 and still held that rank in 1918 RAF Muster Roll. Of course as a fitter he was earning 4/- per day whilst Sgt Perry (No. 316) was only earning 3/3d. He was not awarded his RAF L.S.&G.C. until 17 October, 1934 which makes one ask if his earlier service did not contain the element of good conduct necessary or perhaps he was discharged and then rejoined. In any event he was a Sergeant by that date. He served on during and after WW2 earning Defence and War medals and a bar to his RAF L.S.&G.C. Originally came from Oldham. Medals known in a private collection:— 1914 Star and bar trio, Defence and War Medals and RAF L.S.&G.C. Medal (GV) and bar.

318. JOSEPH EDWARD DUSTING

Enlisted 23 August, 1912, directly into RFC. Served with 3 Squadron. Proceeded overseas 24 July, 1915 and earned 1914/15 trio. Promoted WO (T) 1 November, 1916 and was Chief Master Mechanic (T) in 1918 RAF Muster Roll. RAF L.S.&G.C. *w.e.f.* 25 August, 1930 as SM1 and fifth senior RAF Warrant Officer in 1931 *A.F.L.* Awarded 1935 Silver Jubilee

Medal. Group of five medals sold at Christies in 1990, all named to SM or WO.

319. ALBERT LEVICK

Born Thetford, Norfolk 17 July, 1880. Formerly in the Royal Engineers he was a Sergeant Major at the Central Flying School at Upavon from 17 August, 1912. Awarded Royal Aero Club Aviators' Certificate No. 583 on 8 August, 1913 at Upavon in a Short of the Central Flying School. No record of a 1914 nor 1914/15 Star have been traced. He was commissioned Lieutenant and Quartermaster 1 March, 1915 and was promoted Captain 1 March, 1918. He is shown as a Major (Technical Branch) in 1918 *A.F.L.*, and was a Squadron Leader in 1921 *A.F.L.* with an O.B.E. and listed as 'Staff Officer' serving from 1 April, 1920 at Inland Area Command HQ, Uxbridge. He retired a Wing Commander on 15 August, 1925. In the 1937 *A.F.L.* he was employed as Assistant to the Officer in charge of RAF School of Aeronautical Engineering at Henlow Camp. Last noted in 1946 *A.F.L.* as 01191 Wing Commander O.B.E. (Retd) (GD).

★ 320. HENRY JAMES

Enlisted 16 March, 1906. Formerly 42762 Gunner 56 Battery RFA. Posted to 2 Squadron 16 August, 1912 on transfer to RFC. As Sergeant in 4 Squadron he served in France from 12 August, 1914. He was awarded Military Medal as Flight Sergeant on 3 June, 1916 with 13 Squadron and was promoted WO (T) on 12 October, 1916. He was Chief Master Mechanic (T) in 1918 RAF Muster Roll. Awarded RAF Meritorious Service Medal for service in France in the first such list of the award in *L.G.* 3 June, 1918, as Sergeant Major, and shown as coming from Eltham, Kent. Awarded RAF L.S.&G.C. Medal *w.e.f.* 16 March, 1924 as SM1. Fourth senior RAF WO in 1931 *A.F.L.* His Military Medal only was reported as for sale in 1989.

★ 321. A. JARMAN

Enlisted 3 November, 1906. Formerly 32788 Gunner 67 Company RGA. Posted to 2 Squadron 16 August, 1912 on transfer to Corps. As Sergeant 2 Squadron earned 1914 Star and bar in France from 12 August, 1914. Promoted T/SM (T) on 1 May, 1916 and was Chief Master Mechanic (Technical) in 1918 RAF Muster Roll. Awarded RAF M.S.M. for services in France with 5 Squadron in *L.G.* 3 June, 1918. He came from Plumstead.

322. H. Bullock

As 2AM was discharged with ignominy 1 December, 1913.

323. G. Wathen

As 2AM was transferred to 52 (MT) Company, ASC 11 December, 1912.

* 324. T. Ford

Direct enlistment into RFC 28 August, 1912. As 2AM Airship Detachment earned 1914 Star and bar being transferred to RNAS 18 October, 1914 as Air Mechanic First Class No. 696. C.P.O. 3, 15 December, 1916. Was Chief Mechanic (Rigger Airships) in 1918 RAF Muster Roll as 200696.

* 325. H. R. Bayne

Direct enlistment into RFC 28 August, 1912. As 2AM Airship Detachment earned 1914 Star and bar being transferred to RNAS 18 October, 1914 as Air Mechanic First Class No. 690. Chief P.O. 3, 15 December, 1916. Was Chief Mechanic (Rigger Airships) in 1918 RAF Muster Roll as No. 200690.

* 326. Fredrick Thomas McElwee

Formerly 28 Company RE. A long serving soldier for in March, 1914 he re-engaged to continue beyond 21 years. He was a Sergeant at CFS at this time. Posted overseas on 16 April, 1915, earning 1914/15 Star. Commissioned 2 Lieutenant 7 December, 1916. Flying Officer in November, 1921 *A.F.L.* (Stores List) serving from 12 November, 1919 at RAF Cranwell. He was promoted Flight Lieutenant (E) 1 January, 1922 and retired in that rank 21 September, 1927. Flight Lieutenant RAFO, 1 January, 1936 and serving as Adjutant at RAF Digby, No. 12 Fighter Group in 1937 *A.F.L.*

327. Alfred Jukes

Born 6 June, 1881. Enlisted 1899. Was a Flight Sergeant in 1914 and was posted overseas on 20 August, 1915 earning 1914/15 Star. Awarded Army L.S.&G.C. Medal October, 1917 in Army Order 312. Commissioned 2 Lieutenant 29 December, 1917. Was Flight Lieutenant in November, 1921

A.F.L. (Stores List) with an M.B.E., and seniority of 30 June, 1921, employed from 24 May, 1921 at Irish Stores and Repair Unit, No. 11 (Irish) Wing, Clondalkin. He retired 24 June, 1929. He was an Equipment Officer at RAF Hendon in January, 1938 *A.F.L.* (Flt Lieut retired). Recalled 1 September, 1939 to 12 December, 1945. Squadron Leader 1 June, 1940. Last noted in April, 1968 *A.F.L.*

⋆ 328. H. O. SMITH

Enlisted 11 August, 1909 and served in the Air Battalion RE, transferring to the RFC 24 August, 1912. A Corporal with 2 Squadron in France from 12 August, 1914. Awarded Royal Aero Club Aviators' Certificate No. 1412 on 18 July, 1915. Awarded Military Medal as Sergeant 18 Squadron in *L.G.* 29 September, 1917. Reverted to Sergeant (Pilot) from Flight Sergeant 23 May, 1917 and was shot down when in 20 Squadron and captured, being a POW from 25 January, 1918. Shown as Sergeant Mech (Pilot) in 1918 RAF Muster Roll. See *'Cross and Cockade,'* volume 4, No. 1, page 40. He came from Acton, London.

⋆ 329. FRANK WILKES GODDARD

Enlisted 19 February, 1908. Formerly 8087, Pte 2 Wilts Regiment. Posted to 3 Squadron 23 August, 1912 on transfer to RFC. 1AM 5 Squadron in France from 14 August, 1914. Mentioned by McCudden V.C. in *'Flying Fury'* as SM 20 Squadron. Promoted T/SM (D) 1 February, 1916 and was SM1 in RAF (1918) RAF Muster Roll. RAF L.S.&G.C. Medal *w.e.f.* 19 February, 1926 as SM1. 10th senior RAF Warrant Officer in 1931 *A.F.L.*

330. F. J. KNIGHT

Enlisted 4 November, 1910. Formerly 4023 A/Cpl 1 Rifle Brigade. Obtained Acting Schoolmaster's Certificate in July, 1912 on his transfer to RFC on 4 July, 1912. 1AM in 1914. Posted overseas 3 March, 1915 when a Sregeant and earned 1914/15 Star. Promoted Flight Sergeant (Misc. Discip) 1 December, 1915 and retained that rank in 1918 RAF Muster Roll. 1914/15 Star trio in Olivant collection.

331. R. KEITH BARLOW

A keen flyer. 1AM with 3 Squadron when he served with McCudden (V.C.) at Netheravon in 1913 (nicknamed 'Cuth'). Was accidentally killed on 12 August, 1914 at Netheravon flying as a passenger to Dover *en route* to France. The pilot, 2 Lieutenant Skene, 'C' Flight was also killed. The aircraft, a Blériot, crashed into trees. Buried Bulford Cemetery, Wiltshire.

★ 332. WILLIAM HENRY ROBERTS

Earned 1914 Star in France with 2 Squadron as 1AM. Corporal/Aerial Photographer with 3 Squadron in August, 1915. Was an Air Gunner with 16 Squadron 29 October, 1915. Wounded in thigh in three places. Awarded Royal Aero Club Aviators' Certificate No. 4670 16 May, 1917 as a Sergeant. Killed in Action 11 September, 1917 as a Sergeant Pilot with 20 Squadron. Buried Longvenesse (St Omer) Souvenir Cemetery (IV. D. 76).

★ 333. A. R. BAUGHAN

Enlisted 30 November, 1905. Formerly 40410 Staff Sgt. 142nd Battery RFA. Posted to 2 Squadron 22 August, 1912 on transfer to the Corps. As a Sergeant in 6 Squadron earned 1914 Star and bar in France from 10 September, 1914. T/SM (T) 1 May, 1916. Awarded D.C.M. in *L.G.* 13 February, 1917 as Acting Sgt Major, 'For conspicuous gallantry and devotion to duty. He has been conspicuous for great resourcefulness, unfailing hard work and cheerfulness during a period of continuous strain.' CMM (Tech) in 1918 RAF Muster Roll. Awarded RAF L.S.&G.C. *w.e.f.* 30 November, 1923 as SM1 and an Indian General Service Medal (clasp Waziristan 1921-1924), with No. 28 Squadron. See group photograph No. 2. Later married a French woman, then was killed testing a car.

★ 334. FREDERICK CHARLES VICTOR LAWS

Born 22 January, 1887. Formerly 6112 Pte 3/Coldstream Guards. Posted to 1 Squadron 27 August, 1912. As a Sergeant in 3 Squadron earned 1914 Star and bar in France from 12 August, 1914. (Joined the experimental photographic branch set up in France in early 1915. This section came under No. 1 Wing then commanded by Trenchard. Lieutenant J.T.C. Moore-Brabazon, later Lord Brabazon of Tara, was in charge with Lieutenant C.D.M. Campbell, Flight Sergeant Laws and 2AM Gorse completing the team. Their first aerial camera was a Thornton-Pickard.) Commissioned 2 Lieutenant Lincolnshire Regt and RFC. Squadron Leader (T) in November, 1921 *A.F.L.* with an O.B.E. seniority 1 August, 1918 serving at the Air Ministry as a Junior Assistant in charge of Sections and Officers serving in RAF (Dept. of Dir-Gen of Supply and Research).

A Wing Commander in February, 1931, *Air Force List* seniority 1 January, 1927. (Qualified at Specialist Photographic Course), commanding Aircraft Depot, Iraq Command Hinaidi from 7 October, 1930. Retired as Wing Commander, 1 September, 1933. Re-called 24 November, 1939. Promoted to Group Captain in 1943 (No. 01185). Retired in that rank 12 May 1946. Last noted in April, 1975 *Air Force List* as C.B., C.B.E., and still on retired list. See group photograph No. 2.

335. S. G. DARKE

Enlisted 17 August, 1903. Formerly 5768 Pte 3/Coldstream Guards. Posted to 3 Squadron 27 August, 1912 on transfer to Corps. Was Sergeant with 1 Squadron when posted overseas from Netheravon 3 March, 1915 earning 1914/15 Star. Promoted T/SM (D) 1 November, 1915 still with No. 1 Squadron as a Flight Sergeant. Awarded Military Medal in *L.G.* 11 October, 1916. SM1 (D) in 1918 RAF Muster Roll, when No. 1 Squadron had just completed three years at Bailleul.

336. R. PLUMBE

Formerly 9340 Pte 3/Coldstream Guards. Posted to 2 Squadron 28 August, 1912 on transfer to Corps. Deserted in 1913. Re-joined 1 September, 1913. Discharged 23 December, 1913 under *K.R.* 392 (ix) 'Unfitted for the duties of the Corps.'

★ 337. G. E. BULLEN

Enlisted 26 August, 1912 directly into RFC. As 1AM Aircraft Park served in France from 16 August, 1914. Wounded as 1AM in May, 1915. Promoted Corporal (Storeman) 1 February, 1917. Was Corporal (Clerk) in 1918 RAF Muster Roll. Awarded RAF L.S.&G.C. *w.e.f.* 26 August, 1930 as Flight Sergeant. His group of five medals is in the RAF Museum at Hendon:— 1914 Star (2AM RFC), British War Medal and Victory medal (1AM RFC), 1935 Silver Jubilee medal, RAF L.S.&G.C. Medal (F/ Sgt RAF). (See No. 132.)

338. A. FOX

As a Sgt was discharged 18 August, 1913 under *K.R.* 392 (ix) 'Unfitted for duties in the Corps.'

* 339. FREDERICK JOHN ARCHER WILLIS

Enlisted 3 September, 1912 directly into RFC. As 2AM 5 Squadron earned 1914 Star and bar in France from 14 August, 1914. Promoted T/SM (T) 1 December, 1916 and was CMM (Tech) in 1918 RAF Muster Roll. Awarded RAF L.S.&G.C. Medal *w.e.f.* 3 September, 1930 as SM1 (seniority 15 March, 1929). Awarded 1935 Silver Jubilee Medal. On 18 May, 1937 was commissioned Flying Officer (CEO) and was posted to No. 3 Flying Training School, South Cerney, Cirencester. Group of five medals known in a private collection.

* 340. FREDERICK KERCHEY

Born 3 October, 1893. Enlisted 3 September, 1912 directly into RFC. As 2AM in Airship Detachment earned 1914 Star, transferred to RNAS 18 October, 1914 as No. 700. C.P.O. 3 1 August, 1916, and was Chief Mechanic (Airship Rigger) No. 200700 in 1918 RAF Muster Roll. RAF L.S.&G.C. Medal as Sergeant Major 2 September, 1930. Awarded 1935 Silver Jubilee Medal. Was Commissioned Engineering Officer (Flying Officer) seniority 23 August, 1937. On 4 October, 1937 was posted to Home Aircraft Depot at Henlow Camp, Biggleswade. Personal No. 35136. Promoted Squadron Leader 1 June, 1942. Retired 4 December, 1946. Died 17 December, 1978.

341. FREDERICK ADAMS

Born 24 October, 1888 at Coventry. Formerly of Allesley Old Rd, Coventry. Awarded Royal Aero Club Aviators' Certificate No. 903 on 20 August, 1914. A Sergeant with No. 1 Squadron. Posted overseas 3 March, 1915 and earned 1914/15 Star. Commissioned 2 Lieutenant 16 December, 1916 and was Killed in Action 12 May, 1917 as 2 Lieutenant, over the German lines near Messines, flying in an RE8 No. 3243 of 53 Squadron. He was the tenth victim of Lieutenant Max Ritter Von Muller. He was re-buried in 1924 in Oosttaverne Wood Cemetery, Wytschaete.

★ 342. A. FERNEYHOUGH

Enlisted 25 March, 1912. Formerly 6270, RAMC, transferred to RFC 24 August, 1912. As 1AM with the Aircraft Park in France from 16 August, 1914. Still Air Mechanic 1st Class (Misc) in 1918 RAF Muster Roll.

★ 343. FREDRICK ELLIS WINTER

Enlisted 5 September, 1912 directly into RFC. As 1AM No. 2 Squadron earned 1914 Star and bar in France from 12 August, 1914. Promoted Temporary Sergeant Major (Technical) 1 September, 1916 and was mentioned in despatches in *London Gazette* 24 February, 1917 as Sergeant Major. Listed in the *Times* 'B' Press Release of 27 March, 1917. Was Chief Master Mechanic (Technical) in 1918 RAF Muster Roll. Served with No. 97 Squadron in Waziristan post WW1. Promoted Sergeant Major 13 September, 1929. Awarded RAF L.S.&G.C. Medal *w.e.f.* 5 September, 1930. His group of five medals were sold by Holditch in 1986 for £295:— 1914 Star and bar (Sergeant RFC), British War Medal and Victory Medal with oakleaf, (Temporary Sergeant Major RAF), Indian General Service Medal (Waziristan 1919-21 Sergeant Major 2 RAF) and RAF L.S.&G.C. Medal (Sergeant Major 1 RAF).

344. H. COLEMAN

Formerly 7271 Lance Sergeant 3/Coldstream Guards. Posted to RFC HQ 3 September, 1912 on transfer to Corps. Promoted Sergeant 4 February, 1913. Died at Netheravon 19 May, 1914.

★ 345. F. LITTLE

Rigger at Newcastle 10 August, 1914 with 6 Squadron detachment. As 1AM No. 6 Squadron served in France from 6 October, 1914. Commissioned 2 Lieutenant 25 June, 1917.

★ 346. MICHAEL KEEGAN

Formerly 2515 Lance Sergeant 1/Irish Guards. Posted to No. 3 Squadron 20 July, 1912 on transfer to RFC. As Sergeant No. 5 Squadron posted to France on 12 August, 1914. Mentioned in despatches 8 October, 1914 as Sergeant and 30 November, 1915 as Acting Sergeant Major, with 5 Squadron having earlier been awarded Royal Aero Club Aviators' Certificate No. 1071 on 29 January, 1915. As a Flight Sergeant was awarded Military Medal in *L.G.* 3 June, 1916, having already been commissioned 2 Lieutenant Royal Dublin Fusiliers and RFC on 23 April, 1916. Mentioned for a third time in *L.G.* 5 June, 1919 for services in Egypt as Captain/Acting Major RAF. In 1921 (November) *A.F.L.* was Flight Lieutenant O.B.E., M.M. (T) seniority 1 August, 1919, serving from 1 April, 1921 at RAF Cranwell (Boy's Wing). Retired as a Squadron Leader 1 June, 1926. Last noted in 1937 *A.F.L.*

★ 347. H. WEBB

Direct entry into RFC 10 September, 1912. To France 16 August, 1914 as 1AM Aircraft Park. Mentioned in despatches in *L.G.* 4 January, 1917 as *Sergeant* acting Flight Sergeant having just been promoted to T/SM (T) on 1 January, 1917. Awarded Army M.S.M. in *L.G.* 1 January, 1918 as Sgt (T/SM) 'for Valuable Services with the Armies in the Field.' He was originally from Finsbury Park, North London. Was Ch Mr Mch (Tech) in 1918 RAF Muster Roll.

★ 348. HENRY EDWARD BETHELL

Direct entry into RFC 10 September, 1912. 1AM with RFC HQ in France from 16 August, 1914. Mentioned in despatches as Sergeant in *L.G.* 1 January, 1916 and awarded Army M.S.M. as Flight Sergeant in *L.G.* 11 November, 1916 'For Valuable Services with the Armies in the Field.' Promoted T/SM (Superintending Clerk) 1 February, 1918 and was a Master Clerk in 1918 RAF Muster Roll. Again mentioned in despatches as Sergeant Major in *L.G.* 11 July, 1919. RAF L.S.&G.C. Medal awarded *w.e.f.* 10 September, 1930 as SM1 (seniority 1 April, 1918). Still serving in 1931.

BE2/2A

★ 349. FREDERICK CHARLES WHENMAN

Direct entry into RFC 10 September, 1912. As Corporal 3 Squadron earned 1914 Star and bar in France from 13 August, 1914. Promoted T/SM (T) on 25 August, 1917 and was Ch Mr Mch (Tech) in 1918 RAF Muster Roll. Awarded RAF M.S.M. for services in France in *L.G.* 3 June, 1919. Originally from Kingston on Thames. Awarded RAF L.S.&G.C. Medal *w.e.f.* 10 September, 1930 as SM1 (seniority 1 April, 1918). Awarded 1935 Silver Jubilee Medal. Commissioned Flying Officr (CEO) *w.e.f.* 19 September, 1935. On 1 February, 1937 was posted to the Packing Depot, Sealand, Queensferry, Cheshire (No. 35030). Promoted Squadron Leader 1 September, 1940. Last noted as retired in 1946 *A.F.L.*

★ 350. J. G. RICHARDSON

Enlisted 29 March, 1909 into the Air Battalion RE. As 1AM, Aircraft Park, served in France from 16 August, 1914. Promoted Flight Sergeant (KBS) 1 July, 1916 and mentioned in despatches in *L.G.* 13 March, 1918 'For Valuable Services in the United Kingdom in the War.' Also mentioned in the *Times* 'B' List of 16 March, 1918. Still Flight Sergeant (Labourer) in 1918 RAF Muster Roll. His 1914 Star trio is known in a private collection.

★ 351. THOMAS FREDERICK BOYD CARLISLE

Born Hebburn-on-Tyne 26 December, 1893. As 1AM, 2 Squadron, served in France from 13 August, 1914. Awarded Royal Aero Club Aviators' Certificate No. 1619 on 20 August, 1915 when a Sergeant.
RFC Communiqué No. 31, 19 March, 1916.

Piloting a Morane Parasol, of No. 1 Squadron with Lt. J. McKelvie as observer, escorting an artillery Morane over Oostaverne, he observed an Albatros diving to attack. He turned and attacked at 500 yards, closing to 150. The EA did not return fire, dived steeply out of control from 500 feet.
RFC Communiqué No. 35, 29 April, 1916.

In a Morane bi-plane, 1 Squadron engaged a hostile machine at 20 yards. It dived steeply for its own lines and did not return fire.

30 April, 1916. In a Nieuport Scout between Warneton and Hollebeke

at 5 am observed an Aviatik at 13,000 feet. He attacked from 50 yards and fired a full drum. The EA was hit and dived steeply, he lost it at 4000 feet. Later he saw another Aviatic at 12,000 feet and attacked it near Ploegsteert, fired three drums into it and drove it towards Hollebeke. *RFC Communiqué No. 36, 18 May 1916.*

Flying a Nieuport Scout he attacked two Aviatics between Ypres and Ploegsteert. They turned and returned fire. He fired three drums from 100 yards. One hostile was hit and dived vertically and was destroyed. The other dived and turned towards the German lines.

Wounded 4 July, 1916 as Flight Sergeant (pilot) 23 Squadron and died of wounds 8 July, 1916. Awarded a Military Medal posthumously in *L.G.* 19 February, 1917.

★ 352. F. TARR

Enlisted 2 January, 1905. Formerly 21939 Gunner, 34 Company RGA when he was posted to 3 Squadron on 31 August, 1912 on transfer to RFC. As 1AM 3 Squadron earned 1914 Star and bar in France from 13 August, 1914. Promoted Flight Sergeant (Driver MT) 1st August, 1916 and was Chief Mechanic in 1918 RAF Muster Roll. Awarded RAF L.S.&G.C. Medal *w.e.f.* 2 January, 1923 as Flight Sergeant.

★ 353. S. NICHOLLS

Direct entry into RFC on 12 September, 1912. As 1AM, 3 Squadron, served in France from 13 August, 1914. Promoted Flight Sergeant (Fitter General) on 1 August, 1916 and was Chief Mechanic in RAF Muster Roll (1918).

★ 354. S. C. GRIGGS

Enlisted 29 September, 1909. Formerly 19349 Sapper, 59 Company, RE posted to 2 Squadron 28 August, 1912 on transfer to RFC. 1AM, 4 Squadron in France from 9 September, 1914. Awarded D.C.M. as Corporal in *L.G.* 3 June, 1915 'For Gallant conduct and exceptionally good work on 10-11 March, 1915, in assisting to repair one of our aeroplanes close to the front line of trenches, under heavy shell fire.' Awarded 3rd class Russian Medal of St. George in *London Gazette* 25 August, 1915 as Sergeant, 2 Wing, 5 Squadron. Promoted Flight Sergeant (Painter) *w.e.f.* 1 September, 1916. Was Chief Mechanic in 1918 RAF Muster Roll. Awarded RAF L.S.&G.C. Medal *w.e.f.* 29 September, 1927 as Flight Sergeant.

★ 355. B. E. GOODGAME

Direct entry into RFC 11 September, 1912. As 1AM 4 Squadron, served in France from 12 August, 1914. Promoted Flight Sergeant (Fitter General) *w.e.f.* 24 July, 1917, and was Chief Mech, in 1918 RAF Muster Roll. Mentioned in despatches 'for service at home' in *L.G.* 14 June, 1918, and next day in the *Times* 'B' List.

★ 356. J. N. BIBBY

Direct entry into RFC 11 September, 1912. As 1AM, 4 Squadron served in France from 9 September, 1914. Promoted Sergeant (Carpenter) 1 May, 1916 and was Sergeant Mechanic in 1918 RAF Muster Roll. Awarded General Service Medal (clasp Southern Desert Iraq) and RAF L.S.&G.C. Medal as Flight Sergeant *w.e.f.* 11 September, 1930.

357. G. W. LESTER

Direct entry into RFC 2 September, 1912. Deserted as 2AM on 25 September, 1913 but with no loss of service shown as 3 AM on 1918 RAF Muster Roll. No trace of issue of 1914 nor 1914/15 Stars.

★ 358. S. KIDDELL

As 1AM 5 Squadron served in France from 14 August, 1914. He was discharged as unfit on 11 December, 1914.

★ 359. JOHN DEWBERY

Enlisted 17 September, 1912 directly into RFC. As 1AM 5 Squadron served in France from 14 August, 1914. Aerial Gunner in 11 Squadron during 1915. Wounded 7 December, 1915. Royal Aero Club Aviators' Certificate No. 4182 on 31 January, 1917 as a Corporal. Promoted Sergeant (1st class Pilot) 18 April, 1917. Was Sgt Mech (Pilot) in 1918 RAF Muster Roll.

★ 360. G. H. COWDERY

Enlisted 23 September, 1912 initially into RE. Transferred to 1 Squadron RFC on 13 November, 1912. As 1AM Airship Detachment earned 1914 Star and bar, transferred to RNAS 18 October, 1914 as Air Mechanic 1st

Class No. 693. Petty Officer (Rigger Airships) 1 June, 1915. Was Sergeant Mechanic (Rigger-Airships) No. 200693 in 1918 RAF Muster Roll.

★ 361. WILLIAM ARTHUR CURTIS

Enlisted 17 September, 1912 directly into RFC. As 1AM 2 Squadron earned 1914 Star and bar in France fom 12 August, 1914. Promoted T/ SM (D) 1 May, 1916 and was SM1 (Discip) in 1918 RAF Muster Roll. Warrant Officer Class 1 finally on 15 March, 1929, RAF L.S.&G.C. awarded *w.e.f.* 17 September, 1930 as SM1. Still serving in 1937 when from 17 February, 1931 he was serving with No. 1 Apprentice Wing, No. 1 School of Technical Training at Halton Camp, Aylesbury. In March, 1938 *A.F.L.* he was the 27th senior RAF Warrant Officer. His group of five medals is known as extant in a private collection:— 1914 Star and bar (1AM), British War Medal and Victory medal (SM1 RFC), 1935 Silver Jubilee Medal (unnamed) and RAF L.S.&G.C. (GV Fixed suspender type) (SM1 RAF).

362. A. HERBERT

As 1AM deserted 21 March, 1914.

363. WILLIAM HENRY DRUMM

Enlisted 14 September, 1912 directly into RFC. No trace of 1914 nor 1914/15 Star found. Promoted Sergeant (1st Class Pilot) on 1 February, 1916. Royal Aero Club Aviators' Certificate No. 5609 on 13 May 1917 nearly 16 months later. Sergeant Mechanic (Pilot) in 1918 RAF Muster Roll.

★ 364. GEORGE THORNTON

Born 16 January, 1891. Enlisted 16 September, 1912 directly into RFC. As Corporal in 6 Squadron earned 1914 Star and bar in France from 7 October, 1914. Initially reported KIA October, 1915 when shot down by

Immelman (observer to Sgt/Pilot Courtney) but subsequently confirmed as wounded 21 October, 1915.

RFC Communiqué No. 16, 21 October, 1915.

Sgt. Courtney and Sgt. Thornton, 3 Squadron, in a Morane, when dropping hand grenades and flechettes on La Bassee were attacked by a Fokker monoplane with deflector propellor. Sgt. Thornton was hit in the hand and had his face grazed. When getting out his rifle he was hit in the other hand and the pilot dived towards our lines followed by the Fokker. The pilot was then hit through the leg and a bullet put the engine out of action. On the approach of a BE2c the hostile machine abandoned the chase.

(After more than a year of war some RFC aircraft were still operating with the observer's rifle as the only armament. 'Fletchettes' were small steel darts, dropped in clusters, as a primitive anti-personnel weapon.)

Awarded Military Medal in the *London Gazette* of 27 October, 1916 as Flight Sergeant but was then promoted to Temporary Sergeant Major (Disciplinarian) from 1 August, 1916. Mentioned in despatches 4 January, 1917 and awarded Medal of St. George, 1st Class as Sergeant Major in the *London Gazette* of 15 February, 1917. Was Sergeant Major 1 (Disciplinarian) in 1918 RAF Muster Roll. RAF L.S.&G.C. *w.e.f.* 16 September, 1930 as Sergeant Major 1 with seniority of 1 April, 1918. In 1931 *Air Force List* was the 24th senior Warrant Officer in RAF. Commissioned Flying Officer 10 April, 1932. In 1938 *Air Force List* shown as stationed at Cardington from 5 January, 1938 (No. 31021). Was a Squadron Leader in August, 1939 and retired 16 January,1941. Re-employed until 5 December, 1946. Last noted as still on retired list in April, 1967.

MAURICE FARMAN MFII

170

★ 365. A. EDWARDS

Enlisted 12 August, 1903. Formerly 12892 2nd Corporal 'G' Company RE. Posted to Flying Depot 29 August, 1912 on transfer to RFC. As Sergeant in No. 2 Squadron earned 1914 Star and bar in France from 12 August, 1914. Temporary Sergeant Major (Technical) 1 February, 1916, and Chief Master Mechanic (Technical) in 1918 RAF Muster Roll. Awarded RAF L.S.&G.C. *w.e.f.* 12 August, 1921 as Sergeant Major 1st Class.

★ 366. A. H. CUMMINGS

Enlisted 13 December, 1906. Formerly 45331 Driver, 136 Battery, RFA. Posted to No. 1 Squadron 13 September, 1912 on transfer to RFC. As Corporal Airship Detachment earned 1914 Star. Transferred to RNAS 18 October, 1914 as No. 667. Chief Petty Officer 2nd Class (Engineer) 1 August, 1916. In 1918 RAF Muster Roll was 200667 Master Mechanic (Fitter Aero). Mentioned in Despatches in the *London Gazette* of May 1918.

367. L. G. BRITTON

As 2AM was discharged medically unfit on 2 December, 1913.

368. F. WARWICK

Enlisted directly into RFC 18 September, 1912. Promoted Sergeant (Fitter-Engines) 1 May, 1915. Posted overseas 6 September, 1915 earning 1914/15 Star. Was Sergeant Mech (Fitter AE) in 1918 RAF Muster Roll.

★ 369. A. BOLTON

Enlisted directly into RFC 14 September, 1912. 1AM with RFC HQ in France from 12 August, 1914. Promoted Flight Sergeant (Wireless Operator) 1 February, 1917 and was Chief Mech (W/Op.) in 1918 RAF Muster Roll.

★ 370. E. WOOLAWAY

Enlisted 20 September, 1912 directly into RFC. Was 1AM with 3 Squadron in France from 13 August, 1914. Promoted T/SM (T) 1 March, 1916 and was CMM in 1918 RAF Muster Roll. Awarded RAF M.S.M.

SERGEANT MAJOR R. H. NASH

in *L.G.* 1 January, 1919 for services in France as Chief Master Mech. He came from Berkshire. Rejoined during WW2. His medal group came up in auction at Sothebys in 1986 with an estimation of £320:— 1914 Star (Sgt RFC), British War Medal and Victory medal (SM1 RAF), Defence and War Medals (M.I.D. oakleaf) and RAF M.S.M.

★ 371. REGINALD HENRY NASH

Enlisted into RFC 20 September, 1912. As 1AM 5 Squadron he served in France from 14 August, 1914. Promoted T/SM (T) on 1 September, 1917 and was Chief Master Mechanic (Technical) in 1918 RAF Muster Roll. He was awarded an RAF L.S.&G.C. Medal on 10 September, 1930 as SM2. Copies of his discharge documents (Forms 856, 280 and 2067) have been traced together with a number of photographs including those of Colonel Cody's funeral, at which

time he formed part of the procession. The forms state that he was born at Frimley, Aldershot on 24 July, 1890 and was by trade a carpenter on enlistment. He attained his Army Education Certificate (3rd class) on 31 January, 1913. He served with the BEF in France from 14 August, 1914 to 12 October, 1914 and again from 16 January, 1916 to 20 August, 1916. He served with the Egyption Expeditionary Force from 16 March, 1917 to 11 November, 1918. In the RFC he was employed as a carpenter and his character was 'very good.' In the

THE FUNERAL OF COLONEL CODY

RAF he was by trade a rigger-aero, and his degree of ability was shown as 'superior.' He also completed a course of Instruction in Practical Inspection and Flying and one of Instruction in Drill. He was discharged 19 August, 1936 'with a view to pension,' 5ft. 6in. tall and aged 46. He had completed 23 years and 11 months service.

372. J. WHITFORD

As 2AM discharged 17 October, 1913 under *K.R.* 392 (ix) 'Unfitted for duties in the Corps.'

★ 373. H. E. CHITTENDEN

Enlisted directly into RFC on 17 September, 1912. As 2AM 4 Squadron, he served in France from 9 September, 1914. Promoted Flight Sergeant (Electrician), 1 July, 1916 and was Chief Mech (Elec.) in 1918 RAF Muster Roll.

★ 374. E. E. HOWARD

Enlisted directly into RFC 18 September, 1912. Was 1AM with 5 Squadron in France from 14 August, 1914. Promoted Sergeant (Carpenter), 1 September, 1915 and was Sergeant Mech (Carpenter) in 1918 RAF Muster Roll.

★ 375. J. E. SMITH

Enlisted directly into RFC 18 September, 1912. Was 1AM in 5 Squadron in France from 14 August, 1914. Promoted Flight Sergeant (Fitter-engines) 1 October, 1916 and was Chief Mech (Fitter AE) in 1918 RAF Muster Roll.

★ 376. JOHN F. W. LITTLE

Enlisted directly into RFC 18 September, 1912. As 2AM, Aircraft Park in France from 12 August, 1914 and earned 1914 Star and bar. Promoted Sergeant (Fitter-General) 1 October, 1917 and was Sergeant Mech (Fitter-General) in 1918 RAF Muster Roll. His medals were returned to RAF Records Office on 27 June, 1929.

★ 377. ERNEST JOSEPH WILLIAMS

Enlisted directly into RFC 18 September, 1912. As Corporal in 3 Squadron earned 1914 Star and bar in France from 13 August, 1914. Promoted T/SM (T) 1 February, 1917 and was Chief Master Mechanic (Tech) in 1918 RAF Muster Roll. Awarded RAF L.S.&G.C. *w.e.f.* 18 September, 1930 as SM1, seniority 1 April, 1918. In 1931 *A.F.L.* was 41st senior RAF Warrant Officer. Awarded 1935 Silver Jubilee Medal. In December, 1937 he was serving as Station Warrant Officer at No. 3 Flying Training School, South Cerney, Cirenster, Glos. Not in January, 1938 *A.F.L.*

VICKERS FB5 GUN BUS

176

★ 378. D. H. WHATLEY

Enlisted directly into RFC on 20 September, 1912. As 2AM with Aircraft Park was in France from 16 August, 1914. Promoted Sergeant (Fitter-General) 1 October, 1917 and was Sergeant Mech (Fitter-Gen.) in 1918 RAF Muster Roll.

379. W. DAVIDSON

As 2AM was discharged 15 July, 1913 under *K.R.* 392 (ix) 'Unfitted for the duties of the Corps.'

★ 380. F. EARLE

Enlisted 24 February, 1911. Formerly 21208 Sapper 4th Field Troop RE. Posted to No. 1 Squadron 5 September, 1912 on transfer to the Corps. As 1AM, Aircraft Park served in France from 16 August, 1914. Promoted Flight Sergeant (Carpenter) 1 July, 1916 and was Chief Mech (Carpenter) in 1918 RAF Muster Roll. Awarded RAF L.S.&G.C. *w.e.f.* 24 February, 1929 still a Flight Sergeant.

★ 381. C. W. CHANDLER

Enlisted directly into RFC 21 September, 1912. As 2AM 2 Squadron served in France from 12 August, 1914. Promoted Flight Sergeant (Fitter-Gen.) 1 January, 1916 and was Chief Mech (Fitter-Gen) in 1918 RAF Muster Roll. Awarded Indian General Service Medal (clasp Afghan N.W. Frontier, 1919) as Flight Sergeant (see also Nos. 390 and 416).

382. A. MIDDLETON

As a 2Am with RFC HQ transferred to Field Troop, RE, 17 January, 1913.

383. T. BARNETT

2AM, discharged 5 July, 1913 under *K.R.* 392 (ix) 'Unfitted for duties in the Corps.'

★ 384. R. C. DOWNER

Enlisted directly into Corps 23 September, 1912 (as did No. 385, presumably his brother?). Stationed at Newcastle 13/14 August, 1914 (to Squadron detachment). As 1AM 6 Squadron served in France from 7

October, 1914. Promoted Flight Sergeant (Fitter-turner) 1 April, 1917 and was CM (Turner) in 1918 RAF Muster Roll.

★ 385. MAURICE DOWNER

Born 23 June, 1893. Enlisted directly into Corps 23 September, 1912. (see 384 above) As 1AM 6 Squadron served in France from 7 October, 1914 and earned 1914 Star and bar. Promoted T/SM (T) 1 January, 1918 and was Chief Master Mech (Tech) in 1918 RAF Muster Roll. Mentioned in despatches in *L.G.* 1 January, 1919 serving with 60 Squadron. Awarded RAF L.S.&G.C. *w.e.f.* 23 September, 1930 as SM1 (Seniority 1 April, 1918). Awarded 1935 Silver Jubilee Medal. Commissioned Flying Officer (CEO) 19 September, 1935 and serving at No. 1 (General Engineering) Home Aircraft Depot, Henlow Camp, Biggleswade. Promoted to Squadron Leader 1 September, 1940. Retired 1 March, 1943. Last noted in 1973 *A.F.L.* as No. 35025 (retired).

★ 386. H. J. GARNER

Enlisted 23 September, 1912 directly into RFC. As 1AM, 3 Squadron, served in France from 13 August, 1914. Awarded French Médaille Militaire in *L.G.* 9 November, 1914 for Gallantry 21 to 30 August, 1914 as 1AM. Promoted Flight Sergeant (Fitter-Gen) on 1 June, 1916 and was Chief Mech in 1918 RAF Muster Roll.

★ 387. C. P. W. BROWNING

2AM in 2 Squadron in France from 12 August, 1914. Having been a watchmaker in civilian life, he was made 'armourer.' Transferred to Tank Corps as No. 307891 after being wounded in January, 1917 as a Corporal. His group of medals was sold in 1979 for £355. Military Medal (Sergeant Tank Corps), 1914 Star and bar (2AM RFC, the bar is not verified), British War Medal and Victory Medal (Sgt. RFC), Defence and War Medals WW2, Regular Army L.S.&G.C. (Staff Sgt RTC) and Army M.S.M. (GVI 2nd type WO1 RTC). The recommendation for his M.M. is as follows: '16 Battalion. In Action 29 September, 1918 at Guillemont Farm. His officer was wounded by armour piercing bullet. He therefore assumed command of the tank until it received several direct hits and burst into flames. He evacuated all the crew and the hotchkiss guns and formed a strong point with the infantry until dark.' Other men who served prior to or subsequent to their RFC service in other branches of the Army, (see 296 Hoffman above) and who earned annuity MSMs are known. Two others are:— F. H. Hawksford, O.B.E. (1st type, military, *L.G.* 3.6.1919 Major RAF), Indian General Service Medal 1854-94 (Burma 1885-87 and Burma 1887-89 Sgt RB), British War Medal (Major RAF), Victorian L.S.&G.C. (C Sgt RB) and M.S.M. (GV1 1st Type AO March, 1939 C Sgt RB) and J. Maxwell, Queen's South Africa Medal (Cape Colony, Orange Free State and Transvaal) (Sgt Coldstream Guards, King's South Africa Medal (usual two clasps), British War Medal and Victory Medal (SM1 RAF), 1939-45 War Medal, GV Coronation Medal 1911, Army L.S.&G.C. (GV Coldstream Guards) and M.S.M. (GV1 2nd type Sgt C.G.).

★ 388. C. BOND

Enlisted 6 June, 1912. Formerly 20147 Sapper 57 Company RE to 2 Squadron 29 August, 1912. As 1AM 4 Squadron earned 1914 Star and bar in France from 14 August, 1914. On 1 September, 1915 was in England at Hounslow when 24 Squadron was formed. Left the Squadron, 18 November, 1916, from Bertangles, France where he had returned in February, 1916. Promoted Flight Sergeant (Carpenter) 26 October, 1917 and was Chief Mechanic in 1918 RAF Muster Roll. Address in 1920: 236, Oak St., Abingdon, Berks.

★ 389. F. ROYSTON

Enlisted 25 September, 1912 directly into RFC. As 1AM Aircraft Park served in France from 16 August, 1914. Promoted Flight Sergeant (Fitter-General) 1 February, 1917 and was CM (F-G) in 1918 RAF Muster Roll.

★ 390. ALBERT EDWARD CHANDLER

(See also Nos. 381 and 416) Formerly served in the Air Battalion RE and transferred to the RFC 18 September, 1912. As Corporal Airship Detachment, earned 1914 Star and bar, transferring to RNAS on 18 October, 1914 as No. 694, leading Mechanic. Chief Petty Officer (3rd Class) 15 December, 1916. In 1918 RAF Muster Roll was No. 200694 Master Mechanic (Rigger Airships). Appointed Warrant Officer class 1 18 May, 1930 (see 1931 *A.F.L.*). RAF L.S.&G.C. Medal 18 September, 1930. Awarded 1935 Silver Jubilee Medal. No. 55516 Flight Lieutenant (Signals) 12 August, 1947.

* 391. C. G. GRIMES

Enlisted directly into RFC 25 September, 1912. Promoted Corporal 6 August, 1914. Earned 1914 Star and bar with 3 Squadron in France from 13 August, 1914. Promoted T/SM (T) 1 February, 1916 and was CMM (Tech) in 1918 RAF Muster Roll. Mentioned in despatches in *L.G.* 14 June, 1918 as Acting Sgt. Major for services in Palestine.

392. F. READ

As 2AM discharged 30 July, 1913 under *K.R.* 392 (xvi) 'No longer physically fit for war service.'

* 393. J. P. POWELL

Enlisted 25 September, 1912 directly into RFC. As 2AM 3 Squadron served in France from 12 August, 1914. Was second in charge of 3 Squadron's wireless operators under Sergeant Ellison in October, 1915 (see No. 814). Promoted Sergeant (MT Driver) 1 January, 1917. Military Medal gazetted in *L.G.* 28 September, 1917 as Corporal. He came from Market Drayton. Was Sergeant Mech (Driver) in 1918 RAF Muster Roll.

* 394. H. HURDLE

Enlisted directly into RFC 27 September, 1912. As 1AM 5 Squadron served in France from 14 August, 1914. Promoted Flight Sergeant (MT Driver) 1 March, 1916 and was Chief Mech (Driver) in 1918 RAF Muster Roll.

395. R. BLACKMORE

Not finally enlisted into RFC until December, 1912, and discharged 15 July, 1913 under *K.R.* 392 (ix) 'Unfitted to the duties of the Corps.'

* 396. D. W. MOTTRAM

Enlisted directly into RFC 25 September, 1912. Was 2AM with Airship detachment earned 1914 Star and bar, transferring to RNAS 18 November, 1914 as No. 699 Air Mechanic 1st Class. Chief Petty Officer (3rd Class) 15 October, 1916. In 1918 RAF Muster Roll was Flight Sergeant (Disciplinarian) No. 200699.

397. F. G. ANKRETT

Enlisted directly into RFC 25 September, 1912. Stationed at Montrose as 1AM Rigger to Lieutenant de Havilland and then was Corporal in 6 Squadron in August, 1914 but only proceeded overseas on 3 April, 1915 earning 1914/15 trio. Was Corporal Mechanic (Rigger Aero) in 1918 RAF Muster Roll which gives the date of his last promotion (to Corporal) as being 1 March, 1918. Thus sometime before this he must have been reduced and then re-promoted.

398. J. ECCLES

As 2AM discharged 31 March, 1914 under *K.R.* 392 (ix) 'Unfitted for the duties of the Corps.'

★ 399. WALLIS ST. JOHN LITTLEWOOD

As 1AM with 2 Squadron served in France from 13 August, 1914. Promoted 2 Lieutenant 25 November, 1917. However he was mentioned in despatches in *L.G.* 13 March, 1918, 'for valuable services in the War' (ie in UK), in his former NCOs rank of Flight Sergeant. Also mentioned in *Times* 'B' List of 16 March, 1918. Flying Officer in November, 1921 *A.F.L.* (Stores List), seniority 20 July, 1920, from 31 May, 1920 stationed at MT Repair Depot, Shrewsbury, Flight Lieutenant in February, 1931 *A.F.L.*, seniority 1 January, 1927, qualified on Commissariat Course and from 2 November, 1930 serving in a supernumerary capacity at RAF Depot, Uxbridge. He retired a Squadron Leader in December, 1935 but was awarded a Coronation Medal in that rank in 1937.

★ 400. W. McFARLAND

Enlisted directly into RFC 25 September, 1912. As 2AM in 4 Squadron served in France from 12 August, 1914. Discharged under *K.R.* 392 (xvi) 30 November, 1915 sick. Silver war badge No. 50563 issued.

★ 401. A. SMITH

Enlisted directly into RFC 30 September, 1912. As 2AM 5 Squadron served in France from 14 August, 1914. Promoted Corporal (MT Fitter) 1 January, 1917 and was Corporal Mechanic in 1918 RAF Muster Roll.

402. A McKay

As 2AM discharged in October, 1913 under *K.R.* 392 (xi) 'Unfitted for the duties of the Corps.'

★ 403. A. E. Hobson

Enlisted directly into RFC 2 October, 1912. As 1AM, 2 Squadron served in France from 13 October, 1914. Promoted T/SM (D) 1 December, 1917 and was SM1 (Discip) in 1918 RAF Muster Roll. Mentioned in despatches for home service in *L.G.* 14 June, 1918, and next day in the *Times* 'B' List.

★ 404. E. F. Prewett

Enlisted directly into RFC 2 October, 1912. As 2AM, Aircraft Park, served in France from 16 August, 1914. Promoted Flight Sergeant (Photographer) on 1 June, 1916 and was Chief Mech (Phot) in 1918 RAF Muster Roll. As Sergeant with 20 Squadron he earned an Indian General Service Medal (clasp Waziristan 1919/21).

★ 405. Robert George Brown

Enlisted directly into RFC 30 September, 1912. As 1AM with RFC HQ served in France from 12 August, 1914. Promoted T/SM (T) 1 June, 1917 and was Chief Master Mech (Tech) in 1918 RAF Muster Roll. Awarded RAF L.S.&G.C. Medal *w.e.f.* 30 September, 1930 as SM1 (seniority as WO1 April, 1918).

406. Richard Lano Pearce

Enlisted directly into RFC 3 October, 1912. Was 1AM in 7 Squadron at. the outbreak of WW1. Posted overseas 3 April, 1915 earning 1914/15 trio. T/SM (T) 24 October, 1916 and SM1 (Discip) in 1918 RAF Muster Roll. Awarded RAF L.S.&G.C. *w.e.f.* 3 October, 1930 as SM1. In February, 1931 *A.F.L.* was the 34th senior RAF Warrant Officer. Awarded both the 1935 Silver Jubilee and the 1937 Coronation Medals. In December, 1937 *A.F.L.* was shown as stationed from 29 March, 1935 at HQ No. 1 Bomber Group, Abingdon. In March, 1938 *A.F.L.* was the second senior RAF Warrant Officer, and the same in November, 1941 and in October, 1944. Retired in 1945/46.

★ 407. E. R. CARR

Enlisted directly into RFC on 30 September, 1912. Was 1AM, 5 Squadron in France from 14 August, 1914 but was reduced to 2AM on 4 September, 1916 and was only 3AM on 1918 RAF Muster Roll where his trade was given as Fitter (Gen.).

408. A. SKINNER

As 2AM with 2 Squadron he deserted 27 May, 1913. However, he rejoined 16 March, 1915 and was only allowed to count service from that date. Posted overseas 5 December, 1915 earning 1914/15 trio. A cook, he was promoted 1AM on 1 July, 1916 but was shown as only Private 1st class on 1918 RAF Muster Roll.

★ 409. G. E. KIRKHAM

Enlisted directly into RFC 30 September, 1912. As Corporal, 4 Squadron, served in France from 12 August, 1914. Promoted Acting WO (D) from 1 March, 1918 and shown as Acting SM1 (paid) in 1918 RAF Muster Roll.

★ 410. ALFRED SPRINGATE

Enlisted directly into RFC 2 October, 1912 and as 1AM 4 Squadron earned 1914 Star and bar in France from 12 August, 1914. Promoted Flight Sergeant (Fitter-turner) 1 May, 1917 and listed as Chief Mech (Turner) in 1918 RAF Muster Roll. Earned Indian General Service Medal (clasp Waziristan 1919-21) as Flight Sergeant. Awarded RAF L.S.&G.C. Medal 2 October, 1930 still as Flight Sergeant. Appointed WO1 15 February, 1934. Awarded 1935 Silver Jubilee Medal. On 1 January, 1937 stationed at RAF Bicester. Served on through WW2 and in the 1946 *A.F.L.* was still serving then the seventh senior WO in RAF. Retired January, 1948.

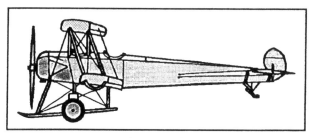

AVRO 504A

411. R. CUDMORE

Killed 15 May, 1914, as 2AM in a flying accident at Northallerton when landing in fog. Lieutenant Empson, the pilot, was also killed. Both were in No. 2 Squadron, flying South from Montrose, Scotland to Netheravon. Both are buried at Northallerton.

BE2A OF 2 SQN. AT SEATON CAREW, 15 MAY, 1914, TAKING OFF
ON THE FATAL FLIGHT.

* 412. A. ADAMS

Enlisted directly into RFC on 3 October, 1912. As 1AM, 4 Squadron, served in France from 9 September, 1914. Promoted Flight Sergeant (Observer) on 1 February, 1916 and was Chief Mech (Observer) in 1918 RAF Muster Roll.

413. C. I. COLLETT

Formerly Bombadier, Warwickshire RHA (TF) 5 April, 1909 to 2 October, 1912. Enlisted directly into RFC on 3 October, 1912. Colletts experience as a recruit at Farnborough followed the usual pattern, but he surprised us very much with his story about the RFC walking-out dress. He was issued with one of a dozen of the new RFC walking out uniforms consisting of Half-Wellington boots, tight dark-blue overalls down which ran a broad red stripe, a light blue buttoned-up-to-the-neck tunic with crossed silver cords, and a dark-blue peaked cap with a red band carrying the RFC crest. Was 1AM, 5 Squadron, in August, 1914. Served overseas from 3 April, 1915 earning 1914/15 trio. Promoted T/SM (T) on 1 September, 1916. Qualified as Sergeant Major Gunner/Observer 29 September, 1916, but shown in his original NCO rank of Flight Sergeant in *L.G.* 27 December, 1916 for the award of a Military Medal, for recovering a crashed aeroplane under fire when serving with 12 Squadron. Chief Master Mechanic (Technical) in 1918 RAF Muster Roll. Group of four medals known:— M.M. (413 Flt Sjt 12/Squadron RFC), 1914-15 Star (Cpl RFC) British War Medal and Victory Medal (T.S.M. RFC) (Brother of Nos. 289 and 415).

414. WALTER THORNE

Enlisted as No. 8624 Oxfordshire & Buckinghamshire L.I. in 1907 aged 17, born 20 February, 1890. Transferred to RFC 2 October, 1912 and made Sergeant in 1 Squadron. Posted overseas 2 March, 1915 earning 1914/15 Star trio. Commissioned 2 Lieutenant 16 November, 1916. Flight Lieutenant in November, 1921 *A.F.L.* seniority 1 January, 1921 on Stores List. Serving from 12 April, 1920 at No. 1 Group HQ, Kenley. Squadron Leader in 1931 (February) *A.F.L.* seniority 1 January, 1927 in Stores Branch, from 25 May, 1927 serving at HQ Wessex Bombing Area, Andover, Hants. Promoted Wing Commander (E) 1 July, 1936 and from 30 June, 1936 serving at the Air Ministry (Dept. of Director of Equipment). Promoted Group Captain 1939, Air Commodor 1942 and Air Vice-Marshal 1946. Served with Bomber Command 1939-42; Maintenance Command, 1942-47. Retired 1947. Lived at Eastbourne to his death on 5 October, 1960. Awarded Order of British Empire (Commander) in 1940 and appointed a Companion of the Bath in 1946.

★ 415. S. S. COLLETT

Enlisted directly into RFC 4 October, 1912 and as 1AM Aircraft Park served in France from 14 August, 1914. Discharged under *K.R.* 392 (xvi) 'Sick' *w.e.f.* 4 February, 1916. Silver War Badge No. 69432. (See also Nos. 289 and 413.)

★ 416. CECIL HUGH CHANDLER

Enlisted directly into RFC on 4 October, 1912. As 1AM in Aircraft Park served in France from 16 August, 1914. Promoted Flight Sergeant (Fitter-engines) 1 February, 1918 and was CM (Fitter (AE)) in 1918 RAF Muster Roll. Appointed WO1 *w.e.f.* 1 September, 1929 and awarded RAF

L.S.&G.C. 4 October, 1930. Served in India and awarded Indian General Service Medal (NW Frontier 1930-31). From 15 April, 1935 was WO at Reception Depot, West Drayton. Awarded 1935 Silver Jubilee Medal. In March, 1938 *A.F.L.* was 30th senior RAF Warrant Officer.

★ 417. A. H. BARNETT

Enlisted directly into RFC 5 October, 1912. As 2AM with 2 Squadron served in France from 12 August, 1914. Promoted A/WO (D) 1 March, 1918 and was Act SM1 (paid) in 1918 RAF Muster Roll.

★ 418. T. REEVES

Enlisted directly into RFC 30 September, 1912. As 2AM 3 Squadron served in France from 12 August, 1914. Promoted Corporal (Fitter-engines) 1 February, 1918 and was Cpl Mech (Fitter AE) in 1918 RAF Muster Roll.

★ 419. T. F. RANDLES

Enlisted directly into RFC 2 October, 1912. As 2AM 2 Squadron earned 1914 Star and bar in France from 12 August, 1914. Promoted Flight Sergeant (Fitter-gen) on 1 January, 1918 and was CM (Fitter-gen) in 1918 RAF Muster Roll.

420. A. SEARLE

When 2AM in 4 Squadron died of tubercular meningitis, at Swindon Hospital, on 26 December, 1912.

★ 421. W. G. ASHDOWN

Enlisted directly into Corps on 3 October, 1912. Was 2AM Airship Detachment, earned 1914 Star and bar, transferring to RNAS 18 October, 1914 as No. 698, Air Mechanic 1st Class. C.P.O. 3, 30 April, 1917. In 1918 RAF Muster Roll was 200698 Chief Mechanic (Rigger-Airships).

★ 422. C. LITTLEJOHN

Enlisted in 1910. Formerly 21803, No. 5 Company RE. Transferred to RFC 2 October, 1912. As 1AM, 3 Squadron, served in France from 16 August, 1914. Awarded Military Medal as Flight Sergeant No. 1 Squadron in *L.G.* 31 June, 1916. Commissioned 2 Lieutenant 19 February, 1918. His group of four medals was sold in 1974 for £165:— M.M. (A/S.M. RFC), 1914 Star (1AM RFC), British War Medal and Victory Medal (Lieutenant RAF) (with M.I.D. oakleaf).

★ 423. F. A. BURTON

Enlisted 9 March, 1911. Formerly 10029 Private, 2/KRRC. Was Corporal in 5 Squadron and served in France from 14 August, 1914. Promoted Flight Segeant (Fitter-Gen) 1 May, 1917. Chief Mech (Fitter-Gen) in 1918 RAF Muster Roll. Mentioned in the *Times* 'B' Press Release of 29 August, 1919.

★ 424. F. C. PHILLIPS

Enlisted directly into RFC 16 September, 1912. As 1AM 2 Squadron earned 1914 Star and bar in France from 12 August, 1914. Acting WO (Superintending Clerk) from 1 December, 1917 and was Acting Master Clerk (paid when necessary) in 1918 RAF Muster Roll. Commissioned 16 November, 1918. Shown in 1937 *A.F.L.* as Pilot Officer (retired).

★ 425. H. D. LANE

Enlisted 7 October, 1912 into RE. Posted to Airship Detachment as 1AM on transfer to RFC. Earned 1914 Star on transfer to RNAS 18 October, 1914 as No. 692. 2 Lieutenant (Airships) in RAF 8 May, 1918.

★ 426. ALBERT FRANK LANG

As 1AM HQ Squadron RFC served in France from 12 August, 1914. Promoted Flight Sergeant, 5 May, 1916. Commissioned 2 Lieutenant 12 October, 1916. Flying Officer (T) in November, 1921 *A.F.L.* with an M.B.E. Seniority 1 August, 1919 in General List. Stationed from 1 March, 1921 at No. 2 Flying Training School, No. 1 Group. Royston. Flight Lieutenant in 1931 *A.F.L.* (February) seniority 1 January, 1923 (Qualified at Specialist Signals Course) stationed from 1 March, 1928 at the Air Ministry (Deputy Directorate of Staffs Dept) as a Junior Asst in the Signals Branch.

* 427. A. L. GODDEN

Enlisted 14 November, 1906. Formerly 7002 Pte 3/Coldstream Guards. Posted to RFC on 30 September, 1912. As 1AM, 5 Squadron, earned 1914 Star and bar in France from 14 August, 1914. Promoted T/SM (D) 1 October, 1916, although in *L.G.* 7 December, 1917 he was mentioned in despatches as Sergeant Acting Flight Sergeant. SM1 (Disciplinarian) in 1918 RAF Muster Roll. Awarded RAF L.S.&G.C. Medal as SM1 *w.e.f.* 14 November, 1924.

* 428. G. C. BROWN

Enlisted 7 October, 1903. Formerly 36608 Gunner 72 Battery RFA. Posted to 3 Squadron on transfer to RFC on 10 September, 1912. As 1AM 3 Squadron earned 1914 Star and bar in France from 13 August, 1914. Returned to UK and again to France 24 November, 1914. Promoted Sergeant (Rigger) *w.e.f.* 1 November, 1917 and was Sergeant Mechanic (Rigger-Aero) in 1918 RAF Muster Roll. Awarded RAF L.S.&G.C. 7 October, 1921 as Sergeant. Trio and RAF L.S.&G.C. known in a private collection (1AM and Cpl RFC and Sgt RAF).

429. G. E. JOEL

Enlisted directly into RFC on 7 October, 1912. As 1AM posted overseas on 7 March, 1915 earning 1914/15 trio. Promoted Flight Sergeant (Driver MT) 1 September, 1916 and was Chief Mech, (Driver) in 1918 RAF Muster Roll.

430. J. W. GATENBY

Enlisted into RE 7 October, 1912 and transferred to 1 Squadron RFC from RE Depot 13 November, 1912. 1AM with 6 Squadron August, 1914. No trace of entitlement to either 1914 or 1914/15 Star. Promoted Sergeant (Rigger) 15 September, 1915 and was Sergeant Mechanic (Rigger-Aero) in 1918 RAF Muster Roll.

* 431. F. G. CRACKNELL

Enlisted directly into RFC 9 October, 1912. As 1AM in Aircraft Park earned 1914 Star and bar in France from 16 August, 1914. Promoted Corporal (Rigger) 1 May, 1916 and was Corporal Mech (Rigger-Aero) in 1918 RAF Muster Roll. RAF L.S.&G.C. Medal awarded *w.e.f.* 1 January,

1934 as Sergeant. In view of the four years delay in awarding L.S.&G.C., one wonders if he was discharged post war then re-enlisted or if at some time his actions barred him counting his first four years service towards the Good Conduct element of the medal.

* 432. C. WILKIN

As 2AM with 2 Squadron earned 1914 Star and bar in France from 16 August, 1914. Discharged unfit 16 January, 1915.

433. A. Y. RICHARDS

Enlisted 7 October, 1912 directly into RFC. No record of entitlement to either 1914 nor 1914/15 Star. Promoted Corporal (Vulcanizer) 1 March, 1916 and was Corporal Mechanic (Vulcanizer) in 1918 RAF Muster Roll.

* 434. M. H. DOYLE

Formerly 10431 Pte Royal Irish Fusiliers. Transferred from their Depot to RFC 24 September, 1912. As 1AM, 5 Squadron, served in France from 14 August, 1914. Promoted Sergeant (Air Gunner) in August, 1917. Commissioned 2 Lieutenant 31 October, 1917. (As Observer/Sergeant served in 100 Squadron in July, and August, 1917 flew on 13 occasions mainly with 2 Lieutenants Kent and Prosser, mostly bombing raids against enemy airfields.)

435. J. NASH

As 2AM was discharged at his own request on 8 May, 1913 on payment of £18 within three months of enlistment, under *K.R.* 392 (v).

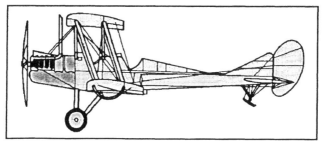

BE2C

★ 436. A. H. SIMPSON

Enlisted directly into RFC 2 October, 1912. Was a Corporal in 4 Squadron in France from 13 August, 1914. Mentioned in despatches with 5 Squadron in *L.G.* 15 May, 1917 as Flight Sergeant (Acting Sergeant Major). Commissioned 2 Lieutenant 5 October, 1917.

★ 437. H. F. TRAILL

Enlisted 7 February, 1907. Formerly 7809 Sergeant 1/Cameron Highlanders. Transferred to RFC 8 October, 1912. Was Sergeant in Corps HQ in France from 16 August, 1914. Promoted T/SM (D) 1 March, 1916 and was SM1 (D) in 1918 RAF Muster Roll. See group photograph No. 2.

★ 438. R. A. J. FILEY

Enlisted 24 October, 1908. Formerly 30086 RGA. Transferred to RFC 9 October, 1912. As 1AM, 5 Squadron, served in France from 14 August, 1914. Promoted Corporal (Fitter MT) 15 September, 1914. Was reported as being a POW. Still Corporal Mechanic (Fitter MT) in 1918 RAF Muster Roll.

★ 439. W. GREGORY

Enlisted 13 September, 1911. Formerly 21987 Sapper, Air Battalion RE.Transferred to 1 Squadron RFC on 13 October, 1912. As 1AM, Aircraft Park served in France from 16 August, 1914. Promoted Sergeant (Sailmaker) 1 May, 1917 and was Sergeant Mech (Fabric Worker) in 1918 RAF Muster Roll. Awarded RAF L.S.&G.C. Medal as SM1 *w.e.f.* 13 September, 1929.

440. J. W. HARLEY

As 2AM discharged at his own request, 23 December, 1912, on payment of £10 within three months of enlistment (*vide K.R.* 392 (v)).

★ 441. S. HAIRE

Enlisted directly into RFC on 14 October, 1912. With 4 Squadron as 1AM earned 1914 Star and bar. Promoted Sergeant (Driver MT) 1 September, 1916 and was Sergeant Mech (Driver) in 1918 RAF Muster Roll.

442. J. J. McCarthy

Enlisted 2 November, 1904. Formerly 34978 Bombardier RFA, posted to RFC HQ 2 October, 1912 and appointed Sergeant-Master-Tailor that day. No record of a 1914 Star or a 1914/15 Star traced. No further promotions. Still same rank and trade in 1918 RAF Muster Roll. See group photograph No. 2.

443. R. H. Bright

2AM 2 Squadron in 1914. As QMS promoted 2 Lieutenant 23 December, 1916. No trace of issue of 1914 or 1914/15 Stars.

444. J. R. Graham

Transferred to 1 Squadron from RE Depot 13 November, 1912. As 2AM discharged at his own request on payment of £18 on 9 May, 1913.

445. H. Campbell

Enlisted 25 August, 1908. Formerly No. 65, Cpl 1/Gordon Highlanders. Transferred to RFC on 4 October, 1912. Was a Sergeant in 5 Squadron when his leg was broken in an aeroplace crash on 20 July, 1914. The pilot, Lieutenant L. Hordern, was killed. Promoted Flight Sergeant (Fitter-General) 1 March, 1915. No entitlement to 1914 or 1914/15 Star traced. Taken POW at Kut in 1916. D.C.M. awarded 12 December, 1917 (no citation) the *L.G.* entry states he was from Auckland, New Zealand. See group photograph No. 2.

★ 446. Edward James Spearing

Enlisted 5 December, 1905. Was 1AM in the Airship Detachment in August, 1914. Earned 1914 Star and bar, having tansferred to RNAS 18 October, 1914 as No. 663, Air Mechanic 1st Class. CPO2 15 December, 1916. Was Master Mechanic (Rigger Airship) in 1918 RAF Muster Roll as No. 200663. Commissioned Flying Officer 1 January, 1920. Retired 18 March, 1928.

★ 447. E. Clarke

Enlisted 17 November, 1909. Formerly 20982 Driver, Air Battalion RE. Posted to 3 Squadron on 14 November, 1912 on transfer to RFC. 1AM with Aircraft Park in France from 16 August, 1914 and still 1AM (Rigger Aero) in 1918 RAF Muster Roll. (See also 302).

448. T. BENNETT

Enlisted directly into RFC on 15 October, 1912. As 1AM, 2 Squadron, earned 1914 Star and bar in France from 13 August, 1914. Awarded D.C.M. as Corporal in *L.G.* 9 October, 1915 'For conspicuous bravery and skill on 13 September, 1915 over Bois de Biez while on patrol duty with 2 Lieut H. S. Shield. At an elevation of about 10,000 feet a German Albatross was sighted. The Officer dived towards it and engaged at about 7,000 feet. Whilst diving they were subjected to heavy anti-aircraft gun fire. The Germans used, during the engagement, a machine gun very conveniently mounted, but Corporal Bennett handled his gun with great coolness and skill, and succeeded in disabling the German machine, which side-slipped, nose-dived, and came to ground in our lines.'
RFC Communiqué No. 10 13 September, 1915.

Shield and Bennett were in a BE2c with Lewis gun. The German pilot, Lt Suwelach, 24 Flieger Abteilung attached to XIXth (Saxon) Corps, and the observer, Lt Oskar Teuchmann, 2nd Photographic Section, were both killed by bullets. Three cameras were found in the aeroplane.
RFC Communiqué No. 12 28 September, 1915.

Shield and Bennett, both of 16 Squadron, again in a BE2c on a reconnaissance North East of Vavrin at 7.05 am observed a small Albatross approaching from Lille. At very close range they exchanged fire and the enemy aircraft flew back at a very low altitude with smoke from the engine.
RFC Communiqué No. 16 22 October, 1915.

Flying with Lieut Greenwood in a BE2c of 16 Squadron, encountered an Albatross in the vicinity of Don. The German fired a white light and the anti aircraft guns ceased firing. The two observers exchanged fire and the Albatross dived steeply and made off Eastwards. Re-crossing the line near Bois Grenier, they were hit by a shell and Bennett was wounded in the elbow.

Promoted Sergeant Observer, 22 October, 1915 on the same day that he was hit by an anti-aircraft shell and wounded. Promoted Flight Sergeant (NCO Observer) 1 April, 1917 and was Chief Mechanic (Observer) in 1918 RAF Muster Roll.

* 449. A. COOPER

Enlisted directly into RFC 17 October, 1912. As 2AM, RFC HQ, in France from 12 August, 1914. Promoted 1AM 1 December, 1917 and was Private 1 (Discip) in 1918 RAF Muster Roll.

450. (NOT TRACED, SEE 88)

Possibly Sergeant Borne, 2 Sqn in January, 1914. See group photograph No. 3.

* 451. PERCIVAL G. BARTLETT

Enlisted into RE 16 October, 1912. Transferred to No. 1 Squadron from RE Depot 13 November, 1913. Was 1AM Airship Detachment in August, 1914. Earned 1914 Star and bar being transferred to RNAS 18 October, 1914 as No. 688 Air Mechanic 1st Class. Chief Petty Officer 3rd Class 1 August, 1916. Was Chief Mechanic (Rigger Airships) No. 200688 in 1918 RAF Muster Roll. RAF L.S.&G.C. Medal as Sergeant Major 2nd Class *w.e.f.* 16 October, 1930. WO1, from 5 January, 1931. Awarded 1935 Silver Jubilee Medal. In March, 1938 *Air Force List*. Commissioned Flying Officer, 1 October, 1942 (Administration and Miscellaneous Duties).

452. F. MATTHEWS

As 2AM was discharged 20 April, 1914 under *K.R.* 392 (ix) 'Unfitted for duties in the Corps.'

* 453. J. MCLEAN

Enlisted 18 October, 1912 directly into RFC. As 1AM, Aircraft Park, served in France from 16 August, 1914. Promoted Temporary Sergeant Major (Technical) 1 August, 1917 and was Chief Master Mechanic (Technical) in 1918 RAF Muster Roll.

* 454. HENRY JAMES DANN

Enlisted 16 October, 1912, directly into RFC. As Corporal, No. 5 Squadron earned 1914 Star and bar in France from 14 August, 1914. Promoted WO1 2 May, 1917 and commissioned 2 Lieutenant 16 November, 1917. Flying Officer in 1921 (November) *Air Force List*, seniority 20 July, 1920 in Stores List. Stationed from 6 October, 1921 at No. 1

School of Technical Training (Boys), Halton. Dismissed by Court Martial 30 June, 1924.

★ 455. A. T. MARTIN

Enlisted directly into RFC on 16 October, 1912. Was 2AM, Airship Detachment in August, 1914. Earned 1914 Star and bar, being transferred to RNAS on 18 October, 1914 as No. 658, Air-Mechanic 1st Class. Chief Petty Officer 3rd Class, 30 April, 1917. Was Chief Mechanic (Hydrogen Worker) No. 200658 in 1918 RAF Muster Roll.

★ 456. H. GRIGG

Enlisted 15 November, 1911. Formerly 7330 Private 3/Coldstream Guards. Transferred to RFC 17 October, 1912. As 2AM, No. 2 Squadron served in France from 12 August, 1914. Promoted 1AM (cook) 1 November, 1916 and was Private 1st Class (cook) in 1918 RAF Muster Roll. (See also No. 302.)

★ 457. WILLIAM WHIDDON HART

Born 15 November, 1887. Formerly 6887 Private 3/Coldstream Guards. Transferred to RFC 21 October, 1912. As Corporal served in France from 12 August, 1914 with RFC HQ. Commissioned 21 September, 1915. Served as 2 Lieutenant with 4 Squadron. Flight Lieutenant (T) in 1921 (November) *A.F.L.*, with M.B.E., seniority 1 August, 1919 stationed at No. 2 Indian Wing HQ Amdala from 20 July, 1920. As an acting local Wing Commander earned Indian General Service Medal (clasp Waziristan 1921-24). Squadron Leader in 1931 (February) *A.F.L.*, seniority 1 January, 1925 in GD Branch (Qualified in Specialist Signalling Course). Stationed from 28 January 1926 on Signals Duties at Coastal Command HQ, Tavistock Place, London. In 1937 *A.F.L.* was Squadron Ldr (retired) but from 16 July 1937 was Flight Lieutenant RAFO. Recalled 1 September, 1939 to 19 June, 1946. Last noted in the 1962 *A.F.L.* as Squadron Leader retaining the rank of Wing Commander (retired).

★ 458. J. E. JONES

Enlisted 15 April, 1907. Formerly 9334 Private 2/Welsh Regt. As 1AM served in 2 Squadron in France from 13 August, 1914. Promoted Flight Sergeant (Carpenter) 1 March, 1916 and was CM (Carpenter) in 1918 RAF Muster Roll. Mentioned in the *Times* 'B' Press Release of 29 August,

1919. Awarded RAF L.S.&G.C. medal as Flight Sergeant *w.e.f.* 15 April 1925.

459. T. G. RAWDON

Enlisted directly into RFC 25 October, 1912. 2AM in August, 1914. No trace of entitlement to 1914 or 1914/15 Star. Promoted 1AM (Carpenter) 1 September, 1917 and no futher promotion in RFC. Awarded RAF L.S.&G.C. medal as Sergeant *w.e.f.* 25 October, 1930.

460. R. MITCHELL

As 2AM discharged 9 September, 1913 under *K.R.* 392 (ix) 'Unfitted for the duties of the Corps.'

★ 461. JAMES YOUNG

Enlisted 26 October, 1912 directly into RFC. As 1AM, 2 Squadron, served in France from 12 August, 1914. Promoted Temp SM (T) 1 April, 1916 and was Chief Master Mech (Tech) in 1918 RAF Muster Roll. 'Mentioned' for his services at the Air Ministry 22 January, 1919 and next day in the *Times* 'B' List. Went to North Russia that year with 'Syren Force' as Sergeant Major and in *L.G.* 22 December, 1919, was awarded an RAF M.S.M., as CMM, one of only 29 such awarded for this theatre.

★ 462. A. J. BIRD

Enlisted 26 October, 1912, directly into RFC. Was 2AM, Airship Detachment in August 1914. Earned 1914 Star, being transferred to RNAS on 18 October, 1914 as No. 686. Leading Mechanic (Engineer) 15 December, 1916. Was Corporal Mechanic (Fitter general) No. 200686 in 1918 RAF Muster Roll.

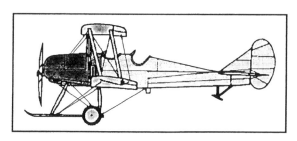

RE5

★ 463. L. A. G. BUTCHER

Enlisted 16 December, 1910. Served in the Air Battalion of RE. Was 2AM, Airship Detachment in August, 1914. Earned 1914 Star and bar, being transferred to RNAS on 18 October, 1914 as No. 675, 1AM. Petty Officer 1 June, 1915. Was Sergeant (Discip) in 1918 RAF Muster Roll, No. 200675. Brother of No. 1175.

★ 464. ROBERT EDWARD KELLY

Transferred to No. 1 Squadron RFC on 28 November, 1912 from RE Depot. As 1AM 4 Squadron served in France from 12 August, 1914. Died 20 February, 1915, aged 27. Buried at St. Omer (Longnevesse Souvenir Cemetery I.A. 42). Son of Edward and Lucy Kelly, 35, Seaford Ave, Sandymor, County Dublin.

465. C. E. JEFFORD

As 2AM was discharged free under Article 1130 (i) of the Pay Warrant on 27 February, 1914, suggesting that he was a long service soldier transferred to RFC and not a recruit.

★ 466. A. B. HEMMINGS

Enlisted 28 October, 1912 directly into RFC. As 1AM, 4 Squadron, served in France from 13 August, 1914. Promoted Flight Sergeant (Blacksmith) 1 November, 1916, and was CM (Blacksmith) in 1918 RAF Muster Roll. Awarded Indian General Service Medal as Flight Sergeant (clasp Waziristan 1919-21) in 20 Squadron.

★ 467. E. SMALLEY

Enlisted 21 October, 1912 directly into RFC from the Merchant Navy. As 1AM, 2 Squadron, served in France from 12 August, 1914 as a fitter. Promoted Temp SM (T) 1 May, 1917 and was CMM (T) in 1918 RAF Muster Roll. Awarded RAF M.S.M., for services in France, in the first gazetting of this award in *L.G.* 3 June, 1918. He came from Liverpool. See *'Cross and Cockade'* Volume 6, No. 3, page 122 for a photograph and *'The Forgotten Ones.'*

Opposite: SGT.-MAJ. SMALLEY (extreme right) WITH CAPTURED GERMAN AEROPLANE

★ 468. W. H. CLOVER

As Sergeant, 4 Squadron, earned 1914 Star and bar, in France from 13 August, 1914. Commissioned 2 Lieutenant, 1 July, 1916.

469. F. BAST

As 2AM was discharged 25 September, 1913 under *K.R.* 392 (ix) 'Unfitted for the duties of the Corps.'

★ 470. N. V. PIPER

Son of a Master Mariner. Enlisted directly into RFC 22 October, 1912, at the age of 18, and trained as a fitter/rigger with S. F. Cody. As Corporal, No. 4 Squadron, earned 1914 Star and bar, in France from 9 September, 1914, flying as passenger with Captain Chinnery and survived a crash at Poperinghe in November, 1914. Promoted Sergeant (Fitter general) 1 May, 1915. With 15 Squadron, 17 January, 1916 as a gunner/observer was reported 'Killed in Action' but later confirmed as POW at Giessen. Repatriated to Holland in May, 1918. Served from 1935 to 1958 at Halton Apprentice School as a Civilian Instructor. Alive in July, 1977 living at 45 Beaconsfield Road, Tring, Herts. He had a British Empire Medal awarded in 1957. See *'Cross and Cockade'* Volume 4, No. 2, pages 54 and 70. '15 Squadron's first casualty occurred in the morning of 17 January, 1916 when Captain V. N. H. Wadham (OC A Flight) and Sergeant Piper in a BE2c were escorting another BE on a recce. At approximately 0830 over the Houlhulst Forest a Fokker monoplane attacked the recce BE and Wadham dived to the rescue. In a subsequent letter home Sergeant Piper told how Wadham was shot in the neck and killed instantly. Piper at once climbed into the pilots cockpit where, sitting on the dead Wadhams lap, he took the controls and tried to fly the BE to safety. Soon realising this was impossible, he landed in German lines. Deliberately crashing the BE to render it useless, he managed to jump clear before the impact.'

★ 471. L. WRIGHT

Enlisted directly into RFC 31 October, 1912. As 2AM, No. 4 Squadron, earned 1914 Star and bar, in France from 9 September, 1914. On 30 October, 1917 he was re-classified and reduced to 3AM (Driver MT) and retained that rank and trade in 1918 RAF Muster Roll.

★ 472. ALFRED BOX

Born 17 October, 1890. Enlisted directly into RFC on 4 November, 1912. As 1AM, with No. 2 Squadron served in France from 14 August, 1914. Promoted Temporary Sergeant Major (Disciplinarian) 1 April, 1917 and was Sergeant Major 1st Class (Disciplinarian) in 1918 RAF Muster Roll. Awarded M.B.E. in *London Gazette* of 3 June 1930 and RAF L.S.&G.C. medal with effect from 4 November, 1930. In 1931 *Air Force List* was 47th senior RAF Warrant Officer. Awarded 1935 Silver Jubilee Medal. On 25 May, 1937 he was appointed SWO, RAF Reception Depot, West Drayton, Middlesex, and in March, 1937 was the fifth senior RAF Warrant Officer. Commissioned (No. 43595) 7 March, 1940 Flight Lieutenant 1 March, 1942. Retired 31 May 1944. Last noted on retired list of April, 1960 *Air Force List*.

473. J. BRAITHWAIT

As 2AM was discharged 3 February, 1913 under *K.R.* 392 (v) 'Having claimed his discharge with 3 months of enlistment.'

474. W. MACRAE

As 2AM discharged 3 February, 1913 at own request under *K.R.* 392 (v).

475. W. GRANT

As 2AM discharged 3 December, 1912 at own request, under *K.R.* 392 (v) on payment of £10.

★ 476. H. C. STRICKLAND

Enlisted 11 November, 1912. Previously served in the Air Battalion RE. As 1AM 4 Squadron, earned 1914 Star and bar in France from 9 September, 1914. Promoted Temp SM (T) 1 July 1916 and was CMM (T) in 1918 RAF Muster Roll. 1914 Star trio known in a private collection.

★ 477. S. R. CALLINGHAM

Enlisted 11 November, 1912 directly into RFC. As 2AM, 2 Squadron earned 1914 Star. Promoted Flight Sergeant (Rigger) 1 December, 1917 and was CMM (Rigger Aero) in 1918 RAF Muster Roll.

⋆ 478. H. ROOK

Enlisted 7 November, 1912, directly into RFC. As 1AM served in France from 16 August, 1914 with Aircraft Park. Discharged 'sick' under *K.R.* 392 (xvi) 10 March 1915. Silver War Badge No. 203512 issued.

479. P. DOBBINS

Born 12 April, 1893. Enlisted originally 11 November, 1912 directly into RFC. However he deserted 22 March, 1914 but returned 29 April, 1914. He was then only allowed to count his service from 4 May, 1914 and this date is shown in 1918 RAF Muster Roll as his date of joining. He was 2AM in August, 1914. No trace of any entitlement to either 1914 or 1914/15 Stars has been found. Promoted 1AM (Fitter AE) 1 December, 1916 and held this rank and trade in RAF Muster Roll (1918). He must have made good his lost service however, for as Flight Sergeant his RAF L.S.&G.C. medal was awarded *w.e.f.* 11 November, 1930. Commissioned into Technical Branch 12 June, 1939, Flight Lieutenant 12 June, 1942. Retired Acting Wing Commander 12 June, 1949. Last noted on the retired list in the 1964 *A.F.L.*

⋆ 480. GEORGE C. ALDERTON

A recruit 15 November, 1912. As 2AM with 2 Squadron in France from 12 August, 1914, having previously been serving in Limerick. He drove a lorry in the retreat from Mons and took wounded RFC men to Paris. He helped load bombs onto Lt. Rhodes-Moorhouse's plane prior to the flight that won him a posthumous V.C. Promoted Corporal (Fitter Engines) 1 November, 1917 was Corporal Mech (Fitter AE) in 1918 RAF Muster Roll. (see No. 481)

⋆ 481. H. W. ALDERTON

A recruit from 15 November, 1912. As 2AM with 2 Squadron in France from 12 August, 1914. Promoted Sergeant (Driver MT) 1 January, 1918 and was Sergeant Mech (Driver) in 1918 RAF Muster Roll (see No. 480).

⋆ 482. GEORGE FREDERICK DRUDGE

A recruit 18 November, 1912. As 1AM with 6 Squadron earned 1914 Star and bar in France from 12 August, 1914. He must have been attached to another Squadron, as 6 Squadron as a unit did not serve in France until

October, 1914. Commissioned 2 Lieutenant 28 May, 1916. Promoted Lieutenant 1 May, 1917. In November, 1921 *A.F.L.* was Flying Officer (T) seniority 24 October, 1919 serving from 12 August, 1921 at No. 2 Flying Training School, Royston.

★ 483. A. FLOWER

A recruit on 16 November, 1912. As 2AM, 4 Squadron, served in France from 12 August, 1914. Promoted Sergeant (Telephonist) 1 November, 1916 and retained that trade and rank in 1918 RAF Muster Roll.

★ 484. ARCHIBALD JOSEPH SHIMMONS

Born 14 November, 1894. A recruit on 14 November, 1912. 2AM, 2 Squadron, in France from 12 August, 1914. Promoted Sergeant (Fitter MT) 1 September, 1916 and retained that trade and rank in 1918 RAF Muster Roll. Awarded RAF L.S.&G.C. medal *w.e.f.* 14 November, 1930 as Flight Sergeant. Awarded 1935 Silver Jubilee Medal as Warrant Officer. Commissioned Flying Officer (CEO) 6 April, 1938. Promoted Wing Commander 1 July, 1942. Retired 15 November, 1949. (No. 35188) Last noted on retired list in 1978 *A.F.L.*

★ 485. ERNEST DOUGLAS JACKSON

Born 7 August, 1892. A recruit on 7 November, 1912. As Corporal, 4 Squadron, earned 1914 Star and bar in France from 12 August, 1914. Promoted Temp SM (T) 1 May 1917 and was mentioned in despatches 13 March, 1918 as Sergeant Major 'for Valuable services in the War' (*i.e.* in UK). Chief Master Mech (Tech) in 1918 RAF Muster Roll. Awarded RAF L.S.&G.C. medal *w.e.f.* 7 November 1931 when he was 52nd senior RAF Warrant Officer. Commissioned Flying Officer (CEO) on 18 May, 1937 and was then serving at Home Aircraft Depot, Henlow Camp, Biggleswade. Retired 12 July, 1946. As No. 35078, he is last listed as Squadron. Ldr. (Tech) (E) (retired) retaining the rank of Wing Commander in 1968 *A.F.L.*

★ 486. JOHN JOSEPH HARRINGTON

A recruit on 20 November, 1912. As 1AM RFC HQ served in France from 12 August, 1914. KIA at Ypres 13 November, 1914. Originally buried at a farm 1000 yds North of Zillebeke, Belgium, now in Burr Cross Roads Cemetery (II D. 17). Born Newport Monmouth 24 February, 1886.

Educated St. Mary's R.C. School, Newport. Served in Royal Monmouthshire Royal Engineers 1905-08. Son of John Harrington, Master Plasterer of 6 King St, Newport. Prior to his enlistment he had driven the mail between Tredegar and Newport and was later employed by British and Colonial Aeroplane Co. Filton Works, Bristol.

★ 487. W. E. JONES

A recruit on 19 November, 1912. 2AM with Airship Detachment in August, 1912. Earned 1914 Star transferring to RNAS 18 November, 1914 as No. 687 1AM. Hon. 2 Lieut in April 1918 *A.F.L.*

★ 488. W. L. BAGLEY

A recruit on 18 November, 1912. 1AM with Aircraft Park in France from 16 August, 1914. Reverted to Sergeant (Fitter MT) from Flight Sergeant 11 August, 1917 and had this trade and rank in 1918 RAF Muster Roll.

489. ARTHUR JAMES LOCKER

Born Darlington 7 August, 1889. Enlisted 16 November, 1912. Originally in RE. Awarded Royal Aero Club Aviators' Certificate No. 775 on 28 April 1914 as an Air Mechanic at the Bristol School of Flying, in a Bristol aeroplane, on Salisbury Plain. As a 2AM with 4 Squadron he earned a 1914 Star and bar serving in France from 9 September, 1914. However, on 19 February, 1915 he was discharged for misconduct and forfeited his entitlement to the medal.

490. W. E. UNDERHILL

A recruit on 22 November, 1912. As 2AM he deserted on 20 January, 1913.

★ 491. W. H. BOWKER

A recruit on 25 November, 1912. As Sergeant with 4 Squadron served in France from 14 August, 1914. Awarded M.M. as Flight Sergeant in *L.G.* 11 October, 1916. He had already been commissioned 2 Lieutenant 4 June, 1916 and promoted Lieutenant 1 September, 1916.

492. H. J. R. GUPPY

A recruit on 25 November, 1912. Discharged 16 February 1914 under *K.R.* 392 (ix) 'Unfitted for the duties of the Corps.'

493. A. W. C. STENTIFORD

A recruit. Discharged 20 April, 1914 under *K.R.* 392 (ix) 'Unfitted for the duties of the Corps.'

★ 494. VICTOR CLARANCE JUDGE

Born Portsmouth 29 June, 1891. A recruit on 29 November, 1912. Awarded Royal Aero Club Aviators' Certificate No. 855 on 21 July, 1914 as 1st Class Air Mechanic in a Maurice Farman of Central Flying School at Upavon. As 1AM in 4 Squadron served in France from 9 September, 1914. Promoted Corporal (1st Class Pilot) on 19 December, 1914. As a pilot in a Voisin, still in 4 Squadron, he was shot down near Bapaume 21 July, 1915 and taken prisoner. The observer, Lieut J. Parker died of wounds. Transferred to Holland May, 1918. (The Germans dropped a message the next day into the British airfield advising them of Cpl. Judge's capture and Lieut. Parker's death.)

★ 495. J. A. SMITH

A recruit 25 November, 1912. As 1AM, 2 Squadron earned 1914 Star and bar in France from 12 August, 1914. Promoted Flight Sergeant (Rigger) 1 January, 1917 and was Chief Mech (Rigger Aero) in 1918 RAF Muster Roll.

★ 496. G. E. PANKHURST

A recruit 27 November, 1912. As 2AM, 4 Squadron, served in France from 9 September, 1914. Promoted Corporal (Fitter Engine) 1 August, 1917 and was Corporal Mech (Fitter MT) in 1918 RAF Muster Roll.

⋆ 497. E. E. HALES

A recruit 2 December, 1912. Was 2AM in 2 Squadron in France from 12 August, 1914. Promoted A/WO (T) 1 December, 1918 and was A/Chief Master Mech (Paid when necessary) in 1918 RAF Muster Roll.

⋆ 498. SIDNEY RASTALL GOLDTHORPE

A recruit 2 December, 1912. As 2AM in Aircraft Park served in France from 16 August, 1914. Promoted Flight Sergeant (Storeman) on 1 April, 1916. Awarded Army M.S.M. in *L.G.* 11 November, 1916 'For Valuable Service with the Armies in the Field.' Flight Clerk in 1918 RAF Muster Roll. RAF L.S.&G.C. medal as SM2 *w.e.f.* 2 December, 1930. Appointed WO1 1 September, 1931. Awarded 1935 Silver Jubilee Medal. On 4 September, 1935 serving at No. 3 Flying Training School, South Cerney, Cirencester (*A.F.L.* 1937). In March, 1938 *A.F.L.* was the 49th most senior RAF Warrant Officer.

⋆ 499. E. HOWELL

A recruit 2 December, 1912. Was 2AM with Airship Detachment in August, 1914. Earned 1914 Star and bar transferring to RNAS 18 October, 1914 as No. 680 1AM. Leading Mechanic 15 December, 1916. In 1918 RAF Muster Roll was 200680 Corporal Mechanic (Rigger Airships).

⋆ 500. THOMAS EDWARD WHITTAKER

A recruit 30 November, 1912. As 1AM, 4 Squadron, served in France from 12 August, 1914. Promoted Sergeant (Carpenter) 22 July, 1917, and was same rank and trade in 1918 RAF Muster Roll. Mentioned in despatches 10 October, 1919 'For distinguished services in the Field as Flight Sgt.'

⋆ 501. TOM LLEWELLIN THOMAS

A recruit on 26 November, 1912. As 1AM, 4 Squadron, earned 1914 Star and bar serving in France from 12 August, 1914. Transferred to RNAS later in 1914 but transferred back to RFC prior to promotion to Flight Sergeant (Fitter Turner) on 1 September, 1916. Chief Mech (Turner) in 1918 RAF Muster Roll. Appointed WO Class 1 on 1 August, 1929. Awarded RAF L.S.&G.C. medal *w.e.f.* 26 November, 1930. Awarded 1935 Silver Jubilee Medal. Commissioned as Flying Officer (CEO) on 23 August, 1937. Then stationed at No. 1 School of Tech Training, Halton

Camp, Aylesbury. No. 35120 promoted to Wing Commander 1 September, 1942. Still serving in that rank in 1946 *A.F.L.*

* 502. W. E. HAM

A recruit on 5 December, 1912. As 2AM, 4 Squadron, served in France from 12 August, 1914. Then transferred to Argyll and Sutherland Highlanders as No. 250001.

* 503. C. DONOVAN

A recruit 5 December, 1912. 2AM serving with 6 Squadron, in early August, 1914. Posted to France with Aircraft Park 14 August, 1914 and earned 1914 Star and bar. Promoted 1AM (Fitter-Turner) 1 March, 1918 and was that rank and trade in 1918 RAF Muster Roll.

* 504. FREDERICK WILLIAM NUNN

A recruit on 10 December, 1912. As 1AM in No. 3 Squadron served in France from 12 August, 1914. On 19 December 1914 was Court Martialled and given 2 years hard labour for quitting his post. However, he was promoted to Sergeant (Fitter general) 1 December, 1917 and at the end of the war in Europe served with the RAF in South Russia, where, as Flight Sergeant he was awarded both an RAF Meritorious Service Medal (*London Gazette* 1 April, 1920) and the Russian Medal of Zeal with the ribbon of St. Stanislas. (See also No. 995).

* 505. E. EDWARDS

A recruit on 30 November, 1912. As 2AM No. 2 Squadron he served in France from 12 August, 1914 and earned 1914 Star and bar. Promoted to Sergeant (Fitter general) 1 November, 1916 and was Sergeant Mechanic (Fitter general) in 1918 RAF Muster Roll. Awarded RAF L.S.&G.C. medal with effect from 30 November, 1930 as Sergeant Major 2nd Class. Still serving in 1935. His group of five medals are in the Webb collection:— 1914 Star and bar trio (2AM RFC and F. Sgt. RAF), 1935 Silver Jubilee medal and RAF L.S.&G.C. medal (GV) (SM2).

* 506. SYDNEY ASHBY

Born Balham London, son of Henry Ashby, 208 Queens Rd, Battersea. A recruit on 9 December, 1912. As 2AM No. 2 Squadron served in France from 12 August, 1914. Awarded Military Medal, 7 August, 1917 as aerial gunner to 2 Lieutenant F.D. Holder for shooting down an enemy airship (L48). Took off from Aeroplane Experimental Establishment Orford Ness in an FE26 No. B. 401 at 01.55 and landed at 04.05. See *'Cross and Cockade,'* pp 104-6, Volume 7, No. 3. The pilot was awarded Military Cross. Ashby was accidentally killed in a crash on 16 March, 1918 at Martleshaw Heath when a Flight Sergeant and is buried in Ipswich Cemetery, Suffolk.

★ 507. S. L. NICHOLS

A recruit 9 December, 1912. As 2AM, 2 Squadron, earned 1914 Star and bar, in France from 12 August, 1914. Commissioned 2 Lieutenant 25 April, 1917 and killed in action 12 August, 1917 (19 Squadron).

★ 508. J. MOOREY

A recruit 11 December, 1912. 2AM with Airship Detachment in August, 1914. Earned 1914 Star and bar, transferring to RNAS on 18 October, 1914 as 1AM, No. 691. Chief Petty Officer 3rd Class (Driver) 1 September, 1917. In 1918 RAF Muster Roll was Chief Mechanic (Driver (P)) No. 200691. Awarded RAF L.S.&G.C. as Flight Sergeant with effect from 11 December, 1930.

★ 509. CHARLES EDWARD LEE

A recruit 11 December, 1912. Was 2AM with Aircraft Park serving in France from 16 August, 1914. Promoted Flight Sergeant (Clerk general) on 1 November and was Flight Clerk in 1918 RAF Muster Roll. Awarded RAF M.S.M. in *L.G.* 3 June, 1919, King's Birthday Honours, 'For service in France' as Flight Sergeant. Came originally from Dover.

★ 510. F. RODGERS

Enlisted 4 August, 1903 into Lancashire Fusiliers. Was 2AM, 4 Squadron, earning 1914 Star and bar, for service in France from 12 August, 1914. Promoted 1AM (Carpenter) on 19 December, 1914 and retained that rank and trade throughout the war. (See also No. 302) Awarded RAF L.S.&G.C. medal as Sergeant *w.e.f.* 28 March, 1923. (Lost 18 months at some point towards his medal.)

* 511. W. H. JENKINS

A recruit on 13 December, 1912. As 2AM, 4 Squadron, earned 1914 Star and bar for service in France from 12 August, 1914. Transferred to Tank Corps as No. 309101 then was Corporal No. 786925. His medals were forfeited. They were probably restored 13 August, 1940.

* 512. H. J. ANSDELL

A recruit 7 December, 1912. As 2AM, 6 Squadron, served in France from 6 October, 1914. Promoted Sergeant (Driver M.T.) 1 September, 1916 and retained this rank and trade in the 1918 RAF Muster Roll. Awarded General Service Medal (Southern Desert Iraq), and then RAF L.S.&G.C. medal *w.e.f.* 3 December, 1930 as Flight Sergeant.

* 513. E. W. C. SAUNDERS

A recruit on 20 December, 1912. As 2AM earned 1914 Star. Promoted Temp SM (T) 1 June, 1917. Was Chief Master Mechanic (Technical) in 1918 RAF Muster Roll. 'Mentioned' for service at the Air Ministry 22 January, 1919, and next day in the *Times* 'B' List.

* 514. HERBERT PARKER

A recruit 30 December, 1912. As 2AM in 2 Squadron, earned 1914 Star and bar in France from 13 August, 1914. Commissioned 2 Lieutenant 10 January 1918. Flying Officer in 1921 (November) *A.F.L.*, seniority 20 July, 1920 in Stores List, serving from 22 March, 1921 on board HMS '*Argus*,' a sea-plane carrier. Flight Lieutenant in 1931 (February) *A.F.L.*, seniority 1 January, 1929, serving from 12 October, 1928 at No. 4 Stores Depot, Ruislip, Middlesex. Shown as retired in January 1938 *A.F.L.*

* 515. A. McCULLOCH

Enlisted 10 January, 1911, formerly 20992 Driver, Air Battalion, RE. Posted to No. 1 Squadron. on transfer to RFC on 20 November, 1912. Was 1AM with Airship Detachment in August, 1914. Earned 1914 Star and bar, transferring to RNAS 18 October, 1914 as No. 669 1AM. P.O. 1 August, 1916. In 1918 RAF Muster Roll was Sergeant (Discip) No. 200669.

Fred Karno's Army

(After a popular music hall artist of the time.)
(Tune: 'The Church's one Foundation')

We are Fred Karno's Army,
We are the RFC,
We cannot fight, we cannot shoot,
What earthly use are we?
But when we get to Berlin
The Kaiser he will say,
'Hoch! Hoch! Mein Gott!
What a wunderschoen lot
Are the boys of the RFC.'

Part 3
Numbers 516 to 1013
January—December 1913

Those who enlisted directly into or were transferred to the RFC in 1913 (Nos. 558 to 569 were RFC Reservists recalled in August 1914).

★ 516. W. H. WING

Formerly 14154 Driver, with the Air Battalion, RE from its mobilisation. Transferred to RFC 3 January, 1913. As 2AM, Aircraft Park, served in France from 16 August, 1914. Discharged under *K.R.* 392 (xvi) 'Sick' 30 September, 1915. Silver War Badge No. 88926.

★ 517. W. H. PERRY

A recruit 3 January, 1913. As 1AM, 2 Squadron, served in France from 13 August, 1914. Awarded Royal Aero Club Aviators' Certificate No. 1620 on 20 August, 1915. Promoted A/WO (T) 1 December, 1917 and was Acting Chief Master Mechanic in 1918 RAF Muster Roll. Awarded Air Force Medal in *L.G.* 8 February 1919.

★ 518. G. W. SKERRETT

A recruit 4 January, 1913. As 2AM, 2 Squadron, earned 1914 Star and bar in France from 13 August, 1914. Was an Observer/Gunner from 20 September, 1915. Promoted Flight Sergeant (Rigger) on 1 September, 1916 and was Chief Mech (Rigger Aero) in 1918 RAF Muster Roll.

519. C. BURT

A recruit 9 January, 1913. As 2AM discharged 16 February, 1913 under *K.R.* 392 (ix) 'Unfitted for the duties of the Corps.'

★ 520. G. DURRANT

A recruit on 10 January, 1913. As 2AM, 2 Squadron, served in France from 12 August, 1914. Transferred to 112th Tank Regiment, later No. 116779 Pte Machine Gun Corps.

★ 521. F. POWELL

A recruit 8 January, 1913. As Corporal, 2 Squadron, served in France from 12 August, 1914. Awarded French Médaille Militaire as Sergeant for Gallantry between 21 and 30 August, 1914 in *L.G.* 9 November, 1914. Commissioned 2 Lieutenant 28 October, 1917.

★ 522. F. W. CARPENTER

A recruit on 13 January, 1913. As 2AM, No. 2 Squadron, served in France from 12 August, 1914. Promoted Sergeant (Sailmaker) 1 December, 1916. Was Sergeant (Fabric Worker) in 1918 RAF Muster Roll.

★ 523. H. G. EGGAR

A recruit on 14 January, 1913. Was 1AM with the Aircraft Park in France from 16 August, 1914. Commissioned 2 Lieutenant 17 August, 1917. Lieutenant (Technical) in April, 1918 *Air Force List.*

★ 524. FRANCIS EDWIN DARVILL

Born London, 6 June, 1890. A recruit on 15 January, 1913. 2AM, No. 2 Squadron, in France from 12 August, 1914. Promoted Sergeant (Fitte -MT) 27 September, 1915. Awarded Royal Aero Club Aviators' Certificate No. 2772 on 21 April, 1916. Went to France 2 August, 1916 with No. 40 Squadron. Injured in a flying accident 13 November, 1916 when Sergeant/Pilot, 40 Squadron. Sergeant Mechanic (Fitter MT) in 1918 RAF Muster Roll.
RFC Communiqué No. 61, 9 November, 1916.
Encountered 3 hostile machines over Souchez, drove one down out of control. Observers of 61st A.A. battery reported it fell in a vertical nose dive and crashed. He was flying in an FE8a No. 7629.

* 525. GEORGE KIMBER MARCHMONT

Born Sydenham, Surrey 22 May, 1883. In 1908 he trained as a Mechanic in one of Britain's first flying schools. A recruit on 15 January, 1913. As 2AM, No. 2 Squadron, served in France from 12 August, 1914 to 27 March, 1917. Sergeant (Rigger-Aero) 1 June, 1917 and retained that rank and trade in 1918 RAF Muster Roll. Discharged 15 January, 1921. Joined Handley Page Transport, dropping newspapers by parachute to Scottish towns. Then worked at Croydon Airport until 1943. He had joined the RAF Reserve as 2AM on 24 May, 1927 as 559040 for four years and re-engaged for another four, taking his final discharge on 25 May, 1935. In June 1967 he celebrated his Golden Wedding Anniversary in Wallington where he had lived for 46 years (See No. 60.). His 1914 Star trio named to Cpl. RFC are known in a private collection.

* 526. MARK FRANK TOMKINS

Born 11 December, 1893. A recruit on 14 January, 1913. Was 2AM, No. 2 Squadron, in August, 1914. Served overseas from 24 July, 1915 earning 1914/15 Star trio. Commissioned 2 Lieutenant, 30 November, 1917. Flying Officer (Technical) in 1921 (November) *Air Force List*, seniority 5 December, 1919, in General List, stationed from 20 May, 1920 at RAF Aircraft Depot, Aboukir, Egypt. Still Flying Officer (E) in February, 1931 *Air Force List* in the Stores Branch from 1 October, 1926, from 1 July, 1929 stationed at the Marine Aircraft Experimental Establishment, Felixstowe, Suffolk. Flight Lieutenant (E) seniority 1 June, 1932. At the Air Ministry from 12 October, 1936 (Department of Directorate of Equipment). Still there in 1938. (No. 21075) Wing Commander 11 March, 1940. Retired 11 December, 1946. Re-employed 11 December, 1946 to 26 September, 1947. Noted as still on retired list in 1970.

* 527. C. W. WILSON

A recruit on 16 January, 1913. As 2AM, No. 4 Squadron earned 1914 Star and bar. Promoted Flight Sergeant (Driver MT) 1 September, 1917 and was Chief Mechanic (Driver) in 1918 RAF Muster Roll. Medals returned to RAF Records Office 27 June, 1929.

528. W. FROST

A recruit on 15 January, 1913. As 2AM was discharged 14 April, 1913 under *K.R.* 392 (iii) 'Not likely to become an efficient soldier.'

★ 529. H. V. COULTER

A recruit on 17 January, 1913. As 2AM, 2 Squadron, earned 1914 Star and bar in France from 12 August, 1914. Promoted Corporal (Carpenter) 1 May, 1915 and retained that rank and trade in RAF 1918 Muster Roll. Awarded RAF L.S.&G.C. medal *w.e.f.* 17 January, 1931 as Flight Sergeant. Awarded 1935 Silver Jubilee Medal. Appointed Warrant Officer 18 March, 1936 and was the 113th senior WO in November, 1941 *A.F.L.*, and 58th in October, 1944.

★ 530. L. T. FIDLER

A recruit on 17 January, 1913. As 1AM with Aircraft Park served in France from 16 August, 1914. Promoted Temp SM (D) on 1 February, 1918 and was SM1 (Disciplinarian) in 1918 RAF Muster Roll.

★ 531. HERBERT CLARANCE BAKER

A recruit on 15 January, 1913. As Corporal, 2 Squadron, earned 1914 Star and bar in France from 12 August, 1914. Promoted T/SM (T) 1 March, 1916. Was Chief Master Mechanic (Technical) in 1918 RAF Muster Roll. Awarded M.B.E. as SM1 in King's Birthday Honours in *L.G.* 3 June, 1923. Probationary Flying Officer (Stores Branch) 5 January, 1931. Not in 1938 *A.F.L.*

★ 532. A. E. TOMLIN

A recruit 16 January, 1913. Was 2AM, Airship Detachment in August, 1914. Earned 1914 Star and bar, transferring to RNAS on 18 October, 1914 as 1AM No. 684. Petty Officer 15 December, 1916. In 1918 RAF Muster Roll was No. 200684 Sergeant Mechanic (Hydrogen Worker).

★ 533. W. H. CANDY (OR MINTER-CANDY)

A recruit on 18 January, 1913. As 1AM, 4 Squadron, served in France from 9 September, 1914. Promoted Corporal (Fitter general) 1 July 1915. Listed as a prisoner of war at Kut-al-Amarah 30 May, 1916, one of 41 RFC ORs captured. Shown as same rank and trade in 1918 Muster Roll, still a P.O.W. He died in captivity later that year.

* 534. W. BARKER

A recruit 14 January, 1913. Shown in Routine Orders of 8 April, 1914 as discharged under *K.R.* 392 (ix). However as 1AM, 3 Squadron served in France from 13 August, 1914 and then was killed on 12 March, 1915 in an accidental explosion loading bombs at Merville Aerodrome as 1AM (see also 194, 582, 589, 872 and 1192). Buried Chocques Military Cemetery (1.A.41).

535. W. CURRIER

A recruit on 14 January, 1913. As 2AM deserted 19 April, 1914.

* 536. H. WARE

A recruit on 20 January, 1913. As 1AM, in Aircraft Park, served in France from 12 August, 1914. To Central Flying School on a Riggers course in September, 1914. Promoted Flight Sergeant (Rigger) 1 October, 1917 and was Chief Mech (Rigger Aero) in 1918 RAF Muster Roll.

* 537. JOHN GOLDSMITH

A recruit on 20 January, 1913. As 2AM, 2 Squadron, served in France from 12 August, 1914. Promoted Sergeant (Driver MT) 1 May, 1916. Was Sergeant Mech (Driver) in 1918 RAF Muster Roll. Awarded RAF M.S.M. in King's Birthday Honours *L.G.* 3 June, 1919 'For services in France.' Came originally from Brighton. Promoted WO1 *w.e.f.* 15 June, 1933. Awarded 1935 Silver Jubilee Medal. In July, 1935 was stationed at RAF Reception Depot, West Drayton. No trace of a L.S.&G.C. medal found. In March, 1938 *A.F.L.* was the 70th most senior RAF Warrant Officer, but in November, 1941 *A.F.L.* he was the 74th most senior with seniority for 1 August, 1934. In October, 1944 he was the 33rd most senior.

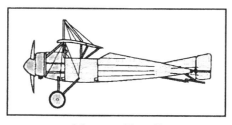

MORANE TYPE P

538. T. FIELD

A recruit on 18 January, 1913. Proceeded overseas 3 April, 1915 earning 1914/15 Star trio. Promoted Sergeant (Fitter general) 1 December, 1917 and held this rank and trade in RAF Muster Roll (1918).

539. A. J. SPELLER

A recruit 14 January, 1913. As 2AM discharged 8 April, 1914 under *K.R.* 392 (ix) 'unfitted for the duties of the Corps.'

* 540. H. MARTIN

A recruit on 17 January, 1913. As 2AM, with Aircraft Park, served in France from 16 August, 1914. Promoted Sergeant (Fitter general) 1 October, 1917 and held that trade and rank in 1918 RAF Muster Roll.

* 541. C. E. GARDINER

A recruit on 17 January, 1913. As 2AM, 5 Squadron, served in France from 14 August, 1914. Reverted to Flt Sergeant (Electrician) 29 January, 1918 and was Chief Mech (Elec) in 1918 RAF Muster Roll.

* 542. T. STONE

A recruit 17 January, 1913. As 2AM, 2 Squadron, earned 1914 Star and bar in France from 12 August, 1914. Promoted Sergeant (Machinist) 1 October, 1916 and held this trade and rank in 1918 RAF Muster Roll.

543. J. T. CASLAKE

A recruit on 18 January, 1913. No issue of 1914 or 1914/15 Stars traced. Promoted Flight Sergeant (Joiner) 1 August, 1916. Was Chief Mech (Carpenter) in 1918 RAF Muster Roll.

544. W. CROSTHWAITE

A recruit on 18 January, 1913. As 2AM was discharged 4 March, 1913 under *K.R.* 392 (iii) 'Not likely to become an efficient soldier.'

★ 545. WILFRED ARTHUR CLAYDON

Born 11 May, 1893. A recruit 20 January, 1913. As 1AM, 5 Squadron, served in France from 14 August, 1914. Promoted A/SM (D) (paid when necessary) 1 March, 1918 but was A/SM1 (Discip) (paid) in 1918 RAF Muster Roll. Awarded RAF L.S.&G.C. medal *w.e.f.* 20 January, 1931 as SM1 and awarded both the 1935 Silver Jubilee and 1937 Coronation Medals. In December 1937 *A.F.L.* was serving as Station Warrant Officer at RAF Station Halton from 11 February that year. In March, 1938 RAF Muster Roll was the twelfth senior RAF Warrant Officer. Commissioned 21 March, 1940. Flight Lieutenant 1 September, 1945. Retired 2 December, 1947. Last noted in 1966 *A.F.L.* (Admin and Special Duties Branch).

★ 546. C. R. S. EVANS

A recruit 20 January, 1913. As 1AM, 4 Squadron, served in France from 13 August, 1914. Was awarded French Médaille Militaire, in *L.G.* 9 November, 1914 as Corporal 'For gallantry between 21 and 30 August 1914. Mentioned in despatches as Corporal *L.G.* 22 June, 1915. Promoted Flight Sergeant (Fitter-engines) on 1 December, 1916 and was Chief Mechanic (Fitter AE) in 1918 RAF Muster Roll.

★ 547. C. R. MILLS

A recruit 24 January, 1913. As 2AM, 2 Squadron, served in France from 12 August, 1914. A/WO (T) 1 February, 1918. Was A/Chief Master Mech (Tech) (Paid when necessary) in 1918 RAF Muster Roll.

★ 548. F. W. HALL

A recruit 24 January, 1913. As 2AM, 2 Squadron, served in France from 13 August, 1914. Discharged under *K.R.* 392 (xvi) 'Sick' 11 December 1917, aged 27 years 11 months, when a Flight Sergeant. Silver War Badge No. 288067 issued.

★ 549. A. A. HOBBS

A recruit 24 January, 1913. As 2AM, 2 Squadron, earned 1914 Star and bar in France from 12 August, 1914. Promoted Flight Sergeant (Fitter general) 1 February, 1917 and was Chief Mech in 1918 RAF Muster Roll.

550. E. J. HARRISON

A recruit 23 January, 1913. As 2AM in Aircraft Park, served in France from 16 August, 1914. Promoted Sgt (Coppersmith) 1 July, 1917. Forfeited 1914 Star under *K.R.* 392 (xiii) 'Having been discharged with ignominy' when Sergeant Mechanic RAF.

★ 551. A. V. SNITCH

A recruit 24 January, 1913. As 1AM with RFC HQ served in France from 12 August, 1914. Promoted Flight Sergeant (Inst. Repr) 18 October, 1917 and was Chief Mech in 1918 RAF Muster Roll.

★ 552. W. E. MOODY

A recruit on 24 January, 1913. As 1AM, 2 Squadron, served in France from 12 August, 1914. Promoted Corporal (Fitter general) on 1 February, 1918 and was Cpl Mech in 1918 RAF Muster Roll.

★ 553. F. H. BEER

A recruit 27 January, 1913. As 1AM, 2 Squadron, served in France from 12 August, 1914. Awarded French Médaille Militaire 6 November, 1915. Commissioned Lieutenant 12 March, 1917 and promoted Captain 22 January, 1918. (see 555)

★ 554. J. J. DUFFEY

A recruit 27 January, 1913. As 1AM, 2 Squadron, served in France from 12 August, 1914. Promoted A/SM (T) on 1 March, 1918 and was mentioned in despatches on 13 March, 1918 'For valuable services in the War.' (*i.e.* U.K.) and again on 14 June, 1918 'For service at Home,' and next day in the *Times* 'B' List. A/Chief Master Mechanic (Paid when necessary) in 1918 RAF Muster Roll.

555. (FIRST) L. C. SLANEY

A recruit 27 January 1913. Discharged 29 January 1913 under *K.R.* 392 (iii). On this occasion and perhaps because of the two day service, his number was not discounted but was re-used. The one and only time this has been noted.

555. (SECOND) A. A. J. BEER

A recruit on 27 January, 1913. See 553 above. As 1AM with the Aircraft Park served in France from 12 August, 1914. Mentioned in despatches 1 January, 1916 and awarded French Médaille Militaire as Sergeant in *L.G.* 24 February, 1916. Promoted Temp SM (T) on 1 October, 1917 and was Chief Master Mechanic (Technical) in 1918 RAF Muster Roll. Again mentioned in despatches, *L.G.* 28 October, 1921 this time for Mesopotamia and awarded a General Service Medal (clasp Iraq). Later awarded an Indian General Service Medal (clasp North West Frontier 1930/31). As Flight Sergeant after seemingly 20 years and nine months service, he was awarded an RAF L.S.&G.C. medal *w.e.f.* 26 October, 1933. It is not known if at some stage he lost the 33 months for less than 'V.G.' conduct, or perhaps, left the service then re-enlisted.

* 556. A. BARTER

A recruit 28 January, 1913. As 1AM, 4 Squadron, served in France from 10 September, 1914. Mentioned in despatches as Corporal in *L.G.* 22 June, 1915. Promoted T/SM (T) 1 September, 1917 and was Chief Master Mech (Tech) in 1918 RAF Muster Roll.

* 557. F. HARRIS

Enlisted 27 February, 1904. As 2AM, 2 Squadron, earned 1914 Star and bar in France from 13 August, 1914. Promoted Sergeant (Fitter AE) 1 March, 1918 and retained that rank and trade in 1918 RAF Muster Roll. He was awarded a General Service Medal (clasp Kurdistan) as Flight Sergeant. Certainly he had long service but perhaps the fact that he was only an Air Mechanic 2nd class after 10 years service in 1914 explains why no trace of an award of an RAF L.S.&G.C. medal has been found. Group in a private collection, 1914 Star and bar (2AM), British War Medal and Victory (2AM RFC) General Service Medal (Kurdistan Flight Sergeant).

* 558. ARTHUR GEORGE ALCOCK

Enlisted 4 March, 1902. Formerly 10696 Sapper (Balloonist and Engine Driver) No. 1 Company, Balloon School RE on mobilisation of the Air Battalion in 1911. An RFC Reservist who re-joined 5 August, 1914. As 1AM, with the Aircraft Park served in France from 16 August, 1914. Promoted Flight Sergeant (Fitter-millwright) on 1 March, 1918, he was Chief Mechanic (Millwright) in 1918 RAF Muster Roll. Awarded RAF

M.S.M. in King's Birthday Honours *L.G.* 3 June, 1919 'for service in France' as Flight Sergeant. Originally from Wood Green, North London.

★ 559. W. G. BLACK

Enlisted 7 March, 1907. An RFC Reservist who re-joined 5 August, 1914. As 1AM with the Aircraft Park served in France from 16 August, 1914. Promoted Corporal (Sailmaker) on 1 September, 1915 and was Corporal (Fabric Worker) on the 1918 RAF Muster Roll.

560. G. F. COOLING

Enlisted 30 October, 1902. Formerly 11824 Sapper (Balloonist) he was shown on the July, 1910, RE Balloon Company Roll as 'a Dismounted, Reservist. No. 2 Company.' His RFC rank of 1AM (Rigger Aero) is shown as being gained on 1 January, 1913 and it did not change throughout the war. As an RFC Reservist he re-joined on 5 August, 1914 and 1AM with Aircraft Park. Proceeded overseas on 3 April, 1915 and earned 1914/15 Star trio. Wounded 23 September, 1918. (see also No. 302).

★ 561. W. CHITTENDEN

Enlisted 13 July, 1903. Formerly 12844 Sapper (Blacksmith) RE. Shown on No. 1 Balloon Company Roll of July 1910 as 'Dismounted Reservist.' As an RFC Reservist he re-joined 5 August, 1914 and as 1AM with the Aircraft Park served in France from 16 August, 1914. Promoted Flight Sergeant (Blacksmith) 1 November, 1916 and was Chief Mech (Blacksmith) in 1918 RAF Muster Roll.

★ 562. G. DENYER

An RFC Reservist, rejoined 5 August, 1914. As 1AM with Aircraft Park, served in France from 16 August, 1914. Discharged 10 March, 1917 'On Termination of Engagement.'

★ 563. J. GRUNDY

Enlisted 2 July, 1903. An RFC Reservist who re-joined 5 August, 1914. As 1AM with Aircraft Park served in France from 16 August, 1914. Promoted Flight Sergeant (Fitter general) 1 November, 1917 and was Chief Mechanic in 1918 RAF Muster Roll.

★ 564. E. G. GRAHAM

Enlisted 1 January, 1906. An RFC Reservist who re-joined 5 August, 1914. As 1AM with the Aircraft Park served in France from 16 August, 1914. Promoted Flight Sergeant (Painter) 1 April, 1917 and was Chief Mechanic in 1918 RAF Muster Roll.

★ 565. JOSEPH JAMES LAKE

Enlisted 29 March, 1904. An RFC Reservist who re-joined 5 August, 1914. As 1AM with the Aircraft Park served in France from 16 August, 1914. Promoted Flight Sergeant (Fitter general) 1 November, 1917. Was Chief Mechanic in 1918 RAF Muster Roll. Awaded RAF M.S.M. in the King's Birthday Honours *L.G.* 3 June, 1919 'for services in Egypt.' Originally from Upper Tooting, London SW.

★ 566. D. B. McFARLANE

Enlisted 28 June, 1899. An RFC Reservist who re-joined on 5 August, 1914. As 1AM with the Aircraft Park served in France from 16 August, 1914. Promoted Sergeant (Machinist) 1 February, 1917. Was mentioned in despatches in *L.G.* 7 December, 1917. Sergeant Mechanic in 1918 RAF Muster Roll.

567. W. A. TURNBULL

Enlisted 16 January, 1900. His rank of 1AM (Rigger Aero) in the 1918 RAF Muster Roll is shown as being gained on 1 January, 1913 and he retained it throughout the war. An RFC Reservist who re-joined 5 August, 1914 with the Aircraft Park. Proceeded overseas 3 April, 1915 and earned 1914/15 trio. (see also No. 302)

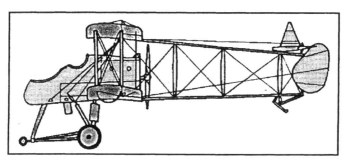

FE2A

* 568. F. A. C. VOISEY

Enlisted 12 April, 1904. Formerly 18443 Sapper (Balloonist and Blacksmith). 1 Balloon Company, Balloon School, RE in July, 1910. An RFC Reservist who re-joined 5 August, 1914. As 1AM with the Aircraft Park served in France from 16 August, 1914. Promoted Flight Sergeant (Storeman), 1 May, 1917 and was Flight Clerk in 1918 RAF Muster Roll. Was mentioned in despatches in *L.G.* 11 July 1919.

* 569. JOHN WALLS

Enlisted 25 January, 1909. Formerly 13614 Sapper (Fitter). 2 Balloon School RE on 12 January, 1911. An RFC Reservist who re-joined on 5 August, 1914. As 1AM with the Aircraft Park served in France from 16 August, 1914. Promoted A/WO (T) 1 December, 1917 and was A/Chief Master Mech (paid when necessary) in 1918 RAF Muster Roll. 'Mentioned' for services at the Air Ministry 22 January, 1919 and next day in the *Times* 'B' List. Awarded RAF L.S.&G.C. medal with effect from 6 August, 1929 as SM1 (seniority 1 April 1918) which indicates that taking into account his original date of enlistment and his date of re-

joining from the reserve, he must have been transferred to the reserve in late January, 1912. He was still listed in 1931 *A.F.L.* as a serving Warrant Officer.

* 570. F. F. CROCOMBE

A recruit on 29 January, 1913. As 2AM, 2 Squadron, served in France from 12 August, 1914. Promoted Flight Sergeant (Fitter Turner) 19 September, 1916. Was Chief Mechanic (Turner) in 1918 RAF Muster Roll. Awarded RAF L.S.&G.C. medal *w.e.f.* 29 January, 1931 as SM2.

* 571. H. LAWES

A recruit on 31 January, 1913. As 1AM, 4 Squadron, earned 1914 Star and bar in France from 12 August, 1914. Promoted Sergeant (Fitter, engines) 1 August, 1916. Was Sergeant Mechanic (Fitter AE) in 1918 RAF Muster Roll. Earned General Service Medal (clasp Kurdistan) as Acting Sergeant in 1924.

M.T. LINES

* 572. A. L. WILLIAMS

A recruit on 31 January, 1913. As 2AM, 4 Squadron, served in France from 9 September, 1914. Promoted Corporal (Driver MT) 1 June, 1917 a rank and trade he retained in 1918 RAF Muster Roll.

* 573. P. E. WRIGHTON

A recruit on 1 February, 1913. As 1AM with the Aircraft Park served in France from 16 August, 1914. Discharged as 'unfit' 23 January, 1915.

* 574. S. W. PYNE

A recruit 30 January, 1913. As 1AM 3 Squadron, earned 1914 Star and bar in France from 12 August, 1914. Reverted to Sergeant (Inst. Rep.) on 4 September, 1917 a rank and trade he retained in 1918 RAF Muster Roll.

575. J. W. GARNER

A recruit 28 January, 1913. Discharged 23 March, 1914 under *K.R.* 392 (ix) 'Unfitted for the duties of the Corps.'

* 576. T. C. A. OCKENDEN

A recruit 30 January, 1913. 1AM, 5 Squadron in France from 14 August, 1914. Promoted Corporal (Rigger Aero) 1 September, 1915 and retained that rank and trade in the 1918 RAF Muster Roll.

BRISTOL SCOUT D, FLOWN BY McCUDDEN, V.C.

577. W. PICKETT

A recruit 6 February, 1913. 2AM, 6 Squadron, in August, 1914. Served overseas from 24 November, 1915 earning 1914/15 Star trio. Promoted Sergeant (Driver MT) 1 May, 1917 and retained that rank and trade in 1918 RAF Muster Roll.

* 578. W. HAMMOND

A recruit on 20 January, 1913. As Corporal, 4 Squadron, served in France from 9 September, 1914. Promoted Temp SM (T) 1 November, 1916 and was Chief Master Mech (Tech) in 1918 RAF Muster Roll. 1914 Star and bar trio (AM1 RFC) in a private collection, with his brother's British War Medal and Victory Medal as a Private in the Liverpool Regt.

★ 579. THOMAS EWART GUTTERY

Born Brierley Hill, Birmingham, 3 December, 1896. Served as a Boy in S/Staffs R. A recruit on 3 February 1913. A clear illustration of the path by which a fascination with both flight and engines led to the RFC is shown by the early career of T. E. Guttery who was to be drafted to No. 3 Squadron at Larkhill on Salisbury Plain. With the fortunate start of many hours in his uncle's engineering workshop in Cradley Heath, the next step on leaving school was his local engineering works. Inspired by the Blériot cross-channel flight in 1909 and by making flying models which were initially using twisted elastic as their motive power before he devised a relay system to lengthen the duration of the flight, Guttery and some friends actually made their own aeroplane. It did lack certain all too essential elements, an engine, housing for engine assembly and testing and not least, somewhere from which it could fly! The line of development was no cul de sac but an avenue to the RFC. Guttery had become totally convinced of the application in war of the flying machine. There were opportunities in the newly-established RFC for young men with his interests and experience and, after recruits' training, he was appointed as an air mechanic. As No. 3 Squadron was equipped with Nieuport, Deperdussin, Blériot and Bristol monoplanes and Avro and Bristol biplanes, he was not to lack for variety in engine maintenance work. (This quotation and the next come from Wing Commander Guttery's recollections as recorded by Mr. P. H. Liddell.) As 1AM, 5 Squadron, served in France from 14 August, 1914. So precipitate was the great retreat from Mons that it is recorded in Guttery's memoirs that two of

his officers landed and borrowed two cavalry horses to deliver more swiftly the intelligence they had learned but on return to their machine found it under shellfire and were fortunate in being able to take-off safely. It was intended, however ineffectually, to form a defensive laager of the transport vehicles around the parked aircraft if the squadron were to be in danger of being overtaken. Such a measure was taken but the anticipated night attack did not occur and in point of fact, the worst damage to the squadron's machines was done by torrential rain and high winds in mid-September as the Germans took their stand on the Aisne. Promoted Temp SM (T) 1 October 1916. Was Chief Master Mech (Tech) in 1918 RAF Muster Roll. Mentioned in despatches *L.G.* 14 June 1918 'For services in the war' (*i.e.* in UK), and the next day in the *Times* 'B' List. RAF L.S.&G.C. medal awarded *w.e.f.* 3 February 1931 when he was the 29th senior RAF Warrant Officer. Commissioned Flying Officer

FLYING OFFICER GUTTERY (*left*) LEAVING BUCKINGHAM PALACE IN 1932 AFTER BEING INVESTED WITH THE MB.E.

(CEO) 19 April 1932. M.B.E. in *L.G.* 3 June, 1932. In 1937 serving at RAF Reception Depot West Drayton. Flight Lieutenant 19 April 1938 No. 35002. Squadron Leader 1 March, 1940. Wing Commander 1 December 1941. Retired 12 April, 1950. The following obituary was published in *'Cross and Cockade,'* Vol. 9, No. 3, 1978:—

Wing Commander Thomas Ewart Guttery, M.B.E., C. Eng., A.F.R.Ae.S., died at his home at Pulloxhill near Bedford on June 1st, 1978 aged 82. He had enlisted as a 'Boy' with the South Staffordshire Regiment but transferred to the Royal Flying Corps on its formation in 1912 (*N.B.* Not so — see above.). He originally served with No. 3 Squadron but transferred with its 'C' Flight to form No. 5 Squadron. With that Squadron, he went to France in 1914 serving there until he returned to the UK for technical duties in connection with flying training. Whilst serving with 23 Wing at South Carlton, he devised modifications to the Sopwith Camel to produce two-seater dual control versions.

His post war service included time at Drigh Road in India and a tour of duty at the Apprentice School then at Cranwell. Various other postings during the 'twenties' saw him in a variety of roles connected with technical and flying training, repair and maintenance units and trade testing. In 1932 he was awarded the M.B.E. having by then been commissioned from the rank of WO1. During the Second World War he served on various staff appointments with Technical and Flying Training Commands and at the Ministry of Aircraft Production. His post war career included duties at the Air Ministry and he retired from the active list in 1950.

This did not sever his connection with the service as he was employed in a civilian capacity at the RAF Technical College and at HQ Bomber Command for a further eleven years finally retiring in 1961. He then joined the staff of the 'Shuttleworth Collection' as archivist, researcher and author of their publications. (These include a life of Richard Shuttleworth, the 'Guide' to the collection and various educational pamphlets on the workings of aero engines.)

His passing leaves a sad gap in the ranks at 'Old Warden;' he was most instructive and entertaining with his tales of early service life. He was always ready to assist all with their research, from school children simply wanting lists of collection aircraft to serious researchers delving into the histories of service units and their equipment.

(R. W. Elliot, Shuttleworth Collection Librarian)

★ 580. CYRIL ERNEST BUTCHERS

A recruit 4 February 1913. As 2AM, 4 Squadron, earned 1914 Star and bar in France from 12 August, 1914. Accidentally killed 13 May 1916, 33 Squadron at Bramham Moor, Beverley, Yorkshire. Born 1895, son of James and Mary Priscilla Butchers, Bishopsworth, Bristol. Buried Fulford Water Burial Ground, York (Row H, Group 1).

★ 581. H. F. BOOTH

A recruit 6 February 1913. As 2AM with RFC HQ served in France from 12 August 1914. Promoted Sergeant (Driver MT) 1 October 1917 and retained this rank and trade in 1918 RAF Muster Roll.

★ 582. O. T. V. BOWYER

A recruit on 1 February 1913. As 1AM, 3 Squadron, served in France from 13 August 1914. In January 1915 was at the La Rhone works near Paris with Sgt Dunn (1372). He was accidentally killed 12 March 1915 when a Corporal in a bomb explosion at Mervill Aerodrome (see also Nos. 194, 534, 589, 872 and 1192). Buried Chocques Military Cemetery (I,A,41). Single 1914 Star sold in 1990 for £60.

583. H. S. CROWHURST

A recruit 6 February 1913. Was a Sergeant in 7 Squadron in August 1914. Served overseas from 2 April 1915, earning 1914/15 trio when he was an observer/gunner still with 7 Squadron. Discharged 'sick' 24 November 1917 aged 31 years and 4 months. Silver War Badge No. 276346 issued.

★ 584. W. V. BRITTAIN

A recruit on 4 February 1913. As 1AM, 5 Squadron, earned 1914 Star and bar in France from 14 August 1914. Promoted Temp SM (T) 1 September 1917. Was Chief Master Mech (Tech) in 1918 RAF Muster Roll.

★ 585. L. F. FAGG

Enlisted 1 August, 1911 as No. 21748 into 57 Company Royal Engineers. As 1AM, 2 Squadron, served in France from 12 August, 1914 earning 1914 Star and bar. Was Flight Sergeant (Fitter general) on 1 January, 1918 and was Chief Mech (Fitter general) in 1918 RAF Muster Roll.

★ 586. W. C. IBBOTT

A recruit 1 February, 1913. As Corporal, 2 Squadron, served in France from 12 August, 1914. As Flight Sergeant was mentioned in despatches 1 January, 1916 with 8 Squadron. Promoted QMS then commissioned 2 Lieutenant 23 November, 1917.

★ 587. LESLIE WALTER WILMOT CASWELL

A recruit 6 February, 1913. As 1AM with the Aircraft Park served in France from 16 August, 1914. Promoted Flight Sergeant (Fitter-turner) 1 January 1917 and was Chief Mechanic (Turner) in 1918 RAF Muster Roll. Warrant Officer 1st Class 15 March, 1929. Awarded RAF L.S.&G.C. medal 6 February, 1931. Awarded 1935 Silver Jubilee Medal. In 1937 *A.F.L.* was serving at No. 1 School of Tech Training, Halton Camp, Aylesbury in No. 4 Apprentice Wing. 26th senior RAF Warrant Officer in March 1938 *A.F.L.* and 23rd senior in November, 1941, and 12th senior in October, 1944.

★ 588. W. FENNING

A recruit 5 February, 1913. As 2AM, 5 Squadron, served in France from 14 August, 1914. Promoted Flight Sgt (Fitter General) on 14 August, 1917 and was Chief Mech in 1918 RAF Muster Roll.

FE2B

★ 589. G. COOK

A recruit 7 February, 1913. As 2AM, 3 Squadron, served in France from 13 August, 1914. Killed when 1AM, 12 March, 1915, accidentally when loading bombs at Merville Aerodrome (see also Nos. 194, 534, 582, 872 and 1192). Buried Chocques Military Cemetery (I.A.30).

★ 590. V. J. THOMSON

Enlisted 5 June, 1909. As 2AM, 3 Squadron, served in France from 13 August, 1914. Promoted Flight Sergeant (Driver MT) 1 May, 1917 and was Chief Mechanic in 1918 RAF Muster Roll.

★ 591. W. J. L. WILLIAMS

A recruit 7 February, 1913. As 1AM, 3 Squadron, served in France from 12 August, 1914. Promoted Sergeant (Fitter general) 1 August, 1916 and was mentioned in despatches *L.G.* 24 February, 1917. Listed in the *Times* 'B' Press Release of 27 March, 1917. Sergeant Mechanic in 1918 RAF Muster Roll.

★ 592. E. A. SMITH

A recruit on 8 February, 1913. As 1AM, 4 Squadron, earned 1914 Star. Promoted Flight Sergeant 1 May, 1916. Awarded Royal Aero Club Aviators' Certificate No. 3438 of 2 August, 1916. Was Chief Mechanic (Pilot) in 1918 RAF Muster Roll.

★ 593. D. McINTYRE

A recruit 6 February, 1913. As 1AM, 5 Squadron, earned 1914 Star and bar in France from 14 August, 1914. Awarded French Médaille Militaire for Gallantry as 1AM in *L.G.* 9 November, 1914. Promoted Acting WO (T) 1 April, 1917 and was C.M.M. (T) in 1918 RAF Muster Roll.

★ 594. A. TURNER (NICKNAMED 'BATCHY')

A recruit on 10 February, 1913. After recruit training at Farnborough, he was posted to No. 3 Squadron at Lark Hill, Salisbury Plain. As 1AM with the Aircraft Park served in France from 16 August, 1914. Promoted Flight Sergeant (Carpenter) 1 October, 1917 and was Chief Mech in 1918 RAF Muster Roll. See *'The Forgotten Ones.'*

595. J. LIGHTFOOT

A recruit 4 February, 1913. Discharged 'Sick' 26 July, 1917 under *K.R.* 392 (xvi). Silver War Badge No. RFC 124136 issued. No overseas service.

★ 596. ROBERT MORTIMER ADAMS

Born Aberdeen 29 September, 1890. A recruit 11 February, 1913. As 2AM, 3 Squadron, earned 1914 Star and bar from 12 August, 1914. Promoted Flight Sergeant 1 April, 1916. Royal Aero Club Aviators' Certificate No. 3172 on 1 July, 1916. Was Chief Mech (Pilot) in 1918 RAF Muster Roll. In 1976 his medal trio was sold by Dyas of Birmingham.

★ 597. W. J. WEEKS

A recruit on 8 February, 1913. Was posted from 6 Squadron to the Aircraft Park 12 August, 1914 and went to France on 16 August, 1914. Promoted Flight Sergeant (Fitter AE) 1 August, 1917 and was CM in 1918 RAF Muster Roll.

★ 598. WILLIAM ERNEST LEDNOR

A recruit 7 February, 1913. As 1AM, 4 Squadron, earned 1914 Star and bar in France from 9 September, 1914. Promoted Temp SM (Discip) 1 August, 1917 and was SM1 in 1918 RAF Muster Roll. RAF L.S.&G.C. medal awarded *w.e.f.* 7 February, 1931. His Star and bar only are known in a private collection.

★ 599. FREDERICK GEORGE MAYES

(See also Nos. 304 and 785; most likely this is the middle brother.) A recruit 10 February, 1913. As 1AM, 3 Squadron, earned 1914 Star and bar in France from 13 August, 1914. In October, 1915 he was serving as a Sergeant Observer at the same time as Sergeant McCudden (No. 892). Promoted Acting WO (T) 1 December, 1917 and was Acting CMM (T) (paid when necessary) in 1918 RAF Muster Roll. RAF L.S.&G.C. medal awarded 10 February, 1931. In 1931 *A.F.L.* shown as SM1 seiority 1 April, 1918.

★ 600. WILLIAM HENRY WARD

A recruit 13 February, 1913. As 2AM, 5 Squadron, served in France from 14 August, 1914. Died 4 September, 1915 serving at No. 1 Reserve Aircraft Depot, when a Corporal, aged 24. Son of William Henry and Frances Ann Ward, 39 Cross St., Erith. Buried, St. John the Baptist Church yard, Erith.

★ 601. A. F. DEVERILL

A recruit 13 February, 1913. As 1AM, 4 Squadron, served in France from 9 September, 1914. Promoted Flight Sergeant (Electrician) 21 September, 1916 and was Chief Mech in 1918 RAF Muster Roll.

★ 602. W. J. PRESS

A recruit 17 February, 1913. As 1AM, 3 Squadron, earned 1914 Star and bar in France from 13 August, 1914. Promoted Flight Sergeant (Discip) 1 January, 1916 and retained that rank in 1918 RAF Muster Roll.

★ 603. A. G. BERRY

A recruit 17 February, 1913. As 2AM, 4 Squadron, served in France from 12 August, 1914. Promoted Sergeant (Rigger Aero) 1 May, 1917. Sergeant (Mechanic) in 1918 RAF Muster Roll. Mentioned in despatches on 28 October, 1921 'for services in Mesopotamia' when he earned General Service Medal (clasp Iraq). Awarded RAF L.S.&G.C. medal *w.e.f.* 8 January, 1933 as Sergeant, so he 'lost' almost two years at some time — or left the service and re-joined.

★ 604. W. J. MORRIS

A recruit 17 February, 1913. As 2AM, 3 Squadron, served in France from 12 August, 1914. Promoted Corporal (Cook) 1 September, 1916 and retained that rank and trade in 1918 RAF Muster Roll.

* 605. G. FELSTEAD

Served originally as 11128, Sergeant in 3/Grenadier Guards. Transferred to RFC 9 January, 1913. Was a Sgt in 2 Squadron, in France from 12 August, 1914 and earned 1914 Star and bar. Mentioned in despatches *L.G.* 1 July, 1916 'for services with the Egyptian Expeditionary Force.' Awarded D.C.M. as Sergeant Major, 14 Squadron, in *L.G.* 27 July, 1916 'For consistent good work. His devotion to duty has been invaluable in promoting the efficiency of the squadrons.' Awarded Army M.S.M., again as S.M. in *L.G.* 11 November, 1916 'for valuable service with the Armies in the Field.' Commissioned 2 Lieutenant 19 December, 1916, and promoted Lieutenant 19 June, 1918. Was again mentioned in despatches for Egypt in *L.G.* 5 June, 1919 as 2 Lieutenant RAF. Promoted Flying Officer 20 July, 1920 and retired 6 April, 1921. See group photographs Nos. 2 and 3.

* 606. A. G. MOUNT

A recruit 17 February, 1913. As 2AM, 3 Squadron, served in France from 13 August, 1914. Promoted Flight Sergeant (Driver MT) 1 November, 1917 and was Chief Mechanic in 1918 RAF Muster Roll.

* 607. T. HYLAND

A recruit 15 February, 1913. As 2AM, 4 Squadron, served in France from 14 August, 1914. Awarded Army M.S.M. as a Corporal in 101 Squadron in *L.G.* 11 November, 1916 'For Valuable Services with the Armies in the Field.' Later known to be Sergeant. However, in 1918 RAF Muster Roll he is shown as Corporal Mech (Fitter general) having attained that rank only on 1 January, 1918.

* 608. R. A. ARNOLD

A recruit 17 February, 1913. As 1AM, 3 Squadron, served in France from 12 August, 1914. Reverted to Corporal (Fitter engines) 23 January 1917 and retained that rank and trade in 1918 RAF Muster Roll.

609. A. MOLYNEUX

A recruit 17 February, 1913. Discharged 22 April, 1913 under *K.R.* 392 (iii) 'Not likely to become an efficient soldier.'

* 610. P. A. RICH

A recruit 18 February, 1913. As 2AM, 3 Squadron, earned 1914 Star and bar in France from 13 August, 1914. Commissioned 2 Lieutenant 1 October, 1916.

* 611. W. G. MILNER

A recruit 18 February, 1913. As 1AM, 3 Squadron, served in France from 12 August, 1914. Promoted Sergeant (Electrician) 1 March, 1917 and retained that rank and trade in 1918 RAF Muster Roll.

* 612. P. D. WIGGETT

A recruit 17 February, 1913. As 1AM, 5 Squadron, served in France from 14 August, 1914. Promoted Sergeant (Draughtsman) 1 November, 1915 and retained that rank and trade in 1918 RAF Muster Roll.

* 613. J. W. KNOTT

A recruit 19 February, 1913. As 2AM, 4 Squadron, earned 1914 Star and bar in France from 12 August, 1914. Promoted Sergeant (Rigger-Aero) 1 December, 1916 and retained that rank and trade in 1918 RAF Muster Roll.

614. N. L. WINSTONE

A recruit 19 February, 1913. As 2AM discharged 6 March, 1913 under *K.R.* 392 (v), on payment of £5.

615. T. LEEDING

A recruit 20 February, 1913. Later 2AM, 3 Squadron, sentenced to six months hard labour 27 May, 1914 for forgery. Served his time in Winchester Prison then discharged from RFC.

* 616. W. E. ('BILL') WATSON

A recruit 21 February, 1913. As 2AM, 4 Squadron, served in France from 9 September, 1914. Promoted Acting Flight Sergeant (paid) (Fitter MT)

1 March 1918, and was CM in 1918 RAF Muster Roll. Born in Woking in the house next door to 1175 Butcher. Son of the village blacksmith and limped badly from a kick on the thigh by a horse in his childhood. He was a skilled designer and craftsman in wrought iron.

617. J. OLDHAM

A recruit 17 February, 1913. 2AM, 3 Squadron, in August, 1914. Served overseas from 2 April, 1915 earning 1914/15 trio. Was Sergeant Pilot with 57 Squadron before reverting, on 3 October, 1917 to Corporal (Fitter general). Retained that trade and rank in 1918 RAF Muster Roll.

★ 618. S. J. HARRIS

A recruit on 19 February, 1913. As 1AM, with the Aircraft Park served in France from 16 August, 1914. Reverted to Sergeant (Fitter general) 17 April, 1916, and retained that rank and trade in 1918 RAF Muster Roll.

619. SIDNEY GIBSON BOWLES

A recruit on 21 February, 1913. Was 1AM, 7 Squadron, in August, 1914. Served overseas from 3 April, 1915 and earned 1914/15 trio. Promoted Flight Sergeant (NCO Observer) 1 June, 1916. Was CM (Observer) in 1918 RAF Muster Roll. Awarded RAF L.S.&G.C. medal *w.e.f.* 21 February, 1931 as Flight Sergeant. Appointed WO1 18 March, 1936. In 1938 *A.F.L.* shown as supernumary at RAF Gosport. His group of five medals including that for the 1935 Jubilee are known in a private collection.

★ 620. S. TALBOT

A recruit on 24 February, 1913. As 1AM, 4 Squadron, earned 1914 Star and bar in France from 12 August, 1914. Injured in a road accident 21 November, 1915. Promoted Temp SM (D) 1 July, 1917 and was SM1 in 1918 RAF Muster Roll.

621. F. LEONARD

A recruit 17 February, 1913. As 2AM discharged 8 December, 1913, under K.R. ̋392 (ix) 'Unfitted for the duties of the Corps.'

★ 622. F. H. HARRISON

A recruit 25 February, 1913. As 1AM, 5 Squadron, served in France from 14 August, 1914. Permitted to change his name to 'Francis Harrison Harley' 16 February, 1916. Promoted Temp SM (T) 1 August, 1917 and was Chief Master Mechanic in 1918 RAF Muster Roll.

★ 623. R. E. WHARTON

A recruit 24 February, 1913. As 2AM, with the Aircraft Park served in France from 16 August, 1914. Wounded in May, 1915. Promoted Flight Sergeant (Instr. Rep.) 1 April, 1917 and was Chief Mech in 1918 RAF Muster Roll.

★ 624. F. C. LACEY

A recruit 27 February, 1913. As 2AM, with the Aircraft Park served in France from 16 August, 1914. Promoted Sergeant (Fitter AE) 1 June, 1917 and retained that rank and trade in 1918 RAF Muster Roll.

★ 625. A. F. SUNMAN

A recruit 1 March, 1913. As 1AM, with the Aircraft Park served in France from 16 August, 1914. Promoted Flight Sergeant (Draughtsman) 1 July, 1916 and was Chief Mechanic in 1918 RAF Muster Roll.

★ 626. REGINALD JAMES MOODY

A recruit, 1 March, 1913. As 1AM, 3 Squadron, served in France from 12 August, 1914. Reported missing 12 March, 1916 (observer). Awarded Royal Aero Club Aviators' Certificate No. 3889 on 27 November, 1916 as Flight Sergeant. Killed in Action flying with 2 Lt. E. E. Horn on 4 March, 1917 when a Flight Sergeant Pilot with 8 Squadron. Shot down by Lt. Werner Voss. Their aircraft, BE2d No. 6252, fell in flames at 10.30 a.m. He was then aged 32. Son of Charles and Ellen Moody of Church St, Odiham, Hants. Buried Warlincourt Halte Military Cemetery (VI B 10). See 'Cross and Cockade,' Vol. 6, No. 1, page 40 and Vol. 6, No. 3, page 103.

AN OFFICER AND SENIOR NCOS OF NO 56 SQUADRON AT LONDON COLNEY
IN 1916
(Left to right): UNKNOWN, 626 MOODY, 711 QUICKE, UNKNOWN, 1224
BASTABLE, 1364 NEVILL.

★ 627. C. V. YEA

A recruit, 5 March, 1913. As 2AM, with the Aircraft Park served in France from 16 August, 1914. Promoted Sergeant Carpenter, 1 August, 1917 and retained that rank and trade in 1918 RAF Muster Roll.

628. R. W. AMEY

A recruit, 3 March, 1913. Was Corporal, 7 Squadron, in August, 1914. Served overseas from 3 April, 1915 earning 1914/15 Star trio. An Observer 4 April, 1916. Promoted Temp SM (T) 16 September, 1917. Was Chief Master Mech in 1918 RAF Muster Roll. Mentioned in despatches *L.G.* 11 July, 1919 as Sergeant Major.

★ 629. H. CARRINGTON

A recruit, 4 March, 1913. As 1AM, 4 Squadron, earned 1914 Star and bar in France from 12 August, 1914. Promoted Temp SM (T) 1 April, 1917. Was Chief Master Mech in 1918 RAF Muster Roll. Awarded RAF M.S.M. in *L.G.* 3 June, 1918 (King's Birthday Honours) as T/SM 'for services in France.' He came originally from Norwich.

★ 630. WILLIAM SIDNEY ARTHUR STEWART

A recruit 5 March, 1913. As 1AM with the Aircraft Park served in France from 16 August, 1914. Promoted Temp SM (T) 1 October, 1917 and was CMM in 1918 RAF Muster Roll. Indian General Service Medal (clasp Afghanistan, North West Frontier 1919). Awarded RAF L.S.&G.C. medal *w.e.f.* 18 February, 1932 as Flight Sergeant, having 'lost' 11 months on the way. Promoted WO Class 1, 15 May, 1934. Awarded 1935 Silver Jubilee Medal. On 3 February, 1937 appointed Station WO RAF, Hawkinge, Folkstone, Kent. Awarded 1937 Coronation Medal.

★ 631. D. INGLIS

A recruit, 3 March, 1913. 1AM (Fitter) at Montrose in August, 1914, servicing the aircraft of Lt de Havilland. As 1AM, 6 Squadron, served in France from 7 October, 1914 and was CMM (Tech) in 1918 RAF Muster Roll.

★ 632. THOMAS WRIGHT CUMMINS

A recruit 12 March, 1913. As 2AM, 4 Squadron served in France from 12 August, 1914. At Hounslow, September, 1915, when 24 Squadron were formed. Served in France with them from February, 1916 and left 7 May, 1916 when at Bertangles. Promoted Temporary Sergeant Major (Technical) 1 November, 1916, and awarded Army Meritorious Service Medal as Sergeant (acting Sergeant Major) in *London Gazette* of 1 January, 1918 'For Valuable Services with the Armies in the Field.' He was CMM (Technical) in 1918 RAF Muster Roll. Originally from Bristol. Commissioned prior to the end of the war and served overseas as an officer. Released in 1920. His group of four medals is known in a private collection – 1914 trio (2AM and 2 Lieutenant RAF) and Army M.S.M. (A.S.M.). (See also Nos. 220 and 1174.)

★ 633. FREDERICK CHARLES ROOT

A recruit 12 March, 1913. As 2AM, with the Aircraft Park served in France from 16 August, 1914. Promoted Flight Sergeant (Disciplinarian) 7 November, 1917, retaining this rank in 1918 RAF Muster Roll. Awarded RAF Meritorious Service Medal in the *London Gazette* of 3 June, 1919 for services in France as Flight Sergeant (King's Birthday Honours). Awarded RAF L.S.&G.C. medal with effect from 12 March, 1931 still a Flight Sergeant. Originally from Earlfield, London S.W. Promoted

Warrant Officer 1st Class with effect from 25 January, 1935. Awarded 1935 Silver Jubilee Medal. Still serving in 1938 *A.F.L.* and was 80th Senior RAF Warrant Officer in November, 1941 *A.F.L.*

⋆ 634. ARTHUR EDWARD SMITH

A recruit, 15 March, 1913. As 1AM, No. 5 Squadron, served in France from 14 August, 1914, and earned 1914 Star and bar. Reverted to Sergeant (Fitter AE) 27 December, 1917 and retained that rank and trade in 1918 RAF Muster Roll. Served in North Russia in 1919 and awarded Air Force Medal in the *London Gazette* of 22 December, 1919. He was then posted as Flight Sergeant to the North West Frontier of India earning Indian General Service Medal (Afghanistan North West Frontier 1919). On 4 October, 1933 as Warrant Officer 2nd Class he was posted to No. 1 School of Technical Training at Halton Camp. Promoted to Warrant Officer Class 1 with effect from 6 April, 1935. Awarded 1935 Silver Jubilee Medal. Still serving there in 1938 *A.F.L.*

⋆ 635. P. M. VEITCH

A recruit, 17 March, 1913. As 1AM, No. 4 Squadron, served in France from 12 August, 1914. Mentioned in despatches as 1AM on 1st January, 1915 and again on 30 November, 1915. Promoted Sergeant (1st Class Pilot) 1 March, 1916. Awarded French Croix de Guerre as Sergeant in the *London Gazette* of 1 May, 1917. Was Sergeant Mechanic (Pilot) in 1918 RAF Muster Roll.

636. R. S. C. FARQUETT

A recruit on 15 March, 1913. As 2AM, was discharged 18 April, 1914 under *K.R.* 392 (ix) 'Unfitted for the duties of the Corps.'

⋆ 637. W. McCULLAGH

A recruit on 15 March, 1913. As 1AM, 4 Squadron, earned 1914 Star and bar in France from 12 August, 1914. Commissioned 2 Lieutenant 5 January, 1918.

⋆ 638. A. R. BOURNE

A recruit 26 March, 1913. As 2AM, 3 Squadron, served in France from 13 August, 1914. Promoted 1AM (Sailmaker) 1 November, 1916 and was Private 1st Class in 1918 RAF Muster Roll.

639. J. V. YATES

A recruit 27 March, 1913, and gained Army 2nd Class Flying Certificate 1 October, 1913. A pilot at Farnborough in 1913. As Sergeant, 3 Squadron, served in France from 12 August, 1914. Promoted Temp SM (T) 1 January, 1917 and was CMM (Tech) in 1918 RAF Muster Roll. See group photograph of pre-War RFC pilots under No. 7. Note he is not at this time wearing Sergeants tapes. See *'Cross and Cockade,'* Vol. 7, No. 3, page 135. (A 2 Lieutenant of this name was awarded Royal Aero Club Aviators' Certificate No. 4924 on 23 June, 1917.)

* 640. GEORGE LAING

Born 1884. Formerly 9562 Sergeant 1/Gordon Highlanders. Transferred to RFC 9 October, 1912. (Yet his number is amongst all those who were recruits in March, 1913. Perhaps their date of joining is their final acceptance and they were given their numbers on initial interview [?]) As Sergeant Major with the Aircraft Park served in France from 16 August, 1914. Lieutenant and Quarter Master 21 September, 1915. Major 1 November, 1916. Was Major (Tech) in 1918 (April) *A.F.L.* Mentioned in despatches. O.B.E. in 1919. Wing Commander in 1921 (November) *A.F.L.*, seniority 1 January 1921 on Stores List (Second most senior, behind Wing Commander Frank Howard Kirby, V.C., O.B.E., D.C.M., who won both his V.C. and his D.C.M. in the Boer War and was the Quarter Master of RFC in 1912). He was then serving at the Air Ministry (Department of Directorate of Equipment). Promoted Group Captain (E) 1 January, 1927. Awarded C.B.E. 1928 serving as Officer Commanding No. 1 Stores Depot Kidbrook. On 1 December, 1931 he was appointed Deputy Director in Directorate of Equipment at the Air Ministry. Awarded both the 1935 Jubilee and 1937 Coronation Medals. Air Officer Commanding 41 Group 1939-44 (Air Commodore). CB 1941. Air Vice Marshal 1944. KCB 1945. Sir George died 1 May, 1956.

* 641. A. PATERSON

A recruit 26 March, 1913. As 1AM, RFC HQ earned 1914 Star and bar in France from 12 August, 1914. As Sergeant was awarded Royal Aero Club Aviators' Certificate No. 1452 on 19 July, 1915. Ceased flying December, 1915 with 22 Squadron. Commissioned 2 Lieutenant 14 October, 1917.

* 642. B. R. ALLEN

A recruit 29 March, 1913. As 2AM, 5 Squadron, earned 1914 Star and bar from 14 August, 1914 in France. Promoted Temp SM (T) 1 November, 1917 and was CMM (Tech) in 1918 RAF Muster Roll. His 1914 Star and bar trio (1AM RFC on all three) sold 1986 by Beadle Medals.

643. C. E. LEXIUS-LAWSON

A recruit 27 March, 1913. In August, 1914 was 2AM. Promoted Coporal (Fitter AE) 1 January, 1918. No record of entitlement of either 1914 or 1914/15 Star.

* 644. G. LEGGATT

A recruit 28 March 1913. As 2AM, 3 Squadron, served in France from 13 August, 1914. Promoted Sergeant (Driver MT) 1 June, 1917 and retained that rank and trade in 1918 RAF Muster Roll.

* 645. H. P. CHICK

A recruit 31 March, 1913. As 2AM, 3 Squadron, served in France from 12 August, 1914. Promoted Flight Sergeant (Fitter general) 27 March 1917. Was Chief Mech in 1918 RAF Muster Roll.

646. B. J. BULPITT

A recruit 1 April, 1913. Died 19 January, 1914 at Alexandra Hospital, Cosham of peritonitis, when 2AM.

647. A. M. OSBORNE-ELLIS

A recruit 3 April, 1913. Discharged 16 August, 1913 under Article 1058 (i).

648. L. R. SYDENHAM

A recruit 1 April, 1913. 2AM, 6 Squadron, in August 1914. Earned 1914/15 Star trio. Sergeant (Driver MT) 1 October, 1916 and held this rank and trade in April 1918 RAF Muster Roll.

649. ERNEST N. HAXTON

A recruit on 1 April, 1913. No issue of 1914 or 1914/15 Star recorded. As a Sergeant passed out of CFS Farnborough with Sergeants McCudden (V.C., D.S.O., M.C., M.M., No. 892), Mottershead (V.C., D.C.M., No. 1396) and Pateman (later 2 Lieut). All four were to die in crashes. His Royal Aero Club Aviators' Certificate was No. 3223. He was killed in action on 10 October, 1916 when he came down in flames near Bapaume, a Flight Sergeant, No. 11 Squadron, aged 23. His observer was 3023 Cpl. B.G.F. Jeffs. Son of James G. Haxton and Margaret Haxton of 7, East Hadden Road, Dundee. Buried Douchy-les-Ayette British Cemetery (III. D. 6).

★ 650. ERNEST O. DRUDGE

Born 4 March, 1894. Enlisted 4 April, 1913 as a recruit. Served in France from 13 August, 1914 as 2AM, No. 2 Squadron. Later a photographer in 11 Squadron. Commissioned 2 Lieutenant 12 October, 1916 and mentioned in despatches 1 January, 1917. M.B.E. 1 January, 1919 as Captain RAF. In 1921 *A.F.L.* was Flight Lieutenant M.B.E. (Technical) at the School of Photography Farnborough. In 1931 *A.F.L.* shown as Observer Officer, qualified Photographer seniority 1 April, 1918 from 19 April, 1930 stationed at Basra, Iraq with 203 (Flying Boat) Squadron. In 1937 *A.F.L.* was shown as Flight Lieutenant M.B.E. (retired 4 March, 1934). Later Adjutant, RAF Station Tangmere (11, Fighter, Group) as Flight Lieutenant (Reserve of Air Force Officers). Served in WW2 in RAFVR from 1 September, 1939 to 17 March, 1947. Promoted to Wing Commander (No. 02123) 1 July, 1945 and last shown as retired in 1967 *A.F.L.*

★ 651. F. R. J. COOPER

Enlisted originally 13 June, 1906. Formerly No. 6812 3/Coldstream Guards. Transferred to RFC 23 November, 1912. As 1AM, served in France from 16 August, 1914 (earning 1914 Star and bar) with Aircraft Park. Promoted Sergeant (Rigger) 1 October, 1917. Was Sergeant Mechanic (Rigger/Aero) in 1918 RAF Muster Roll. Awarded RAF Meritorious Service Medal in the *L.G.* of 1 January, 1919. Originally from Bethnel Green. Entitled to India General Service Medal (clasp Waziristan, 1925). Awarded RAF L.S.&G.C. medal as Sergeant with effect from 13 June, 1924.

★ 652. A. T. MOTTRAM

Enlisted 30 December, 1905. Formerly 1117 Lance Corporal, Military Foot Police. Transferred to RFC 23 October, 1912. As Sergeant, served in France from 12 August, 1914 No. 2 Squadron earning 1914 Star and bar. Promoted Temporary Sergeant Major (Disciplinarian) 1 December, 1916 and was Sergeant Major 1st Class (Disciplinarian) in 1918 RAF Muster Roll. Awarded RAF L.S.&G.C. medal with effect from 30 December, 1923 as Sergeant Major 1st Class. See group photograph No. 2.

★ 653. F. J. JEFFREY

Enlisted 19 October, 1906. Formerly 16094 Lance/Corporal 2nd Balloon Company (Mounted) (in June 1910). Transferred to newly formed Air Battalion RE. Transferred to RFC 8 November, 1912. As 1AM, No. 3 Squadron, served in France from 13 August, 1914 earning 1914 Star and bar. Promoted Quarter Master Sergeant (Technical) 1 July, 1917 and was Master Mechanic in 1918 RAF Muster Roll. Awarded RAF L.S.&G.C. medal with effect from 19 October 1924 as SM2.

★ 654. THOMAS ARTHUR HANSON

Enlisted 17 October, 1910. Formerly 20650 Sapper, Air Bn, RE. Transferred to RFC 17 March, 1913. As 1AM, with 5 Squadron, earned 1914 Star and bar, serving in France from 14 August, 1914. Promoted Temp SM (D) 1 January, 1918. Was SM1 (Discip) in 1918 RAF Muster Roll. Awarded RAF L.S.&G.C. medal *w.e.f.* 17 October, 1928 as SM1. Still serving in 1931.

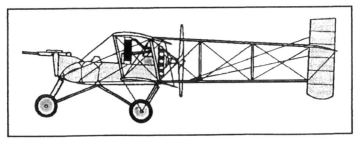

VOISIN 5

* 655. S. T. C. ROBERTS

A recruit, enlisted 9 April, 1913. As 1AM, 4 Squadron, served in France from 13 August, 1914. Commissioned 2 Lieutenant 24 January, 1918. Killed 30 July, 1918 when with 52 Squadron. Buried at Varennes, France.

* 656. W. RAWSTHORNE

A recruit, enlisted 3 April, 1913. As 1AM, with Aircraft Park served in France from 16 August, 1914. Promoted Corporal (Fitter-Engines) 1 October, 1917 and was Corporal Mechanic (Fitter Aero Engines) in 1918 RAF Muster Roll.

657. J. V. CORP

A recruit, enlisted 14 April, 1913. As 2AM, was discharged 23 April, 1914 under *K.R.* 392 (ix) 'Unfitted for the duties of the Corps.'

* 658. H. HIGGS

A recruit, enlisted 14 April, 1913. As 1AM, with 4 Squadron, served in France from 12 August, 1914. Promoted Temp SM (T) 1 February, 1917 and was Chief Master Mechanic (Technical) in 1918 RAF Muster Roll. Listed in the *Times* 'B' Press Release of 29 August, 1919.

* 659. C. H. CONDON

A recruit, enlisted directly into the Corps on 15 April, 1913. As 1AM 5 Squadron, served in France from 15 April, 1915, earning 1914/15 Star trio. Promoted Sergeant (Driver MT) 1 November, 1916. Was Sergeant Mechanic (Driver) in 1918 RAF Muster Roll. Awarded RAF M.S.M. for services in France in *L.G.* 3 June, 1919 (King's Birthday Honours) as Sergeant (acting Flight Sergeant) and RAF L.S.&G.C. medal *w.e.f.* 15 April, 1931 as Flight Sergeant.

* 660. A. HARRISON

A recruit, enlisted directly into RFC 11 April, 1913. As 2AM, 2 Squadron, served in France from 26 September, 1914. Promoted Corporal (Clerk-General) 1 December, 1916 and was Corporal Clerk in 1918 RAF Muster Roll. Awarded RAF L.S.&G.C. medal *w.e.f.* 11 April, 1931 as Sergeant. Still serving in 1935. His group of five medals are known in a private collection:—1914 Star and bar (660 2AM RFC), British War Medal and VM (660 Cpl RFC), Jubilee Medal 1935, RAF L.S.&G.C. Medal (660 Sgt RAF).

★ 661. H. H. Lane

A recruit enlisted directly into RFC on 16 April, 1913. As 2AM, 4 Squadron, served in France from 9 September, 1914. Promoted Flight Sergeant (Electrician) 1 May, 1917 and was Chief Mechanic (Electrician) in 1918 RAF Muster Roll.

★ 662. W. Simpson

A recruit, enlisted directly into RFC on 18 April, 1913. As 2AM, 4 Squadron, served in France from 12 September, 1914 earning 1914 Star and bar trio. Promoted Temp SM (D) 1 October, 1917 and was SM1 (Discip) in 1918 RAF Muster Roll. Awarded Army M.S.M. in *L.G.* 17 December, 1917 as Flight Sergeant. Originally from Sunderland.

663. F. J. Russell

A recruit, enlisted directly into RFC 17 April, 1913. Was 2AM, 6 Squadron, inAugust, 1914. Posted overseas 21 March, 1915, earning 1914/15 Star trio. Promoted Sergeant (Fitter Engines) 1 December, 1916 and was Sergeant Mechanic (Fitter AE) in 1918 RAF Muster Roll.

★ 664. G. R. Payne

A recruit, a direct entrant into RFC, 17 April, 1913. As 2AM with No. 2 Squadron served in France from 13 August, 1914. Promoted to Temporary Sergeant Major (Technical) 1 June, 1916 and was Chief Master Mechanic in 1918 RAF Muster Roll.

665. O. H. Price

A recruit a direct entrant into RFC, 21 April, 1913. As 1AM with No. 4 Squadron served in France from 12 August, 1914. He was discharged for misconduct on 19 February, 1915 and forfeited his 1914 Star. However, Butcher, in *'Skill and Devotion,'* says he was killed at Reading Aerodrome learning to fly. See photograph under No. 812.

666. S. L. YOUNG

A recruit into RFC 23 April, 1913. Discharged 9 July, 1913 under *K.R.* 392 (v) on payment of £10.

★ 667. A. E. CLACK

A recruit into RFC 23 April, 1913. As 2AM in No. 4 Squadron served in France from 12 August, 1914. Promoted Flight Sergeant (Rigger) 1 May, 1917 and was Chief Mechanic (Rigger Aero) in 1918 RAF Muster Roll.

★ 668. J. H. HAYWARD

A recruit, a direct entrant into RFC 23 April, 1913. As 2AM in No. 3 Squadron served in France from 13 August, 1914. Promoted to Temporary Sergeant Major (Technical) 1 February 1917 and was Chief Master Mechanic (Technical) in 1918 RAF Muster Roll.

669. S. C. HILLIER

A recruit, a direct entrant into RFC 23 April, 1913. As 2AM was discharged on 30 June, 1914 under *K.R.* 392 (xiv) at his own request, on payment.

670. R. HOLT

A recruit, a direct entrant into RFC 25 April, 1913. 2AM in August 1914. No record of issue of either 1914 or 1914/15 Stars. Promoted 1AM (Blacksmith) 27 January, 1918 and held this rank and trade in 1918 RAF Muster Roll.

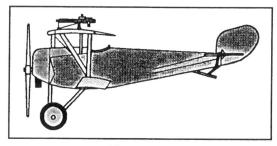

NIEUPORT II

★ 671. W. HARPER

A recruit, a direct entrant into RFC 22 April, 1913. As 1AM in No. 4 Squadron served in France from 12 August, 1914. Awarded Distinguished Conduct Medal as 1AM. In the *London Gazette* of 30 June, 1915 his citation read:— 'For gallant conduct and coolness when carrying out his duties under fire; also for the conspicuous thoroughness and efficiency for which his work has been noticeable.' Promoted Flight Sergeant (Fitter and Turner) 1 December, 1916 and was Chief Mechanic (Turner) in 1918 RAF Muster Roll.

★ 672. WILLIAM STUART DOBBIE

A recruit, a direct entrant into RFC on 22 April, 1913. As 2AM with 2 Squadron earned 1914 Star and bar in France from 12 August, 1914. As Corporal earned D.C.M. in *L.G.* 30 June, 1915:— 'For gallant conduct and coolness when carrying out his duties under fire; also for the conspicuous thoroughness and efficiency for which his work has been noticable.' Promoted Sergeant 1 December, 1916. Awarded Royal Aero Club Aviators' Certificate No. 5802 on 24 October, 1917, and classified as 1st class Pilot. Was Sergeant Mechanic (Pilot) in 1918 RAF Muster Roll.

673. A. E. VICKERY

A recruit, a direct entrant, into RFC 26 April, 1913. As 2AM was discharged 15 September, 1913, under *K.R.* 392 (ix) 'Unfitted for the duties of the Corps.'

★ 674. J. SMITH

Enlisted originally 3 September, 1908 and transferred into RFC in April, 1913. Formerly served as No. 9873 in Welsh Regiment. As 2AM served in 2 Squadron in France from 12 August, 1914 as servant to Major Lowcroft. Promoted 1AM (motor cyclist) 1 January, 1915 and was Private 1st Class (motor cyclist) in 1918 RAF Muster Roll (see also No. 302). Mentioned in despatches in *L.G.* 11 July 1919 as Leading Aircraftman.

675. L. LEWIS

Formerly served as 21549 Sapper RE. Original enlistment date not known. May have transferred to RFC as early as November, 1912. However, he was discharged 16 March, 1914 under *K.R.* 392 (xiv) on payment of £18 at his own request. (See also 676 and 677.)

676. J. W. WILLERTON

Formerly 31019 Driver, Army Service Corps, who enlisted originally 18 December, 1911. He was transferred to RFC 15 November, 1912 (see 675 and 677 – and note date of issue of RFC number, *i.e.* August 1913). 2AM with 2 Squadron in August, 1914. First posted overseas 24 July, 1915, earning 1914/15 Star trio. Promoted Corporal (Fitter Engines) 1 January, 1917. Was Corporal Mechanic (Fitter AE) in 1918 RAF Muster Roll.

* 677. T. A. BULLOCK

Formerly 9195 1st Bn, Somerset Light Infantry, enlisted 27 July, 1911. Transferred to RFC 18 November, 1912 (see 675 and 676). As 2AM in 5 Squadron, served in France from 14 August, 1914. Promoted 1AM (Driver M.T.) 1 April, 1915 and held this rank and trade in 1918 RAF Muster Roll (see 302). He was wounded 25 August, 1918 serving with 1st Brigade RAF.

* 678. C. A. W. JOHNSON

A recruit, a direct entrant into RFC, 25 April, 1913. As 2AM 4 Squadron earned 1914 Star and bar. He was discharged as unfit 17 June, 1915.

* 679. M. C. DUDDING

A recruit, a direct entrant into RFC 1 May, 1913. Was 1AM with 6 Squadron, until early August, 1914. Served in France from 16 August, 1914, with the Aircraft Park. Promoted Sergeant (Fitter, general) 1 September, 1916 and was Sergeant Mechanic (Fitter, general) in 1918 RAF Muster Roll.

680. R. B. FULLER

A recruit, a direct entrant into RFC 28 April, 1913. Discharged 9 June, 1913 under *K.R.* 392 (v).

* 681. J. A. LATHAEN

A recruit, a direct entrant into RFC 29 April, 1913. As 2AM 4 Squadron served in France from 12 August, 1914. The squadron Nominal Rolls for the period state 'accidentally shot dead at Ostend,' then 'Reported here 15 August, 1914.' However he was mentioned in despatches 30 April, 1916 and 15 June, 1916 as 1AM and was promoted Corporal (NCO Observer) 1 September, 1916. He was Corporal Mechanic (Observer) in 1918 RAF Muster Roll. Vide *RFC Communiqué No. 27, 17 January, 1916.* 'Flying in a BE2c of 15 Squadron piloted by 2 Lt. Wilson, drove off a Fokker attacking a reconnaissance aeroplane and exchanged fire with another which fired through the propeller.' 15 Squadron went to France late December, 1915.

682. W. HANNAH

Enlisted 9 December, 1903. Was 1AM in 6 Squadron in August, 1914. First served overseas on 2 April, 1915 earning 1914/15 Star trio. Reverted to Armourer Sergeant 7 May, 1917 and was Sergeant Mechanic (Armourer) in 1918 RAF Muster Roll. Served in South Russia until 9 July, 1919 with 47 Squadron and awarded Russian Medal of St. Stanislas. Awarded RAF L.S.&G.C. medal as Flight Sergeant *w.e.f.* 25 April, 1924 after 20 years four months service.

* 683. W. D. CORMACK

A recruit, a direct entrant into RFC on 28 April, 1913. As 2AM, 4 Squadron, earned 1914 Star and bar in France from 12 August, 1914. Promoted Corporal (Observer) 4 February, 1916. Promoted WO (Technical) 1 December, 1916 and was mentioned in despatches for Anti-Aircraft work in England in *L.G.* 20 December, 1917 as T/Sgt. Major. He was listed in the *Times* 'B' Press Release of 21 December, 1917. 'For services in the Air Defence of Great Britain.' Was Chief Master Mechanic in RAF Muster Roll (1918).

* 684. CHARLES MAYNARD

Born 5 January, 1893. A recruit, a direct entrant into RFC 5 May, 1913. As 2AM, 4 Squadron, served in France from 12 August, 1914. Mentioned in despatches as Sergeant *L.G.* 7 November, 1917, with 59 Squadron for 'salvaging an aeroplane from no mans land.' Promoted Flight Sergeant (Fitter engines) 1 June, 1917. Was Chief Mechanic (Fitter AE) in 1918

RAF Muster Roll. Appointed Sergeant Major 1st Class 20 August, 1930. Awarded RAF L.S.&G.C. medal *w.e.f.* 5 May, 1931. Awarded 1935 Silver Jubilee Medal. Commissioned Probationary Flying Officer (CEO) 23 August, 1937 and in October, 1937 was stationed at Andover (No. 2 Bomber Group HQ). Promoted Squadron Leader, 1 September, 1941 (No. 35140). Retired in February, 1947. Noted on retired list in 1965 *A.F.L.*

★ 685. J. LEWIS

A recruit, a direct entrant into RFC 2 May, 1913. As 1AM, 4 Squadron served in France from 12 August, 1914. Promoted Sergeant (Carpenter) 1 June, 1917 and held this rank and trade in 1918 RAF Muster Roll. Awarded India General Service Medal (clasp Afghanistan North West Frontier 1919) as Flight Sergeant.

686. G. N. COOMBS

A recruit, a direct entrant into RFC 29 April, 1913. Discharged 15 July, 1913 under *K.R.* 392 (v).

★ 687. STANLEY HERBERT GRAHAM

Born St. Mary's, Chatham, Kent, 29 September, 1892. Next of kin mother, home address 33 Henry St., Chatham. A recruit, a direct entrant into RFC 29 April, 1913, signing for four years and four on the reserve. Third class Certificate of Education in May, 1913 and second class in August the same year. As 2AM with 3 Squadron served in France from 12 August, 1914 earning 1914 Star and bar. Served in 15 Squadron in 'A' Flight, servicing RE8s. Promoted Flight Sergeant (Rigger) on 1 October, 1916, and served in France until 20 May, 1917. Was Chief Mechanic (Rigger, Aero) in RAF Muster Roll, April, 1918. Mentioned in the *Times* 'B' List of 29 August, 1919. Served in Egypt from December, 1919 to November, 1924, in Aden from December, 1928 to March, 1931, when again posted to Egypt. Awarded RAF L.S.&G.C. medal as SM1 *w.e.f.* 29 April, 1931. Awarded 1935 Silver Jubilee Medal. In December, 1937 *A.F.L.* is shown as Warrant Officer since 15 June, 1930 and was serving at RAF Reception Depot from 18 May, 1934. In March, 1938 *A.F.L.* was the 38th most senior RAF Warrant Officer. See *'Cross and Cockade,'* Volume 5, No. 1, Page 1A. Commissioned (No. 43493) 14 March 1940 Flight Lieutenant (T) 3 November, 1942. Retired Squadron Leader 3 April, 1946. Alive in 1970.

NO. 687 GRAHAM WITH AN RE8

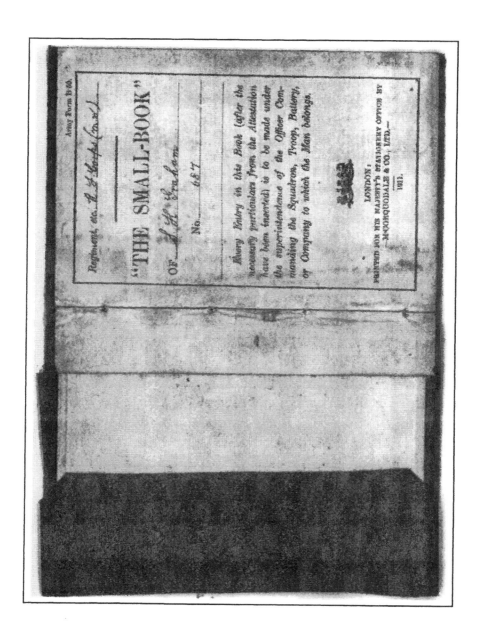

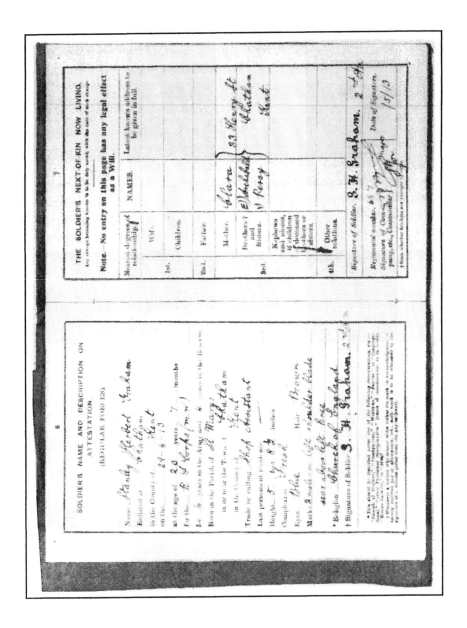

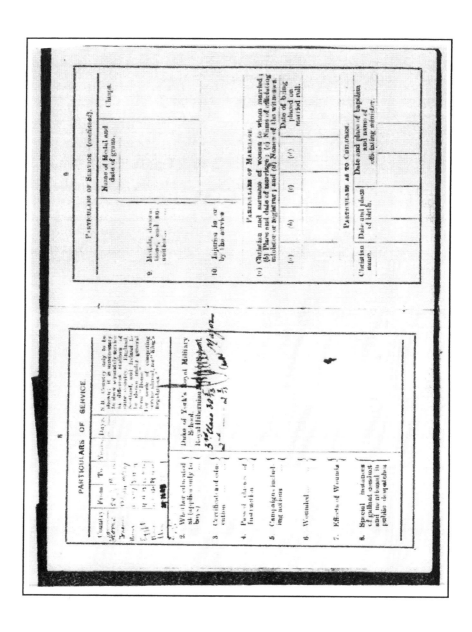

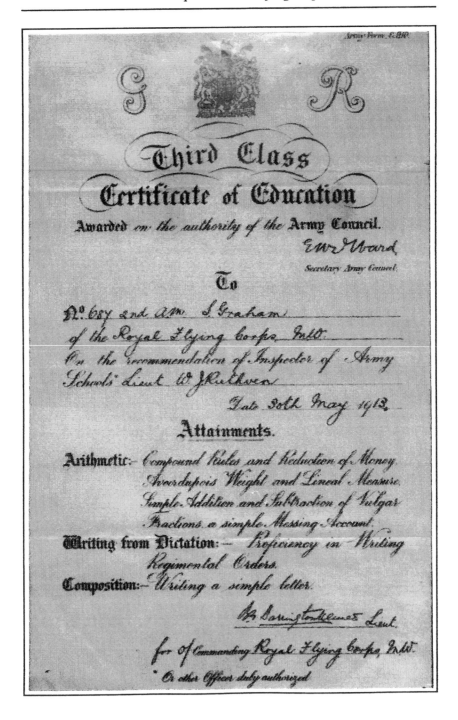

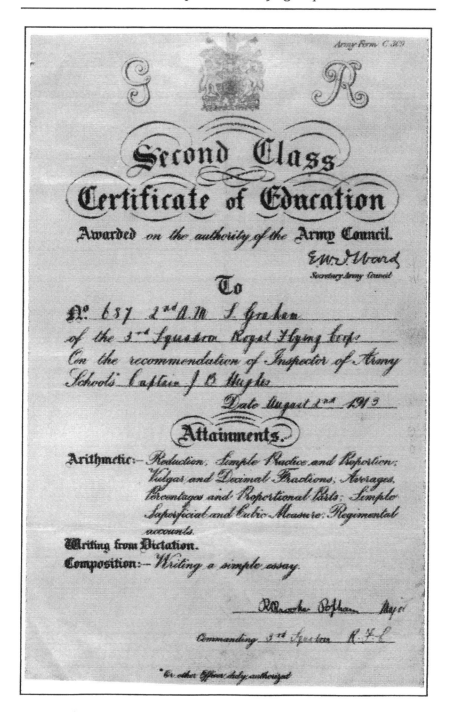

★ 688. T. W. GOODMAN

A recruit, a direct entrant into RFC 29 April, 1913. As 2AM with 4 Squadron served in France from 9 September, 1914. Promoted Corporal (Rigger) 1 October, 1917 and was Corporal Mech (Rigger, Aero) in April 1918 RAF Muster Roll.

★ 689. C. EDWARDS

A recruit, a direct entrant into RFC 5 May, 1913. As 2AM with 3 Squadron served in France from 12 August, 1914. Was 1AM (Fitter, engines) from 29 September, 1917 and retained that rank and trade in 1918 RAF Muster Roll. Awarded RAF L.S.&G.C. *w.e.f.* 14 November, 1931 as Leading Aircraftman, having 'lost' seven months towards his entitlement somewhere in his service. Only one other RAF L.S.&G.C. was awarded to a pre-war airman below the rank of Corporal up to this time. (See No. 74 LAC S. H. Whittaker.)

★ 690. G. CRAVEN

A recruit, a direct entrant into RFC on 5 May, 1913. As 2AM with 2 Squadron, served in France from 12 August, 1914 earning 1914 Star and bar trio. In RFC Communiqué No. 14 of 11 October, 1915 he is mentioned thus: '2nd Lieutenant Medlicott and Sergeant Craven of No. 2 Squadron, in a BE2c with Lewis gun, when testing the aeroplane at 10.00 AM, observed a hostile machine over La Bassée and engaged it. After 14 rounds from an automatic pistol had been fired at 130 yards range the hostile machine went off in an Easterly direction.' Promoted Temp SM (T) *w.e.f.* 1 January, 1917 and was Chief Master Mechanic in April, 1918 RAF Muster Roll.

★ 691. W. JINMAN

A recruit, a direct entrant into RFC 7 May, 1913. As 2AM 4 Squadron served in France from 12 August, 1914. Promoted Sergeant (Fitter, engines) *w.e.f.* 1 August, 1917 and was Sergeant Mechanic (Fitter AE) in April 1918 RAF Muster Roll.

692. G. D. LAURAINE

Formerly 19291, Private RAMC. Transferred to RFC 4 April, 1913. Re-transferred to No. 1 Company, RAMC 25 February, 1914.

★ 693. H. F. DIBDEN

A recruit, a direct entry into RFC 9 May, 1913. As 2AM, 4 Squadron served in France from 12 August, 1914. Promoted Sergeant (Fitter, general) 1 May, 1917 and retained that rank and trade in RAF Muster Roll in April, 1918.

★ 694. C. E. SKIPPEN

A recruit, a direct entrant into RFC 13 May, 1913. As 1AM served in France from 16 August, 1914 with the Aircraft Park. Promoted Flight Sergeant (Sailmaker) on 1 May, 1916 and was Flight Sergeant (Fabric Worker) in April, 1918 RAF Muster Roll.

★ 695. A. WOOLRIDGE

A recruit, a direct entrant into RFC on 14 May, 1913. As 2AM served in France from 12 August, 1914 with RFC HQ. Promoted 1AM (Batman) 1 January, 1916 and was Private (1st Class) (Batman) in April, 1918 RAF Muster Roll.

696. W. H. ELLARD

Formerly 13056 Lance Sergeant 1/Grenadier Guards. Transferred to RFC 14 December, 1912. In August, 1914 was 1AM. No entitlement to medals traced. Not shown in 1918 RAF Muster Roll. (See also Nos. 197 and 967.)

★ 697. A. H. CARE

A recruit, a direct entrant into RFC on 14 May, 1913. As 1AM with Aircraft Park, served in France from 16 August, 1914. Promoted Sergeant (Fitter, general) on 1 September, 1916. Mentioned in despatches in *L.G.* 20 December, 1917. Listed in the *Times* 'B' Press Release of 21 December, 1917 'For services in the Air Defence of Great Britain.' Was Sergeant Mechanic (Fitter, general) in April, 1918 RAF Muster Roll.

698. G. TOON

A recruit, a direct entrant into RFC 14 May, 1913. Discharged 31 May, 1913 under *K.R.* 392 (v) 'having claimed his discharge within three months of enlistment on payment of £10.'

699. C. A. MILLINGTON

A recruit, a direct entrant into RFC 14 May, 1913. Discharged 25 July, 1913 under *K.R.* 392 (v) 'having claimed his discharge within three months of enlistment on payment of £10.'

★ 700. R. H. TANNER

A recruit, a direct entrant into RFC 5 May, 1913. As 1AM 4 Squadron served in France from 12 August, 1914. Promoted Temp SM (D) 1 December, 1916 and joined 24 Squadron at Bertangles in France, 5 December, 1916 and left them 24 February, 1918 from Maligney. Was SM1 (Disciplinarian) in April, 1918 RAF Muster Roll. Address on discharge in 1920: 26 Viola St, Bootle, Liverpool.

★ 701. C. W. H. NEWBY

A recruit, a direct entrant into RFC 19 May, 1913. As 1AM with 3 Squadron served in France from 13 August, 1914 earning 1914 Star and bar trio. Reported to have been wounded by a bomb at St. Omer in December, 1914. Promoted Sergeant (Storeman) 25 October, 1916 and was Sergeant Clerk in April, 1918 RAF Muster Roll.

★ 702. H. C. JEFFRIES

Served in the Army prior to transferring to RFC. Originally enlisted 13 March, 1911. As 2AM, 4 Squadron, served in France from 12 August, 1914 earning 1914 Star and bar trio. Promoted 1AM (Fitter general) and retained that rank and trade in April, 1918 RAF Muster Roll (see No. 302).

★ 703. J. W. SAMPSON

Formerly 27156 Wheeler/Gunner RGA. Transferred to RFC 26 November, 1912. As Sergeant 4 Squadron served in France from 12 August, 1914. Accidentally killed in a road accident 30 May, 1915, when serving in No. 3 Wing, aged 24. He was the son of Thomas Jesse and Alice Maud Amelia Sampson of 42 Cragford Road, Holloway, London. Buried Lonquenesse (St. Omer) Cemetery (I.A.144).

⋆ 704. F. T. Swain

Formerly 11586 Private 2/Notts and Derby Regt. Transferred to RFC 11 December, 1912. As 2AM with 3 Squadron, served in France from 13 August, 1914 earning 1914 Star and bar trio. Reduced to Corporal (Storeman) 28 September, 1917 and was Corporal Clerk in April, 1918, RAF Muster Roll.

⋆ 705. A. Ledger

Formerly 20756 Shoeing Smith Corporal RFA. Transferred to RFC 20 December, 1912. A Sergeant in 4 Squadron he served on a Riggers course at the Central Flying School in early September, 1914 and then was posted to France on 9 September, 1914 and earned a 1914 Star and bar trio. He was recommended for, but not awarded a French Médaille Militaire in October, 1915. He was commissioned 2 Lieutenant 10 September, 1917. See group photograph No. 2. (See also No. 261.)

⋆ 706. W. A. C. Elsby

A recruit, a direct entrant into RFC 17 May, 1913. As 1AM with 4 Squadron, served in France from 9 September, 1914. Promoted Flight Sergeant (Carpenter) 1 May, 1917 and was Chief Mechanic (Carpenter) in April 1918 RAF Muster Roll. Awarded RAF L.S.&G.C. *w.e.f.* 17 May, 1931 as Flight Sergeant.

⋆ 707. M. Robertson

A recruit, a direct entrant into RFC 12 May, 1913. As 2AM with 3 Squadron served in France from 12 August, 1914. Promoted 1AM (Driver M.T.) *w.e.f.* 1 May, 1915 and retained that rank and trade in April 1918 RAF Muster Roll.

⋆ 708. W. Ryan

A recruit, a direct entrant into RFC 15 May, 1913. As 2AM with Airship Detachment earned 1914 Star and bar trio. Transferred to RNAS 18 October, 1914 as No. 702 Petty Officer Mechanic (E). Was 200702 Sergeant Mechanic (Blacksmith) in April, 1918 RAF Muster Roll.

★ 709. W. H. DYSON

A recruit, a direct entrant into RFC 20 May, 1913. As 1AM with 3 Squadron earned 1914 Star and bar trio in France from 12 August, 1914. Promoted Temp SM (T) from 1 October, 1916 and was Chief Mechanic (Technical) in April, 1918 RAF Muster Roll. Sergeant Major with 100 Squadron when discharged. Home address 16, Penny Farthing St., Salisbury.

★ 710. E. J. ROBSON

A recruit, a direct entrant into RFC 21 May, 1913. As Corporal with Aircraft Park served in France from 16 August, 1914. Promoted 1AM (Fitter, aero) 1 June, 1916 and retained that rank and trade in RAF Muster Roll (April, 1918). Possibly the 1AM Robson 55 Squadron on a bombing raid to Boue at 3.50 p.m. when he was wounded and shot down, 23 April, 1917, flying in DH4 No. A7410 with Captain A.T. Greg as pilot. Machine wrecked at Urvillers.

★ 711. SIDNEY HERBERT QUICKE

A recruit, a direct entrant into RFC 21 May, 1913. As 1AM, 4 Squadron, served in France from 12 August, 1914. Qualified as an observer 31 March, 1916, and obtained his Royal Aero Club Aviators' Certificate (No. 3890) on 27 November, 1916 as a Flight Sergeant (Observer). He died of wounds when a Flight Sergeant, of 16 Squadron, on 22 March, 1917. He was piloting a BE2e the previous day when attacked by hostile aircraft at 4.30 pm, and fell out of control. Buried in Broavy Communal Cemetery Extension (D12). See 'Cross and Cockade,' Vol. 6, No. 1, page 42 and photograph under No. 626.

★ 712. G. L. EVANS

A recruit, direct entrant into RFC 22 May, 1913. As 2AM, 5 Squadron, he served in France from 14 August, 1914. He reverted to Sergeant (Fitter general) on 3 July, 1917 and retained that rank and trade in April, 1918 RAF Muster Roll.

713. S. C. HOGG

A recruit, a direct entrant into RFC 21 May, 1913. Discharged 12 March, 1914 under *K.R.* 392 (ix) 'Unfitted for the duties of the corps.' However, an M.S.M. was awarded to 713 Sergeant Major S.C. Crawford and is shown in *L.G.* 3 June, 1919 (note same initials). No number 713 is shown in April 1918 RAF Muster Roll. No trace of an issue of either 1914 or 1914/15 Stars.

* 714. WILLIAM FREDERICK LEECH

A recruit, a direct entrant into RFC 27 May, 1913. As 1AM with 3 Squadron, served in France from 12 August, 1914. He was a Sergeant Observer in 9 Squadron in October, 1916. Mentioned by McCudden V.C. in *'Flying Fury.'* Commissioned 2 Lieutenant 27 October, 1916. Wounded 16 August, 1917 and died of those wounds 18 August, 1917. Appointed posthumously to the Distinguished Service Order in *L.G.* 26 September, 1917 as Temporary 2 Lieutenant. Details are found in *L.G.* 9 January, 1918:— 'For conspicuous gallantry and devotion to duty. He carried out a number of valuable reconnaissance flights under difficult conditions, bringing back information which was invariably correct. When the situation was obscure during an attack he correctly reported on it during the morning, in doing so was wounded in the arm. In spite of that he went out in the afternoon and was severely wounded.'

* 715. E. A. SMITH

A recruit, a direct entrant into RFC 27 May, 1913. As 1AM in the Aircraft Park, served in France from 16 August, 1914. Commissioned 2 Lieutenant, 13 March 1917.

* 716. WILLIAM MILLETT

Appears to have been a re-enlisted, time served soldier, or a very experienced tradesman. Enlisted into RFC 27 May, 1913 and posted directly to Flying Depot that day. Promoted 1AM the next day. As a Sergeant with RFC HQ earned 1914 Star and bar in France from 12 August, 1914. Commissioned Lieutenant 23 June, 1916 (Equipment Officer). Promoted Squadron Leader 20 July, 1920 and was Stores Officer No. 7 Group HQ at Andover from 15 September, 1921. Appointed Officer of the Order of the British Empire. Wing Commander O.B.E. from 1 July, 1928, in Stores Branch. Serving in Iraq Command as Wing Commander,

Stores Staff Duties from 7 October, 1930. Awarded 1935 Silver Jubilee Medal. With effect from 13 July, 1936 was Equipment Staff Officer, Bomber Command, Uxbridge and in the 1937 *Air Force List* was Group Captain (Equipment) *w.e.f.* 1 January, 1937. Shown as retired in 1944 *A.F.L.* See group photograph No. 2.

★ 717. L. F. BRIANT

A recruit, a direct entrant into RFC 24 May, 1913. As 2AM, 3 Squadron served in France from 12 August, 1914 earning 1914 Star and bar. Promoted Acting Flight Sergeant (paid) M.T. 1 December, 1917 and was Chief Mechanic (Driver) in April, 1918 RAF Muster Roll.

★ 718. F. J. HELLYER

A recruit, a direct entrant into RFC 29 May, 1913. As 2AM, 4 Squadron served in France from 12 August, 1914. As Flight Sergeant with 17 Squadron he was awarded a Distinguished Conduct Medal in *L.G.* 27 June 1916:— 'For conspicuous good work. He worked night and day to keep the aeroplanes in working order. The skill he displayed and the example he set enabled this detachment to carry out its duties with success.' Again as Flight Sergeant he was mentioned in despatches on 25 September, 1916 and in *L.G.* 11 November, 1916 was awarded an Army M.S.M. 'For Valuable Services with the Armies in the Field,' one of 23 awarded in the Gazette to RFC, and one of only 134 in total to the Corps. He reverted to Sergeant (1st Class Pilot) on 29 April, 1917 and was Sergeant Mechanic (Pilot) in April, 1918 RAF Muster Roll. (The D.C.M., M.S.M. and mention were all for services with the Egyptian Expeditionary Force).

★ 719. J. V. GASCOYNE

A recruit, a direct entrant into RFC 28 May, 1913. As 2AM, 3 Squadron earned a 1914 Star and bar trio in France from 12 August, 1914. Promoted Corporal (MT Driver) 1 September, 1915 and was Corporal Mechanic (Driver) in April, 1918, RAF Muster Roll.

★ 720. B. MORTER

A recruit, a direct entrant into RFC 28 May, 1913. Earned 1914 Star and bar with Airship Detachment as 2AM. Transferred to RNAS 18 October, 1914 as No. 685, 1AM. Leading Mechanic 1 March, 1916. Was 200685 Corporal (Disciplinarian) in April, 1918 RAF Muster Roll.

721. W. DALTON

A recruit, a direct entrant into RFC 28 May, 1913. No issue of 1914 or 1914/15 Star traced. Promoted Temp SM (D) 1 January, 1918 and was SM1 (Disciplinarian) in April, 1918 RAF Muster Roll.

722. C. G. MARCH

A recruit, a direct entrant into RFC 26 May, 1913. Discharged 31 July, 1913 under *K.R.* 392 (v) 'Having claimed his discharge within three months of enlistment.'

★ 723. H. A. GAMON

A recruit, a direct entrant into RFC 27 May, 1913. As 1AM, Aircraft Park, served in France from 16 August, 1914. Awarded Distinguished Conduct Medal, in *L.G.* 13 February, 1917 as Flight Sergeant:— 'For conspicuous gallantry and devotion to duty. He worked extremely long hours under arduous conditions, and has maintained throughout a high standard.' Promoted Temp SM (T) 1 June, 1917 and was Chief Master Mechanic (Technical) in April, 1918 RAF Muster Roll. He was awarded an Air Force Medal in *L.G.* 12 July, 1920 for service in Palestine, as Sergeant Major in 216 Squadron. Only 48 AFMs were awarded between 1920 and 1929 (see *British Gallantry Awards*, by P. E. Abbott and J. M. A. Tamplin) making this a very rare combination. Prior to this, and for services in WW1, only 102 AFMs had been awarded since its introduction in June, 1918.

★ 724. F. J. PHILLIPS

A recruit, a direct entrant into RFC 2 June, 1913. As 1AM, served in France with the Aircraft Park, from 16 August, 1914. Promoted Acting Flight Sergeant (paid) (Blacksmith) on 14 March, 1918, and was Chief Mechanic in April, 1918 RAF Muster Roll. He was listed in the *Times* 'B' Press Release of 29 August, 1919.

★ 725. HERBERT EDWARD PARFITT

A recruit, a direct entrant into RFC 27 May, 1913. As 2AM, 3 Squadron served in France from 13 August, 1914. However, three days later on the 16th whilst flying as a passenger in a BE8, serial No. 625, piloted by 2 Lieutenant E.W. Copeland Perry, he was burned to death in an accidental crash at Amiens. The pilot was also killed. Parfitt was aged 21 and was the son of William James and Clara Parfitt of 48 St. John's Hill Grove, Clapham Junction, London. He was a native of Croydon. He is buried in St. Acheul (French National) Cemetery, Amiens.

★ 726. W. J. BRIDGES

A recruit, a direct entrant into RFC 31 May, 1913. As 2AM with 4 Squadron, he served in France from 14 August, 1914. He reverted to Sergeant (Fitter, general) on 8 April, 1916 and was Sergeant Mechanic (Fitter, general) in April, 1918 RAF Muster Roll. He died of enteric 30 November, 1918 in Salonika.

★ 727. B. N. ASPREY

Enlisted in June, 1908. Formerly 8250 Corporal, 1st Grenadier Guards. Transferred to RFC 13 December, 1912. As a Corporal in 4 Squadron served in France from 14 August, 1914. He was recommended for a commission in September 1914 and was commissioned 2 Lieutenant West Yorks Regt. on 4 October, 1914. He was killed in action 23 February, 1915. His 1914 Star named to Corporal RFC is in the RAF museum collection at RAF Hendon.

★ 728. G. S. CHAPMAN

A recruit, a direct entrant into RFC 2 June, 1913. As 1AM, 4 Squadron served in France from 13 August, 1914. Mentioned by McCudden V.C. in *'Flying Fury'* as having driven him, three other ranks and Lieutenant Cruikshank from Boulogne to Amiens on the 14th. He was mentioned in despatches in *L.G.* 1 January, 1916 as a Corporal in 4 Squadron. In *RFC.*

MORANE PARASOL

Communiqué No. 37 of 20 May, 1916 he is again noted:— 'When flying as observer to Captain Adams in an F.E. of 23 Squadron, he attacked an Aviatik at 9000 feet, the hostile machine crashed into trees east of Adinfer Wood.' He was promoted A.WO (T) on 1 December, 1917 and was Acting Chief Master Mechanic (paid when necessary) in April, 1918 RAF Muster Roll.

★ 729. A. BARTON

A recruit, a direct entrant into RFC 6 June, 1913. As 2AM with RFC HQ earned 1914 Star and bar trio, in France from 12 August, 1914. Promoted 1AM (Driver M.T.) on 1 August, 1917 and retained that rank and trade in April, 1918 RAF Muster Roll.

★ 730. J. F. GRANT

A recruit, a direct entrant into RFC 6 June, 1913. As 2AM, 5 Squadron, served in France from 14 August, 1914. Promoted 1AM (Driver M.T.) on 1 February, 1916 and retained that rank and trade in April, 1918 RAF Muster Roll.

★ 731. A. G. SUTTON

A recruit, a direct entrant into RFC 7 June, 1913. As 2AM with RFC HQ served in France from 12 August, 1914. Promoted Corporal (Driver M.T.) 1 November, 1917 and retained that rank and trade in April, 1918 RAF Muster Roll. Awarded India General Service Medal (clasp Afghanistan North West Frontier 1919) as Corporal.

★ 732. G. P. SMITH

A recruit, a direct entrant into RFC 3 June, 1913. As 2AM, 2 Squadron served in France from 12 August, 1914. Promoted 1AM (Electrician) 2 February, 1915 and retained that rank and trade in April, 1918 RAF Muster Roll. His medals were returned to RAF Records 27 June, 1929.

★ 733. G. C. BURDETT

A recruit, a direct entrant into RFC 10 June, 1913. As 2AM, 3 Squadron, earned 1914 Star and bar trio in France from 13 August, 1914. Promoted Sergeant (Driver MT) 1 October, 1917 and was Sergeant Mechanic ~river) in April, 1918 RAF Muster Roll.

734. THOMAS FRANCIS BEERE

A recruit, a direct entrant into RFC 9 June, 1913. No trace of issue of 1914 or 1914/15 Stars found. As Sergeant (T/Sgt. Major) was mentioned in despatches in *L.G.* 7 December, 1917. He had already been commissioned 2 Lieutenant from 15 October, 1917. In November, 1921 *A.F.L.* he is shown as Flying Officer on Stores List *w.e.f.* 20 July, 1920, and was shown on the Non-effective list from 2 January, 1921. He retired on 13 December, 1922. Still shown on retired list in 1937.

735. A. J. BOOKER

A recruit, a direct entrant into RFC 11 June, 1913. No trace of issue of 1914 or 1914/15 Stars found. He was promoted Temp SM (T) 1 July, 1917, and was C.M.M. (Technical) in April, 1918 RAF Muster Roll. Noted in the *Times* 'B' Press Release 29 August, 1919.

★ 736. D. ABRAHAM

A recruit, a direct entrant into RFC 10 June, 1913. As 2AM 3 Squadron served in France from 12 August, 1914 when, with McCudden V.C., he was rigger on Lt Conran's machine. In September, 1914 flying as observer with Lt. Conran he unsuccessfully attempted to bomb a German kite balloon. He was promoted to Flight Sergeant (Carpenter) 1 September, 1917 and was Chief Mechanic (Carpenter) in April, 1918 RAF Muster Roll.

★ 737. JOHN GREENER

Born in 1894. A recruit, a direct entrant into RFC 11 June, 1913. As 2AM, 4 Squadron earned 1914 Star and bar trio in France from 12 August, 1914. Promoted Temp SM (T) 1 June, 1917 and was Chief Master Mechanic (Technical) in April, 1918 RAF Muster Roll. As Sergeant Major earned Indian General Service Medal (clasp Waziristan 1925) and was awarded RAF L.S.&G.C. as SM1 *w.e.f.* 11 June, 1931. Awarded both the 1935 Jubilee and 1937 Coronation Medals. Shown in the December, 1937 *A.F.L.* as Station Warrant Officer at RAF Kenley (11 Fighter Group) from 19 November 1935. In March, 1938 *A.F.L.* was the ninth senior RAF Warrant Officer. Recalled in WW2, commissioned and promoted to Flight Lieutenant. He was alive in 1989 and living in Blackpool.

738. G. F. THOMAS

A recruit, a direct entrant into RFC 16 June, 1913. No trace of issue of 1914 or 1914/15 Star found. Commissioned 2 Lieutenant 5 April, 1917.

★ 739. T. E. IRELAND

A recruit, a direct entrant into RFC 9 June, 1913. As 2AM, 4 Squadron, served in France from 12 August, 1914. Promoted Acting Corporal (paid) (Fitter, turner) 1 March, 1918 and was Corporal Mechanic (turner) in April, 1918 RAF Muster Roll.

★ 740. REGINALD JOHN CAMERON TANSLEY

A recruit, a direct entrant into RFC 13 June, 1913. As 2AM, 4 Squadron served in France from 12 August, 1914. As a Flight Sergeant he was posthumously mentioned in despatches in *L.G.* 21 July 1917. He had died of wounds received in an air raid when aged 23 on 27 February, 1917, serving with 47 Squadron in Salonika. He was the son of William Henry and Margaret Shaw Cameron Tansley of 19 Kingston Terrace, Kingston-on-Sea, Sussex. He is buried in Sarigol Military Cemetery, Greece (Row B. Grave 203).

★ 741. ERNEST GEORGE FENTON HALL

A recruit, a direct entrant into RFC 12 June, 1913. As 2AM, 5 Squadron, he served in France from 14 August, 1914. Accidentally shot in the stomach in September, 1915. He was an aerial photographer prior to his being commissioned 2 Lieutenant, 28 August, 1916. Mentioned in despatches in May, 1918. Noted in November, 1921 *A.F.L.* as Temp Flying Officer (General List) . As Lieutenant R.G.A. he was under instruction as a pilot at No. 6 Flying Training School, Ramsgate from September, 1921. His 1914 Star trio (2AM and 2nd Lieutenant) are in the Webb collection.

★ 742. M. W. WINTERBOTTOM

A recruit, a direct entrant into RFC 17 June, 1913. As 2AM, Airship Detachment earned a 1914 Star and bar. He transferred to the RNAS 18 October, 1914 as No. 689 1AM. Chief Petty Officer 3rd Class (Engineer) 1 August, 1916. He was No. 200689 Chief Mechanic (Winch driver and fitter) in April, 1918 RAF Muster Roll.

⋆ 743. E. Pyke

A recruit, a direct entrant into RFC 19 June, 1913. As 2AM in 4 Squadron, he earned a 1914 Star and bar, in France from 12 August, 1914. Promoted Sergeant (Driver MT) 1 March, 1917, he was a Sergeant Mechanic (Driver) in April, 1918 RAF Muster Roll.

⋆ 744. H. McQueen

A recruit, a direct entrant into RFC 12 June, 1913. As 2AM, 3 Squadron, served in France from 13 August, 1914. He was promoted SM (T) 1 August, 1917 and was Chief Master Mechanic (Technical) in April, 1918 RAF Muster Roll. Awarded a Royal Air Force M.S.M. in *L.G.* 1 January 1919 for services in France. He came from Leicester.

⋆ 745. J. B. Hartnett

A recruit, a direct entrant into RFC 19 June, 1913. As 1AM with the Aircraft Park he served in France from 16 August, 1914. He died in an aeroplane accident at Dover on 23 January, 1917 when serving as a Flight Sergeant in 49 Squadron. He is buried in St. James's Cemetery, Dover, Kent (Plot E, Row V, grave 24).

⋆ 746. J. Spallen

A recruit, a direct entrant into RFC 17 June, 1913. As 1AM, 2 Squadron, served in France from 13 August, 1914. Promoted Flight Sergeant (Electrician) 1 August, 1916, and was Chief Mechanic (Electrician) in April, 1918 RAF Muster Roll. His 1914 Star trio was bought some years ago from his son who lived in New Jersey, U.S.A. The Star is named to 1AM, the British War Medal and Victory medal to Flt. Sgt.

747. J. E. Taylor

A boy recruit, the first such direct entry into RFC, joining on 24 June, 1913. However, he was discharged 13 December, 1913, under *K.R.* 392 (xxv) 'His services no longer required,' *i.e.* a boy discharged for misconduct. The vagueness of the wording was probably considered less detrimental to the boys' future employment prospects than any more specific reason might be.

748. H. J. HARBEN

A boy recruit who enlisted directly into RFC 24 June, 1913. No further trace has been found. However, a Private P.J. Browning, 1/East Yorks Regt was killed in action 23 August, 1918 and is shown as being previously 748 Air Mechanic RFC. This number may, of course, be incorrect.

* 749. G. A. BALDWIN

A recruit, a direct entrant into RFC on 18 June, 1913. As 1AM, 4 Squadron he served in France from 12 August, 1914. Promoted Flight Sergeant (Carpenter) 1 May, 1917, and was Chief Mechanic (Carpenter) in April, 1918 RAF Muster Roll. Previously awarded the British Red Cross Society Medal for the Balkan Wars, for services as a Nursing Orderly in Unit III with the Turkish Army. The medal was presented to him by Queen Alexandra on 8 July, 1913. OC RFC (Military Wing) on 21 July, 1913, requested permission for him to wear the award in uniform. Refused 16 December, 1913. See also 772 Harris.

* 750. S. ABRAM

A recruit, a direct entrant into RFC on 21 June, 1913. As 1AM, 4 Squadron he served in France from 13 August, 1914. Reverted to Sergeant (Fitter engines) 6 April, 1917. He was Sergeant Mechanic (Fitter AE) in April, 1918 RAF Muster Roll.

* 751. FRED FARRER

Born in Milton Ernest in Bedfordshire on 9 April, 1882. Enlisted 18 December, 1906. Formerly an Armourer Staff Sergeant in Army Ordnance Corps (No. 350). Transferred to RFC May, 1913. He earned his Royal Aero Club Aviators' Certificate No. 685 in a Maurice Farman aircraft of the Central Flying School at Upavon and was then a Sergeant. Appointed '2nd class flyer' with effect from 17 December, 1913. He was a Sergeant in the Aircraft Park in France on 16 August, 1914. He was commissioned 2 Lieutenant 2 March, 1917. He was killed, still a 2 Lieutenant 28 November 1917. Photograph taken from *Army Ordnance Gazette*, Christmas 1913. See also group photograph No. 2. He had been an Armament Artificer in the AOC; after passing examinations this trade was recruited directly into the corps as Staff Sergeants. Their main task was the repair of artillery pieces.

★ 752. H. V. Page

Formerly 3331 'H' Company, RE. Transferred to RFC 23 January, 1913. He was a Sergeant with the Aircraft Park, in France from 16 August, 1914. Commissioned 2 Lieutenant 15 May, 1917. See group photograph No. 2.

★ 753. W. J. Southgate

Enlisted 17 March, 1905. Formerly 22658 Gunner RGA. Transferred to RFC 22 June, 1913. As 1AM, No. 2 Squadron earned 1914 Star and bar in France from 12 August, 1914. Promoted Temporary Sergeant Major (Technical) 1 March, 1916 and was Chief Master Mechanic in April, 1918 RAF Muster Roll. He was awarded RAF Meritorious Service Medal for services with 52 Squadron in France in *L.G.* 1 January, 1919, where he is shown as coming from Highgate, North London. He earned an Indian General Service Medal (clasp Mahsud 1919-20). Only appoximately 175 such clasps were awarded the RAF (27 November, 1919 to 7 May, 1920).

MAHSUD CAMPAIGN
THE FIRST PLANE EVER TO LAND IN WAZIRISTAN

★ 754. C. CALOW

A recruit, a direct entrant into RFC 23 June, 1913. As 1AM with the Aircraft Park served in France from 16 August, 1914. Promoted Sergeant (Motor Cyclist) 1 October, 1917 and retained that rank and trade in April, 1918 RAF Muster Roll.

755. WILLIAM GORDON BATES

Born 7 February 1898. A boy recruit, a direct entrant into RFC 20 June, 1913. Was still a Boy with the Aircraft Park in August, 1914. However, no trace of entitlement to 1914 or 1914/15 Star has been found. He was promoted Sergeant (Fitter engines) 1 June, 1917 and was Sergeant Mechanic (Fitter AE) in April 1918 RAF Muster Roll. He was awarded an RAF Meritorious Service Medal in the *L.G.* of 11 June, 1924, for services in Kurdistan during 1923 (only 18 RAF MSMs awarded for this theatre). Also entitled to General Service Medal (Kurdistan). Three RAF Squadrons were present:— 6, 30 and 63. During the operations two companies of 1/11th Sikhs were moved by air on 21 February, 1923. This was the first such occasion. He was awarded his RAF L.S.&G.C. medal as Sergeant Major 2nd Class *w.e.f.* 20 June, 1931, thus all his boy service was allowed to count. In the December, 1937 *A.F.L.* he is shown as Sergeant Major 1st Class *w.e.f.* 1 November, 1933 and from 21 March, 1936 was Station Warrant Officer, No. 9 Flying Training School, Hullavington, Chippenham. In March, 1938 *A.F.L.* was then the 82nd most senior RAF Warrant Officer. Commissioned (No. 44373) (T) 5 August, 1940. Flight Lieutenant 1 September, 1941. Retired 7 October, 1945. Last noted in 1964 *A.F.L.* Trio of medals sold at Spinks, December, 1990: General Service Medal (Kurdistan), RAF Meritorious Service Medal and RAF Long Service & Good Conduct Medal.

756. H. F. WALKER

Formerly 50506 'M' Battery RHA. Transferred to RFC 27 January, 1913. Was 2AM, 2 Squadron in August, 1914 but no entitlement to 1914 or 1914/15 Stars has been found. Possibly commissioned 2 Lieutenant 5 September, 1916.

757. A. W. GILLIAT

A boy recruit, a direct entrant into RFC 27 June, 1913. Was 2AM in August, 1914. No entitlement to 1914 or 1914/15 Stars has been found.

Promoted 1AM (Fitter general) 1 March, 1917 and retained that rank and trade in April, 1918 RAF Muster Roll.

* 758. W. E. ELLIOTT

A recruit, a direct entrant into RFC 30 June, 1913. As 1AM, Aircraft Park served in France from 16 August, 1914. Promoted Corporal (Shoemaker) 1 May, 1916, retaining this rank and trade in April, 1918 RAF Muster Roll. Awarded RAF L.S.&G.C. medal as Sergeant, with effect from 30 June, 1931.

* 759. A. H. REFFELL

A recruit, a direct entrant into RFC 30 June, 1913. As 2AM with RFC HQ served in France from 12 August, 1914. Awarded French Médaille Militaire in October, 1914. Awarded Royal Aero Club Aviators' Certificate No. 1259 on 17 May, 1915 as 1AM. Promoted Sergeant (1st class pilot) 1 May, 1916 and retained that rank and trade in April, 1918 RAF Muster Roll.

* 760. GEORGE FREDERICK PAICE

A recruit, formerly 25178 Training Battalion RE, enlisted 1913. Transferred to RFC 26 January, 1914. Awarded 1914 Star for service in France from 1 October, 1914. Promoted Flight Sergeant (Sailmaker) on 1 October, 1916 and was Flight Sergeant (Fabric Worker) in April, 1918 RAF Muster Roll. Awarded India General Service Medal (clasp Waziristan 1919-21) with 99 Squadron. Awarded RAF L.S.&G.C. medal, *w.e.f.* 30 June, 1931 as SM2. Awarded both the 1935 Jubilee and 1937 Coronation Medals. In March, 1938 *A.F.L.* is shown as a Warrant Officer *w.e.f.* 1 October, 1935 and as Station Warrant Officer, RAF Worthy Down, 2nd Bomber Group, from 28 November, 1935. Was the 99th Senior RAF Warrant Officer in November, 1941 *A.F.L.*

* 761. P. COOK

A recruit, a direct entrant into RFC 27 June, 1913. As 2AM, 3 Squadron served in France from 13 August, 1914. Promoted Flight Sergeant (Machinist) 1 December, 1916 and was Chief Mechanic (Machinist) in April, 1918 RAF Muster Roll. Awarded RAF L.S.&G.C. medal *w.e.f.* 27 June, 1931 as SM1. Commissioned Flying Officer (CEO) 23 August, 1937.

762. F. L. B. BURNS

A boy recruit, a direct entrant into RFC 23 June, 1913. In August, 1914 he was a Boy, serving in 2 Squadron. No entitlement to either 1914 or 1914/15 Stars has been found. Promoted 2AM (MT Driver) 26 November, 1916 but was downgraded to 3AM (Driver) in April, 1918 RAF Muster Roll.

763. H. B. RICHARDSON

A boy recruit, a direct entrant into RFC on 4 July, 1913. Served in Egypt from 15 November, 1914 and awarded 1914/15 Star trio. Promoted 1AM (Sailmaker) 1 September, 1917 and was Private 1 (Fabric Worker) on April, 1918 RAF Muster Roll.

★ 764. J. W. EDWARDS

Formerly No. 1710 Corporal in the 1/Black Watch, he transferred on probation to RFC 10 March, 1913. As a Corporal with the Aircraft Park served in France from 16 August, 1914. He was discharged 'sick' 24 July, 1915 when a Sergeant and awarded Silver War Badge No. 59278.

★ 765. W. A. BONE

A recruit, a direct entrant into RFC 2 July, 1913. As 2AM, 3 Squadron served in France from 13 August, 1914. Reverted to Corporal (Fitter Engines) 25 February, 1918 and was Cpl. Mech (Fitter AE) in April 1918 RAF Muster Roll.

A FLIGHT OF DH2 AIRCRAFT

273

* 766. LEONARD SPENCER

Born 3 January, 1889. A recruit, a direct entrant into RFC 3 July, 1913. As 1AM with the Aircraft Park served in France from 16 August, 1914. Was on a Fitters course at Central Flying School in September, 1914. Mentioned in despatches as Sergeant, *L.G.* 4 January, 1917. Promoted Temp SM (T) 1 October, 1917, was Chief Master Mechanic in April, 1918 RAF Muster Roll. Awarded RAF L.S.&G.C. medal as SM1, 3 July, 1931. Awarded 1935 Silver Jubilee Medal. In 1937 *A.F.L.* was Flying Officer (CEO) *w.e.f.* 23 August, 1937 and from 1 October 1937 was serving at No. 3 School of Technical Training, Manston. Appointed an Officer of the Order of the British Empire. Was Wing Commander (No. 35137) 1 September, 1942. Retired 4 November, 1947. Noted, still on retired list in 1967 *A.F.L.*

767. J. R. WRIGHT

A recruit, a direct entrant into RFC 7 July, 1913. As 2AM discharged 9 May, 1914 under *K.R.* 392 (ix) 'Unfitted for the duties of the Corps.' A 767 Sergeant Trumpeter C. J. Ellington is reported as killed in action in March 1917 but it is not felt that the number given was correct.

* 768. P. T. GINGELL

A recruit, a direct entrant into RFC 7 July, 1913. As 2AM, 3 Squadron earned 1914 Star and bar, serving in France from 12 August, 1914. Promoted Sergeant (Storeman) 1 June, 1917 and retained this rank and trade in April, 1918 RAF Muster Roll.

* 769. THOMAS FREDERICK STEPHENSON

A recruit, a direct entrant into RFC 7 July, 1913. As 2AM, 2 Squadron served in France from 12 August, 1914. Awarded Distinguished Conduct Medal in *L.G.* 4 March, 1918 as Sergeant:— 'For conspicuous gallantry and devotion to duty. While flying over the enemy's lines, he was attacked by twelve hostile scouts and engaged four of them, one of which he destroyed. He was then attacked by another of the enemy machines, and, though his observer had been wounded he succeeded in destroying it. His machine was then rendered almost uncontrollable by a shell, the right wing being almost shot off, but he succeeded in landing it in our front line wire. He has destroyed five hostile machines and shown splendid courage and determination.' As a Sergeant Pilot with 11 Squadron he is again reported as having crash landed, this time 31 October, 1917, possibly this is the date of the incident described above. On 20 November, 1917 he was reported missing and subsequently killed in action. He was then aged 23. His name is on the Arras Memorial of missing aircrew. He was the son of George Frederick and Annie Georgina Stephenson. He came originally from Peterboro.'

★ 770. F. C. HEATH

A recruit, a direct entrant into RFC 5 July, 1913. As 2AM, 3 Squadron served in France from 13 August, 1914. Promoted 1AM (Driver MT) 1 July, 1917 and retained that rank and trade in April 1918 RAF Muster Roll.

★ 771. T. MURNEY

A recruit, a direct entrant into RFC 4 July, 1913. As 2AM with the Aircraft Park, served in France from 16 August, 1914. Promoted Sergeant (Fitter general) 1 March, 1917 and was Sergeant Mechanic (Fitter general) in April, 1918 RAF Muster Roll.

★ 772. CHRISTIAN COLES HARRIS

A recruit, a direct entrant into RFC 4 July, 1913. As 2AM, 3 Squadron he served in France from 13 August, 1914. Died 1 November, 1914 aged 19. Son of Coles Lewis and Christine Harris of 88, Philbeach Gdns, Earls Court, London. He is buried in Béthune town Cemetey (III, A, 32). See also 749 Baldwin. Served in the British Red Cross Society as an Orderly in Unit I with the Montenegran Army. Medal presented 8 July, 1913. Permission to wear requested 21 July, and was refused 16 December, 1913.

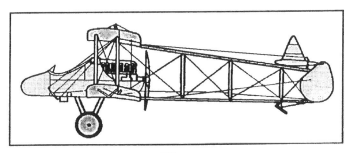

FE2C

773. A. R. THOMAS

A long service soldier joined RFC 7 July, 1913. Dischaged at his own request on payment of £10 on 29 September, 1913 under *K.R.* 392 (xiv) under article 1130 (i) of the pay warrant. This clause applied to men wishing to leave the Army before expiry of their period of enlistment.

774. HORACE BARNES

Born 16 June, 1898 (which made him an under age entrant). A recruit, a direct entrant into RFC 24 June, 1913. He was a 2AM in August, 1914. No entitlement to either 1914 or 1914/15 Stars have been traced. Promoted Sergeant (Rigger) 1 August, 1917. He was Sergeant Mechanic (Rigger aero) in April, 1918 RAF Muster Roll. Awarded RAF L.S.&G.C. medal *w.e.f.* 24 June, 1931 as a Flight Sergeant. Awarded 1935 Silver Jubilee Medal. He was commissioned Flying Officer, (CEO) 23 August, 1937, and from 30 August, 1937 was stationed at RAF Cranfield, No. 1 Bomber Group. In the 1946 *A.F.L.* he is shown as No. 35131 Wing Commander, seniority 1 January 1945. Retired 1 June, 1948. Still noted on retired list in 1978.

* 775. SAMUEL THOMAS KEMP

Formerly 5629 Lance Sergeant 11 Hussars and transferred to RFC 6 February, 1913. As Corporal, 2 Squadron served in France from 12 August, 1914. Mentioned in Despatches as Corporal 19 November, 1914 and as Sergeant Major 25 January, 1917. Commissioned 2 Lieutenant 28 August, 1917. In April, 1918 *A.F.L.* shown as 2 Lieutenant (Technical). Promoted Flying Officer 28 February, 1919. In the November 1921 *A.F.L.* he is shown as serving at No. 1 School of Technical Training (Boys) Halton as Technical F/O from 1 October, 1921. He retired 17 January, 1926.

* 776. THOMAS FAWDRY

Born 10 April, 1891, eldest son of the late A. Fawdry of Maidenhead. Educated at Abingdon. Enlisted into the Oxfordshire & Buckinghamshire L.I. in July, 1909. Bought himself out to join RFC 10 July, 1913. As a Corporal with RFC HQ served in France from 12 August, 1914, earning 1914 Star and bar. He was commissioned 2 Lieutenant Loyal North Lancaster Regt. 17 December, 1914 and was mentioned in despatches. Staff Captain RAF, Middle East, 1918 to 1919. Appointed a Member of the Order of the British Empire 3 June, 1919 (M.B.E.). Flight Lieutenant in 1920, serving then at Cairo, HQ Middle East Area. Promoted Squadron Leader, 1 July, 1924, he served on the Staff in Iraq from 1926 to 1928. He was promoted Wing Commander in 1931 after serving on Stores Staff Duties at RAF Cranwell and was again on the Staff of Middle East Command from 1933 to 1936, when he was awarded the O.B.E. He was next serving at No. 1 Equipment Depot, Kidbrooke, London S.E.3. He was promoted Group Captain in 1938. In the War of 1939-45 he was first on the Staff of Maintenance Command and in 1942 was promoted Air Commodore on the Staff of Bomber Command, where he was mentioned in despatches, and appointed to C.B.E. in 1944 and C.B. 1946 when he retired. He died 4 July, 1968 in Andover, Hampshire. Group of eight medals sold at Christies in 1990 for £572 consisted of C.B. (Military Division) silver gilt and enamel neck badge, C.B.E. (Military Division) 2nd Type, 1914 Star and bar (Cpl RFC), British War Medal and Victory Medal (Capt RAF), Defence and War Medals and 1935 Silver Jubilee Medal.

* 777. CHARLES WILLIAM GOODCHILD

A recruit, a direct entrant into the RFC 10 July, 1913. As 2AM, 3 Squadron served in France from 12 August, 1914. Mentioned in despatches as Flight Sergeant *L.G.* 25 January, 1917. Promoted Temp SM (D) 1 February, 1917 and was SM1 (Disciplinarian) in April, 1918 RAF Muster Roll. Listed in the *Times* 'B' Press Release 29 August, 1919. Appointed M.B.E. 3 June, 1929. Still serving as WO in February 1931 *A.F.L.* Commissioned and then promoted Flight Lieutenant 1 September, 1937. Since 31 March, 1936 in the Equipment Branch Middle East Depot, Aboukir, with No. 836. Promoted to Wing Commander in 1941. Last noted in 1944 *A.F.L.*

778. W. W. SINCLAIR

A boy recruit, a direct entrant into RFC 8 July, 1913. Still a Boy with 2 Squadron in August, 1914, no trace of entitlement to 1914 and 1914/15 Stars found. Promoted Sergeant (Rigger) 1 September 1917 and was Sergeant Mechanic (Rigger aero) in April, 1918 RAF Muster Roll.

779. E. F. GILL

A recruit, a direct entrant into RFC 14 July, 1913. No trace of entitlement to either 1914 or 1914/15 Stars found. Promoted Temp Flight Sergeant (paid) 1 January, 1918 and was Chief Mechanic (Draughtsman) in April, 1918 RAF Muster Roll.

* 780. GEORGE WALKER HEPPLE

A recruit, a direct entrant into RFC 14 June, 1913. As 2AM with Aircraft Park served in France from 16 August, 1914. Mentioned in despatches as Corporal in *L.G.* 15 June, 1916. Awarded Army M.S.M. in *L.G.* 11 November, 1916 'For Valuable Services with the Armies in the Field,' as a Sergeant. Promoted Flight Sergeant (Fitter, engines) 1 January, 1917 and was Chief Mechanic (Fitter AE) in April, 1918 RAF Muster Roll. As a Sergeant he was awarded an RAF M.S.M. in *L.G.* 28 October, 1921 for services in Mesopotamia but this subsequently cancelled in November 1921 as it was not considered appropriate that he should be awarded both an Army and a Royal Air Force M.S.M. Presumably as a consolation, in *L.G.* 10 Oc-

tober, 1922 he was again mentioned in despatches and was awarded a General Service Medal (clasp Iraq), for service there between 10 December, 1919 and 17 November, 1920 with one of the following RAF Squadrons: 6, 30, 55, 63, 84. In the King's Birthday Honours of 3 June, 1927 as Flight Sergeant he was awarded a British Empire Medal. Up until this award only two other 2nd type BEMs of the Military Division had been awarded. Awarded RAF L.S.&G.C. medal as Flight Sergeant *w.e.f.* 14 July, 1931. He received one of approximately 1,350 clasps to the RAF for North West Frontier 1930-31 for services between 23 April, 1930 and 22 March, 1931 with either 5, 11, 20, 27, 28, 39 or 60 Squadrons and in 1935 received the King's Jubilee Medal as Warrant Officer which appointment he had received on 15 May, 1934, when he was serving at RAF Abingdon. In the 1937 *A.F.L.* he was serving at RAF Dishforth, Thirsk with No. 4 Bomber Group. He served in WW2 so would be entitled to some 1939-45 medals. (However, he was not shown amongst the RAF Warrant Officers in the November, 1941 *A.F.L.* He was later recalled but discharged before October, 1944.) As can be seen in the photograph, his medals are extant, strangely mounted as worn with the B.E.M. last! They are in a private collection, being sold by Liverpool Coins and Medals in February, 1984 for in excess of £1000. See photograph under No. 812.

* 781. L. R. J. Halcro

A recruit, a direct entrant into RFC 14 July, 1913. As 2AM with 6 Squadron earned 1914 Star. Reverted to Sergeant (Clerk general) 29 November, 1917 and retained that rank and trade in April, 1918 RAF Muster Roll. Listed in the *Times* 'B' Press Release of 29 August, 1919.

782. E. F. Pointing

A boy entrant into the RE transferring to RFC 14 July, 1913. Was still a Boy with 2 Squadron in August, 1914. No trace of entitlement to either 1914 or 1914/15 Stars has been found. Promoted Sergeant (Rigger) 1 October, 1917 and was Sergeant Mechanic (Rigger aero) in April, 1918 RAF Muster Roll.

783. A. E. Cartland

A Boy at the Recruit Depot in August, 1914. Served overseas from 17 April, 1915 and entitled to 1914/15 Star trio.

784. S. V. Burdett

An RE Boy Recruit. Transferred to RFC 17 July, 1913. No trace of entitlement to either 1914 or 1914/15 Stars found. Promoted Acting Corporal (paid) (Fitter engines) 1 December, 1917 and was Corporal Mechanic (Fitter AE) in April, 1918 RAF Muster Roll.

785. H. D. Mayes

An RE Boy Recruit. Transferred to RFC 17 July, 1913. Was 2AM in August, 1914. Promoted 1AM (Rigger) 1 June, 1917 and was 1AM (Rigger aero) in April, 1918 RAF Muster Roll. Possibly the younger brother of numbers 304 and 599. No entitlement to Stars traced.

786. H. J. S. Leslie

A boy recruit, a direct entrant into RFC 17 July, 1913. Was 2AM in August, 1914. No entitlement to Stars traced. Promoted 1AM (Rigger) 1 May, 1917. Was 1AM (Rigger Aero) in April, 1918 RAF Muster Roll.

787. H. J. Phillips

An RE Boy Recruit. Transferred to RFC 18 July, 1913. Was 2AM in August, 1914. No entitlement to Stars traced. Promoted 1AM (Rigger) 1 June, 1917 and was 1AM (Rigger aero) in April, 1918 RAF Muster Roll.

★ 788. Ernest Cousins

A recruit, a direct entrant into RFC 16 July, 1913. As 2AM with Airship Detachment earned 1914 Star. Transferred to RNAS 18 October, 1914 as No. 683. Petty Officer 1 March, 1916. In April, 1918 RAF Muster Roll was No. 200683 Sergeant Mechanic (Rigger Airships). Awarded RAF L.S.&G.C. as SM2 *w.e.f.* 16 July, 1931.

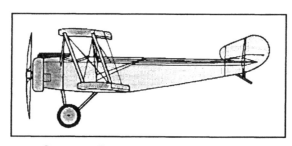

Sopwith One-and-a-Half Strutter

789. H. A. LYON

A recruit, a direct entrant into RFC 17 July, 1913. No trace of entitlement to 1914 or 1914/15 Stars found. Promoted Flight Sergeant (Instr. Rep.) 10 July, 1917 and was Chief Mechanic (Instr. Rep.) in April, 1918 RAF Muster Roll. Awarded RAF L.S.&G.C. medal SM2 *w.e.f.* 17 July, 1931.

★ 790. E. E. KING

A recruit, a direct entrant into RFC 17 July, 1913. As 2AM, 5 Squadron earned 1914 Star and bar in France from 13 August, 1914. Promoted Sergeant (Fitter general) 1 July, 1916 and was Sergeant Mechanic (Fitter general) in April, 1918 RAF Muster Roll. Awarded RAF L.S.&G.C. medal as Flight Sergeant *w.e.f.* 17 July, 1931.

★ 791. H. PRETTY

A recruit, a direct entrant into RFC 21 July, 1913. As 2AM with Aircraft Park served in France from 16 August, 1914. Promoted 1AM (Driver MT) 1 September, 1915 and retained this rank and trade in April, 1918 RAF Muster Roll.

★ 792. FREDERICK JAMES SMITH

A recruit, a direct entrant into RFC 19 July, 1913. As 2AM, 4 Squadron earned 1914 Star and bar in France from 9 September, 1914. Awarded Military Medal in *L.G.* 27 October, 1916 as Flight Sergeant Air Gunner. Promoted Temp SM (T) 1 February, 1918 and was Chief Master Mechanic (Technical) in April, 1918 RAF Muster Roll. Awarded RAF L.S.&G.C. medal as SM1 *w.e.f.* 19 July, 1931. Awarded both the 1935 Jubilee and 1937 Coronation Medals. In December, 1937 *A.F.L.* shown as WO serving from 23 February, 1932 at No. 3 Apprentice Wing, No. 1 School of Technical Training (Apprentices) Halton Camp, Aylesbury, Bucks. In March, 1938 *A.F.L.* was the eleventh senior RAF Warrant Officer, and in that of November, 1941 he was the fifth.

793. S. D. FRANCIS

Enlisted 4 January, 1911. Formerly 20908 Sapper 59 Company RE. Transferred to RFC 10 February 1913. No trace of entitlement to 1914 or 1914/15 Stars found. Promoted Flight Sergeant (Carpenter) 8 August, 1917 and was Chief Mechanic (Carpenter) in April, 1918 RAF Muster

Roll. Awarded RAF L.S.&G.C. medal as Flight Sergeant, *w.e.f.* 4 January, 1929.

* 794. H. MORRISON

Enlisted 19 April, 1911. Formerly 21496, Sapper, 59 Company RE. Transferred to RFC 10 February, 1913. As 1AM, 3 Squadron earned 1914 Star and bar in France from 12 August, 1914. Promoted to Sergeant (Sailmaker) 1 December, 1915 and was Sergeant (Fabric Worker) in April, 1918 RAF Muster Roll. Awarded Medal of Zeal with the ribbon of St. Stanilas in March, 1920 for services in South Russia. Awarded RAF L.S.&G.C. medal as Sergeant *w.e.f.* 19 April, 1929.

* 795. A GRANGE

A recruit, a direct entrant into RFC 21 July, 1913. As 2AM, 5 Squadron served in France from 14 August, 1914 earning 1914 Star and bar. Promoted 1AM (Fitter engines) 1 June, 1915 and retained that rank and trade in April, 1918 RAF Muster Roll.

* 796. W. HOLMES

A recruit, a direct entrant into RFC 22 July, 1913. As 2AM, 5 Squadron earned 1914 Star and bar in France from 14 August, 1914. Promoted Sergeant (Ftr Eng Er (MT)) 1 September, 1917, and was Sergeant Mechanic (Fitter MT) in April, 1918 RAF Muster Roll.

* 797. R. A. LEVY

A recruit, a direct entrant into RFC 24 July, 1913. As 2AM, 5 Squadron served in France from 13 August, 1914. Sergeant (Observer/Gunner) 7 Squadron, in 1915. Promoted Flight Sergeant (Painter) 1 July, 1916 and was Chief Mechanic (Painter) in April, 1918 RAF Muster Roll.

798. FRANK LAMDIN

A recruit, a direct entrant into RFC 26 July, 1913. Served overseas from 8 February, 1915 earning 1914/15 Star trio. Promoted Temp SM (D) 15 August, 1916 and mentioned in despatches in *L.G.* 24 February, 1917. Listed in the *Times* 'B' Press Releases 27 March, 1917. Awarded M.B.E. as SM1 *L.G.* 3 June, 1930 (King's Birthday Honours). Probationary Flying

Officer 5 January, 1931 (vide November, 1931 *A.F.L.*) Stores Branch. Not in 1938 *A.F.L.*

★ 799. CHARLES HAWKSWORTH TUTING

A recruit, a direct entrant into RFC 28 July, 1913. As 2AM, an officer's servant, with Aircraft Park served in France from 16 August, 1914. Promoted Sergeant (Driver MT) 1 May, 1916 and was Sergeant Mechanic (Driver) in April, 1918 RAF Muster Roll. Served in WW2. W.O. on 15 October, 1941. His group of five known as extant in a private collection: 1914 Star trio, Defence and War Medals.

800. C. G. BOORE

A recruit, a direct entrant into RFC 28 July, 1913. No trace of entitlement to 1914 or 1914/15 Stars found. Promoted Corporal (Motor Cyclist) 1 July, 1916 and retained that rank and trade in April, 1918 RAF Muster Roll.

★ 801. R. J. ROBINSON

A recruit, a direct entrant into RFC 26 July, 1913. As 2AM, 5 Squadron served in France from 14 August, 1914. Promoted 1AM (Fitter-turner) 18 September, 1916. Wounded 22 July, 1917. 1AM (Turner) in April, 1918 RAF Muster Roll.

802. C. P. BOWRING

A recruit, a direct entrant into RFC 1 August, 1913. As 2AM served overseas from 24 January, 1915 and earned 1914/15 Star trio. Promoted 1AM (Rigger) 1 January, 1918 and retained that rank and trade in April, 1918 RAF Muster Roll.

★ 803. A. S. NOVELL

A recruit, a direct entrant into RFC 1 August, 1913. As 2AM, 5 Squadron served in France from 14 August, 1914. Promoted Acting Sergeant (paid) (Storeman) 1 December, 1917 and was Sergeant Clerk in April, 1918 RAF Muster Roll.

★ 804. F. BULLOCK

A recruit, a direct entrant into RFC 6 August, 1913. As 2AM, 4 Squadron earned 1914 Star in France.

805. J. WHITE

Boy recruit, a direct entrant into RFC 7 August, 1913. Still a Boy at RFC HQ in August, 1914. No entitlement to Stars traced. Promoted 1AM (Rigger-aero) 1 April 1917 and retained that rank and trade in April, 1918 RAF Muster Roll.

★ 806. JOSEPH RICHARD EAVES

Boy recruit, a direct entrant into RFC 7 August, 1913. Man's service commenced 11 August, 1914. As 2AM, 5 Squadron, served in France from 14 August, 1914. As 1AM listed as a prisoner of war at Kut in 1916 and died in captivity 7 May 1916 aged 19. His name is on the Basra Memorial, Iraq. Brother of Mrs. F. E. Booker, 21 Jessel House, Page St., Westminster, London.

807. F. DALY

Boy recruit, direct entrant into RFC 8 August, 1913. Discharged 9 October, 1913 under *K.R.* 392 (xxv).

★ 808. E. J. PARKER

Formerly 8308 Lance Sergeant 1/Grenadier Guards. Transferred to RFC 2 April, 1913, and was Sergeant Major at Gosport *w.e.f.* 3 September, 1913. As Sergeant Major of 5 Squadron served in France from 14 August, 1914. Mentioned in Despatches *L.G.* 8 October, 1914. Awarded Military

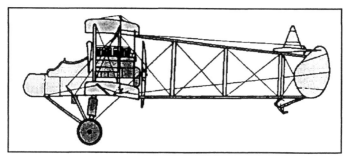

FE2D

Cross in the *L.G.* of 1 January, 1915. This was the first gazetting of this award, 99 issued including 27 to Warrant Officers, of whom three were RFC (see No. 3 Ramsey and No. 9 Jillings). Commissioned Lieutenant and Q.M. 1 June, 1915 and was Temporary Major RFC 1 June, 1915. See Group Photographs No. 1 and 2. (See reference under No. 979.)

809. OLIVER THORNTON STONE

Formerly 7298 Lance Sergeant 2/Coldstream Guards. On probation to RFC 28 February, 1913 and accepted in August, 1913. Nicknamed 'Ginger' he was Drill Instructor at the recruit Depot at Aldershot. No further references noted until found as Flying Officer on stores List of November, 1921 *A.F.L.* with seniority of 20 July, 1920 and a commission date of 6 December, 1918. Since 20 May, 1921 he had been serving at No. 4 Flying Training School, Palestine. C. R. King (No. 874) said of him in '*The Forgotten Ones*,' 'When I first joined the recruit depot at Aldershot we had a Lance-Sergeant Stone from the Coldstream Guards as our Drill Instructor. He was exactly the man to take over young men from civilian life. He was tall and smart and his voice held you to instant obedience to his commands. After parade he would talk to us in an informal way, and make us understand that discipline was a thing to make service life run smoothly. Many of us owed our happiness in the service to 'Ginger' Stone's advice and example.'

★ 810. W. G. BIAS

A recruit, a direct entrant into RFC 12 August, 1913. As 2AM, 4 Squadron served in France from 10 September, 1914 earning 1914 Star and bar. Promoted Flight Sergeant (Carpenter) 1 July, 1917 and was Chief Mechanic (Carpenter) in April, 1918 RAF Muster Roll.

★ 811. H. W. BARKER

Born 13 November, 1893. A recruit, a direct entrant into RFC 8 August, 1913. As 2AM, 5 Squadron served in France from 14 August, 1914 and earned 1914 Star and bar. Promoted Temp SM (T) 1 July, 1917 and was Chief Master Mechanic (Technical) in April, 1918 RAF Muster Roll. Awarded General Service Medal (Clasp Kurdistan). Awarded RAF L.S.&G.C. medal as Flight Sergeant *w.e.f.* 26 November, 1932 after 19 years 3 months service. Appointed WO1 1 April, 1936. Shown in March 1938 *A.F.L.* as serving at No. 11 FTS Wittering with No. 54, J. C. Jones D.C.M. M.M. Commissioned into Technical Branch 6 April, 1938. Flight

Lieutenant 6 April, 1941. Retired as acting Wing Commander 12 January, 1949. (See 1970 *A.F.L.*).

★ 812. GORDON BROWN

Enlisted 6 February, 1912. Formerly 22523 Pioneer 'B' signal Company RE. Transferred to RFC 21 February, 1913. As 1AM with Aircraft Park served in France from 16 August, 1914. Mentioned in despatches as Flight Sergeant in *L.G.* 1 January, 1916. Promoted Temp SM (D) 1 August, 1916 and mentioned again in *L.G.* 7 December, 1917. Was SM1 (Disciplinarian) in April, 1918 RAF Muster Roll. Awarded General Service Medal (clasp Kurdistan). Awarded RAF L.S.&G.C. medal *w.e.f.* 6 February, 1930 as SM1. 24th Senior RAF WO in 1931 *A.F.L.*

Standing (left to right): 1181 RIPLEY, 1175 BUTCHER, 1173 TAIT, UNKNOWN, 1174 CUMMINS, 1171 BIRD. *Seated:* UNKNOWN, UNKNOWN, 812, UNKNOWN, 1165 CAMPBELL. *Front:* 665 PRICE, 780 HEPPLE.

★ 813. W. FREEGARD

Enlisted 13 January, 1912. Formerly 68319 Gunner 138 Battery, RFA. Transferred to RFC 15 May, 1913. As 2AM, 3 Squadron served in France from 12 August, 1914. Was a 2AM motor cyclist right through to April 1918 RAF Muster Roll when he is shown as Private 1st Class (See No. 302).

★ 814. WILFRED VICTOR ELLISON

Enlisted 19 June, 1908. Formerly 1324 Trooper, Royal Horse Guards. Transferred to RFC 25 February, 1913. Mentioned many times by McCudden V.C. in *'Flying Fury.'* Known as Fonso because of his resemblance to King Alphonso of Spain. He served with McCudden from May, 1913 in 3 Squadron. As a 1AM he went to France with RFC HQ 12 August, 1914. However, once there he was appointed second in charge of 3 Squadron's portable wireless plant. This plant was accommodated in two high sided horse drawn carts. Promoted Sergeant in October, 1915 and awarded a French Croix de Guerre in *L.G.* 24 February, 1916. Sergeant-Air Gunner with 34 Squadron in early 1917. Promoted Temp SM (D) 1 August, 1917 and was SM1 (Disciplinarian) in April, 1918 RAF Muster Roll. Awarded RAF L.S.&G.C. medal *w.e.f.* 19 June, 1926. Still serving as a Warrant Officer Class 1 in February, 1931 *A.F.L.*

★ 815. JOHN CHEFFY HALLETT

Enlisted 28 April, 1902. Formerly 8558 Private, 2/Royal Sussex Regiment. Transferred to RFC 26 February, 1913. As 1AM with the Aircraft Park served in France from 16 August, 1914. Promoted Flight Sergeant (Rigger) 1 April, 1917 and was Chief Mechanic (Rigger aero) in April, 1918 RAF Muster Roll. Awarded RAF L.S.&G.C. as SM1 with effect from 28 April, 1920, which would have been amongst the earliest awarded (see No. 835 for details of the first six). This group of four medals are known as extant in a private collection with a bar on the 1914 Star (1AM RFC and SM1 RAF).

★ 816. ARTHUR MYRTLE SAYWOOD

Born 14 March, 1882. Formerly 15962 Sergeant 'C' Company, Army Service Corps. As Sergeant served in France from 12 August, 1914 with RFC HQ and earned 1914 Star and bar. Mentioned in despatches in *L.G.* 19 October, 1914 as Flight Sergeant. Commissioned 2 Lieutenant 1 November, 1916 and promoted Lieutenant 30 August, 1917. Was Lieutenant (Technical) in the first *A.F.L.* of April, 1918. Flying Officer 20 July, 1920 a Stores Officer at the Aeroplane Experimental Establishment Ipswich in November, 1921 *A.F.L.* Promoted Squadron Leader 1 January, 1930 serving from 6 February, 1928 at No. 1 Stores Depot Kidbrooke, London (see February, 1931 *A.F.L.*). In 1937 *A.F.L.* he was shown as retired from 14 March, 1932 and serving as a Barracks Officer at Home Aircraft Depot, Henlow Camp. Beds. Recalled 1 October, 1939 to 14 September, 1943. Last noted in 1963 *A.F.L.* as No. 10143, Squadron Leader (retired) (Equipment Officer).

★ 817. H. MORGAN

A recruit, a direct entrant into RFC 13 August, 1913. As 2AM, 5 Squadron served in France from 14 August, 1914. Promoted 1AM (Fitter Eng) 1 December, 1916 and retained that rank and trade in April, 1918 RAF Muster Roll.

★ 818. J. LANE

A recruit, a direct entrant into RFC 8 August, 1913. As 2AM posted into 5 Squadron 14 August, 1914 and went to France that day. Promoted Temp SM (T) 1 September, 1917 and was Chief Master Mechanic (Technical) in April, 1918 RAF Muster Roll.

819. N. W. B. BOVEY

A recruit, a direct entrant into RFC 14 August, 1913. Was 2AM, '2nd man on lorry' with No. 6 Squadron detachment at Newcastle in August, 1914 and was posted to Reserve Aeroplane Squadron. Served overseas as 1AM with 7 Squadron from 3 April, 1915 earning 1914/15 Star trio. Promoted Temp SM(T) 1 February, 1917 and was Chief Master Mechanic (Technical) in April, 1918 RAF Muster Roll. However, he had been commissioned 2 Lieutenant on 27 March, 1918 so in truth should not have appeared in the Muster Roll.

★ 820. A. K. HAMILTON

Enlisted 24 January, 1910. Formerly 1766 Corporal 1/Black Watch. Transferred to RFC 24 February, 1913. As 1AM with RFC HQ served in France from 12 August, 1914. Awarded Military Medal in *L.G.* 22 January, 1917 as Flight Sergeant. Promoted Temp SM (T) 1 February, 1917 and was Chief Master Mechanic (Technical) in April, 1918 RAF Muster Roll.

★ 821. A. D. MONK

A recruit, a direct entrant into RFC 18 August, 1913. As 2AM, 5 Squadron served in France from 14 August, 1914. Promoted Temp SM (T) 1 February, 1918 and was Chief Master Mechanic (Technical) in April, 1918 RAF Muster Roll.

822. A. G. LITTLE

A recruit, a direct entrant into RFC 16 August, 1913. As 2AM discharged 21 July, 1914 under *K.R.* 392 (xvi) 'no longer physically fit for war service.'

★ 823. REUBEN HOLLINGSWORTH

A recruit, a direct entrant into RFC 18 August, 1913. As 1AM, 5 Squadron served in France from 14 August, 1914 and earned 1914 Star and bar. Promoted Acting Flight Sergeant (paid) (Fitter Engines) 1 February, 1918 and was Chief Mechanic (Fitter AE) in April, 1918 RAF Muster Roll. Awarded RAF M.S.M. as Flight Sgt *L.G.* 3 June, 1919 for services in France. Shown as being from Lincoln. Awarded RAF L.S.&G.C. medal *w.e.f.* 18 August, 1931 as Flight Sergeant and 1935 Silver Jubilee Medal. Appointed WO 31 December, 1935. Awarded 1937 Coronation Medal. In March, 1938 *A.F.L.* had been stationed at No. 2 Air Armament School, Grimsby from 14 August, 1937. Alive in July 1975.

★ 824. E. C. BROADHURST

A recruit, a direct entrant into RFC 16 August, 1913. As 2AM, 5 Squadron served in France from 14 August, 1914 earning a 1914 Star and bar. In the retreat from Mons had to burn a Henri Farman near Le Cateau to stop it falling into enemy hands after he and 871 Knight failed to re-start its engine. Promoted Flight Sergeant (Fitter Engines) 1 February, 1917 and was Chief Mechanic (Fitter AE) in April, 1918 RAF Muster Roll.

★ 825. J. A. STRICKLAND

A recruit, a direct entrant into RFC 16 August, 1913. As 2AM, 5 Squadron served in France from 14 August, 1914. Promoted Sergeant (Fitter-General) 1 May, 1917 and was a Sergeant Mechanic (Fitter general) in the April, 1918 RAF Muster Roll.

826. C. E. MILLER

Formerly 22162 56 Company RE. Transferred to RFC 12 March, 1913. As 2AM transferred back to 5th (Field) Company RE 5 June, 1914.

★ 827. W. D. JEFFERIES

A recruit, a direct entrant into RFC 18 August, 1913. As 2AM, 5 Squadron served in France from 14 August, 1914. Discharged as unfit 9 March 1915.

★ 828. B. A. T. DIBBLE

A recruit, a direct entrant into RFC 20 August, 1913. As 2AM, 3 Squadron served in France from 13 August, 1914. Promoted Flight Sergeant (Driver MT) 1 October, 1917. Was Chief Mechanic (Driver) in April, 1918 RAF Muster Roll.

★ 829. T. CARROLL

A recruit, a direct entrant into RFC 15 August, 1913. As 2AM, 3 Squadron earned 1914 Star and bar in France from 12 August, 1914. Promoted Sergeant (Fitter gen.) 1 May, 1917, and was Sergeant Mech (Fitter gen.) in April, 1918 RAF Muster Roll. Awarded RAF L.S.&G.C. medal as Flight Sergeant *w.e.f.* 15 August, 1931.

★ 830. J. THOMAS

A recruit, a direct entrant into RFC 19 August, 1913. As 2AM, 4 Squadron served in France from 12 August, 1914. Promoted Flight Sergeant (Rigger) 10 October, 1917. Was Chief Mechanic (Rigger Aero) in April, 1918 RAF Muster Roll.

831. J. HUGHES

A recruit, a direct entrant into RFC 22 August, 1913. Discharged 2 May, 1914 under *K.R.* 392 (ix) 'unfitted for the duties of the Corps.'

832. F. C. BORST

A recruit, a direct entrant into RFC 22 August, 1913. Deserted 9 May, 1914.

★ 833. C. R. TINDALE

A recruit, a direct entrant into RFC 25 August, 1913. As 2AM 6 Squadron served in France from 6 October, 1914. As 2AM was wounded in May,

1915. A Fitter (general) he was reduced to 3AM in April, 1918 RAF Muster Roll.

★ 834. J. McINTYRE

Formerly 242 1/Black Watch. Transferred to RFC 27 June, 1913. As Sergeant, 5 Squadron earned 1914 Star and bar, in France from 14 August, 1914. Discharged as unfit 9 December, 1915.

★ 835. L. FURRENTS

Enlisted 11 December, 1900. Formerly 12116, 124 Battery, RFA. Transferred to RFC 16 April, 1913. As 2AM, 5 Squadron earned 1914 Star and bar in France from 14 August, 1914. Promoted Corporal (Driver MT) 1 November, 1915. Was Corporal Mechanic (Driver) in April, 1918 RAF Muster Roll. He was awarded RAF L.S.&G.C. medal in A.M.O. 1123, October, 1919 with effect from 11 December, 1918 as Corporal. This was one of the first six such medals awarded. The other five were: two SM1s, a Chief Master Mech, a Master Mech, and a Flight Sergeant (see No. 28). With the exception of Nos. 74 and 689 (both L.A.C.s) this was the only RAF L.S.&G.C. awarded to a pre-war RFC man in a rank below that of Sergeant, and thus the only one to a Corporal.

★ 836. RICHARD EDWIN PENDARVIS PAYNTER

Born 25 May, 1895. A recruit, a direct entrant into RFC 25 August, 1913. As 2AM served in France from 16 August, 1914 with Aircraft Park. As a Corporal was awarded a Distinguished Conduct Medal in the *L.G.* of 22 June, 1915:— 'For gallant conduct and coolness when carrying out his duties under fire, and also for the conspicuous thoroughness and efficiency for which his work has been noticeable.' Promoted Temporary Sergeant Major (Technical) 1 September, 1916 and was Chief Master Mechanic in April, 1918 RAF Muster Roll. 26th Senior RAF Warrant Officer 1st Class in February, 1931 *A.F.L.* Commissioned and then promoted Flight Lieutenant 1 September, 1937. In January, 1938 *A.F.L.* shown as serving at RAF Middle East Depot Aboukir from 26 September, 1931 as Equipment Officer serving with No. 777 Goodchild. Wing Commander 1 October, 1946. Retired 10 December, 1947. Last noted in 1975 retired list., but not that of 1977

★ 837. W. G. WOOLRIDGE

A recruit, a direct entrant into RFC 25 August, 1913. As 1AM No. 5 Squadron served in France from 14 August, 1914. He was accidentally killed by a hand grenade exploding in a hanger, 9 November, 1914 at Longnesse (St. Omer). Buried Souvenir Cemetery, St. Omer (Plot I. Row A Grave 19).

838. H. BUTTERWORTH

A recruit, a direct entrant into RFC 18 August, 1913. As 1AM No. 7 Squadron served overseas from 3 April, 1915 earning 1914/15 Star trio. Promoted Temporary Sergeant Major (Disciplinarian) 1 December, 1916. Was Sergeant Major 1st Class (Disciplinarian) in April, 1918 RAF Muster Roll.

★ 839. WAINWRIGHT DONALD BEARD

(See four page article and photograph in 'Cross and Cockade,' Vol. 7, No. 2, 1976 by R. Vann.) Born Sandbach, Cheshire, 20 May, 1895. A recruit, a direct entrant into RFC 20 August, 1913. Served with No. 4 Squadron at Netheravon. As 1AM (Mechanic) with No. 4 Squadron served in France from 14 August, 1914. By Summer 1916 he was Flight Sergeant 'B' Flight at Baizieux near Arras. Flew as an Observer with Captain Copeland, a Canadian on 20 July, 1916 in a BE2c on artillery spotting duties. After one-and-a-half hours they were attacked by four Pfalz scouts. Beard fired his .303 Lewis gun at 80 yards. The BE2c was hit many times, and an explosive bullet hit Captain Copeland's upper arm, knocking him unconscious. At 200 feet, Beard clipped into the socket the spare joy-stick used for dual control, eased the aircraft out of its dive, arrived over the airfield and touched down. The pilot lost his arm and Beard learned that he had shot down one of the Pfalz and was to be recommended for a Military Medal, which was gazetted 9 December, 1916. Beard was returned to C.F.S. Upavon for pilot training gaining his pilots certificate, first class, 26 July, 1917. Posted to 11 Squadron, 26 November, 1917 at Bellevue flying Bristol FB2 fighters. Force-landed 30 November, 1917 with engine failure. Flew with No. 1058 Corporal V. H. Davis as his observer. Hit by A.A. fire Christmas week 1917. Beard scored five more victories in March 1918, one on 9 March when the squadron attacked seven E.A.; three on the 15 March when one of 25 Albatross scouts the squadron attacked broke up in the air, after Beard hit the pilot, another stalled and sideslipped out of control, and a third was hit at 30 yards by his observer's fire, turned upside down and crashed. Finally on 22 March on an evening recce mission the Squadron attacked 8 E.A.s and Beard sent one down in flames. He was commissioned 2 Lieutenant in April, 1918, having been shown as Sergeant Mechanic (Pilot) on April, 1918 RAF Muster Roll, a rank he had reverted to on 27 April, 1917. Throughout May and June he flew many photographic missions but on 9 June, 1918 scored two more victories again with 1058 Sergeant H. V. Davis as

'R.F.C. Nuts'
852 Ripley   Unidentified
888 Collins   839 Beard   853 Clarke

observer. The official report states, 'After two attempts and 50 rounds the first E.A., a Pfalz, fluttered wing tip over wing tip to crash and at 9000 feet and from very close range he fired a further 100 rounds and a second E.A. turned on its back and crashed one mile east of Combles.' In Autumn 1918 2 Lieutenant Beard was posted as an instructor to Ireland and left the RAF on 10 December, 1919.

★ 840. T. E. HACCHE

A recruit, a direct entrant into RFC 22 August, 1913. As 2AM, 5 Squadron served in France earning 1914 Star and bar from 14 August, 1914. Promoted Flight Sergeant (Driver MT) 1 February, 1917 and was Chief Mechanic (Driver) in April, 1918 RAF Muster Roll.

841. W. E. STREEK

A boy recruit, a direct entrant into RFC 27 August, 1914. 2AM in August 1914 but no trace of entitlement to 1914 or 1914/15 Stars found. Promoted 1AM (Vulanizer) 1 August, 1917 and retained that rank and trade in April, 1918 RAF Muster Roll.

★ 842. G. GRAHAM

Enlisted 21 October, 1911 into the Air Battalion. Formerly 22115 Boy RE. Transferred to RFC 20 August, 1913. Was at Montrose in August, 1914, 2AM, (Sailmaker) with Lieutenant de Havilland then posted to 6 Squadron. As 2AM, 6 Squadron served in France from 7 October, 1914. Transferred to 1/Royal West Kents as L/11664 Sergeant.

★ 843. J. WELCH

Enlisted 21 October, 1911 into the Air Battalion. Formerly 22116 Boy RE. Transferred to RFC 20 August, 1913. Man's service commenced 28 May, 1914. As 2AM, 5 Squadron served in France from 14 August, 1914. The following *RFC Communiqué No. 16* appeared 26 October, 1915. Capt. Porter and Cpl. Welch, 2 Squadron, in a BE2c whilst engaged in artillery observation over Vermelles, attacked a Albatros which, at the time, was about 200 feet above them and a quarter-of-a-mile away on their left front. A running fight was kept up as far as Arras where Capt Porter, having used up his ammunition and running short of petrol, broke off the fight and returned to his aerodrome. Was Corporal (Fabric worker) in April,

1918 RAF Muster Roll. Awarded RAF L.S.&G.C. medal as Sergeant *w.e.f.* 21 October, 1929.

844. ERNEST SALTER

Enlisted 6 November, 1911 into the Air Battalion. Formerly 22187 Boy RE. Transferred to RFC 20 August, 1913. Man's service commenced 11 July, 1914. Was 2AM, 6 Squadron in August, 1914. No trace of entitlement to 1914 or 1914/15 Stars. Promoted 1AM (Fitter general) 1 December, 1914, and retained that rank and trade in April, 1918 RAF Muster Roll (see No. 302). Awarded RAF L.S.&G.C. medal *w.e.f.* 6 November, 1929 as Flight Sergeant. Awarded 1935 Silver Jubilee Medal. Commissioned Flying Officer (CEO) 23 August, 1937. 30 August, 1937 was stationed at RAF Driffield, No. 4 Bomber Group. Promoted Squadron Leader on 1 September, 1941. Still shown thus, No. 35129 in 1946 *A.F.L.*

845. J. S. ELEY

Enlisted 31 January, 1911 into Air Battalion. Formerly 21069 Boy RE. Transferred to RFC 20 August, 1913. Was still a Boy with 3 Squadron in August, 1914. No trace of entitlement to 1914 or 1914/15 Stars. In England (Hounslow) September, 1915 when 24 Squadron was formed. As Corporal served in France with them 2 February to 18 June, 1916 at St. Omer and Bertangles. Promoted Flight Sergeant (Driver MT) 1 September, 1917. Was Chief Mechanic (Driver) in April 1918 RAF Muster Roll. Awarded Indian General Service Medal (Waziristan 1919/21) and RAF L.S.&G.C. medal as SM1 31 January, 1929. Awarded 1935 Silver Jubilee Medal. Commissioned Flying Officer (E) 12 April, 1937. In March, 1938 *A.F.L.* at the Packing Depot Queensferry, Cheshire. Retired as a Wing Commander (No. 31108) seniority 1 January, 1944.

* 846. P. V. W. FENN

A recruit, a direct entrant into RFC 28 August, 1913. As 2AM, 4 Squadron served in France from 12 August, 1914. Promoted 1AM (Fitter, general) 1 October, 1916 and retained that rank and trade in April, 1918 RAF Muster Roll.

* 847. W. F. CLARK

A recruit, a direct entrant into RFC 22 August, 1913. As 2AM, 4 Squadron was on Fitters course at Central Flying School September, 1914, having already served in France with the Aircraft Park from 16 August, 1914. Promoted Corporal (Ftr Eng Er MT) 1 September 1917 and was Corporal Mechanic (Fitter MT) in April, 1918 RAF Muster Roll.

★ 848. WILLIAM SQUIRES

Born 8 June, 1892. Enlisted 26 February, 1912. Formerly 22608 Sapper, 30 Company RE. Transferred to RFC 26 March, 1913. As 2AM, 2 Squadron served in France from 12 August, 1914 earning 1914 Star and bar. Promoted Temp SM (D) 1 March, 1916. Was SM1 (Disciplinarian) in April, 1918 RAF Muster Roll. Awarded RAF L.S.&G.C. *w.e.f.* 9 March, 1931 as SM2, after over 19 years. Awarded 1935 Silver Jubilee Medal as WO 1st Class. Commissioned Flying Officer (CEO) 18 May, 1937. From 3 June, 1937 was stationed at No. 6 Flying Training School, Netheravon, Salisbury. Appointed to Order of British Empire as Officer. Promoted Wing Commander O.B.E. 1 June, 1942. Retired 11 February, 1948 and was still shown thus in 1970 *A.F.L.* (No. 35079).

★ 849. JOHN DUNCAN HOLT

Enlisted 14 October, 1911. Formerly 9286 Private 3/Coldstream Guards. Transferred to RFC 14 July, 1913. As 2AM, 4 Squadron served in France from 12 August, 1914. Promoted Sergeant (Machinist) 1 March, 1917. Was Sergeant Mech (Machinist) in April, 1918 RAF Muster Roll. Awarded RAF M.S.M. as Sergeant in *L.G.* 3 June, 1919 (King's Birthday Honours) for services in France. Awarded RAF L.S.&G.C. medal *w.e.f.* 14 October, 1929 as Flight Sergeant. Came from Ashby de la Zouch.

★ 850. D. BLAIR

A recruit, a direct entrant into RFC 29 August, 1913. As 1AM, with the Aircraft Park served in France from 16 August, 1914. He must have been reduced and promoted again, as he is shown as 1AM (Electrical) 1 March, 1918 and retained that rank and trade in April, 1918 RAF Muster Roll.

851. F. JOHNSTON

A boy recruit, a direct entrant into RFC 28 August, 1913. As Boy discharged 23 July, 1914 under *K.R.* 392 (xxv) 'His services no longer required.'

★ 852. E. A. RIGBY

A recruit, a direct entrant into RFC 28 August, 1913. As 2AM, 4 Squadron served in France from 13 August, 1914. Promoted Temp SM (D) 1 February, 1917. Was SM1 (Disciplinarian) in April, 1918 RAF Muster Roll.

★ 853. W. CLARKE

A recruit, a direct entrant into RFC 30 August, 1913. As 2AM, 4 Squadron served in France from 12 August, 1914. Promoted 1AM (Driver MT) 18 January, 1915 and retained that rank and trade in April, 1918 RAF Muster Roll. Mentioned in despatches for services in France in *L.G.* 3 June, 1919, as 1AM. See photograph under No. 839.

★ 854. H. AINSWORTH

A recruit, a direct entrant into RFC 29 August, 1913. As 2AM, 5 Squadron served in France from 14 August, 1914. Promoted Flight Sergeant (Acet Wldr) 1 July, 1917 and was Chief Mechanic (Acet Wldr) in April, 1918 RAF Muster Roll.

855. E. FRANKLIN

A recruit, a direct entrant into RFC 1 September, 1913. Discharged 17 September, 1913 under *K.R.* 392 (xiv) on payment of £10.

★ 856. GEORGE WILLIAM HALSTEAD

A recruit, a direct entrant into RFC 2 September, 1913. As 1AM, 4 Squadron served in France from 13 August, 1914.
RFC Communiqué No. 57: 9 October, 1916:
On the Reserve Army front 26 points including hostile battery positions, were registered. Capt. Walser and Flight Sergeant Halstead, 4 Squadron, after directing the fire of a battery and obtaining a direct hit on a hostile battery target, directed shrapnel fire on a collection of the enemy in the trenches near Pys. On another occasion they flew low and fired six drums on the enemies *[sic]*

infantry.

RFC Communiqué No. 63: 23 November, 1916:

Captain Walser and Flt. Sgt. Halstead, 4 Squadron, engaged three hostile batteries with the 13th Siege Battery. One battery position was practically destroyed, and in the others, one pit was destroyed, two were damaged, and one lot of ammunition exploded.

RFC Communiqué No. 65: 4 December, 1916:

2nd Lieut H.D. Crompton and Flt. Sgt. Halstead were brought down in our lines as a result of an aerial combat. The pilot was killed and the observer wounded.

Awarded Military Medal in *L.G.* 19 February, 1917. Awarded Royal Aero Club Aviators' Certificate No. 4462 3 April, 1917 as Flight Sergeant. Commissioned 2 Lieutenant 1 March, 1918. Accidentally killed 31 January, 1919.

★ 857. W. E. T. TAYLOR

A recruit, a direct entrant into RFC 2 September, 1913. As 2AM, 4 Squadron served in France from 9 September, 1914 earning 1914 Star and bar trio. Promoted Acting Flight Sergeant (paid) (Storeman) 1 January, 1918 and was Flight Clerk (Storeman) in April, 1918 RAF Muster Roll.

★ 858. F. F. J. BAKER

Enlisted 3 January, 1913. Formerly 38475 Gunner, 24 (Heavy) Battery RGA. Transferred to RFC 12 March, 1913. To France 16 August, 1914 with the Aircraft Park. Promoted 1AM (Driver MT) 2 September, 1917 and retained that rank and trade in April 1918 RAF Muster Roll.

★ 859. A. CORDEAUX

Enlisted 7 May, 1901. Formerly 6167 Sergeant, Royal West Kents. Transferred to RFC 6 May, 1912 but not confirmed and not given a number until September, 1913. A note states that all 12 years previous service was allowed to count but he dropped to 1AM and in this rank earned 1914 Star and bar in France with RFC HQ from 12 August, 1914. Appointed WO Class 1, 2 May, 1917. Mentioned in despatches as T/Sgt Major *L.G.* 13 March, 1918. Listed in the *Times* 'B' Press Release of 16 March, 1918. Commissioned 2 Lieutenant 10 March, 1918.

860. L. S. Mendes

A recruit, a direct entrant into RFC 1 September, 1913. As 2AM, RFC HQ discharged medically unfit 5 December, 1913.

861. H. L. Young

A recruit, a direct entrant into RFC 5 September, 1913. Discharged 6 October, 1913 under *K.R.* 392 (iii) 'not likely to become an efficient soldier.'

862. Alfred Reid

A recruit, a direct entrant into RFC 1 September, 1913. 2AM, 4 Squadron in August, 1914, but no trace of entitlement to 1914 or 1914/15 Stars found. Listed as a prisoner of war at Kut as a Corporal, No. 1 Reserve Squadron. Died in a Turkish Prison, 5 May, 1916. His name is on the Basra Memorial, Iraq. He was aged 23, the son of Edward and Elizabeth Reid of 38 Canal St., Castleton, Manchester.

★ 863. E. T. Symons

A recruit, a direct entrant into RFC 6 September, 1913. As 2AM, 5 Squadron served in France from 14 August, 1914. Promoted Flight Sergeant (Joiner) 1 October, 1917 and was Chief Mechanic (Carpenter) in April, 1918 RAF Muster Roll.

★ 864. C. F. R. Bunting

A recruit, a direct entrant to RFC 9 September, 1913. As 1AM with the Aircraft Park served in France from 16 August, 1914. Promoted Acting Flight Sergeant (paid) 1 December, 1917 and was Chief Mechanic (Fitter general) in April, 1918 RAF Muster Roll. Awarded RAF M.S.M. as Flight Sergeant in *London Gazette* 28 October, 1921 for Mesopotamia and was mentioned in despatches in *L.G.* 10 October, 1922 for services in Iraq in 1921 (30 Squadron). Entitled to a General Service Medal for Iraq and N.W. Persia (see also No. 950).

★ 865. A. J. Reeves

A recruit, a direct entrant into RFC 5 September, 1913. As 2AM, 6 Squadron served in France from 5 October, 1914. Promoted to Sergeant

(Telephonist) 1 July, 1916 and was Sergeant (Tel Op) in April, 1918 RAF Muster Roll.

866. C. J. HARRIS

A recruit, a direct entrant into RFC 8 September, 1913. Discharged 25 September, 1913 under *K.R.* 392 (xiv) on payment of £10.

867. L. HOLGATE

A recruit, a direct entrant into RFC in August, 1913. Posted to 5 Squadron 11 September, 1913. Discharged 5 May, 1914, under *K.R.* 392 (ix) 'unfitted to the duties of the Corps.'

868. C. E. KEAY

Formerly 56399, 141 Battery, RFA. Transferred to RFC 7 April, 1913. Discharged (not free) under Article 1130 (i) of the Pay Warrant, 20 February, 1914.

* 869. W. W. CLARKE

Enlisted 3 December, 1907. Formerly 31003, 17 Company, Army Service Corps. Transferred to RFC 14 April, 1913. As Corporal, 3 Squadron served in France from 12 August, 1914 and earned 1914 Star and bar. QM Sgt (T) 1 March, 1916. In *RFC Communiqué No. 54*, 17 September, 1916 he is mentioned with 2 Lieutenant Lynch of 3 Squadron who forced an enemy machine to land near Bapaume. He was awarded a Military Medal in *L.G.* 28 September, 1917 as QMS Master Mech (T) in April, 1918 RAF Muster Roll. He came from Wanstead. Awarded General Service Medal (clasp Iraq) as WO2.

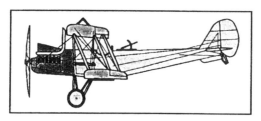

RE8

870. S. J. HITCHCOCK

A recruit, a direct entrant into RFC 9 September, 1913. Discharged 18 March, 1914 under *K.R.* 392 (ix).

★ 871. H. H. KNIGHT

A recruit, a direct entrant into RFC 8 September, 1913. As 2AM, 5 Squadron served in France from 14 August, 1914. See also 824 Broadhurst. He was promoted QMS (T) 1 March, 1917 and was Master Mechanic (T) in April, 1918 RAF Muster Roll.

★ 872. ALBERT T. J. MORGAN

Formerly 10111 Lance Corporal 2/K.R.R.C. Transferred to RFC 12 April, 1913. As 1AM, 3 Squadron served in France from 13 August, 1914. Was killed 12 March, 1915 in an accidental bomb explosion (see Nos. 194, 534, 582, 589) at Merville Aerodrome. Buried Chocques Military Cemetery (Plot I, row A, grave 41).

873. R. BAKER

A recruit, a direct entrant into RFC 17 September, 1913. No trace of entitlement to 1914 or 1914/15 Stars found. Promoted Flight Sergeant (Rigger) 1 September, 1916. Mentioned in despatches *L.G.* 20 December, 1917 for Anti Aircraft services in U.K. as Sergeant. Listed in the *Times* 'B' Press Release 21 December, 1917 for services in the Air Defence of Great Britain. Chief Mechanic (Rigger aero) in April 1918 RAF Muster Roll. Awarded General Service Medal (clasp Kurdistan).

874. CECIL R. KING

A recruit, a direct entrant into RFC 16 September, 1913. As 2AM, No. 5 Squadron served in France from 14 August, 1914 and earned 1914 Star and bar. The reactions of the British airman, drilled and disciplined in the manner of the Brigade of Guards, to his early experiences in France and the rather sloppy appearance of the French troops are described by Air Mechanic C. R. King, of the R.F.C in *'The Forgotten Ones.'*

> 'When we got to France we took rather a poor view of the French soldiers with their rusty aeroplanes, dirty ungroomed artillery horses and unshaven faces, but the civilians welcomed us and were always kind and helpful. They often helped me picket down my

aircraft, and would hump tins of petrol when I was filling up. A very pretty girl helped me one day so I allowed her to sit in the pilot's seat for a moment, as she had never seen an aeroplane on the ground before.'

On one occasion when he arrived at a field by air his pilot was told to take off at once with another officer. King was ordered to take up a defensive position in a nearby farm with the remainder of the squadron and transport. They were supposed to be surrounded by Uhlans and had to hold the farm till help came from some of our cavalry. How he longed for a rifle! But he had only a revolver, the same as the rest of his comrades. They had just settled down in their positions when one of the officers came along and examined the ammunition. It was mostly flat-nosed, the same as had been used for target shooting in England. Quickly the ammunition was buried deep in the farmyard manure. The men were told that if they were captured using the ammunition by the enemy they could have been shot right away, so, quite unarmed, they just waited to see what happened. There was a Lewis-gun, (it might have been the only one in the RFC at that time), and one of the officers fired a few bursts with it. The Uhlans drew off after a time and the party got out of it safely, but intensely disappointed at not being able to fire a single shot.

Promoted Flight Sergeant (Rigger) 1 September, 1915. As Flight Sergeant mentioned in despatches in *L.G.* of 14 October, 1916 for services with the Egyptian Expeditionary Force. Was Chief Mechanic (rigger aero) in April, 1918 RAF Muster Roll. Mentioned by Air Chief Marshal de la Ferté as being alive in 1960.

★ 875. A. H. BUTLIN

A recruit, a direct entrant into RFC 15 September, 1913. As 2AM 5 Squadron served in France from 14 August, 1914 earning 1914 Star and bar. Discharged under *K.R.* 392 (ix) 16 February, 1915 'unfitted for the duties of the Corps.'

★ 876. J. CHILTON

A recruit, a direct entrant into RFC 22 September, 1913. As 2AM, 5 Squadron served in France from 14 August, 1914 earning 1914 Star and bar. A Fitter (MT) he was reported as a prisoner of war 12 September,

1914. Shown as 3AM in April, 1918 RAF Muster Roll, presumably still a P.O.W.

★ 877. S. F. FRASER

Born in 1895, he was a recruit, a direct entrant into RFC 22 September, 1913. As 1AM, Aircraft Park served in France from 16 August, 1914. Promoted Corporal (Driver MT) 1 June, 1917 and was Corporal Mechanic (Driver) in April, 1918 RAF Muster Roll. Awarded Indian General Service Medal (with 3 clasps, North West Frontier Afghanistan 1919, Waziristan 1919-21 and Mahsud) as Corporal 28 Squadron. This last medal only is known as a single with the last two clasps in a private collection. However in July, 1986 when aged 90 he was re-issued with all four medals which had been lost in the London Blitz. He died in 1987 a resident of Warstones House, Wolverhampton.

★ 878. F. G. BEALE

A recruit, a direct entrant into RFC 23 September, 1913. As 2AM, 5 Squadron earned 1914 Star and bar, in France from 14 August, 1914. Promoted Sergeant (Fitter, engines) 1 December, 1915 and was Sergeant Mechanic (Fitter AE) in April, 1918 RAF Muster Roll.

★ 879. A. E. SCHOFIELD

A recruit, a direct entrant into RFC 24 September, 1913. As 2AM, with the Aircraft Park served in France from 16 August, 1914. Promoted Sergeant (Sailmaker) 1 November, 1916 and was Sergeant (Fabric Worker) in April, 1918 RAF Muster Roll.

★ 880. A. H. LAW

A recruit, a direct entrant into RFC 25 September, 1913. As 2AM, 4 Squadron served in France from 12 August, 1914. Promoted Sergeant (Driver MT) 1 September, 1916 and was Sergeant Mechanic (Driver) in April, 1918 RAF Muster Roll. Mentioned in despatches in *L.G.* 1 November, 1918 and 30 January, 1919 as Sergeant Mechanic, 17 Squadron both times for services in Salonika.

★ 881. R. H. MORGAN

A recruit, a direct entrant into RFC 25 September, 1913. As 2AM, 5 Squadron served in France from 14 August, 1914. Acting Flight Sergeant (paid) (Carpenter) 14 March, 1918 and was Chief Mechanic (Carpenter) in April, 1918 RAF Muster Roll.

★ 882. E. TAYLOR

A recruit, a direct entrant into RFC 26 September, 1913. As 2AM, with the Aircraft Park served in France from 16 August, 1914. As Sergeant joined 24 Squadron 11 December, 1916 at Chipilly, Flez and Baisieux and left 14 February, 1917. Commissioned 2 Lieutenant, 23 September, 1917.

★ 883. J. W. H. BAKER

Enlisted 20 May, 1912. Formerly 6905, 4th Dragoon Guards. Transferred to RFC 26 April, 1913. As 2AM, 3 Squadron served in France from 12 August, 1914. Promoted Flight Sergeant (Driver MT) 1 August, 1916 and was Chief Mechanic (Driver) in April, 1918 RAF Muster Roll.

★ 884. P. F. LARGE

A recruit, a direct entrant into RFC 27 September, 1913. As 2AM, with the Aircraft Park served in France from 16 August, 1914. Promoted T/ SM (D) 1 June, 1917 and was SM1 (Disciplinarian) in April, 1918 RAF Muster Roll.

★ 885. E. N. HILL

A recruit, a direct entrant into RFC 25 September, 1913. As 2AM, 5 Squadron served in France from 14 August, 1914. Promoted T/SM (T) 1 July, 1917 and was Chief Master Mechanic (Technical) in April, 1918 RAF Muster Roll. Listed in the *Times* 'B' Press Release for services at the Air Ministry 22 January, 1919. Awarded RAF L.S.&G.C. medal as WO1 *w.e.f.* 29 April, 1932 some six months later than might be expected.

★ 886. ROBERT GEORGE BROBSON

A recruit, a direct entrant into RFC 27 September, 1913. As 2AM, 4 Squadron served in France from 14 August, 1914. Awarded French Croix de Guerre as Sergeant, still in 4 Squadron in *L.G.* 24 February, 1916.

Promoted Flight Sergent (Carpenter) 1 September, 1916 and was Chief Mechanic (Carpenter) in April, 1918 RAF Muster Roll.

* 887. J. H. WOODLEY

A recruit, a direct entrant into RFC 2 October, 1913. As 2AM, 5 Squadron earned 1914 Star and bar in France from 14 August, 1914. Promoted 1AM (Fitter engines) 1 October, 1915 and retained that rank and trade in April, 1918 RAF Muster Roll.

* 888. J. COLLINS

A recruit, a direct entrant into RFC 23 September, 1913. As 2AM, 4 Squadron earned 1914 Star and bar in France from 12 August, 1914. Promoted 1AM (Fitter general) 1 July, 1916 and retained that rank and trade in April, 1918 RAF Muster Roll.

* 889. A. S. HOLMES

Formerly 8060 Lance Corporal 2/Suffolk Regt. Transferred to RFC 28 April, 1913. As 2AM, Aircraft Park served in France from 16 August, 1914. As Sergeant killed at Lincoln, 18 June, 1917. Buried in Woodbridge Cemetery, Suffolk (Plot A, Row 12, grave 40).

* 890. E. E. KIRBY

Enlisted 30 March, 1911. Formerly 9554 Lance Corporal 1/Buffs. Transferred to RFC 28 April, 1913. As 2AM, with the Aircraft Park in France from 16 August, 1914. Promoted T/SM (T) 1 July, 1917 and was Chief Master Mechanic (Technical) in April, 1918 RAF Muster Roll.

* 891. F. TINDALE (ALIAS F. ELDERIDGE)

Enlisted 20 June, 1910. Formerly 41767 Acting Bomdardier I Battery, RHA. Transferred to RFC 28 April, 1913. As Corporal with the Aircraft Park, earned 1914 Star in France. Promoted T/SM (D) 1 April, 1916. Changed his name to Elderidge sometime prior to being awarded a Distinguished Conduct Medal as Acting Sergeant Major in *L.G.* 13 February, 1917. 'For conspicuous gallantry and devotion to duty. He has shown exceptional organising ability and energy as Sergeant-Major and has been on continuous service for over 15 months.' Was SM1 in April, 1918 RAF Muster Roll. However, there is now some confusion as 891

Sergeant F. Elderidge was awarded his RAF L.S.&G.C. medal *w.e.f.* 13 February 1927, seemingly after less than 17 years service and having come down three ranks from SM1 to Sergeant.

★ 892. James Thomas Byford McCudden

Born 28 March, 1895 in Gillingham, the son of an RE QMS from County Carlow, Ireland. He enlisted in 1910 as a Boy Bugler into 6 Company RE, formerly No. 20083. Younger brother of No. 61 Flight Sergeant W. T. J. McCudden. Followed him into RFC 28 April, 1913 when 18 years of age. Promoted 1AM, 1 April, 1914. As 1AM he made a number of flights as passenger with his brother and other pilots. Went to France on 12 August, 1914 after driving down to Southampton from Netheravon in a *Sunbeam* touring car with Lieutenant Cruikshank and four Air Mechanics of 3 Squadron. The Squadron sailed in a very small tramp steamer, the *'Dee.'* McCudden flew from Maubeuge to Le Cateau with Lieutenant de la Ferté 24 August, 1914 in a Blériot and two days later to St. Quentin with Captain Charlton D.S.O. On a number of occasions from October, 1914 to January, 1915 he flew with Lieutenant Conran, acting as gunner, armed with a rifle, initially as 1AM but from 20 November, 1914 as Corporal. He was promoted Sergeant 1 April, 1915 and was shown as Observer from July, 1915. He was awarded a French Croix de Guerre on 21 January 1916, which he received from General Joffre the French Commander in Chief, and two days later was promoted Flight Sergeant. In mid-February, he was posted to Royal Aircraft Park, Farnborough, as Pilot trainee flying a Henri Farman. On 16 April, 1916 he gained his Royal Aero Club Aviators' Certificate, No. 2745, on a 'Longhorn' Maurice Farman at Gosport in 41 Squadron, and was posted back to France flying over in a BE2d to St. Omer

on 4 July after a spell as instructor at the Central Flying School, having only eight hours 'solo' when he took up his first pupil. In France he was posted to 20 Squadron and had his first war flight as a pilot on 10 July, 1916. His second decoration was awarded in *L.G.* 10 December, 1916, a Military Medal, and he was commissioned 2 Lieutenant on 1 January, 1917. Very quickly afterwards, on 16 February, 1917 his third decoration, a Military Cross, was gazetted and this was followed by a bar to his M.C. in *L.G.* 3 October, 1917, the citation for which reads:

> 'For conspicuous gallantry and devotion to duty, he took part in many offensive patrols, over thirty of which he led. He destroyed five enemy machines and drove down three others out of control. He showed the greatest gallantry, dash and skill.'

McCudden and Bristol Scout

He had been promoted to acting Captain 1 May, 1917 and in that rank he was appointed to the Distinguished Service Order in *L.G.* 15 December, 1917 and gained a bar to his D.S.O. in *L.G.* 3 January, 1918:— The two citations appeared in *London Gazettes* of 5 and 18 July, 1918. *D.S.O.:*

> 'For conspicuous gallantry and devotion to duty. He attacked and brought down an enemy two-seater machine inside our lines, both the occupants being taken prisoner. On another occasion he encountered an enemy two-seater at 2000 feet. He continued to fight down to a height of 100 feet in very bad weather conditions and destroyed the enemy machine. He came down to within a few feet of the ground on the enemy's side of the lines and finally crossed the line at a very low altitude. He has recently destroyed seven enemy machines, two of which fell within our lines and he has set a spendid example of pluck and determination to his squadron.'

Bar to D.S.O.:

'For Conspicuous Gallantry and Devotion to Duty. He attacked enemy formations both when leading his patrol and single handed. By his fearlessness and clever manœuvering he has brought down 31 enemy machines, ten of which have fallen in our lines. His pluck and determination have had a marked effect on the efficiency of the Squadron.'

It would have come to no surprise to his contemporaries in the RFC to learn that he had been awarded the Victoria Cross in *L.G.* 2 April, 1918. After all he had shot down four aircraft in one day—twice! His citations tell the story of an exceptional man. Major McCudden was killed whilst flying from Auxi-le-Petit aerodrome not far from Warans, a few kilometers N.E. of Abbeville and just South of Agincourt. He is buried in Warans Military Cemetery, a small, lonely little graveyard in the west side of the village. He had just been awarded the Medal of Honor and Merit of the Aero Club of America. Major J. T. B. McCudden, V.C., D.S.O., and bar, M.C. and bar, M.M., Croix de Guerre, formerly No. 892 2AM RFC was killed whilst flying 9 July, 1918 aged 23 at Marquise, France.

Citation for Victoria Cross:

'For most conspicuous bravery, exceptional perseverance, keenness, and a very high devotion to duty.

Captain McCudden has at the present time accounted for 54 enemy aeroplanes. Of these 42 have been definitely destroyed, 19 of them on our side of the lines. Only 12 out of the 54 have been driven down out of control.

On two occasions he has totally destroyed four two-seater enemy aeroplanes on the same day, and on the last occasion all four machines were destroyed in the space of one hour and thirty minutes.

While in his present squadron he has participated in 78 offensive patrols, and in nearly every case has been the leader. On at least 30 occasions, whilst with the same squadron, he has crossed the lines alone, either in pursuit or in quest of enemy aeroplanes.

The following incidents are examples of the work he has done recently:

On the 23rd December, 1917, when leading his patrol, eight enemy aeroplanes were attacked between 2.30 p.m. and 3.50 p.m. Of these two were shot down by Captain McCudden in our lines. On the morning of the same day he left the ground at 10.50 and encountered four enemy aeroplanes; of these he shot two down.

On the 30th January, 1918, he, single-handed, attacked five enemy scouts, as a result of which two were destroyed. On this occasion he only returned home when the enemy scouts had been driven far east; his Lewis gun ammunition was all finished and the belt of his Vickers gun had broken.

As a patrol leader he has at all times shown the utmost gallantry and skill, not only in the manner in which he has attacked and destroyed the enemy, but in the way he has during several aerial fights protected the newer members of his flight, thus keeping down their casualties to a minimum.

V.C. KILLED

Captain James Byford McCudden, V.C., D.F.C., M.C., M.M., the famous airman, who has met with a fatal accident while flying in France. Only two or three days ago his award of the Distinguished Flying Cross was announced.

This officer is considered, by the record which he has made, by his fearlessness, and by the great service which he has rendered to his country, deserving of the very highest honour.'

The *Daily Mirror* of 11 July, 1918 records:—

'Airmans VC's Tragic End—Major McCudden, the famous air V.C., who had downed fifty-four Huns, has been killed accidentally just after flying back to France. He left the aerodrome to rejoin his squadron but hit some trees and crashed to the ground.

News reached London yesterday that Major James Byford McCudden, V.C., D.S.O. and bar, M.C. and bar, M.M., Mons Medal and Croix de Guerre, the British Air Star, had been accidentally killed in France. When he took off from the Aerodrome he was starting very low down when for some unexplained reason, he was seen to go down and hit some trees and crash on to the ground.

When the ambulance reached him he was found to be dead.

Major McCudden was very cheery on the eve of his departure for France and had expressed his hopes of getting 100 Huns.

Officially Major McCudden had accounted for fifty-four German aeroplanes, and unofficially the score was put at seventy. He was anxious to beat Fonck's record, which unofficially is placed at eighty.

For some time before getting his majority Captain McCudden had been acting as an instructor, and he was most patient with his pupils.

On three occasions he fought duels with the great German Airman Immelmann now also dead.'

There is a memorial to him in Sheerness Parish Church. He is named on the War Memorial at Gillingham, Kent. He is buried in Warans British Cemetery, France.

★ 893. J. H. STAMP

Enlisted 8 February, 1912. Formerly 22519 Sapper, RE. Transferred to RFC 22 April, 1913. As 2AM with the Aircraft Park served in France from 16 August, 1914. Promoted Corporal (Fitter general) 1 September, 1917 and retained that rank and trade in April, 1918 RAF Muster Roll.

894. A. JAMES

A recruit, a direct entrant into RFC 3 October, 1913. He deserted 12 January, 1914.

★ 895. P. A. WICKS

Enlisted 23 June, 1908. Formerly 3188 Private, 3 Hussars. Transferred to RFC 1 May, 1913. As 2AM, 4 Squadron served in France from 12 August, 1914. Reverted to Sergeant (Driver MT), 10 December, 1917 and was Sergeant Mechanic (Driver) in April, 1918 RAF Muster Roll.

★ 896. ERNEST JAMES FARLEY

A recruit, a direct entrant into RFC 5 October, 1913. As 1AM, 4 Squadron earned 1914 Star and bar serving in France from 9 September, 1914. Promoted Flight Sergeant (Rigger) 1 March, 1917. Awarded French Croix de Guerre 1 May, 1917 in his previous rank of Sergeant. Was Chief Mechanic (Rigger, aero) in April, 1918 RAF Muster Roll.

★ 897. W. G. BORRETT

Enlisted 19 August, 1911. Formerly 10194 Lance Corporal 2/KRRC. Transferred to RFC 1 May, 1913. As 1AM, 3 Squadron earned 1914 Star and bar, in France from 13 August, 1914. One morning after the victory on the Marne, he had a hangover, swung his pilots propeller, the engine backfired and the propeller caught his shoulder and hospitalised him. Promoted Flight Sergeant (Rigger) 1 June, 1916. Awarded Military Medal 27 October, 1916 as Flight Sergeant. Chief Mechanic (Rigger aero) in April, 1918 RAF Muster Roll. Mentioned in despatches *L.G.* 22 January, 1919 for Egypt and listed the next day in the *Times* 'B' Air Ministry Press Release. RAF L.S.&G.C. medal awarded *w.e.f.* 26 April, 1929 as Sergeant Major 1st Class.

★ 898. M. T. WILLIAMS

A recruit, a direct entrant into RFC 7 October, 1913. As 2AM, 2 Squadron earned 1914 Star and bar in France from 12 August, 1914. Promoted Sergeant (Ftr Eng Er MT) 1 April, 1917 and was Sergeant Mechanic (Fitter MT) in April, 1918 RAF Muster Roll.

899. J. S. STRETTON

A recruit, a direct entrant into RFC 7 October, 1913. Discharged 6 January, 1914 under *K.R.* 392 (xiv) on payment of £10.

★ 900. J. SMITH

Enlisted 4 May, 1900. See also 954 J. Smith one formerly 5858 3/Worcs transferred to RFC 6 May, 1913. The other formerly 12015 2/Worcs transferred to RFC 30 May, 1913. As 2AM, 2 Squadron earned 1914 Star and bar in France from 12 August, 1914. Promoted Flight Sergeant (Armourer) 1 March, 1918, and was Chief Mechanic (Armourer) in April, 1918 RAF Muster Roll.

★ 901. DUNCAN MITCHELL

Born Dumfries 28 November, 1881. Enlisted in 1896. As Sergeant Drummer earned Queen's South Africa Medal (clasps Orange Free State, Transvaal, South Africa 1901 and South Africa 1902). Formerly 6298 Colour Sergeant, 1/Black Watch. Transferred to RFC 27 May, 1913. Awarded Royal Aero Club Aviators' Certificate No. 701 at Upavon on 11 December, 1913 in a Maurice Farman of the Central Flying School. Shown as '2nd Class flyer' *w.e.f.* 17 December, 1913. As Sergeant, 5 Squadron served in France from 14 August, 1914. Awarded Army L.S.&G.C. as Sergeant in *A.O.* 12 October, 1914. Appointed Sgt. Major 12 March, 1915. Commissioned 2 Lieutenant 3 March, 1917. In 1937 *A.F.L.* shown as Flight Lieutenant (E) (retired 16 October, 1926) seniority 1 January, 1921 then employed at RAF Halton. See group photograph No. 2.

313

★ 902. OLIVER L. DAY

Completed a seven year apprenticeship as a marine engineer and, as a recruit, was a direct entrant into RFC 10 October, 1913. As 2AM, 2 Squadron earned 1914 Star and bar in France from 12 August, 1914 (in charge of B flight workshop lorry). With 16 Squadron on 6 October, 1915 an Aerial Gunner. Promoted T/SM (T) 1 April, 1917 and was Chief Master Mechanic (Technical) in April, 1918 RAF Muster Roll. Commissioned and promoted to Flight Lieutenant in WW2. Alive in 1960. Flight Lieutenant Day of No. 2 Squadron also has something to say on the attitude of the French civilians in *'The Forgotten Ones.'*

'We sailed from Glasgow in the S.S. *Dogra* and as we steamed down the Clyde the shipyard workers gave us a tremendous send-off by beating on steel plates with their rivetting hammers.

At Boulogne the local ladies gave us a warm reception, but it was noticeable that they were wearing badges of regiments which had passed through ahead of us. Already the owners of these badges were forgotten. For the ladies the interest was the man on the spot!'

From Boulogne No. 2 Squadron moved to Amiens and then to Maubeuge. Soon aircraft were needing repair from enemy action and Day and his lorry were busy. At night the glare from burning villages showed in the northern sky and the realities of war were coming home to the airmen, whose trip to France had hitherto been in the nature of a holiday.

On Sunday, 23rd August, it was clear that the RFC would have to leave Maubeuge and move south-west. Through Aulnoye the column of vehicles trundled along, halting from time to time, their drivers hoping

NIEUPORT SCOUT 17 *(above and right)*

that darkness would see them comfortably encamped. This was not to be. Late that night orders came for a further move, and head to tail, each driving on his predecessor's red tail-light, the transport nosed its way towards safety. By next day exhaustion was setting in and Day had little recollection of what was happening. He remembered the crowds of refugees. Did he see perhaps the famous crippled old lady being pushed down the road on her bed which fortunately was provided with castors? How devoted must have been her family!

One night when the transport was parked in a field a heavy rainstorm broke. The officer in charge at once ordered all the vehicles on to the road in case they got bogged down and so might fall into German hands. The language of the troops as they were dug out from their hiding-holes must have been in a class by itself! Next night their sleep was broken again by the invasion of a herd of cattle. The owners had decided to drive them south to escape the Germans and had started the operation well before dawn.

Baths were an unknown quantity. Passing a big château surrounded by a deep moat, the O.C. Transport decided that the moment had arrived for an all-over wash. Stripping on the bank the troops plunged in—into a foot or so of water and several of mud! They emerged black and stinking and any thought of using the one towel that they possessed was soon discarded. Lying in the sun, they dried out. The mud caked on them and had to be removed by scraping with grass and leaves. All told, it was not a successful bathe, but Day and others have recorded that it was six months before they had the chance of another cleansing.

The retreat ran its course, and after the battle for Paris the RFC started its move to cover the Channel ports. Day seems to have kept his workshop lorry in serviceable condition because it reached St. Omer in one piece. Here, he says, 'The workshops were opened up, major repairs were done and discipline enforced.' Good old RFC!

Day writes of Christmas Day, 1914, when by consent of the troops on either side of the line there was an 'Armistice'—the last until 1918! The miseries of war and weather had already struck deep into the souls of the common men of all races and there were a number of instances of fraternization. Civilization still had a hold which soon was to be loosened!

'The weather was very wet that winter,' says Day, 'and what was very bad, all airmen including myself were lousy. We were sleeping on straw, in our clothes and under one blanket. Our laundry, such as it was, had been done by French women but soon they refused to accept it because of the lice.'

When a peasant from the Pas de Calais at this date became so finicky the louse situation must have been fantastically bad. Ovens for baking out the vermin had been sent out to France but their efficiency was doubtful. A story was current about two Jocks who were examining their clothes after these had passed through the ovens. 'Fergus—they're a' there yit!' 'Aye, mon! But they must h' got a awfu' frecht!'

'In January, 1915,' says Day, 'we were told we would go in batches to bathe and get clean underclothes at a laundry in Estaires, part of which had been turned into a bathing pool. Into the pool we went, stripped, and on coming out we were given clean underclothes. Part of the laundry was still being used for its original purpose, and sacking had been put around the pool to shield our modesty. But while we were washing we could see the sacking moving and hear the girls from the laundry commenting on our appearance!'

Soon, dozens of holes had been made in the sacking and salaciously inclined young Frenchwomen were peeping and squeaking at this vision of young British manhood in the nude!

Day was once asked to go up as observer. He was at first delighted, but after the aircraft had crossed the trench line he noticed the engine was failing. He signalled to the pilot who made back for home, reaching the edge of the airfield with a useless engine and confronted by a flock of sheep. The aircraft was written off completely in a whirl of oil, petrol and bits of sheep, but no one was much hurt and the squadron enjoyed fresh mutton as a change from the never-ending bully beef.

Day returned to England in early 1915 on promotion to Flight Sergeant and was posted to No. 40 Squadron. He seems to have spent a year in

England before going back to France to be stationed with the squadron at Aire. That winter of 1916-17, though not so bitter as the 1917-18 abomination, was quite cold enough. No. 40 was equipped with engines using vegetable oil as a lubricant. On return from a flight this oil was immediately emptied into a drum which was then placed next to a stove as near as safety permitted. The oil would then remain sufficiently fluid to be poured back into the engines next day. This was back-breaking and finger-freezing work at a temperature of zero Fahrenheit. Day speaks with feeling about this task. What seems to have struck him as particularly unfortunate was that even the beer froze solid, and in those days beer had some alcohol in it!

★ 903. J. H. O'DONOGHUE

A recruit, a direct entrant into RFC 7 October, 1913. As 2AM, No. 2 Squadron served in France from 12 August, 1914. Promoted to Corporal (Fitter turner) 1 October, 1917 and was Corporal Mechanic (Turner) in April, 1918 RAF Muster Roll. Later in 1918 he was an NCO Observer in 100 Squadron, promoted Sergeant in June, 1918, flew on 15 bombing flights against German aerodromes mainly with 2 Lieutenant Dickins. Discharged 1919. Home address 12 Ingrestre St., Stafford.

★ 904. E. L. TAYLOR

Formerly 6995 Sergeant No. 1 Signalling Company, RE. Transferred to RFC 9 July, 1913. Served as a Sergeant with RFC HQ in France from 12 August, 1914. Awarded a French Médaille Militaire for gallantry between 21 and 24 August, 1914 in *L.G.* 9 November, 1914. Commissioned 2 Lieutenant 29 August, 1915. Was Captain (Tech) in April, 1918 *A.F.L.*

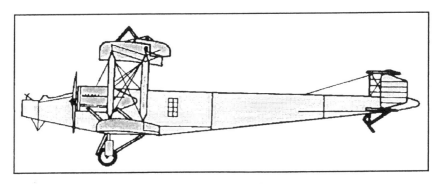

HANDLEY-PAGE O/100

★ 905. J. McKenzie

A recruit, a direct entrant into RFC 10 October, 1913. As 2AM, with Aircraft Park served in France from 16 August, 1914. Promoted Corporal (Fitter general) 1 March, 1917 and retained that rank and trade in April, 1918 RAF Muster Roll.

★ 906. W. J. Henry

A recruit, a direct entrant into RFC 1 October, 1913. As 2AM, 4 Squadron served in France from 12 August, 1914. Discharged, 24 July, 1915 under *K.R.* 392 (xiv) from wounds. Awarded Silver War Badge No. 10145.

907. W. H. Perrott

Enlisted 12 March, 1909. Formerly 22564 RE (Training Depot). Transferred to RFC 18 June, 1913. As 2AM, was on a Riggers course at CFS in September, 1914. Posted overseas 19 January, 1915 earning 1914/ 15 Star trio. He was an Aerial Gunner in 1915 with 5 Squadron. Promoted Flight Sergeant (Rigger) 19 September, 1916. He was Chief Mechanic (Rigger Aero) in April, 1918 RAF Muster Roll.

★ 908. Thomas Burns Williams

A recruit, a direct entrant into RFC 6 October, 1913. As 2AM, 6 Squadron served in France from 6 October, 1914. Promoted Flight Sergeant, (Fitter general) 1 July, 1917 and was Chief Mechanic (Fitter general) in April, 1918 RAF Muster Roll. Appointed Warrant Officer (Class 1) 19 March, 1930. Awarded RAF L.S.&G.C. medal *w.e.f.* 6 October, 1931.

909. G. L. Collins

A boy recruit, a direct entrant into RFC 13 October, 1913. No trace of entitlement to 1914 or 1914/15 Stars. Promoted 1AM (Rigger Aero) 1 July, 1917 and retained that rank and trade in April, 1918 RAF Muster Roll.

910. Sidney Richard Pegg

Born 4 September, 1898. A boy recruit, a direct entrant into RFC 13 October, 1913. No trace of entitlement to 1914 or 1914/15 Stars found. 2AM (Fitter general) 4 September, 1916 but reduced to 3AM in April,

1918 RAF Muster Roll. In March, 1924 sailed as a Flight Sergeant (fitter) in HMS *Pegasus*, a sea plane carrier for Singapore and Hong Kong. Awarded RAF L.S.&G.C. medal as Flight Sergeant *w.e.f.* 13 October, 1931. Awarded 1935 Silver Jubilee Medal. Appointed WO1 July, 1937. In January, 1938 *A.F.L.* shown as serving at No. 6 Armament Training Camp Dorchester from 1 July, 1937. Wherever he served he ran the station band, being very musical. He continued to serve all through WW2 as a Warrant Officer and was awarded a bar to his L.S.&G.C. in 1949. He was not discharged until 13 September, 1953. He was then commissioned as Flight Lieutenant (RAFVR) in the Air Training Corps. He died in 1980. Sadly, his medals were stolen in 1990, together with those of his father and his son. The full family group is M.B.E., War and Victory Medals, Defence and War Medals, 1935 Jubilee Medal and RAF L.S.&G.C. (and bar); Queen's South Africa and King's South Africa (ASC, Father); Africa General Service Medal (Kenya) and Campaign Service Medal (Northern Ireland) (RAF, Son). See *'The Forgotten Ones.'* He would appear to have been the last serving pre-war RFC man serving when he finally retired (See 1015).

911. W. W. S. STANLEY

A boy recruit, a direct entrant into RFC 13 October, 1913. No trace of entitlement to 1914 or 1914/15 Stars found. 2AM (Fitter engines) 17 August, 1917, but reduced to 3AM in April, 1918 RAF Muster Roll.

912. H. T. INGLIS

A boy recruit, a direct entrant into RFC 13 October, 1913. No trace of entitlement to 1914 or 1914/15 Stars found. 2AM (Fitter engines) 16 August, 1917, but reduced to 3AM (Fitter AE) in April, 1918 RAF Muster Roll. Awarded a George V (second type) Air Force Medal as Flight Sergeant Pilot in *L.G.* 3 June, 1931 (King's Birthday Honours). Of the 150 AFMs awarded in George V's reign only 20 were of this type (1930-37). Awarded RAF L.S.&G.C. medal as Flight Sergeant *w.e.f.* 3 November, 1931, 21 days later than one might have expected.

913. W. H. HILLS

A boy recruit, a direct entrant into RFC 13 October, 1913. No trace of 1914 or 1914/15 Stars found. Promoted 1AM (Fitter AE) 9 January, 1918 and retained that rank and trade in April, 1918 RAF Muster Roll. Served in South Russia until 9 July, 1919 with 47 Squadron, earning a British War Medal and a Victory Medal.

914. E. L. J. SAVILLE

A boy recruit, a direct entrant into RFC 13 October, 1913. No trace of entitlement to 1914 or 1914/15 Stars found. Promoted 1AM (Bomber) 1 November, 1917 and was 1AM (Miscellaneous) in April, 1918 RAF Muster Roll.

★ 915. W. STRUGNELL

Enlisted 1 January, 1912. Formerly 8062 15th Hussars. Transferred to RFC 13 May, 1913. A not very common surname, perhaps related to No. 71 (later Group Captain) W. V. Strugnell. As 1AM, with RAF HQ served in France from 12 August, 1914. Promoted Corporal (Fitter MT) 1 March, 1917 and retained that rank and trade in April, 1918 RAF Muster Roll. A Sergeant Strugnell, 7 (Bomber) Squadron won the 'Laurence Minot Memorial Trophy' in 1930.

★ 916. E. H. S. BICKHAM

Enlisted 8 November, 1912. Formerly 14333 Private 4th Middlesex Regt. Transferred to RFC 13 May, 1913. As 2AM, 4 Squadron earned 1914 Star and bar in France from 10 September, 1914, Promoted 1AM (Driver MT) 15 March, 1915 and retained that rank and trade in April, 1918 RAF Muster Roll.

★ 917. FREDERICK JAMES SHAW

Born 17 April, 1892 in Uttoxeter, Staffs. A recruit, a direct entrant into RFC 15 October, 1913. As 2AM, 5 Squadron served in France from 14 August, 1914. An Observer/Gunner with 16 Squadron from 4 October, 1915, after obtaining Royal Aero Club Aviators' certificate No. 3386 3 June, 1915, when a Sergeant. Missing then reported killed in action as Sergeant Pilot 15 Squadron, 4 February, 1917. His observer was 2 Lieutenant G. W. B. Bradford also killed. They were shot down in flames and were the 11th

accredited victory of Obltn. Erwin Bohme of Jägdstaffel Boelke. He was aged 25. His name is on the Arras Memorial of Missing Airmen. Son of Albert Edward and Alice Shaw of 6, Bow St, Rugeley, Staffordshire.

RFC Communiqué 11, 19 September, 1915:

Lt. Powell (pilot) and 1AM Shaw (observer), 5 Squadron, in a Vickers with a Lewis gun, when patrolling east of Polygon Wood at 6.00 a.m. and at a height of 9,000 feet saw an L.V.G. at a height of 6,000 feet. The Vickers dived at the German who also dived firing upwards over his tail. The Vickers followed firing until he had dived so low that it was impossible to follow him further. He was last seen flying very low towards Menin. Immediately afterwards Lt. Powell looked around and saw a large machine (German), an unknown type, coming up behind him. The machine was a three-seater with two engines, single fuselage, propellers behind main plane, two machine-guns. The machine was very much larger than a F.E.2, (probably a Rumpler G1 powered by two 150 hp Benz or 150 hp Mercedes engines. It had a wing span of 63 feet). Lt. Powell turned to engage it when he was about 100 yards away coming straight on and some 30 feet above the Vickers. The German was firing both his machine guns. When he was about 50 feet away 1AM Shaw emptied a drum into him and he dived straight down just over the tail of the Vickers. One of his engines had stopped and a cloud of smoke was seen coming from the other engine.

Another machine was seen flying westwards alaong the River Lys. When the Vickers turned towards him this machine went away.

While regaining height over Ypres Lt Powell observed an Albatros east of Poelcapelle. The last two drums of the Lewis gun were fired at him at a range of 200 yards. The German replied with his machine-gun but continued to fly eastwards. Having no more ammunition Lt Powell gave up the pursuit.

(Information has been received that on the 19th instant a German aeroplane fell at Lawe, pilot and observer both being killed. It is probable that the machine was brought down by Lt Powell and 1AM Shaw.)

RFC Communiqué No. 13, 3 October 1915:

Lt Powell (pilot) and 1AM Shaw (observer), of 5 Squadron, in a Vickers with Lewis gun when patrolling south-west of Passchendaele and Becelaere at 5.50 a.m. attacked an L.V.G. which dived, pursued by the Vickers. An Albatros then appeared on the scene and opened machine gun fire at about 300 yards range and then turned away. The Vickers followed the Albatros down to about 2,000 feet.

RFC Communiqué No. 15, 11 October 1915:

Lt Powell and 1AM Shaw, 5 Squadron, in a Vickers with Lewis gun, when patrolling near Hooge at 10 a.m., observed a German machine flying at a height of about 5,000 feet apparantly ranging. The German avoided action by flying eastward. As he was getting further away owing to his superior speed fire was opened on him at a range of about 300 yards. The pursuit had then to be broken off as a shell from an anti-aircraft gun burst not more than 3 feet to the left of the nacelle hitting 1AM Shaw in the leg and knocking three holes in the petrol tank just behind the pilot.

★ 918. L. Murphy

A recruit, a direct entrant into RFC 27 September, 1913. As 2AM, 2 Squadron earned 1914 Star and bar in France from 13 August, 1914. Commissioned 2 Lieutenant 12 May, 1915.

★ 919. S. Hill

Enlisted 27 June, 1908. Formerly 50779 RFA. Transferred to RFC 15 May, 1913. As 2AM, 5 Squadron served in France from 14 August, 1914 earning 1914 Star and bar. Promoted T/SM (D) 1 November, 1917 and was SM1 (Disciplinarian) in April, 1918 RAF Muster Roll.

★ 920. S. E. Eels

A recruit, a direct entrant into RFC 16 October, 1913. As 2AM, 5 Squadron served in France from 14 August, 1914. Promoted Corporal (Blacksmith), 1 August, 1917 and retained that rank and trade in April, 1918 RAF Muster Roll.

★ 921. R. Herrick

A recruit, a direct entrant into RFC 16 October, 1913. As 2AM, with the Aircraft Park served in France from 16 August, 1914. Promoted Sergeant (Rigger aero) 1 December, 1917 and retained that rank and trade in April, 1918 RAF Muster Roll. Awarded RAF L.S.&G.C. medal *w.e.f.* 16 October, 1931 as Flight Sergeant.

★ 922. W. Bailey

Enlisted into RFC 16 October, 1913. As 2AM, 5 Squadron served in France from 16 August, 1914. Possibly the W. J. Bailey who gained Royal

Aero Club Aviators' Certificate 3252 of 20 July, 1916. Commissioned 2 Lieutenant 29 September, 1917.

923. JAMES DENNIS PAYNE

Born 22 July, 1887. Enlisted into RFC 10 October, 1913. As 2AM, in 6 Squadron served overseas from 2 March, 1915 earning 1914/15 Star trio. Gained Royal Aero Club Aviators' Certificate No. 1415 of 10 July, 1915, as an NCO. Commissioned 2 Lieutenant 30 October, 1916. Joined 41 Squadron 12 June, 1917. Posted to 29 Squadron 6 August, 1917. Military Cross 23 August, 1917. Promoted to Flight Commander and in January, 1918 posted to Home Establishment, by which time he had shot down fourteen enemy aircraft.

924. G. H. COTTELL

Enlisted into RFC 18 October, 1913. As 2AM, discharged 29 January, 1914, free under article 1131 of the Pay Warrant.

★ 925. J. LENNOX

A recruit, a direct entrant into RFC 17 October 1913. As 2AM, 2 Squadron served in France from 12 August, 1914. Promoted Corporal (Blacksmith) 1 March, 1916 and retained that rank and trade in April, 1918 RAF Muster Roll.

★ 926. G. BROWN

Enlisted 6 March, 1912. Formerly 1509, Royal Horse Guards. Transferred to RFC 13 May, 1913. As 1AM, 3 Squadron served in France from 12 August, 1914. Promoted Flight Sergeant (Blacksmith) 1 May, 1916 and was Chief Mechanic (Blacksmith) in April, 1918 RAF Muster Roll.

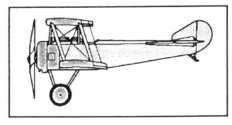

SOPWITH PUP

★ 927. J. LAWRENCE

Enlisted 1 July, 1912. Formerly 9651 2/Coldstream Guards. Transferred to RFC 13 May, 1913. As 2AM, 3 Squadron earned 1914 Star. Promoted Corporal (Electrician) 1 October, 1916 and retained that rank and trade in April, 1918 RAF Muster Roll.

928. S. EDWARDS

A recruit, a direct entrant into RFC 2 October, 1913. Serving with CFS in August, 1914. No trace of entitlement to 1914 or 1914/15 Stars found. Promoted Flight Sergeant (Rigger Aero) 1 May, 1917. He was Chief Mechanic in the April, 1918 RAF Muster Roll. Alive in July, 1977 living at Wellingore Hall, Wellingore, Lincoln.

★ 929. E. W. RUMSEY

A recruit, a direct entrant into RFC 18 October, 1913. As 2AM in the Aircraft Park served in France from 16 August, 1914. Mentioned in despatches as a Flight Sergeant 24 February, 1917. Discharged 12 August, 1917 when T/Sergeant Major, under *K.R.* 392 (xvi) 'sick' Silver War Badge No. 219138.

930. J. V. HALL

A recruit, a direct entrant into RFC 17 October, 1913. As 2AM, discharged 23 June, 1914 under *K.R.* 392 (xvi) 'no longer physically fit for war service.'

★ 931. EDWIN CECIL ('DARKY') RUMFORD

A recruit, a direct entrant into RFC 18 October, 1913. As 2AM, served with RFC HQ from 12 August, 1914 in France, and earned 1914 Star and bar. Mentioned in despatches 22 June, 1915 as Sergeant and awarded Russian 2nd Class Medal of St. George on 25 August, 1915 serving with 2 Squadron, 1 Wing. Commissioned 2 Lieutenant, 8 November, 1916. Lieutenant (Technical) in *A.F.L.* of 1 April, 1918.

★ 932. CHRISTOPHER WILLIAM HENRY BOWERS

A recruit, a direct entrant into RFC 17 October, 1913. As 2AM, 2 Squadron served in France from 12 August, 1914. Observer/ Gunner 13 October, 1915, with 2 Squadron. As a Corporal awarded Royal Aero Club Aviators' Certificate No. 3960, 8 December, 1916. Died 1 May, 1917, a Sergeant at No. 2 School of Aerial Gunnery. Buried Girvan Cemetery Strathclyde (Row D. Grave 1).

933. G. C. F. LESTER

A recruit, a direct entrant into RFC 18 October, 1913. No trace of entitlement to 1914 or 1914/15 Stars found. Promoted Flight Sergeant (Fitter general) 15 September, 1916, and was Chief Mechanic in April, 1918 RAF Muster Roll.

★ 934. ERIC A. HENRY DOBSON

Born Keele, Staffs, 2 December, 1894. A recruit, a direct entrant into RFC 13 October, 1913. As 1AM with RFC HQ served in France from 12 August, 1914 earning a 1914 Star and bar. Awarded Royal Aero Club Aviators' Certificate No. 1587 on 13 August, 1915 in a de Havilland aircraft, when a Corporal. Joined 24 Squadron as Sergeant on its formation at Hounslow in September, 1915. Served with them in France from 7 February to 28 March, 1916, at St. Omer and Bertangles. Posted to 32 Squadron and reported missing believed killed 12 August, 1916 flying as a pilot. *RFC Communiqué No. 48* states that haze limited observations on artillery targets on that day. His name is on the Arras Memorial of Missing Airmen. Son of Frederick and Esther Dobson of 141 Poplar Ave, Edgbaston, Birmingham, aged 22.

* 935. J. H. Davis

A recruit, a direct entrant into RFC 23 October, 1913. As 2AM, 2 Squadron served in France from 12 August, 1914. Promoted Sergeant (Rigger Aero) 1 November, 1917 and retained that rank and trade in April, 1918 RAF Muster Roll.

* 936. A. A. Winder

Enlisted into RFC 24 October, 1913. As 2AM, with the Aircraft Park served in France from 16 August, 1914. Promoted 1AM (Driver MT) and retained that rank and trade in April, 1918 RAF Muster Roll. Died in South Australia. Buried in Central Park Cemetary, Adelaide, under a headstone which reads, '936 Corporal A. A. Winder, Royal Flying Corps. 29 May, 1959 aged 64.'

* 937. Samuel Bingham

Enlisted into RFC 16 October, 1913. As 2AM, 2 Squadron served in France and awarded 1914 Star. Promoted Sergeant (Clerk General) 7 January, 1917. Recommended in 2 Squadron, twice, unsuccessfully for Army M.S.M. September and December, 1917. Sergeant Clerk in April, 1918 RAF Muster Roll. Commissioned. No. 53943 in 1921 (November) *A.F.L.* shown on Stores List as Flying Officer from 12 September, 1919. Since 29 December, 1920 he had been stationed at RAF Aircraft Park Iraq which was commanded by Wing Commander A Fletcher C.M.G., C.B.E., M.C. (See No. 4 on this roll). Promoted Flight Lieutenant 1 July, 1927. In February, 1931 *A.F.L.* he had been serving from 20 March 1929 at No. 4 Flying Training School, Abu Sueir (Middle East) which was then equipped with Atlas, Avro, Bristol Fighter and Vimy aircraft. Promoted to Squadron Leader 1 February, 1936. Since 28 September, 1937 stationed at Home Aircraft Depot, Biggleswade, Beds.

* 938. H. H. Winton

Enlisted into RFC 28 October, 1913. As 2AM, 2 Squadron served in France and earned 1914 Star. Promoted Flight Sergeant (Fitter Engines) 1 October, 1917 and was Chief Mechanic (Fitter AE) in April, 1918 RAF Muster Roll.

★ 939. H. JONES

A recruit, a direct entrant into RFC 25 October, 1913. As 2AM, 2 Squadron served in France from 26 September, 1914, earning 1914 Star and bar. Promoted Corporal (Armourer) 1 September, 1916 and retained that rank and trade in April, 1918 RAF Muster Roll.

★ 940. GEORGE FARMER

A recruit, a direct entrant into RFC 27 October, 1913. As 2AM, 5 Squadron served in France from 14 August, 1914. Promoted Corporal (Photographer) 1 July, 1916 and retained that rank and trade in April, 1918 RAF Muster Roll. Wounded 5 August, 1918, as Corporal, 5 Squadron with 20 others.

★ 941. G. A. LEMON

A recruit, a direct entrant into RFC 15 October, 1913. As 2AM with the Aircraft Park served in France from 16 August, 1914. Reverted to Sergeant (Fitter Engines) 7 March, 1917 and was Sergeant Mechanic (Fitter AE) in April, 1918 RAF Muster Roll.

★ 942. C. J. O'TOOLE

A recruit, a direct entrant into RFC 18 October, 1913. As 1AM, 5 Squadron earned 1914 Star and bar in France from 14 August, 1914. Promoted T/SM (T) 1 February, 1916 and was Chief Master Mechanic (Technical) in April, 1918 RAF Muster Roll. Awarded RAF Meritorious Service Medal as Sergeant (Temporary Sgt Maj.) in *L.G.* 3 June, 1918 for services in France. He originated from Dublin.

★ 943. J. ROBINSON

A recruit, a direct entrant into RFC 3 November, 1913. As 2AM, 4 Squadron served in France from 12 August, 1914. Promoted T/SM (D) 1 September, 1916 and was SM1 (Disciplinarian) in April, 1918 RAF Muster Roll. Awarded RAF Meritorious Service Medal as T/SM in *L.G.* 3 June, 1918 for services in France. Originally from Gillingham. 1914 Star, Victory Medal (SM RAF) and RAF M.S.M. in McInnes collection.

★ 944. THOMAS CHRISTOPHER GEORGE BIRD

Born Solihull 25 December, 1895. A recruit, a direct entrant into RFC 31 October, 1913. As 2AM, 5 Squadron earned 1914 Star and bar in France from 14 August, 1914. Mentioned in despatches as a Corporal 22 June, 1915. Promoted Flight Sergeant, 1st Class Pilot 1 March, 1916. Awarded Royal Aero Club Aviators' Certificate No. 2617 24 March, 1916. Was Chief Mechanic (Pilot) in April, 1918 RAF Muster Roll.

★ 945. A. F. WILKINSON

Enlisted 27 June, 1905. Formerly 23530, Royal Garrison Artillery. Transferred to RFC 22 May, 1913. As 1AM Airship Detachment earned 1914 Star and bar. Transferred to RNAS 18 October, 1914 as 1AM No. 665. CPO3 (Engineer) 6 September, 1916. Was Chief Mechanic (Fitter general) No. 200665 in April, 1918 RAF Muster Roll. Awarded RAF L.S.&G.C. medal as Flight Sergeant 27 June, 1923.

★ 946. L. LINDOP

A recruit, a direct entrant into RFC 3 November, 1913. As 2AM, 2 Squadron served in France from 12 August, 1914. As Sergeant, discharged 'sick' under *K.R.* 392 (xvi) 30 June, 1916. Silver War Badge No. 161049 issued.

947. W. WRIGHT

A recruit. Discharged 17 November, 1913 under *K.R.* 392 (v) on payment of £10.

★ 948. WILLIAM LODGE

A recruit, a direct entrant into RFC 4 November, 1913. As 2AM, 2 Squadron earned 1914 Star and bar in France from 12 August, 1914. Promoted Flight Sergeant (Photographer) 1 November, 1917 and was Chief Mechanic (Photographer) in April, 1918 RAF Muster Roll. Awarded RAF M.S.M. in *L.G.* 1 January, 1919 as Chief Mechanic, for services in France. Came originally from Brighton. Awarded RAF L.S.&G.C. medal as SM2 *w.e.f.* 4 November, 1931. Awarded 1935 Silver Jubilee Medal. Commissioned (CEO) Flying Officer, *w.e.f.* 23 August, 1937. In 1937 *A.F.L.* was shown as serving, from 30 August, 1937 with 3 Apprentice Wing at No. 1 School of Technical Training Halton Camp. Promoted through to Squadron Leader 1 September, 1941 and to Wing Commander by 1 September, 1942. In 1946 *A.F.L.* still serving (No. 35128). His 1914 Star (only) is known in a private collection.

★ 949. W. JOHNSON

A recruit, a direct entrant into RFC 4 November, 1913. As 2AM, 4 Squadron served in France, earning 1914 Star and bar, from 12 August, 1914. Promoted Corporal (Fitter general) 1 April, 1917 and retained that rank and trade in April, 1918 Muster Roll.

★ 950. C. E. H. BUNTING

A recruit, a direct entrant into RFC 6 November, 1913. As 1AM, with the Aircraft Park served in France from 16 August, 1914. Promoted T/ SM (T) 1 March, 1917. Awarded Army Meritorious Service Medal as A/ Sgt. Maj. 10 Squadron in *L.G.* 4 July, 1917. Was Chief Master Mechanic (Technical) in April, 1918 RAF Muster Roll. Listed in the *Times* 'B' Press Release of 23 January, 1919 by the Air Ministry. Mentioned in despatches for services in Somaliland, in *L.G.* 12 July, 1920 and awarded African General Service Medal (clasp Somaliland 1920). This clasp was awarded for services between 21 January, and 12 February of that year, 36 RAF officers and 189 other ranks, under command of Group Captain R. Gordon with a flight of DH9 bombers, receiving the medal. Two of Bunting's medals are known in a private collection, having been sold at Glendining in 1981 for £650, his Army M.S.M. and his African General Service Medal. (See also No. 864.)

★ 951. C. S. W. JOHNCOCK

A recruit, a direct entrant into RFC 3 November, 1913. As 2AM, with Aircraft Park served in France from 16 August, 1914. Promoted Corporal (Fitter engines) 1 September, 1917 and was Corporal Mechanic (Fitter AE) in April, 1918 RAF Muster Roll.

952. F. GILL

A recruit, a direct entrant into RFC 6 November, 1913. Deserted 19 April, 1914.

★ 953. JOHN W. FAULKNER

Enlisted 19 January, 1912. Formerly 8808 1/Wilts. Regt. Transferred to RFC 29 May, 1913. As 2AM, 3 Squadron earned 1914 Star and bar in France from 13 August, 1914. Promoted Flight Sergeant (Fitter Engines) 1 November, 1917 and was Chief Mechanic (Fitter AE) in April, 1918 RAF Muster Roll. Awarded General Service Medal (clasp Kurdistan). Awarded RAF L.S.&G.C. medal *w.e.f.* 19 January, 1930 as Flight Sergeant. Awarded 1935 Silver Jubilee Medal. Appointed WO Class 1 *w.e.f.* 1 May, 1935. In 1937 *A.F.L.* shown as serving from 17 June, 1935 at Old Sarum, Salisbury (No. 16 Army Co-operation Squadron).

954. J. SMITH

See No. 900. Probably formerly 12015 2/Worcs Regt. As 1AM with 3 Squadron deserted 5 June, 1914.

★ 955. A. R. HARVEY

A recruit, a direct entrant into RFC 7 November, 1913. As 2AM, 5 Squadron served in France from 14 August, 1914. In *RFC Communiqué No. 36* of 18 May, 1916 he is noted as flying as Corporal Observer in a BE2c with 2 Lieutenant Williams of 5 Squadron on patrol at 11500 feet over Hooge and being attacked by a German Fokker aircraft. He fired one full drum into it at close range and it fell out of control. Promoted Flight Sergeant (Fitter general) 1 April, 1917 and was Chief Mechanic in April, 1918 RAF Muster Roll.

★ 956. W. TOOKE

A recruit, a direct entrant into RFC 10 November, 1913. As 2AM, with the Aircraft Park served in France from 16 August, 1914. Promoted Flight Sergeant (Photographer) 1 February, 1917 and was Chief Mechanic in April, 1918 RAF Muster Roll.

★ 957. DAVID PATTERSON

Born Bailiebourough, Cavan, Ireland, 26 May, 1883. Enlisted 20 February, 1899. Promoted Sergeant 8 August, 1907. Formerly 7942 Sergeant, 1/Grenadier Guards. Transferred to RFC 16 August, 1913. Awarded Royal Aero Club Aviators' Certificate No. 677 on 4 November, 1913 in a Short aircraft of the Central Flying School at Upavon. Appointed 2nd class Flyer *w.e.f.* 17 December, 1913 (Certificate No. 51). As Sergeant, 5 Squadron served in France from 14 August, 1914. Appointed Warrant Officer (Technical) 12 March, 1915 and awarded Army L.S.&G.C. medal in Army Order 312 of October, 1917. He was a Chief Master Mechanic (Technical) in April, 1918 RAF Muster Roll. Appointed Warrant Officer 1 July, 1934 and was the 73rd senior RAF Warrant Officer in November, 1941 *A.F.L.* He served on during WWII and as a Flight Lieutenant (RAFVR) aged 59 in June, 1942 was appointed a Member of the Order of the British Empire. In 1951 in *A.O.* 156 he was awarded a Meritorious Service Medal in respect of his services in the Guards prior to WW1. (See also No. 296 Hoffman.) His group of nine medals were sold at auction by Sothebys in 1980: M.B.E. (2nd type, military ribbon), 1914 Star and bar, British War Medal and Victory Medal (oakleaf), 1939/45 Star, Defence, 1939/45 War Medal, Army L.S.&G.C. (GV. WO RFC), Army M.S.M. (GV1 WO1 Gren. Gds.) Belgian Croix de Guerre. His

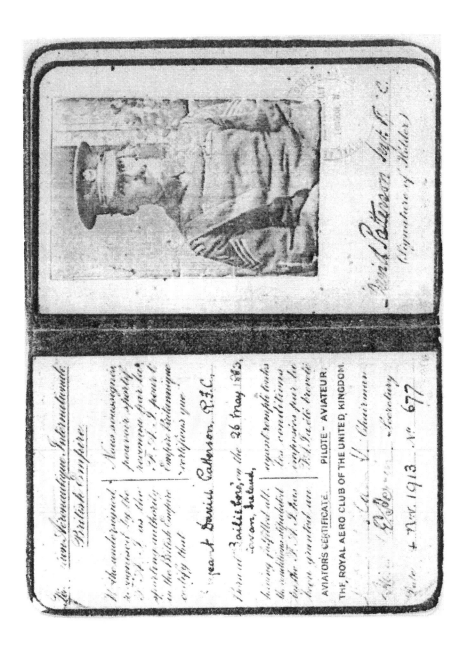

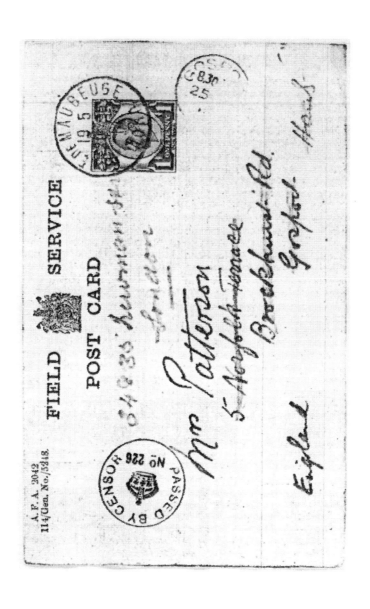

NOTHING is to be written on this except
the date and signature of the sender. Sentences
not required may be erased. If anything else
is added the post card will be destroyed.

I am quite well.

~~I have been admitted into hospital~~

{ ~~sick~~ } ~~and am going on well.~~

{ ~~wounded~~ } ~~and hope to be discharged soon.~~

~~I am being sent down to the base.~~

~~I have received your~~ { ~~letter.~~
~~telegram.~~
~~parcel.~~ }

Letter follows at first opportunity.

I have received no letter from you

{ ~~lately.~~
~~for a long time.~~ }

Signature }
only. } David Patterson

Date 19th August '14

[Postage must be prepaid on any letter or postcard addressed
to the sender of this card.]

B.

Certificate No. *51.*

ROYAL FLYING CORPS.

(Flying Certificate—Warrant, Petty and Non-Commissioned Officers, and Men.)

CENTRAL FLYING SCHOOL,

UPAVON,

17ᵗ December 1913.

THIS IS TO CERTIFY that *No 957 Sergeant.*

D. Patterson, R. F. C.

has graduated at the Central Flying School, and is qualified as a* *second*
class flyer in the Royal Flying Corps.

Captain Rᵂ.
Commandant. *6·7·5*

* Here insert " First " or " Second."

W 2557—2015 500 6/12 H W V G. 12
66¹

entitlement to this last medal has not been traced. See group photograph
No. 2.

★ 958. GEORGE WIRTH EDDINGTON

A recruit, a direct entrant into RFC 12 November, 1913. As 2AM, 2 Squadron earned 1914 Star and bar in France from 12 August, 1914. Awarded Royal Aero Club Aviators' Certificate No. 4465 on 4 April, 1917 as Corporal and was promoted Sergeant (1st class pilot) 30 April, 1917. Awarded Military Medal in *L.G.* 12 December, 1917. He was wounded in January, 1918. Shown as Sergeant Mechanic (Pilot) in April, 1918 RAF Muster Roll. He came from Tottenham, London.

★ 959. R. S. GUDE

A recruit, a direct entrant into RFC 14 November, 1913. As 2AM, No. 5 Squadron served in France from 14 August, 1914. Awarded Royal Aero Club Aviators' Certificate No. 4461 on 2 April, 1917 as Corporal. Promoted Sergeant (1st class Pilot) 27 May, 1917 and was Sergeant Mechanic (Pilot) in April, 1918 RAF Muster Roll. As Sergeant Pilot, 211 Squadron he was reported missing 27 July, 1918. In fact he made a forced landing in Holland after bombing raid and was interned.

★ 960. JOHN GRANT MCKENZIE MARTIN STRONACH

Born 6 July, 1891 at Huntley, Aberdeen. A recruit, a direct entrant into RFC 7 November, 1913. As 2AM No. 2 Squadron served in France from 12 August, 1914. Awarded Royal Aero Club Aviators' Certificate 2252 1 May 1916, in a Maurice Farman Bi-plane at the Military School Shoreham. Mentioned in Despatches 24 February, 1917 as Flight Sergeant and listed in the *Times* 'B' Press Release of 27 March, 1917. Promoted Temporary Sergeant Major (Technical) 1 July, 1917 and was Chief Master Mechanic (Technical) in April, 1918 RAF Muster Roll. Served in France and the Adriatic. Later Commissioned and as a 2 Lieutenant, RAF appointed a Member of the Order of the British Empire in *L.G.* 3 June, 1919. His group of medals is known in a private collection: M.B.E. (1st

George R. I.

George the Fifth by the Grace of God of the United Kingdom of Great Britain and Ireland, and of the British Dominions beyond the Seas, King Defender of the Faith, Emperor of India, and Sovereign of the Most Excellent Order of the British Empire to Our trusty and well beloved John Grant McKenzie Martin Stronach Esquire Second Lieutenant in Our Army

Greeting whereas We have thought fit to nominate and appoint you to be a Member

of the Military Division of Our said Most Excellent Order of the British Empire,

Grant of the dignity of a Member
of the Military Division of the Order of the British Empire
to Second Lieutenant John Grant McKenzie Martin Stronach

We do by these presents grant unto you the Dignity of a   Member   of Our said Order and hereby authorise you to have hold and enjoy the said Dignity and Rank of a   Member   of Our aforesaid Order together with all and singular the privileges thereunto belonging or appertaining.

Given at Our Court, at Saint James's under Our Sign Manual and Seal of Our said Order, this   Third   day of June   1919, in the Tenth year of Our Reign.

By the Sovereign's Command.

Edward P

Grand Master.

Type, military ribbon), 1914 Star (2AM RFC) British War Medal and Victory Medal (Flight Sergeant RFC) with oakleaf and a French Croix de Guerre. His entitlement to this last award has not been traced.

★ 961. A. H. JACOBS

A recruit, a direct entrant into RFC 14 November, 1913. As 2AM, No. 5 Squadron served in France from 14 August, 1914. Promoted Corporal (Driver MT) 1 November, 1917 and was Corporal Mechanic (Driver) in April, 1918 RAF Muster Roll.

962. ERIC NORMAN DEANE

Formerly 18862, Sergeant 3 Field Troop, Royal Engineers. Transferred to RFC 4 July, 1913. He was killed in a flying accident 8 April, 1914, while learning to fly at Brooklands, with British and Colonial Aeroplanes Ltd. He was in a Bristol pusher bi-plane and whilst making a steep gliding turn, not being strapped in, he fell out. Buried 11 April, 1914 at Gillingham, Kent. He was a pupil of Warren F. Merrian. He fell several hundred feet and the 'box kite' aircraft wallowed to a crash landing. Shortly afterwards safety belts were fitted to all service machines.

★ 963. R. M. WILDBORE

A recruit, a direct entrant into RFC 6 November, 1913. As 2AM, 2 Squadron earned 1914 Star and bar in France. Promoted Sergeant (Carpenter) 1 February, 1916. Mentioned in despatches, 24 February,

1917. Listed in the *Times* 'B' Press Release of 27 March, 1917. Was Sergeant Mechanic (Carpenter) in April, 1918 RAF Muster Roll. Awarded RAF L.S.&G.C. medal *w.e.f.* 6 November, 1931 as SM2. Awarded Indian General Service Medal (clasp Waziristan 1925). Appointed WO 15 May, 1934 and in March, 1938 *A.F.L.* shown as stationed at No. 10 FTS Tern Hill.

964. W. BRERETON

Formerly a boy signaller in an RE company of the Territorial Force. A boy recruit, a direct entrant into RFC 19 November, 1913. Still a Boy at the Recruit Depot in August, 1914. Served overseas as 2AM from 30 September, 1914, probably in Egypt and awarded 1914/15 Star. Reverted to Sergeant (Miscellaneous) 25 May, 1917 and was Sergeant (Disciplinarian) in April, 1918 RAF Muster Roll. At the outbreak of WW2 he was a Flight Sergeant parachute instructor at RAF Ringway, Manchester and was later a Wing Commander. His quite remarkable group of medals are in the Airborne Forces Museum at Aldershot:— M.B.E., A.F.C., 1914/15 trio, Defence and War Medals and RAF L.S.&G.C. medal.

★ 965. A. MANDEVILLE

A recruit, a direct entrant into RFC 18 November, 1913. As 2AM, with Aircraft Park served in France from 16 August, 1914. Promoted Sergeant (MT Driver) 1 January, 1918 and retained that rank and trade in April, 1918 RAF Muster Roll.

★ 966. MAURICE WALKER PIERCEY

Born London, 27 May, 1891. A recruit, a direct entrant into RFC 22 November, 1913. As 1AM, with the Aircraft Park served in France from 16 August, 1914. As a Corporal he was awarded Royal Aero Club Aviators' Certificate No. 1842, 7 October, 1915. In *RFC Communiqué No. 44* dated 21 July, 1916 it states that as a Sergeant, he was one of five pilots in De Havilland aircraft and that they were attacked by five Rolands and five Fokkers which were driven off. They then attacked four LVGs, breaking up the hostile formation. *RFC Communiqué No. 46* of 3 August, 1916 says he was piloting one of four DH aircraft of 24 Squadron when they encountered seven hostile machines near Flers. Five were driven down and the other two scattered East. The fight lasted 45 minutes. During this encounter Sergeant Piercey engaged another hostile aircraft, high above the remainder preventing it from attacking. Promoted Flight Sergeant (1st Class Pilot) 1 November, 1916 he was Chief Mechanic (pilot) in April, 1918 RAF Muster Roll, though he had been commissioned 2 Lieutenant 27 March, 1918.

★ 967. JOHN SHEPHERD ELLARD

Enlisted 18 August, 1910. Formerly 14874 Lance Corporal 3/Grenadier Guards. Transferred to RFC 21 June, 1913. As 1AM, 6 Squadron earned 1914 Star and bar in France from 7 October, 1914. Promoted TempSM (D) 1 February, 1918 and was SM1 (Disciplinarian) in April, 1918 RAF Muster Roll. Listed in the *Times* 'B' Press Release of 29 August, 1919. Awarded RAF L.S.&G.C. medal *w.e.f.* 18 August, 1928 as SM1. 77th Senior RAF Warrant Officer in February, 1931 *A.F.L.*, out of a total of 209. See also Nos. 197 and 696.

★ 968. W. H. HARVEY

A recruit, a direct entrant into RFC 22 November, 1913. As 2AM, 5 Squadron served in France earning 1914 Star and bar from 14 August, 1914. Promoted 1AM (Fitter, general) 1 April, 1915 and retained that rank and trade in April, 1918 RAF Muster Roll.

★ 969. R. A. TALLBOYS

A recruit, a direct entrant into RFC 24 November, 1913. As 2AM, 2 Squadron earned 1914 Star and bar in France. Promoted Sergeant (Rigger) 1 October, 1917 and was Sgt Mech (Rigger aero) in April, 1918 RAF Muster Roll.

970. L. U. HENDERSON

A recruit, a direct entrant into RFC 24 November, 1913. 2AM, 5 Squadron in August, 1914 but did not proceed overseas until posted to Egypt in October; 1914. His entitlement to a 1914/15 Star is stated as dating from 15 November, 1915. Commissioned 2 Lieutenant 20 November, 1917. Died 29 October, 1918.

★ 971. F. HOCKLEY

A recruit, a direct entrant into RFC 28 November, 1913. As 2AM, 2 Squadron earned 1914 Star and bar in France from 12 August, 1914. Promoted Sergeant (MT Driver) 1 November, 1917 and was Sergeant Mech (Driver) in April, 1918 RAF Muster Roll.

★ 972. D. EVANS

A recruit, a direct entrant into RFC 28 November, 1913. As 2AM, 2 Squadron served in France from 12 August, 1914. Promoted Sergeant (Fitter general) 1 April, 1917 and retained that rank and trade in April, 1918 RAF Muster Roll.

973. WILLIAM ROBERT McCLEERY

A Boy recruit, a direct entrant into RFC 1 December, 1913. Was 2AM, in August, 1914 but no trace of entitlement of either 1914 or 1914/15 Stars has been found. Awarded Royal Aero Club Aviators' Certificate No. 4971, 12 July, 1917, as 1st Class Air Mechanic. Promoted Sergeant (1st Class Pilot) 15 August, 1917. Wounded February, 1918. Was Sergeant Mechanic (Pilot) in April, 1918 RAF Muster Roll. Awarded French Croix de Guerre 17 August, 1918. Would of course also have been entitled to British War Medal and Victory Medal, Awarded General Service Medal (clasp Kurdistan). Awarded RAF L.S.&G.C. medal *w.e.f.* 1 December, 1931 as Flight Sergeant. Awarded Air Force Medal as Flight Sergeant in *L.G.* 4 June, 1934 (this would be GV second type). Awarded 1935 Silver Jubilee Medal. Came from Swindon. Commissioned and promoted Flying Officer (E) 8 January, 1937. In March 1938 *A.F.L.* stationed at 'C' Equipment Depot, Coventry.

974. H. R. C. CURGENVEN

A recruit, a direct entrant into RFC 29 November, 1913. Was 2AM, 5 Squadron in August, 1914. No trace of entitlement to either 1914 or 1914/15 Stars has been traced. Reduced to 1AM (Fitter engines) 1 June, 1916 and retained this rank and trade in April, 1918 RAF Muster Roll.

975. H. J. HIATT

Enlisted 29 July, 1911. Formerly 15386 Drummer 2/Grenadier Guards. Transferred to RFC 20 August, 1913. Still a Boy with the Aircraft Park in August, 1914. Served overseas from 20 December, 1915, just being entitled to 1914/15 Star. Promoted to Temp SM (T) 1 October, 1917. Was Chief Master Mechanic (Technical) in April, 1918 RAF Muster Roll. (See also No. 1353.)

* 976. J. FALDON

A recruit, a direct entrant into RFC 29 November, 1913. As 2AM, 5 Squadron served in France from 14 August, 1914. Reverted to Corporal (Fitter general) 5 June, 1917 and retained that rank and trade in April, 1918 RAF Muster Roll. 1914 Star Trio known in a private collection, later (in 1989) sold for £250. See group photograph under No. 979.

* 977. A MAGOOKIN

A recruit, a direct entrant into RFC 29 November, 1913. As 2AM, with the Aircraft Park served in France from 16 August, 1914. Promoted Corporal (Fitter Engines) 1 November, 1916, and retained that rank and trade in April, 1918 RAF Muster Roll.

978. C. HOOD

A recruit, a direct entrant into RFC 1 December, 1913. Deserted 25 April, 1914. Re-joined 9 August, 1914 and given a free pardon. Served overseas from 3 December, 1914, being thus entitled to 1914/15 Star trio. Discharged 17 December, 1915.

* 979. ERIC G. SHREWSBURY

Born 6 January, 1894, his father was born in 1869 and was a School master before he enlisted aged 46 in 1915 into the King's Royal Rifle Corps. He was killed in action in 1917. Shrewsbury himself was a boy scout in 1903. Joined the TA in 1912 (20th London Regt) then the regular army, initially attempting to join the ASC and being recommended by the recruiting Sergeant to consider 'the new flying corps.' A recruit, a direct entrant into RFC 29 November, 1913. As 2AM, 5 Squadron shared a room with No. 47 Geard (killed in France August, 1914) No. 57 Kidd and No. 71 Strugnell (later Group Captain M.C. and bar). Served in France as 2AM,

5 Squadron from 14 August, 1914. In Febuary, 1915 invalided to England and served as a Corporal at Netheravon in the MT Repair Depot, with 48 Squadron. He went with them to France from 7 March, 1917 to 17 November, 1917 as Sergeant in Charge of Motor Transport. Promoted Temp SM (T) 1 November, 1917 and was Chief Master Mechanic (Technical) in April, 1918 RAF Muster Roll. He originally enlisted for four years and four years reserve service. Once the war was over he was discharged, but not until June, 1921. He took his pilots' license between the wars in the Civil Air Guard, in a Swallow and a Gypsy Moth. Was a Major in the Home Guard in WW2 at the Woolwich

Works of Standard Telephones. In November, 1988 he appeared in a TV documentary 'Cavalry in the Clouds' and sent the following letter to the authors in January 1989 when he was 95 years of age:

'At the time I joined the Royal Flying Corps, in 1913, it was still run like a regiment of the old Victorian army, when class distinction was rife throughout, where in regular units of the line, Officers were gentlemen while the 'other ranks' were considered riff-raff, out-of-works, often joining the army instead of prison.

In the beginning, RFC Officers, being 'seconded' from other regiments, brought some of this with them.

The Adjutant of the RFC was one Barrington Kennett, of the Grenadier Guards and the powers-that-be decided (in the interest of flying?) that one should be instructed on how to salute with walking-out cane and without walking-out cane.

We were given lectures, on being ordered, how to 'fall-in' to put a man under arrest.

Refusal to do so, was by far the worse crime.

All the drill instructors were, of course, Grenadier Guardsmen. The exception being our drill Sergeant Major, who was late of the Prison Service (No. 984 Wilford).

Barrington Kennett's favourite hobby was to order a squadron on parade and then put everybody, but everybody, on a charge of some sort, 'To smarten them up.'

The charge I was put on was 'Shaving the upper lip,' although at that time, I had never shaved in my life.

When the RFC was first formed, No. 1 was the airship squadron, made up mostly of naval ratings.

Nos. 2, 3 and 4 were composed from the Kite Balloon and Air Battalion sections of the Royal Engineers and transfers from other regiments, whereas, No. 5 tended to be largely 'direct trade entries' like myself.

No. 2 was away at Montrose, with Nos. 3 and 4 at Larkhill or Netheravon while No. 5 stayed at Farnborough, the Headquarters.

With hindsight, on reading the narratives of other members, Nos. 2, 3 and 4 squadrons seem to have been more well knit squadrons of old soldiers and because they were away on their own, commanders took more interest in their 'rank and file' and the 'other ranks' were more used to looking after themselves.

While No. 5 seemed to be a hotchpotch of ex-civilians, with not too much notice being taken of them, with the squadron, as a whole, being overshadowed by the comings and goings at HQ and the awakened publicity of the Royal Aircraft Factory close by.

No. 5 had no quarters of its own, but shared blocks of the Blenheim and Malplaquet Barracks in Aldershot.

Aldershot, the wholly military town, steeped in army tradition and lore, where mainly 'Pubs' provided entertainment for the troops.

On Saturday afternoons, there being no general duties, it was an unwritten law among the troops 'In bed or out of barracks.'

At such times, as a young teetotaller, I used to wander down to Laffans Plain and help myself to Bowden fittings from Cody's wrecked and abandoned machine.

Our block had the Black Watch, practicing with their bagpipes, on the one side and the Munster Fusiliers who tried to sell us their comrades boots, on the other.

Each barrack room accommodated 12 or so men, with a partitioned off Sergeants' room at one end and a coal fire-place at the other with a prescribed amount of fuel which might be burned in winter.

Two or three bare light bulbs hung from the ceiling. Furniture consisted of plain wooden plank tables (which had to be scrubbed) on iron trestles, likewise wooden similar stools the same length along each side.

Beds were iron frames, with three stuffed pallets, the whole folding up into a sort of chair, during the daytime (not to be sat on, until after the Orderly Officer's inspection).

A rack over each bed, on which ones kit had to be folded and packed in the prescribed manner.

Our kit comprised, Cap, Tunic, Breeches and Slacks, 2 pairs Boots and socks, Short Great Coat, Two grey back flannel shirts, which had to double as night shirt, open-bladed razor and brushes.

Two brown blankets, with a tunic or other clothing folded as a pillow.

There was no sanitary arrangement of any sort in the barrack rooms, 'ablutions' so called, were in a separate block, some hundred or more yards away, where those old enough to shave had to do so in cold water with cut-throat razors.

A large container, for night use, was brought in each night and the orderly man had to get it away sharp in 'reveille' each morning, otherwise it was used to over-flowing.

976 FALDON (*back row, right*), 979 SHREWSBURY (*second row from back, left*), 983 BRASSINGTON (*second row from back, right*), 984 SGT. MAJ. WILFORD (*sitting, second from left*).

Likewise the cookhouse was in a separate block some distance away and the orderly man of the day brought the food to the room in a large open two handled pan, so, even if it was palatable at the cookhouse, it was cold and barely edible when it was dished out to us in the barrack room, but we had to eat it or starve.

As well as an orderly to clean the room and bring the food etc., there were other fatigues, such as coal fatigue, delivering coal to married quarters, cook house fatigue, peeling spuds, guard duties at the hangers and Church parades with near fatigues in the form of kit inspections.

Mention of Sergeants earlier reminds me that originally the only ranks in the RFC were 2nd Class Air Mechanic, 1st Class ditto, Sergeants, and in the squadrons two Sergeant Majors, one technical and the other disciplinarian.

Corporal rank was brought in during the war [sic].

The machines No. 5 had were mostly 80 HP Henri Farmans with one or two 50 HP warped wing Avros and later 80 HP 504 type Avros.

There were two mechanics per machine, engine man and rigger.

Maybe because I had passed a mechanical trade test (fitter and turner) I was put down as engine man although I was never told anything about the Gnome rotary engine involved, the only instruction received was to take a wing tip when our machine was taxying in, fill up with oil and petrol, then help the rigger wipe off the sticky castor oil on the machine parts, thrown out from the engine (due to total loss lubrication) before it set and hardened.

On this particular day, the machine came in, the officer pilot got out and went away, without a word, as usual. I had filled up and was helping the rigger wipe off, when he came back with another officer, soon after, inspected the engine and I heard him say 'Priceless.'

It turned out that the back plate of the nacelle, supporting the engine, with sections cut out to lighten, had started to crack at the perforations.

I was held to blame, narrowly missed being court-martialled and was demoted to rigger.

(Much later in life, when training for pilot, it was impressed on me to report any roughness in running or anything untoward noticed in flight, to the maintenance men on landing).

In May 1914, No. 5 had a flying accident, a collision in the air, resulting in Captain Anderson and a mechanic in the other machine being killed. Captain Anderson was given a full military gun carriage funeral, with detachments from all squadrons carrying wreaths in the cortage.

No. 5 – Commanding Officer Major Higgins (complete with eye glass) – together with the other aeroplane squadrons foregathered in June, 1914 at Netheravon in what was termed 'the concentration camp.' No. 5 under canvas.

Although I was unaware at the time (or don't remember) several notables were said to have visited the camp. McCudden in his book says Lord Roberts. Butcher in his, says Kitchener.

On the break up, No. 5 seems to have slipped away without fuss to Fort Grange, Gosport, while other squadrons were having group photos taken, No. 2 complete with Colonel Sykes commanding the RFC.

The squadron, as stated, went to Fort Grange but for some reason, I was sent to the British and Colonial Company, at Bristol on a course (my very first) for rigging the BE8, nicknamed 'Bloater,' because of its shape, a R. A. Factory design, as I understand, then coming on production.

On being assigned to an employee erecting a machine, I noticed fitting the engine in place, he was awkwardly using packing strips with his spanners.

Enquiring why, he explained that his spanners were British Imperial size while the units on the engine were metric size.

I said, if he could find an old 10″ flat file I would make him a metric spanner, which I did (and still have one). The word got round and for the rest of the time there, I was making metric spanners for all and sundry. Although I did not get much done on rigging, I was reported on, very favourably, by those at the works, supervising the course.

Was hoping to go on leave from Bristol, but had a telegram saying return to squadron. It turned out war was on the eve of being declared.

At Fort Grange, found the squadron busy collecting various civilian vehicles, to bring the transport up to strength, collected were several small Pickford vans, larger furniture vans etc. and one large load lorry taken from the coach builders painted bright red, with half finished letters 'HP,' on one side. Where the notion 'The Worlds Appetiser' came from, I do not know. It was before the days of camouflage and they were left as they were, as it happened, just as well.

Lieutenant Strange, who had joined No. 5 at Gosport, was keen on fitting a machine gun to his Henri Farman. Having gained permission, with the help of ground staff, proceeded to fit a Vickers (maxim) belt fed infantry machine gun complete with water jacket (empty) on a ¾" plank across the front of the nacelle.

(Pity they did not think of fixing the gun and flying the machine as a single seater).

In his book, he refers to it as a Lewis gun. The Lewis gas operated gun was an American invention, offered all round but only the Belgian Government accepted and used it, prior to the war. During the war, it was made in England under licence by the Birmingham Small Arms Co. (BSA)

The transport of No. 5, including yours truly, went over to France, via Southampton—Boulogne, on the good ship SS *Chevington*, not impressed with the first French troops we saw on the quayside, but they were probably reservists.

After St. Omer, am not sure what route we took, but eventually arrived at a flying field, outside Maubeuge, where we found our machines already there.

It was while we were there, that Strange had the chance to try out his 'gun bus.' An enemy machine came over us, at a guess 5000 ft and the Henri Farman took off to attack it but the weight of the two occupants plus the weight of the machine gun and ammuition, reduced its ceiling to some 3000 feet. When he landed again he had to take the gun off the machine.

Speaking of Strange reminds me that in his book he calls the HP red box lorry 'Red van with BOVRIL painted in black letters all over it.'

The RFC was only a few days at the Maubeuge field before we were on retreat, after the battle of Mons. From then on, not stopping for more than a night, all the way down to Melun, beyond Paris, in many cases having to clear corn fields, fortunately cut, to make landing grounds for the machines.

One transport item sticks in my mind, one of the small Pickfords ran a big end so the transport Sergeant took out the con rod and it ran on 3 cylinders. From then on, it was allowed to make its own time, going like hell down hill, to the cheers of the rest and at a walking pace up the next rise.

Digressing pro tem, although the RFC did well, in the short time since its formation, to be able to send four squadrons to France on the outbreak of war, it had no field experience at least as far as the men were concerned.

The PBI although they suffered tremendously, did have mobile field kitchens and could occasionally get a hot meal.

Whereas the RFC had to survive on 'hard tack' alone, at least 'other ranks' of No. 5 did.

'Hard tack,' a large and thick dry oatmeal biscuit carried in your pocket, needed tools to break it. (McCudden in his book mentions bacon and biscuit). I had heard, not to drink any water without boiling, as we had no time to make a fire, no drinking. To counter the effect of this dry diet, one stuck a finger in the tin of lubricating castor oil and sucked it. Again at Gosport, we were only issued with a water-proof sheet, nothing to keep us warm at night, out in the open, under the machines. In France, No. 5 was issued with a large French blanket, one between two. (McCudden again, says they were issued, one each.)

Standing: 454 DANN, 511 JENKINS, 979 SHREWSBURY.

351

The Officers were either billeted, where possible or had their valises to sleep in, carried for them by the batman. The Sergeant Majors slept in the workshop lorry. At Mélun we stayed for a while and I think it was there that I tried to take my socks off, but found the skin started to come away with them. I had to wait until I could soak them off in warm water.

After the battle of the Marne, we commenced to move back up again. It was while I was passenger in a Crossley light tender, moving up to Fère-en-Jardenois, we were stopped by Major Brooke-Popham, who had been directing traffic. Told me to get down and send all vehicles to the left, took my place and away they went.

I dutifully did as I was told, until there were no more vehicles passing only troops marching, so 'fell in' and marched with them until night fall. Detecting the outline of aircraft I 'fell out,' found the remains of a barn still standing and had a very good nights rest, not hearing the storm that arose and wrecked four of No. 5's Henri Farmans. Come morning, found they had been up most of the night trying to save the machines, so said nothing.

Such was the mixed up state of affairs, the tender in front of ours took the wrong turning, ran into the German army, was captured, complete with its load of spares.

It was intended, I believe, to arm the RFC with Webley Scott automatic pistols, with webbing equipment to suit. We received the webbing but not the pistol, so had to hang on to the old short barrel revolvers, with flat nosed ammunition, which rumour had it, the enemy regarded as dum-dum, so it was discreetly lost, but on the advance we were able to re-arm ourselves with abandoned items, including webbing equipment with ammunition, rifles and bayonets.

I forget where it was, but we came across a Belgian armoured car, ditched and abandoned, with its Lewis gun aboard, which we annexed plus the ammunition, the only thing was it fired recessed rim cartridges, so after that it was necessary to scrounge Belgian ammo.

Thinking back, the above must have been after we left Fère-en-Jardenois, where we stayed some two or three weeks, enabling partially wrecked buildings to be found and made use of, likewise the 'cook house' to get going, solely brewing and serving out raw tea.

There, I had found an enamelled barrel shaped mug with wire loop handle and going for my raw tea one evening the 'cook' said

'Rum issue caught up with us, shall I pour it into your tea?' – with that he did.

The lads had found a room in an Establishment, which could be used, so went there to munch my biscuit and sip my strong raw tea.

As the evening wore on, I felt the room was hot and stuffy so got up and went out. That's all I remember. We were sleeping in the part of a barn left standing, in the morning complaining of my head, yes, they said, you came in last night fighting mad drunk and we had to knock you out.

So that was my first (and last) real drink.

No. 5 eventually got back up to Bailleul and settled there until I left the squadron.

But not before Lieutenants Strange and Small, with the gun we had found, brought down and captured an Aviatik. On the 504 Avro, a bar was fixed across the two rear fuselage struts, from which the gun was hung, the gunner kneeling in the front seat, firing back over the pilot's head, so the ploy was to get below and in front of the enemy machine.

Later in the year King George V visited the squadron. The landing field at Bailleul was very soggy, with several small ditches, marked with flags on sticks.

One windy night, I was on guard duty, when I became aware of dark shapes, in the distance, with the sound of padding footfalls. The shapes disappeared and the sounds ceased, presumably, I thought, by whoever it was, dropping to the ground. There they were again, I considered – should I turn out the Guards? No, my first shot at the intruders would do that, again there they were. I waited for them to come closer, but they never did, so creeping forward I found it was the flags round the ditches. When the wind sprang up, the flags spread and being wet rustled in the breeze, when it stopped they folded and fell.

The place I chose on night sentry duty (two hours on, four hours off) was standing close to the rudder, under the rear wing of a Henri Farman. To stop me dozing off, which was very serious in war time, one stood with the bayonet just under your chin, so if your head drooped forward, the point would sharply bring one back to consciousness.

Another night I was on, the disciplinary Sergeant Major (808 SM Parker) was snooping around, obviously trying to catch the sentry out, I kept out of sight by the rudder, and let him creep around, until he passed where I stood, then stepped out and stopped him on the point of my bayonet 'Halt who goes there.' Thoroughly put the wind up him.

He mumbled something and sloped off.

This same Sergeant Major started to check for dirty boots when the men had been in the wind most of the night.

There was an accident when the old guard was being stood down one evening, alongside the workshop lorry, which had a light showing through the canvas awning. The guard had been ordered to 'empty magazine' and on the command 'ease Springs' a shot rang out and the bullet went through the workshop lorry canvas, one of the rifles had not been completely emptied, most unfortunate, as the disciplinary Sergeant Major was in the lorry at the time.

The last night I was on screw picket duty, as said earlier, the ground was very soggy and the screw pickets holding the machines down tended to pull loose and needed screwing in further. On this night the gusts were particularly strong, as soon as I had got one machine firmly anchored another was lifting.

In tackling the screw pickets on a machine that was lifting, I slipped in the mud and part of the under-carriage must have come down on my leg. I felt a sharp pain in my knee but managed to hobble round and continue.

In the morning, I couldn't use my leg, it was so swollen, the medical orderly had to cut my breeches away. He thought it was dislocated and so it turned out.

So in February 1915, I left No. 5 squadron by the light tender on ambulance duty.

On the hospital ship, I felt ashamed and quite an imposter, to be among all those badly wounded infantry men from the trenches.

One last coincidence, I finally landed up at Sturminster Marshal in Dorset, in a large house taken over as a VAD hospital, by the locality where the nurses were daughters of the Vicar and round-about farmers. One of them was the sister of Lieutenant Strange.'

980. A. WATKIN

Enlisted 20 July 1896. Formerly 5893 Drill Sergeant, 1/Grenadier Guards, a rank unique to the Brigade of Guards, equivalent to W.O.2. Awarded Queen's South Africa Medal (Cape Colony, Transvaal, Wittebergen) as Lance Sergeant and King's South Africa Medal as Sergeant. Awarded Bronze Royal Victorian Medal for the funeral of Edward VII. Transferred to RFC 2 September 1913. L.S.&G.C. in October 1913 in *A.O.* 333 as Drill Sergeant and seemingly as Grenadier Guards and not as RFC as one would expect. Sergeant, 1 Squadron in August 1914. Promoted WO(D) 24 September 1914. Served overseas from 3 March 1915 and awarded 1914/15 Star trio. Was *SMI* (Disciplinarian) in April 1918 RAF Muster Roll. Served in South Russia, with 47 Squadron until 9 July 1919 and awarded Medal of Zeal with the ribbon of St. Stanislas in March 1920. Discharged 18 January, 1921. Awarded Army 'annuity' M.S.M. in *A.O.* 18 of 1948. Died 29 November, 1956 in Brighton. His GVI M.S.M. (only) is known, named 5891 WO1, Grenadier Guards.

5893   W.O.CL .1 A. WATKIN. G. GDS.

EDGE NAMING ON MERITORIOUS SERVICE MEDAL.

★ 981. R. HILL

A recruit, a direct entrant into RFC 2 December 1913. As 2AM, Aircraft Park served in France from 16 August, 1914. Promoted Corporal (Fitter Engines) 1 February 1917 and was Corporal Mechanic (Fitter AE) in April 1918 RAF Muster Roll.

★ 982. W. H. NIXON

A recruit, a direct entrant into RFC 1 December 1913. As 1AM, RFC HQ served in France from 12 August 1914. Commissioned 2 Lieutenant, King's Own (Royal Lancaster Regt) 14 February 1915.

★ 983. CHARLES EDWARD BRASSINGTON

A recruit, a direct entrant into RFC 4 December 1913. As 2AM, 5 Squadron earned 1914 Star. Promoted Acting Corporal (paid) (Clerk general) 1 February 1918. Was Corporal Clerk in April 1918 RAF Muster Roll. Awarded Royal Aero Club Aviators' Certificate No. 4260 on 17 February 1917 as Corporal. See group photograph under No. 979.

984. JAMES HENRY WILFORD

Enlisted April 1896. Formerly 1353 Quarter Master Sergeant, Military Provost Staff Corps. Transferred to RFC 5 December 1913. Appointed Warrant Officer 6 December 1913 at South Farnborough, awarded Army L.S.&G.C. medal in April 1914 in AO 99 and permitted to serve beyond 21 years 6 April 1914. Was Sergeant Major of RFC HQ in August 1914 and served in France from 24 November 1914 being awarded 1914/15 trio. Commissioned Quartermaster and Lieutenant 1 March 1915 and was mentioned in despatches in *L.G.* 24 February 1917. Promoted to Honorary Captain and Quartermaster 1 March 1918 and was Major (Administration) in April 1918 *A.F.L.* He retired as a Squadron Leader (acting Wing Commander) 7 November 1925 and was shown thus in 1946 *A.F.L.* See group photographs 1 and 2. As can be seen, he wore a pair of medal ribbons in addition to the L.S.&G.C. which appear to be the Queen's and Khedive's Sudan Medals. Also in group photograph under No. 979.

★ 985. F. G. MORRIS

A recruit, a direct entrant into RFC 2 December 1913. As 2AM 5 Squadron earned 1914 Star and bar in France from 14 August 1914. Promoted Corporal (Carpenter) 1 May 1915 and retained that rank and trade in April 1918 Muster Roll.

★ 986. W. J. BEADLE

A recruit, a direct entrant into RFC 3 December 1913. As 1AM with the Aircraft Park served in France from 16 August 1914. Reverted to Sergeant 1st Class Pilot on 14 December 1916 and was awarded a Royal Aero Club

Aviators' Certificate No. 5126 on 26 April, 1917 as Sergeant. Was in a Military Hospital on 27 July 1917. Was Sergeant Mechanic (Pilot) in April 1918 RAF Muster Roll.

★ 987. B. HARRISON

Enlisted 7 August 1908. Formerly 6395 Private 2/Connaught Rangers. Transferred to RFC 4 July 1913. Was 2AM 5 Squadron in France from 20 August 1914. Promoted 1AM (Fitter Engines) 1 April 1917 and was 1AM (Fitter AE) in April 1918 RAF Muster Roll.

★ 988. J. DEEGAN

A recruit, a direct entrant into RFC 5 December, 1913. As 2AM, Aircraft Park he earned a 1914 Star and bar in France from 16 August, 1914. He had transferred from 6 Squadron to the Aircraft Park on 12 August, 1914. Promoted 1AM (Driver MT) 1 October, 1915 and retained that rank and trade in April, 1918 RAF Muster Roll.

★ 989. WILLIAM J. STANDFORD

Enlisted 28 October, 1907. Formerly 59362, L Battery, RHA Transferred to RFC 4 July, 1913. As 1AM with the Airship Detatchment earned 1914 Star. To RNAS 18 October, 1914 as No. 666, a Leading Mechanic. Died 23 April, 1915 at Royal Naval Air Station, Kingsworth. Buried at Gillingham, Kent.

990. J. SEMPLE

A recruit, a direct entrant into RFC 4 December, 1913. As 2AM, 6 Squadron served overseas from 2 April, 1915 earning a 1914/15 Star trio. Promoted Sergeant (Storeman) 1 January, 1917 and was Sergeant Clerk in April, 1918 RAF Muster Roll.

★ 991. J. H. BRYANT

A recruit, a direct entrant into RFC 4 December, 1913. As 1AM, with the Aircraft Park served in France from 16 August, 1914. Reduced to 2AM (Armourer) 30 October, 1916, and was given the new rank of 3AM (Armourer) in April, 1918 RAF Muster Roll.

992. A MASON

A recruit, a direct entrant into RFC 8 December, 1913. Deserted 29 June, 1914.

993. ADRIAN MOODY

A recruit, a direct entrant into RFC 8 December, 1913. Deserted 29 June, 1914 but re-joined and served overseas from 16 April, 1915 earning 1914/15 Star trio. Died 16 February, 1917 when a Corporal in 59 Squadron, aged 26. Son of Alexander and Mary Moody. Buried Bois Guillaume Cemetery (Plot II, Row C, Grave 11).

994. W. TURNER

Formerly 4171 Lance Corporal 1/Irish Guards. Transferred to RFC 3 July, 1913. Discharged with ignominy, 11 March, 1914, under *K.R.* 392 (xii) for stealing from an officer.

★ 995. A. B. McALLISTER

Enlisted 17 January, 1906. Transferred to RFC 12 December, 1913. As 2AM, 3 Squadron served in France from 13 August, 1914. On 19 December, 1914, he was sentenced to 2 years hard labour for leaving his post as a sentinel before being relieved. However, some of his sentence must have been commuted for he was promoted 1AM (Rigger-aero) 1 July, 1915 and retained that rank and trade in April, 1918 RAF Muster Roll. As Sergeant, 31 Squadron awarded Indian General Service Medal (clasps Waziristan 1919/21 and Mahsud). (See also No. 504.) (Photograph in *'First in India's Skies'*)

★ 996. A. C. MAITLAND-ADDISON

A recruit, a direct entrant into RFC 11 December, 1913. As Corporal, 2 Squadron earned 1914 Star. Commissioned 2 Lieutenant 5 October, 1914 in 1/Cheshire Regt. Died of wounds 27 October, 1914, after the First Battle of Ypres, when effectively the battalion ceased to exist.

★ 997. W. F. KEEL

A recruit, a direct entrant into RFC 15 December, 1913. As Corporal, 5 Squadron served in France from 6 November, 1914 being thus just entitled to 1914 Star. Promoted Flight Sergeant (Blacksmith) 1 May, 1917 and was Chief Mechanic (Blacksmith) in April, 1918 Muster Roll.

★ 998. R. W. FOOTMAN

A recruit, a direct entrant into RFC 12 August, 1914. As 2AM, 4 Squadron earned 1914 Star and bar in France from 12 August, 1914. Promoted Corporal (Driver MT) 1 October, 1916, and retained that rank and trade in April, 1918 RAF Muster Roll.

★ 999. W. F. NORTHWAY

A recruit, a direct entrant into RFC 15 December, 1913. As 2AM, 6 Squadron was transferred and served in France from 16 August, 1914, probably with the Aircraft Park. He remained a 2AM (Wireless Operator) all through his RFC service, never being promoted, and indeed in the April, 1918 RAF Muster Roll, was reduced in rank to 3AM.

1000. G. BUCHANNAN

A recruit, a direct entrant into RFC 15 December, 1913. Deserted 27 May, 1914 but re-joined and served in France from 7 October, 1915. However, the medal roll states that his former service was forfeited for desertion and his engagement was only reckoned from 22 August, 1916. Not found in April, 1918 RAF Muster Roll.

★ 1001. R. T. LAUNDER

A recruit, a direct entrant into RFC 15 December, 1913. Posted from 6 Squadron to Aircraft Park 12 August, 1914 and as 2AM with Aircraft Park served in France from 16 August, 1914. Promoted Temp SM (Tech) 1 September, 1917 and was Chief Master Mechanic (Tech) in April, 1918 RAF Muster Roll.

★ 1002. F. L. PANRUCKER

A recruit, a direct entrant into RFC 16 December, 1913. As 2AM, 5 Squadron served in France from 14 August, 1914. Promoted Corporal (Driver MT) 1 September, 1915 and was Corporal Mechanic (Driver) in April, 1918 RAF Muster Roll. He served in Mesopotamia in 1920 and 1921 as a Corporal in 30 and 55 Squadrons. Awarded General Service Medal (Iraq).

1003. T. G. BRICKNELL

A recruit, a direct entrant into RFC 16 December, 1913. Discharged 14 March, 1914 under *K.R.* 392 (iii) 'Not likely to become an efficient soldier.'

1004. W. SPOURS

A recruit, a direct entrant into RFC 13 December, 1913. As 2AM, 5 Squadron served in France from 14 August, 1914. His 1914 Star was forfeited for desertion 8 July, 1917.

1005. G. RUSSELL

A recruit, a direct entrant into RFC 17 December, 1913. Was 2AM with 6 Squadron in August, 1914. Served overseas from 24 July, 1915 earning 1914/15 Star trio. Promoted Flight Sergeant (Fitter general) 1 May, 1917 and was Chief Mechanic (Fitter general) in April, 1918 RAF Muster Roll.

* 1006. G. COOKE

A recruit, a direct entrant into RFC 18 December, 1913. As 1AM, 5 Squadron, served in France from 14 August, 1914. Promoted Flight Sergeant (Fitter general) 1 January, 1918 and was Chief Mechanic (Fitter general) in April, 1918 RAF Muster Roll. Mentioned in despatches in *L.G.* 14 June, 1918 for services in Palestine.

* 1007. C. MAY

A recruit, a direct entrant into RFC 18 December, 1913. As 2AM, 2 Squadron served in France from 14 August, 1914. Discharged as unfit 11 January, 1915.

* 1008. F. LINN

A recruit, a direct entrant into RFC 17 December, 1913. As 2AM, 5 Squadron served in France from 14 August, 1914 and earned 1914 Star and bar. Promoted Sergeant (Photogapher) 1 April, 1917 and was Sergeant Mechanic (Photographer) in April, 1918 RAF Muster Roll.

1009. J. McArthur

Enlisted 30 July, 1901. Formerly 7666 Private 2/Royal Scots. Transferred to RFC 25 July, 1913. Was 2AM with the Aircraft Park in August, 1914 but did not serve overseas until 3 March, 1915 earning 1914/15 Star Trio. Promoted Flight Sergeant (Driver MT) 1 July, 1916 and was Chief Mechanic (Driver) in April, 1918 RAF Muster Roll. Awarded one of the first six RAF L.S.&G.C. medals as Flight Sergeant *w.e.f.* 30 July, 1919 *vide A.M.O.* 1123 of October, 1919 (see No. 28). Served in Mesopotamia in 1920 as Flight Sergeant with 30 Squadron. Awarded General Service Medal (Iraq).

1010. G. Naylor

A recruit, a direct entrant into RFC 16 December, 1913. As 2AM, was on a Riggers course at CFS in September, 1914. No trace of entitlement to 1914 or 1914/15 Stars found.

★ 1011. W. E. Chalfont

A recruit, a direct entrant into RFC 22 December, 1913. As 2AM, 2 Squadron served in France from 12 August, 1914, and earned 1914 Star and bar. Promoted Corporal (Driver MT) 1 December, 1916 and was Corporal Mechanic (Driver) in April, 1918 RAF Muster Roll.

1012. T. J. Owen

A recruit, a direct entrant into RFC 31 December, 1913. No trace of entitlement to 1914 or 1914/15 Stars found. Commissioned and promoted Lieutenant 1 December, 1917.

★ 1013. W. J. Townsend

A recruit, a direct entrant into RFC 31 December, 1913. As a 2AM, (Sailmaker) with 6 Squadron was stationed with the Newcastle detachment 10-14 August, 1914. As 1AM No. 6 Squadron served in France from 6 October, 1914. Promoted Corporal (Fitter, turner) 1 June, 1917 and was Corporal Mechanic (Turner) in April, 1918 RAF Muster Roll.

The Young Aviator

(Tune: Originally 'The Dying Lancer,' but mainly associated
with 'Tarpaulin Jacket.' Of the many versions of this tune
and lyrics published over the years, this is perhaps one of
those most commonly used.)

The Young Aviator lay dying,
And as in the hangar he lay, he lay,
To the mechanics who round him were standing
These last parting words he did say—

Chorus:
Take the cylinders out of my kidneys.
The connecting rod out of my brain, my brain.
The cam box from under my backbone
And assemble the engine again.

Then go ye and get me a school bus
And bury me out on the Plain, the Plain*
And get them to write on my tombstone
Some formulæ out of Duchesne.

When the Court of Inquiry assembles
To find out the reason I died, I died.
Then say I forgot 'twice Iota'
Was the minimum angle of glide.

Oh had I the wings of an Avro
Then far into Holland I'd fly, I'd fly,
I'd stop there until the war's over
And laugh at you blighters on high.

And now I suppose I'll be joining
The Flying Corps up in the sky, the sky,
Where they all understand 'twice Iota',
And they all have got wings that will fly!

* Salisbury Plain, Wiltshire, home of the original RFC Central
Flying School.

Part 4
Numbers 1014 to 1400
January—August 1914

Those who enlisted directly into or were transferred to the RFC between 1 January, 1914 and 10th August, 1914 when the RFC joined the BEF in France (Nos. 1369—72 and 1376 were members of the Air Battalion Reserve).

1014. CHARLES LITTLEPROUD

A recruit, a direct entrant into RFC 1 January, 1914. No trace of entitlement to 1914 or 1914/15 Stars found. Promoted Sergeant (Fitter general) on 1 May, 1917 and was Sergeant Mechanic in April, 1918 RAF Muster Roll. Recommended for an M.S.M. for gallantry with No. 34 Squadron but not awarded. Awarded Indian General Service Medal (clasp North West Frontier 1930/31) and in the *London Gazette* of 31 July, 1931 was awarded a Military British Empire Medal as Flight Sergeant, for operations on North West Frontier of India, between 23 April, 1930 and 12 September, 1930. Awarded RAF L.S.&G.C. medal as Sergeant Major 2nd Class, with effect from 1 January, 1932. Awarded both the 1935 Silver Jubilee and the 1937 Coronation Medals. In 1937 *A.F.L.* is shown as Warrant Officer 1st Class, with effect from 1 April, 1936 and was stationed at RAF Leconsfield from 16 March, 1937 (Nos. 97 and 166 Bomber, Squadrons). In November, 1941 *A.F.L.* he was the 114th senior RAF Warrant Officer and in October, 1944 the 59th.

1015. A. R. CLARK

Born 8 February, 1898. A boy recruit, a direct entrant into RFC 3 January, 1914. Served overseas in Egypt from 15 November, 1914 earning 1914/15 trio. Promoted to Corporal (Rigger) 1 April, 1917. Was Corporal Mechanic (Rigger Aero) in April, 1918 RAF Muster Roll. Served in India with 31 Squadron and awarded India General Service Medal (clasp Waziristan 1921-24). Awarded RAF L.S.&G.C. as Flight Sergeant with effect from 3 January, 1932. Awarded both the1935 Silver Jubilee Medal and the 1937 Coronation Medal as Flight Sergeant. Commissioned (No.

35255) 12 June, 1939. Wing Commander 1 July, 1949. Retired 15 February, 1953. He would appear to have been the second last of the pre-war RFC men to be serving when he finally retired aged 55 (see 910). Died 18 March, 1979.

1016. WILLIAM HARRAWAY

A recruit, a direct entrant into RFC 3 January, 1914. No trace of entitlement to WW1 medals found and not shown in 1918 RAF Muster Roll. Warrant officer *w.e.f.* 1 December, 1933. Still serving in March 1938 (*A.F.L.*). Since 23 March, 1937 was stationed at RAF Gosport.

1017. R. G. SMITH

A recruit, a direct entrant into RFC 5 January, 1914. Discharged 11 March, 1914 under *K.R.* 392 (v) on payment of £10.

1018. WALTER ROGERS

A recruit, a direct entrant into RFC 2 January, 1914. Was 2AM with 6 Squadron in August, 1914. Served overseas from 24 July, 1915 earning 1914/15 Star trio. Promoted Sergeant 1 January, 1917. Awarded Royal Aero Club Aviators' Certificate No. 5800 of 7 September, 1917. To hospital, injured, 24 February, 1918. Was Sergeant Mechanic (Pilot 1st Class) in April, 1918 RAF Muster Roll. Awarded Air Force Medal in *L.G.* 1 January, 1919. Originally from Vauxhall, London.

★ 1019. HENRY DAVID BEAUMONT

Enlisted 19 February, 1912. Formerly 68695 49 Bty. RFA. Transferred to RFC 23 July, 1913. As 2AM, 3 Squadron served in France from 12 August, 1914 and earned 1914 Star and bar. Charged by Flight Sergeant Ridd (No. 26) along with McCudden (No. 892) with looting. Actually they had raided an orchard and stolen some apples. He later, after hearing of his officers aircraft going missing, 'aquired' some of his kit. When the missing officer turned up safely, he only just managed to return the clothes. Posted back to UK in the winter of 1914-15 to 15 Squadron at

Farnborough, then Dover. He crossed the elevator wire of a Bleriot and was almost demoted from Corporal. He was sent to the RNAS Station at Eastbourne. He returned to 15 Squadron and to France in August, 1915. Promoted Acting Flight Sergeant (paid) (Rigger) 1 December, 1917. Was Chief Mechanic (Rigger Aero) in April, 1918 RAF Muster Roll. Awarded RAF L.S.&G.C. medal *w.e.f.* 19 February, 1930 as SM2. Warrant Officer *w.e.f.* 1 February, 1934. Awarded 1935 Silver Jubilee Medal. Since 3 February, 1936 had been stationed at No. 4 Apprentice Wing. Halton Camp. In November, 1941 he was the 57th senior RAF WO and in October, 1944 the 22nd. Appointed an M.B.E. in 1944. Still serving in 1946 and was then 6th most senior WO in RAF. Retired in 1949 the senior WO in the RAF.

1020. ROBERT DONALDSON

A recruit, a direct entrant into RFC 5 January, 1914. Was 2AM (Fitter) with Lieutenant de Havilland at Montrose in August, 1914. Transferred from 6 Squadron to Aircraft Park 12 August, 1914. Served overseas from 3 April, 1915 earning 1914/15 Star trio. Mentioned in despatches in February, 1917 as Flight Sergeant. Appointed Temp. SM (T) 24 April, 1917 and was Ch Mr Mech (Technical) in April, 1918 RAF Muster Roll. Awarded RAF L.S.&G.C. medal as SM1 5 January, 1932. Station WO Marine Aircraft Experimental Establishment, Felixstowe, Suffolk, from 22 September, 1933. Awarded 1935 Silver Jubilee Medal. In March, 1938 *A.F.L.* he was the sixth most senior RAF Warrant Officer. In the November, 1941 *A.F.L.* he was the third. Not traced in 1944 *A.F.L.*

∗ 1021. A. MACKLAM

A recruit, a direct entrant into RFC 8 January, 1914. As 2AM 6 Squadron served in France from 7 October, 1914. Promoted Sergeant (MT Driver) 1 December, 1917 and was Sergeant Mechanic (Driver) in April, 1918 RAF Muster Roll. His trio was offered by Liverpool Coins and Medals in 1982 for £145 and by Beadles in 1986 for £175. His 1914 Star was named to 2AM and his British War Medal and Victory medal to Sergeant RAF. They were sold by Spink in 1990 for £90.

∗ 1022. W. C. TURNER

A recruit, a direct entrant into RFC 8 January, 1914. Was 2AM, 6 Squadron initially, transferred to Aircraft Park 12 August, 1914 and served in France from 16 August, 1914. Mentioned in the *Times* 'B' Press

Release of 27 March, 1917. As Sergeant posted to 38 (Training) Squadron at Rendcombe, and was killed in a flying accident on 3 June, 1917. An enquiry was held on 4 June, 1917 which found that whilst making his first solo flight as a pilot, his aircraft nose dived into the ground and burst into flames. His body was badly burned before it could be pulled clear of the wreckage. He died of a fractured skull, and a dislocation of the neck (*vide* Flight 14 June, 1917). He was buried in Brecon Cemetery Powys in grave No. 3690.

1023. S. HESKETH

A recruit, a direct entrant into RFC 9 January, 1914. Was 2AM, 6 Squadron in August, 1914. Served overseas from 3 April, 1915 earning 1914/15 Star trio. Promoted Corporal (Aerial Gunner) No. 7 Squadron in July, 1915. Promoted Temp. SM (T) 1 September, 1917. Was Ch Mr Mech (Technical) in April, 1918 RAF Muster Roll.

1024. J. LEECH

A recruit, a direct entrant into RFC 9 January, 1914. Was 2AM, 6 Squadron in August and served overseas from 3 March, 1915 earning 1914/15 Star trio. Promoted Temp SM (D) 1 November, 1917 and was SM1 (Disciplinarian) in April, 1918 RAF Muster Roll.

* 1025. THOMAS ALEC GORDON HAWLEY

A recruit, a direct entrant into RFC 9 January, 1914. As 2AM in the Aircraft Park served in France from 16 August, 1914. Mentioned in despatches as Corporal 1 January, 1916. Awarded Army M.S.M. as Flight Sergeant in *L.G.* 11 November, 1916. Commissioned 12 October, 1916. Promoted Lieutenant 17 August, 1917. Again mentioned in despatches in January, 1919. Promoted Flight Lieutenant 30 June, 1922, and was then Supplies Officer at RAF HQ Iraq. Retired 5 April, 1930. Still shown in 1938 *A.F.L.* His M.S.M. only was sold by Capital Medals in 1988 for £225.

* 1026. C. DONALDSON

A recruit, a direct entrant into RFC 10 January, 1914. As 2AM, with the Aircraft Park served in France from 14 August, 1914. Promoted Acting Flight Sergeant (paid) (Rigger) 1 December, 1917 and was Chief Mechanic (Rigger Aero) in April, 1918 RAF Muster Roll.

★ 1027. CYRIL RAPLEY

Born 10 November, 1895, his father served in the Royal Navy. A recruit, a direct entrant into RFC 10 January, 1914. As 2AM with the Aircraft Park served in France from 16 August, 1914. Mentioned in despatches 15 June, 1916 for services with No. 1 Aircraft Park. As Acting Sergeant Major awarded Army M.S.M. in *L.G.* 11 November, 1916 for valuable services with the Army in the Field. Commissioned 2 Lieutenant 21 December, 1917. Flying Officer (Technical) 21 June, 1919. Stationed from 16 August, 1920 at Central Flying School, Upavon. Married 1924. Flight Lieutenant (E) 1 January, 1927. Stationed from 27 January, 1928 at No. 4 Apprentice Wing, Halton Camp, Bucks. Squadron Leader 1 July, 1936. Stationed from 5 October, 1937 at the Aircraft Depot Dhibban, Group Captain (No. 04186) 1 March, 1942. In 1946 *A.F.L.* shown as Air Commodore CEng., AFRAeS; created C.B.E. 1946. Promoted substantive Group Captain 1 July, 1947. Retired 26 January, 1950. See Debrett's 1972/73 when he was living at Chilterns, World's End, Wendover, Bucks. Noted as still alive in 1978 *A.F.L.*

★ 1028. ARTHUR MAXWELL

Enlisted 19 December, 1912. Formerly 23737 'E' Company RE. Transferred to RFC 11 August, 1913. As 2AM, 5 Squadron served in France from 14 August, 1914. Promoted Corporal (Photographer) 1 April, 1917 and retained that rank and trade in April, 1918 RAF Muster Roll. Awarded RAF M.S.M. as Flight Sergeant, in *L.G.* 3 June, 1919. He came originally from Ealing West.

★ 1029. GEORGE FILMER

A recruit, a direct entrant into RFC 10 January, 1914. As 2AM, with the Aircraft Park earned 1914 Star and bar in France from 16 August, 1914. Promoted Flight Sergeant (Painter) 1 March, 1917 and was Chief Mechanic (Painter) in April, 1918 RAF Muster Roll. Appointed Warrant Officer 4 June, 1930. Awarded RAF L.S.&G.C. medal *w.e.f.* 10 January, 1932 as SM1. From 15 February 1933 was stationed at the Equipment Section, HQ Middle East Command. Commissioned Flying Officer (Equip) 3 January, 1938 and posted to 207 (Bomber) Squadron, Worthy Down, Winchester, Hants.

1030. R. Dobson

A recruit, a direct entrant into RFC 9 January, 1914. Discharged 4 April, 1914 under *K.R.* 392 (iii) 'Not likely to become an efficient soldier.'

1031. John (Jack) North Rogers

Born Duston, Northants 1895. A recruit, a direct entrant into RFC 13 January, 1914. Was 2AM, 6 Squadron in August, 1914. Served overseas from 3 April, 1915 and entitled to 1914/15 Star trio. An aerial gunner with 16 Squadron from 2 May, 1915. As Corporal he was awarded a Distinguished Conduct Medal in *L.G.* 19 June, 1915 'For conspicuous gallantry on 10 May, 1915, when he was acting as a gunner with an officer as pilot in the neighbourhood of Lille. A German aeroplane, armed with a machine gun, was attacked at a height of about 10,000 feet. The hostile pilot was hit, and his aeroplane dived, but was followed, and the fight continued until at an altitude of about 1,500 feet it turned on its back and fell to the ground.' During the D.C.M. action, Lieutenant W. H. D. Acland was the pilot flying a Vickers Gun Bus, of No. 5 Squadron, on a patrol of the Ypres salient. At the time, he was a 1AM. The German observer returned fire with a pistol. Awarded Russian Cross of St. George (4th Class) 25 August, 1915 when with 2 Squadron, 1 Wing RFC, as a Corporal. He died in the U.K. a Sergeant, 20 May, 1917. Son of A. and M. Rogers of 20 Althorpe Rd., St. James, Northampton. Buried St. Lukes Churchyard, Duston, Northants.

1032. Sidney George Dean

A recruit, a direct entrant into RFC 13 January, 1914. Was 2AM, 6 Squadron in August, 1914. Served overseas from 3 December, 1914 earning 1914/15 Star trio. Promoted Sergeant (Fitter engines) 1 April, 1917 and was Sergeant Mechanic (Fitter A.E.) in April, 1918 RAF Muster Roll. Awarded Indian General Service Medal (clasp NW Frontier 1930/

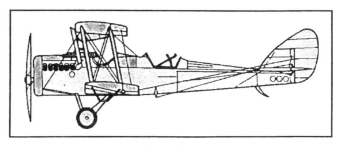

Airco DH4

368

31) and RAF L.S.&G.C. *w.e.f.* 13 January, 1932 as Flight Sergeant. Awarded 1935 Silver Jubilee Medal as Flight Sergeant. Commissioned Flying Officer (CEO) *w.e.f.* 18 May, 1937. Stationed at No. 5 FTS Queen's Ferry, Chester in March, 1938.

⋆ 1033. H. C. GRAY

A recruit, a direct entrant into RFC 13 January, 1914. Posted from 6 Squadron to Aircraft Park 12 August, 1914. As 2AM, with Aircraft Park, served in France from 16 August, 1914. Promoted Sergeant (Fitter general) 1 February, 1916 and retained that rank and trade in April, 1918 RAF Muster Roll.

⋆ 1034. R. S. H. LANG

A recruit, a direct entrant into RFC 16 January, 1914. As 2AM, with the Aircraft Park served in France from 16 August, 1914. Transferred to Argyll and Sutherland Highlanders as No. 24866.

⋆ 1035. R. J. SADLER

A recruit, a direct entrant into RFC 16 January, 1914. As 2AM, 4 Squadron served in France from 12 August, 1914. Promoted Corporal (Fitter engines) 1 August, 1917 and was Corporal Mechanic (Fitter AE) in April, 1918 RAF Muster Roll.

⋆ 1036. C. J. MATTEN

A recruit, a direct entrant into RFC 15 January, 1914. As 2AM, 2 Squadron served in France from 12 August, 1914. Promoted 1AM (Driver MT) 1 April, 1916 and retained that rank and trade in April, 1918 RAF Muster Roll.

⋆ 1037. A. C. ABBOTT

A recruit, a direct entrant into RFC 13 January, 1914. As 2AM, with the Aircraft Park served in France from 16 August, 1914 earned 1914 Star and bar. Discharged 2 January, 1915.

★ 1038. E. R. STOODLEY

A recruit, a direct entrant into RFC 17 January, 1914. As 2AM, 6 Squadron served in France from 6 October, 1914. Discharged 'unfit' 16 February, 1915.

★ 1039. D. L. DIMENT

Enlisted into RFC 19 January, 1914. As 2AM, 2 Squadron served in France from 12 August, 1914. Promoted Sergeant (Fitter Engines) 1 November, 1917. Was Sergeant Mechanic (Fitter AE) in April, 1918 RAF Muster Roll. Awarded RAF L.S.&G.C. medal *w.e.f.* 19 January, 1932 as Flight Sergeant.

★ 1040. ROBERT SHERWOOD

Enlisted into RFC 13 January, 1914. As 2AM with the Aircraft Park served in France from 16 August, 1914. Commissioned 2 Lieutenant 12 September, 1917. Killed in action 26 February, 1918.

★ 1041. A. F. QUINLAN

Enlisted into RFC 16 January, 1914. As 2AM with the Aircraft Park served in France from 12 August, 1914. Returned to UK and served on a Riggers course at CFS in September, 1914. Commissioned 2 Lieutenant 10 February, 1915 as an Observer.

★ 1042. F. C. WILKINSON

A recruit, a direct entrant into RFC 15 January, 1914. As 2AM 6 Squadron served in France from 7 October, 1914 earning a 1914 Star and bar. Promoted 1AM (Blacksmith) 1 December, 1916 and retained that rank and trade in April 1918 RAF Muster Roll.

★ 1043. S. KING

Enlisted 20 November, 1908. Formerly 9939 Private 1/Royal Lancs. Regt. Transferred to RFC 8 August, 1913. As 2AM, 3 Squadron served in France from 12 August, 1914, earning 1914 Star and bar. Promoted Corporal (Driver MT) 1 August, 1917 and retained that rank and trade in April, 1918 RAF Muster Roll. His medals are known in a private collection:— 1914 Star and bar (2AM) British War Medal and Victory Medal (Cpl RAF) 1939/45 Star and Defence and War Medals.

★ 1044. A. E. PHIPPS

A recruit, a direct entrant into RFC 19 January, 1914. Was 2AM, with 6 Squadron but transferred to Aircraft Park 12 August, 1914. Served in France from 16 August, 1914. Promoted Acting Sergeant Major (Paid) (Disciplinarian) 1 March, 1918. Retained that rank and trade in April, 1918 RAF Muster Roll.

★ 1045. R. T. WALTER

Enlisted 26 February, 1908. Formerly 8822 2/Ox and Bucks L.I. Transferred to RFC 12 August, 1913. In 1914 was the servant to Captain Holt. As 2AM, 1 Squadron served in France from 1 November, 1914. Promoted 1AM (Batman) 1 May, 1917 but reverted to Private 1st class (Batman) in April, 1918 RAF Muster Roll. (See No. 302).

★ 1046. F. W. G. RAVENHILL

A recruit, a direct entrant into RFC 20 January, 1914. As 2AM, 6 Squadron served in France from 30 September, 1914. Promoted Sergeant (Fitter general) 1 December, 1917. Injured 6 January, 1918. Was Sergeant Mechanic (Fitter general) in April, 1918 RAF Muster Roll.

★ 1047. W. CHURCHILL

A recruit, a direct entrant into RFC 22 January, 1914. As 2AM, 4 Squadron served in France from 12 August, 1914. Never promoted, and indeed reverted to 3AM in April, 1918 RAF Muster Roll. A fitter (general). His 1914 Star (only) was sold in 1976 by Dyas for £7.50.

★ 1048. R. STEWART

Enlisted 7 April, 1913. Formerly 24436 Sapper RE. Transferred to RFC 23 July, 1913. As 2AM with the Aircraft Park served in France from 16 August, 1914. Promoted Temp SM (T) 1 December, 1917 but was mentioned in despatches in *L.G.* 7 December, 1917 as Sergeant (acting Flight Sergeant). Was Ch Mr Mech (Technical) in April, 1918 RAF Muster Roll.

★ 1049. B. E. HANLEY

A recruit, a direct entrant into RFC 24 January, 1914. As 2AM with the Aircraft Park served in France from 16 August, 1914. Promoted 1AM (Joiner) 1 June, 1915 and was 1AM (Carpenter) in April, 1918 RAF Muster Roll. His trio of medals were sold by Hall's in 1986 for £140:— 1914 Star (2AM) British War Medal and Victory Medal (1AM RAF).

★ 1050. P. GREEN

A recruit, a direct entrant into RFC 24 January, 1914. As 2AM, Aircraft Park, served in France from 16 August, 1914. Promoted 1AM (Joiner) 1 May, 1915 and was 1AM (Carpenter) in April, 1918 RAF Muster Roll.

★ 1051. H. BISHOPS

A recruit, a direct entrant into RFC 22 January, 1914. As 2AM, Aircraft Park, served in France from 16 August, 1914. Promoted Acting Corporal (paid) (Carpenter) 1 March, 1918 and was Corporal Mechanic (Carpenter) in April, 1918 RAF Muster Roll.

★ 1052. T. BOSTON

A recruit, a direct entrant into RFC 22 January, 1914. As 2AM, No. 4 Squadron served in France from 12 August, 1914. Promoted 1AM (Motor Cyclist) 1 February, 1916 and was Private 1 (Motor Cyclist) in April, 1918 RAF Muster Roll.

★ 1053. EDMUND JOHN ALGERNON KNIGHT

Born 18 May, 1895. A recruit, a direct entrant into RFC 22 January, 1914. As 2AM, Aircraft Park, served in France from 16 August, 1914. Mentioned in despatches as Corporal 30 November, 1915. Promoted Flight Sergeant (Rigger) 1 October, 1916 and was Chief Mechanic (Rigger aero) in April,

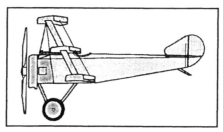

SOPWITH TRIPLANE

1918 RAF Muster Roll. Awarded RAF L.S.&G.C. medal as SM2 *w.e.f.* 22 January, 1932. Awarded 1935 Silver Jubilee Medal. Commissioned Flying Officer (CEO) 19 September, 1937, and in 1938 (March) *A.F.L.* was shown as stationed at No. 1 School of Technical Training (Apprentices) (No. 4 Wing) Halton Camp, Aylesbury, Bucks. Promoted Squadron Leader 1 September, 1940. Re-employed 18 May, 1945 to 18 January, 1946. In 1946 *A.F.L.* shown as No. 35027 Wing Commander (E) (acting Group Captain) (retired). Last noted in 1973 *A.F.L.* as retired.

⋆ 1054. A. G. SHEPHERD

Enlisted 26 August, 1913 at the RE Training Depot, formerly 24819 Pioneer. Transferred to RFC that same day. As 2AM, No. 5 Squadron served in France from 14 August, 1914. Killed in action, 2 June, 1917 as a Flight Sergeant Observer still in 5 Squadron.

⋆ 1055. A. MATTHEWS

A recruit, a direct entrant into RFC 23 January, 1914. Transferred from 6 Squadron to Aircraft Park 12 August, 1914. As 2AM with the Aircraft Park served in France from 16 August, 1914. Promoted 1AM (Fitter, turner) 1 January, 1916 and retained that rank and trade in April, 1918 RAF Muster Roll. Awarded RAF L.S.&G.C. medal as Flight Sergeant *w.e.f.* 23 January, 1932. Appointed WO 3 June, 1937 and shown in March 1938 *A.F.L.* as serving at RAF Honington (No. 3 Bomber Group) Bury St. Edmunds (77 and 102 Squadrons were then stationed there).

⋆ 1056. H. J. BEARD

A recruit, a direct entrant into RFC 24 January, 1914. As 2AM, No. 2 Squadron earned 1914 Star and bar in France from 12 August, 1914. Promoted Sergeant (Fitter engines) 1 May, 1917 and was Sergeant Mechanic (Fitter AE) in April, 1918 RAF Muster Roll. Recorded as serving with 145 Squadron in November, 1918. Awarded Indian General Service Medal (clasp Waziristan 1921-24). Awarded RAF L.S.&G.C. medal as Flight Sergeant *w.e.f.* 24 January, 1932.

⋆ 1057. G. E. COOK

A recruit, a direct entrant into RFC 27 January, 1914. Transferred from 6 Squadron to Aircraft Park 12 August, 1914. As 2AM, Aircraft Park served in France from 16 August, 1914. Promoted Flight Sergeant (Fitter general) 1 November, 1917 and was Chief Mechanic (Fitter general) in April, 1918 RAF Muster Roll. Last noted in the *Times* 'B' Press Release of 23 January, 1919.

★ 1058. V. H. DAVIS

A recruit, a direct entrant into RFC 27 January, 1914. As 2AM with the Aircraft Park served in France from 16 August, 1914. Corporal (NCO Observer) 15 October, 1917. Flew many times with No. 839 W. D. Beard. In 11 Squadron 1 January, 1918. Promoted Sergeant 7 February, 1918, and was Sergeant Mechanic (Observer) in April, 1918 RAF Muster Roll. Awarded India General Service Medal (clasp Waziristan 1921-24) as Sergeant. See *Cross and Cockade*, Volume 7, No. 2, page 87.

★ 1059. S. DIVALL

A recruit, a direct entrant into RFC 26 January, 1914. As 2AM, Aircraft Park, served in France from 16 August, 1914. Promoted Flight Sergeant (Fitter Turner) 1 January, 1918, and was Chief Mechanic (Turner) in April, 1918 RAF Muster Roll.

★ 1060. H. BREWSTER

Enlisted 25 February, 1908. Formerly 13629 1/Grenadier Guards. Transferred to RFC 30 August, 1913. As 2AM with RFC HQ, served in France from 12 August, 1914. He was the original cook with the RFC HQ in the BEF. Promoted Temp SM (D) 1 July, 1917 and was SM1 (Disciplinarian) in April, 1918 RAF Muster Roll.

ARMSTRONG WHITWORTH F.K.8

374

★ 1061. SYDNEY JAMES

A recruit, a direct entrant into RFC 26 January, 1914. As 1AM with No. 6 Squadron served in France from 7 October, 1914. Reverted to Sergeant 2 January, 1917 then gained Royal Aero Club Aviators' Certificate No. 4380 on 15 March, 1917 as a Flight Sergeant and was appointed 1st class Pilot. Was Sergeant Mechanic (Pilot) in April, 1918 RAF Muster Roll.

★ 1062. CHARLES LEONARD TREVITHICK

Born 22 April, 1893. A recruit, a direct entrant into RFC 22 January, 1914. As 2AM, No. 6 Squadron served in France from 6 October, 1914. Promoted Flight Sergeant (Rigger) 1 February, 1916 and was Chief Mechanic (Rigger Aero) in April, 1918 RAF Muster Roll. 'Mentioned' for services at the Air Ministry 22 January, 1919. Gained Indian General Service Medal (clasp Waziristan 1921-24) and was awarded RAF L.S.&G.C. *w.e.f.* 22 January, 1932 as SM1. Awarded 1935 Silver Jubilee Medal. Commissioned Flying Officer (CEO) 18 May, 1937 and in March, 1938 *A.F.L.* shown as serving at No. 10 Flying Training School, Tern Hill, Market Drayton, Shropshire. Promoted Squadron Leader *w.e.f.* 1 June, 1941. Retired 27 October, 1946. Still shown thus in 1960 *A.F.L.* (No. 35056).

1063. W. T. BOVETT

A recruit, a direct entrant into RFC 27 January, 1914. No record of an issue of either 1914 or 1914/15 Stars found. Promoted to Sergeant (Fitter engines) 1 October, 1917 and was Sergeant Mechanic (Fitter AE) in April, 1918 RAF Muster Roll.

★ 1064. W. DAKAYNE

A recruit, a direct entrant into RFC 30 January, 1914. As 2AM, with RFC HQ served in France from 12 August, 1914 and awarded 1914 Star and bar. Promoted Corporal (Draughtsman) 12 April, 1917 and retained that rank and trade in April, 1918 RAF Muster Roll. Mentioned in despatches in the *London Gazette* of 11 July, 1919, when still a Corporal.

★ 1065. B. HARRISON

A recruit, a direct entrant into RFC 2 February, 1914. As 1AM with No. 6 Squadron, served in France from 6 October, 1914. Promoted Flight Sergeant (Rigger) 1 July, 1917 and was Chief Mechanic (Rigger aero) in April, 1918 RAF Muster Roll.

★ 1066. R. BRAZIER

A recruit, a direct entrant into RFC, 2 February, 1914. Transferred from the Aircraft Park to No. 6 Squadron as 2AM 12 August, 1914. Served in France with 6 Squadron from 16 August, 1914 earning 1914 Star and bar. Promoted Sergeant (Rigger) 1 January, 1917 and was Sergeant Mechanic (Rigger aero) in April, 1918 RAF Muster Roll.

★ 1067. J. R. SALSBURY

A recruit, a direct entrant into RFC 31 January, 1914. As 2AM with the Aircraft Park, served in France from 16 August, 1914. Reverted to 1AM (Storeman) 29 June, 1916 and was Clerk 1st Class in April, 1918 RAF Muster Roll.

★ 1068. A. T. LIVINGSTONE

A recruit, a direct entrant into RFC 30 January, 1914. 2AM (Carpenter) on detachment from No. 6 Squadron at Newcastle in August, 1914. Served in France from 7 October, 1914 as 2AM, No. 6 Squadron, and awarded 1914 Star and bar. Noted as an Aerial Gunner on 19 September, 1915. Promoted Corporal (Carpenter) 1 November, 1916 and retained that rank and trade in April, 1918 RAF Muster Roll.

★ 1069. L. A. GOODMAN

A recruit, a direct entrant into RFC 29 January, 1914. As 2AM, No. 2 Squadron served in France from 12 August, 1914. Transferred to the Tank Corps as No. 309368 prior to formation of RAF.

★ 1070. F. S. JOHNSON

A recruit, a direct entrant into RFC 2 February, 1914. Was '2nd Man on Lorry' at Montrose in August, 1914 with Lieutenant de Havilland and then as 2AM transferred to the Reserve Aero Squadron. As 2AM with

No. 6 Squadron served in France from 8 October, 1914. Promoted Sergeant (Fitter general) 1 August, 1917 and retained that rank and trade in April, 1918 RAF Muster Roll.

★ 1071. ERNEST RICHARD WOOD

Born 29 January, 1894. A recruit, a direct entrant into RFC 30 January, 1914. As 2AM with the Aircraft Park served in France from 16 August, 1914. Mentioned in despatches in March, 1916 and awarded Army M.S.M. in *L.G.* 11 November, 1916 as Flight Sergeant 'For Valuable Services with the Armies in the Field.' Commissioned, 2 Lieutenant, RFC, 1 February, 1918. Promoted Flying Officer 20 July, 1920 and as a Stores Officer was serving with No. 4 Squadron at South Farnborough from 10 May, 1921. Promoted Flight Lieutenant (Stores Branch) 1 January, 1928 and shown in February 1931 *A.F.L.* as serving from 10 September, 1929 at No. 4 Stores Depot, Ruislip, Middlesex. Promoted Squadron Leader (E) 1 February, 1936 and shown in 1937 *A.F.L.* as serving from 20 June, 1936 at the Air Ministry (Supply and Org.) (No. 10168) Wing Commander 1 April, 1939. Group Captain 1 September, 1941. Retired 20 April, 1948. Last noted in 1978 *A.F.L.* Awarded C.B.E. in 1946.

★ 1072. R. MORGAN

Enlisted 8 February, 1909. Formerly 8924 Private 2/Royal Munster Fusiliers. Transferred to RFC 1 December, 1913. As 2AM with No. 3 Squadron, served in France from 13 August, 1914. Promoted 1AM (Fitter general) 1 January, 1916 and retained that rank and trade in April, 1918 RAF Muster Roll (see No. 302).

★ 1073. T. DREWERY

Enlisted 21 November, 1908. Formerly 14082 Drummer 1/Grenadier Guards. Transferred to RFC 3 September, 1913. As 2AM with No. 5 Squadron, awarded 1914 Star and bar for services in France from 14 August, 1914. Promoted but reverted back to 2AM (Driver MT) 16 August, 1917. Down graded further to 3AM (Driver) in April, 1918 RAF Muster Roll. (See 302).

1074. A. H. TURNER

A recruit, a direct entrant into RFC 2 February, 1914. Was 2AM with No. 6 Squadron in August, 1914. Served overseas from 24 July, 1915 earning 1914/15 Star trio. Promoted Sergeant (Blacksmith) 1 October, 1917 and retained that rank and trade in RAF Muster Roll of April, 1918.

* 1075. V. H. ROSER

A recruit, a direct entrant into RFC 2 February, 1914. As 2AM with No. 5 Squadron served in France from 14 August, 1914. Promoted Sergeant (Blacksmith) 1 March, 1917 and retained that rank and trade in April, 1918 RAF Muster Roll.

* 1076. JOHN MICHAEL GRENNAN

Born 30 October, 1893. A recruit, a direct entrant into RFC 3 February, 1914. As 2AM, with No 4 Squadron served in France from 12 August, 1914 and earned a 1914 Star and bar. Promoted Acting Corporal (paid) (Rigger) 1 February, 1918 and was Corporal (Rigger aero) in April, 1918 RAF Muster Roll. Awarded RAF L.S.&G.C. as Flight Sergeant *w.e.f.* 3 February, 1932. Appointed Warrant Officer 15 May, 1934 and still serving in 1938, when he was Commissioned (No. 35170 C.E.O.) Flight Lieutenant 6 April, 1941. Wing Commander O.B.E., 1 July, 1944. Retired 15 November, 1948. Alive in 1963. His group of medals was sold by Lusted in 1973 for £62:— O.B.E. (Military, 2nd issue), 1914 Star and bar, British War Medal and Victory Medal (all 1AM RFC), Africa Star, Defence and War Medals (M.I.D.) and RAF L.S.&G.C. (GV F/Sgt).

* 1077. G. HICKLING

A recruit, a direct entrant into RFC 5 February, 1914. As 2AM with No. 4 Squadron served in France from 9 September, 1914. Promoted Sergeant (Rigger) 1 August, 1916 and retained that rank and trade in April, 1918 RAF Muster Roll.

1078. F. J. FOWLER

A recruit, a direct entrant into RFC 4 February, 1914. Discharged 3 March, 1914 under *K.R.* 392 (v) on payment of £10.

1079. J. H. ELLIS

A recruit, a direct entrant into RFC 6 February, 1914. Was a 2AM (Rigger) at Montrose in August, 1914 with Lieutenant de Havilland's detachment, (No. 6 Squadron). Served overseas from 2 April, 1915 earning 1914/15 Star trio. Promoted Flight Sergeant (Rigger) 1 March, 1917 and was Chief Mechanic (Rigger Aero) in April, 1918 RAF Muster Roll.

★ 1080. C. T. WRIGHT

Enlisted 24 July, 1908. Formerly 8681 Private 1/Somerset Light Infantry. Transferred to RFC 4 December, 1913. As 2AM with No. 3 Squadron served in France from 12 August, 1914. Promoted Sergeant (Storeman) 1 September, 1917, and was Sergeant Clerk in April, 1918 RAF Muster Roll.

★ 1081. J. THOMASSON

A recruit, a direct entrant into RFC 3 February, 1914. As 2AM transferred from No. 6 Squadron to the Aircraft Park on 12 August, 1914 and served with this unit in France from 16 August, 1914. Sent on a fitters course at Central Flying School in September, 1914, still a 2AM. Promoted Flight Segeant (Driver MT) 1 April, 1917 and was Chief Mechanic (Driver) in April, 1918 RAF Muster Roll.

★ 1082. HARRY JAMESON

A recruit, a direct entrant into RFC 9 February, 1914. Served in France from 12 August, 1914 as 2AM with the RFC HQ and earned 1914 Star and bar. Awarded French Médaille Militaire as 1AM 20 September, 1914 (see *L.G.* 9 November, 1914 'For Gallantry 21-30 August, 1914.' He said of the award 'It seems the Medal Militaire is very highly prized by the French.' It was presented to him by Brigadier-General Henderson, at that time in command of the RFC in France. Awarded Distinguished Conduct

Medal in *L.G.* 22 June, 1915 when a Corporal. 'For conspicuous coolness and gallantry on several occasions in connection with wireless work under fire.' He wrote at the time 'I got it for working the wireless in an aeroplane, over the German lines, when a shell from one of their anti-aircraft guns exploded near us and blew part of our main inlet valve away and cut the pilot's hand. The pilot was Lieutenant Lewis, now a Captain, and he was doing some very fine work with the wireless.' Commissioned 2 Lieutenant 30 October, 1915, and was killed in action with No. 6 Squadron 5 January, 1917 still a 2 Lieutenant having also been awarded a Military Cross. His group of six medals is in the RAF Museum at Hendon to whom they were donated in 1972 by his sister.

1083. J. R. W. SLADDEN

(See also No. 212) Enlisted 1 April, 1913, a boy entrant into the Royal Engineers. Formerly No. 2433 transferred to the RFC from the RE Training Depot 21 August, 1913. Was 2AM in August, 1914 but no trace of entitlement to either 1914 or 1914/15 Stars has been found. Promoted 1AM (Fitter engines) 1 October, 1917 and retained that rank and trade in April, 1918 RAF Muster Roll. Awarded RAF L.S.&G.C. medal as Sergeant *w.e.f.* 1 April, 1931.

★ 1084. W. W. PYLE

Enlisted 15 March, 1912. Formerly 22655, 26 Company RE Transferred to RFC 25 August, 1913. As 2AM with the Aircraft Park served in France from 16 August, 1914. Promoted to Acting Sergeant Major (Tech) (paid when necessary) 1 March, 1918 and was Acting Ch Mr Mech (paid when necessary) in the April, 1918 RAF Muster Roll.

★ 1085. M. O'CONNOR

Enlisted 11 February, 1910. Formerly 14642 L/Cpl 1/Grenadier Guards. Transferred to RFC 11 September, 1913. As 1AM with the Aircraft Park served in France from 16 August, 1914. Promoted Temp SM (D) 1 September, 1916 and awarded an Army M.S.M. as Flight Sergeant (Act. S.M.) with No. 4 Squadron in *L.G.* 4 June, 1917 for 'Valuable Services with the Army in France and Flanders.' He was SM1 (Disciplinarian) in April, 1918 RAF Muster Roll and was then mentioned in despatches in *L.G.* 11 July, 1918.

1086. W. H. RANDALL

A recruit, a direct entrant into RFC 9 February, 1914. Discharged 27 February, 1914 under *K.R.* 392 (v) on payment of £10.

1087. C. W. BROWN

Formerly 13106 L/Sergeant 1/Grenadier Guards. Transferred to RFC 11 October, 1913. Was 2AM in August, 1914. Served in France with No. 32 Squadron of 5 Brigade from 28 May 1916 to 2 September, 1917 and awarded an Army M.S.M. as Flight Sergeant in *L.G.* 4 July, 1917. He was recommended 15 March 1917 by Brig. General C. A. H. Longcroft 'For conspicuous good work and devotion to duty. This Warrant Officer (note:— *L.G.* says Flight Sergeant) by his excellent example has materially increased the discipline and general efficiency of the Squadron.' Commissioned 2 Lieut. RFC 3 September, 1917. He must have had overseas service after 1 April, 1918 as his two war medals are named to him as 2 Lieutenant, RAF. His trio of medals are known in a private collection (British War Medal, Victory medal and Army M.S.M.).

★ 1088. W. H. DAY

Formerly 15691 L/Cpl 1/Grenadier Guards, Transferred to RFC 11 September, 1913. As 2AM with the Aircraft Park served in France from 16 August, 1914. Commissioned 2 Lieutenant, RFC and Hampshire Regt, 18 November, 1914. In the 1937 *A.F.L.* he is shown as a Flight Lieutenant in the Reserve of Air Force Officers and as the Adjutant at RAF Lymne from 1 September, 1937. He served in WW2 and was promoted to Wing Commander in 1941. No. 75178. Still shown thus in 1946 *A.F.L.*

★ 1089. F. ESPLIN

A recruit, a direct entrant into RFC 11 February, 1914. As 2AM with the Aircraft Park served in France from 16 August, 1914. Promoted Corporal (Fitter general) 1 January, 1918, he retained that rank and trade in April, 1918 RAF Muster Roll.

1090. E. GABBUTH

A recruit, a direct entrant into RFC 14 February, 1914. He was discharged 24 February, 1914 under *K.R.* 392 (v) on payment of £10.

1091. W. BODKIN

A recruit, direct entrant into RFC 16 February, 1914. He deserted 6 June, 1914.

1092. H. S. HUGHES

A recruit, a direct entrant into RFC 16 February, 1914. No trace of entitlement to 1914 or 1914/15 Stars found. Promoted Sergeant (Fitter general) 1 April, 1917, and retained that rank and trade in April, 1918 RAF Muster Roll.

* 1093. C. F. WILSON

A recruit, a direct entrant into RFC 13 February, 1914. As 2AM with No. 2 Squadron served in France from 12 August, 1914. Promoted Flight Sergeant (Fitter engines) 1 October, 1917 and was Chief Mechanic (Fitter A.E.) in April, 1918 RAF Muster Roll.

1094. F. BULLIMORE

A recruit, a direct entrant into RFC 16 February, 1914. Discharged 28 April, 1914 under *K.R.* 392 (iii) 'Not likely to become an efficient soldier.'

* 1095. F. G. RUMSEY-WILLIAMS

A recruit, a direct entrant into RFC 16 February, 1914. As 2AM with the Aircraft Park served in France from 16 August, 1914. Promoted Temp SM (T) 1 May, 1917 and was mentioned in despatches for services in Egypt. He was shown as Ch Mr Mech (Technical) in April, 1918 RAF Muster Roll and was mentioned in the *Times* 'B' list of Press Releases of 23 January, 1919.

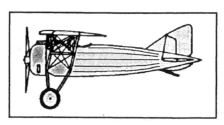

MORANE PARASOL AI

* 1096. H. G. B. Thomas

A recruit, a direct entrant into RFC 10 February, 1914. As 1AM with No. 4 Squadron served in France from 12 August, 1914. Promoted Flight Sergeant, (Fitter general) 1 December, 1916 and was Chief Mechanic (Fitter general) in April, 1918 RAF Muster Roll. He was mentioned for services rendered by the Air Ministry on 22 January, 1919.

* 1097. F. W. Bailey

A recruit, a direct entrant into RFC 17 February, 1914. As 2AM with the Aircraft Park served in France from 16 August, 1914. Promoted Flight Sergeant (Carpenter & Joiner) 1 October, 1916 and was Chief Mechanic (Carpenter) in April, 1918 RAF Muster Roll.

1098. S. V. Winney

A recruit, a direct entrant into RFC 13 February, 1914. No trace of entitlement to 1914 or 1914/15 Stars found. Promoted Flight Sergeant (General Clerk) 21 November, 1916. Mentioned in despatches *L.G.* 13 March, 1918 'For Valuable Services in the War' (*i.e.* in United Kingdom). Mentioned in the *Times* 'B' Lists of Press Releases on both 16 March, 1918 and 29 August, 1919. Was Flight Clerk in April, 1918 RAF Muster Roll.

* 1099. B. Byrne

A recruit, a direct entrant into RFC 17 February, 1914. As 2AM with No. 4 Squadron, served in France from 14 August, 1914. He was discharged as unfit 23 March, 1915.

1100. G. W. O. Harvey

A recruit, a direct entrant into RFC 21 February, 1914. Was 2AM in No. 6 Squadron in August, 1914 and served overseas from 5 March, 1915 earning a 1914/15 Star Trio. Promoted 1AM (Driver MT) 1 July, 1915 and retained that rank and trade in April, 1918 RAF Muster Roll.

* 1101. R. Barnett

A recruit, a direct entrant into RFC 18 February, 1914. As 1AM with No. 6 Squadron served in France from 6 October, 1914. Promoted to

Flight Sergeant (Fitter MT) 1 September, 1916 and was Chief Mechanic (Fitter MT) in April, 1918 RAF Muster Roll.

★ 1102. J. STOCKLER

A recruit, a direct entrant into RFC 12 February, 1914. He was transferred from No. 6 Squadron to the Aircraft Park 12 August, 1914, and as a 2AM served with that unit in France from 14 August, 1914 earning a 1914 Star and bar. Promoted to 1AM (Driver MT) 1 August, 1915, but for some reason, although he appears in the April 1918 RAF Muster Roll in that rank and trade an official note against his name says 'Delete Entry.'

★ 1103. W. HATHAWAY

A recruit, a direct entrant into RFC 21 February, 1914. Was a 2AM (Fitter) at Montrose in August, 1914 with Lieut. de Havilland then posted back to No. 6 Squadron. He went on a Fitters course at the Central Flying School in September, 1914 and was then posted to France 6 October, 1914. Promoted to Temp SM (T) 1 April, 1917 and was Ch Mr Mech (Technical) in April 1918 RAF Muster Roll.

★ 1104. F. E. SKELLAND

Enlisted 8 September, 1911. Formerly 15462 Private 1/Grenadier Guards. As 2AM with No. 5 Squadron, served in France from 14 August, 1914 earning 1914 Star and bar. Promoted to Temp SM (D) 1 November, 1917 and was SM1 (Disciplinarian) in April, 1918 RAF Muster Roll.

1105. S. POINTON

A recruit, a direct entrant into RFC 21 February, 1914. Discharged 25 March, 1914 under *K.R.* 392 (v) on payment of £10.

★ 1106. W. W. CROSTON

A recruit, a direct entrant into RFC 18 February, 1914. As 2AM with the Aircraft Park, served in France from 16 August, 1914. Promoted to Temp SM (T) 1 August, 1917 and was Ch Mr Mech (Technical) in April, 1918 RAF Muster Roll.

1107. A MITCHENER

Enlisted into RFC 17 February, 1914. However he was not a recruit for a note in the records state that he was allowed to count his previous service of 6 years and 292 days in the RHA. No trace of entitlement to 1914 or 1914/15 Stars has been found. Promoted to Corporal (Driver MT) 1 December, 1915 and was Corporal Mechanic (Driver) in April, 1918 RAF Muster Roll.

★ 1108. C. H. CLARKE

A recruit, a direct entrant into RFC 23 February, 1914. As 2AM served with the Aircraft Park in France from 16 August, 1914 earning a 1914 Star and bar. Promoted to Temp SM (T) 1 October, 1917 and was Ch Mr Mech (Technical) in April, 1918 RAF Muster Roll.

★ 1109. H. BEETLESTONE

A recruit, a direct entrant into RFC 23 February, 1914. As 2AM with No. 2 Squadron served in France from 12 August, 1914. Promoted to Temp SM (T) 1 October, 1917 and was Ch Mr Mech (Technical) in April, 1918 RAF Muster Roll.

★ 1110. A. A. RIDEOUT

A recruit, a direct entrant into RFC 26 February, 1914. As 2AM with No. 6 Squadron served in France from 5 October, 1914 earning 1914 Star and bar. As a Corporal he was wounded in November, 1916 and was discharged 11 September, 1917 aged 26 under the terms of *K.R.* 392 (xvi) 'No longer physically fit for war service.' A Silver War Service Badge, No. 249377, was issued to him.

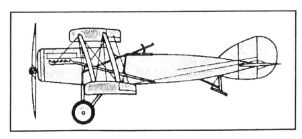

BRISTOL F.2B

★ 1111. W. H. LINNELL

A recruit, a direct entrant into RFC 26 February, 1914. As 2AM with No. 3 Squadron served in France from 13 August, 1914 earning a 1914 Star and bar. He was an 2AM (Armourer) all his RFC service and was down graded to 3AM (Armourer) in the April, 1918 RAF Muster Roll.

★ 1112. J. FULTON

Enlisted 13 March, 1905. Formerly 22953, 53 (MT) Company A.S.C. Transferred to RFC 19 January, 1914. As a Sergeant with the Aircraft Park served in France from 16 August, 1914. Mentioned twice in despatches, 22 June, 1915 and 15 June, 1916, the second time for Egypt. Awarded an Army M.S.M. *L.G.* 11 November, 1916 'For Valuable Services with the Armies in the Field,' as Acting Sergeant Major. He had been promoted to Temp SM (T) 1 December, 1915 and was Ch Mr Mech (Technical) in April, 1918 RAF Muster Roll. 'Mentioned' for services by the Air Ministry 22 January, 1919, in a *Times* 'B' press release. He was awarded his RAF L.S.&G.C. *w.e.f.* 13 March, 1923 as SM 1st Class. See group photograph No. 2.

★ 1113. F. J. COLE

Enlisted 16 March, 1910. Formerly 61131, 86 Battery, RFA. Transferred to RFC 13 September, 1913. As 1AM with No. 6 Squadron, served in France from 6 October, 1914. Promoted Sergeant (Wireless Operator) 1 September, 1916 and retained that rank and trade in April, 1918 RAF Muster Roll.

★ 1114. G. McKEE

A recruit, a direct entrant into RFC 24 Februry, 1914. As 2AM with the Aircraft Park served in France from 16 August, 1914, earning 1914 Star and bar. Promoted Sergeant (Fitter MT) 1 December, 1917 and retained that rank and trade in April, 1918 RAF Muster Roll.

★ 1115. S. O. CROSSLEY

A recruit, a direct entrant into RFC 24 February, 1914. As 2AM with the Aircraft Park served in France from 16 August, 1914. Discharged under *K.R.* 392 (xvi) 4 February, 1916. 'No longer physically fit for war service.'

1116. R. WHEELDON

A recruit, a direct entrant into RFC 24 February, 1914. Discharged 18 May, 1914 under *K.R.* 392 (v) on payment of £10.

★ 1117. H. T. T. NIAS

A recruit, a direct entrant into RFC 26 February, 1914. As 2AM with No. 2 Squadron served in France from 12 August, 1914 earning a 1914 Star and bar. Promoted to Acting Sergeant (paid) (Armourer) 1 December, 1917 and was a Sergeant Mechanic (Armourer) in April, 1918 RAF Muster Roll.

1118. G. A. COMER

A recruit, a direct entrant into RFC 27 February, 1914. Nothing more has been traced on this airman.

★ 1119. E. H. BRADDER

A recruit, a direct entrant into RFC 28 February, 1914. As 2AM with the Aircraft Park served in France from 16 August, 1914. Promoted to Flight Sergeant (Storeman) 1 May, 1917 and was a Flight Clerk in April, 1918 RAF Muster Roll.

CROSSLEY TENDER AND PHELAN & MOORE MOTORCYCLE

★ 1120. A. L. H. WILLEY

A recruit, a direct entrant into RFC 27 February, 1914. As 2AM with RFC HQ served in France from 12 August, 1914. Promoted Flight Sergeant (Clerk General) 1 April, 1917 and was a Flight Clerk in April, 1918 RAF Muster Roll.

★ 1121. H. R. HARLAND

A recruit, a direct entrant into RFC 27 February, 1914. As 2AM with No. 6 Squadron served in France from 6 October, 1914 earning 1914 Star and bar. Promoted to Flight Sergeant (Rigger) 1 September, 1916 and was Chief Mechanic (Rigger Aero) in April, 1918 RAF Muster Roll. He was a Yorkshireman. His trio is known in a private collection:— 1914 Star and bar (2AM RFC) British War Medal and Victory (Flt. Sgt. RAF).

★ 1122. E. F. G. SHARP

A recruit, a direct entrant into RFC 26 February, 1914. As 2AM with the Aircraft Park served in France from 16 August, 1914. Promoted to Sergeant (Rigger) 1 February, 1918 and was Sergeant Mechanic (Rigger Aero) in April, 1918 RAF Muster Roll.

1123. D. MACRAE

A recruit, a direct entrant 25 February, 1914 but his enlistment was not finally approved and less than a week later on 2 March, 1914 he was discharged as not likely to become an efficient soldier.

1124. V. J. CALLUS

Enlisted 23 August, 1906. Formerly 9238 Private 1/Royal Welsh Fusiliers. Transferred to RFC 29 December, 1913. As Corporal with No. 5 Squadron served in France from 14 August, 1914 earning a 1914 Star and bar. Promoted to Temp SM (T) 1 May, 1916 and was Ch Mr Mech (Technical) in April, 1918 RAF Muster Roll. Awarded RAF L.S.&G.C. *w.e.f.* 23 August, 1924 as SM 1st Class.

★ 1125. H. SCARR

A recruit, a direct entrant into RFC 24 February, 1914. As 2AM with No. 2 Squadron served in France from 12 August, 1914. Promoted to 1AM (Fitter and turner) 2 May, 1915 and retained that rank (as Turner) in April, 1918 RAF Muster Roll.

★ 1126. W. C. LANGSTAFF

A recruit, a direct entrant into RFC 28 February, 1914. As 2AM with No. 5 Squadron served in France from 14 August, 1914 earning a 1914 Star and bar. Promoted to Flight Sergeant (Carpenter) in November, 1917 and Chief Mechanic (Carpenter) in April, 1918 RAF Muster Roll.

★ 1127. E. J. GOODWIN

A recruit, direct entrant into RFC 2 March, 1914. As 2AM with No. 2 Squadron, served in France from 12 August, 1914. Promoted to Sergeant (Fitter Engines) 1 December, 1916 and was a Sergeant Mechanic (Fitter AE) in April, 1918 RAF Muster Roll. Received a Military Medal in King's Birthday Honours of 3 June, 1918 for services as a former air gunner in No. 59 Squadron.

★ 1128. ALBERT JOHN GARDNER

A recruit, a direct entrant into RFC 27 February, 1914. As 2AM with the Aircraft Park, served in France from 16 August, 1914. Awarded Royal Aero Club Aviators' Certificate No. 5036 as 2AM, 5 August, 1917. He died on 6 November, 1917 in the United Kingdom, still a 2AM. Buried Abney Park Cemetery, Stoke Newington (Plot D3, Row 1, Grave No. 18858). Son of Mr. T. E. Gardner, 174 High St., Deptford, London.

1129. SAMUEL BROOKS

A recruit, a direct entrant into RFC 2 March, 1914. No record of entitlement to 1914 or 1914/15 Stars traced. Drowned in Alexandria, Egypt, 21 March, 1917 when a Sergeant with the No. 23 (Reserve) Squadron. Buried in the Hadra War Memorial Cemetery, Egypt (Row D, Grave 98). He was the son of James and Lucy Brooks of Stretton Sugwar, Herefordshire. Entitled to British War Medal and Victory Medal.

1130. FRANK RUSSELL

Born in Brighton on 13 July, 1894. Enlisted into the RFC 28 February, 1914. No record of entitlement to 1914 or 1914/15 Stars traced. Awarded Royal Aero Club Aviators' Certificate No. 3482 of 27 August, 1916 as 1AM. Killed in action as 1AM (Observer) whilst flying in a one-and-a-half strutter, 16 April, 1917, aged 22, when with 'A' Flight 43 Squadron. Son of Mr. and Mrs. Russell of 65 Elm Grove, Brighton. Buried Douai Communal Cemetery (Row A, Grave 13). He would have been entitled to British War Medal and Victory medal. See *'Cross and Cockade'* Vol. 6, No. 2, p. 79.

1131. W. R. STEVENS

Enlisted into RFC 26 February, 1914. No record of entitlement to 1914 or 1914/15 Stars traced. Promoted to Corporal (Fitter MT) 1 October, 1916 and retained that rank and trade in April, 1918 RAF Muster Roll.

★ 1132. R. F. SEGROTT

Enlisted into RFC 27 February, 1914. As 2AM with No. 2 Squadron served in France from 12 August, 1914. Promoted Corporal (Kite Balloon Winch Driver and Fitter) 1 February, 1917 and was Corporal Mechanic (Winch D.F.) in April, 1918 RAF Muster Roll.

★ 1133. H. FULCHER

A recruit, a direct entrant into RFC 3 March, 1914. As 2AM with the Aircraft Park served in France from 16 August, 1914. Promoted to Flight Sergeant (Fitter general) 1 December, 1917 and was Chief Mechanic (Fitter general) in April, 1918 RAF Muster Roll.

★ 1134. WILLIAM A. G. GOLDSWORTHY

Enlisted 15 July, 1908. Formerly 9371 Private 1/Loyal North Lancashire Regt. Transferred to RFC 5 November, 1913. As 1AM with No. 4 Squadron served in France from 9 September, 1914 and earned 1914 Star and bar. Promoted to Temp SM (D) 1 December, 1916 and was SM1

(Disciplinarian) in April, 1918 RAF Muster Roll. Commissioned 2 Lieutenant 14 November, 1918. In 1921 he was a Stores Officer serving at 10 Group HQ, Lee-on-Solent. In 1931 he was stationed at RAF Hawkinge, nr Folkstone, Kent with No. 25 (Fighter) Squadron, and he is shown in 1937 Air Force List as Flying Officer (E) (retired) seniority from 23 December, 1919.

★ 1135. J. W. Fox

A recruit, a direct entrant into RFC 4 March, 1914. As 2AM with RFC HQ served in France from 12 August, 1914. Promoted Sergeant (Photographer) 1 March, 1918 and retained that rank and trade in April, 1918 RAF Muster Roll. His 1914 Star trio named to 2AM RFC was sold by Beadles in 1986 for £175.

★ 1136. H. G. Henderson

A recruit, a direct entrant into RFC 5 March, 1914. As 2AM with RFC HQ earned 1914 Star in France. Promoted to 1AM (Rigger) 1 January, 1916 and retained that rank and trade in April, 1918 RAF Muster Roll.

1137. C. J. A Thomas

A recruit, a direct entrant into RFC 3 March, 1914. No record of entitlement to either 1914 or 1914/15 Star traced. Promoted to 1AM (Fitter MT) 26 January, 1915 and retained that rank and trade in April, 1918 RAF Muster Roll.

★ 1138. E. Hart

Enlisted into RFC 27 February, 1914. As 2AM with 5 Squadron served in France from 14 August, 1914. Promoted to Flight Sergeant (Coppersmith) 1 October, 1917 and was Chief Mechanic (Coppersmith) in April, 1918 RAF Muster Roll.

1139. G. P. Mills

Enlisted into RFC 7 March, 1914. Deserted 27 March, 1914.

1140. D. W. ROSS

Enlisted into RFC 7 March, 1914. Was 2AM with No. 7 Squadron in August, 1914. Not issued with 1914 or 1914/15 Star. Promoted to 1AM (Rigger) 1 October, 1916 and retained that rank and trade in April, 1918 RAF Muster Roll.

1141. T. COATES

Enlisted into RFC 3 March, 1914. Was 2AM in August. No record of entitlement to 1914 or 1914/15 Stars traced. Promoted to Flight Sergeant (Rigger) 1 October, 1917 and was Chief Mechanic (Rigger Aero) in April, 1918 RAF Muster Roll.

1142. A. CHILVER

Enlisted into RFC 7 March, 1914. Was 2AM in August. No record of entitlement to 1914 or 1914/15 Stars traced. Promoted Acting Sergeant (paid) (Rigger) 1 December, 1917 and was Sergeant Mechanic (Rigger Aero) in April, 1918 RAF Muster Roll.

1143. A. A. SANDERSON

Enlisted into RFC 5 March, 1914. No record of entitlement to 1914 or 1914/15 Stars traced. Promoted Sergeant (2nd class Pilot) 1 July, 1916 and was Sergeant Mechanic (Pilot) in April, 1918 RAF Muster Roll.

★ 1144. JOHN WILLIAM MITCHELL

A recruit, a direct entrant into RFC 6 March, 1914. As 2AM with the Aircraft Park served in France from 16 August, 1914. Promoted Sergeant (Rigger) 1 September, 1916 and was Sergeant Mechanic (Rigger Aero) in April, 1918 RAF Muster Roll. Awarded RAF L.S.&G.C. as Flight Sergeant *w.e.f.* 6 March, 1932. Appointed WO April, 1937.

★ 1145. F. N. SLINGSBY

A recruit, a direct entrant into RFC 9 March, 1914. As 2AM with No. 6 Squadron served in France from 6 October, 1914 and earned 1914 Star and bar. Awarded a Military Medal 12 March, 1917 as a Flight Sergeant for bringing back an aeroplane when the pilot had been wounded. Promoted to Acting Sergeant Major (paid) (D) 1 March, 1918 and retained that rank and trade in April, 1918 RAF Muster Roll.

1146. S. CLARKE

A recruit, a direct entrant into RFC 10 March, 1914. Discharged 4 April, 1914 under *K.R.* 392 (iii) 'Not likely to become an efficient soldier.'

* 1147. A. C. WILSON

Formerly 18090 Private 2 Company RAMC. Transferred to RFC 9 October, 1913. As 1AM with No. 2 Squadron served in France from 12 August, 1914. Discharged 14 July, 1916 as Corporal at the Recruit Depot, Montrose and died 25 August, 1916 aged 40. Husband of Ethel Wilson, 68 Ferry St, Montrose. Buried Montrose (Sleepy Hillock) Cemetery, Tayside, Scotland, Row A6, Grave 195).

* 1148. N. HEMSLEY

A recruit, a direct entrant into RFC 11 March, 1914. As 2AM with No. 6 Squadron served in France from 9 September, 1914 earning a 1914 Star and bar. Commissioned 2 Lieutenant 17 September, 1917.

* 1149. S. G. ROWLEY

Enlisted 27 August, 1907. Formerly 9477 Private 2/Welsh Regt. Transferred to RFC 11 October, 1913. He was the first 2AM to be posted to No. 7 Squadron on its formation on 1 May, 1914. Transferred back to No. 6 Squadron in August, 1914 and served in France from 6 October, 1914. Promoted to Temp SM (D) 1 September, 1916 and was SM 1st Class (Disciplinarian) in April, 1918 RAF Muster Roll.

* 1150. S. A. COX

Enlisted 23 September, 1911. Formerly 67386 39 Battery RFA. Transferred to RFC 11 October, 1913. As 2AM with No. 4 Squadron, served in France from 12 August, 1914. Promoted to Temp SM (T) 1 September, 1917 and was Ch Mr Mech (Technical) in April, 1918 RAF Muster Roll. Mentioned in despatches for Mesopotamia in *L.G.* 12 January, 1920. See *Cross and Cockade*, Volume 3, No. 3, p. 113, which notes him serving as Temp. Sgt. Major in 97 Squadron.

1151. E. DRACUP

A recruit, a direct entrant into RFC 9 March, 1914. No record of entitlement to 1914 or 1914/15 Stars traced. Promoted to Flight Sergeant (Machinist) 1 July, 1916, and was Chief Mechanic (Machinist) in April, 1918 RAF Muster Roll. Awarded RAF L.S.&G.C. *w.e.f.* 9 March, 1932 as Flight Sergeant.

1152. C. A. BAKER

A recruit, a direct entrant into RFC 11 March, 1914. No record of entitlement to 1914 or 1914/15 Stars traced. Promoted to Temp SM (D) 1 November, 1917 and was SM1 (Disciplinarian) in April, 1918 RAF Muster Roll.

★ 1153. R. J. SOULSBY

A recruit, a direct entrant into RFC 13 March, 1914. As 2AM with the Aircraft Park served in France from 16 August, 1914. Promoted to Corporal (Blacksmith) 1 May, 1917 and retained that rank and trade in April, 1918 RAF Muster Roll.

1154. V. H. COLEMAN

A recruit, a direct entrant into RFC 16 March, 1914. No record of entitlement to 1914 or 1914/15 Stars traced. Promoted Corporal (Carpenter & Joiner) 1 December, 1916 and was Corporal Mechanic (Carpenter) in April, 1918 RAF Muster Roll. (See No. 1155)

1155. P. E. COLEMAN

A recruit, a direct entrant into RFC 16 March, 1914. No record of entitlement to 1914 or 1914/15 Stars traced. Was an 2AM observer with 2 Lieut Castle (11 Squadron) when shot down 30 March, 1916 on

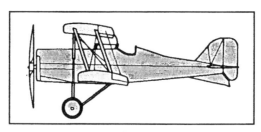

SE5

photographic duties between Fampoux and Monchy le Preux (*vide RFC Communiqué No. 32*). Awarded Military Medal 9 July, 1917 as Corporal in 11 Squadron. Promoted to Sergeant (Storeman) 1 October, 1917 and was Sergeant Clerk in April, 1918 RAF Muster Roll (see No. 1154).

★ 1156. G. W. HUNNISETT

A recruit, a direct entrant into RFC 16 March, 1914. As 2AM with No. 6 Squadron served in France from 7 October, 1914 and earned 1914 Star and bar. Promoted to Acting Warrant Officer (Disciplinarian) (paid when necessary) 1 January, 1918 and was Act. SM1 (paid) (D) in April, 1918 RAF Muster Roll.

1157. W. F. NEWLAND

A recruit, a direct entrant into RFC 12 March, 1914. No record of entitlement to 1914 or 1914/15 Stars traced. Promoted to Sergeant (Fitter-engines) 1 June 1917 and was Sergeant Mechanic (Fitter AE) in April, 1918 RAF Muster Roll.

★ 1158. A. JONES

A recruit, a direct entrant into RFC 12 March, 1914. As 2AM with the Aircraft Park served in France from 16 August, 1914. Promoted to Flight Sergeant (Driver MT) 1 November, 1917 and was Chief Mech (Dvr. MT) in April, 1918 RAF Muster Roll.

1159. H. BERE

A recruit, a direct entrant to RFC 11 March, 1914. No record of entitlement to 1914 or 1914/15 Stars traced. Promoted to Flight Sergeant (Rigger) 1 November, 1916. Mentioned in despatches *L.G.* 24 February, 1917. Listed in the *Times* 'B' Press Release of 27 March, 1917. He was Chief Mechanic (Rigger Aero) in April, 1918 RAF Muster Roll.

★ 1160. FRANK WILLIAM HENRY GEE

A recruit, a direct entrant into RFC 6 March, 1914. As 2AM with RFC HQ served in France from 12 August, 1914 and earned a 1914 Star and bar. He was a Corporal (Aerial Gunner) from 20 October, 1915. Promoted Flight Sergeant, (Fitter general) 1 September, 1916. He was a Chief Mechanic (Fitter general) in April, 1918 RAF Muster Roll. Awarded

General Service Medal (clasp Southern Desert, Iraq) for services between 8 January and 3 June, 1928 against the Akhwan in either 30, 55, 70 or 84 Squadrons. (See No. 123 Lee.) He was awarded his RAF L.S.&G.C. *w.e.f.* 6 March, 1932 as SM1 and was commissioned, Flying Officer (C.E.O.) 20 July, 1934. In 1937 *A.F.L.* he was shown as serving from 9 August, 1935 at No. 3 School of Technical Training, Manston, Ramsgate.

★ 1161. LOUIS F. BOWLER

A recruit, a direct entrant into RFC 16 March, 1914. As 2AM with No. 3 Squadron served in France from 13 August, 1914. Promoted to 1AM (Driver MT) 1 April, 1915 and retained that rank and trade in April, 1918 RAF Muster Roll. As Corporal he was awarded a RAF M.S.M. in *L.G.* 3 June, 1919 for services in France (he originally came from Bedford).

★ 1162. ARTHUR JAMES VALENTINE PARISH

A recruit, a direct entrant into RFC 16 March, 1914. As 2AM with the Aircraft Park served in France from 16 August, 1914. Promoted to Corporal (Fitter and turner) 1 October, 1916 and was Corporal Mechanic (Fitter) in April, 1918 RAF Muster Roll. Awarded RAF L.S.&G.C. medal *w.e.f.* 16 March, 1932 as SM2. Commissioned Flying Officer (CEO) 15 July, 1937. In 1937 *A.F.L.* stationed at RAF Station Leconsfield. Promoted to Wing Commander (No. 35096) 1 June, 1942. Still serving in 1946.

1163. CHARLES JACKSON

A recruit, a direct entrant into RFC 18 March, 1914. A 2AM with No. 7 Squadron in August, 1914. No record of entitlement to 1914 or 1914/15 Stars traced. Accidentally killed, 11 November, 1917 when Sergeant, Engine Repair Shop, aged 24. Son of Alice and William Hardy Jackson of 124 Hollingbury Park Ave, Brighton. Buried St. Sever Communal Cemetery, France (PIII N. 14B). Entitled to British War Medal and Victory medal.

★ 1164. W. A. ELSTOW

A recruit, a direct entrant into RFC 5 March, 1914. As 2AM with the Aircraft Park served in France from 16 August, 1914. Mentioned in despatches 1 January, 1916 as 1AM. Promoted Sergeant (Ftr Eng Er MT)

1 March, 1918 and was Sergeant Mechanic (Fitter MT) in April, 1918 RAF Muster Roll.

★ 1165. H. G. CAMPBELL

A recruit, a direct entrant into RFC 14 March, 1914. Was on a Fitters course at CFS in September, 1914. As 2AM served in France from 7 November, 1914. Promoted to Sergeant (Fitter and turner) 1 January, 1917 and was Sergeant Mechanic (Turner) in April, 1918 RAF Muster Roll. His 1914 Star (only) was sold in 1990. See photograph under 812.

★ 1166. CHARLES JAMES COMERFORD

Enlisted 11 October, 1907. Formerly 16855, 17 Company, RE. Transferred to RFC 28 October, 1913. As 2AM with No. 4 Squadron served in France from 12 August, 1914 and earned 1914 Star and bar. Reverted to Sergeant (1st Class Pilot) 8 October, 1916 and was awarded Royal Aero Club Aviators' Certificate No. 4295 on 22 February, 1917. Reported 'Missing' 18 August, 1917 (57 Squadron). Sergeant Mechanic (Pilot) in April, 1918 RAF Muster Roll. Presumably then a POW.

★ 1167. A. W. DORRANCE

Enlisted 27 March, 1913. Formerly 11455 2/Royal Scots. Transferred to RFC 17 October, 1913. As 2AM with No. 4 Squadron served in France from 3 November, 1914. Reverted to 1AM (Fitter and Turner) 14 April, 1917 and was 1AM (Turner) in April, 1918 RAF Muster Roll.

1168. H. O. EDWARDS

A recruit, a direct entrant into RFC 20 March, 1914. 2AM in August, 1914. No record of entitlement to 1914 or 1914/15 Stars traced. Promoted Acting Flight Sergeant (Fitter engines) (paid) 1 December, 1917, and was Chief Mechanic (Fitter AE) in April, 1918 RAF Muster Roll. Was mentioned in despatches in *L.G.* 5 June, 1919 for services in Egypt.

⋆ 1169. JAMES HUDSON

A recruit, a direct entrant into RFC 23 March, 1914. As 2AM with the Aircraft Park served in France from 16 August, 1914. Promoted to Temp SM (D) 1 December, 1917 and was SM1 (Disciplinarian) in April, 1918 RAF Muster Roll. Awarded RAF M.S.M. in *L.G.* 10 October, 1919. Brother of No. 77, one of a family of twelve.

⋆ 1170. C. R. WOODERSON

A recruit, a direct entrant into RFC 23 March, 1914. As 2AM with No. 3 Squadron served in France from 13 August, 1914. As Flight Sergeant, discharged 'sick' under *K.R.* 392 (xvi) 26 May, 1917. Silver War Badge 194727 issued.

⋆ 1171. S. BIRD

A recruit, a direct entrant into RFC 23 March, 1914. As 2AM with No. 3 Squadron served in France from 14 August, 1914. Wounded 12 March 1915 in an accidental bomb explosion (see No. 194). Promoted to Sergeant (Driver MT) 1 September, 1916 and was Sergeant Mechanic (Driver) in April, 1918 RAF Muster Roll. See photograph under No. 812.

⋆ 1172. G. A. PYLE

A recruit, a direct entrant into RFC 23 March, 1914. As 2AM with No. 6 Squadron served in France from 7 October, 1914. Promoted to Corporal (Electrician) 1 February, 1917 and retained that rank and trade in April, 1918 RAF Muster Roll. Deserted 23 July, 1921.

⋆ 1173. S. E. TAIT

A recruit, a direct entrant into RFC 20 March, 1914. As 2AM with No. 3 Squadron served in France from 12 August, 1914. Promoted to Temp SM (T) 1 August, 1917 and was Ch Mr Mech (Technical) in April, 1918 RAF Muster Roll. See photograph under No. 812.

⋆ 1174. ALFRED GEORGE CUMMINS

A recruit, a direct entrant into RFC 24 March, 1914. As 2AM with No. 3 Squadron served in France from 13 August, 1914. Posted back to UK on a Riggers' Course at CFS in September, 1914. Promoted but reverted to 2AM (Carpenter & Joiner) 31 January, 1918 and reduced to 3AM in April, 1918 RAF Muster Roll. He was a Sergeant with 98 Squadron when he died of pneumonia on 21 November, 1918, aged 22. Son of Patrick and Sarah Cummins of Norman Court, Stud West, Tytherley, Salisbury. Buried in Auberqcourt British Cemetery (I D 20). See photograph under No. 812.

★ 1175. P. E. BUTCHER

Born in 1896 in Woking. Brother of No. 463. A recruit, a direct entrant into RFC 27 March, 1914. As 2AM with the Aircraft Park served in France from 16 August, 1914. Wounded 23 September, 1914. Promoted to Sergeant (Fitter engines) 1 October, 1917 and was Sergeant Mechanic (Fitter A.E.) in April, 1918 RAF Muster Roll. Discharged 27 April, 1920. In 1971 he wrote his autobiography *'Skill and Devotion (1913-1918).'* In it he states he was awarded a D.C.M., an M.S.M. and was mentioned in despatches, but the authors can trace none of the three in the *London Gazettes*.

The following are some extracts from his book.

'With my apprenticeship incomplete, but my training in engineering to date culminating in passing those examintions I had taken and also the London County Council Tests, I was in a confident mood when, about the middle of February, I cycled all the way from Woking to Farnborough, some 15 miles, for my tests as a volunteer for the RFC. These were carried out at the Royal Aircraft Factory, where I was taken by an Officer and handed over to a Mr. Measures, who was to supervise the practical fitness tests (see No. 12).

These began by his giving me a three inch length of mild steel bar, from which he told me to make a hexagonal 1/4 inch BSF nut. This sort of test went on, until the officer re-appeared with a Crossley tender. He explained that I must attempt to drive it backwards between posts set out in a figure of eight pattern, and then I had to take him in it through Farnborough and Aldershot.

The NCO in charge of our instruction was a very august person in our young eyes, having the much-coveted brevet on his tunic. He had transferred from the Royal Engineers and seen service on balloons, airships and aeroplanes. A man who knew his work thoroughly, and who made sure that those under him progressed rapidly, by the clarity of his lectures.

My job, after sufficient instruction, was that of engine fitter on a Maurice Farman and it was on this machine that I had my first flight, in May, 1914, when taken on a trip from Farnborough to Brooklands, a thrilling and awe-inspiring event.

Swinging the propeller was also among a fitter's duties and we all received instruction in how to carry out this dangerous job. Pre-ignition was the chief menace, because, if the engine was hot, it would fire back, catching one's knees, hands or even oneself.

Starting a Beardmore was an experience in itself. Four of us made a human chain and, while the pilot operated the CAV magneto, at the word 'Contact' we all gave a strong pull. You knew when she started – the whole bunch were sent flying every time!

At this period fitters and riggers had plenty of flights and very little attention was paid to their flying hours. Being only some eight stone in weight, I came in for all of my share of this, especially on Maurice and Henri Farmans. Every flight was an experience and an adventure, for although many difficulties were surmounted you never knew how your engine would behave itself.

By the evening of August 12th we were all ready for the Channel crossing and I was standing on the makeshift airfield on the cliffs when a familiar figure came towards me; it was Captain Picton Warlow, the officer whose car I had driven so frequently; he came up and said that his mechanic was not available and he wanted me as his fitter. I told him that I was in No. 2 Squadron, and he was, I think, in No. 3. 'We'll sort that out when we get to Amiens,' he said, adding 'if we ever do!.' So the machine that took us to France was a Henri Farman, with an 80hp Gnome engine that had a tendency to oil up. This trip was no exception and we were forced to land at Wimereux by Napoleon's Monument. Next morning we set off again passing over Arras and leaving Albert on our starboard side. A little later I spotted Amiens, where we landed safely. I was at Amiens long enough to see a fatal accident, the second to No. 3 Squadron. The machine, a BE8 came down and burst into flames as I watched. Lieutenant Copland Penny and my friend whom I had last met at Netheravon, Air Mechanic Parfit, were both burnt to death as I watched, unable to approach because of the heat. (See No. 725).

Our passage was that of a carnival, the inhabitants of the towns lining the streets and cheering us, handing out fruit and gifts. All the other machines we saw in the air as we pushed forward along the dusty roads were those of the RNAS which was officially formed as a separate unit on July 1st, although it had begun to take shape at the beginning of the year, two months before I joined the service. Then, out of the blue as far as we were concerned, fate turned on us. We had thrust forward, half-way across France it seemed, and had arrived at Maubeuge and gone right through the aerodrome about four miles out, without having seen any troops in the town. We, as you will have gathered, were all over the place, wherever the machines had landed, on places made by the advance party, and marked by a white sheet on the ground. However, reports began to come in saying that the Germans were pressing hard only five miles away, and we were ordered back to the town. It was on our return thence that we saw our first troops in the area, in the early hours of the morning of August 24th. By now we could see the black smoke, hear the gunfire and watching our infantry going forward, we understood well enough when Major Brooke Popham told us to make our way back as best we could, but at all times to keep an eye open for our machines and give them every attention. With some of us going back by road transport and others left behind to look after the machines, it was going to be every man for himself. As we finally left the crowds in Maubeuge via the City

RE5 OF 6 SQN COMING ASHORE IN FRANCE, OCTOBER 1914.

401

Gate at one end, the grey-clad German troops were marching in at the other.

On our way we ran into a detachment of French Cuirassiers looking like something from another age, as they trotted by in their full-dress uniforms with the late summer sun blazing on their breast plates and jingling accoutrements. An incident which remains in my mind concerning our passage through this part of France, where the nuns gave us long loaves of bread as we passed along, was when an Intelligence Officer approached me, being in charge of the guard, and said, 'I want you to stop a dray with a priest on board: don't understand anything he says, just hold him until I arrive.' It is sufficient to say that, in the early hours of the following morning, with myself as witness, the man died a spy's death before a French firing squad in Béthune Square. On the improvised landing grounds which the advance parties cut, the fitters and riggers tried to help each other, only to find that we had to rely on the tools in our pockets, anything else being on the transport lorries which were, no one knew where. Men like Lauri Kiesler, Freddie Trailer, Joey Kemper, 'Darky' Romford, 'Smuggler' Smith, Woolsey, Craven and Sgt-Maj Rumbold (Nos. 56, 72, 251, 931, ?, 168, 690 and 162), working and travelling until they were literally dead on their feet from fatigue, to keep the machines in the air. Although we were issued with six-chamber Webley Scott revolvers and dum-dum bullets, and were thus capable of taking care of ourselves, at least we did not have to fight the hideous rear-guard actions of the troops.

It was while we were still at Melun that word filtered through that the French had evacuated Juvisy aerodrome. Now we had Renault engines for which spares were very low, so it was decided that someone should fly over and see if there was anything useful there, left behind. The party which went found Juvisy to be a very nice aerodrome just off the Fontainebleau road, lying in a large basin surrounded by hills. Here in the hangars were found old machines which I had never seen before, and plenty of spares for our Renault engines. With this booty we made good the motors of our BEs which, being air cooled, got very hot and required parts to be renewed frequently. Thus were the machines serviced and we waited to see what were the next cards that Fate would play. Coulommiers, where we were at last able to have a sponge down was, I think the last time the old squadrons were together, although for most of the war, we worked as a team. I remember Christmas

1914 being spent on a strip landing ground alongside Zillebeke Lake, where the Belgian Air Force were operating. One of our BEs had landed there, and the rigger and I shared the Christmas dinner we had been brought, under its wing.

He died in October, 1973, aged 78. See photograph under No. 812.

★ 1176. W. A. APPEL

A recruit, a direct entrant into RFC 30 March, 1914. As 2AM with No. 3 Squadron, served in France from 13 August, 1914 and earned 1914 Star and bar. Promoted to Corporal (Fitter MT) 1 September, 1915 and retained that rank and trade in April, 1918 RAF Muster Roll.

1177. G. W. LLOYD

A recruit, a direct entrant into RFC 1 April, 1914. Served overseas from 24 July, 1915 earning a 1914/15 Star trio. Discharged 'sick' 20 June, 1917. Silver War Badge No. 203507 issued.

1178. W. F. RANDALL

A recruit, a direct entrant into RFC 31 March, 1914. Was 2AM with No. 7 Squadron in August, 1914. Served overseas from 3 April, 1915 and earned 1914/15 Star trio. Noted as an aerial gunner with No. 7 Squadron in August, 1915. Promoted to Flight Sergeant (Fitter engines) 1 October, 1916 and was Chief Mechanic (Fitter AE) in April, 1918 RAF Muster Roll.

★ 1179. E. A. FOX

A recruit, a direct entrant into RFC 3 April, 1914. As 2AM with No. 6 Squadron, served in France from 7 October, 1914. Reverted to Corporal (Rigger) 22 September, 1917 and was Corporal Mechanic (Rigger Aero) in April, 1918 RAF Muster Roll.

★ 1180. J. McHARDY

Enlisted 2 December, 1901. Formerly 8482 1/Black Watch. Transferred to RFC 3 November, 1913 as a Corporal in No. 5 Squadron. Promoted Sergeant 10 August, 1914. Served in France with No. 5 Squadron from 14 August, 1914. Promoted to Temp SM (D) 1 November, 1915 and was

SM1 (Disciplinarian) in April, 1918 RAF Muster Roll. Awarded RAF L.S.&G.C. as SM1 with effect from 20 October, 1919.

1181. CHARLES RIPLEY

A recruit, a direct entrant into RFC 4 April, 1914. No record of entitlement to either 1914 or 1914/15 Star has been traced. Promoted to Temp SM (D) 1 August, 1916 and was SM1 (Disciplinarian) in April, 1918 RAF Muster Roll. Awarded RAF L.S.&G.C. medal as SM2 on 4 April, 1932. Appointed WO with effect from 15 February, 1934. Awarded 1937 Coronation Medal and in the March, 1938 *A.F.L.* is shown as serving from 27 August, 1936 at No. 3 Apprentice Wing at No. 1 School of Technical Training, Halton Camp, Aylesbury. See photograph under No. 812.

★ 1182. C. E. HYDE

A recruit, a direct entrant into RFC 2 April, 1914. As 2AM with the Aircraft Park, served in France from 16 August, 1914. Awarded a Military Medal as 1AM in No. 1 Wing in *L.G.* 25 September, 1917. He came originally from Malton. Promoted Sergeant (Fitter general) 1 December, 1917 and retained that rank and trade in April, 1918 RAF Muster Roll.

SE5A (McCUDDEN, V.C.)

* 1183. F. H. STIRLING

A recruit, a direct entrant into RFC 6 April, 1914. As 1AM with RFC HQ served in France from 12 August, 1914. Promoted Sergeant (Carpenter & Joiner) 1 February, 1916 and was Sergeant Mechanic (Carpenter) in April, 1918 RAF Muster Roll.

1184. ALFRED SCOTT

Enlisted 27 May, 1905. Formerly 7299 Private 1/Wiltshire Regiment. Transferred to RFC 14 January, 1914. Was 2AM with No. 6 Squadron in August, 1914. Served overseas from 24 July, 1915 with No. 10 Squadron and earned 1914/15 Star trio. Promoted to Sergeant (Rigger) 1 December, 1917 and was Sergeant Mechanic (Rigger Aero) in April, 1918 RAF Muster Roll. Awarded RAF M.S.M. for services in France in *L.G.* 3 June, 1919 as a Flight Sergeant. The *Gazette* gives his home town as Montrose. Mentioned in despatches in *L.G.* 11 July, 1919. Awarded RAF L.S.&G.C. medal *w.e.f.* 27 May, 1923 still a Flight Sergeant.

* 1185. J. MURRAY

A recruit, a direct entrant into RFC 1 April, 1914. As 2AM with the Aircraft Park served in France from 16 August, 1914. Promoted Corporal (Tinsmith) 1 April, 1917 and was Corporal Mechanic (Tinsmith and Sheet Metal Worker) in April, 1918 RAF Muster Roll.

* 1186. F. WILLMORE

A recruit, a direct entrant into RFC 8 April, 1914. As 2AM with No. 3 Squadron, served in France from 12 August, 1914. Promoted but reverted to 2AM (Tinsmith) 12 April, 1916 and was further reduced to 3AM (Tinsmith and Sheet Metal Worker) in April 1918 RAF Muster Roll.

* 1187. ARTHUR HENRY GEE

A recruit, a direct entrant into RFC 8 April, 1914. As 2AM with No. 6 Squadron, served in France from 7 October, 1914 earning 1914 Star and bar. Mentioned in despatches as Flight Sergeant in *L.G.* 15 May, 1917 serving with 25 Squadron, when his home town is given as Leicester. Promoted Temp SM (D) 1 June, 1917 and was SM1 (Disciplinarian) in April, 1918 RAF Muster Roll. Awarded French Médaille Militaire in *L.G.*

17 August, 1918 still with No. 25 Squadron. Awarded RAF L.S.&G.C. w.e.f. 8 April, 1932 as SM1 when he was the 55th senior RAF Warrant Officer.

★ 1188. L. F. BRUNNING

A recruit, a direct entrant into RFC 11 April, 1914. Was 2AM with No. 6 Squadron and served in France from 9 September, 1914. Promoted to Flight Sergeant (Fitter general) 1 May, 1916 and was Chief Mechanic (Fitter general) in April, 1918 RAF Muster Roll.

★ 1189. P. F. HARPER

A recruit, a direct entrant into RFC 14 April, 1914. As 2AM with No. 6 Squadron, served in France from 7 October, 1914. Promoted to Flight Sergeant (Fitter general) 1 December, 1917 and was Chief Mechanic (Fitter general) in April, 1918 RAF Muster Roll.

★ 1190. G. ROBINSON

A recruit, a direct entrant into RFC 15 April, 1914. As 2AM with No. 3 Squadron, served in France from 13 August, 1914. Promoted to 1AM (Driver MT) 1 June, 1915 and retained that rank and trade in April, 1918 RAF Muster Roll.

1191. FREDERICK PETCH

Born 8 January, 1882. Formerly 8532 Sergeant 2/Highland Light Infantry to which rank he was promoted 6 January, 1906. Transferred to RFC 13 March, 1914. (See group photograph No. 2.) Was a Sergeant in No. 6 Squadron on a Riggers' Course in September, 1914 and served overseas from 4 April, 1915 earning 1914/15 Star trio. Commissioned 2 Lieutenant 23 June, 1916 and promoted to Lieutenant (No. 11003) 27 July, 1917. Awarded M.B.E. *L.G.* 3 June, 1919. In 1921 *A.F.L.* shown as Flight Lieutenant on *Stores List* seniority 1 January, 1921 serving from 16 November, 1920 in Iraq at Middle East Area HQ. In the February, 1931 *A.F.L.* he is shown as Squadron Leader O.B.E., seniority 1 January, 1927 serving from 25 February, 1927 at 22 Group HQ, South Farnborough, Hants. Squadron Leader in WW2 from 16 August, 1940, having retired, 3 January, 1932 and having been recalled from 27 September, 1939 to 8 October, 1940. Died in 1973.

★ 1192. A. H. C. CUFF

A recruit, a direct entrant into RFC during April, 1914. As 2AM with No. 3 Squadron served in France from 13 August, 1914. Promoted 1AM then accidentally killed loading bombs 12 March, 1915 (see No. 194). Buried Chocques Military Cemetery (I, A, 38).

★ 1193. R. J. KIRWIN

A recruit, a direct entrant into RFC 31 March, 1914. As 2AM with RFC HQ served in France from 12 August, 1914. Wounded 12 May, 1915 when serving with No. 6 Squadron. Promoted Flight Sergeant (Wireless Operator) 8 August, 1917 and then Chief Mechanic (Wireless Opeator) in April, 1918 RAF Muster Roll. His 1914 Star was sold by Dyas in 1988 for £75.

★ 1194. ALBERT JAMES BRADFORD

A recruit, a direct entrant into RFC 16 April, 1914. As 2AM with the Aircraft Park, served in France from 16 August, 1914. Awarded French Croix de Guerre 24 February, 1916 as 1AM. Promoted to Sergeant (Wireless Operator) 1 June, 1916 and retained that rank and trade in April, 1918 RAF Muster Roll.

1195. H. GIBBARD

A recruit, a direct entrant into RFC 20 April, 1914. Was 2AM with No. 6 Squadron in August, 1914 and first served overseas from 17 April, 1915 earning 1914/15 Star trio. Transferred to the Northamptonshire Regiment as No. 50392.

★ 1196. C. W. WAITT

A recruit, a direct entrant into RFC 20 April, 1914. As 2AM with RFC HQ served in France from 12 August, 1914. Awarded Military Medal as Sergeant in *L.G.* 11 October, 1916. Commissioned 2 Lieutenant 16 May, 1917. His Military Medal (only) known to be in a private collection in 1989.

★ 1197. R. E. TOLLERFIELD

A recruit, a direct entrant into RFC 20 April, 1914. As 2AM with No. 6 Squadron served in France from 9 September, 1914. Wounded 22 April, 1917 as a Corporal (Observer) in No. 11 Squadron flying in a BE2f No. A3168, piloted by 2 Lieut. Welsh. Promoted Sergeant (1st Class Pilot) 16 May, 1917. Awarded Military Medal in *L.G.* 9 July, 1917 in his previous rank of Corporal. Was a Sergeant Mechanic (Pilot) in April, 1918 RAF Muster Roll.

★ 1198. F. W. CARR

A recruit, a direct entrant into RFC 24 April, 1914. Was 2AM in No. 6 Squadron then served in France from 30 September, 1914. Wounded 6 July 1917. Promoted to 1AM (Driver MT) 1 October, 1917 and retained that rank and trade in April, 1918 RAF Muster Roll.

★ 1199. N. RIDING

A recruit, a direct entrant into RFC 23 April, 1914. As 2AM with the Aircraft Park served in France from 16 August, 1914. Promoted to Sergeant (Driver MT) 1 October, 1916 and retained that rank and trade in April, 1918 RAF Muster Roll. 1914 Star only sold Beadles 1986 for £45, named to 2AM.

1200. E. HEATH

A recruit, a direct entrant into RFC 23 April, 1914. No record of entitlement to either 1914 or 1914/15 Stars traced. As a Corporal in No. 4 (Reserve) Squadron he was discharged 11 April, 1916.

★ 1201. H. J. BARDSLEY

A recruit, a direct entrant into RFC 23 April, 1914. Was 2AM with No. 6 Squadron and earned 1914 Star and bar in France from 6 October, 1914. Discharged under *K.R.* 392 (xvi) 'sick' 7 November, 1916. Silver War Badge No. 76790 issued. 1914 Star and bar (1AM), British War and Victory Medals (Pte) known in a private collection.

★ 1202. A. BURDEN

A recruit, a direct entrant into RFC 25 April, 1914. Was 2AM No. 6 Squadron then served in France from 9 September, 1914. Transferred to the Tank Corps as No. 309238. His 1914 Star trio all named to 2AM RFC sold Beadles 1986 £175.

★ 1203. J. CROOK

A recruit, a direct entrant into RFC 21 April, 1914. As 1AM with No. 6 Squadron served in France from 5 October, 1914. Promoted to Flight Sergeant (Fitter general) 31 October, 1916 and was Chief Mechanic (Fitter general) in April, 1918 RAF Muster Roll.

★ 1204. R. WHITE

A recruit, a direct entrant into RFC 28 April, 1914. Was 2AM with No. 6 Squadron then served in France from 5 November, 1914 having first served briefly in Egypt during October. Promoted to Sergeant (Rigger) 1 June, 1916 and was Sergeant Mechanic (Rigger Aero) in April, 1918 RAF Muster Roll.

* 1205. ARCHIBALD STILES

A recruit, a direct entrant into RFC 29 April, 1914. As 2AM with No. 5 Squadron served in France from 14 August, 1914 earning a 1914 Star and bar. Promoted 1AM (Blacksmith) 1 June, 1915 and retained that rank and trade in April, 1918 RAF Muster Roll. A family group of eight medals are known in a private collection in 1988:— South African Medal (clasp 1879 W. Stiles Pte RM, HMS *Boadicea*) and RN L.S.&G.C. medal (Victorian, William Stiles Pte No. 10 Company RMLI); 1914 Star and bar (1205 2AM RFC) and British War Medal and Victory Medal (both 1AM RFC); 1939/45 Star, Air Crew Europe Star and 1939/45 War Medal (in box of issue to 639949 Sgt. Royston Charles Edward Stiles 57 Squadron RAF KIA 26 August, 1940, aged 18. Failed to return from a sweep over the North Sea flying in a Blenheim. The WW2 medals were sent to his father A. Stiles Esq, 3 Hastings Ave, Brockhurst, Gosport, Hants.

* 1206. W. J. BRAMBLEY

A recruit, a direct entrant into RFC 30 April, 1914. Was 2AM (Motor-Cyclist) with the No. 6 Squadron detachment at Newcastle in August, 1914. Served in France from 6 October, 1914. Appointed Warrant Officer 1st Class 1 June, 1917. Commissioned 2 Lieutenant 13 October, 1917.

* 1207. A. A. SIMPSON

A recruit, a direct entrant into RFC 30 April, 1914. As 2AM with No. 5 Squadron served in France from 14 August, 1914. Promoted to Sergeant (Misc Discip) 1 July, 1917 and was Sergeant (Disciplinarian) in April, 1918 RAF Muster Roll.

1208. T. F. HICKEY

A recruit, a direct entrant into RFC 28 April, 1914. Discharged under *K.R.* 392 (v) 22 July, 1914 on payment of £10.

* 1209. H. GREEN

A recruit, a direct entrant into RFC 1 May, 1914. As 2AM with the Aircraft Park served in France from 17 August, 1914. Discharged under *K.R.* 392 (ix) 23 March, 1915 'unfitted for the duties of the Corps.'

★ 1210. DOUGLAS ALWYN ROUGIER CHAPMAN

Born London, 26 August, 1894. A recruit, a direct entrant into RFC April, 1914. As 2AM with No. 3 Squadron served in France and earned 1914 Star. Awarded Royal Aero Club Aviators' Certificate No. 1711 on 25 May, 1915 as 1st Class Air Mechanic.

RFC Communiqué No. 39, 18 June, 1916:
'Two FE's of 25 Squadron flown by Capt. Gralton Bellow and 2 Lieutenant Armstrong with Lt. Lewes and Sergeant Chapman as observers, encountered two Fokkers east of Lens at 4.15 p.m. at 9000 feet. They chased them down and Sergeant Chapman shot one down from 4000 feet which was seen to crash.'

Wounded 4 July, 1916 when a Sergeant Pilot in 25 Squadron. Commissioned 2 Lieutenant 12 October, 1916.

★ 1211. A. E. TAYLOR

Enlisted 9 September, 1908. Formerly served in the Royal Garrison Artillery as 37399. Transferred to RFC 1 December, 1913. As 2AM with No. 5 Squadron served in France from 14 August, 1914 and earned a 1914 Star and bar. Promoted to Temp SM (D) 1 October, 1916 and was SM1 (Disciplinarian) in April, 1918 RAF Muster Roll. Awarded RAF L.S.&G.C. medal *w.e.f.* 9 September, 1926 as SM1.

★ 1212. HERBERT JOHN WAKELING

A direct entrant into RFC 30 April, 1914 but allowed to count previous R.E. service of 4 years and 213 days. Was 2AM in 6 Squadron and served in France from 9 September, 1914. Promoted to Flight Sergeant (Misc Discip) 1 March, 1917 in Major Hawker V.C.'s 24 Sqn ('B' Flight) and was Flight Sergeant (Discip) in April, 1918 RAF Muster Roll. Served in India with No. 31 Squadron post war. See photograph in *'First in Indian Skies.'* Awarded RAF L.S.&G.C. medal as SM1 *w.e.f.* 29 September, 1927. In the February, 1931 *A.F.L.* he is shown as Warrant Officer, Class 1, with seniority from 1 June, 1918. In November, 1941 *A.F.L.* he was the eighth most senior RAF Warrant Officer. Commissioned (No. 113938) Flight Lieutenant 1 September, 1942. Posted to Air Ministry (Directory of Organisation and Establishment) 31 May, 1943.

★ 1213. G. H. WALLIS

A recruit, a direct entrant into RFC 30 April, 1914. Was 2AM with No. 6 Squadron and served in France from 9 September, 1914 earning a 1914 Star and bar. Reverted to Corporal (Fitter general) 22 February, 1917 and retained that rank and trade in April, 1918 RAF Muster Roll.

1214. E. STEWART

A recruit, a direct entrant into RFC 30 April, 1914. Nothing more traced regarding this airman.

★ 1215. JOHN WILLIAM HONEYBONE

Enlisted 11 February, 1911. Formerly served in Royal Engineers as No. 21119. Transferred to RFC 4 December, 1913. As 2AM with No. 5 Squadron served in France from 14 August, 1914. Promoted to Flight Sergeant (Rigger) 15 April, 1916 and was Chief Mechanic (Rigger Aero) in April, 1918 RAF Muster Roll. Awarded RAF M.S.M. for services in Mesopotamia in *L.G.* 28 October, 1921 as Flight Sergeant. Also awarded General Service Medal (clasp Iraq).

1216. E. RAMSDEN

Enlisted 1 October, 1908. Formerly served in 1/Coldstream Guards as No. 2168. Transferred to RFC 2 December, 1913. No record of entitlement to either 1914 or 1914/15 Stars traced. Promoted Temp SM (D) 1 January, 1916. Mentioned in despatches 24 February, 1917 as Acting Sergeant Major and listed in the *Times* 'B' Press Release of 27 March, 1917. SM1 (Disciplinarian) in April, 1918 RAF Muster Roll. Awarded India General Service Medal (Afghan NWF 1919 and Waziristan 1919/21). This last medal is known in a private collection as a single. He is also on the roll for Mahsud 1919-21 but this clasp is not on the medal. Awarded RAF L.S.&G.C. medal *w.e.f.* 1 October, 1926 as SM1.

★ 1217. FREDERICK MAWBY

Enlisted 30 August, 1908. Formerly served in 3/Grenadier Guards as No. 2168. Transferred to RFC 2 December, 1913. As 1AM with the Aircraft Park served in France from 16 August, 1914. Promoted to Temp SM (D) 1 January, 1917 and was SM1 (Disciplinarian) in April, 1918 RAF Muster Roll. Awarded RAF L.S.&G.C. *w.e.f.* 31 August, 1926 as SM1. 38th Senior RAF Warrant Officer in February, 1931 *A.F.L.*

1218. S. J. CROAD

A recruit, a direct entrant into RFC, 28 April, 1914. No record of entitlement to either 1914 or 1914/15 Stars traced. Promoted to Temp SM (D) 1 August, 1916 and was SM1 (Disciplinarian) in April, 1918 RAF Muster Roll.

★ 1219. G. V. HUNTER

A recruit, a direct entrant into RFC 29 April, 1914. Was 2AM with No. 6 Squadron, then served in France from 10 September, 1914. Promoted Corporal (Aerial Gunner) 1 June, 1917 and retained that rank and trade in April, 1918 RAF Muster Roll.

1220. L. R. BACKSHALL

A recruit, a direct entrant into RFC 8 May, 1914. No record of entitlement to either 1914 or 1914/15 Stars traced. Promoted to 1AM (Fitter engines) 1 September, 1916 and retained that rank and trade in April, 1918 RAF Muster Roll. (A 2160 W. Backshall served as a reservist (mounted) in 3 Balloon Company RE in 1910. A relation perhaps?)

1221. W. J. F. GOLDING

A recruit, a direct entrant into RFC 8 May, 1914. Served overseas from 17 April, 1915 earning 1914/15 Star trio. Promoted to Flight Sergeant (Electrician) 1 September, 1917 and was Chief Mechanic (Electician) in April, 1918 RAF Muster Roll. Awarded Army M.S.M. in *L.G.* 11 April, 1918 for 'Distinguished Services in Jerusalem in connection with Military Operations,' when a Flight Sergeant (noted as being from Kensington). Fifteen Army M.S.M.s were awarded to members of the RFC for services in Jerusalem, none of the 14 others were awarded to pre-war members of the Corps. Five Army M.S.M.s were also awarded to the Australian Flying Corps for services in Jerusalem.

★ 1222. B. J. W. WINTER

A recruit, a direct entrant into RFC 8 May, 1914. As 2AM with No. 5 Squadron served in France from 14 August, 1914 earning a 1914 Star and bar. Discharged as unfit 16 February, 1915.

★ 1223. F. T. MICKLEWRIGHT

A recruit, a direct entrant into RFC 9 May, 1914. As 2AM with 3 Squadron served in France from 12 August, 1914. Fraudulently enlisted as C. J. Forrester into Army Service Corps 12 May, 1915. Later he transferred into East Surrey Regiment and was then commissioned 2 Lieutenant in ASC 5 June, 1917.

★ 1224. WALTER EDWARD BASTABLE

A recruit, a direct entrant into RFC 11 May, 1914. As 2AM in No. 6 Squadron served in France from 6 October, 1914. Awarded Royal Aero Club Aviators' Certificate No. 3884 on 26 November, 1916. Killed in Action as a Sergeant Pilot, still with No. 6 Squadron 17 March, 1917. Son of Walter and Alice Bastable of 13 Eldon Terrace, Swanage, Dorset. Buried Lijssenthoek Military Cemetery, Belgium (Plot XI, Row C, Grave 2). See group photograph under No. 626.

1225. H. HERBERT

A boy recruit, a direct entrant into RFC 14 May, 1914. No record of entitlement to 1914 or 1914/15 Stars. Promoted 1AM (Fitter engines) 1 August, 1917 and was 1AM (Fitter AE) in April, 1918 RAF Muster Roll.

1226. H. J. R. HARRIS

A boy recruit, a direct entrant into RFC 14 May, 1914. No record of entitlement to 1914 or 1914/15 Stars. Was 2AM (Coppersmith) from 20 August, 1917 but was 3AM (Coppersmith) in April, 1918 RAF Muster Roll. Awarded RAF L.S.&G.C. as Sergeant *w.e.f.* 14 May, 1932, thus all his boy service was allowed to count towards the medal.

1227. H. A. CLARK

A boy recruit, a direct entrant into RFC 14 May, 1914. No record of entitlement to 1914 or 1914/15 Stars. Was 2AM (Fitter engines) from 21 December, 1917 but was 3AM (Fitter AE) in April, 1918 RAF Muster Roll. In 1921 served as A/Cpl in 30 Squadron in Mesopotamia and awarded General Service Medal (clasp Iraq).

1228. P. W. Bloxham

A boy recruit, a direct entrant into RFC 14 May, 1914. No record of entitlement to either 1914 or 1914/15 Stars. Still a Boy on one shilling a day in April, 1918 RAF Muster Roll.

1229. R. A. Whyte

A boy recruit, a direct entrant into RFC 15 May, 1914. No record of entitlement to either 1914 or 1914/15 Stars. Promoted to 1AM (Rigger) 1 October, 1916 and retained that rank and trade in April, 1918 RAF Muster Roll. See No. 1230.

1230. A. R. Whyte

A boy recruit, a direct entrant into RFC 15 May, 1914. No record of entitlement to either 1914 or 1914/15 Stars. Still a Boy in April, 1918 RAF Muster Roll but a subsequent note says:— 'Delete entry.' See No. 1229.

1231. S. H. F. Jones

A boy recruit, a direct entrant into RFC 15 May, 1914. No record of entitlement to either 1914 or 1914/15 Stars. Commissioned 2 Lieutenant 2 February, 1918.

1232. James McKinley Hargreaves

Enlisted 24 May, 1905. Formerly 9245 Sergeant Royal Scots. Transferred to RFC 15 May, 1914 as Sergeant. First served overseas on 24 July, 1915, earning 1914/15 Star trio, and awarded Royal Aero Club Aviators' Certificate No. 1887 on 13 October, 1915. Awarded Distinguished Conduct Medal in *L.G.* 16 November, 1915 as an Observer with 11 Squadron. 'For conspicuous gallantry and skill on several occasions notably the following:— On 21st September, 1915 when in a machine armed with one machine gun and piloted by Captain Rees, a large German Biplane armed with two machine guns was sighted 2,000 feet below. Our machine spiralled down and engaged the enemy, who, being faster, manœuvered to get broadside on and then opened fire. The attack,

however, was pressed, and the engine of the enemy's biplane was apparently struck, for after a quick turn it glided down some distance then fell just inside the German lines. On 31st August, Captain Rees, with Flight Sergeant Hargreaves, fought a powerful German machine for three-quarters of an hour. They then returned for more ammunition and went out again to the attack. Finally the enemy's machine was brought down apparently wrecked.' He was discharged 'sick' 30 May, 1917 and issued with Silver War Badge No. 187645. The Captain Rees mentioned above was temp Major L. W. B. Rees RA and RFC who was awarded a Victoria Cross in the *London Gazette* of 5 August, 1916. See group photograph No. 2. The following three RFC Communiqués are of interest. (Also see No. 1389.)

RFC Communiqué No. 8, 31 August, 1915:

Capt. Rees and Flt. Sgt. Hargreaves on a Vickers came across an LVG at 7000 feet between Budquoy and Bapaume when patrolling. The hostile machine was much faster than the Vickers, but throttled down and allowed them to approach to 200 yds. when the enemy observer fired a few rounds, with an automatic rifle then accelerated, this occurred five or six times. The Vickers having expended four drums, returned to the aerodrome for more ammunition. It then came back to look for the hostile aeroplane, and found it in the same place. It was 1000 feet lower, they dived at it and fired one drum. The LVG dived into clouds. It was reported by another aircraft as coming down in spirals, and irregular 'S' turns, apparently badly hit.

RFC Communiqué No. 11, 21 September, 1915:

Capt. Rees and Flt. Sgt. Hargreaves of 11 Squadron. in a Vickers Fighter, with Lewis gun and pistol when photographing at 11 am between Dompierre and Flancourt, observed a twin engined twin fuselaged tractor German biplane, armed with two machine guns, 2000 feet below. The Vickers engaged it at a height of 7000 feet. The German's engine was hit and he glided down towards Péronne, smoke coming from one engine. Later that day they patrolled S.E. of Albert, and engaged an Albatross. It went down steeply at 150 mph its engine running full on.

RAF Communiqué No. 12, 30 September, 1915:

Again flying with the same pilot he attacked an Albatross biplane near Gommecourt. After firing one drum the enemy dived into cloud, and after another drum it spiralled and nose dived. Its right wing fell off at 5000 feet. The pilot had been hit in the head by a MG bullet.

1233. L. EDWARDS

A boy recruit, a direct entrant into RFC 20 May, 1914. No record of entitlement to either 1914 or 1914/15 Stars. Was 2AM (Fitter and turner) 18 October, 1916, but was reduced to 3AM (Turner) in April, 1918 RAF Muster Roll.

1234. F. J. A. NUNN

A boy recruit, a direct entrant into RFC 20 May, 1914. No record of entitlement to either 1914 or 1914/15 Stars. Was 2AM (Tinsmith) 25 October, 1917 but was reduced to 3AM (Tinsmith and Sheet Metal Worker) in April, 1918 RAF Muster Roll.

1235. W. CLACK

A recruit, a direct entrant into RFC 20 May, 1914. Discharged 22 May, 1914 under *K.R.* 392 (iii) 'not likely to become an efficient soldier.'

1236. H. HUDSON

A recruit, a direct entrant into RFC 21 May, 1914. No record of entitlement to either 1914 or 1914/15 Stars. Promoted to Corporal (Fitter general) 14 August, 1917 and retained that rank and trade in April, 1918 RAF Muster Roll.

1237. A. E. WILLIS

A recruit, a direct entrant into RFC 25 May, 1914. Served overseas from 6 December, 1914 and awarded 1914/15 Star trio. Discharged 'sick' 4 February, 1916 aged 21 years, 9 months. Silver War Badge No. 298508 issued.

1238. H. SMITH

A recruit, a direct entrant into RFC 22 May, 1914. Was 2AM with No. 6 Squadron in August. Served overseas from 3 April, 1915 earning a 1914/15 Star trio. Promoted to Acting Corporal (paid) (Fitter general) 1 March, 1918 and was Corporal Mechanic (Fitter general) in April, 1918 RAF Muster Roll.

★ 1239. H. COPE

A recruit, a direct entrant into RFC 25 May, 1914. As 2AM with No. 6 Squadron served in France from 7 October, 1914. Promoted to Acting Flight Sergeant (paid) (Fitter engines) 1 February, 1918 and was Chief Mechanic (Fitter AE) in April, 1918 RAF Muster Roll.

★ 1240. G. TUGWELL

A recruit, a direct entrant into RFC 26 May, 1914. As 2AM with the Aircraft Park, served in France from 16 August, 1914. Promoted to Corporal (Driver MT) 1 September, 1916 and was Corporal Mechanic (Driver) in April, 1918 RAF Muster Roll.

1241. J. PARK

A recruit, a direct entrant into RFC 15 May, 1914. Discharged 10 July, 1914 under *K.R.* 392 (ix) 'Unfitted for the duties of the Corps.'

1242. C. B. DANIEL

A recruit, a direct entrant into RFC 29 May, 1914. No record of entitlement to either 1914 or 1914/15 Stars. Promoted to acting Corporal (paid) (Rigger) 1 December, 1917 and was Corporal Mechanic (Rigger Aero) in April, 1918 RAF Muster Roll. Awarded India General Service Medal (Clasp North West Frontier 1930-31) as Flight Sergeant, and RAF L.S.&G.C. medal in the same rank *w.e.f.* 9 May, 1933.

★ 1243. T. C. VIGGERS

A recruit, a direct entrant into RFC 28 May, 1914. Was 2AM with No. 6 Squadron, then served in France from 9 September, 1914. Promoted to Flight Sergeant (Fitter engines) 1 November, 1917 and was Chief Mechanic (Fitter AE) in April, 1918 RAF Muster Roll.

★ 1244. G. W. HUGHES

A recruit, a direct entrant into RFC 1 June, 1914. As 2AM with No. 5 Squadron served in France from 14 August, 1914. Promoted to Corporal (Driver MT) 1 April, 1917 and was Corporal Mechanic (Driver) in April, 1918 RAF Muster Roll.

★ 1245. D. FORBES

A recruit, a direct entrant into RFC 30 May, 1914. As 2AM with No. 3 Squadron served in France from 13 August, 1914. Discharged 'sick' under the terms of *K.R.* 392 (xvi) 9 September, 1917 aged 28 years 11 months. Silver War Badge 249924 issued.

1246. J. D. RATTRAY

A recruit, a direct entrant into RFC 22 May, 1914. Posted to Egypt 15 November, 1914 and awarded 1914/15 Star trio. Promoted to Sergeant (1st class Pilot) 6 September, 1917 and was Sergeant Mechanic (Pilot) in April, 1918 RAF Muster Roll.

★ 1247. J. S. MARKS

A recruit, a direct entrant into RFC 3 June, 1914. As 2AM with No. 5 Squadron served in France from 14 August, 1914. 2AM (Fitter MT) from 1 October, 1917, he is shown as 3AM (Fitter MT) on April, 1918 RAF Muster Roll.

★ 1248. ROY ALBERT QUESTED

Born in Paddington, London, 15 December, 1895. A recruit, a direct entrant into RFC 2 June, 1914, at Blenheim Barracks, Aldershot. As 2AM (Rigger) with No. 6 Squadron served in France from 7 October, 1914 and earned a 1914 Star and bar. Promoted to Corporal (Carpenter & Joiner) 1 February, 1917 and was a Corporal Mechanic (Carpenter) in April, 1918 RAF Muster Roll. He was interviewed in 1970 for *'Cross and Cockade'* and the following are extracts from Volume 1, No. 2, pages 33–36.

'As a rigger, I drew 2 pairs of pliers, a spike for wire splicing, thimbles for the cable ends, a leather palm and a hammer with a tempered face. Later we had Squadron use of Abney Levels and Tensiometers.

I finally reached the Squadron in the month of July, 1914, at that time based at Laffan's Plain. On the day that war was declared I was on duty. 'Guard,' to be exact. When I set out on this duty I left all my kit in one of the new huts that was being built for the RFC. When I returned the next morning all of my kit, and that of my hutmates, was outside wrapped in a blanket. Our quarters were taken over by the Army, and we occupied new Barrack buildings. We had on that station the SE4 which was a very rapid machine in its day. Another was the BE8 or Bloater. There was also the RE5 and BE2. We were brought up to strength about mid August, and I suppose that we were considered operational. There were the old faithful Maurice Farmans, BE2's and I recall that there was a BE8 or two. I can well remember that the BE's suffered from the undercarriage collapsing with anything over the lightest landings. The BE8's were left behind when we sailed for France.

The aircraft took off for Ostend on the 7th October, 1914 and all reached there safely. Quite a feat then! In all I think we had eight machines on the race-course there. On arrival we were issued with revolvers and ammunition; made us realise that the war was not too far away. Life was very hard indeed and the normal thing was to sleep under the wings of the aircraft. Some did manage to get a bit of comfort in the back of lorries. When the evacuation of Antwerp started, we went to St. Pol near Dunkirk. At this time we had Hales rifle grenades fitted with aircraft fabric streamers to straighten the fall from aircraft. There were also flechettes but I cannot recall tht we used them in No. 6. Other Squadrons did though. I remember that a BE2 No. 488 came down rather close to the front and I was in the party sent out to effect a salvage operation. We reached the machine alright, only to be tackled by a Cavalry Officer who told us that we were quite likely to be taken prisoner ... it appeared that the Germans were still advancing in this sector ... so we set it alight and got back too.

During mid July, 1916 I was transferred to No. 16 and at that time they were at La Gorgue, attached to the Canadian Corps. During the battle at Neuve Chappele [*sic*] there had been a lack of communication between front line and rear echelon, mainly due to the telephone wires being cut, and as a consequence HQ was ignorant of the true position. Using the system of white panels being shown on the ground some 40 or so messages were transmitted from the air to a receiving centre.

I did have the opportunity to fly as a Gunner in an RE8; the two flights were entirely without incident. I was sent to have flight training towards the end of the war. I applied to the CO on the 14th May, 1918, I did not really think I would get far. In June I was posted to Hamstead [*sic*] to take the necessary tests, then on to Hastings for yet more. From here I went to No. 8 School of Aeronautics at Cheltenham where we were taught the art of wireless operation, navigation, and rigging. I started my flying time at Northolt but prior to that I had a session at the School of Armament at Uxbridge. Naturally the old 504K was the aircraft. I had about 3 hours in the air — dual control.

As luck would have it, I started cross country running during my stay here and as a result eventually made the RAF team. I represented the Service against the Universities and the other branches of the Armed Forces. I left the RAF in 1921 as a Corporal Rigger. In 1939, in the role of Driver/MT, having been recalled as a Class E reservist, I was attached to HQ Staff. I was promoted to Ft. Sgt. in 1942 which rank I kept until the end of the war. I finally left the Service in 1945 to spend a well earned peacetime life in London.

(See also *Cross and Cockade*, Vol. 1, No. 2.)

1249. R. H. SHEPHERD

A recruit, a direct entrant into RFC 5 June, 1914. 2AM at the Recruit Depot in August. No record of entitlement to either 1914 or 1914/15 Star. Reverted to 1AM (Fitter engines) 4 December, 1917 and was 1AM (Fitter AE) in April, 1918 RAF Muster Roll.

★ 1250. C. P. O'FLANAGAN

A recruit, a direct entrant into RFC 5 June, 1914. As 2AM with No. 6 Squadron served in France from 6 October, 1914. Promoted to Sergeant (Wireless Operator) 8 August, 1917 and retained that rank and trade in April, 1918 RAF Muster Roll.

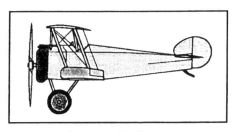

SOPWITH F1 CAMEL

★ 1251. W. G. EDWARDS

A recruit, a direct entrant into RFC 12 June, 1914. As 2AM with No. 3 Squadron served in France from 12 August, 1914. He is mentioned in the *RFC Communiqué, No. 58*, of 20 October, 1916 when flying in an F.E. of 22 Squadron with Lieutenant Hackwill, he brought down a hostile machine out of control near Grevillers. Promoted to Sergeant (NCO Observer) 1 November, 1917 and was Sergeant Mechanic (Observer) in April, 1918 RAF Muster Roll.

★ 1252. A. W. HAINES

A recruit, a direct entrant into RFC 12 June, 1914. Was 2AM, with No. 6 Squadron, then served in France from 10 September, 1914. Promoted to Acting Corporal (paid) (Electrician) 1 January, 1918 and was Corporal Mechanic (Electrician) in April, 1918 RAF Muster Roll.

★ 1253. MAURICE LYLE

A recruit, a direct entrant into RFC 12 June, 1914. As 2AM with No. 6 Squadron served in France from 6 October, 1914. Died 10 December, 1914 and buried in Lonquenesse (St. Omer) Souvenir Cemetery (Plot 1, row A, grave 26).

1254. C. H. SPONG

A recruit, a direct entrant into RFC 15 June, 1914. Was 2AM with No. 3 Squadron in August. First served overseas 24 July, 1915 earning 1914/15 Star trio. Promoted to Temp SM (T) 1 January, 1917 and was Ch Mr Mech (Technical) in April, 1918 RAF Muster Roll. Twice mentioned in despatches, 1 January, and 3 June, 1919, both times for services with 'I' Force in France.

AIRCO DH9

1255. J. COLCUTT

A recruit, a direct entrant into RFC 3 June, 1914. Was 2AM at the Recruit Depot in August. No record of entitlement to either 1914 or 1914/15 Stars. Reverted to 1AM (Blacksmith) 23 May, 1916 and retained that rank and trade in April, 1918 RAF Muster Roll.

★ 1256. J. TURNER

A recruit, a direct entrant into RFC 11 June, 1914. Was 2AM with No. 6 Squadron, then served in France from 9 September, 1914. Promoted to 1AM (Rigger) 1 December, 1917 and retained that rank and trade in April, 1918 RAF Muster Roll.

1257. E. A. SILLITOE

A recruit, a direct entrant into RFC 15 June, 1914. First served overseas 8 March, 1915 earning 1914/15 Star trio. Promoted to Corporal (Ftr Eng Er MT) 1 April, 1917 and was Corporal Mechanic (Fitter MT) in April, 1918 RAF Muster Roll. Awarded RAF L.S.&G.C. medal as Flight Sergeant 15 June, 1932 and commissioned (C.E.O.) as Flying Officer 6 April, 1938 (No. 35162). Wing Commander 1 July, 1944.

1258. H. F. TAYLOR

A recruit, a direct entrant into RFC 15 June, 1914. Discharged 25 July, 1914 under *K.R.* 392 (ix) 'unfitted for the duties of the Corps.'

★ 1259. G. L. OWEN

A recruit, a direct entrant into RFC 15 June, 1914. As 2AM with No. 6 Squadron then served in France and earned 1914 Star, but returned to England 1 October, 1914 as the Servant to Major Becke of No. 2 Squadron. Promoted to Sergeant (Fitter general) 1 June, 1917 and retained this rank and trade in April, 1918 RAF Muster Roll.

★ 1260. H. T. VAUGHAN

A recruit, a direct entrant into RFC 17 June, 1914. As 2AM with the Aircraft Park served in France from 16 August, 1914. Promoted to Flight Sergeant (Fitter MT) 1 June, 1917 and was Chief Mechanic (Fitter MT) in April, 1918 RAF Muster Roll.

* 1261. H. A. E. BURLINGHAM

Enlisted 19 May, 1911. Formerly 4250 L/Corporal 1/Rifle Brigade. Transferred to RFC 14 January, 1914. As 2AM with No. 5 Squadron served in France from 14 August, 1914. Promoted to Temp SM (D) 1 March, 1918 and was SM1 (Disciplinarian) in April, 1918 RAF Muster Roll.

1262. W. GARTH

A recruit, a direct entrant into RFC 13 June, 1914. First served overseas 3 April, 1915 earning 1914/15 Star trio. Promoted to Flight Sergeant (Coppersmith) 1 September, 1917 and was Chief Mechanic (Coppersmith) in April, 1918 RAF Muster Roll.

* 1263. H. M. GRAY

A recruit, a direct entrant into RFC 15 June, 1914. As 2AM with No. 6 Squadron served in France from 7 October, 1914. Promoted to Sergeant (Motor Cyclist) 1 January, 1917 and retained that rank and trade in April, 1918 RAF Muster Roll.

1264. A. ERSKINE

A recruit, a direct entrant into RFC 16 June, 1914. 2AM at the Recruit Depot in August. No record of entitlement to either 1914 or 1914/15 Stars. Warrant Officer 1st Class 1 August, 1917. No further references traced.

1265. T. A. McGREGOR

A recruit, a direct entrant into RFC 16 June, 1914. 2AM at the Recruit Depot in August. First served overseas 17 April, 1915 earning 1914/15 Star trio. Promoted to Sergeant (Fitter engines) 1 December, 1917 and was Sergeant Mechanic (Fitter AE) in April, 1918 RAF Muster Roll. Awarded Indian General Service Medal (clasp Afghan, NWF, 1919) as Sergeant.

* 1266. P. HEADRIDGE

A recruit, a direct entrant into RFC 18 June, 1914. As 2AM with No. 6 Squadron served in France from 7 October, 1914. Discharged 'unfit' 17 March, 1916.

1267. ROBERT JOHN HAYNE HOLLAND

Born 13 February, 1894 in Dorchester. A recruit, a direct entrant into RFC 13 June, 1914. 2AM at the Recruit Depot in August. First served overseas 3 April, 1915 earning 1914/15 Star trio. Awarded Royal Aero Club Aviators' Certificate No. 3385 of 2 August, 1916 as a Sergeant. Mentioned in despatches as Sergeant 28 June, 1917. Commissioned 2 Lieutenant 8 December, 1917. Awarded Army M.S.M. in his original rank of Sergeant in *L.G.* 17 December, 1917 'For valuable services with the Armies in the Field' (*Gazette* gives his home town as Branksome). Again mentioned in despatches, for Egypt, *L.G.* 12 January, 1918. No. 07155 Flying Officer (Aeroplane officer, *i.e.* pilot) 5 December, 1919. In November, 1921 *A.F.L.* shown as serving at No. 5 Flying Training School, Chester, from 16 June, 1921. Flight Lieutenant 1 January, 1926 and in the February, 1931 *A.F.L.* is shown as serving at No. 1 F.T.S. Netheravon from 24 November, 1930. Retired 11 March, 1934. In the 1937 *A.F.L.* is shown as Flight Lieut. (retired) working as an Accountant at RAF Abingdon. Recalled 1 September, 1939 to 19 April, 1945. Squadron Leader (T) 1 September, 1941. Alive in 1970. In 1987 his medals were noted as extant in a private collection:— 1914/15 trio (Sergt RFC – Lieut RAF) A/M.S.M. (Sgt RFC).

1268. H. MATTHEWS

A recruit, a direct entrant into RFC 20 June, 1914. No record of entitlement to either 1914 or 1914/15 Stars. Was a Corporal on 27 May, 1916 when he joined 24 Squadron in France at Bertangles. He left the squadron on 10 September, 1916. Reverted to Sergeant (Fitter general) 25 June, 1917 and retained that rank and trade in April, 1918 RAF Muster Roll. Entitled to British War Medal and Victory Medal.

1269. FRED COLLIS FREEMANTLE

Born 1 June, 1893. A recruit, a direct entrant into RFC 22 June, 1914. No record of entitlement to either 1914 or 1914/15 Stars. Promoted to Flight Sergeant (Rigger) 1 April, 1916 and was Chief Mechanic (Rigger Aero) in April, 1918 RAF Muster Roll. Appointed Warrant Officer 1st

Class 1 May, 1929. Awarded RAF L.S.&G.C. medal *w.e.f.* 22 June, 1932. Awarded 1935 Silver Jubilee Medal. Posted 10 June, 1937 to RAF Duxford (12 Fighter Group HQ) as Station Warrant Officer. 28th Senior RAF Warrant Officer in March 1938 *A.F.L.* Commissioned as Flying Officer (CEO) 6 April, 1938. Flight Lieutenant 6 April, 1941. No. 35185 Retired Acting Wing Commander 27 June, 1948. See 1978 *A.F.L.*

1270. J. S. NICHOLLS

A recruit, a direct entrant into RFC 20 June, 1914. Was 2AM at Recruit Depot in August. No record of entitlement to either 1914 or 1914/15 Stars. Promoted to 1AM (Driver MT) 1 January, 1915. Served overseas from a date in 1916 and was wounded that October. 1AM (Driver) in April, 1918 RAF Muster Roll. Killed in an air crash as Sergeant Pilot 12 November, 1918 aged 22 (note just one day after the Armistice) when serving with 203 Squadron. Son of Mrs. M. J. Ferrari, 149 Cline Road, West Dulwich, London. Buried Valenciennes Communal Cemetery (Plot 1, Row C, Grave 38). Entitled to British War Medal and Victory Medal.

1271. H. MILLIKIN

A recruit, a direct entrant into RFC 22 June, 1914. 2AM at the Recruit Depot in August. No further references to this airman traced.

1272. W. EGAN

A recruit, a direct entrant into RFC 18 June, 1914. 2AM at the Recruit Depot in August. First served overseas 27 December, 1915 just being entitled to a 1914/15 Star trio. Promoted to Corporal (Fitter general) 1 July, 1917 and retained that rank and trade in April, 1918 RAF Muster Roll.

* 1273. T. HODGSON

A recruit, a direct entrant into RFC 23 June, 1914. As 2AM with No. 6 Squadron served in France from 6 October, 1914. Promoted to Temp ŠM (T) 1 November, 1916. Mentioned in despatches in *L.G.* 13 March, 1918 as Acting Sgt. Major. Listed in the *Times* 'B' Press Release of 16 March, 1918. Ch Mr Mech (Technical) in April, 1918 RAF Muster Roll.

★ 1274. R. HINDS (OR HYNES)

A recruit, a direct entrant into RFC 23 June, 1914. As 2AM with No. 6 Squadron served in France from 6 October, 1914. Promoted Temp SM (T) 1 May, 1917 and was Ch Mr Mech (Technical) in April, 1918 RAF Muster Roll. Listed in the *Times* 'B' Press Release of 29 August, 1919.

1275. WILLIAM GEORGE BENNETT

A recruit, a direct entrant into RFC 20 June, 1914. Was 2AM at the Recruit Depot in August. Served in France from 6 October, 1914. Promoted to Sergeant 10 February, 1916. Awarded Royal Aero Club Aviators' Certificate No. 3726 on 20 October, 1916. Flying with 15 Squadron on 4 April, 1917 he was wounded in the leg by machine gun fire. (See *Cross and Cockade*, Vol. 4, No. 2, pp. 64 and 70.) He was Sergeant Mechanic (Pilot) in April, 1918 RAF Muster Roll.

★ 1276. W. WOOD

Formerly 39873 4 Depot RGA. Transferred to RFC 22 January, 1914. As 2AM with RFC HQ served in France from 12 August, 1914. Commissioned 2 Lieutenant Royal Irish Rifles 12 March, 1916.

1277. N. C. T. WILKINSON

A recruit, a direct entrant into RFC 24 June, 1914. First served overseas 1 January, 1915 earning 1914/15 Star trio. Promoted to 1AM (Instr Rep.) 1 February, 1917 and retained that rank and trade in April, 1918 RAF Muster Roll.

★ 1278. HARRY ALEXANDER DINNAGE

A recruit, a direct entrant into RFC 20 June, 1914. As 2AM served in France from 6 November, 1914. Commissioned 2 Lieutenant 24 September, 1917. In November, 1921 *A.F.L.* shown as Technical Officer, a Flying Officer seniority 24 March, 1919, who from 18 August, 1921 was serving at the School of Naval Co-operation and Aerial Navigation, Coastal Area No. 10 Group at Fawley, Southampton. Transferred as

Flying Officer to Class B of the Reserve of Air Force Officers 12 December, 1926 (*vide* 1931 *A.F.L.*).

1279. BENJAMIN WILLIAM WRIGHT

A recruit, a direct entrant into RFC 24 June, 1914. As 2AM with No. 6 Squadron served in France from 19 Janury, 1915 earning 1914/15 Star trio. Promoted to Flight Sergeant (Fitter general) 1 December, 1916 and was Chief Mechanic in April, 1918 RAF Muster Roll. As a Flight Sergeant of No. 5 Squadron was awarded in *L.G.* 25 July, 1918 both a Belgian Croix de Guerre and appointed a Chevalier of the Order of Léopold II. He came from Lutterworth.

1280. R. G. NICHOLS

A recruit, a direct entrant into RFC 24 June, 1914. To France 6 December, 1914 earning a 1914/15 Star trio. Promoted to Flight Sergeant (Rigger) 1 September, 1917 and was Chief Mechanic (Rigger Aero) in April, 1918 RAF Muster Roll.

★ 1281. A. MOORE

A recruit, a direct entrant into RFC 27 June, 1914. As 2AM with No. 6 Squadron served in France from 6 October, 1914. Discharged 25 June, 1915 under *K.R.* 392 (xvi) 'no longer physically fit for war service.'

★ 1282. A. WRIGHT

A recruit, direct entrant into RFC 26 June, 1914. As 2AM with the Aircraft Park served in France from 6 November, 1914. Promoted Sergeant (Rigger) 1 October, 1916 and retained that rank and trade in April, 1918 RAF Muster Roll.

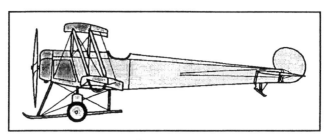

AVRO 504K

★ 1283. G. BREBNER

Enlisted 3 April, 1907. Formerly 46489, Fitter 47 Battery RFA. Transferred to RFC 26 January, 1914. As 2AM with the Aircraft Park served in France from 16 August, 1914. Promoted to Sergeant (Turner and fitter) 1 October, 1917 and retained that rank and trade in April, 1918 RAF Muster Roll.

★ 1284. FRANCIS TALBOT PARKER

Enlisted 1 March, 1910. Formerly 14663 Pte 1/Grenadier Guards. Transferred to RFC 26 January, 1914. As 2AM with No. 5 Squadron served in France earning 1914 Star and bar from 14 August, 1914. Promoted Temp SM (D) 1 June, 1916 and was SM1 (Disciplinarian) in April, 1918 RAF Muster Roll. Mentioned in the *Times* 'B' Press Release 22 January, 1919 for services in Egypt. Awarded RAF L.S.&G.C. *w.e.f.* 1 March, 1928. 19th Senior RAF Warrant Officer in February, 1931 *A.F.L.* when he is shown as entitled to M.B.E. Commissioned and served in W.W.2. Squadron Leader, 1 July, 1944.

1285. C. GRANT

A recruit, a direct entrant into RFC 24 June, 1914. 2AM at the Recruit Depot in August. Nothing more has been traced of this man.

1286. A. ALLAN

A recruit, a direct entrant into RFC 24 June, 1914. Discharged 5 August, 1914 under *K.R.* 392 (ix) 'Unfitted for the duties of the Corps.'

★ 1287. JAMES KEMP TOUGH

A recruit, a direct entrant into RFC 24 June, 1914. Served in France from 26 September, 1914. Promoted Sergeant (Rigger) 1 March, 1917 and was Sergeant Mechanic (Rigger Aero) in April, 1918 RAF Muster Roll. Awarded the Medal of the Order of the British Empire (*i.e.* first pattern medal) *L.G.* 1 January, 1923 to be dated from 28 December, 1922. This medal was often issued for bravery, instituted in 1917. 2014 were issued until it was superceded on 29 December, 1922 by the B.E.M. for Gallantry (Empire Gallantry Medal) and the B.E.M. for Meritorious Service. Only 510 of this first type B.E.M. were in the Military Division, this award to Tough was in the final gazetting of 12 such military division awards.

Awarded RAF L.S.&G.C. medal 24 June, 1932 as Flight Sergeant. Awarded 1935 Silver Jubilee Medal as a Warrant Officer. Commissioned (CEO) as Flying Officer 18 March, 1936. In the 1937 *A.F.L.* he is shown as serving from 5 October, 1937 at the Aircraft Depot, Dhibdan, Iraq. Promoted Squadron Leader 1 September, 1940. Not in 1944 *Air Force List*.

1288. R. J. HONE

A recruit, a direct entrant into RFC 27 June, 1914. 2AM at the Recruit Depot in August. Nothing more traced.

* 1289. WILLIAM JAMES LOUGHEAD

Born 22 September, 1894. A recruit, a direct entrant into RFC 3 July, 1914. 2AM at the Recruit Depot in August. Served in France and awarded 1914 Star. Promoted Temp SM (T) 1 June, 1916. Mentioned in despatches as Acting Sergeant Major in *L.G.* 24 February, 1917. Listed in the *Times* 'B' Press Release 27 March, 1917. Ch Mr Mech (Technical) in April, 1918 RAF Muster Roll. 18th Senior RAF Warrant Officer in 1931 *A.F.L.* Awarded RAF L.S.&G.C. *w.e.f.* 3 July, 1932. Commissioned (CEO) as Flying Officer 11 September, 1933. In 1937 *A.F.L.* shown as serving from 13 November, 1936 at RAF Depot, Aboukir, Middle East Command. Promoted to Squadron Leader 1 September, 1940 and to Wing Commander (No. 35005) 1 December, 1941. Still serving in 1946 with an O.B.E. Retired 22 February, 1949. Noted as still on the retired list in 1960 *A.F.L.*

1290. W. FISHER

A recruit, a direct entrant into RFC 3 July, 1914. 2AM at Recruit Depot, in August. Nothing more traced.

1291. W. RAWBONE

A recruit, a direct entrant into RFC 3 July, 1914. 2AM at Recruit Depot in August. Nothing more traced.

1292. J. TABERNER

A recruit, a direct entrant into RFC 3 July, 1914. First served overseas 3 March, 1915 earning 1914/15 Star trio. Promoted to 1AM (Fitter general) 1 January, 1916 and retained that rank and trade in April, 1918 RAF Muster Roll.

1293. B. SOUTHWELL

A recruit, a direct entrant into RFC 3 July, 1914. First served overseas 3 April, 1915 earning 1914/15 Star trio. Promoted to Sergeant (Fitter general) 1 August, 1917 and retained that rank and trade in April, 1918 RAF Muster Roll.

1294. ALGRED JAMES NICHOLAS

Born 3 July, 1896. A recruit, a direct entrant into RFC 6 July, 1914. Posted to Egypt 19 November, 1914 and awarded 1914/15 Star trio. Promoted to Sergeant (Rigger) 1 October, 1917 and retained that rank and trade in April, 1918 RAF Muster Roll. Awarded RAF L.S.&G.C. medal *w.e.f.* 6 July, 1932 as SM2. Commissioned (CEO) as Flying Officer, 18 March, 1936. Since that date serving at No. 1 Apprentice Wing, Halton Camp. Promoted to Squadron Leader 1 September, 1940 and promoted to acting Wing Commander (No. 35033) *w.e.f.* 1 December, 1941 and War Substantive Wing Commander 7 August, 1943. Retired 16 March, 1951 as A.F.R.Ae.S. Noted as still on the retired list in 1978 *A.F.L.*

★ 1295. D. E. ROPER

A recruit, a direct entrant into RFC 2 July, 1914. As 2AM with No. 6 Squadron served in France from 6 October, 1914. Discharged 16 February, 1915 under *K.R.* 392 (ix) 'Unfitted for the duties of the Corps.'

1296. J. H. CREASEY

A recruit, a direct entrant into RFC 29 June, 1914. As 1AM served in France from 24 November, 1914 earning 1914/15 Star trio. Reverted to Sergeant (Rigger) 26 June, 1917 and retained that rank and trade in April, 1918 RAF Muster Roll.

1297. W. J. TOOKE

A recruit, a direct entrant into RFC 7 July, 1914. No record of entitlement to 1914 or 1914/15 Stars. Promoted to Sergeant (Fitter general) 1 December, 1916 and retained that rank and trade in April, 1918 RAF Muster Roll.

1298. R. AITKEN

A recruit, a direct entrant into RFC 27 June, 1914. Was 2AM at the Central Flying School in August. Served overseas from 16 April, 1915 earning a 1914/15 Star trio. Reverted to 1AM (Rigger) 6 September, 1915 and retained that rank and trade in April, 1918 RAF Muster Roll.

★ 1299. L. V. CLARIDGE

A recruit, a direct entrant into RFC 2 July, 1914. Was 2AM at the Recruit Depot in August. Served in France from 7 November, 1914. Promoted to 1AM (Fitter general) 1 September, 1915. Listed as a prisoner of war at Kut in 1916 and reported as 'died' May, 1916. However, he is still listed as 1AM in April, 1918 RAF Muster Roll.

★ 1300. C. H. MATTHEWS

A recruit, a direct entrant into RFC 8 July, 1914. As 2AM with No. 6 Squadron served in France from 7 October, 1914. Promoted to Sergeant (Fitter general) 1 August, 1917 and retained that rank and trade in April, 1918 RAF Muster Roll.

1301. H. T. G. SMITH

A recruit, a direct entrant into RFC 8 July, 1914. Was 2AM at the Recruit Depot in August. No record of entitlement to either 1914 or 1914/15 Stars. Promoted to Corporal (Fitter engines) in 1917 and retained that rank and trade in April, 1918 RAF Muster Roll.

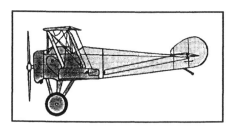

SOPWITH 2F1 CAMEL

1302. JACK AUSTEN LUCK

A recruit, a direct entrant into RFC 14 July, 1914. Was 2AM at the Recruit Depot in August. No record of entitlement to either 1914 or 1914/15 Stars. As Corporal awarded Royal Aero Club Aviators' Certificate No. 3767 on 24 October, 1916 serving with No. 6 Squadron. Accidentally killed 3 November, 1916. Buried Ramsgate Cemetery, Kent (Row DC, grave 297).

1303. H. C. HALL

A recruit, a direct entrant into RFC 3 July, 1914. Was 2AM at the Recruit Depot in August. First served overseas 24 July, 1915 earning 1914/15 Star trio. Promoted to 1AM (Fitter and turner) 1 July, 1915 and was 1AM (Turner) in April, 1918 RAF Muster Roll.

1304. H. R. POWELL

A recruit, a direct entrant into RFC 11 July, 1914. First served overseas 14 March, 1915 earning 1914/15 Star trio. Promoted to Corporal (Clerk general) 1 July, 1916 and retained that rank and trade in April, 1918 RAF Muster Roll. His medals were returned to RAF Records Office 27 June, 1929.

1305. J. S. CLARK

A recruit, a direct entrant into RFC 6 July, 1914. Was 2AM at the Recruit Depot in August. Served overseas from 17 April, 1915 earning 1914/15 Star trio. Awarded Military Medal as 1AM (Observer) with No. 8 Squadron 'For consistent good work as aeroplane observer and gunner from 10 June, 1915 to 1 June, 1916. He has always shown great coolness and skill in engagements in the air. His work on the ground has also been very satisfactory.' See *London Gazette* 27 October, 1916. He must have been promoted for he reverted to 1AM (Rigger) 29 April, 1917 and retained that rank and trade in April, 1918 RAF Muster Roll.

1306. F. T. TYRRELL

A recruit, a direct entrant into RFC 15 July, 1914. Was 2AM at the Recruit Depot in August. Served overseas from 3 March, 1915 earning 1914/15 Star trio. Promoted to Corporal (Rigger) 1 September, 1916 and retained that rank and trade in April, 1918 RAF Muster Roll.

* 1307. ARTHUR CHARLES HAWKINS

A recruit, a direct entrant into RFC 15 July, 1914. Was 2AM at the Recruit Depot in August. Served in France from 7 November, 1914 with No. 4 Squadron. Died of septicaemia 5 February, 1915 aged 21. Son of Charles and Alice Mary Hawkins of 107 Station Rd, Addlestone, Surrey. Buried Longuenesse (St. Omer) Souvenir Cemetery (Plot I, row A, grave 8). See War Office Casualty list dated 11 March, 1915. His 1914 Star, British War Medal, Victory Medal and Next of Kin plaque are known in the Webb collection.

1308. F. HARFLEET

Enlisted 19 September, 1907. Formerly 7433 Corporal 1/Coldstream Guards. Transferred to RFC 16 February, 1914. Served overseas from 7 December, 1915 earning 1914/15 Star trio. Promoted Sergeant (Machinist) 1 June, 1916 and retained that rank and trade in April, 1918 RAF Muster Roll. Awarded RAF L.S.&G.C. medal as Flight Sergeant *w.e.f.* 19 September, 1925.

1309. A. W. LAWRENCE

A recruit, a direct entrant into RFC 16 July, 1914. Discharged 30 July, 1914 under *K.R.* 392 (iii) 'Not likely to become an efficient soldier.'

1310. E. W. BEALE

A recruit, a direct entrant into RFC 16 July, 1914. Was 2AM at the Recruit Depot in August. No record of entitlement to either 1914 or 1914/15 Stars. Promoted Sergeant (Fitter engines) 1 July, 1917 and retained that rank and trade in April, 1918 RAF Muster Roll. Served in Mesopotamia in 1920-21 as a Flight Sergeant in 30 Squadron and awarded General Service Medal (clasp Iraq).

1311. D. T. MUMFORD

A recruit, a direct entrant into RFC 17 July, 1914. Was 2AM at the Recruit Depot in August. Served overseas from 3 March, 1915 earning 1914/15 Star trio. *RFC Communiqué No. 41* of 3 July, 1916 states: 'Lieut. T. A. Oliver and Sergeant Mumford in a Morane biplane of No. 1 Squadron encountered five hostile aeroplanes, driving four off with little trouble. The fifth showed more fight, but was last seen diving vertically with engines full on, and is believed to have been destroyed.' Reverted to Corporal (Fitter general) 1 January, 1917 and retained that rank and trade in April, 1918 RAF Muster Roll.

★ 1312. CECIL PERCY JOHN BROMLEY

Born Dover, 15 July, 1896. A recruit, a direct entrant into RFC 15 July, 1914. As 2AM with No. 6 Squadron served in France from 6 October, 1914. Awarded Royal Aero Club Aviators' Certificate No. 3350 on 13 August, 1916, when a Sergeant. He was 20 years of age when on 2 November, 1916 he was killed in action. Flying as Sergeant Pilot of No. 7 Squadron with 2 Lieut. Wood as Observer, they were brought down in combat falling to the west of the line. The observer was wounded. Sergeant Bromley's name is on the Arras Memorial to missing airmen. Son of Percy R. and Mrs. A. A. Bromley of 55 High St, Dover.

1313. R. S. BAYLEY

A recruit, a direct entrant into RFC 17 July, 1914. Was 2AM at the Recruit Depot in August. Nothing further traced regarding this man.

1314. THOMAS JAMES WILLIAM SAMUEL PEARCE

Born 27 May, 1892. A recruit, a direct entrant into RFC 15 July, 1914. Was 2AM at the Recruit Depot in August. No record of entitlement to 1914 or 1914/15 Stars. Promoted to Flight Sergeant (Fitter general) 1 March, 1917 and was Chief Mechanic (Fitter general) in April, 1918 RAF Muster Roll. Appointed Warrant Officer 10 February, 1930. Awarded RAF L.S.&G.C. medal as SM1 *w.e.f.* 15 July, 1931. In October, 1937 was posted to RAF Station Ismailia, Middle East Command as the Senior Warrant Officer there. In the March 1938 *A.F.L.* he was the 33rd senior RAF Warrant Officer. Commissioned in WW2. Flight Lieutenant 12 June, 1942. Promoted to Squadron Leader (Technical Engineer) (No. 35293) 1 July, 1944. Retired 23 June, 1949. (See Nos. 406 and 1315). Last noted in 1968 *A.F.L.*

1315. ALBERT EDWARD PEARCE

A recruit, a direct entrant into RFC 15 July, 1914. Served overseas from 23 July, 1915 earning 1914/15 Star trio. Reverted to Sergeant 24 July, 1917 and was Sergeant Mechanic (Rigger Aero) in April, 1918 RAF Muster

Roll. Awarded RAF L.S.&G.C. as Flight Sergeant *w.e.f.* 15 July, 1932. Awarded 1937 Coronation Medal. Commissioned (CEO) as Flying Officer (No. 35081) 18 May, 1937. Posted 1 July, 1937 to RAF Tangmere (No. 11 Fighter Group HQ). Promoted to Squadron Leader 1 June, 1941 and to Wing Commander 1 June, 1942 and was still serving in 1946 (see No. 1314).

1316. HAROLD OLIVER BARTON MAWDSLEY

A boy entrant into RFC 21 July, 1914. Still in boy service in April, 1918 RAF Muster Roll. No record of any medal entitlement WW1. Awarded RAF L.S.&G.C. medal *w.e.f.* 21 July, 1932 as Flight Sergeant. Awarded 1937 Coronation Medal. Commissioned (CEO) as Flying Officer (No. 35107) 18 May, 1937 and posted 29 July, 1937 to No. 9 Flying Training School, Hullavington, Chippenham. Shown in 1946 *A.F.L.* as retired.

★ 1317. H. WILSON

A recruit, a direct entrant into RFC 21 July, 1914. Was 2AM Lorry Driver at Montrose in August with Lieutenant de Havilland of 6 Squadron then posted to the Reserve Aeroplane Squadron. Served in France from 6 October, 1914. Promoted Temp SM (T) 1 March, 1917 and was Ch Mr Mech (Technical) in April, 1918 RAF Muster Roll.

★ 1318. C. L. SANDERSON

Enlisted 2 September, 1913. Formerly 13643, Gunner Royal Marine Artillery. Transferred to RFC 16 July, 1914. As 2AM with the Aircraft Park served in France from 16 August, 1914. Promoted to Corporal (Inst. Rep.) 1 August, 1916 and retained that rank and trade in April, 1918 RAF Muster Roll.

★ 1319. S. G. RIDGERS

A recruit, a direct entrant into RFC 20 July, 1914. Was 2AM in No. 6 Squadron then served in France from 10 September, 1914. Promoted to 1AM (Driver MT) 1 December, 1916 and retained that rank and trade in April, 1918 RAF Muster Roll.

★ 1320. F. P. ATKINS

A recruit, a direct entrant into RFC 21 July, 1914. As 2AM with No. 6 Squadron served in France from 6 October, 1914. Promoted to Sergeant (Fitter engines) 1 September, 1916 and was Sergeant Mechanic (Fitter AE) in April, 1918 RAF Muster Roll.

★ 1321. RICHARD NICHOLLS

Born 31 December, 1895. A recruit, a direct entrant into RFC 21 July, 1914. Was 2AM with No. 6 Squadron then served in France and earned 1914 Star and bar from 10 September, 1914. Aerial Gunner, 5 Squadron in 1915.

RFC Communiqué No. 5 dated 18 August, 1915:

'On a Vickers Fighter with 2nd Lieutenant Grey near Boesinghe at 11,000 feet saw an Albatross at 9000 feet heading south. 2 Lieut Grey got to within 300 yards and fired a drum. The Albatross opened fire and dived. The machine was hit in several places by the enemy's guns.'

Injured as an aerial gunner 26 October, 1915. Promoted to Flight Sergeant (Fitter Engines) 1 September, 1917. Mentioned in despatches 20 December, 1917 'For Anti Aircraft Services in U.K.' Listed in the *Times* 'B' Press Release of 21 December, 1917 for services in the Air Defence of Great Britain. Was Chief Mechanic (Fitter AE) in April, 1918 RAF Muster Roll. Listed in the *Times* 'B' Press Release 23 January, 1919. Awarded Indian General Service Medal (clasp Waziristan 1921-24). Awarded RAF L.S.&G.C. medal *w.e.f.* 21 July, 1932 as SM2. Appointed WO class 1, 1 October, 1932. On 13 August, 1936 was S. W. O. at RAF Station Hornchurch (No. 11 Fighter Group). Awarded 1937 Coronation Medal. Noted also in March 1938 *A.F.L.* as the 62nd Senior RAF Warrant Officer. Commissioned (No. 35350) 12 June, 1939. Promoted to Squadron Leader (Tech.) 1 December, 1941. Retired 10 March, 1949. Last noted in 1978 *A.F.L.*

AIRCO DH9A

1322. R. VILLENDER

A recruit, a direct entrant into RFC 22 July, 1914. 2AM at the Recruit Depot in August, 1914. Nothing further traced.

1323. W. COOK

A recruit, a direct entrant into RFC 22 July, 1914. 2AM at the Recruit Depot in August. No record of entitlement to either 1914 or 1914/15 Stars. Promoted to Sergeant (1st class Pilot) 31 May, 1917 and was Sergeant Mechanic (Pilot) in April, 1918 RAF Muster Roll. Awarded 1937 Coronation Medal. 29th senior RAF Warrant Officer in November, 1941 with seniority from 1 October, 1930.

1324. H. DAVIES

A recruit, a direct entrant into RFC 15 June, 1914. No record of entitlement to either 1914 or 1914/15 Stars. Promoted to Sergeant (Rigger) 1 December, 1917 and was Sergeant Mechanic (Rigger Aero) in April, 1918 RAF Muster Roll.

★ 1325. W. S. YOUNG

Enlisted 24 October, 1912. Formerly 15382 Private, 4/Royal Fusiliers. Transferred to RFC 14 February, 1914. As 2AM with No. 4 Squadron served in France, and awarded a 1914 Star and bar, from 12 August, 1914. Promoted to 1AM (Rigger Kite Balloon Service) 1 November, 1915 and was 1AM (Rigger, Airships) in April, 1918 RAF Muster Roll.

★ 1326. E. V. HICK

A recruit, a direct entrant into RFC 20 July, 1914. As 2AM with No. 6 Squadron served in France from 7 October, 1914. Promoted to Sergeant (Blacksmith) 1 December, 1916 and retained that rank and trade in April, 1918 RAF Muster Roll.

1327. D. ROBERTS

A recruit, a direct entrant into RFC 16 July, 1914. Discharged 28 July, 1914 under *K.R.* 392 (iii) 'Not likely to become an efficient soldier.'

1328. E. E. PAGE

A recruit, a direct entrant into RFC 22 July, 1914. No record of entitlement to either 1914 or 1914/15 Stars. Commissioned 2 Lieutenant 30 August, 1917. Demobilised December, 1918 as Acting Captain RAF.

1329. J. J. STONE

A recruit, a direct entrant into RFC 20 July, 1914. 2AM at the Recruit Depot in August. Served overseas from 3 April, 1915 and earned 1914/15 Star trio. Was Corporal (Aerial Gunner) with No. 7 Squadron in August, 1915. Promoted to Flight Sergeant (Fitter general) 1 August, 1916 and was Chief Mechanic (Fitter general) in April, 1918 RAF Muster Roll.

1330. W. H. SWEETING

A recruit, a direct entrant into RFC 27 July, 1914. Served overseas from 12 December, 1915 as a Flight Sergeant earning 1914/15 Star trio. Awarded Army Meritorious Service Medal in *L.G.* 1 January, 1918 still a Flight Sergeant 'For Valuable Services with the Armies in the Field.' (He came from Cirencester). Promoted to Temp SM (T) 1 February, 1918 and was Ch Mr Mech (Technical) in April, 1918 RAF Muster Roll. His group of four medals are known in a private collection in U.S.A.:- 1914/15 Star (Flight Sergeant RFC) British War Medal and Victory Medal (T/SM RAF) and Army M.S.M. (Flt. Sgt. RFC).

1331. A. A. SPICER

A recruit, a direct entrant into RFC 27 July, 1914. No further references found on this man.

1332. A. ARNOLD

A recruit, a direct entrant into RFC 27 July, 1914. Was 2AM at the Recruit Depot in August. No record of entitlement to either 1914 or 1914/15 Stars. Promoted to Corporal (Fitter general) 1 April, 1916 and retained that rank and trade in April, 1918 RAF Muster Roll.

1333. RICHARD ARTHUR LLOYD

A recruit, a direct entrant into RFC 29 July, 1914. 2AM at the Recruit Depot in August. No record of entitlement to either 1914 or 1914/15 Stars. Awarded Royal Aero Club Aviators' Certificate No. 3693 of 29 September, 1916, as a Corporal. However on 2 May, 1917 he reverted to 1AM (Fitter general) and retained that rank and trade in April, 1918 RAF Muster Roll.

★ 1334. GEORGE BAXTER HARRIES

Enlisted 10 March, 1911. Formerly 7116 Lance Corporal, 18 Hussars. Transferred to RFC 21 May, 1914. As 2AM with RFC HQ served in France from 16 August, 1914 and earned a 1914 Star and bar. Mentioned in despatches *L.G.* 15 May, 1917 as a Flight Sergeant with No. 9 Wing Head Quarters. Promoted to Temp SM (D) 1 November, 1917 and was SM1 (Disciplinarian) in April, 1918 RAF Muster Roll. Awarded RAF L.S.&G.C. *w.e.f.* 10 March, 1929 as SM1. He was the 66th senior RAF Warrant Officer in February, 1931.

★ 1335. L. BARTLETT

Enlisted 11 July, 1913. Formerly10317, 18 Hussars. Transferred to RFC 29 April, 1914. As 2AM with No. 3 Squadron served in France from 13 August, 1914. Promoted to 1AM (Sailmaker) 1 March, 1915 and was Private 1 (Fabric Worker) in April, 1918 RAF Muster Roll.

★ 1336. D. R. BAXTER

Enlisted 2 July, 1908. Formerly 35487, 30 Company RE. Transferred to RFC 29 April, 1914. As 2AM with No. 3 Squadron served in France from 13 August, 1914. In *RFC Communiqué No. 60* of 31 October, 1916 mentioned as flying with Lieutenant T. S. Green in No. 3 Squadron and attacking an LVG enemy aircraft and driving it down in a nose dive. However, its destruction was not confirmed. Awarded Distinguished Conduct Medal as Sergeant in *L.G.* 1 January, 1917 and the citation in *L.G.* 13 February, 1917 says 'For conspicuous gallantry in action. On three occasions he came to a very low altitude to attack infantry on the ground. He has displayed great courage and determination throughout.' Promoted to Flight Sergeant (NCO Observer) 1 May, 1917 and was Chief Mechanic (Observer) in April, 1918 RAF Muster Roll.

★ 1337. H. DEWHURST

Enlisted 4 November, 1909. Formerly 39453 48 Battery RGA. Transferred to RFC 8 June, 1914. As 2AM with No. 3 Squadron served in France from 12 August, 1914 and earned a 1914 Star and bar. Promoted to Sergeant (Carpenter) 1 February, 1917 and retained that rank and trade in April, 1918 RAF Muster Roll. Awarded RAF L.S.&G.C. medal as Flight Sergeant *w.e.f.* 4 November, 1927.

★ 1338. J. W. LUCY

Enlisted 4 April, 1913. Formerly 2789 Private 2/Lancashire Fusiliers. Transferred to RFC 15 July, 1914. As 2AM with No. 3 Squadron served in France from 13 August, 1914 and earned a 1914 Star and bar. Promoted to 1AM (Cook) 1 September, 1916 and was Private 1st Class (Cook) in April, 1918 RAF Muster Roll. However a later note says:— 'delete entry.'

★ 1339. J. LINDSAY

Enlisted 20 November, 1908. Formerly 58 Company RGA. As 2AM with No. 4 Squadron served in France from 12 August, 1914. Promoted to Corporal (Driver MT) 1 February, 1918 and retained that rank and trade in April, 1918 RAF Muster Roll.

1340. FREDERICK JAMES ANDREWS

Enlisted 3 August, 1907. Formerly 34904 63 Company RGA. Transferred to RFC 7 May, 1914. Was 1AM with No. 7 Squadron in August. Served overseas from 3 April, 1915 and awarded 1914/15 Star trio. Promoted to Temp SM (T) 1 August, 1917 and was Ch Mr Mech (Technical) in April, 1918 RAF Muster Roll. He is noted as having served as a Flight Sergeant in No. 100 Squadron where his home address is given as 11 Waterloo Road, Shoeburyness. Awarded RAF L.S.&G.C. medal as SM1 *w.e.f.* 3 August, 1925. 59th senior RAF Warrant Officer in 1931 *A.F.L.*

✶ 1341. W. LEDDRA

Enlisted 22 July, 1908. Formerly 35776 16 Company RGA. Transferred to RFC 2 July, 1914. Transferred from No. 6 Squadron to Aircraft Park 12 August, 1914. As 2AM with the Aircraft Park served in France from 16 August, 1914. Promoted to Corporal (Armourer) 1 May,. 1916 and retained that rank and trade in April, 1918 RAF Muster Roll.

✶ 1342. C. SMITH

Enlisted 15 January, 1909. Formerly 36701, 21 Company RGA. Transferred to RFC 2 July, 1914. As 2AM with No. 6 Squadron served in France from 7 October, 1914. Promoted to Flight Sergeant (Blacksmith) 1 August, 1917 and was Chief Mechanic (Blacksmith) in April, 1918 RAF Muster Roll. Awarded RAF L.S.&G.C. medal 15 January, 1927 as Flight Sergeant.

✶ 1343. E. G. WEST

Formerly 37396, 18 Company RGA. Transferred to RFC 2 July, 1914. As 2AM with No. 6 Squadron served in France from 6 October, 1914. Accidentally killed whilst flying at Central Flying School as a Flight Sergeant on 31 May, 1916, aged 22. Son of Enos and Leah Lovisa West of 52 Kingsley Road, Milton, Portsmouth. Buried in Upavon Cemetery, Wiltshire (grave 4). His 1914 Star trio are known to be in a private collection with his father's medals.

1344. S. W. COCKRAM

Enlisted 2 September, 1907. Formerly 32776, 33 Company RE. Transferred to RFC 4 May, 1914. No record of entitlement to either 1914 or 1914/15 Stars. Mentioned in despatches *L.G.* 24 February, 1917 as Flight Sergeant and listed in the *Times* 'B' Press Release of 27 March, 1917. Promoted to Temp SM (T) 1 September, 1917 and was Ch Mr Mech (Technical) in April, 1918 RAF Muster Roll. However he was awarded an Indian General Service Medal (Waziristan 1925) as a Flight Sergeant and was awarded his RAF L.S.&G.C. medal as Flight Sergeant *w.e.f.* 5 July, 1926 after 18 1/2 years service.

* 1345. J. T. TANSLEY

Enlisted 2 September, 1911. Formerly 2158 Private 2/Manchester Regt. Transferred to RFC 8 June, 1914. As 2AM with No. 2 Squadron, served in France from 12 August, 1914 earning 1914 Star and bar. Promoted to Corporal (Fitter general) 1 August, 1917 and retained that rank and trade in April, 1918 RAF Muster Roll. His 1914 Star (2AM) and British War Medal (Cpl RAF) were offered by Beadle in 1986 for £100.

* 1346. J. E. HUNNISETT

Enlisted 10 March, 1914. Formerly 15985 Private 4/Royal Fusiliers. Transferred to RFC 11 May, 1914. As 2AM with No. 2 Squadron served in France from 12 August, 1914 and earned 1914 Star and bar trio. Promoted to Corporal (Acet. Welder) 1 October, 1916 and retained that rank and trade in April, 1918 RAF Muster Roll. His 1914 Star trio (2AM and Cpl RFC) were offered by Beadle in 1986 for £125.

* 1347. J. H. FERGUSON

Formerly 15925 Sergeant ASC. Transferred to RFC 30 June, 1914. As a Sergeant with No. 6 Squadron, served in France from 6 October, 1914. Commissioned 2 Lieutenant, 1 August, 1917.

* 1348. T. C. LOCK

Enlisted 6 June, 1908. Formerly 11257 Private 3/Worcs. Regt. Transferred to RFC 2 May, 1914. As 2AM with No. 4 Squadron served in France from 9 September, 1914 and earned 1914 Star and bar. Promoted Sergeant (Carpenter) 3 September, 1917 and retained that rank and trade in April, 1918 RAF Muster Roll. Awarded RAF L.S.&G.C. medal with effect from 6 June, 1926 as Sergeant.

* 1349. SYDNEY CHARLES MURTON

Enlisted 11 December, 1907. Formerly 8855 Private 1/Somerset Light Infantry. Transferred to RFC 12 May, 1914. As 2AM with RFC HQ served in France from 11 August, 1914 (NB one day before the main body arrived) and earned 1914 Star and bar. Promoted to Corporal (Rigger) 1 May, 1916 and was Corporal Mechanic (Rigger Aero) in April, 1918 RAF Muster Roll. Awarded a Distinguished Flying Medal in *L.G.* 28 October, 1921 for services in Mesopotamia and was also mentioned in despatches for Iraq 1921-1922 as a Corporal in No. 30 Squadron. Awarded General Service Medal (Iraq) Awarded RAF L.S.&G.C. medal with effect from 11 December, 1925 as Acting Sergeant. The D.F.M. was instituted in 1918 for 'acts of valour, courage or devotion to duty performed whilst flying in active operations against the enemy.' Only 167 medals and 3 bars were awarded with George V obverse from 1918 to 1937 of which 22 were probably the 2nd type. Of the 145 1st type 102 were for the Great War. Six were for Mesopotamia, making this one not only a very rare award but the only D.F.M. to one of the pre-war RFC NCOs and OR's.

★ 1350. W. HILL

Formerly 10373 Private Royal Inniskilling Fusiliers. Transferred to the RFC 25 April, 1914. As 2AM with No. 5 Squadron served in France from 14 August, 1914. Discharged 18 February, 1916 under *K.R.* 392 (xvi) 'No longer physically fit for war service.'

1351. L. H. ROBERTSON

Enlisted 2 June, 1909. Formerly 37398, 108 Heavy Battery RGA. Transferred to RFC 27 June, 1914. Was 1AM with No. 5 Squadron in August, 1914. Served overseas from 23 July, 1915 earning 1914/15 Star trio. Promoted to Flight Sergeant (Rigger) 13 March, 1918 and was Chief Mechanic (Rigger Aero) in April, 1918 RAF Muster Roll. Awarded General Service Medal (clasp Kurdistan) as Flight Sergeant and RAF L.S.&G.C. medal with effect from 2 June, 1927 also as Flight Sergeant. At Sothebys in 1984 his group was auctioned:— 1914/15 Star trio (re-issues), General Service Medal (Kurdistan), RAF L.S.&G.C.

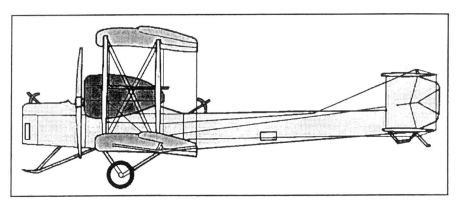

VICKERS VIMY

★ 1352. W. JOHNSON

A boy entrant, joined RFC 29 July, 1914. As 2AM with No. 6 Squadron served in France from 6 October, 1914 and earned 1914 Star and bar. Promoted to Corporal (Vulcanizer) 1 January, 1917 and retained that rank and trade in April, 1918 RAF Muster Roll.

1353. G. A. H. HIATT

A boy entrant, joined the RFC 31 July, 1914. No record of entitlement to 1914 or 1914/15 Star. Out of boy service and made 2AM (Fitter engines) 7 December, 1917 but was 3AM (Fitter AE) in April, 1918 RAF Muster Roll. (See also No. 975.)

★ 1354. A. T. WAY

A recruit, a direct entrant into RFC 6 August, 1914. As 2AM with No. 6 Squadron served in France from 7 October, 1914. Promoted to Corporal (Fitter/Turner) 1 November, 1916 and was Corporal Mechanic (Turner) in April, 1918 RAF Muster Roll.

★ 1355. W. F. BARKHAM

A recruit, a direct entrant into RFC 30 July, 1914. Was 2AM with No. 6 Squadron in August then served in France from 10 September, 1914. Promoted to Flight Sergeant (Fitter/Turner) 1 March, 1917 and was Chief Mechanic (Turner) in April, 1918 RAF Muster Roll.

★ 1356. S. A. J. ROWLAND

A recruit, a direct entrant into RFC 30 July, 1914. As 2AM with No. 6 Squadron served in France from 7 October, 1914. Promoted to Corporal (Fitter MT) 1 May, 1917 and retained that rank and trade in April, 1918 RAF Muster Roll. Brought to notice in the *Times* 'B' Press Release of 29 August, 1919.

★ 1357. JOHN BARRATT

A recruit, a direct entrant into RFC 29 July, 1914. As 2AM with No. 6 Squadron served in France from 6 October, 1914. Promoted to Acting Sergeant (paid) (Fitter general) 1 January, 1918 and was Sergeant Mechanic (Fitter general) in April, 1918 RAF Muster Roll. Awarded Air

Force Medal in *L.G.* 10 October, 1919 as SM2 and was mentioned in despatches in *L.G.* 22 December, 1919 for services in North Russia as Sergeant Major.

★ 1358. V. J. HUTCHINSON

A recruit, a direct entrant into RFC 3 August, 1914. As 2AM with No. 6 Squadron served in France from 7 October, 1914. Discharged 'unfit' 16 February, 1915.

1359. J. F. C. HENSTRIDGE

Recruited under Special Order of 4 August, 1914 at 4/- per day and enlisted on 7 August, 1914 for the Duration of the War. Served overseas from 19 November, 1915 earning 1914/15 Star trio. Promoted to Flight Sergeant (Storeman) 1 September, 1916 and was Flight Clerk (Storeman) in April, 1918 RAF Muster Roll.

1360. D. R. TAYLOR

A recruit, a direct entrant into the RFC 25 July, 1914. Nothing further recorded on this man.

1361. T. HARRY

A recruit, a direct entrant into RFC 5 August, 1914. Served overseas from 25 June, 1915 earning 1914/15 Star trio. Promoted to 1AM (Electrician) 1 October, 1917 and retained that rank and trade in April, 1918 RAF Muster Roll.

1362. W. E. SCRAGG

A recruit, a direct entrant into RFC 7 August, 1914. Served overseas from 3 March, 1915 earning a 1914/15 Star trio. Promoted to Corporal (Fitter general) 1 March, 1917 and retained that rank and trade in April, 1918 RAF Muster Roll.

★ 1363. E. G. HONE

A recruit, a direct entrant into RFC 8 August, 1914. As 2AM with No. 6 Squadron served in France from 5 October, 1914. Mentioned in despatches in *L.G.* 16 January, 1918 for services in Egypt. Promoted to

Flight Sergeant (Rigger) 1 February, 1918 and was Chief Mechanic (Rigger Aero) in April, 1918 RAF Muster Roll.

* 1364. RICHARD THORNTON NEVILL

Enlisted 8 August, 1914 under the Special Order of 4 August for the Duration of the War. As 2AM with No. 3 Squadron served in France from 12 August, 1914 just four days later. Commissioned 2 Lieutenant 17 November, 1914. Promoted to Captain (Experimental Officer 1st Class) 3 October, 1917. In November, 1921 *A.F.L.* shown as Flight Lieutenant (Technical) seniority 1 August, 1919 serving from September, 1921 at Iraq Group HQ, Middle East Area. 'For Disposal.' Transferred to 'B' Reserve of Air Force Officers 25 August, 1923 as Flight Lieutenant (GD) (*vide* 1931 *A.F.L.*). See group photograph under No. 626.

* 1365. JAMES KEIL WALSH

A recruit, a direct entrant into RFC 5 August, 1914. As 2AM with No. 6 Squadron served in France from 6 October, 1914 and earned a 1914 Star and bar. Promoted to Temp SM (T) 1 February, 1917 and was Ch Mr Mech (Technical) in April, 1918 RAF Muster Roll. Awarded RAF L.S.&G.C. medal *w.e.f.* 5 August, 1932. From 3 December, 1934 was Station Warrant Officer at Odiham, Basingstone Hants (No. 4 Army Co-operation Squadron). In the March 1938 *A.F.L.* was the fourth senior RAF Warrant Officer.

1366. S. G. CLOAKE

A recruit, a direct entrant into RFC 5 August, 1914. As 2AM served overseas from 2 April, 1915 earning 1914/15 Star trio. Promoted to Corporal (Instr Rep.) 1 December, 1917 and retained that rank and trade in April, 1918 RAF Muster Roll.

1367. A. E. NUNN

A recruit, a direct entrant into RFC 5 August, 1914. As 2AM served overseas from 3 April, 1915 earning a 1914/15 Star trio. Promoted to Sergeant (Fitter engines) 1 June, 1916 and was Sergeant Mechanic (Fitter AE) in April, 1918 RAF Muster Roll.

★ 1368. C. PERRIN

A recruit, a direct entrant into RFC 5 August, 1914. As 2AM with No. 3 Squadron served in France from 12 August, 1914. Discharged under *K.R.* 392 (xvi) 'Sickness' 20 March, 1915. Silver War Badge 147869 issued.

1369. LEWIS W. F. TURNER

Born Dorsetshire 7 January, 1884. A member of the Air Battalion Reserve. Awarded Royal Aero Club Aviators' Certificate No. 66 on 4 April, 1911, in a Henri Farman at Hendon. Before the war he was Chief Flying Instructor at Graham White's Flying School. Enlisted into RFC as a Sergeant Pilot 8 August, 1914 and served in UK with the Reserve Aeroplane Squadron. No record of entitlement to either 1914 or 1914/15 Stars. Commissioned 2 Lieutenant 27 April, 1915 and promoted Captain 1 March, 1916.

★ 1370. REGINALD HUGH CARR

Born Walthemstow 9 September, 1886. A member of the Air Battalion Reserve. Awarded Royal Aero Club Aviators' Certificate No. 504 on 2 June, 1913 in a Graham White Machine at Hendon. He was a competition flyer pre-war for the Graham White Company. Enlisted 8 August, 1914 and posted as a Sergeant-Pilot to Montrose with Lt de Havilland's No. 6 Squadron detachment. As Sergeant-Pilot served in France from 30 September, 1914 employed on artillery observation duties. McCudden V.C. mentions him in *'Flying Fury'* and describes him as a Chief Mechanic of Graham-White's, then stationed with No. 3 Squadron at Abbeville (October, 1914). Awarded Distinguished Conduct Medal in *L.G.* 22 June, 1915 'For conspicuous gallantry and devotion to duty. He has shown great courage and initiative throughout the campaign, and has been on continuous service since the commencement of hostilities.' He was commissioned 2 Lieutenant in the Special Reserve 27 April, 1915.

Promoted to Captain 7 December, 1915. Awarded Air Force Cross as Major D.C.M. in *L.G.* 2 November, 1918. Retired in 1919. His 1914 Star is in the RAF Museum Collection at Hendon.

★ 1371. C. F. M. CHAMBERS

Born Middleburg, South Africa 27 March, 1892. A member of the Air Battalion Reserve. Awarded Royal Aero Club Aviators' Certificate No. 168 on 12 December, 1911 in a Valkyme monoplane of Aeronautical Services at Hendon. Enlisted 8 August, 1914. Was a Sergeant Pilot with the Reserve Aeroplane Squadron then served in France from 10 October, 1914. Commissioned 25 April, 1916 as Flight Sub-Lieutenant RNAS.

★ 1372. F. G. DUNN

Awarded Royal Aero Club Aviators' Certificate No. 728 on 23 January, 1914 as a civilian. A member of the Air Battalion Reserve. He was an Instructor at Hendon. Enlisted 8 August, 1914 and served as a Sergeant Pilot at Newcastle with No. 6 Squadron detachment, then transferred to the Reserve Aeroplane Squadron. On 3 October, 1914 posted to France with No. 3 Squadron at Abbeville. In January, 1915 he went with McCudden, Webb and Bowyer to the Le Rhone works in Paris for engineering instruction. Commissioned 2 Lieutenant 27 April, 1915 and promoted to Captain 1 December, 1915.

1373. A. M. GODFREY

Enlisted 8 August, 1914 for the duration of the War under Special Order of 4 August. No record of entitlement to either 1914 or 1914/15 Stars. Promoted to Flight Sergeant (Fitter MT) 1 June, 1916 and was Chief Mechanic (Fitter MT) in April, 1918 RAF Muster Roll.

1374. G. JAPPE

Enlisted 8 August, 1914 for the duration of the War under the terms of the Special Order of 4 August. No record of entitlement to either 1914 or 1914/15 Stars. Awarded Army M.S.M. *L.G.* 4 June, 1917 as Flight Sergeant 'For Valuable Services with the Army in France and Flanders' serving with 19 Squadron. Promoted to Temp SM (T) 1 July, 1917 and was Ch Mr Mech (Technical) in April, 1918 RAF Muster Roll. His British War Medal and Victory Medal together with his M.S.M. are in the Webb Collection.

1375. H. E. WRIGHTON

A recruit, a direct entrant into RFC 8 August, 1914. Served overseas from 3 April, 1915 earning 1914/15 Star trio. Promoted to Corporal (Sailmaker) 1 May, 1917 and was Corporal (Fabric Worker) in April, 1918 RAF Muster Roll.

1376. EDWARD RODOLPH CLEMENT SCHOLEFIELD

A member of the Air Battalion Reserve. Awarded Royal Aero Club Aviators' Certificate FR819 of 16 April, 1912. Enlisted 8 August, 1914 as a Sergeant Pilot. Served in France from early 1915 earning 1914/15 Star trio. Awarded Distinguished Conduct Medal as Sergeant in *L.G.* 22 June, 1915 'For conspicuous gallantry and ability with which he has carried out

the duties of a pilot.' He had already been commissioned on 27 April, 1915 as 2 Lieutenant in the Special Reserve of Officers. On 1 September, 1915 serving with No. 8 Squadron he was shot down (unharmed) and taken prisoner of war. His observer, Captain F. J. C. Wilson was also captured unhurt. In the November, 1921 *A.F.L.* he is shown as a Flying Officer *w.e.f.* 31 January, 1920 serving as a pilot at the Experimental Section of the Royal Aircraft Establishment. His group of five medals are in the RAF Museum at Hendon:— Air Force Cross, D.C.M. (Sergt RFC) 1914/15 Star (Sgt RFC) British War Medal and Victory (Lieutenant RAF). In *RFC Communiqué No. 6* of 23 August, 1915 he is mentioned as 2 Lieutenant, IIIrd Wing on a Bristol Scout he intercepted a hostile machine near Albert going North. He opened fire with his Lewis gun and exchanged fire for several minutes. At 3000 feet above Péronne he turned for Albert, got above the hostile and emptied his last drum into it.

1377. ROBERT JOHN LILLYWHITE

Born Chichester 12 April, 1893. Awarded Royal Aero Club Aviators' Certificate No. 720 on 1 January, 1914 in a Graham White machine at Hendon. He then worked as an instructor for Graham White. Enlisted 8 August, 1914 for the duration of the War under the terms of the Special Order of 4 August. Was a Sergeant Pilot. Served in France from December, 1914, earning 1914/15 Star trio. Commissioned 2 Lieutenant 28 September, 1915. Flying in No. 3 Squadron in January, 1916 with McCudden as his observer. Promoted Captain 1 September, 1916. Killed in a flying accident 26 November, 1917.

RFC Communiqué No. 16 26 October, 1915

2 Lt. Lillywhite and 2 Lt Fielding Johnston, 3 Squadron, in a Morane Parasol on escort duty to photographic reconnaissance, when flying at 10,000 feet saw an Aviatik 500 feet below them and dived towards it opening fire. The Aviatik turned towards its own lines. The Morane was now attacked from behind by two more Aviatiks which both opened fire at about 150 yards. On fire being returned both the hostile machines dived in opposite directions apparantly undamaged. A fourth Aviatik now opened fire from above and glided past the Morane into the German lines with its propellor stopped. As Lt. Lillywhite was returning to the aerodrome he met yet another Aviatik which he chased for about 15

minutes over the lines, the German eventually turning and going down into its own lines.

RFC Communiqué No. 22 November 18, 1915

2 Lt. Lillywhite and Lt. Sherwin (Morane, 3 Squadron) returning from photography encountered an Aviatik over Béthune. Fire opened at about 400 feet as the hostile machine passed immediately over the Morane, but the Lewis gun jammed after the sixth round. The Aviatik crossed the lines apparantly undamaged.

RFC Communiqué No. 25 19 December, 1915

Lt. Lillywhite and Lt. Long (Morane, 3 Squadron) fired one drum at a range of about 250 feet into an Aviatik which dived steeply, flattened out near the ground and then turned over and crashed just east of Salome. Later with Sgt. J. B. McCudden as his air gunner he escorted a Morane Parasol flown by Capt. Mealing on a reconnoitring flight to Valenciennes. Over the airfield at Douai, the main base for Fokkers, sixteen aircraft were reported as leaving the ground.

★ 1378. ALFRED EDWARD BARRS

Born Loughborough 22 June, 1886. Awarded Royal Aero Club Aviators' Certificate No. 749 on 7 March, 1914 in a Graham White machine at Hendon. Enlisted 8 August, 1914 under Special Order of 4 August, as a Sergeant Pilot. Served in France from 10 October, 1914. Crashed 22 October, 1914. Discharged under *K.R.* 392 (xvi) 'Sick' 12 October, 1915. Silver War Badge 52252 issued.

★ 1379. H. F. TIDY

Enlisted 9 August, 1914 under the terms of Special Order of 4 August for the duration of the War. Was 2AM in No. 6 Squadron, then served in France from 9 September, 1914. Reverted to Sergeant (Fitter general) and retained that rank and trade in April, 1918 RAF Muster Roll.

★ 1380. J. R. B. WEEDING

Enlisted under the terms of the Special Order of 4 August, 1914 for the duration of the War. As 2AM with No. 5 Squadron served in France from

14 August, 1914. Commissioned 2 Lieutenant 2/Welsh Regt 17 November, 1914. Killed in Action 22 December, 1914.

★ 1381. R. C. SMITH

Enlisted 4 August, 1914. As 2AM with No. 6 Squadron served in France from 6 October, 1914. Discharged 30 November, 1917 aged 22 1/2 under *K.R.* 392 (xvi) from injuries. Silver War Badge No. 277577 issued.

1382. GLENDON GODFREY NICHOLAS MARSHALL

A recruit, a direct entrant into RFC 10 August, 1914. No record of entitlement to either 1914 or 1914/15 Stars. Promoted to Temp SM (D) 1 February, 1916 and was SM1 (Disciplinarian) in April, 1918 RAF Muster Roll. Mentioned in despatches for services in Egypt and brought to notice in the *Times* 'B' Press release of 23 January, 1919. Appointed Member of the Order of British Empire (M.B.E.) in King's Birthday Honours of 3 June, 1931 as SM1. Awarded RAF L.S.&G.C. medal *w.e.f.* 10 August, 1932. 11th Senior RAF Warrant Officer at this time.

1383. L. J. MITCHELL

Enlisted 10 August, 1914 for the duration of the War under the terms of Special Order of 4 August, 1914. Was 1AM with No. 6 Squadron and served in France from 3 April, 1915 earning 1914/15 Star trio. Promoted to Flight Sergeant (Fitter Motor Cycle) 1 December, 1916 and was Chief Mechanic (Fitter MT) in April, 1918 RAF Muster Roll.

1384. S. EDGINGTON

Enlisted 10 August, 1914 for the duration of the War under the terms of Special Order of 4 August. No record of entitlement to either 1914 or 1914/15 Stars. Reverted to Sergeant (1st Class Pilot) 9 January, 1917. Killed in action 11 September, 1917 as Sergeant Pilot.

★ 1385. H. E. LOWREY

Enlisted 10 August, 1914 under the terms of the Special Order of 4 August for the duration of the War. As 2AM with No. 6 Squadron served in France from 6 October, 1914 and earned a 1914 Star and bar. Promoted to Temp SM (T) 1 July, 1917 and was Ch Mr Mech (Technical) in April, 1918 RAF Muster Roll.

1386. C. C. HANN

Enlisted 10 August, 1914. Served overseas from 3 March, 1915, earning 1914/15 Star trio. Commissioned 2 Lieutenant 17 October, 1915. Killed in action 22 October, 1916.

★ 1387. SAMUEL JOHN FROST

Born London 3 April, 1885. Enlisted 10 August, 1914. As 2AM with No. 6 Squadron served in France from 7 October, 1914. Awarded Royal Aero Club Aviators' Certificate No. 2828 on 4 May, 1916. Captain 5 October, 1916. Flight Lieutenant 2 March, 1920. Stationed from 15 September, 1920 at Aircraft Depot, Egypt. To 'C' Reserve of Air Force Officers 15 February, 1923.

★ 1388. H. MAYNARD

A recruit, a direct entrant into RFC 10 August, 1914. Served overseas from 3 December, 1914 earning 1914/15 Star trio. Promoted to Corporal (Aerial Gunner) 1 May, 1917 and was serving with 59 Squadron from 21 August, 1917. Retained the same rank and trade in April, 1918 RAF Muster Roll.

1389. H. A. COOPER

Enlisted into RFC 10 August, 1914 directly as a Sergeant. Commissioned 2 Lieutenant 10th London Regt and RFC in 1915 and flew as an Observer (see the following RFC Communiqués).
RFC Communiqué No. 8 31 August 1915:
Capt Rees and Flt Sgt Hargreaves came across an LVG at a height of 7,000 feet between Bucquoy and Bapaume when patrolling. The hostile machine was much faster than the Vickers but throttled down and allowed the Vickers to approach to 200 yards,

when the enemy observer fired a few rounds with an automatic rifle and then accelerated. This occurred five or six times. The Vickers having expended four drums, returned to the aerodrome for more ammunition. It then went back to look for the hostile aeroplane, and found it near the same place. It was 1,000 feet lower than the Vickers, which dived at it and fired one drum. The LVG dived into clouds. The engine of the Vickers cut out owing to the steep angle of glide, causing the petrol to run into the top of the tank. This second encounter was seen by 2 Lt Cooper (pilot) and 2 Lt Insall (observer), who were patrolling near Achiet-le-Petit. They report that the German machine came down in spirals and irregular 'S' turns, apparently badly hit, but owing to thick clouds they could not see it come to earth.

(This was with 2 Lt G. S. M. Insall who was awarded a Victoria Cross in *L.G.* 23 December, 1915 for an action on 7 November, 1915.)

RFC Communiqué No. 9 5 Sept 1915:

2 Lt Cooper (pilot) and 2 Lt Insall (observer), 11 Squadron, in a Vickers Fighter when patrolling near Gommecourt, sighted an LVG at 7,500 feet, they themselves being at 9,000 feet. The Vickers intercepted the LVG and got in front of it, and above it. The hostile aeroplane then came straight at the Vickers and passed underneath, opening fire with a machine-gun. The LVG then turned so as to get the Vickers on his broadside and dived past it. During this manœuvre, he was fired on and then assumed a steeper angle (80). When last seen, smoke and bright yellow flames were coming from his exhaust pipe above the engine. The Vickers could not follow owing to engine failing to pick up. Reports of eye witnesses of this encounter indicate that the German machine struck the ground while still in a nose dive.

RFC Communiqué No. 10 Sept. 8, 1915:

2 Lt Cooper (pilot) and 2 Lt Insall (observer) of 11 Squadron, on a Vickers chased an LVG near Hebuterne. The German machine avoided action and tried to draw the Vickers over his own A. A. guns.

RFC Communiqué No. 21 November 26, 1915:

2 Lt Cooper and 2 Lt Insall (Vickers, 11 Squadron) while on Army patrol and photography over Bray observed an Albatross flying 200 feet above them. The Vickers was turned and about 15 shots fired from the Lewis gun without effect. The German opened fire apparantly from a trap door in the floor of the machine, and accelerating, made for the lines. Another drum was fired without effect. Engine failure forced the Vickers to give up the chase and when last seen the German was heading for Péronne.

RFC Communiqué No. 33 April 10, 1916:

There were eight combats in the air. Capt. H. A. Cooper and 2 Lt. Vickery (Vickers fighter, 11 Squadron) whilst engaged in taking photographs near Bailleul, saw an LVG at 8,000 feet flying east. The Vickers dived with the engine off and engaged the hostile machine at a range of 40 yards at 6,000 feet. The observer of the hostile machine was seen to fall back in his seat, and the LVG immediately dived steeply and was lost sight of still diving through the clouds.

Promoted Hon. Captain 1 January, 1916 and mentioned in despatches the same date. Awarded Royal Aero Club Aviators' Certificate No. 3978 on 12 September, 1916 when he is shown as 2 Lieut 1/10th London Regt. Awarded Military Cross in *L.G.* 22 June, 1918 for shooting down three enemy aeroplanes as an Observer. Entitled to 1914/15 Star trio.

1390. E. LINDSAY

Enlisted into RFC 10 August, 1914 and as 2AM served overseas from 20 December, 1914 earning a 1914/15 Star trio. Discharged 3 February, 1915.

★ 1391. LEONARD SIDNEY GOSS

Born Fulham 1892. Educated at King's College. Enlisted into RFC 10 August, 1914 and two days later on 12 August, 1914 was serving in France as 2AM with No. 3 Squadron. Was a Corporal (Aerial gunner and observer) with No. 3 Squadron on 19 September, 1917 when he was killed in action aged 25. Son of Ida Goss of 81 Deodar Road, Putney and the late Sidney Francis Goss. Buried in Caudry British Cemetery (Plot iv, Row C, Grave 11).

1392. HENRY COCKERELL

Enlisted 10 August, 1914. Served in France from 3 April, 1915 and earned 1914/15 Star trio. Commissioned 2 Lieutenant 13 February, 1916. *RFC Communiqué No. 36* of 5 May, 1916 records him as Observer on a flight of three hours with Lieutenant Wigglesworth of No. 7 Squadron. They successfully ranged a battery onto six targets. In November, 1921 he is shown as Flight Lieutenant O.B.E. seniority 1 August, 1919, serving as a Technical Officer at the Marine and Armament Experimental Establishment on the Isle of Grain from 17 December, 1920. In 1931 *A.F.L.* he is shown as Squadron Leader seniority 1 January, 1926 (qualified at Specialist Armament Course) and serving from 13 April, 1926 at the Armament and Gunnery School, Eastchurch, Sheerness, Kent. In the 1937 *A.F.L.* he is shown as a retired officer working at the Air Ministry (Department of Personnel).

* 1393. H. N. BARNARD

Enlisted into RFC 10 August, 1914 and as a 2AM with RFC HQ was serving in France two days later on 12 August, 1914. Injured 21 July, 1917 when as a Sergeant Pilot he crash landed whilst serving with 54 Squadron. Commissioned 2 Lieutenant 17 November, 1917.

1394. A. J. STRINGER

Enlisted 10 August, 1914 and as 1AM was accidentally killed on 7 October, 1914. Aged 23. Son of the late Richard Stringer, he was buried in Hove Cemetery, Sussex (Plot PB, Row B, Grave 55).

1395. E. E. MOORE

Enlisted 10 August, 1914 for the duration of the War under the terms of Special Order of 4 August, 1914. He was a recruit, employed as a lorry driver with the No. 6 Squadron detachment at Newcastle and was then transferred to the Reserve Aeroplane Squadron. No record of entitlement to either 1914 or 1914/15 Stars. Promoted to Flight Sergeant (Fitter engines) 1 July, 1916 and was Chief Mechanic (Fitter AE) in April, 1918 RAF Muster Roll. Brought to notice in the *Times* 'B' Press Release of 23 January, 1919.

1396. THOMAS MOTTERSHEAD

Born 17 January, 1892 in Widnes, Lancashire. Enlisted 10 August, 1914. No record of entitlement to either 1914 or 1914/15 Stars. Posted to France in 1916 as a Sergeant Pilot with No. 25 Squadron he was awarded a Distinguished Conduct Medal in *L.G.* 14 November, 1916:— 'For conspicuous gallantry when on a bombing raid. He dived down to 1,500 feet, blew up one ammunition train with bombs, and attacked another with machine gun fire. On rising he was attacked by a Fokker from behind, but by skilful and daring manœuvring he enabled his observer to destroy it by fire.'

He died of wounds, 12 January, 1917, received in winning the Victoria Cross as a Sergeant Pilot in an FE2D with No. 20 Squadron. *RFC Communiqué No. 55* of 22 September, 1916 contains a shorter version of the D.C.M.

citation. *Cross and Cockade*, Volume 4, No. 1, pages 34 to 44 contains many details of his Victoria Cross action which took place near Ploegsteert Wood, Belgium, as does the following:—

Extract from Commonwealth War Graves Commission Roll for Bailleul Communal Cemetery Extension, where he is buried in Plot III, Row A, Grave 126:—

1396, 20th Sqdn. Royal Flying Corps. Died age 27 on 12 January, 1917 of injuries received on 7 January. Son of Thomas and Lucy Mottershead, of Widnes; husband of Lilian Medlicott Mottershead of 31, Lilac Avenue, Widnes, Lancs.

An extract from the *London Gazette*, No. 29937, dated 9th Feb, 1917, records the following:—

'For most conspicuous bravery, endurance and skill, when attacked at an altitude of 9,000 feet; the petrol tank was pierced and the machine set on fire. Enveloped in flames, which his Observer Lt. Gower was unable to subdue, this very gallant soldier succeeded in bringing his aeroplane back to our lines, and though he made a successful landing, the machine collapsed on touching the ground, pinning him beneath wreckage from which he was subsequently rescued. Though suffering extreme torture from burns, Sergt. Mottershead showed the most conspicuous presence of mind in the careful selection of a landing place, and his wonderful endurance and fortitude undoubtably saved the life of his Observer. He has since succumbed to his injuries.'

They were shot down by VZFW Gottseh of Jasta 8. His observer was thrown clear. There is an obelisk in Victoria Park, Widnes, dedicated to him.

A group of miniatures: Victoria Cross, Distinguished Conduct Medal, British War Medal and Victory Medal were sold at Sotheby's in June 1985. These were from the collection of the late Major General A. C. Shortt, C.B., O.B.E., Colonel Commandant, Intelligence Corps. They were of course simply a representative group made up for display. However it is believed that the full size medals were at one time in the General's collection.

1397. W. J. WILLIAMS

Enlisted 10 August, 1914 for the duration of the War under the terms of the Special Order of 4 August, 1914. No record of entitlement to 1914 or 1914/15 Stars. Promoted to Corporal (Fitter and turner) 1 September, 1916 and was Corporal Mechanic (Turner) in April, 1918 RAF Muster Roll. (See No. 1398)

* 1398. P. S. WILLIAMS

Enlisted 10 August, 1914 as 2AM with No. 2 Squadron served in France four days later on 14 August, 1914, earning a 1914 Star and bar. Commissioned 2 Lieutenant 2 July, 1916 (see No. 1397).

* 1399. HERBERT LEE

Enlisted 10 August, 1914 and as 2AM earned 1914 Star for services in France. SM1 4 June, 1930. RAF L.S.&G.C. medal 10 August, 1932. On 17 October, 1937 was SWO No. 6 FTS Netheravon. In March 1938 was the 37th most senior RAF Warrant Officer, and was the 28th most senior in November, 1941 and the 14th in October, 1944.

1400. FRANK RICHARD HAYNES

Enlisted 10 August, 1914 for the duration of the war. As 1AM with No. 6 Squadron served overseas from 3 December, 1914 earning 1914/15 Star trio. Promoted to Temp SM (D) 1 February, 1917 and was SM1 (Disciplinarian) in April, 1918 RAF Muster Roll. Mentioned in despatches as WO1 for Egypt and brought to notice in the *Times* 'B' Press Release of 23 January, 1919. Awarded RAF L.S.&G.C. medal *w.e.f.* 10 August, 1932. Awarded 1935 Silver Jubilee Medal. On 25 May, 1936 he was posted as Station Warrant Officer to No. 1 RAF Depot, 24 Training Group, Uxbridge. Awarded 1937 Coronation Medal. In the March, 1938 he was the 3rd senior RAF Warrant Officer.

The Village Blacksmith
(RFC Version)

Under the spreading hangar roof
The serjeant-major stands,
A fierce, imposing monster he,
All quake at his commands;
And the thunder of his booming voice
Is worse than German bands.

His hair is cropped beyond recall,
His face is like a boot;
His brow is wet with thoughts of debt
Incurred when a recruit;
He looks nobody in the face
(If so, they'd have to scoot!)

He goes at midday to the Mess
And sits among the swells,
Then drags defaulters by the necks
And dumps them in the cells,
While his massive fists are tightly clenched
Like those of Billy Wells.*

Week in, week out, from morn till night,
You can hear him curse the day
When he started out on his maiden flight
And a beastly strut gave way,
When (according to his own account)
He was foremost in the fray.

Strafing, abusing, bellowing,
Onward through life he goes;
Each morning he contrives to add
To many a A/M's woes.
Something attempted, Someone 'run'†
Will earn him a damaged nose.

---

* Heavyweight boxing champion of Britain.
† Service term for being put on a disciplinary charge.

Part 5
Numbers SR1 to SR25
The Special Reservists

The following 25 men can certainly be said to qualify for inclusion in this book. They were the Special Reservists who enlisted into the Reserve on the formation of the Royal Flying Corps and who were recalled at the outbreak of the war for the duration. A number of officers on the Special Reserve in other Corps and in Regiments also joined the RFC but these are the other ranks:—

SR1. S. MILLS

Recalled 5 August, 1914. Initially was 2AM with No. 1 Squadron. Promoted through to Acting Sergeant Major then commissioned 2 Lieutenant 30 July, 1916. No record of issues of either 1914 or 1914/15 Star.

★ SR2. F. J. BLACKWELL

Recalled 5 August, 1914. As 2AM with No. 6 Squadron served in France from 6 October, 1914. Promoted Flight Sergeant (Fitter MT) 1 November, 1916 and was Chief Mechanic (Fitter MT) in April, 1918 RAF Muster Roll. His medals were returned to RAF Records 27 June, 1929.

SR3. J. BENNETT

Recalled 5 August, 1914. Initially was 2AM with No. 6 Squadron. Nothing more traced.

SR4. CHARLES WHEELER

Recalled 5 August, 1914. Initially was 2AM with No. 6 Squadron. Served overseas from 2 April, 1915, he was entitled to 1914/15 trio. Promoted to Sergeant (Fitter general) 1 December, 1916 and retained that rank and trade in April, 1918 RAF Muster Roll. Remained in the RAF after the war and was awarded his RAF L.S.&G.C. as a Flight Sergeant with effect from 5 August, 1932. Appointed Warrant Officer, 27 January, 1935 and in 1938 (March) *A.F.L.* is shown as serving at RAF Abingdon (HQ, No. 1 Bomber Group) from 22 February, 1937. 81st senior RAF Warrant Officer in November, 1941 *A.F.L.* and 39th senior in October, 1944.

★ SR5. W. A. H. TREAVIS

Recalled 5 August, 1914. Initially was 2AM in No. 6 Squadron. First served overseas from 6 October, 1914 earning 1914 Star. He was in England in September, 1915 at Hounslow when 24 Squadron was first formed and went to France with them in Febuary, 1916. Appointed Temp SM (T) 1 November, 1916 and left the Squadron on 3 November, 1916. He was Ch Mr Mech (Technical) in April, 1918 RAF Muster Roll. His civilian address in 1920 was 10 Marion Terrace, Doncaster. See SR6, probably his brother.

SR6. H. L. TREAVIS

Recalled 5 August, 1914. Initially was 2AM with No. 6 Squadron. Served overseas from 3 April, 1915, earning 1914/15 Star trio. Promoted Corporal (Rigger) 13 April, 1917 and was Corporal Mechanic (Rigger Aero) in April, 1918 RAF Muster Roll. See SR5, probably his brother.

★ SR7. C. WILLS

Recalled 5 August, 1914. Initially was 2AM with No. 6 Squadron. Served in France from 7 October, 1914 earning 1914 Star and bar. As a Corporal with No. 9 Wing was awarded a Military Medal on 9 December, 1916. Promoted Sergeant (Fitter general) 1 March, 1917 and retained that rank and trade in April, 1918 RAF Muster Roll.

SR8. J. ROSS

Recalled 7 August, 1914. Initially was 2AM with No. 1 Squadron, promoted 1AM (Cook) 2 November, 1914. Served overseas from 3 March, 1915 and earned a 1914/15 Star trio. These were sold by Capital Medals in 1986, for £35 and are now known in a private collection. He is shown as Private 1st class (Cook) in April, 1918 RAF Muster Roll.

SR9. F. G. ELLIOTT

Recalled for the duration of the war on 11 August, 1914. 2AM with 1 Squadron initially. Served overseas from 3 March, 1915 earning 1914/15 Star trio. Sergeant (Vulcaniser) 1 November, 1917 and retained that rank and trade in April, 1918 RAF Muster Roll.

SR10. P. COULTATE

Recalled for the duration of the war on 6 August, 1914. Initially 2AM with No. 1 Squadron. Served overseas from 3 March, 1915 earning 1914/15 Star trio. Promoted Sergeant (Motor Mechanic) 1 October, 1917 and was Sergeant Mechanic (Fitter MT) in April, 1918 RAF Muster Roll.

SR11. A. LUFF

Recalled for the duration of the war on 12 August, 1914. Initially was 2AM with the Reserve Aeroplane Squadron. Served overseas from 7 March, 1915 earning 1914/15 Star trio. Promoted Sergeant (Driver MT) 1 August, 1916 and was Sergeant Mechanic (Driver) in April, 1918 RAF Muster Roll.

ORDERLY ROOM

SR12. W. C. WARNER

Recalled for the duration of the war from 12 August, 1914. Initially was 2AM with No. 1 Squadron. Served overseas from 3 March, 1915 earning 1914/15 Star trio. Promoted Sergeant (Fitter engines) 1 June, 1917 and was Sergeant Mechanic (Fitter A.E.) in April, 1918 RAF Muster Roll.

SR13. W. A. C. SNOOK

Recalled for the duration of the war from 12 August, 1914. Initially 2AM in the Reserve Aeroplane Squadron. Served overseas from 2 April, 1915 earning 1914/15 Star trio. He was an aerial gunner in No. 7 Squadron in 1915 and was mentioned in despatches in *L.G.* 4 January, 1917 as a Flight Sergeant. Promoted Temp SM (T) from 1 December, 1916 and was again mentioned in despatches in *L.G.* 20 December, 1917 as Sergeant Major for Anti Aircraft work in England. He was listed in the *Times* 'B' Press Release of 21 December, 1917 'For work associated with the Air Defence of Great Britain.' Ch Mr Mech (Technical) in April, 1918 RAF Muster Roll.

SR14. F. HOLLINGSHEAD

Recalled for the duration of the war from 12 August, 1914. Initially was 2AM with the Reserve Aeroplane Squadron. Served overseas from 7 March, 1915 and earned 1914/15 Star trio. Before being posted overseas he had been promoted then reverted to 2AM (Driver MT) on 4 March, 1915 and was never again promoted. Indeed in April, 1918 RAF Muster Roll he had been reduced further to 3AM (Driver).

SR15. F. B. ANWELL

Recalled for the duration of the war from 12 August, 1914. Initially 2AM with No. 1 Squadron. Served overseas from 2 March, 1915 earning 1914/15 Star trio. Promoted to Flight Sergeant (Fitter general) 1 July, 1916 and was Chief Mechanic (Fitter general) in April, 1918 RAF Muster Roll.

SR16. A. H. HOOD

Recalled for the duration of the war from 12 August, 1914 but as 2AM discharged 17 August, 1914 as unfit.

SR17. SAMSON REGINALD BROWN

Recalled for the duration of the war from 13 August, 1914. Initially was 2AM with No. 1 Squadron. No record of entitlement to either 1914 or 1914/15 Stars has been traced. Promoted Flight Sergeant (Fitter MT) 1 January, 1918 and was Chief Mechanic (Fitter MT) in April, 1918 RAF Muster Roll. Appointed WO *w.e.f.* 1 December, 1933. On 22 September, 1937 was posted as an Accountant to Fighter Command HQ at Stanmore. He was the 84th Senior RAF WO in the March 1938 *A.F.L.* Commissioned in WW2 and promoted to Squadron Leader on 1 December, 1941 (*vide* 1944 *A.F.L.*).

SR18. H. WARBOYS

Recalled for the duration of the war from 13 August, 1914. Initially 2AM with Reserve Aeroplane Squadron. No record of entitlement to either 1914 or 1914/15 Stars has been traced. As a Flight Sergeant he was mentioned in despatches in *L.G.* 21 February, 1917. He is listed in the *Times* 'B' Press Releases of 27 March, 1917 and 29 August, 1919. Promoted Temp SM (T) 1 September, 1917 and was Ch Mr Mech (Technical) in April, 1918 RAF Muster Roll.

★ SR19. W. A. LAWRENCE

Recalled for the duration of the war from 13 August, 1914. Initially was 2AM with No. 1 Squadron. Posted overseas 6 October, 1914 and was thus only the fourth of these 25 Special Reservists to earn a 1914 Star (See Nos. SR2, SR5 and SR7). Promoted to Sergeant (Fitter engines) 1 February, 1918 and was Sergeant Mechanic (Fitter A.E.) in April, 1918 RAF Muster Roll.

SR20. J. BRAITHWAITE

Recalled for the duration of the war from 13 August, 1914. Initially 2AM with No. 1 Squadron. Nothing more has been traced of this airman.

SR21. B. D. CROSSLEY

Recalled for the duration of the war from 14 August, 1914. Initially was 2AM in No. 1 Squadron. Served overseas from 3 March, 1915 and earned 1914/15 Star trio. In the *RFC Communiqué No. 29* of 7 February, 1916 he is noted as an observer to Sergeant J. Noakes in 29 Squadron when they attacked on Aviatik in a BE2c. Promoted Sergeant (Fitter engines) 1 October, 1917 and was Sergeant Mechanic (Fitter AE) in April, 1918 RAF Muster Roll.

SR22. ERNEST LEOPOLD

Recalled for the duration of the war from 14 August, 1914. Initially was 2AM in No. 1 Squadron. Served overseas from 3 March, 1915 and earned a 1914/15 trio. Promoted Sergeant (Fitter MT) 1 August, 1917 and retained that rank and trade in April, 1918 RAF Muster Roll. Awarded RAF L.S.&G.C. as Flight Sergeant *w.e.f.* 14 August, 1932. Appointed Warrant Officer 1 May, 1935 and in July, 1935 was serving at RAF Odiham, Basingstoke with No. 13 (Army Co-operation) Squadron. Still serving in March, 1938. Not shown in 1941 (November) *A.F.L.*

SR23. H. I WILLIAMS

Recalled for the duration of the war from 14 August, 1914. Initially 2AM with No. 1 Squadron. Served overseas from 3 March, 1915 and earned a 1914/15 Star trio. Promoted Corporal (Tinsmith) 1 January, 1917 and was Corporal Mechanic (Tin. SMW) in April RAF Muster Roll.

SR24. W. R. SPENCER

Recalled for the duration of the war on 14 August, 1914. Initially was 2AM with No. 1 Squadron. Served overseas from 3 April, 1915, and earned 1914/15 Star trio. Promoted Sergeant (Coppersmith) 1 March, 1918 and retained that rank and trade in April, 1918 RAF Muster Roll.

SR25. H. M. THOMPSON

Recalled for the duration of the war on 15 August, 1914. Initially was 2AM with No. 1 Squadron. Served overseas from 3 March, 1915 and earned 1914/15 Star trio. Applied for a commission in October, 1917 but was refused. Promoted Sergeant (Fitter general) 1 March, 1918 and retained that rank and trade in April RAF Muster Roll.

When this bleedin' war is over,
No more soldierin' for me.
When I gits mi civvy clo's on,
Oh, 'ow 'appy I will be.
No more church parades on Sundays,
No more askin' for a pass,
You can tell the Sergeant-Major,
To stick it up 'is bloody arse!

Appendix 1

Statistics

For those interested in statistics, the following figures are listed:—

1. Of the 1426 men on the roll (including two with No. 555), 138 had left the Corps prior to the outbreak of WW1. Some had died, some had been killed accidentally, some had bought themselves out, some were court martialled and some discharged with ignominy. Some had deserted, some discharged as unfit and some transferred to other units. Some had simply disappeared from the records.

2. Of the balance of 1288 men, 812 were awarded a 1914 Star for service with the original BEF, and 254 of these were also awarded a bar. (NB, the official figure is given as 755 O.R.'s) In addition, 158 men were also awarded a 1914 Star for service in later drafts in September, October and November including 31 who were awarded bars.

3. Later 157 men earned 1914/15 Stars, making a total of 1127 men with trios. It is not known how many of the balance of 161 earned a British War Medal and a Victory Medal.

4. The following casualties have been noted:—

> 26 were killed in action
> 25 were accidentally killed
> 1 was drowned
> 23 died
> 7 died of wounds
> 1 died of self inflicted wounds
> 33 others were wounded
> 16 became prisoners of war
> At least six others were injured in flying accidents and four were injured in traffic accidents.

5. During the War men left the Corps for a variety of reasons besides those who were fatalities:—

> 10 transferred to other units

4 were discharged with ignominy

5 were discharged as unfitted for the duties of the corps

42 were discharged as 'sick,' 'unfit' or 'no longer physically fit for war service'.

1 was discharged 'time served'

1 deserted.

6. When one hears of the early RFC, one thinks of aircrew and it is interesting to note that at least 126 of these men are noted as pilots and another 83 are known to have been observers, aerial gunners or aerial photographers, but there would certainly have been many who would have seen 'unofficial' aerial action.

7. A very large number of these first RFC men rose to become Sergeant Majors or Warrant Officers, 305 during WW1, another 59 between the wars and two (No. 36 T. A. Grou and No. 799 C. H. Tuting) in WW2.

8. Many of these SMs and WOs (and others who were not appointed to Warrant rank) were subsequently commissioned. 199 in fact during WW1, another 46 between the wars, and a further 18 during WW2.

9. It was unexpected to find that so many of these men were commissioned to such high ranks:—

3 Air Vice Marshals:	271	Storrer C.B.E.
	414	Thorne C.B. C.B.E.
	640	Laing K.C.B. C.B.E.
4 Air Commodores	4	Fletcher C.M.G. C.B.E. M.C.
	307	Archibold C.B.E.
	776	Fawley C.B. C.B.E.
	1027	Rapley C.B.E. (M.S.M.)
10 Group Captains	71	Strugnell M.C. & bar
	107	Bruce O.B.E.
	174	McCrea M.B.E.
	177	Winch
	242	Attwood
	304	Mayes O.B.E. D.S.M. A.F.M. & bar
	334	Laws C.B. C.B.E.
	716	Millett O.B.E.
	1053	Knight (RAF L.S.&G.C.)
	1071	Wood C.B.E. (M.S.M.)

and at least 36 Wing Commanders (of whom 19 had RAF L.S.&G.C. medals and one an Army L.S.&G.C. medal).

10. Continuing on the subject of honours and awards we have noted the following earned by these men:—

2	Victoria Crosses (V.C.)
1	Knight Commander of the Bath (K.C.B.)
3	Commanders of St. Michael and St. George (C.M.G.)
11	Commanders of the Order of the British Empire (C.B.E.)
20	Officers of the Order of the British Empire (O.B.E.)
26	Members of the Order of the British Empire (M.B.E.)
1	Distinguished Service Order & bar (D.S.O.)
1	Distinguished Service Order (D.S.O.)
2	Military Crosses & bar (M.C.)
10	Military Crosses (M.C.)
4	Air Force Crosses (A.F.C.)
30	Distinguished Conduct Medals (D.C.M.)
34	Military Medals (M.M.)
3	Distinguished Service Medals (D.S.M.)
1	Distinguished Flying Medal (D.F.M.)
1	Air Force Medal & bar (A.F.M.)
7	Air Force Medals (A.F.M.)
1	British Empire Medal (B.E.M.) (1st type)
3	British Empire Medals (B.E.M.) (2nd type)
1	Royal Victorian Medal
160	Mentions in Despatches or Brought to Notice in the *Times*
16	Queen's South Africa Medals (Q.S.A.)
3	King's South Africa Medals (K.S.A.)
2	China 1900 Medals
970	1914 Star trios
158	1914/15 Star trios
42	Indian General Service Medals
26	General Service Medals
1	African General Service Medal
3	1911 Coronation Medals
67	1935 Silver Jubilee Medals
21	1937 Coronation Medals
	plus unaccounted numbers of WW2 Stars and medals, and
3	Naval L.S.&G.C. Medals
18	Army L.S.&G.C. Medals
38	Army Meritorious Service Medals (M.S.M.)
46	RAF Meritorious Service Medals (M.S.M.)
234	RAF L.S.&G.C. Medals
3	Belgian Orders of Léopold

4	Belgian Croix de Guerre
21	French Médailles Militaire
1	French Médaille d'Honneur
7	French Croix de Guerre
1	Russian Cross of St. George
5	Russian Medals of St. George
2	Russian Medals of St. Stanislas
1	Serbian Medal of Karageorge
1	Rumanian Barbatie Si Credenta
1	Khedive's Sudan Medal (1910)
2	British Red Cross Society Medals for the Balkan Wars.

Thus 293 honours and awards were made for gallantry and distinguished and meritorious service to officers and men, plus 160 'mentions' of various kinds, and in addition 254 medals were given for long service. Or, with the Jubilee and Coronation Medals, nearly 800 awards to a force of 1288 men, not counting around 3750 campaign medals and stars!

11. In addition to the 'early birds' listed on this roll a number of men enlisted after the war started and were still in time to serve in France and earn a 1914 Star trio. The following have been traced as extant:—

1409	Nash	1914 Star trio (2AM/F.Sgt RFC)
1504	Spargo	D.C.M., 1914 Star, Victory medal and Plaque
1523	Harrison	1914 Star trio
1576	Hall	1914 Star trio, Army M.S.M.
1689	Robarts	M.C., D.F.C., D.C.M., 1914 Star trio, General Service Medal (Kurdistan)

D.C.M. 14 January, 1916 to 'Corporal Royal Flying Corps. For consistent good work as an observer. In September when certain photographs were urgently required, and the clouds were very low, he took the photographs under heavy fire.

M.C. London Gazette 3 March, 1917. '2nd Lieut. Temp. Lieut. Royal Sussex Regiment and Royal Flying Corps. For Conspicuous gallantry in action; he three times dispersed an enemy working party with bombs and machine gun fire from a height of 1000 feet. On another occasion, he shot down an enemy machine. He has shown great determination on many occasions in taking photos under most difficult and trying conditions.'

D.F.C. London Gazette 25 May 1926. 'Flight Lieut., M.C. D.C.M. For gallant and distinguished services during operations in Iraq, Sept.—Nov. 1924' (No. 14 Squadron).

Royal Flying Corps Communiqué No. 14

'Oct. 10th, 1915—Lt. Johnson and Cpl. Roberts of 3 Sqn., in a Morane armed with a rifle, when doing photography over Hulluch at 2.15 p.m. were attacked by a hostile aeroplane which approached close behind them unseen and fired about 20 rounds from a machine-gun hitting Cpl. Roberts in three places. The Morane then returned to our lines.' As observer, Corporal Roberts would have the use of the rifle.

Royal Flying Corps Communiqué No. 56

'Oct. 1st. 1916—Lt. Roberts and Lt. Jones, 3 Sqn., when taking photographs, were attacked by 7 Rolands. The attack was driven off with the assistance of two F.E.s who joined the fight. One of the Rolands, apparently hit by fire from one of the F.E.s, fell in a nose dive and crashed.' Roberts, now commissioned, had gained his wings and, as a pilot, was still serving with No. 3 Sqn.

Ninety-two D.C.M.s were awarded to members of the RFC and Empire Air Forces, of which only 34 were air awards.

Three D.F.C.s were awarded during 1926.

1719	Walston	1914 Star (F/Sgt)
1725	Stott	1914 Star trio
1922	Winter	1914 Star trio (2AM/Pte RFC)
1934	Tugwell	1914 Star trio and plaque
?	Ashford	1914 Star trio (AM RFC/Cpl RAF)
?	Rockwell	1914 Star & bar trio

Appendix 2

Royal Aero Club Certificates

The Royal Aero Club issued certificates for Aviators (i.e aeroplane pilots), Aeronauts (i.e. balloonists) and Airship pilots. Each of these lists started at No. 1.

We have traced the vast majority of these early flyers' certificates for men in this roll, but a few are missing. It may be that they leant to fly in the RFC and did not apply for a civilian certificate.

RFC		RAeC	RFC		RAeC
No.		No.	No.		No.
4	Fletcher	519	151	Wilson	3883
7	Thomas	276	152	James	864
8	Unwin	862	153	Warran	748
9	Jillings	1178	156	Wright	456
10	Waddington	573	158	Dunville	5144
11	Baxter★	(98)	159	Jarvis	524
12	Measures	520	166	O'Giollagain	1299
13	Lanman★	(9/23)	167	May	863
16	Barnes★	(14/28)	174	McCrae	691
19	Vagg	443	178	Gardiner	707
20	McGrane★	861 (12/26)	185	Higginbottom	317
22	Stafford	438	186	McNamara	445
24	Scovell★	(13/27)	188	Copper	674
26	Ridd	227	190	Dismore	580
52	Hobby	757	191	Webb	1330
53	Jerrard	538	196	Rose	964
61	McCudden	269	206	Cardno	??
64	Mullen	522	207	Power	838
67	Protheroe★	(36/21)	208	Hunter	137
71	Strugnell	253	224	Street	439
91	Butt	673	238	Pratt	541
92	Wilson	232	239	Burtenshaw	3894
93	Maskery	3273	242	Attwood	4259
102	Robins	793	247	Bateman	712
107	Bruce	467	251	Kemper	444
109	Collis	412	254	Porter	549
144	Smith	579	263	Robbins	464
RFC		RAeC	RFC		RAeC

No.		No.	No.		No.
269	Parker	850	944	Bird	2617
270	Mead	475	957	Patterson	677
271	Storrer	??	958	Eddington	4465
276	Weare	??	959	Gude	4461
290	Cox	3160	960	Stronach	2252
303	Mepstead	??	966	Piercey	1842
305	Surman	4434	973	McCleery	4971
315	Sharpe	1247	983	Brassington	4260
319	Lovick	583	986	Beadle	5126
328	Smith	1412	1018	Rogers	5800
332	Roberts	4670	1061	James	4380
346	Keegan	1071	1128	Gardner	5036
351	Carlisle	1619	1130	Russell	3482
359	Dewbery	4182	1143	Sanderson	??
363	Drumm	5609	1166	Commerford	4295
489	Locker	775	1197	Tollerfield	??
494	Judge	855	1210	Chapman	1711
517	Perry	1620	1224	Bastable	3884
524	Darvill	2772	1232	Hargreaves	1887
596	Adams	3172	1267	Holland	3385
626	Moody	3889	1270	Nicholls	??
635	Veitch	??	1275	Bennett	3726
639	Yates	??	1302	Luck	3767
641	Paterson	1452	1312	Bromley	3350
672	Dobbie	5802	1333	Lloyd	3693
711	Quick	3890	1369	Turner★★	66
718	Hellyer	??	1370	Carr★★	504
751	Farrer	685	1371	Chambers★★	168
759	Reffell	1259	1372	Dunn★★	1372
769	Stephenson	??	1376	Scholefield★★	FR819
839	Beard	??	1377	Lillywhite	720
856	Halstead	4462	1378	Barrs	749
892	McCudden	2745	1384	Edgington	??
901	Mitchell	701	1387	Frost	2828
917	Shaw	3386	1389	Cooper	3978
932	Bowers	3960	1393	Barnard	??
934	Dobson	1587	1396	Mottershead	??
RFC		RAeC			

★Aeronauts' and Airship Certificate
★★Air Battalion Reserve

For most of these men a photograph exists in the records of the RAF Museum at Hendon in their files of Royal Aero Club Aviators' Certificates. Some have been removed and some are not suitable for reproduction. The better ones are included in the text.

Abbreviations used in Appendices 3 & 4

11	George V Coronation Medal
14	1914 Star
14/15	1914-1915 Star
35	1935 Silver Jubilee Medal
37	Coronation Medal
39/45	1939-1945 Star
	Other dates refer to dated bars
AFC	Air Force Cross
AFM	Air Force Medal
AGSM	Africa General Service Medal
AS	Africa Star
(B)	Belgium
BEM	British Empire Medal
CB	Companion of the Order of the Bath
CBE	Commander of the Order of the British Empire
CdG	Croix de Guerre (France if not stated otherwise)
CSG	Cross of St. George (Russia)
D	Defence Medal
DCM	Distinguished Conduct Medal
DFM	Distinguished Flying Medal
DSM	Distinguished Service Medal
DSO	Distinguished Service Order
(F)	France
GSM	General Service Medal
IGSM	India General Service Medal
KSA	King's South Africa Medal
KSM	Khedive's Sudan Medal (Egypt)
LS&GC	Long Service & Good Conduct Medal
MBE	Member of the Order of the British Empire
MC	Military Cross
MdH	Médaille d'Honneur (France)
Méd Mil	Médaille Militaire (France if not stated otherwise)
MM	Military Medal
MSG	Medal of St. George (Russia)
MSM	Meritorious Service Medal
MZ	Medal of Zeal (Russia)
OBE	Officer of the Order of the British Empire
OL	Order of Léopold (Belgium)
QSA	Queen's South Africa Medal
(R)	Russia
SDI	Southern Desert Iraq
SS	Medal of St. Stanislas (Russia)
V	Victory Medal
VC	Victoria Cross
W	British War Medal (WWI)
W2	War Medal (WWII)

Appendix 3

Extant Medals of 118 Men in the Roll

3	Ramsey	MC QSA 14 W V
4	Fletcher (A/Comm)	CMG CBE MC 14 W V D W2
5	Moore	14/15 (QSA W V Army LS&GC (E VII) RAF MSM MdH Barbatie si Credenta (Rumania) all missing)
10	Warrington	OBE QSA 14 W V
11	Baxter	QSA KSA 14 W V D Army LS&GC
13	Lanman	AFC MBE QSA 14 W V RN LS&GC
18	Cullen	QSA 14 W V D Army LS&GC
22	Stafford	MC DCM China 14/15 W V Army LS&GC El Nahda (Hedjaz)
30	Jones	QSA 14 W V RAF MSM RAF LS&GC Karageorge
34	Little	14 W V RAF LS&GC
38	Attree	14/15 W V IGSM (W25) RAF LS&GC
40	*Bolt	14 W V RAF LS&GC
41	Breading	14 W V RAF LS&GC
60	Marchment	V
62	McClenaghan	14/15 W V D RAF LS&GC
79	Preen	14 W V RAF LS&GC
95	*Shelton	14 W V GSM (K) RAF LS&GC
104	Nethey	MM QSA (CC) 14 W V
123	Lee	14 W V GSM (SDI) 35 RAF LS&GC
130	*Bell	14 W V D W2 35 37 RAF LS&GC
142	McEvoy	14 W V
152	James	MBE 14 W V D W2 RAF MSM RAF LS&GC Méd Mil (F)
157	Bannister	14/15 W V
169	Baker	14 W V D W2 RAF LS&GC
170	Dangerfield	14
178	Gardiner (W/Comm)	14/15 W V 39/45 D W2 Army MSM
181	Chambers	14 W V 39/45 AS D W2 35 RAF LS&GC
196	Rose	14 W
209	Metz	14 W V Army MSM RAF LS&GC
212	Sladden	MBE DCM 14/15 W V KS (D 16)
219	Raynbird	14 W V
230	Rowe	14 W V IGSM (Afg, W, W) RAF LS&GC
241	*Carter	DCM 14 W V
242	Attwood (G/Capt)	14/15 W V GSM (K) A D W2
243	Carlyle	14 W
254	Porter	MBE DCM 14 W V

255	Haywood	DCM 14 W V Army MSM
269	Parker	14 W V IGSM (Afg and W 19/20) Méd Mil
272	Kelly	14 W V RAF LS&GC
283	Hart	14 W V
288	White	14
296	Hoffman	14 W V RAF LS&GC Army MSM (GVI)
297	Angell	14 W V D W2 Méd Mil
317	Beard	14 W V D W2 RAF LS&GC & bar
318	Dusting	14/15 W V 35 RAF LS&GC
320	James	MM
330	Knight	14/5 W V
337	*Bullen	14 W V 35 RAF LS&GC
339	Willis	14 W V 35 RAF LS&GC
343	Winter	14 W V IGSM (W 19/21) RAF LS&GC
350	Richardson	14 W V
361	Curtis	14 W V 35 RAF LS&GC
370	Wollaway	14 W V D W2 RAF MSM
387	Browning	MM 14 W V D W2 R/A LS&GC Army MSM (GVI)
413	Collett	MM 14/15 W V
422	Littlejohn	MM 14 W V
428	Brown	14 W V RAF LS&GC
476	Strickland	14 W V
505	Edwards	14 W V 35 RAF LS&GC
525	Marchmont	14 W V
557	Harris	14 W V GSM (K)
578	Hammond	14 W V
582	Bowyer	14
596	Adams	14 W V
598	Lednor	14
619	Bowles	14/15 W V 35 RAF LS&GC
632	Cummins	14 W V Army MSM
642	Allen	14 W V
660	Harrison	14 W V 35 RAF LS&GC
727	*Asprey	14
737	Greener	14 W V IGSM (Waz 25) D W2 35 37 RAF LS&GC
741	Hall	14
746	Spallen	14 W V
755	Bates	GSM (K) D W2 RAF MSM RAF LS&GC
776	Fawdry (A/Comm)	CB CBE 14 W V D W2 35
780	Hepple	BEM (GV) 14 W V GSM (I) IGSM (NWF '30/1) D W2 35 Army MSM RAF LS&GC
799	Tutting	14 W V D W2
815	Hallett	14 W V RAF LS&GC
877	Fraser	(Missing 14 W V) IGSM (W 19/21 Mahsud)
910	Pegg	MBE W V D W2 35 RAF LS&GC & bar
943	Robinson	14 V RAF MSM
948	Lodge	14
950	Bunting	(Missing 14 W V) AGSM (Som 20) Army MSM

957	Patterson	MBE 14 W V 39/45 Star D W2 Army LS&GC Army MSM CdG (B)
960	Stronach	MBE 14 W V CdG (F)
964	Brereton	MBE AFC 14/15 W V D W2 RAF LS&GC
976	Faldon	14 W V
979	Shrewsbury	14 W V D
980	Watkins	Army MSM(GVI) (Missing QSA KSA 14/15 W V Army LS&GC MZ)
1021	Macklam	14 W V
1025	Hawley	(14 W V missing) Army MSM
1043	King	14 W V
1047	Churchill	14
1049	Hanley	14 W V
1076	Grennan	OBE 14 W V Afr D W2 RAF LS&GC
1082	*Jameson	MC DCM 14 W V Méd Mil
1087	Brown	W V Army MSM
1121	Harland	14 W V
1135	Fox	14 W V
1165	Campbell	14
1193	Kirwin	14
1196	Waitt	MM
1199	Riding	14
1201	Bardsley	14 W V
1202	Burden	14 W V
1205	Stiles	14 W V
1216	Ramsden	(14 W V missing) IGSM (Afg and Waz) (RAF LS&GC missing)
1221	Golding	14/15 W V Army MSM
1267	Holland	14/15 W V Army MSM
1307	Hawkins	14 W V Plaque
1330	Sweeting	14/15 W V Army MSM
1343	West	14 W V
1345	Tansley	14 W
1346	Hunnisett	14 W V
1351	Robertson	14/15 W V GSM (K) RAF LS&GC
1370	*Carr	14 (AFC DCM W V missing)
1374	Jappe	W V Army MSM
1376	*Scholefield	AFC DCM 14/15 W V
SR 8	Ross	14/15 W V

*   In the RAF Museum Collection

Appendix 4

Other Medal Entitlements

(WW1 medals with RAF LS&GC only are excluded)

2	Starling (L/Col)	QSA KSA 14 W V Army LS&GC
6	Squires	AFC QSA 14 W V Army LS&GC
7	Thomas	MC 14 W V
8	Unwin (W/Comm)	OBE 14 W V Méd Mil.
9	Jilling	MBE MC 14 W V D W2
12	Measures (W/Comm)	CBE 14 W V D W2 Méd Mil
14	Edwards	14 W V Army LS&GC
15	Hughes	DCM 14 W V Army LS&GC
17	Mallet	14 W V Army LS&GC
20	McGrane	China 14 W V RN LS&GC
23	Wilkinson	14 W V GSM (K) RAF MSM RAF LS&GC
24	Scovell	AFC QSA RN LS&GC
25	Goodchild	14 W V SS
28	Hatchett	QSA 14 W V RAF LS&GC
29	Taylor	14 W V RAF LS&GC Méd Mil
36	Grou	14/15 W V D W2 RAF LS&GC
37	Arvoy	DSM 14 W V
39	Bell	QSA 14/15 W V Army LS&GC
48	Graham	14/15 W V 11 Army LS&GC
54	Jones	DCM MM 14 W V RAF LS&GC & bar
59	Longhurst	14 W V Army MSM
63	Lewis	14 W V Army MSM
64	Mullen	14 W V Army MSM
65	Nash	14 W V IGSM (W 21/24) RAF LS&GC
71	Strugnell (G/Capt)	MC & bar 14 W V D W2 35 37
80	Fowles	W V Army MSM
83	Harrison	QSA 14 W V
84	Powell	14 W V Méd Mil
85	Price	DSM 14 W V
90	Carden	14 W V RAF MSM RAF LS&GC
96	Hills	14 W V 11
101	Pead	14 W V 11
106	Langfield	14 W V Army MSM RAF LS&GC
107	Bruce (G/Capt)	OBE 14 W V
112	Jenkins	14 W V Méd Mil
116	Bullock	MM 14 W V

118	Hillier (W/Comm)	14 W V
119	Nicholls	14 W V Army LS&GC
120	Sharp	W V Army MSM
122	Ware (W/Comm)	14 W V D W2 35 RAF LS&GC
126	Waeland	14 W V RAF MSM
128	Turner	14/15 W V RAF MSM
132	Bullen	OBE 14 W V Méd Mil
135	Macrostie	MBE 14 W V D W2
136	Green	DCM 14 W V Army MSM
138	Street	14 W V Méd Mil
140	Hare	14/15 W V IGSM (Afg/NWF'19)
145	Ramplin	14 W V GSM (I) RAF MSM RAF LS&GC
147	Mountford	DCM 14 W V
148	Jenkins	14 W V GSM (K) RAF LS&GC Méd Mil
159	Jarvis	14/15 W V RAF MSM RAF LS&GC
161	Bryant (W/Comm)	14 W V D W2
167	May	14 W V RAF MSM RAF LS&GC
168	Woolsey	MM 14 W V RAF LS&GC
173	Payne	14 W V CdG (B)
174	McCrae (G/Capt)	MBE 14 W V 35 37
175	Martin	14 W V RAF MSM RAF LS&GC OL (B) C de G (B)
177	Winch (G/Capt)	14 W V D W2
180	Holder	14 W V IGSM (NWF 30/31) RAF LS&GC
181	Chambers	14 W V D W2 RAF LS&GC
188	Copper	W V D W2 35 RAF MSM RAF LS&GC
190	Dismore	14 W V OL (B)
198	Whilton	DCM 14/15 W V Army MSM
203	Brockbank	MBE 14 W V
208	Hunter	OBE 14 W V FC d G
210	Glidden	14 W V RAF MSM Méd Mil
211	Fidler (W/Comm)	DCM 14 W V D W2
213	Davis	14/15 W V Army MSM
215	Kerr	14 W V RAF MSM RAF LS&GC
217	Newton (W/Comm)	MBE 14 W V Army MSM RAF LS&GC
220	Cummins	14 W V D W2 35 RAF LS&GC
224	Street	14 W V Méd Mil
229	Jones	MBE 14 W V
232	Billing	14 W V RAF MSM
235	Scott	DCM 14 W V
245	Lindon	MBE 14/15 W V
246	Baker	MBE 14/15 W V D W2 35 RAF MSM RAF LS&GC
248	Woods	14 W V Army LS&GC
251	Kemper	MBE 14 W V Méd Mil
252	Martin	MM 14 W V RAF MSM
253	Smyrk	14 W V Army MSM
256	Norman	14 W V D W2 RAF LS&GC & bar
266	Aspinall	14 W V Army MSM RAF LS&GC

270	Mead (W/Comm)	CBE MC 14 W V
271	Storrer (AVM)	CBE 14 W V D W2
275	Kirk	14 W V IGSM (Afg)
276	Weare	MM 14/15 W V
278	Brown	14 W V 35
279	King	DCM 14 W V
282	Punter	14 W V D W2 35 RAF LS&GC
289	Collett	14/15 W V IGSM (NWF 30/31) RAF LS&GC
290	Cox	AFM 14 W V
291	Clark	14 W V Army MSM
299	Bell	MM 14 W V
301	McAllister	14 W V IGSM (W 21/24) RAF LS&GC
304	Mayes (G/Capt)	OBE DSM AFM & bar 14 W V D W2 37
306	Tindale	DCM 14 W V RAF LS&GC
307	Archibold (A/Comm)	CBE 14 W V D W2 35
313	Attrill	14 W V GSM (I) RAF MSM RAF LS&GC
319	Levick (W/Comm)	OBE
320	James	MM 14 W V RAF MSM RAF LS&GC
321	Jarman	14 W V RAF MSM
327	Jukes	MBE 14/15 W V Army LS&GC
328	Smith	MM 14 W V
333	Baughan	DCM 14 W V IGSM (W 21/24) RAF LS&GC
334	Laws (G/Capt)	CB CBE 14 W V D W2
335	Darke	MM 14/15 W V
340	Kerchey	14 W V D W2 35 RAF LS&GC
346	Keegan	OBE MM 14 W V
347	Webb	14 W V Army MSM
348	Bethell	14 W V Army MSM RAF LS&GC
349	Whenman	14 W V 35 RAF MSM RAF LS&GC
351	Carlisle	MM 14 W V
354	Griggs	DCM 14 W V RAF LS&GC MSG (R)
356	Bibby	14 W V GSM (SDI) RAF LS&GC
364	Thornton	MM 14 W V D W2 RAF LS&GC MSG (R)
377	Williams	14 W V 35 RAF LS&GC
381	Chandler	14 W V IGSM (Afg)
385	Downes	14 W V D W2 35 RAF LS&GC
386	Garner	14 W V Méd Mil
390	Chandler	14 W V D W2 35 RAF LS&GC
393	Powell	MM 14 W V
399	Littlewood	14 W V 37
404	Prewitt	14 W V IGSM (W 19/21)
406	Pearce	14/15 W V D W2 35 37 RAF LS&GC
410	Springate	14 W V IGSM (W 19/21) D W2 35 RAF LS&GC
414	Thorne (AVM)	CB CBE 14/15 W V D W2
416	Chandler	14 W V IGSM (NWF 30/31) D W2 35 RAF LS&GC
426	Lang	MBE 14 W V
448	Bennett	DCM 14 W V
451	Bartlett	14 W V 35 RAF LS&GC

457	Hart (W/Comm)	MBE 14 W V IGSM (W 19/21) D W2
461	Young	14 W V RAF MSM
466	Hemming	14 W V IGSM (W 19/21)
467	Smalley	14 W V RAF MSM
470	Piper	BEM (EIIR) 14 W V
472	Box	MBE 14 W V D W2 35 RAF LS&GC
479	Dobbins (W/Comm)	D W2 RAF LS&GC
484	Shimmons (W/Comm)	14 W V D W2 35 RAF LS&GC
485	Jackson (W/Comm)	14 W V D W2 RAF LS&GC
491	Bowker	MM 14 W V
498	Goldthorpe	14 W V 35 Army MSM RAF LS&GC
501	Thomas (W/Comm)	14 W V D W2 35 RAF LS&GC
504	Nunn	14 W V RAF MSM SS (R)
506	Ashby	MM 14 W V
509	Lee	14 W V RAF MSM
512	Ansdell	14 W V GSM (SDI) RAF LS&GC
517	Perry	AFM 14 W V
521	Powell	14 W V Méd Mil
526	Tomkins (W/Comm)	14/15 W V D W2
529	Coulter	14 W V D W2 35 RAF LS&GC
537	Goldsmith	14 W V 35 RAF MSM
545	Clayton	14 W V D W2 35 37 RAF LS&GC
546	Evans	14 W V Méd Mil
553	Beer	14 W V Méd Mil
555	Beer	14 W V GSM (I) IGSM (NWF '30/31) RAF LS&GC Méd Mil
558	Alcock	14 W V RAF MSM
565	Lake	14 W V RAF MSM
571	Laws	14 W V GSM (K)
579	Guttery (W/Comm)	MBE 14 W V D W2 RAF LS&GC
587	Caswell	14 W V D W2 35 RAF LS&GC
593	McIntyre	14 W V Méd Mil
603	Berry	14 W V GSM(I) RAF LS&GC
605	Felstead	DCM 14 W V Army MSM
607	Hyland	14 W V Army MSM
630	Stewart	14 W V IGSM (Afg) 35 37 RAF LS&GC
633	Root	14 W V D W2 35 RAF MSM RAF LS&GC
634	Smith	AFM 14 W V IGSM (Afg) 35
635	Veitch	14 W V CdG (F)
640	Laing (AVM)	KCB CBE 14 W V D W2 35 37
650	Drudge (W/Comm)	MBE 14 W V D W2
651	Cooper	14 W V IGSM (W 1925) RAF MSM RAF LS&GC
659	Condon	14/15 W V RAF MSM RAF LS&GC
662	Simpson	14 W V Army MSM
671	Harper	DCM 14 W V
682	Hannah	14/15 W V RAF LS&GC SS
684	Maynard	14 W V D W2 35 RAF LS&GC
685	Lewis	14 W V IGSM (Afg)
687	Graham	14 W V D W2 35 37 RAF LS&GC

713	Hogg	RAF MSM
714	Leech	DSO 14 W V
716	Millett (G/Capt)	OBE 14 W V 35
718	Hellyer	DCM 14 W V Army MSM
723	Gamon	DCM AFM 14 W V
731	Sutton	14 W V IGSM (Afg)
744	McQueen	14 W V RAF MSM
749	Baldwin	14 W V Balkan War Medal
753	Southgate	14 WW V IGSM (Mahsud) RAF MSM
759	Reffell	14 W V Méd Mil
760	Paice	14 W V IGSM (W 19/21) D W2 35 37 RAF LS&GC
766	Spencer (W/Comm)	OBE 14 W V D W2 35 RAF LS&GC
769	Stephenson	DCM 14 W V
772	Harris	14 W V Balkan WM
774	Barnes (W/Comm)	W V D W2 35 RAF LS&GC
777	Goodchild (W/Comm)	MBE 14 W V D W2
792	Smith	MM 14 W V 35 37 RAF LS&GC
794	Morrison	14 W V RAF LS&GC SS (R)
798	Lamdin	MBE 14/15 W V RAF LS&GC
808	Parker	MC 14 W V
811	Barker	14 W V GSM (K) RAF LS&GC
812	Brown	14 W V GSM (K) RAF LS&GC
814	Ellison	14 W V RAF LS&GC Fr CdG
820	Hamilton	MM 14 W V
823	Hollingworth	14 W V 35 37 RAF MSM RAF LS&GC
836	Paynter (W/Comm)	DCM 14 W V D W2
839	Beard	MM 14 W V
844	Salter	D W2 35 RAF LS&GC
845	Eley (W/Comm)	W V IGSM (Waz 19/21) D W2 35 RAF LS&GC
848	Squires (W/Comm)	OBE 14 W V D W2 35 RAF LS&GC
849	Holt	14 W V RAF MSM RAF LS&GC
856	Halstead	MM 14 W V
864	Bunting	14 W V GSM (I and NWP) RAF MSM
869	Clarke	MM 14 W V GSM (I)
873	Baker	GSM (K)
877	Frazer	14 W V IGSM (Afg Waz 21/24 and Mahsud)
886	Brobson	14 W V CdG (F)
891	Tindall/Eldridge	DCM 14 W V RAF LS&GC
892	McCudden	VC DSO & bar MC & bar MM 14 W V CdG (F)
897	Borrett	MM 14 W V RAF LS&GC
901	Mitchell	QSA 14 W V Army LS&GC
904	Taylor	14 W V Méd Mil
912	Inglis	AFM (GV 2nd) RAF LS&GC
923	Payne	MC 14/15 W V
931	Rumford	14 W V MSG (R)
942	O'Toole	14 W V RAF MSM
948	Lodge (W/Comm)	14 W V D W2 35 RAF MSM RAF LS&GC
953	Faulkner	14 W V GSM (K) 35 RAF LS&GC

958	Eddington	MM 14 W V
963	Wildbore	14 W V IGSM (Waz 25) RAF LS&GC
973	McCleery	AFM (GV 2nd) W V GSM (K) 35 RAF LS&GC CdG (F)
984	Wilford (W/Comm)	14/15 W V Army LS&GC
995	McAllister	14 W V IGSM (W and Mahsud)
1002	Panrucker	14 W V GSM (I)
1009	McArthur	14/15 W V GSM (I) RAF LS&GC
1014	Littleproud	BEM W V IGSM (NWF 30/31) D W2 35 37 RAF LS&GC
1015	Clark (W/Comm)	14/15 W V IGSM (Waz 21/24) D W2 35 37 RAF LS&GC
1018	Rogers	AFM 14/15 W V
1019	Beaumont	MBE 14 W V D W2 35 RAF LS&GC
1020	Donaldson	14/15 W V D W2 35 RAF LS&GC
1027	Rapley (A/Comm)	CBE 14 W V D W2 Army MSM
1028	Maxwell	14 W V RAF MSM
1031	Rogers	DCM 14/15 W V CSG (R)
1032	Dean	14/15 W V IGSM (30/31) 35 RAF LS&GC
1053	Knight (G/Capt)	14 W V D W2 35 RAF LS&GC
1056	Beard	14 W V IGSM (W21/24) RAF LS&GC
1058	David	14 W V IGSM (W21/24)
1062	Trevithick	14 W V IGSM (W21/24) D W2 35 RAF LS&GC
1071	Wood (G/Capt)	CBE 14 W V D W2 Army MSM
1088	Day (W/Comm)	14 W V D W2
1112	Fulton	14 W V Army MSM RAF LS&GC
1127	Goodwin	MM 14 W V
1145	Slingsby	MM 14 W V
1155	Coleman	MM W V
1160	Gee	14 W V GSM (SDI) RAF LS&GC
1161	Bowler	14 W V RAF MSM
1162	Parish (W/Comm)	14 W V D W2 RAF LS&GC
1169	Hudson	14 W V RAF MSM
1182	Hyde	MM 14 W V
1184	Scott	14/15 W V RAF MSM RAF LS&GC
1191	Petch	OBE 14 W V D W2
1194	Bradford	14 W V CdG (F)
1197	Tollerfield	MM 14 W V
1215	Honeybone	14 W V GSM (I) RAF MSM
1232	Hargreaves	DCM 14/15 W V
1242	Daniel	IGSM (30/31) RAF LS&GC
1257	Sillitoe (W/Comm)	14/15 W V D W2 RAF LS&GC
1265	McGregor	14/15 W V IGSM (Afg)
1269	Freemantle (W/Comm)	W V D W2 35 RAF LS&GC
1279	Wright	14/15 W V OL CdG (B)
1284	Parker	MBE 14 W V RAF LS&GC
1287	Tough	BEM (1st type) 14 W V D W2 35 RAF LS&GC
1289	Loughhead (W/Comm)	OBE 14 W V D W2 RAF LS&GC
1294	Nicholas (W/Comm)	OBE 14/15 W V D W2 RAF LS&GC

1305	Clark	MM 14/15 W V
1310	Beale	GSM (Iraq)
1315	Pearce (W/Comm)	14/15 W V D W2 37 RAF LS&GC
1321	Nicholls	14 W V IGSM (W 21/24) D W2 37 RAF LS&GC
1336	Baxter	DCM 14 W V
1344	Cockram	IGSM (Waz 25) RAF LS&GC
1349	Murton	DFM 14 W V IGSM (I) RAF LS&GC
1357	Barratt	AFM 14 W V
1382	Marshall	MBE W V RAF LS&GC
1389	Cooper	MC 14/15 W V
1392	Cockerell	OBE 14/15 W V
1396	Mottershead	VC DCM W V
1399	Lee	14 W V D W2 RAF LS&GC
1400	Haynes	14/15 W V 35 37 RAF LS&GC
SR4	Wheeler	14/15 W V D W2 RAF LS&GC
SR7	Wills	MM 14 W V

Appendix 5

Discharges from the R.F.C.
1912–14

During the period covered by this list, the regulations regarding other ranks leaving the army were codified in paragraph 392 of King's Regulations. The various reasons for a man's discharge, either at his own request or by order of the authorities, were itemised under twenty five sections, which specified the action to be taken, and stated which rank or appointment of officer was responsible for such action.

The sections which apply to men listed in this book were as follows:

iii.   Not likely to become an efficient soldier'. This was used in cases of mental or physical unsuitability.

v.   'Having claimed his discharge within three months of enlistment'. A recruit was entitled to a discharge on payment of £10. In 1914 this was increased to £18, and in July of that year to £30.

ix.   'Unfitted for the duties of the Corps'. A separate sub-section referred specifically to men in the R. F. C.

x.   'Having been convicted by the Civil Power'. *i.e.*, guilty of a civil offence, under civil law.

xii.   'Having been sentenced to penal servitude'.

xiii.   'Having been discharged with ignominy'. This heading could be used for men guilty of military crimes.

xiv.   'At his own request, on payment of —, under Art. 1130 (i) Pay Warrant'. This section referred to long-service men, (as opposed to recruits) who wished to leave the Army before the expiration of their period of enlistment.

xv.   A. 'Free after — year's service, under Art. 1130 (ii) Pay Warrant'. This section enabled men who had finished their long-term enlistment (usually 12 or 18 years), and who had re-engaged for a further short period, to leave the service at short notice.

xvi.   'No longer physically fit for war service'. This section was used for a man wishing to re-engage after completing a term of service.

xviii. 'At his own request after 18 years service, with a view to pension'. This section, unlike xv A, was to be used for a man eligible for a pension for long service and good conduct.

xxv.   'His services no longer required'. This section was used only for:—

1. Men who could not be discharged under any other section, and
2. Boys who were to be discharged for misconduct. Its vagueness was probably considered less detrimental to the boy's future employment prospects than any of the more specific reasons given in other sections.

Appendix 6

Non-Commissioned Ranks in the R.A.F. on 1 April, 1918

Although alterations were made at various later dates the R.A.F. began life with a system of three parallel sets of rank, viz., the Technical branch, the Disciplinary or General Duties branch, and the Clerical branch. Each had its own set of ranks, listed below with their daily rates of pay in April, 1918.

Technical		Disciplinary		Clerical	
Chief Master Mechanic	9/-	Sgt Major 1st Cl	7/6	—	—
Master Mechanic	8/-	Sgt Major 2nd Cl	6/9	Master Clerk	6/9
Chief Mechanic	7/-	Flight Sgt	3/10	Flight Clerk	5/6
Sgt Mechanic	6/-	Sgt	3/3	Sgt Clerk	4/9
Cpl Mechanic	5/-	Cpl	2/4	Cpl Clerk	4/-
Air Mechanic 1st Cl	4/-	Pte 1st Cl	1/8	Clerk 1st Cl	3/-
Air Mechanic 2nd Cl	3/-	Pte 2nd Cl	1/6	Clerk 2nd Cl	2/-
Air Mechanic 3rd Cl	2/-	—	—	Clerk 3rd Cl	1/8
		Boy	1/-		

(Plus, where appropriate, flying pay at 1/6 per day.)

Appendix 7

Establishment of the Air Battalion, R.E. in 1911

PEACE ESTABLISHMENT OF THE AIR BATTALION, R.E., IN 1911

Ranks	HQ	No. 1 Coy	No. 2 Coy	Total
Officers	10	2	2	14
Sgts and Above	19	3	2	24
Cpls and below	67	44	41	152
Total	96	49	45	190

WAR ESTABLISHMENT OF THE AIR BATTALION, 1911

Ranks	HQ	No. 1 Coy	No. 2 Coy	Total
Officers	3	8	18	29
Sgts	5	10	9	24
O/r's	66	199	115	380
Totals	74	217	142	433
	+17 OR attached	+22 OR attached	+12 OR attached	

(From AHB204/85/35)

494

The actual strength of the Air Battalion in April, 1912 is shown in 'Rates of Pay' as:—

	Dismounted	Mounted	Total
WO (Suptg Clk)	1	—	
Sgts	19	2	
Junior NCOs	23	6	
R and F	72	37	
Boys	6	—	
Totals	121	45	166

(AHB204/85/24)

Appendix 8

Establishment Strength of the Royal Flying Corps on its Formation in 1912

Ranks	HQ	No.1 Sqn (Airships & Kites)	2–4 Squns	Flying Depot	Total
C.O. (Lt Col.)	1				1
Sqn Commders		1	3	1	5
Flight Comdr (Major)	1	3	9	–	13
Flying Officers	–	7	75	–	82
Quarter Master	–	–	–	1	1
Total Officers	2	11	87	2	102
Warrant Officers	1	2	6	1	10
Sergeants	3	12	63	7	85
Sgt/Tailor	1	–	–	–	1
Total Sgts	4	12	63	7	86
1st Cl. Air Mechs	10	55	177	9	251
2nd Cl. Air Mechs	7	45	147	7	206
Total Rank and File	17	100	324	16	457
Totals	24	125	480	26	655

Appendix 9

Actual Establishment of the R.F.C. August, 1912

Ranks	HQ	No. 1 Sqn (Airships & Kite)	2–6 Sqns	Flying Depot	Total
C.O. (Lt Col)	1	—	—	—	1
Squad Comdr	1	1	5	1	8
Flight Commdrs	1	3	15	—	19
QM	1	—	—	—	1
Flying Officers	—	7	75	1	83
Total Officers	4	11	95	2	112
Warrant Officers	1	2	10	2	15
Sgt Tailor	1	—	—	—	1
Sgt Cook	1	—	—	—	1
Sgts	6	12	105	6	129
Total Sgts	8	12	105	6	131
1st Cl. Air Mechs	10	55	300	34	399
2nd Cl. Air Mechs	11	45	240	26	322
Total Rank and File	21	100	540	60	721
Totals	34	125	750	70	979

Appendix 10

Peace Establishment of the Royal Flying Corps, 1914-15

AIT 1/782/BOX   Document 204/4/501
(Number proposed in May, 1914)

Ranks	HQ	Aeroplane Squadrons	Aircraft Park	Total
Lt/Col (C.O.)	1	–	–	1
Majors (Sqn Comdrs)	1	8	1	10
Capts (Flt Comdrs)	2	24	2	28
Subs (Flying Offrs)	3	120	2	125
Q/M	1	–	–	1
Total Officers	8	152	5	165
Warrant Officers	1	16	2	19
Sgt/Tailor	1	–	–	1
Sgt/Cook	1	–	–	1
Fl/Sgts	2	40	2	44
Sgts	8	96	6	110
Total Sgts	12	136	8	156
Corporals	10	104	4	118
Ptes 1AM	32	360	35	427
2AM	47	423	30	509
Boys	–	32	3	35
Total Rank & File	89	928	72	1089
Total Numbers	110	1232	87	1429

Appendix 11

Notes on RFC Uniforms, Badges, etc.

UNIFORMS

In Photographs of other ranks, as with officers, taken after the formation of the RFC, one is struck by the wide variety of uniforms worn. Men are seen in both Naval and Army dress and in many of these early photographs the Army dress is usually standard khaki General Service tunic with brass buttons, and GS Cap with an RFC brass badge. The 'maternity jacket' appeared in 1913, worn (mostly) with a side cap, breeches and puttees. However, at Cody's funeral all ORs and NCOs are

in maternity jackets and GS cap. Mechanics seem to wear coveralls when working, and plimsols were also issued. Sergeant Majors did not appear to wear a Sam Browne pre-War, but see the photograph of 371 Sergeant Major Nash. Also issued in 1913 to about 12 Air Mechanics and NCOs on an experimental basis was an RFC walking out uniform, consisting of half-wellington boots, tight dark blue overalls down which ran a broad red stripe (*i.e.* Royal Engineers pattern), a light blue tunic, buttoned up to the neck, with crossed silver cords, and a dark blue peaked cap with a red band carrying the RFC badge. See page 19 for a variant of this on display in the RAF Museum at Hendon.

BADGES

In 1912, since the Military Wing of the RFC was a Part of the Army, standard sergeants' chevrons were issued, *i.e.* khaki on khaki. The brass, other ranks RFC cap badge was approved in *Army Order* 378 of 1913. About the same time the Royal Flying Corps shoulder flash, khaki on a black cloth background, also makes an appearance on the maternity jackets. Inverted khaki chevrons, each denoting satisfactory service, worn above the cuff of the left sleeve, were also the then-standard Army issue. Warrant Officers 1st Class are noted in early photographs wearing a brass crown on each cuff, not the Royal Cypher badge. In May, 1914, the ranks of Flight Sergeant and Corporal were introduced. Again standard Army chevrons indicated the rank, with the addition of a cloth crown above the three chevrons for the Flight Sergeant.

A four-bladed propeller had been introduced in 1913 to indicate that the wearer was a specialist, and in *Army Order* 322 of 1916 a two-bladed propeller was authorised for 1AMs who had qualified for the distinction by trade-testing, and were not eligible for promotion until they had passed.

AIRCREW

The pilots' 'wings' were designed by Generals Sykes and Henderson and approved by H.M. King George V in *A.O.* 40 of February 1913. The observers' badge was not introduced until September, 1915 under *A.O.* 327, initially for officers only but extended to all who qualified in November of that year.

Appendix 12

Principal References Consulted in the Public Record Office

AHB No.	AIR/1 No.	
15/9/169–173	75	5 Group Honours and Awards
15/161/1–178/1	173	Histories of 27–58 Sqdns
15/16/1	502	Increases in Establishment of Mil. Wing 1912–13
21/20/1–216	687, 696	Squadron Histories
21/100/1	725	Sir A Bannerman's Paper on the Air Battalion pre–1914
176/3/1	728	Names of balloons
199/7	733	Reports 1 to 26 by Royal Aero Club, on flying accidents
204/1/1	734	2 Squadron Mobilisation Scheme, 1914
204/2/1	737	3 Squadron Orders, Feb–Aug, 1914
204/2/18	738	3 Squadron Nominal Roll, 1914
204/2/28	739	1 Wing Routine Orders, Nov 1914–March 1916
204/2/29	740	HQ RFC Daily Routine Orders, Aug 1914–Dec 191
204/4/1	750	HQ Mobilisation Returns, 1913–14
204/4/125	758	HQ Personnel to France, Aug–Sep, 1914
204/4/278	771	4 Squadron Personnel to France, Aug 1914
204/4/305	772	4 Squadron Daily Orders, May 1914
204/4/306	772	4 Squadron Daily Orders, June 1914
204/4/377	775	French Decorations to RFC Sep–Nov 1914
204/4/480	780	HQ Airmen for BEF draft, Nov 1914
204/4/500	782	Report on accident to 2AM H. W. Carter
204/4/516	783	Report on accident to Sgt Campbell
204/4/593	787	Report on accident to 2AM Cudmore
204/4/596	787	Proposed establishment of boys, 1912–1914
204/4/613	788	French decorations to RFC, Sep–Dec 1914
204/4/804	793	Nominal rolls of airmen for course at CFS Sept. 1914
204/4/909	795	Boards for Sgt promotions 1913–14
204/4/1073	800	Nominal roll of NCOs holding pilots' certificates, July 1913–July 1914
204/4/1173	804	History of RFC 1910–July 1914
204/4/1187–1195	805–9	HQ Routine Orders, Jan 1913–Aug 1914

204/4/1254	812	Historical record of Balloon School (1907)
204/4/1255	813	Casualties and Communiqués Aug 1915–Jan 1916
204/4/1316	819	Muster Roll of airmen, 1st April 1918
204/5/141	826	Nominal roll of NCOs in 1, 4, 5, 6 and 7 Sqns, Aug 1914
204/5/169	827	Casualty Returns, March 1915
204/5/218–226	829–832	HQ Routine Orders, Aug 1914–Dec 1916
204/5/252–255	835	HQ Routine Orders, Nov 1917–1919
204/5/551–559	871–874	HQ Routine Orders, Jan 1916–Jun 1918
204/5/669	889	Accidental bomb explosion, March 1915
204/5/696–698	892	Lists of POW's in Germany, Turkey and Switzerland, 1916
204/5/857–870	914–916	Casualties, May 1916–Dec 1918
204/5/1097–1102	967–969	Flying casualties in France, June 1915 to April 1919
204/5/1216	993	Recommendations for awards, Oct 1915–Aug 1916
204/5/1433–1434	1030–1033	Honours and Awards, Mar 1916–Dec 1918
204/5/2398	1152	3 Bde recommendations for M.S.M. Dec 1918
204/5/2532	1163	Nominal rolls of pilots and observers, 1918
204/5/2592	1169	Foreign decorations, Nov 1917–April 1918
204/5/2630	1214	Pilots and Observers overseas, 1 Jan 1918
204/5/2634	1216–1228	Combat reports, by Sqns
204/11/171	1303	Casualty returns Feb 1915–Nov 1916
204/17/34	1324	1 Squadron Routine Orders, May 1912–Oct 1914
204/17/36	1325	1 Squadron Routine Orders June 1912–Apr 1913
204/17/38	1326	Daily Orders, Pt II, Jan 1913–Oct 1914
204/17/39–42	1326–1327	Daily Orders, Pt II, July 1913–Dec 1914
204/17/68–78	1336–1338	1 Squadron Daily Routine Orders 1914–1918
204/85/9	1607	Mobilisation rolls, officer and men, 1910–1912
204/85/24	1608	Rates of pay of Air Battalion., Apr 1912, (with roll of surnames and Rank)
204/85/34	1608	Peace and War Establishment of Air Battalion
204/99/12	1666	Nominal roll, all ranks, S Russia 1919–20
204/99/13	1666	Nominal roll, officers, S Russia 1919–20
204/120/52	1690	16 Wing (Salonika) Casualty reports 1917–18
204/246/19	1940	Casualty list, Jan 1915
204/260/12	1957	Recommendations for honours, S Russia 1919–20
209/3/206–208	2150	Casualty returns May–Nov 1915
223/25/3–12	2318	Despatches Sep 1914–Jan 1920 (Printed) with MID's to 1916
306/1	2432	Aviators' Certificates granted by Royal Aero Club, Dec 1914–Apr 1916
WO330/1 & 2		1911 Coronation Medal Roll

Appendix 13

'B' Press Releases in The Times

In the Journal of OMRS, Summer 1978, Major Sainsbury published an excellent and comprehensive account of these lists.

Briefly the Government in the First World War wanted an honour such as the 'mentioned in despatches' for civilians and for troops in non-operational areas (mainly the United Kingdom), but there being no despatches in which such names could appear, instituted the 'A' (Gazetted) lists and the 'B' (Press) lists.

The 'A' lists appeared in the *London Gazette* exactly like the mentions in despatches and entitled the persons listed to wear an oak leaf on their Victory Medal (if they had one for some operational service).

The 'B' lists did not usually appear in the *London Gazettes* and did not entitle those listed to wear an oak-leaf, and (for officers) were not mentioned in their records of service in their personal entries in Army Lists.

Other ranks had the award noted on their service papers, as a sort of second grade M.I.D.

The phrase almost always used in the *Times* is:— 'The following names have been brought to notice for services in connection with the War' except for a couple of short lists which start 'Services in connection with the Air Defences of the U.K.'

On a few occasions men listed in these pages were mentioned both in the *London Gazette* and bought to notice in the *Times* at very close intervals. Perhaps these were 'duplications'?

Appendix 14

Bibliography

ABBOTT, P. E. and TAMPLIN, J. M. A. *British Gallantry Awards*

ADKIN, F. J. *From the Ground Up*. Airlife, England, 1983

BARING, M. *RFC HQ 1914-1918*. Bell 1920

BICKERS, R. T. *The First Great Air War*. Hodder and Stoughton, 1988

BOWYER, C. *AIRMEN OF W.W.I*

BOWYER, C. *For Valour – the Air VCs*

BURKES *Handbook to the most Excellent Order of the British Empire*. 1921

BURGE, Major C. Gordon, O.B.E. *The Annals of 100 Squadron*

BUTCHER, P. E. *Skill and Devotion*

COLE, Christopher. *RAF Communiqués 1918*

COLE, Christopher. *RFC Communiqués 1915-16*

COOMBS, Rose E. B. *Before Endeavours Fade*

CROOK, M. J. *Evolution of the Victoria Cross*. Ogilby Trust 1975

DALZELL, M. and L. *Mention in despatches roll W.O.'s N.C.O.'s and O.R.'s RFC and RAF*

DE LA FERTÉ, A.C.M. Sir Philip Joubert, K.C.B., C.M.G., D.S.O. *The Forgotton Ones*

—— *The Third Service*

FRANKS, N. L. R. *First in Indias Skies (31 Squadron RAF)*

HARVEY, W. F. J. *Pi in the Sky – 22 Squadron RFC*

ILLINGWORTH, Captain A. E. *A History of 24 Squadron RAF*

LEIGH, W. R. and JAMES, H. A. *Official History of the War: The War in the Air*. Clarendon Press 1922-7

LEWIS, C. S. *Sagittarius Rising*. Peter Davies, London, 1936

LIDDLE, P. H. *The Airmans War 1914-18*. Blandford Press 1987

McCUDDEN, J. B., V.C., D.S.O., M.C., M.M. *Flying Fury*. Aeroplane and General Publishing Co. 1918

McINNES, I. *M.S.M. to Aerial Forces*. Picton Publishing 1983

McKEE, Alexander. *The Friendless Sky*

MORRIS, Alan. *The Balloonatics*

NORRIS, G. *A History of the RFC*. Frederick Muller, London, 1965

ROLT, L. T. C. *The Aeronauts*

Scott, A. J. L. *Sixty Squadron R.A.F.* William Heinemann, 1928

TAYLOR, J. W. R. *CFS The Birthplace of Air Power*
WALKER, Percy B. *Early Aviation at Farnborough*
WALKER, R. *Distinguished Conduct Medals*
WEBB, J. V. *MCs to Warrant Officers 1915-1919.* 1989
Air Force Lists. 1918-1980
Cross and Cockade. 1970-1989
Flight
London Gazettes, 1911-1930
Official Directory of the Aldershot Command – October, 1913
ORDERS & MEDALS RESEARCH SOCIETY *Journals*
Regimental Roll of Officers who died in the War
Register of Service Deaths 1914-20. St Katherines House
Royal Aero Club *Year Books,* 1917–18–19
The Aeroplane
The Times Casualty Lists 1914-18
Times History of Great War
Who Was Who.

Index

735	Booker, A. J.	387	Browning, P.	351	Carlisle, T. F. B.
800	Boore, C. G.	107	Bruce, W. R.	243	Carlyle, N.
176	Booth, A. E.	1188	Brunning, L. F.	522	Carpenter, F. W.
581	Booth, H. W.	991	Bryant, J. H.	407	Carr, E. R.
897	Borrett, W. G.	161	Bryant, W. F.	1198	Carr, F. W.
832	Borst, F. C.	218	Buchan, G.	1370	Carr, R. H.
1052	Boston, T.	1000	Buchanan, G.	629	Carrington, H.
309	Bosworth, T.	204	Buckingham, J.	829	Carroll, T.
638	Bourne, A. R.	337	Bullen, G. E.	133	Carter, H. W.
1063	Bovett, W. T.	132	Bullen, T.	241	Carter, L. E.
819	Bovey, N. W. B.	1094	Bullimore, F.	783	Cartland, A. E.
932	Bowers, C. W. H.	804	Bullock, F.	543	Caslake, J. T.
491	Bowker, W. H.	116	Bullock, H.	587	Caswell, L. W. W.
1161	Bowler, L. F.	322	Bullock, H.	43	Caulfield, M.
619	Bowles, S. G.	150	Bullock, J.	1011	Chalfont, W. E.
802	Bowring, C. P.	677	Bullock, T. A.	1371	Chambers, C. F. M.
582	Bowyer, O. F. V.	646	Bulpitt, B. J.		
472	Box, A.	950	Bunting, C. E. H.	181	Chambers, I. F.
1119	Bradder, E. H.	864	Bunting, C. F. R.	390	Chandler, A. E.
1194	Bradford, A. J.	1202	Burden, A.	416	Chandler, C. H.
473	Braithwait, J.	733	Burdett, G. T.	381	Chandler, C. W.
SR20	Braithwait, J.	784	Burdett, S. V.	1210	Chapman, D. A. R.
1206	Brambley, W. J.	1261	Burlingham, A. E.		
983	Brassington, C. E.	762	Burns, F. L. B.	81	Chapman, F. S.
1066	Brazier, R.	100	Burns, W.	728	Chapman, G. S.
41	Breading, G. S.	519	Burt, C.	308	Chenney, F.
1283	Brebner, G.	239	Burtenshaw, W. J.	645	Chick, H. P.
964	Brereton, W.	423	Burton, F. A.	876	Chilton, J.
1060	Brewster, H.	286	Bush, E. M.	1142	Chilver, A.
717	Briant, L. F.	258	Bushell, C.	373	Chittenden, H. E.
1003	Bricknell, T. G.	463	Butcher, L. A. G.	561	Chittenden, W.
726	Bridges, W. J.	1175	Butcher, P. E.	44	Chivers, A.
443	Bright, R.	580	Butchers, C. E.	1047	Churchill, W.
42	Bright, T. H.	875	Butlin, A. H.	667	Clack, A. E.
584	Brittain, W. V.	91	Butt, W. H.	1235	Clack, W.
367	Britton, L. G.	838	Butterworth, H.	1299	Claridge, L. V.
824	Broadhurst, E. C.	1099	Byrne, B.	1015	Clark, A. R.
886	Brobson, R. G.			1108	Clark, C. H.
89	Brock, A. R.	295	Cairns, J. H.	447	Clark, E.
203	Brockbank, C. J.	477	Callingham, S. R.	1227	Clark, H. A.
1312	Bromley, C. P. J.	1124	Callus, V. J.	291	Clark, J. F.
1129	Brooks, S.	754	Calow, C.	1305	Clark, J. S.
1087	Brown, C. W.	445	Campbell, H.	199	Clark, T. W.
812	Brown, G.	1165	Campbell, H. G.	1146	Clarke, S.
926	Brown, G.	533	Candy, W. H. (Minter)	853	Clarke, W.
428	Brown, G. C.			847	Clarke, W. F.
405	Brown, R. G.	90	Carden, C. S.	869	Clarke, W. W.
SR17	Brown, S. R.	206	Cardno, A. S.	545	Claydon, W. A.
278	Brown, W.	697	Care, A. H.	82	Clayton, C. W.

682 Hannah, W.	466 Hemmings, A. B.	670 Holt, R.
654 Hanson, T. A.	1148 Hemsley, N.	1363 Hone, E. G.
748 Harben, H. J.	970 Henderson, L. U.	1288 Hone, R. J.
140 Hare, W. T.	1136 Henderson, N. G.	1215 Honeybone, J. W.
1308 Harfleet, F. W.	906 Henry, W. J.	SR16 Hood, A.
1232 Hargreaves, J. McK.	1359 Henstridge, J. F. C.	978 Hood, C.
1121 Harland, H. R.	780 Hepple, G. W.	374 Howard, E. E.
622 Harley, F. H.	362 Herbert, A.	499 Howell, E.
440 Harley, J. W.	1225 Herbert, H.	1236 Hudson, H.
1189 Harper, P. F.	921 Herrick, R.	1169 Hudson, J.
671 Harper, W.	1023 Hesketh, S.	77 Hudson, T. J.
1016 Harraway, W.	1353 Hiatt, G. A. H.	1244 Hughes, G. W.
1334 Harries, G. B.	975 Hiatt, H. J.	1092 Hughes, H. S.
486 Harrington, J. J.	1326 Hick, E. V.	831 Hughes, J.
772 Harris, C. C.	1208 Hickey, T. F.	15 Hughes, T.
866 Harris, C. J.	1077 Hickling, G.	1156 Hunnisett, G. W.
557 Harris, F.	185 Higginbottom, V. C.	1346 Hunnisett, J. E.
1226 Harris, H. J. R.	658 Higgs, H.	208 Hunter, A.
618 Harris, S. J.	264 Hill, A. C.	1219 Hunter, G. V.
660 Harrison, A.	300 Hill, C. H.	394 Hurdle, H.
1065 Harrison, B.	885 Hill, E. N.	129 Hurst, J.
987 Harrison, B.	981 Hill, R.	1358 Hutchinson, V. J.
83 Harrison, C. W.	919 Hill, S.	1182 Hyde, C. E.
550 Harrison, E. J.	1350 Hill, W.	607 Hyland, T.
622 Harrison, F. H.	118 Hilliar, G.	1274 Hynes *or* Hinds, R.
121 Harrison, G.	669 Hillier, S. C.	
50 Harrison, W. H.	96 Hills, F.	586 Ibbott, W. C.
1361 Harry, T.	913 Hills, W. H.	293 Ingleson, W.
1138 Hart, E.	1274 Hinds, R.	631 Inglis, D.
283 Hart, J.	51 Hinds, T. H. C.	912 Inglis, H. T.
457 Hart, W. W.	870 Hitchcock, S. J.	739 Ireland, T. E.
745 Hartnett, J. B.	549 Hobbs, A. A.	
955 Harvey, A. R.	52 Hobby, C. A.	214 Jack, H. D.
1100 Harvey, G. W. O.	403 Hobson, A. E.	1163 Jackson, C.
968 Harvey, W. H.	971 Hockley, F.	485 Jackson, E. D.
28 Hatchett, W.	110 Hodges, J. E.	961 Jacobs, A. H.
1103 Hathaway, W.	189 Hodgson, T.	894 James, A.
1307 Hawkins, A. C.	296 Hoffman, R. G. F.	152 James, F.
1025 Hawley, A.	713 Hogg, S. C.	320 James, H.
649 Haxton, E.	180 Holder, A. F. J.	1061 James, S.
1400 Haynes, F. R.	867 Holgate, L.	1082 Jameson, H.
668 Hayward, J. H.	1267 Holland, R. J. H.	193 Jansen, J. B.
255 Hayward, W. C.	SR14 Hollingshead, F.	1374 Jappe, G.
1266 Headridge, P.	823 Hollingsworth, R.	321 Jarman, A.
155 Hearne, C. H.	889 Holmes, A. S.	159 Jarvis, C. E.
770 Heath, F. C.	796 Holmes, W.	653 Jeffery, F. J.
1200 Heath, G. E.	849 Holt, J. D.	465 Jefford, C. E.
718 Hellyer, F. J.		702 Jeffries, H. C.

827 Jeffries, W. D.
148 Jenkins, H.
112 Jenkins, S.
511 Jenkins, W. H.
53 Jerrard, H. V.
9 Jillings, D. S.
691 Jinman, W. A.
429 Joel, G. E.
951 Johncock, S. W.
678 Johnson, C. A. W.
1070 Johnson, F. S.
949 Johnson, W.
851 Johnston, F.
1352 Johnston, W.
1158 Jones, A.
229 Jones, H.
939 Jones, H.
54 Jones, J. C.
458 Jones, J. E.
236 Jones, L.
183 Jones, S. A.
1231 Jones, S. H. F.
30 Jones, W.
487 Jones, W. E.
227 Jowitt, W. H.
494 Judge, V. T.
327 Jukes, A.

868 Keay, C. E.
346 Keegan, M.
997 Keel, F. W.
272 Kelly, E. J. P.
464 Kelly, R. E.
775 Kemp, S.
251 Kemper, J.
340 Kerchey, F.
56 Keszler, L. A.
57 Kidd, A.
358 Kiddell, S.
279 King, C. E.
874 King, C. R.
790 King, E. E.
1043 King, S.
237 Kirby, E.
890 Kirby, E.
275 Kirk, R.
409 Kirkham, G. E.
1193 Kirwin, R. J.
216 Kitchen, G. H. L.

1053 Knight, E. J. A
330 Knight, F. J.
871 Knight, H. H.
143 Knight, J. M.
613 Knott, J. W.

624 Lacey, F. C.
182 Lacy
640 Laing, G.
565 Lake, J. J.
798 Lamdin, F.
425 Lane, H. D.
661 Lane, J.
426 Lang, F.
1034 Lang, R. S. H.
106 Langfield, G. J.
1126 Langstaff, W. C.
58 Langton, W.
13 Lanman, A.
884 Large, P. F.
681 Lathaen, J. A.
78 Latimer, O.
1001 Launder, R. T.
692 Lauraine, G. D.
880 Law, A. H.
571 Lawes, H.
1309 Lawrence, A. W.
265 Lawrence, E. W.
225 Lawrence, J.
927 Lawrence, J.
SR19 Lawrence, W. A.
334 Laws, F. C. V.
643 Lawson, C. E. Lexius
1341 Leddra, N.
705 Ledger, A.
598 Lednor, W. E.
509 Lee, C. E.
1399 Lee, H.
123 Lee, P. N.
228 Lee, W. E.
1024 Leech, J.
714 Leech, W. F.
615 Leeding, T.
644 Leggatt, G.
941 Lemon, G. A.
925 Lennox, J.
621 Leonard, F.
SR22 Leopold, E.

786 Leslie, H. J. S.
933 Lester, G. C. F.
357 Lester, G. W.
319 Levick, A.
797 Levy, R. A.
63 Lewis, A. E.
685 Lewis, J.
675 Lewis, L.
643 Lexius-Lawson, C. E.
240 Lightfoot, F. W.
595 Lightfoot, J.
1377 Lillywhite, R.
245 Lindon, A.
946 Lindop, L.
1390 Lindsay, E.
1339 Lindsay, J. F.
171 Ling, E. M.
1008 Linn, F.
1111 Linnell, W. H.
822 Little, A. G.
345 Little, F.
34 Little, L.
422 Littlejohn, C.
376 Littlejohn, F. W.
1014 Littleproud, C.
399 Littlewood, W.
1068 Livingstone, A. T.
1177 Lloyd, G. W.
1333 Lloyd, R. A.
1348 Lock, T. C.
489 Locker, A. J.
948 Lodge, W.
149 Long
59 Longhurst, J.
1289 Loughead, W.
1385 Lowrey, H. E.
1302 Luck, J. W.
1338 Lucy, J. W.
SR11 Luff, A.
1253 Lyle, M.
789 Lyon, H. A.

995 McAllister, A. B.
301 McAllister, G. F.
1009 McArthur, J.
442 McCarthy, J. J.
973 McCleery, W. R.
62 McClenaghan, G.

1085	O'Connor, M.	1044	Phipps, A. E.	418	Reeves, T.
903	O'Donoghue, J. H.	577	Pickett, W.	759	Reffell, A. H.
1250	O'Flanagan, C. P.	966	Piercey, M. W.	862	Reid, A.
166	O'Giollagain, J.	470	Piper, N. V.	310	Reynolds, L.
163	O'Reilly, T.	336	Plumb, R.	610	Rich, P. A.
942	O'Toole, C. J.	137	Plunkett, W. G.	433	Richards, A. Y.
576	Ockenden, T. C. A.	782	Pointing, E.	763	Richardson, H. B.
66	Oldershaw, T.	1105	Pointon, S.	350	Richardson, J. G.
617	Oldham, J.	254	Porter, E. E.	26	Ridd, F.
647	Osborne-Ellis, A. M.	302	Porter, J. W.	1110	Rideout, A. A.
1259	Owen, G. L.	84	Powell, C. H.	1319	Ridgers, S. G.
1012	Owen, T. J.	521	Powell, F. W.	1199	Riding, N.
		1304	Powell, H. R.	852	Rigby, E. A.
1328	Page, E. E.	393	Powell, J. P.	27	Rigby, J.
752	Page, H. V. C.	207	Power, W. B.	1181	Ripley, C.
760	Paice, G. F.	238	Pratt, F.	263	Robbins, H. V.
172	Palmer, A.	79	Preen, F. G.	1327	Roberts, D.
98	Palmer, E. F.	602	Press, W. J.	655	Roberts, S. T. C.
496	Pankhurst, G. E.	791	Pretty, H.	332	Roberts, W. H.
1002	Panrucker, F. L.	404	Prewett, E. F.	1351	Robertson, L. H.
725	Parfitt, H. E.	85	Price, M.	707	Robertson, M.
1162	Parish, A. J. V.	665	Price, O. H.	102	Robins, A. C.
1241	Park, J.	67	Protheroe, E. J.	1190	Robinson, G.
808	Parker, E. J.	282	Punter, V. E.	943	Robinson, J.
1284	Parker, F. T.	743	Pyke, E.	801	Robinson, R. J.
514	Parker, H.	1172	Pyle, G. A.	710	Robson, E. J.
269	Parker, W. P.	1084	Pyle, W. W.	510	Rodgers, F.
139	Parsons, E. W.	574	Pyne, S. W.	1031	Rogers, J. N.
641	Paterson, A.			1018	Rogers, W.
957	Patterson, D.	1248	Quested, R. A.	478	Rook, H.
664	Payne, G. R.	711	Quicke, S. H.	633	Root, F. C.
923	Payne, J. D.	1041	Quinlan, A. F.	1295	Roper, D. E.
173	Payne, S. J.			196	Rose, J. H.
836	Paynter, R. E. P.	145	Ramplin, C.	1075	Roser, V. H.
101	Pead, W. A.	3	Ramsay, J.	1140	Ross, D. W.
1315	Pearce, A. E.	1216	Ramsden, E.	SR8	Ross, J.
406	Pearce, R. L.	1178	Randall, W. F.	230	Rowe, O.
1314	Pearce, T.J.W.S.	1086	Randall, W. H.	1356	Rowland, S. A. J.
910	Pegg, S. R.	419	Randles, T. F.	1149	Rowley, S. G.
1368	Perrin, C.	1027	Rapley, C.	389	Royston, F.
907	Perrott, W. H.	1246	Rattray, J. D.	162	Rumbold, R. S.
517	Perry, H. H.	1046	Ravenhill, F. W. G.	931	Rumford, E. C.
316	Perry, T. H.	1291	Rawbone, W.	929	Rumsey, E. W.
1191	Petch, F.	459	Rawdon, T. G.	1095	Rumsey-Williams, F. G.
424	Phillips, F. C.	656	Rawsthorne, W.	1130	Russell, F.
724	Phillips, F. J.	219	Raynbird, R.	663	Russell, F. J.
787	Phillips, H. J.	392	Read, F.	1005	Russell, G.
		865	Reeves, A. J.	103	Rutterford, F.

708 Ryan, W.	555 Slaney, L. C.	493 Stentiford, A. W.
	1145 Slingsby, F. N.	769 Stephenson, T. F.
1035 Sadler, R. J.	125 Smallbone, J. R.	1131 Stevens, W. R.
1067 Salsbury, J. R.	467 Smalley, E.	1048 Stewart, E.
844 Salter, E.	401 Smith, A.	1214 Stewart, E.
703 Sampson, J. W.	634 Smith, A. E.	630 Stewart, W. S. A.
1143 Sanderson, A. A.	284 Smith, A. V.	1205 Stiles, A.
1318 Sanderson, C. L.	1342 Smith, C.	1183 Stirling, F. H.
513 Saunders, E. W. C.	592 Smith, E. A.	1102 Stockler, J.
165 Saunders, P. H.	715 Smith, E. A.	1329 Stone, J. J.
914 Saville, E. L. J.	792 Smith, F. J.	809 Stone, O. T.
816 Saywood, A. M.	108 Smith, G. F.	542 Stone, T.
146 Scales, W. G.	732 Smith, G. P.	1038 Stoodley, E. R.
1125 Scarr, H.	1238 Smith, H.	184 Storey, J.
879 Schofield, A. E.	328 Smith, H. O.	271 Storrar, S. E.
1376 Scholefield, E. R.	1301 Smith, H. T. G.	841 Streek, W. E.
1184 Scott, A.	674 Smith, J.	224 Street, E. J.
235 Scott, A. E.	900 Smith, J.	138 Street, R.
24 Scovell, B.	954 Smith, J.	899 Stretton, J. S.
1362 Scragg, W. E.	495 Smith, J. A.	476 Strickland, H. C.
187 Seabrook, A. R.	375 Smith, J. E.	825 Strickland, J. A.
420 Searle, A.	1381 Smith, R. C.	70 Strickland, P. C.
261 Sedger	1017 Smith, R. G.	1394 Stringer, A. J.
1132 Segrott, R. F.	144 Smith, W.	980 Stronach, J. G.
990 Semple, J.	253 Smyrk, W. J.	915 Strugnell, W.
315 Sharp, A. E.	551 Snitch, A. V.	71 Strugnell, W. V.
1122 Sharp, E. F. G.	SR13 Snook, W. A. C.	281 Stubbington, W.
120 Sharp, W.	1153 Soulsby, R. J.	625 Sunman, A. F.
917 Shaw, F. J.	753 Southgate, W. J.	305 Sunman, W. E.
95 Shelton, F.	1293 Southwell, B.	731 Sutton, A. G.
1054 Shepherd, A. G.	746 Spallen, J.	704 Swain, F. T.
1249 Shepherd, R. H.	446 Spearing, E. J.	1330 Sweeting, W. H.
1040 Sherwood, R.	539 Speller, A. J.	648 Sydenham, L. R.
484 Shimmons, A. J.	766 Spencer, L.	863 Symons, E. T.
979 Shrewsbury, E. G.	69 Spencer, R.	
1257 Sillitoe, E. A.	SR24 Spencer, W. R.	1292 Taberner, J.
68 Simmons, G. A.	1331 Spicer, A. A.	1173 Tait, S. C.
1207 Simpson, A. A.	1254 Spong, C. H.	620 Talbot, S.
436 Simpson, A. H.	1004 Spours, E. W.	969 Tallboys, R. A.
662 Simpson, W.	410 Springate, A.	700 Tanner, R. H.
778 Sinclair, W. W.	6 Squires, G. J.	1345 Tansley, J. T.
1104 Skelland, F. E.	848 Squires, W.	740 Tansley, R. J. C.
518 Skerrett, G. W.	22 Stafford, W.G.	352 Tarr, F.
408 Skinner, A.	893 Stamp, J. H.	1211 Taylor, A. E.
694 Skippen, C. E.	115 Stanbrook, R. F.	1360 Taylor, D. R.
1083 Sladden, J. R. W.	989 Standford, W. J.	882 Taylor, E.
212 Sladden, R. J.	911 Stanley, W. W. S.	1258 Taylor, H. F.
21 Slade, E.	2 Starling, J.	29 Taylor, J.
	200 Steed, H.	747 Taylor, J. E.

Printed in Great Britain
by Amazon